Real World .NET 4, C#, and Silverlight®

REAL WORLD .NET 4, C#, AND SILVERLIGHT®

Real World .NET 4, C#, and Silverlight®

INDISPENSABLE EXPERIENCES FROM 15 MVPS

Bill Evjen
Dominick Baier
György Balássy
Gill Cleeren
David Giard
Alex Golesh
Kevin Grossnicklaus
Caleb Jenkins
Jeffrey Juday
Vishwas Lele
Jeremy Likness
Scott Millett
Christian Nagel
Christian Weyer
Daron Yöndem

John Wiley & Sons, Inc.

Real World .NET 4, C#, and Silverlight® : Indispensible Experiences from 15 MVPs

Published by
John Wiley & Sons, Inc.
10475 Crosspoint Boulevard
Indianapolis, IN 46256
www.wiley.com

Copyright © 2012 by John Wiley & Sons, Inc., Indianapolis, Indiana

Published simultaneously in Canada

ISBN: 978-1-118-02196-5
ISBN: 978-1-118-22189-1 (ebk)
ISBN: 978-1-118-23619-2 (ebk)
ISBN: 978-1-118-25264-2 (ebk)

Manufactured in the United States of America

10 9 8 7 6 5 4 3 2 1

To Ági, forever.

—György Balássy

To my wife-to-be, Lindsey Broos, and my mother. Thanks for being there…always.

—Gill Cleeren

My work on this book is dedicated to my sons: Nick and Timmy. I am more proud of them than of anything else in my life.

—David Giard

For my lovely wife and daughter. Thanks for endless support.

—Alex Golesh

To Rachel — my strong, confident, and loving wife. I love you, Hunny. To Noah, Emily, Kaitlyn and Abigail — you children are amazing. I am blessed to be your father!

—Caleb Jenkins

To my wife, Sherrill, and daughter, Alexandra. To Thomas Juday, my father, who taught me that "it all starts with taking out the trash."

—Jeffrey Juday

This book is dedicated to S^3.

—Vishwas Lele

To Lyns, without whose never-ending supply of tea, toast, love, and encouragement my chapter would have been finished in half the time.

—Scott Millett

To my loving parents. Without your guidance and unconditional support, I would not have the chance to be who I am.

—Daron Yöndem

ABOUT THE TECHNICAL EDITOR

JAMES MILLER is a senior architect and technical evangelist working on highly scalable, reliable, and usable enterprise applications utilizing the latest Microsoft platforms and technologies. He has worked in multiple industries and capacities in both the public and private sectors, and has nearly 30 years of programming experience under his belt, experiencing almost every aspect of the software life cycle, and is especially skilled in architecting and developing frameworks and tools to aid rapid application development and agile practices. Miller has held the Microsoft Certified Professional Developer certification for several years, as well as earning Technology Specialist certifications in Web, Workflow Foundation (WF), and Silverlight development. He has a B.S.E.E. from the University of Michigan, specializing in computer and digital systems, with a Business minor focused in accounting and finance. He lives in a rural area outside Ann Arbor, Michigan, with his wife, three sons, two daughters, four dogs, and four cats. He fills much of his limited free time as a high school men's varsity lacrosse coach, but still has an electric guitar plugged in over in a corner, a bookshelf filled with tech books, and a comfortable chair near the desk, perfect for watching the deer as they meander by.

CREDITS

ACQUISITIONS EDITOR
Paul Reese

PROJECT EDITOR
Kevin Shafer

TECHNICAL EDITOR
James Miller

PRODUCTION EDITOR
Daniel Scribner

COPY EDITOR
San Dee Phillips

EDITORIAL MANAGER
Mary Beth Wakefield

FREELANCER EDITORIAL MANAGER
Rosemarie Graham

ASSOCIATE DIRECTOR OF MARKETING
David Mayhew

MARKETING MANAGER
Ashley Zurcher

BUSINESS MANAGER
Amy Knies

PRODUCTION MANAGER
Tim Tate

VICE PRESIDENT AND EXECUTIVE GROUP PUBLISHER
Richard Swadley

VICE PRESIDENT AND EXECUTIVE PUBLISHER
Neil Edde

ASSOCIATE PUBLISHER
Jim Minatel

PROJECT COORDINATOR, COVER
Katie Crocker

PROOFREADER
Scott Klemp, Word One

INDEXER
Ron Strauss

COVER DESIGNER
LeAndra Young

COVER IMAGE
© Rayman

ACKNOWLEDGMENTS

You're currently holding a book that came together by the joint effort of a lot of people, all around the world. Thanks to the people at Wrox for helping to put this book together!

—GILL CLEEREN

Thanks to Proaction Mentors for the time and focus to get this done. Thanks to Jef, Todd, Tony, Tim, Dave, Ken and the rest of my friends at Improving Enterprises for instilling an agile mindset and appreciation for true TDD. Thanks to Craig Walls for teaching me DI, and Raymond Lewallen for introducing me to BDD. Special thanks to Microsoft and the whole MVP program. To all of the MVP authors on this book, Paul and the whole staff at Wiley — thanks for pulling this thing together! Finally, my chapter is also dedicated to developers everywhere — deep in the trenches, striving to hone their skills and improve our craft — keep fighting the good fight.

—CALEB JENKINS

Special thanks to Stephen Toub and Microsoft Patterns and Practices for their fine documentation and timely answers to all my questions.

—JEFFREY JUDAY

Thanks to Steve Michelotti and Sajad Deyargaroo for their valuable feedback.

—VISHWAS LELE

Lyns, thanks for all your support and getting on with things while I have been writing my chapter and the last book. Even though it might look like I take you for granted, I really don't. I thank you for all your patience and hard work with the house move, "family-do's," and looking after me. You are truly wonderful.

—SCOTT MILLETT

CONTENTS

CHAPTER 10: SECURING WCF SERVICES USING THE WINDOWS IDENTITY FOUNDATION (WIF)

CHAPTER 15: AUTOMATED UNIT TESTING   569

INTRODUCTION

THIS BOOK IS AN OBVIOUS COMPILATION FROM MANY AUTHORS. When putting together the idea for this book, we thought of putting a different style of book together from the get-go. Many of the computer books on the market today are a thorough explanation of a specific area of technology tackled by one or a handful of dedicated authors. Whether the topic is C#, ASP.NET, Extensible Markup Language (XML), or Windows Communication Foundation (WCF) development, there are books that walk you through the topic from beginning to end. You can find many of these comprehensive references on the market today.

This book has been built *not* to be like that. Instead, we thought, "Let's bring together some of the best folks in the industry today (Microsoft MVPs and Microsoft Regional Directors) and have them write a single chapter on the topic that they know best."

Yes, these authors know a lot about .NET as a whole, but it came down to having them focus on the area that they felt was their area of love and interest — the single area they know best. In total, this book is a series of large articles put together in common areas that do indeed provide quite a bit of coverage across the large landscape of the .NET Framework, but you can find each conversation in each chapter to be held by someone that gives you the ins-and-outs of the topic that is near and dear to their hearts.

The .NET Framework is now so large that it is outright impossible to know everything that you have at your fingertips when working with it. That is also an understanding that many developers take into the building of a development team. They focus on putting together groups of individuals that, as a whole, bring a more holistic understanding of the power they have with the .NET Framework as the basis of their work.

As you start to tackle your work in the various areas of the .NET Framework, hopefully you will find this book to be a resource that serves as an advisor that you need as you work through some of the strange areas you haven't yet spent the time to completely understand.

WHO THIS BOOK IS FOR

This book is for the intermediate-to-experienced developer who is focused on building solutions for utilizing the .NET Framework. In this book, you can find everything from web development, to back-end development, and everything in between.

WHAT THIS BOOK COVERS

This book covers many of the core areas of the .NET Framework. It starts with coverage of the client-side by focusing on ASP.NET before moving into Silverlight. With ASP.NET, you find coverage of working with jQuery, one of the most pursued ways in which to develop web applications today, as well as how to deal with your ASP.NET applications after they are built to get the most out of them. In addition to the coverage of ASP.NET, with Silverlight you can find information on applying patterns to Silverlight using patterns such as Model-View-ViewModel (MVVM). The Silverlight coverage then moves from the client on the PC to the client on the phone. Also, when dealing with the client, you can find a chapter that discusses how to bridge the world of designers and developers.

Moving from client-side development work, the next chapters of the book cover communication technologies such as the WCF, as well as some of the best means to secure your communications using the Windows Identity Foundation (WIF). From there, specific communication protocols such as REST and OData are covered. Another great chapter focuses on the .NET Task Parallel Library.

The next set of chapters cover some key topics that include using Windows Workflow and WPF data binding. Then, the final chapters cover aspects of your development life cycle, including working with user stories and developing with unit testing.

Overall, a tremendous amount is covered in this book, and each chapter provides a dedicated look at what you need to know to succeed with the topic at hand.

WHAT YOU NEED TO USE THIS BOOK

The .NET Framework 4 runs on Windows XP, Windows 2003, Windows 7, and the latest Windows Server 2008 R2. To write code using the .NET Framework, you need to install the .NET 4 SDK.

In addition, unless you intend to write your C# code using a text editor or some other third-party developer environment, you almost certainly want Visual Studio 2010. The full SDK is not needed to run managed code, but the .NET runtime is needed.

Also, although this book shows all its code examples in C#, you can convert many of the examples and do just the same in Visual Basic if your want.

CONVENTIONS

This book uses a number of different styles of text and layout to help differentiate among various types of information. Following are examples of the styles used, and an explanation of what they mean:

- ➤ New words being defined are shown in *italics*.

- ➤ Keys that you press on the keyboard, such as Ctrl and Enter, are shown in initial caps, and spelled as they appear on the keyboard.

- ➤ Filenames and folder names, file extensions, URLs, and code that appear in regular paragraph text are shown in a `monospaced` typeface.

A block of code that you can type as a program and run is shown on separate lines, like this:

```
public static void Main()
{
    AFunc(1,2,"abc");
}
```

or like this:

```
public static void Main()     {          AFunc(1,2,"abc");     }
```

Sometimes, you see code in a mixture of styles, like this:

```
    // If we haven't reached the end, return true, otherwise
   // set the position to invalid, and return false.
   pos++;
   if (pos < 4)
      return true;
   else {
      pos = -1;
      return false;
   }
```

When mixed code is shown like this, the bold code background is what you should focus on in the current example.

We demonstrate the syntactical usage of methods, properties, and so on using the following format:

```
SqlDependency="database:table"
```

Here, the italicized parts indicate *placeholder text*: object references, variables, or parameter values that you need to insert.

Some of the code examples throughout the book are presented as numbered listings that have descriptive titles, like this:

LISTING 1-3: Targeting Devices in Your ASP.NET Pages

Each listing is numbered (for example: *1-3*) where the first number represents the chapter number, and the number following the hyphen represents a sequential number that indicates where that listing falls within the chapter. Downloadable code from the Wrox website (www.wrox.com) also uses this numbering system so that you can easily locate the examples you are looking for.

Boxes with a warning icon like this one hold important, not-to-be-forgotten information that is directly relevant to the surrounding text.

The Pencil icon indicates notes, tips, hints, tricks, or asides to the current discussion.

SOURCE CODE

As you work through the examples in this book, you may choose either to manually type in all the code, or to use the source code files that accompany the book. Some of the source code used in this book is available for download at www.wrox.com. When at the site, simply locate the book's title (use the Search box or one of the title lists) and click the Download Code link on the book's detail page to obtain all the available source code for the book. Code that is included on the website is highlighted by the following icon:

Available for download on Wrox.com

Listings include the filename in the title. If it is just a code snippet, you'll find the filename in a code note such as this:

Code snippet filename

> *Because many books have similar titles, you may find it easiest to search by ISBN; this book's ISBN is 978-1-11-8-02196-5.*

After you download the code, just decompress it with your favorite compression tool. Alternatively, you can go to the main Wrox code download page at www.wrox.com/dynamic/books/download.aspx to see the code available for this book and all other Wrox books.

ERRATA

We make every effort to ensure that there are no errors in the text or in the code. However, no one is perfect, and mistakes do occur. If you find an error in one of our books, such as a spelling mistake or faulty piece of code, we would be grateful for your feedback. By sending in errata, you may save another reader hours of frustration, and at the same time, you will help us provide even higher quality information.

To find the errata page for this book, go to www.wrox.com and locate the title using the Search box or one of the title lists. Then, on the book details page, click the Book Errata link. On this page, you can view all errata that has been submitted for this book and posted by Wrox editors. A complete book list, including links to each book's errata, is also available at www.wrox.com/misc-pages/booklist.shtml.

If you don't spot "your" error on the Book Errata page, go to www.wrox.com/contact/techsupport.shtml and complete the form there to send us the error you have found. We'll check the information and, if appropriate, post a message to the book's errata page and fix the problem in subsequent editions of the book.

P2P.WROX.COM

For author and peer discussion, join the P2P forums at p2p.wrox.com. The forums are a web-based system for you to post messages relating to Wrox books and related technologies, and to interact with other readers and technology users. The forums offer a subscription feature to e-mail you topics of interest of your choosing when new posts are made to the forums. Wrox authors, editors, other industry experts, and your fellow readers are present on these forums.

At http://p2p.wrox.com, you can find a number of different forums that can help you, not only as you read this book, but also as you develop your own applications. To join the forums, just follow these steps:

1. Go to p2p.wrox.com and click the Register link.

2. Read the terms of use and click Agree.

3. Complete the required information to join, as well as any optional information you want to provide, and click Submit.

4. You will receive an e-mail with information describing how to verify your account and complete the joining process.

 *You can read messages in the forums without joining P2P, but to post your own messages, you must join.*

After you join, you can post new messages and respond to messages other users post. You can read messages at any time on the web. If you would like to have new messages from a particular forum e-mailed to you, click the Subscribe to This Forum icon by the forum name in the forum listing.

For more information about how to use the Wrox P2P, be sure to read the P2P FAQs for answers to questions about how the forum software works, as well as many common questions specific to P2P and Wrox books. To read the FAQs, click the FAQ link on any P2P page.

1

ASP.NET and jQuery

by David Giard

Approximately ten years ago, Microsoft introduced ASP.NET — a framework for building web applications using the new .NET platform. ASP.NET was designed to assist developers to build, deploy, and maintain web pages and websites. ASP.NET integrates with Microsoft Internet Information Server (IIS) and provides developers with a rich set of tools to develop dynamic web applications.

When it was introduced, this framework focused on Web Forms. Web Forms abstracted away many of the low-level complexities of HTML and HTTP, giving developers an experience similar to one used to build Windows Forms. By using Web Forms, developers could quickly create an interactive web page, even if they knew little about the underlying technologies of the web. This development experience was similar to the popular Visual Basic language, so it appealed to developers familiar with that language.

Like its predecessor Active Server Pages (ASP), ASP.NET provides a developer with the ability to build web applications using a combination of code and markup.

Unlike the classic ASP, ASP.NET is built on top of the Common Language Runtime (CLR) and uses the power of .NET. Because of this, ASP.NET can take advantage of CLR benefits, such as automatic garbage collection, a rich set of libraries, and a robust security model.

The latest version of ASP.NET includes enhancements to the ASP.NET Web Forms Framework and an updated version of the new ASP.NET Model-View-Controller (MVC) framework. Visual Studio .NET 2010 is also the first version to ship with jQuery libraries, which enable developers to build rich client-side functionality into their websites.

This chapter focuses on what is new in ASP.NET 4. First, you learn about some of the new features and enhancements of ASP.NET 4 Web Forms. Next, you learn about the ASP.NET MVC framework. Finally, this chapter covers how to effectively use jQuery to enhance your application.

Along the way, a sample application provides guidance on how to implement these new features.

UNDERSTANDING WEB FORMS

The Web Forms Framework was introduced with ASP.NET 1.0. Countless websites have been successfully built and deployed using this platform.

Essentially, the Web Forms Framework was designed to abstract away the complexities of Hypertext Markup Language (HTML) and Hypertext Transfer Protocol (HTTP) to make web development feel more like Visual Basic forms development. Following are characteristics of Web Forms application development:

➤ The developer is presented with a design surface that looks like a web page.

➤ Web controls are dragged onto this design surface.

➤ Properties are set on the page and on the controls.

➤ Code is written to manipulate the page, controls, and associated data.

Using Visual Studio, developers can quickly build a web application. A rich set of built-in controls and third-party controls adds to this abstraction and helps cut down on many development tasks.

However, this rapid application development (RAD) comes at a cost. Web Forms and associated controls automatically generate HTML and JavaScript. Sometimes the generated code does not exactly match your needs. To add to the difficulty, different web browsers often render the same HTML in different ways, and understand JavaScript differently — particularly as JavaScript interacts with the web page's Document Object Model (DOM). A common problem is that a page renders properly in one browser but improperly in another.

Using Web Forms, it is difficult to modify the output HTML or JavaScript. This is especially an issue when you target multiple browsers. If you have trouble tweaking HTML, you will have trouble supporting some browsers. For this reason, web developers should learn as much as they can about HTML, Cascading Style Sheets (CSS), and HTTP. Abstractions such as Web Forms are fine, but they do not excuse the responsibility to understand the technologies they abstract.

Microsoft introduced a number of enhancements to ASP.NET with version 4. Following are a few of the most important ones:

➤ Improved handling of `View State` provides users with greater flexibility over the controls that participate in `View State`.

➤ The `web.config` file has been greatly simplified.

➤ A new Web Project template provides greater functionality.

➤ `web.config` transformations make it easier to deploy to a new environment.

Let's take a look at these in a bit more detail.

View State

By default, the web and its underlying transport protocol (HTTP) are stateless. This means that, by default, each request remembers nothing about any previous request. ASP.NET introduced `View State` as a way to maintain state between pages in a web application.

`View State` works by automatically creating an extra, hidden input within an HTML form. To save the state of the submitted fields on a page, ASP.NET encodes `View State` data into a single string and sets the value of this hidden field to that string. This field is created on the server and sent down to the client with the rest of the web page.

This convenience comes at a price. The encoded data is submitted each time the form is submitted and it is returned to the browser with each response. If you have a lot of data stored in `View State`, that data can get quite large, slowing down communication between the client and the server.

Using a previous version of ASP.NET, a developer could turn `View State` on or off at the page level, or at the control level. Prior to ASP.NET 4, you basically had three options for enabling `View State`:

> ➤ *Turn off* `View State` *for the entire page* — If you do this, you do not realize any of the benefits of `View State`.

> ➤ *Turn on* `View State` *for the entire page* — If you do this, you may encode and add unneeded items to `View State`, bloating the payload sent between the server and the browser, slowing your application, and degrading the user experience.

> ➤ *Turn on* `View State` *for the page, and then disable* `View State` *for controls that do not need it* — This strategy works well if you want `View State` for almost every control on the page, but not for a few controls. It can be a real pain if you want `View State` enabled only for a couple controls.

ASP.NET 4 provides two relevant properties to control `View State`: `ViewStateMode` and `EnableViewState`. Only `ViewStateMode` is new in version 4, but the two properties work together.

`EnableViewState` has been around since the first version of ASP.NET. It can be set for an entire page, or for a single control, and it can be set to either `True` or `False`. `EnableViewState` does not turn on `View State` for any controls. Rather, it determines whether `View State` may be turned on for a control, and for any controls below it in the control containership hierarchy. A control's `ViewStateMode` turns on or off `View State`, but only if `EnableViewState` is `True`. `ViewStateMode` can be enabled or disabled explicitly, or by inheriting this property from its parent container.

Setting a Page or Control's `View State` attribute to `False` disables `View State` for that Page/Control and for any controls contained therein.

In previous versions of ASP.NET, the only way to selectively enable and disable `View State` on controls was to set `EnableViewState="True"` on the page, and set `EnableViewState="False"` on the controls for which you did not want to maintain the overhead of passing `View State` between the client and the server.

You can set `ViewStateMode` as an attribute of a page or control, or you can set it in code. Following are the allowable values:

➤ `Enabled` — Turns on `View State` for a control.

➤ `Disabled` — Turns off `View State` for a control.

➤ `Inherit` — Tells ASP.NET to set the `ViewStateMode` to that of the control's parent container. This is the default value for a user control.

`ViewStateMode` is only relevant if `EnableViewState` is set to `True` for a control or the control's parent. If `EnableViewState` is `True`, `ViewStateMode` turns `View State` on or off for a given control. By turning on `View State`, any data associated with a control is encoded on the server, saved with a hidden input field, and rendered to the client, so it will be submitted the next time the form is submitted.

My recommendation is to set `EnableViewState` to `True` on the page and to selectively turn on (set to `Enabled`) `ViewStateMode` for the controls that will benefit from it. This minimizes the payload sent between the client and server and prevents you from accidentally adding to this payload as you add new controls to the page. Following is an example of this:

```
<%@ Page …
    EnableViewState="True" ViewStateMode="Disabled" %>

<asp:Label runat="server" Text="Enter UserName:" ID="EnterUserNameLabel" />
<br />
<asp:TextBox runat="server" ID="UserName" ViewStateMode="true" />
```

web.config Transformations

One of the challenges of application development is migrating configuration files from one environment to another. I typically develop my applications in a Development environment, using a Development database, Development web services, and the files on my own computer. Many of these settings (such as connection strings, file paths, and URLs) are set in the application's `web.config` file.

At some point, I deploy my application to a Test environment, so that testers can try it out. The Test environment can use different connection strings, URLs, and file paths, so I need to modify the `web.config` at the time I deploy the application to this environment. This problem presents itself again when I deploy to a Staging environment, a Production environment, and any other environment my organization or customer uses.

ASP.NET 4 provides an elegant way to handle modifying a `web.config` file as the application is deployed to different environments. Using Transformations, you can create a base `web.config` file and a separate file for each of your environments. Each environment file contains only those elements that vary from the base configuration.

Simplified web.config

In earlier versions of ASP.NET, the `web.config` file tended to become bloated and difficult to manage. Even a newly created empty web project contained a large `web.config` file.

With ASP.NET 4, much of the default configuration has been moved to the `machine.config` file, making the `web.config` much smaller. You can even create an ASP.NET application with no settings in the `web.config` file. Developers are encouraged to add only those settings specific to the application to which the `web.config` file applies.

A smaller `web.config` file makes configuration settings easier to find and to manage.

New ASP.NET Web Forms Templates

Visual Studio 2010 includes a new and improved web template that is designed to get web developers up and running faster. You can find the ASP.NET Web Application template in the New Project dialog under Installed Templates ⇨ Web, as shown in Figure 1-1. From the Visual Studio menu, select File ⇨ New Project to open this dialog.

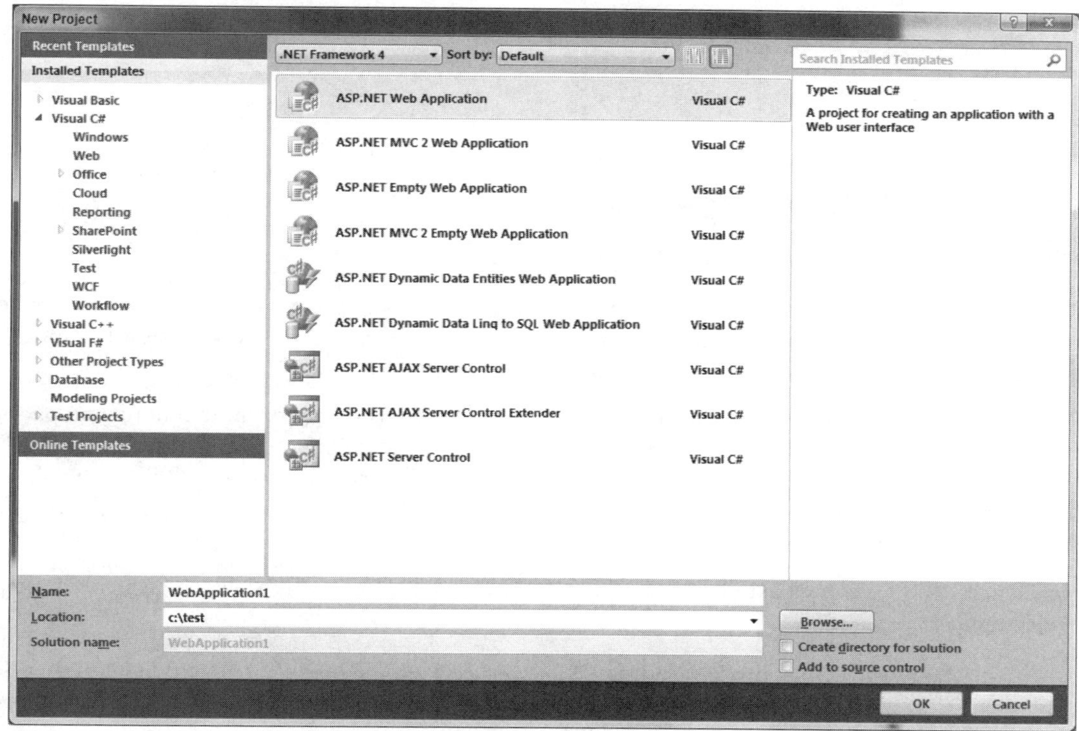

FIGURE 1-1: Locating the ASP.NET Web Application template

This template creates an application that includes Home and About pages, and pages for managing users and roles. The site uses a default stylesheet and master page, giving it a polished look; but developers can modify these files to meet their needs. The application is ready to run and use as soon as it is created. You can add forms and code to the initial site to suit the specific needs of your application. Figure 1-2 shows the structure of an ASP.NET Web Application project as viewed from Solution Explorer.

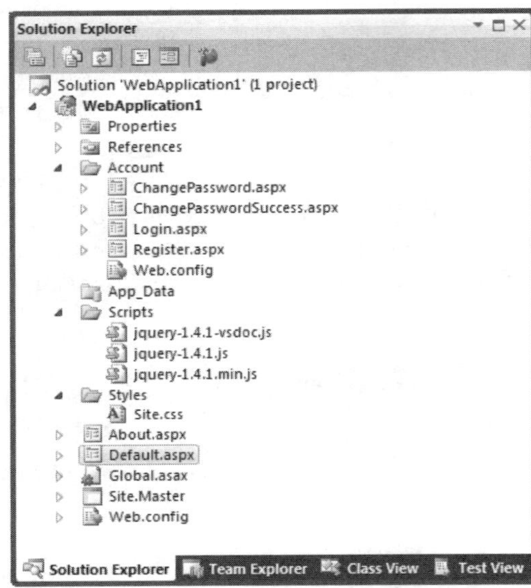

FIGURE 1-2: Structure of an ASP.NET Web Application project

The ASP.NET Web Application template provides a good starting point for developers who are new to ASP.NET and want to see a sample implementation, as well as developers who want to quickly get a site up. Figure 1-3 shows the default page of this application.

The ASP.NET Empty Web Application template takes the opposite approach. It contains no pages or code — only a nearly empty `web.config` file. This template contains only the references required by an ASP.NET website. It is designed to give experienced developers maximum flexibility when building their website. Figure 1-4 shows the structure of an ASP.NET Empty Web Application project as viewed in Solution Explorer.

Developers who want maximum control over their web applications will prefer the ASP.NET Empty Web Application template.

The features discussed thus far allow developers to improve on applications without changing the way they write those applications. However, Microsoft recently released ASP.NET MVC — a set of tools that provide a new way to build web applications.

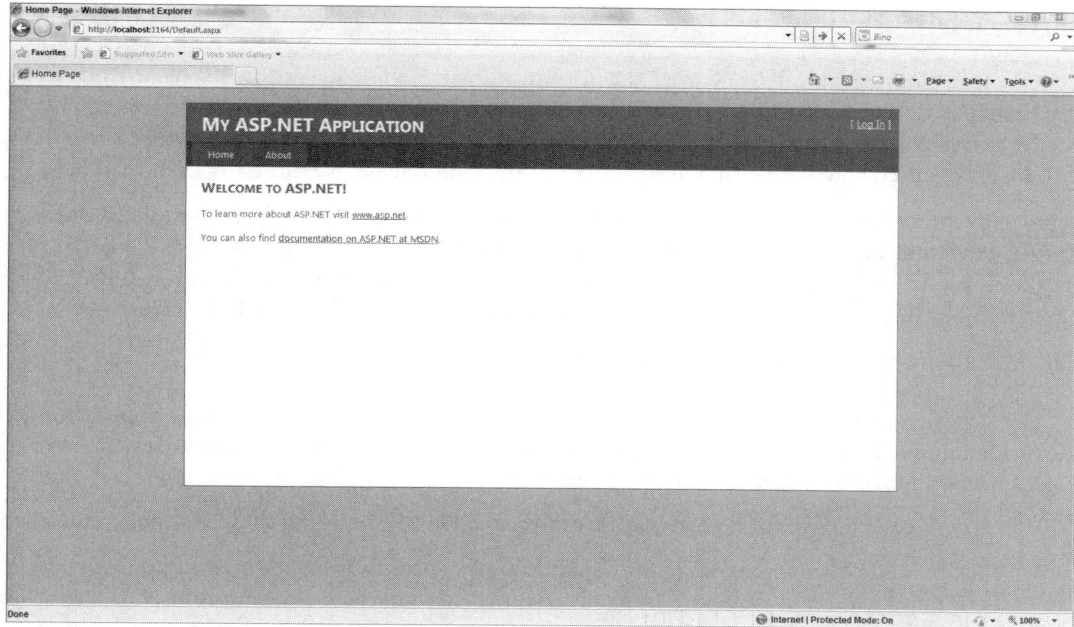

FIGURE 1-3: Default application page

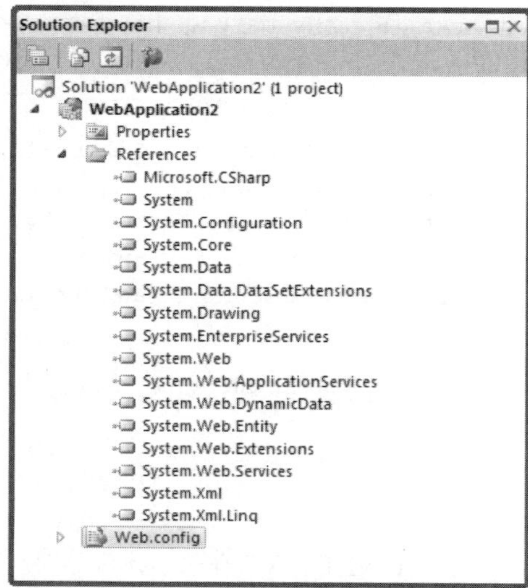

FIGURE 1-4: Structure of an ASP.NET Empty Web Application project

ASP.NET MVC

Strictly speaking, ASP.NET MVC was not introduced with .NET 4. Version 1.0 of ASP.NET MVC (or MVC, as it is referred to here) was an out-of-band release that developers could download for free from Microsoft. Visual Studio 2010 shipped with version 2 of this framework. In 2011, Microsoft released MVC version 3 as another out-of-band release. Version 3 is examined here.

I have built many applications using the ASP.NET Web Forms Framework. I continue to enhance existing websites built with this framework. It has served me well over the years, and many other developers have built countless solid, scalable websites on this framework. However, for new websites built on the .NET platform, I recommend using the newer ASP.NET MVC framework.

The MVC framework has the following advantages:

> ➤ MVC encourages a greater separation of concerns among the parts of your application. For example, each new page has no code-behind file by default, which discourages users from mixing business logic with the user interface.

> ➤ MVC gives a developer greater control over the HTML and CSS that is output to the client.

> ➤ Because MVC encourages greater separation of concerns, it makes it easier to test parts of your application in isolation. In particular, the user interface — a notoriously difficult thing for which to create automated unit tests — is separated from the rest of the application.

In an ASP.NET Web Forms application, a URL typically points to a file on disk. Usually, that file is an `ASPX` page, and that `ASPX` page controls what happens next. Typically, the page life cycle executes, firing a series of page events (`Load`, `PreInit Init`, `Prerender`, `Render`) and runs code associated with each of these events.

In an MVC application, a URL points to a `Controller` method instead of to a file. A `Controller` method is a public method in a `Controller` class. A `Controller` class is a public, concrete class that implements the `IController` interface and has a name that ends with `Controller`. As its name implies, the controller handles all the logic of the request. This may involve accepting input data, applying business logic, retrieving data, deciding which view to render, and sending stateful data (the model) down to the client.

If this sounds complicated, tooling built into the framework can help you quickly create controller classes, controller methods, and views.

Versions of MVC

As of this writing, Microsoft has shipped three versions of the ASP.NET MVC framework. Version 1 shipped out-of-band (that is, between releases of Visual Studio) and was available as a download. Version 2 shipped with Visual Studio 2010. In 2011, Microsoft released version 3 of MVC.

This out-of-band version is available as a download from `www.asp.net/mvc/mvc3`. The install program (shown in Figure 1-5) has one button, labeled Install. Click this button to begin the installation. If you do not already have a version of Visual Studio installed, it will install Visual Studio Express.

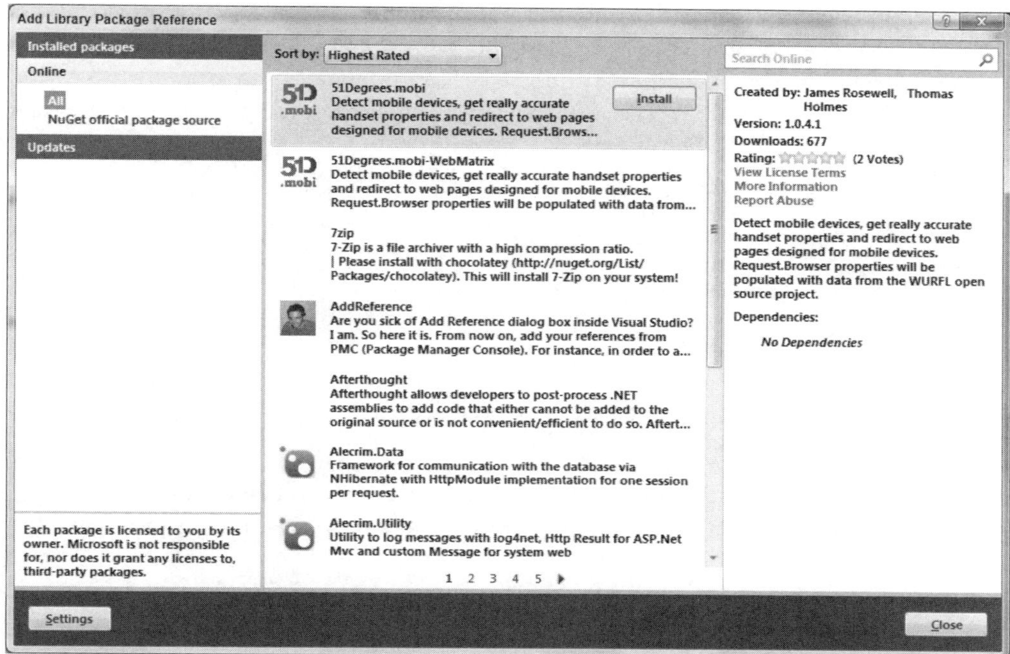

FIGURE 1-5: ASP.NET MVC 3 Install dialog

The most noticeable difference between versions 2 and 3 of MVC is the view engine. MVC versions 1 and 2 used a view engine based on Web Forms. Server-side code in the Web Forms view engine is identified by placing it between the `<%` and `%>` symbols. (I don't know the names of these symbols, so I refer to them as "Bee-Stings.") By default, MVC version 3 uses the new Razor view engine.

In the Razor view engine, server-side code is identified by preceding it with the `@` symbol. MVC figures out from the context when to switch back to client-side code. To me, it seems counter-intuitive that I don't explicitly tell the view engine when server-side code is ending. But I have yet to find an example when Razor did not correctly switch back to client side.

The Pieces of MVC

To better understand the MVC, let's take a closer look at each of the pieces that make up the MVC.

Model

HTTP (and, by association, the World Wide Web) is inherently stateless. Every request from the client to the server is independent of every other request. In other words, when the web server receives a request from a client, the server has no memory of any requests that came before. At least, that's true by default.

But applications tend to be stateful. You want your applications to remember things about users and their data as the user navigates from page to page within your web application. In an MVC application, a *model* is a container for that stateful data.

A model often takes the form of instances of one or more entity classes. An *entity class* is a .NET class that contains properties to hold state information. For example, if you have a page displaying customer information, you may create a `Customer` class with public properties for `FirstName`, `LastName`, `Address`, and so on. This class may also have a public property to hold all orders placed by the customer, as in the following example.

```
public class CustomerDTO
{
    public string FirstName { get; set; }
    public string LastName { get; set; }
    public string Address { get; set; }
    public List<Order> Orders { get; set; }
}
```

An MVC application can instantiate this class to store stateful data about the current customer displayed, and to pass that data between the client and the server.

I prefer to place my model objects in a separate assembly so that they can be used independently of my web application. I refer to such a class as a Data Transfer Object (DTO) because its sole purpose is to maintain stateful data about an object, and transfer that data between pages, or between layers of my application.

The MVC framework provides annotations that allow you to enhance a model class and properties. For example, you can annotate a model property to specify validation rules and a descriptive label to display on a View page, as shown in the following example:

```
[Required(ErrorMessage = "Please enter a Last Name for this customer")]
[Display(Name = "Last Name")]
public string LastName { get; set; }
```

Often, I'll create a ViewModel class for use with a specific view in my application. A ViewModel contains the Model entities that the View requires. This will make more sense after I define a View and walk through a sample application. Following is an example of a ViewModel:

```
public class EditCustomerViewModel
{
    public CustomerDTO Customer { get; set; }
    public List<CustomerTypeDTO> CustomerTypes { get; set; }
}
```

View

A *view* is the markup sent to the client. In most MVC applications, this is HTML, but ASP.NET MVC enables you to create views that pass information as JavaScript Object Notation (JSON), Extensible Markup Language (XML), or almost any other data format. The exact format you choose depends on the client that consumes your application. If a user intends to browse to a view using a web browser, HTML probably makes sense; if a view contains subscription information consumed by a newsreader, The XML format ATOM probably makes sense; and if a web page uses JavaScript to make Ajax call to a server running ASP.NET MVC, JSON might be a preferred format to return.

Controller

A *controller* is a special kind of class in ASP.NET MVC.

The controller is the central nervous system of an MVC application. Everything starts with a controller because it is a controller's action (a method within the class) that the client calls to kick off each request.

In ASP.NET MVC, a controller must meet the following conditions:

> ➤ It must be a concrete class. (No abstract classes or interfaces qualify as controllers.)

> ➤ It must be a public class so that clients can access the controller's methods.

> ➤ It must implement the `IController` interface. The MVC framework provides a base class (`BaseController`) that implements this interface, so I usually inherit from that class.

> ➤ The name of the class must end with the word `Controller`.

The name of the class is important. MVC identifies a controller in part because its name ends with `Controller`. Identifying the functionality of a class by its name is an example of *convention over configuration*. By applying a naming pattern to all controller classes, you don't need to tell your application which classes are controllers: the application can figure this out by the class names.

Action Methods

Within a controller class, you can code one or more `Action` methods. Typically, an `Action` method creates a model (perhaps by querying a database and mapping the results to a stateful data class) and determines the view to render to the client. The `Controller Action` method then returns the view and the model to the client.

Typically, each `Action` method in a `Controller` class returns an `ActionResult`. The runtime then calls the `ExecuteResult` method on this `ActionResult` object, which can either create and send a response to the view engine, or perform some other action (such as redirecting to another `Action` method or raising an exception).

`ActionResult` is an abstract class, so `Action` methods actually return a specific subclass of `ActionResult`.

In a web application, it is common to return the `ViewResult` subclass, which is used to render HTML to a browser. But you can also choose to return the following:

> ➤ `FileResult` — This downloads a file to the client.

> ➤ `HttpUnauthorizedResult` — This returns a 404 error to the client.

> ➤ `JsonResult` — This generates a JSON object that is easily consumed by JavaScript Ajax requests.

> ➤ `RedirectToRouteResult` — This automatically sends the user to a new URL, which should invoke another `Action` method, based on the application's routing rules.

There are several other subclasses, and you can even subclass `ActionResult` in your own custom class to create your own custom behavior.

The MVC `Controller` class contains a number of helper methods to generate these `ActionResult` objects. For example, the `View` method returns a `ViewResult` object, and the `RedirectToAction` method returns a `RedirectToRouteResult` object.

Model Binding

The MVC framework is good at recognizing data and mapping it to appropriate objects. For example, data can be submitted to a Controller `Action` method in a number of ways, including form input values, query string values, and route data. When this data is submitted to an `Action`, the `DefaultModelBinder` kicks in and uses reflection in an attempt to map the values to the properties of a ViewModel. This allows your `Action` method to accept a ViewModel as a parameter, which tends to be much simpler to work with than collections of form or query string values. Working with strongly typed data in your `Action` methods makes it easier to enforce what data may be submitted, and to catch invalid data sooner.

Later in this chapter, you will see an example of such an `Action` method. For now, the following is a sample signature of a Controller `Action` method that accepts a ViewModel parameter:

```
public ActionResult Edit(DepartmentViewModel departmentVm)
```

URL Routing

To understand an ASP.NET MVC application, you need to understand routing.

Most web requests begin with a user typing a URL into a web browser's address bar. In traditional web applications, each URL maps to a physical file on disk containing HTML, scripts, and other markup and code. If the user types **http://MySite.com/CustInfo/CustomerDetails.aspx** into a browser, the web server looks in the `CustInfo` folder of the site `http://MySite.com`, finds a page named `CustomerDetails.aspx`, and processes that page.

URL *routing* allows a developer more flexibility in how to structure a site. It decouples the URL from the location of the physical pages on disk.

This flexibility can allow developers to create URLs that are easier to remember, and that are more easily indexed by search engines. For example, consider the following URL:

```
/OrderDetails.aspx?CustID=123&OrderYear=2010
```

This was a common way to offer data to a customer. In this URL, the `OrderDetails.aspx` file has code that reads the two query string parameters (everything after the question mark) and uses those parameter values to filter the information returned to the user. (In this case, only orders for customer 123 that were placed in 2010 are considered.) One problem with this approach is that it is not optimized for search engines.

Most search engines ignore query string parameters, so the following URLs would be considered the same:

```
/OrderDetails.aspx?CustID=123&OrderYear=2010
/OrderDetails.aspx?CustID=124&OrderYear=2009
```

Of course, you could simply create URLs, such as the following:

```
/OrderDetails123-2010.aspx
/OrderDetails124-2009.aspx
```

However, this requires you to maintain a lot of pages with redundant information, and isn't very flexible. A better solution would be to allow a user to type URLs such as the following:

```
/Order/Details/123/Year/2010
/Order/Details/122/Year/2009
```

These URLs are easier to read and to remember, and will be perceived as two different pages by search engines.

Many people think of ASP.NET routing as it applies to MVC. However, the routing functionality is part of the .NET Framework, and is available to all web applications.

In an ASP.NET MVC application, the URL points to an `Action Controller` method.

You can set up routing in the `Application_Start` method of the `global.asax` file. As the name implies, this method fires when an application first starts, so it's a good place to add startup code. I like to place routing code in its own method, and call it from `Application_Start`. Following is the code added by default to `global.asax` when you create a new ASP.NET MVC project:

```
public static void RegisterRoutes(RouteCollection routes)
{
    routes.IgnoreRoute("{resource}.axd/{*pathInfo}");
    routes.MapRoute(
        "Default", // Route name
        "{controller}/{action}/{id}", // URL with parameters
        new { controller = "Home", action = "Index", id =
            UrlParameter.Optional } // Parameter defaults
    );
}
protected void Application_Start()
{
    RegisterRoutes(RouteTable.Routes);
}
```

In this snippet, the `routes.MapRoute` method defines a `Route` for the application. The `Route` tells MVC how to interpret a URL.

In the previous example, the first parameter (`"Default"`) defines the name of the `Route`.

The second parameter (`"{controller}/{action}/{id}"`) defines the parts of a URL to look for. In this case, the expected URL is split into three parts:

➤ The first part defines the name of a controller.

➤ The second part defines the name of an `Action` method within that controller.

➤ The third part identifies the value of an `id` parameter passed to that `Action` method.

The third parameter of `MapRoute` defines defaults for each part of the URL, which allows you to omit any or all of these parts. If the `controller` is omitted, the *Home* Controller is assumed; if the `Action` is omitted, the *Index* action is assumed; and the `id` parameter is defined as optional, allowing an `Action` method without parameters.

Accessing a Database

Most line-of-business (LOB) applications interact with data in a persistent data store such as Microsoft SQL Server.

The good news about MVC is that the framework does not care how an application stores data, or how it retrieves and updates the data in the database. The bad news is that the framework provides no help interacting with a database.

A developer can use any data-access technology. The developer may write stored procedures and access them via ADO.NET. Or the developer may use an Object Relational Mapper (ORM), such as nHibernate or Entity Framework, to interact with the database. MVC works with any method, as long as the model is populated with .NET entity objects. MVC does not work well with record sets, so there is likely to be some mapping involved.

MVC Tooling

Now that you are familiar with the fundamental building blocks of MVC, let's take a look at how to use the tooling in Visual Studio to quickly create a new MVC project, and add to that project.

Creating a New Project

Creating an ASP.NET MVC application is simple because Visual Studio 2010 ships with built-in templates. As described previously, from the Visual Studio 2010 menu, select File ➪ New ➪ Project. In the Installed Templates section of the New Project dialog, select Web.

On the right side of the New Project dialog (as you learned earlier in this chapter), you can find two relevant templates: ASP.NET MVC 3 Web Application and ASP.NET MVC 3 Empty Web Application. Each of these can create a project with references to assemblies used by the framework, folders expected by the framework, routing code in the `Global.asax`, and assembly and namespace entries in the `web.config` file. The ASP.NET MVC 3 Web Application (let's call it the "nonempty" template) also adds some sample controllers, views, stylesheets, and data. Figure 1-6 shows the New Project dialog. This is the same dialog you saw in the description of the new ASP.NET templates. However, you are now selecting an MVC template.

If you select ASPNET MVC 3 Web Application, Visual Studio prompts you for some more information, as shown in Figure 1-7.

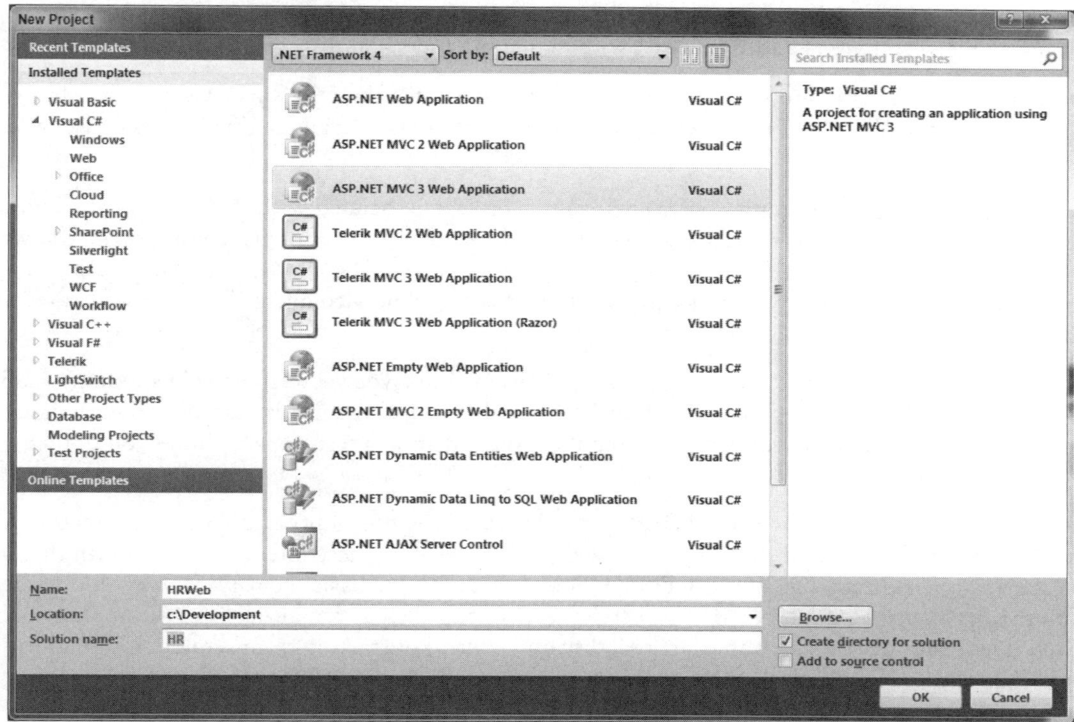

FIGURE 1-6: New Project dialog

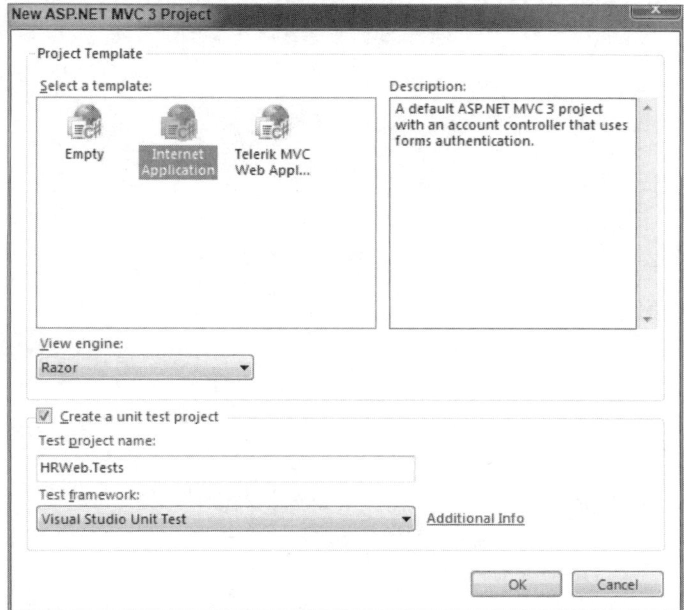

FIGURE 1-7: Project Template dialog

Here you can specify whether you want an "empty" project, or one with a couple of controllers, pages, models, and views added to assist with managing users and displaying basic content.

You also have the option to select a view engine. The default is the new Razor view engine, but you can revert to the older Web Forms view engine if you prefer. The Razor engine is cleaner and would be my recommendation.

Creating MVC project prompts you to create a test project associated with this web application. The default behavior is to create a test project, which encourages you to write unit tests as you write your application code. Some developers jokingly refer to the *No, Do Not Create a Unit Test Project* radio button as the *I Suck* button because clicking it is an acknowledgment that you don't care about unit testing.

You are encouraged to write unit tests because they can make your code more robust, maintainable, and easier to refactor. Also, remember that MVC tends to encourage more testable code because it tends to separate the logical parts of an application. Creating a test project allows you to take advantage of this testability.

If you are new to MVC, you should create a site based on the nonempty template. This creates a site with a couple of controllers and views, allowing you to see how these interact. You can run this site as soon as it is created. The site includes a Home page and some basic security. Start with this site and modify the code, data, HTML, and stylesheets to suit the particular needs of the application. Even if you later decide you want the flexibility and control of starting from scratch, it's good to see this code and use it as a guide for building your own controllers and views.

Referenced Assemblies

Figure 1-8 shows the assemblies referenced by an MVC project.

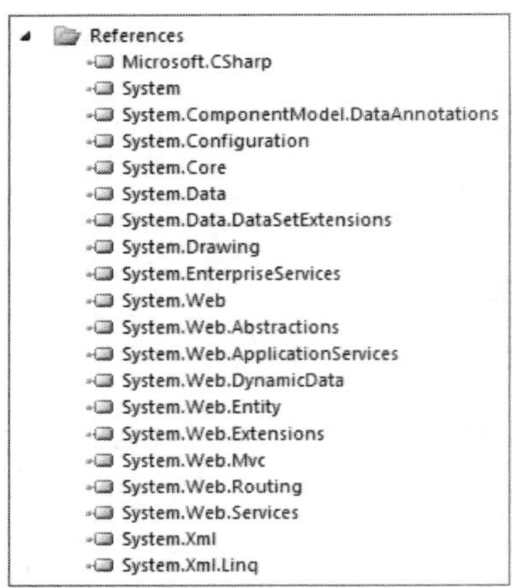

FIGURE 1-8: Assemblies referenced by an MVC project

Following are the important assemblies used by MVC:

➤ `System.Web.Mvc` — This assembly contains the core framework and a number of helper methods.

➤ `System.Web.Routing` — This assembly controls URL routing. It is in its own assembly to make routing available to Web Forms applications as well.

➤ `System.ComponentModel.DataAnnotations` — This assembly contains attributes to decorate model properties. The framework detects these attributes and automatically adds functionality to parts of the application that consume the properties.

Site Structure

Many parts of an MVC application are familiar to Web Forms developers. Take a look at the "empty" MVC project in Figure 1-9.

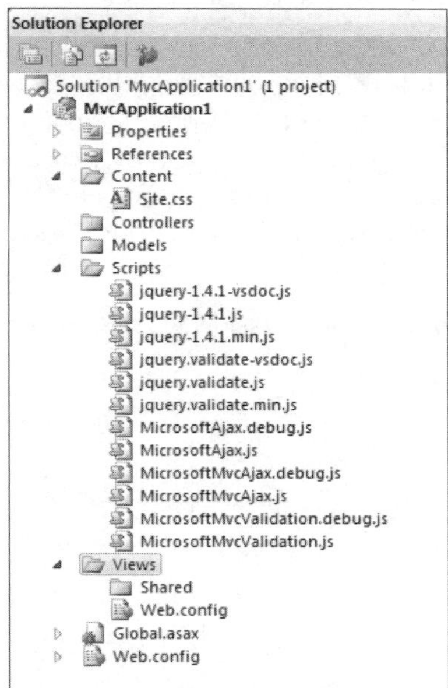

FIGURE 1-9: "Empty" MVC project

The project contains a `web.config` file and — other than references to namespaces and assemblies used by the MVC framework — it looks similar to the `web.config` file in a Web Forms application.

The project contains a `global.asax` file, where you can add code that fires when the application or session starts and stops, as well as other events in the app. MVC adds code in the `Application_Start` event handler to set up a default route, as described earlier.

Under the `Content` folder is a stylesheet file (`Site.css`) that controls fonts, colors, and other visual stylings for the site. Modifying files in this folder changes visual elements throughout the site, giving the site a consistent look and feel.

The `Scripts` folder contains mostly jQuery files. jQuery is an Open Source JavaScript library, useful for adding client-side functionality to a web application. You learn more about jQuery later in this chapter. There are a few other JavaScript files in the `Scripts` folder worth mentioning. `MicrosoftAjax.js` and `MicrosoftMvcAjax.js` provide helper methods for calling server-side code from within your web client application. `MicrosoftMvcValidation.js` provides client-side validation of user input fields.

Some pieces of a new MVC application may be unfamiliar. `Controllers`, `Models`, and `Views` folders exist for developers to add their own custom controllers, models, and views.

The `Models` folder exists as a convenience, so a developer can keep all model classes together, making them easier to find. Because classes are compiled to Intermediate Language (IL), it doesn't matter where they are physically stored. I recommend placing entity objects in a separate project and storing ViewModel classes in the `Models` folder.

Controllers also get compiled to IL, so they need to be saved in the `Controllers` folder. However, MVC provides some tooling that enables you to right-click on this folder and easily create a `Controller` class, so that alone is worth keeping all your controllers there.

By default, each view must be saved to a subfolder of the `Views` folder. MVC uses a convention to find some things, and views are one of those things. When a controller `Action` method looks for a view, there is often no need to specify the name or location of the view. MVC looks for a view with the same name as the `Action` method, and either an `ASPX` or `ASCX` extension. It looks in the `Views` folder — first in the subfolder with the same name as the controller and then in the `Shared` subfolder.

For example, when you specify the Edit view in the `CustomerController` class, MVC will look in the following locations in this order:

1. `Views/Customer/Edit.aspx`

2. `Views/Customer/Edit.ascx`

3. `Views/Shared/Edit.aspx`

4. `Views/Shared/Edit.ascx`

Adding a Controller

It is a simple matter to add a new controller to an MVC project. Right-click the `Controllers` folder in Solution Explorer and select Add ➪ Controller.

The Add Controller dialog displays, as shown in Figure 1-10.

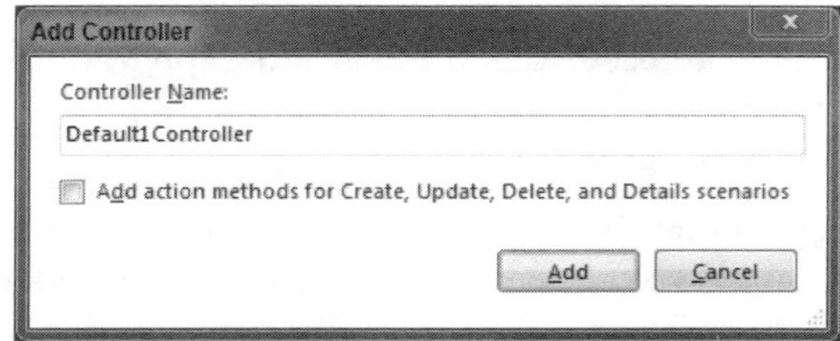

FIGURE 1-10: Add Controller dialog

A controller name must end with the word `Controller`, so the dialog provides a default name (`Default1Controller`) and highlights the first part of this name, enabling you to change it to something more meaningful.

A drop-down menu also gives you the option to allow the framework to automatically generate a set of `Action` methods to create, read, update, and delete (known as CRUD) a model entity. You may allow the tooling to fill in these methods with code that assumes you are using the Entity Framework, or you may tell the tooling to only create method stubs that you can complete later.

In either case, you can modify these `Action` methods and add more `Action` methods to the `Controller` class, as necessary.

Adding a View

When you have a controller `Action` method, the MVC tooling makes it easy to add a default view for that method. Right-click anywhere inside the method, and select Add View from the context menu. The Add View dialog displays, as shown in Figure 1-11.

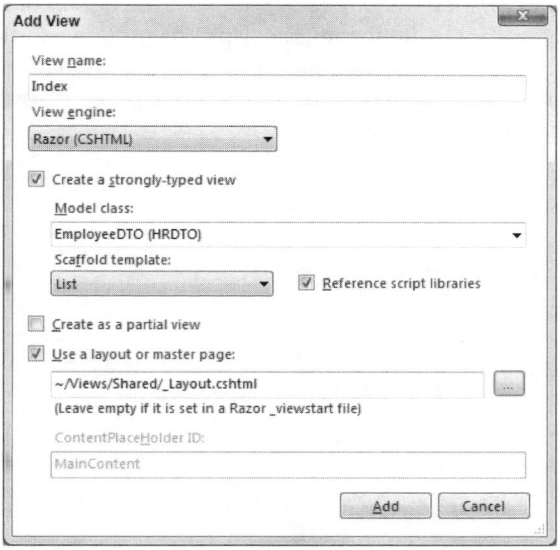

FIGURE 1-11: Add View dialog

The View Name defaults to the name of the `Action` method. This is generally acceptable because, by default, an `Action` method looks for a view matching its name.

The View Engine defaults to Razor, which is a new view engine that shipped with MVC 3. The Razor view engine enables you to create a clean template for a web page. It contains a mixture of HTML and placeholders to be filled in by the model you pass to the view.

For CRUD methods, you need to check the `Create a Strongly Typed View` check box; then select the model class you want to update and the appropriate Scaffold Template. The Scaffold Template generates HTML appropriate for editing, creating, or listing the model.

Click the Add button to create this new view. The view is created in a folder named after the controller. If that folder does not exist, it is also created.

Sample Application

A sample application can illustrate how to use the features of MVC. For this example, you create a simple application called HR designed to track information about a company's employees.

> *You can download this application (file* HR.zip*) from this book's companion website at* www.wrox.com *to see all the code described in this section.*

Sample Application Database

The sample application maintains a database containing two tables: Employees and Departments with primary keys EmployeeId and DepartmentId, respectively. The DepartmentId column of the Employees table points to a row in the Departments table, indicating the department to which the employee is assigned. A foreign key index enforces this relationship, preventing anyone from deleting a department to which any employees are assigned, and from assigning an employee to a department that does not exist. Figure 1-12 shows this relationship.

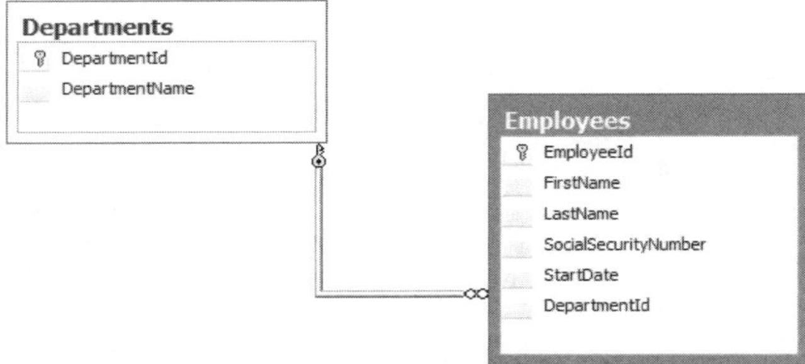

FIGURE 1-12: Relationship between database tables

Departments

Start by writing some code to maintain the Departments table.

The Departments table and the Department entity each contain only two fields — DepartmentId and DepartmentName — so the MVC framework can be demonstrated without writing a lot of business logic code.

Remember that a URL in MVC is a request for a Controller Action method. Therefore, it makes sense to start the web development by creating a Controller class.

The tooling in MVC makes this easy. You can quickly add a new controller by right-clicking the Controllers folder and selecting New ⇨ Controller. The Add Controller dialog displays, providing the option to add some method stubs to read and update data. Regardless of whether you choose to create these method stubs, a public concrete controller class is created, and this class inherits from the `ControllerBase` class, which implements `IController`. In the sample application, this class is named `DepartmentController.cs`.

Details

Take a look at the code in the `DepartmentController` class. Scroll down to the `Details` method. `Details` calls a custom method that retrieves from the database a single department by its ID. The retrieved data is an object of type `DepartmentDTO` and is saved in a variable named `department`. In this method, `department` is the model. Next, the `Action` calls the `View` helper method to generate a `ViewResult` (a subclass of `ActionResult`). By passing the model variable (`department`) to the helper method, MVC makes the model data available to the view. The view can reference this data as part of its `ViewData` before sending a response to the client.

```
public ActionResult Details(int id)
{
    var empBus = new DepartmentBusiness();
    DepartmentDTO department = empBus.GetDepartment(id);
    return View(department);
}
```

To quickly jump to the view, right-click anywhere inside the method, and select "Go to View." The `Details.aspx` page under the `Views\Department` folder opens. This page mostly contains HTML markup. But there are some directives and code that make it dynamic. The first thing to look at is the first line of the file, as shown here:

```
@model HRDTO.DepartmentDTO
```

This directive tells MVC what type of model is passed to the page. In this case, the page expects a model of type `HRDTO.DepartmentDTO`.

Because the page knows what class of model is passed to it, the `Model` variable is strongly typed and has all the properties of a `Department` object. Even IntelliSense works on the page. When you type **Model** and press **.**, the properties of a `Department` (for example, `Id` and `Name`) are listed.

Server-side code in the `ASPX` page is preceded by the special `@` character. As you can see, it is possible to switch back and forth between server-side code and HTML. In the `Details.aspx` page, you have server-side code to render the properties of the model. For example, the following code is in `Department.aspx`:

```
@Model.DepartmentName
```

This outputs to the client browser the `DepartmentName` property of the `DepartmentDTO` object (the model) that was passed to this page.

By default, MVC will `HTMLEncode` any dynamic output before rendering it. This helps to prevent malicious scripting on your site. If the displayed data is retrieved from a database, someone may store malicious JavaScript in that database. When the JavaScript is rendered to a browser, the default behavior is to execute that script. Using `HTMLEncode` reduces this risk by encoding certain characters before rendering them. For example, < is replaced with `<` and > is replaced with `>`. Unless I have a reason not to, I always encode any output generated dynamically for the client.

MVC contains a number of helper methods to make it easier to render objects in a view. This page contains the following code:

```
@Html.ActionLink("Edit", "Edit", new { id=Model.DepartmentId })
```

This code generates a hyperlink with the text "Edit" and a link pointing to the `Edit Action` method in the current controller, and passing in an `id` parameter with a value of the current page's `DeparmentID`.

MVC provides other helper methods. The following methods each generate an HTML element, based on an attribute in a model passed to the view. It should be self-evident what HTML element each method renders.

- `Html.TextBoxFor()`
- `Html.TextAreaFor()`
- `Html.DropDownListFor()`
- `Html.CheckboxFor()`
- `Html.RadioButtonFor()`
- `Html.ListBoxFor()`
- `Html.PasswordFor()`
- `Html.HiddenFor()`
- `Html.LabelFor()`

Index

The `Index Action` method returns a `List` of all the `Department` objects, which is sent to the view engine to be merged with the view.

```
var empBus = new DepartmentBusiness();
List<DepartmentDTO> departments = empBus.GetAllDepartments();
return View(departments);
```

Look at the view and you can see it expects an `IEnumerable<HRDTO.DepartmentDTO>`.

```
@model IEnumerable<HRDTO.DepartmentDTO>
```

This matches the data sent from the action method, which sent down a `List` of `DepartmentDTO` objects with the view. Server-side C# code in this page iterates through this list of departments to output each department individually.

```
<table>
 <tr>
  <th></th>
  <th>Department ID</th>
  <th>Department Name</th>
 </tr>
@foreach (var item in Model) {
    <tr>
        <td>
```

```
            @Html.ActionLink
                ("Edit",
                "Edit",
                new { id=item.DepartmentId }) |
            @Html.ActionLink
                ("Details",
                 "Details",
                 new { id = item.DepartmentId }) |
            @Html.ActionLink
                ("Delete",
                 "Delete",
                 new { id = item.DepartmentId })
        </td>
        <td>
            @item.DepartmentId
        </td>
        <td>
            @item.DepartmentName
        </td>
    </tr>
}
```

The page code switches between server-side C# code and client-side HTML. The Razor view engine knows to begin interpreting code as server-side when it encounters the @ symbol. It figures when to stop based on the context. The server-side code runs first, causing the HTML to be output multiple times — once for each item in the list.

Edit

The `Edit Action` method looks like the details method. It returns a single `Department`. In this case, the `DepartmentDTO` is contained in a `DepartmentViewModel` object. I'll explain more about ViewModels later, but for now, the only thing you need to know is that the `DepartmentViewModel` object contains a `Department` property that is a `DepartmentDTO` object.

```csharp
public ActionResult Edit(int id)
{
    var empBus = new DepartmentBusiness();
    DepartmentDTO department = empBus.GetDepartment(id);
    var deptViewModel = new DepartmentViewModel()
    {
        Department = department
    };
    return View(deptViewModel);
}
```

In this case, you return something called a ViewModel. A ViewModel is data specific to a view. No other application uses the `DepartmentViewModel` other than this MVC application. You can find the `DepartmentViewModel` in the `Models` folder. It looks similar to the `DepartmentDTO`, but special attributes decorate the properties of the ViewModel.

```csharp
public class DepartmentViewModel
{
    [DisplayName("Department ID")]
    public int DepartmentId { get; set; }
```

```
[Required(ErrorMessage="Please provide a name for this department")]
[DisplayName("Department Name")]
public string DepartmentName { get; set; }

}
```

These attributes are recognized by the MVC view engine. Look at the view associated with editing a `Department` (`Views/Department/Edit.aspx`).

```
@using (Html.BeginForm()) {
    @Html.ValidationSummary(true)
    <fieldset>
        <legend>Department</legend>

        @Html.HiddenFor(model => model.Department.DepartmentId)

        <div class="editor-label">
            @Html.LabelFor(model => model.Department.DepartmentId)
        </div>
        <div class="editor-field">
            @Model.Department.DepartmentId
        </div>

        <div class="editor-label">
            @Html.LabelFor(model => model.Department.DepartmentName)
        </div>
        <div class="editor-field">
            @Html.EditorFor(model => model.Department.DepartmentName)
            @Html.ValidationMessageFor
                (model => model.Department.DepartmentName)
        </div>

        <p>
            <input type="submit" value="Save" />
        </p>
    </fieldset>
}
```

The following line uses the MVC attributes:

```
@Html.LabelFor(model => model.Department.DepartmentId)
```

The `LabelFor` helper method outputs an HTML label for the `DepartmentID` property. In this case, the text of the label is determined by the `DisplayName` attribute decorating this property in the ViewModel. So, a label with the text "Department ID" renders. If the model's (or ViewModel's) class is not decorated with an attribute, the property name (`DepartmentId`) displays by default.

Another place where model attributes are used on this page is to validate input. In the ViewModel, the `DepartmentName` property is decorated with the `Required` attribute, as shown here:

```
[Required(ErrorMessage="Please provide a name for this department")]
```

The `Required` attribute comes from the `System.ComponentModel.DataAnnotations` assembly, so you must add a reference to this assembly in your project. This tells the view engine that the user must enter a nonempty `DepartmentName`. If a user tries to submit the form, the submission will be halted.

For the view to take full advantage of this validation, several helper methods output error messages when validation fails. The model property's `Required` attribute includes an error message argument ("Please Provide a Name for This Department"). Below the `DepartmentName`'s textbox in the view, the `ValidationMessageFor` helper method is called to output this message when a user tries to submit a form without a valid `DepartmentName`:

```
@Html.ValidationMessageFor(model => model.DepartmentName)
```

The view also includes a helper method to summarize all validation errors on the page.

```
@Html.ValidationSummary(true)
```

If multiple validation errors occur, all error messages will be listed here in the Validation Summary, so the user can see them all at once and deal with them at the same time.

Following are some `Validation` attributes that you can place on a `Model` property:

➤ `[Required]` — Input is required (see the earlier example).

➤ `[StringLength]` — String properties only. Validation fails if the length of a string is greater than specified.

➤ `[RegularExpression]` — Input must match the pattern defined in a given Regular Expression (regex).

➤ `[Range]` — Numeric properties only. Input must fall within a specified range.

➤ `[DataType]` — Input must be of a given data type.

The other thing to note about the `Edit.aspx` view is this line:

```
@using (Html.BeginForm()) {
```

The content between the beginning and ending braces ({ and }) will be wrapped in an HTML `<form>` tag, defining what will POST back to the same URL.

So, if the form posts to the same URL, it should call the same `Action` method, right? Well…that's almost true. As mentioned earlier, a URL is routed to a given `Action` method. But it is possible to have two `Action` methods with the same name. When MVC posts a form to a URL and two `Action` methods match the routing pattern, it first chooses a method decorated with the `[HttpPost]` attribute. The `DepartmentController` contains an `Edit` method decorated in just this way.

```
[HttpPost]
public ActionResult Edit(DepartmentViewModel departmentVm)
{
    DepartmentDTO department = departmentVm.Department;
    if (ModelState.IsValid)
    {
        try
        {
            var empBus = new DepartmentBusiness();
            empBus.UpdateDepartment(department);
            return RedirectToAction
                ("Details",
                 new { id = department.DepartmentId });
        }
```

```
        catch
        {
            return View(departmentVm);
        }
    }
    else
    {
        return View(departmentVm);
    }
}
```

Several options exist for the signature of this `Action` method. For example, if the method parameter is a `System.Web.Mvc.FormCollection`, it is populated with name-value pairs, matching each of the elements submitted with the form. This is the default MVC uses to auto-generate `Action` methods.

I prefer my `HttpPost` form methods to accept a `ViewModel` object of the same type that was originally passed to the Edit view. This works because MVC looks at the parameters and at the posted form data and then does its best to match them up. With a `ViewModel` parameter (in this case, a `DepartmentViewModel`), all data is strongly typed making the code more type-safe.

The `HttpPost Edit` method is called when the Edit form is posted. The first thing the method does is ensure that validation succeeded, based on the `Data Annotation` attributes added to the model. If so, the `Edit` method calls a helper method to save changes back to the database.

Employees

Maintaining `Employees` is more complex than maintaining `Departments` because the `Department ID` of each `Employee` must be validated against the `Departments` table.

Ideally, when editing or creating an `Employee`, users should select a `Department` from a drop-down list of valid departments, making it impossible to select an invalid `Department`. You can accomplish this by creating a ViewModel that contains information about a single `Employee`, as well as a list of all valid departments, bundling all this data together, and passing it all down to the view.

The `EmployeeViewModel` is just such a ViewModel. It contains both an `Employee` object and a `List` of departments.

```
public class EmployeeViewModel
{
    public EmployeeDTO Employee { get; set; }
    public List<DepartmentDTO> AllDepartments { get; set; }
}
```

The `Edit` action method of `EmployeeController` retrieves the current `Employee` and a `List` of all departments. The `EmployeeViewModel` is populated with these objects before it is sent to the view.

```
public ActionResult Edit(int id)
{
    var empBus = new EmployeeBusiness();
    EmployeeDTO employeeDto = empBus.GetEmployee(id);
    var deptBus = new DepartmentBusiness();
    List<DepartmentDTO> allDepartments = deptBus.GetAllDepartments();
    EmployeeViewModel empVm = employeeDto.TransformToViewModel();
```

```
empVm.AllDepartments = Transformations.
    TransformToViewModelsList(allDepartments);
return View(empVm);
    }
```

The view (`Employee/Edit.aspx`) renders the `Employee` form similar to how the `Department` view was rendered. The difference is in how it constructs a drop-down list containing all departments and binds the selected item to the `Employee`'s `DepartmentID` property.

```
@Html.DropDownListFor(
    model => model.Employee.DepartmentId,
    new SelectList(Model.AllDepartments, "DepartmentId", "DepartmentName"))
```

The `DropDownListFor` helper method renders an HTML drop-down and binds it to a property. The second parameter of this helper method is a `SelectList` — an MVC class that generates a drop-down list given the data, the ID column, and the text column. The data comes from `Model. AllDepartments` because the `EmployeeViewModel` contains an `AllDepartments` property that was populated in the controller action.

The `HttpPost Edit` method looks much like the `HttpPost Edit` method in `DepartmentController`.

```
[HttpPost]
public ActionResult Edit(EmployeeViewModel employeeVm)
{
    if (ModelState.IsValid)
    {
        try
        {
            EmployeeDTO employee = employeeVm.Employee;
            var empBus = new EmployeeBusiness();
            empBus.UpdateEmployee(employee);
            return RedirectToAction
                ("Details", new { id = employee.EmployeeId });
        }
        catch
        {
            return View(employeeVm);
        }
    }
    else
    {
        return View(employeeVm);
    }
}
```

You don't need to do anything special here because all data is automatically bound to the `Employee ViewModel`.

ASP.NET MVC Framework Summary

This section introduced the new ASP.NET MVC framework, explained the advantages of MVC, showed some of the useful features of this framework, and walked through a simple application.

JQUERY

Because web forms have been around for a long time, developers can find countless user controls to enhance their web applications. Microsoft and numerous third-party vendors have produced libraries of rich controls to provide extra functionality to ASP.NET websites.

Many of these Web Forms controls rely on page events and code-behind. Therefore, they do not work with the new ASP.NET MVC paradigm.

Developers can still enhance their applications by adding rich client-side interactions using JavaScript. Many of the same component vendors who built Web Forms controls are working on and releasing controls designed for MVC. In many cases, they use JavaScript to provide client-side interactivity.

JavaScript is an excellent tool to interact with a web page because of the following reasons:

➤   It is a standard language that runs within all modern desktop browsers.

➤   It interacts with the Document Object Model (DOM) exposed by a web page, allowing web developers to manipulate the objects on a page.

➤   It has a rich event model for building interactive applications.

Unfortunately, JavaScript has several disadvantages that have limited its usefulness and popularity, including the following:

➤   The learning curve for JavaScript can be steep for some developers.

➤   Each browser has its own implementation of the DOM, forcing developers to write and test the same functionality multiple times to ensure the code runs correctly in a variety of browsers.

Several libraries have been built on top of JavaScript to address these disadvantages. These libraries abstract away the complexity of JavaScript, and (more important) automatically detect and handle the differences interacting with the variety of DOM implementations among the major browsers.

jQuery is an Open Source JavaScript library that has gained a lot of popularity in recent years, thanks to its rich set of functions and ease of use. With Visual Studio 2010, Microsoft made the decision to include jQuery with the product, which has boosted its popularity even more.

A new ASP.NET MVC project includes a `Scripts` folder that contains a dozen `.js` files. These files contain jQuery functions that the project's web pages can call. You can replace these files with new versions downloaded from `http://jquery.com`. Each filename contains a number (such as `1.4.1`) just before the file extension. This is the version number of jQuery with which the script file is associated. This naming convention makes it easy to tell which version of jQuery a site is running.

To use jQuery in a view page, reference either files in the `Scripts` folder or files hosted on a Content Delivery Network (CDN), such as the one hosted by Microsoft at `http://ajax.microsoft.com/ajax/jquery`. The jQuery script files (for example, `jquery-1.4.4.min.js`) are stored in this folder. Link to each `.js` file you wish to use on your page.

Each location typically contains two versions of each file: one ending in `.js` and one ending in `.min.js`. The `.min.js` version is a minified version of the script, meaning that comments and excess white space have been removed, and variable and function names have been shortened. I always use the minified versions because they are smaller and, therefore, faster to download to the client.

Add the following line to the top of the page to make jQuery functionality available:

```
<script src="[FULL_SCRIPT_PATH]" type="text/javascript"></script>
```

In this snippet, `[FULL_SCRIPT_PATH]` is the path and filename of the script file used by the page.

For example, add the following line to use the main `jquery` file in the project's `Scripts` folder from within the sample site's master page (`Shared_Layout.cshtml`):

```
<script
    src="@Url.Content("~/Scripts/jquery-1.4.4.min.js")"
    type="text/javascript"></script>
```

The `Url.Content` method specifies an absolute path, so that the .js file will be found, regardless which view is rendered, and in which folder that view is found. I prefer to reference this script from my site's master pages.

The jQuery code described in this section is included in the sample applications file (`HR.zip`) available for download on this book's companion website at `www.wrox.com`.

JQuery code is simply JavaScript. Therefore, all jQuery code belongs within `<script language="javascript"></script>` tags.

A common pattern for jQuery syntax is as follows:

```
$(Selector).Event(Action);
```

In this snippet, `$` is simply the dollar sign character, which represents the `jQuery` object; `Selector` is a jQuery selector function (more on this later); `Event` is an event fired by the selected objects; and `Action` is the code to run when the event fires.

Each call to a jQuery function begins with the `$` symbol. This symbol indicates that the JavaScript that follows is jQuery syntax. You can replace the `$` with the keyword `jQuery`, but `$` is far more terse.

A jQuery selector uses syntax similar to the selectors in CSS and always returns a collection of elements that match the selector criteria. The selector syntax can take several forms:

➤ Enclosing a tag name in quotation marks selects all elements of a given tag. For example, `("div")` selects all `div` elements on a page.

➤ Preceding a string with # selects an element by its ID. For example, `("#custIdLabel")` selects an element with the ID `custIdLabel`. It would select multiple elements with this ID if you were foolish enough to have multiple elements on your page with the same ID.

➤ Preceding a string with . selects all elements to which a given class has been applied. For example, (".bodyText") selects an element with the class bodyText.

➤ You can select elements within elements by separating selectors with a space. For example, ("headerDiv a") selects anchor tags contained within an element named headerDiv.

Sometimes, the action might be to bind a function to an event, so that function's code runs when the event is fired. The most common way to do this is to bind an anonymous function to the ready event of the document. For example, the following jQuery code displays an alert message when the user selects the text within a Div with an ID of MyDiv:

```
$("#MyDiv").click(function () {
    alert("You clicked me");
});
```

jQuery code often starts by binding code to the ready event of the document object. The document object represents a page's entire DOM, and the ready event fires when all the elements of the DOM are loaded into memory, making it an ideal time to manipulate elements, or wire up any other events.

Manipulating DOM Elements with jQuery

Take a look at the DemoClick.htm page in the sample project. Following are the relevant parts:

```
<script type="text/javascript" language="javascript">
    $(document).ready(function () {
        $("#Img1").click(function () {
            var newHeight = $(this).height() + 20;
            $(this).height(newHeight);
        });
    });
</script>
...
<img id="Img1" height="50" src="../Images/Grin.png" alt="Click to grow" />
```

The page contains an image tag with the ID "Img1". The JavaScript binds an anonymous function to the document.ready event. The document.ready event fires when the browser has loaded into memory all the objects in the page's DOM. In jQuery, you may shorten $(document) .ready(function() to the more terse syntax $(function(), which I will do in later examples.

This anonymous function binds another function to the click event of the Img1 image.

```
$("#Img1").click(function () {
```

Notice the selector: $("#Img1"). The # symbol preceding "Img1" tells jQuery to search for any elements with an ID of "Img1". A selector returns a set of elements matching the selection criteria. In this case, the selector finds one such element on the page, so it returns a set containing that one matching element. The code then binds an anonymous function to the click event of the matching element. The code of the anonymous function is as follows:

```
var newHeight = $(this).height() + 20;
$(this).height(newHeight);
```

In this code, the variable `newHeight` is declared and assigned. The code uses the keyword `this` to identify the element that fired the event. In this case, it is the image element that fired the `click` event, so `$(this)` refers to the image element. The code retrieves the height of the image element and increments it by 20 pixels before assigning this sum to the `newHeight` variable.

The result is a page that displays an image. Each time the user clicks the image, it grows 20 pixels larger.

Calling Server Code with jQuery

A powerful use of jQuery is its capability to call RESTful web services on the server. This gives a web application the capability to call server code without posting back an entire page.

ASP.NET MVC provides a simple way to expose RESTful services that can be called from jQuery. Recall that each `Controller Action` method returns an `ActionResult` object. The MVC framework provides the `JsonResult` class — a subclass of `ActionResult` that returns data in the JSON format. JSON is a lightweight, text-based data format designed for transmitting data across the web.

The `EmployeeController` class in the `HR` sample application contains a `GetAllEmployees` action method that returns a `JsonResult` object. Following is the code:

```
public JsonResult GetAllDepartments()
{
    var empBus = new DepartmentBusiness();
    List<DepartmentDTO> departments = empBus.GetAllDepartments();
    return Json(departments, JsonRequestBehavior.AllowGet);
}
```

This code looks similar to the `GetAllDepartments` method in the `DepartmentController` class. The difference is that the last line uses the `Json` helper method to pass to the view engine a `JsonResult` object, instead of a `ViewResult` object. The result is that data is sent to the client as JSON — a data format that is small and self-describing, and, therefore, well-suited for passing data between client and server.

```
return Json(departments, JsonRequestBehavior.AllowGet);
```

The `Json` method here passes the list of departments down to the view engine. The second parameter of the method enables this service method to be called via HTTP GET. By default, only POST methods are enabled.

This method can be called directly from a jQuery script on a web page without refreshing that page. The `EditJQ.aspx` page contains the following script:

```
$ (function () {
    var url = "/Employee/GetAllDepartments";
    $.getJSON(
        url,
        null,
        function (data) {
        var options = "";
        for (var i = 0; i < data.length; i++) {
```

```
            options += "<option value=" + data[i].DepartmentId + ">"
            + data[i].DepartmentName + "</option>";
        }
        $("#DepartmentSelect").append(options);
    });
});
```

When the document's `ready` event fires, the script calls the jQuery `getJSON` function, which calls the RESTful web service function `GetAllDepartments`. The last parameter of `getJSON` is a callback function that runs after the web service returns. The `data` parameter is the return value from the web service — in this case, a `List` of departments.

The selector `$("#DepartmentSelect")` selects an empty drop-down list on the page with the ID `DepartmentSelect`. The function loops through the list of departments and builds up an `option` tag for each department. It then appends the list of `option` tags to the empty drop-down list.

jQuery

This section introduced jQuery, described the basic syntax of jQuery, and discussed how use jQuery to call RESTful web services from client-side code.

This discussion has just scratched the surface of this powerful framework by showing a couple of simple examples. You can get more detailed information by exploring the online documentation at `http://docs.jquery.com`.

SUMMARY

This chapter examined some of the new features introduced in ASP.NET 4.0. You learned about enhanced ways of handling `View State` in a web application, the new `web.config` transformations, and improvements to the web application templates (including a simpler `web.config` and more options when creating a new web application).

You also learned about the latest version of the ASP.NET MVC framework. You learned the basic concepts in an MVC application, and saw a sample application built with this framework.

You also learned about jQuery — a tool for enhancing your web applications. The chapter showed how to use jQuery to select and manipulate objects on a web page, and how to call server-side code from client-side script on your web page.

ABOUT THE AUTHOR

David Giard has been developing solutions using Microsoft technologies since 1993. He is a Microsoft Most Valuable Professional (MVP), an International .NET Association (INETA) mentor, and the President of the Great Lakes Area .NET Users Group. He has presented at numerous conferences and user groups. Giard is a recovering certification addict, and holds an MCTS, MCSD, MCSE, and MCDBA, as well as a BS and an MBA. He is the host and producer of the mildly popular online TV show "Technology and Friends." You can read his latest thoughts at `www.DavidGiard.com`. Giard lives in Michigan with his two teenage sons.

2

ASP.NET Performance

by Bill Evjen

It is one thing to know how to build an ASP.NET application and get everything working as you want. It is another thing to get it working well. As you build web applications today, you must also ensure that the choices you make in the construction of the application also work well with regard to the overall performance of the application.

As your web application takes on more user load, you have options for how you want to deal with the growth. The choices you have can be made either via the code of your application, or via actual hardware changes.

This chapter covers a lot of different ground, but all the items mentioned here have a direct impact on the overall performance of your ASP.NET applications.

This chapter includes discussions on how to deal with state management and caching. Also touched upon are hardware considerations and configuration for your server. Finally, this chapter covers how to monitor your application's performance, because this will help you fine-tune what is wrong, or what could be improved.

LOOKING AT HOW ASP.NET HANDLES PAGE REQUESTS

Before starting on some of the items you can do to your applications to help with performance, it is first important to understand how ASP.NET handles page requests. ASP.NET compiles your ASP.NET pages (`.aspx`) as they are referenced (for example, by an end user in the browser).

When an ASP.NET page is referenced in the browser for the first time, the request is passed to the ASP.NET parser that creates the class file in the language of the page. It is passed to the ASP.NET parser based on the file's extension (`.aspx`) because ASP.NET realizes that this file extension type is meant for its handling and processing. After the class file has been created, the class file is compiled into a dynamic link library (DLL) and then written to the disk of the web server. At this point, the DLL is instantiated and processed, and an output is generated for the initial requester of the ASP.NET page. Figure 2-1 shows the details of this process.

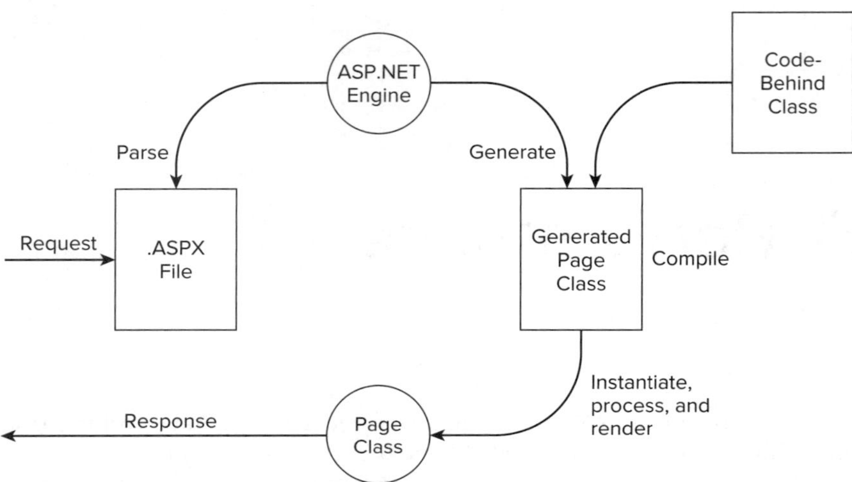

FIGURE 2-1: How ASP.NET handles the initial request

On the next request, great things happen. Instead of going through the entire process again for the second and respective requests, the request simply causes an instantiation of the already-created DLL, which sends out a response to the requester. Figure 2-2 shows how this is done.

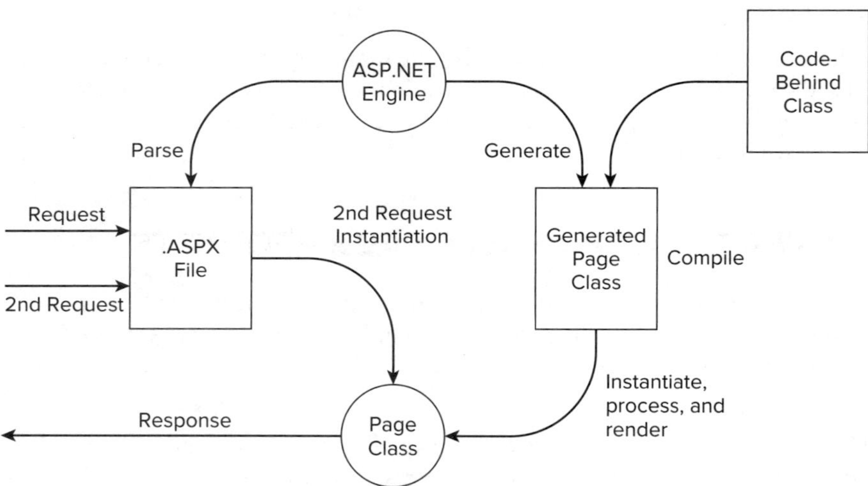

FIGURE 2-2: How ASP.NET handles subsequent requests

Because of the mechanics of this process, if you make changes to your `.aspx` code-behind pages, you must recompile your application. This can be quite a pain if you have a larger site and do not want your end users to experience the extreme lag that occurs when an `.aspx` page is referenced for the first time after compilation. Consequently, many developers have created their own tools that automatically hit every single page within their application to remove this first-time lag hit from the end user's browsing experience.

ASP.NET provides a few ways to precompile your entire application with a single command that you can issue through a command line. One type of compilation is referred to as *in-place precompilation*.

To precompile your entire ASP.NET application, you must use the `aspnet_compiler.exe` tool that comes with ASP.NET. To get to this tool, you will need to navigate to it using the Command window. From the Command window, navigate to `C:\Windows\Microsoft.NET\Framework\v4.0.30319\`. When you are there, you can work with the `aspnet_compiler` tool. You can also get to this tool directly by pulling up the Visual Studio 2010 Command Prompt. Choose Start ➪ All Programs ➪ Microsoft Visual Studio 2010 ➪ Visual Studio Tools ➪ Visual Studio Command Prompt (2010).

After you get the command prompt open, enter the following command:

```
aspnet_compiler -p "C:\Inetpub\wwwroot\WROX" -v none
```

You then get a message stating that the precompilation is successful.

Another great thing about this precompilation capability is that you can also use it to find errors on any of the ASP.NET pages in your application. Because it hits each and every page, if one of the pages contains an error that won't be triggered until runtime, you are notified of the error immediately as you employ this precompilation method.

The next section looks at a couple of the more important aspects of the performance of your applications — state management and caching. Getting these items right from the start is vital for your application.

STATE MANAGEMENT AND CACHING

Simply put, building ASP.NET applications is more difficult than with other types of applications (such as building a Windows Forms application) primarily because web applications are a stateless type of application.

The Internet is *stateless* by nature. You are simply making requests and responses (generally using the Hypertext Transfer Protocol, or HTTP). The server receives an HTTP request for a particular page, and sends the caller the requested page (the response). The server that is sending the response does not keep track of who made the request. Every request is equal in the server's eyes.

When the same calling application makes a second request, the server gives it the second piece of information, but still does not house any information about this calling application. The server does not know that this application is the same one that just recently requested the first piece of logic.

This creates a problem if you want your web application to remember information about the calling application. Remembering the calling application and being able to make a distinction between requests allows end users to work through an application in a continuous manner. You may want your application to retain certain information — who the users are, their preferences, or any other pertinent information about them — as they make multiple requests. You do this by using varying techniques that you can apply throughout your web application's code.

One of the common techniques of the past and present is to use the `Session` object. But by simply using ASP.NET, you have so much more at your disposal. ASP.NET offers a wide variety of features and techniques to apply when working with state management. You might have used many of these techniques with web applications that you developed in the past.

On the other hand, caching, although also focused on storing information, is a means to provide a better experience for your end users by making the application load and perform faster than otherwise. One of the best things you can do for your ASP.NET application is to build an application that has a good caching strategy.

Understanding State in .NET

If you are working with state management in your web application, it is important to understand *state* as it works within .NET as a whole. The .NET Framework and ASP.NET provide a plethora of options when dealing with state. Table 2-1 describes some of your server-side options.

TABLE 2-1: Server-Side Options

SESSION TYPE	DESCRIPTION
Application	Using the `Application` object, you can store state that is applicable to all users. You are unable to use this for providing different state options to different users.
Cache	Using the `Cache` object, you are able to also store state for every user of the application. This object supports the capability to expire the cache, and it also provides the capability to set dependencies on how the cache is expired.
Database-driven Session	This is a means of using the `Session` object and having all the states stored safely on a SQL server.
Session	Using the `Session` object, you are capable of storing state on the server on a per-user basis. The `Session` object allows you to store the state in-process (in the same process as the application), out-of-process (in a different process), or even using the aforementioned database approach.

If it were all about the server-side options, it would not be that long of a story to tell. ASP.NET also includes a good list of client-side state management techniques that make the process of storing state rather easy. Table 2-2 defines your client-side options.

TABLE 2-2: Client-Side Options

SESSION TYPE	DESCRIPTION
`ControlState`	This provides a means of providing state to controls (for the control developer) that is quite similar to `View State`.
`Cookie`	This provides a means of storing state directly in the file system of the client. Cookies can be rejected by clients.
`Hidden Field`	Using hidden fields, you can store state for a user directly in the code of the page to use on subsequent requests that are posted back to the server.
`querystring`	Using the `querystring` capabilities provided, you are able to store state within the actual URL on a per-user basis.
`View State`	This provides the capability to use encoded state within the page code.

As you can see, there are a number of ways to work with state (not even all of them are listed). It is important to understand that there isn't a right or wrong way to work with state. It really has a lot to do with what you are trying to achieve and work with in your application.

Working with Sessions

Sessions within an ASP.NET application enable users to easily maintain application state. Sessions will remain with the user as he or she works through repeated calls to an application for a defined period. Sessions also provide a great way to improve overall performance, as opposed to re-looking up the state over and over again from a data store of some kind.

However, using sessions comes with a warning. One of the best ways to improve the performance of your ASP.NET applications is to fan-out the hardware on which they run (that is, adding additional web servers). Using sessions incorrectly will result in an application that won't work in this fan-out model. If you are taking this approach, you should look at either using *sticky-routing* (making sure that all subsequent requests from the user go to the same machine repeatedly), or using a state server of some kind for central storage of sessions. When using the `Session` object incorrectly (that is, not building them with an anticipation of a fan-out model), the other servers that are dealing with the subsequent requests won't know anything about the stored `Session` request. This will be discussed shortly.

Sessions are easily created, and it is just as easy to retrieve information from them. Use the following code to create a session for the user or calling application that can be accessed later in the application, or to assign a value to an already established session:

```
Session["EmployeeID"] = Value1;
```

This will assign what was being held in the variable `Value1` to the `EmployeeID` `Session` object. To retrieve this information from the session and then use it in your code, use the following:

```
Value2 = Session["EmployeeID"];
```

In ASP.NET, a session would time out on the user after 20 minutes. If the user opened a page within a web application (thereby creating a session), and then walked away for a cup of coffee, when the user came back to the page 40 minutes later, the session would not be there for him or her. You could get around this by going into the server and changing the time allotted to the session timeout property, but this is cumbersome, and requires that you stop the server and then start it again for the changes to take effect. In addition, because sessions are resource-intensive, you would not want to store too many sessions for too long.

ASP.NET allows you to change the session `timeout` property quite easily. On the application level, it is stored in the `web.config` file. The `machine.config` file stores the default timeout setting for the entire server. By changing the setting in the `web.config` file, you can effectively change the `timeout` property of sessions within the application.

The great thing about changing this property within this XML application file is that the server does not have to be stopped and started for the changes to take effect. After the `web.config` file is saved with its changes, the changes take effect immediately. It is important to note though that when you do this, the application domain is indirectly restarted, and all state information is lost, including all the contents of the `Session` object.

Listing 2-1 shows the part of the `web.config` file that deals with session state management — the `<sessionState>` node.

LISTING 2-1: Reviewing the <sessionState> Element in the web.config File

```
<sessionState
   mode="InProc"
   stateConnectionString="tcpip=127.0.0.1:42424"
   sqlConnectionString="data source=127.0.0.1;user id=sa;password="
   cookieless="false"
   timeout="20" />
```

The `<sessionState>` node of the `web.config` file is where session state is managed. The property that you are concerned with now is the `timeout` property.

The `timeout` property is set to `20` (the default setting). This setting represents minutes of time. Therefore, if you want the users' sessions to last for one hour, you set the `timeout` property to `60`.

Running Sessions In-Process

Presently, the default setting for sessions in ASP.NET stores the sessions in the *in-process mode*. Running sessions in-process means that the sessions are stored in the same process as the ASP.NET worker process. Therefore, if Internet Information Services (IIS) is shut down and then brought back up again, all sessions are destroyed and unavailable to users. On mission-critical web applications, this can be a nightmare.

To run the sessions in-process, set the `mode` property in the `<sessionState>` node to `InProc`. Running sessions in-process provides the application with the best possible performance.

Table 2-3 describes all the available session modes.

TABLE 2-3: Available Session Modes

MODE	DESCRIPTION
InProc	Session state is in-process with the ASP.NET worker process. Running sessions InProc is the default setting.
Off	Session state is not available.
StateServer	Session state is using an out-of-process server to store state.
SQLServer	Session state is using an out-of-process SQL Server to store state.

Running Sessions Out of Process

It is possible to run sessions *out of process*. Running a session out of process allows IIS to be stopped and then restarted, while maintaining the user's sessions.

Along with the .NET Framework is a Windows service called ASPState. This service enables you to run sessions out of process, but it must be started in order to use it to manage sessions.

To start the ASPState service, open the command prompt (Start ➪ Programs ➪ Accessories ➪ Command Prompt). At the command prompt, type the following command and press Enter:

```
CD \WINDOWS\Microsoft.NET\Framework\v4.0.30319
```

This changes the directory of the command prompt. After typing that line in the command prompt, enter the following:

```
net start aspnet_state
```

This turns on the session out-of-process capabilities, as shown in Figure 2-3.

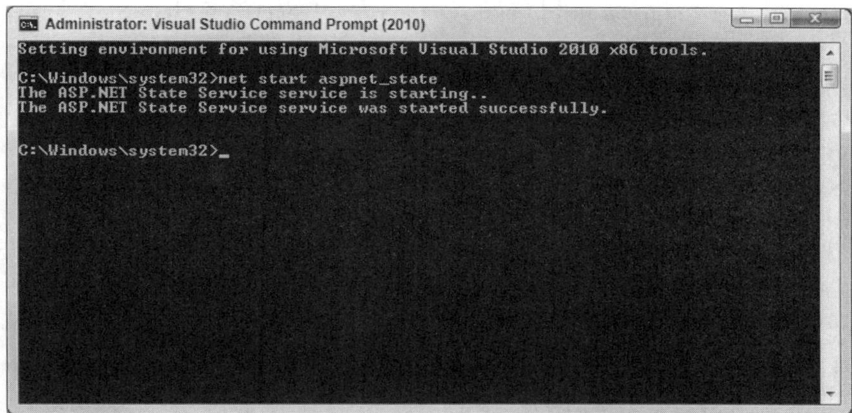

FIGURE 2-3: Turning on the session out-of-process capabilities

Once the out-of-process mode is enabled, you can change the settings in the `<sessionState>` node of the `web.config` file so that all the users' sessions are run in this manner. You do this by setting the `mode` to `StateServer`, as shown in Listing 2-2.

LISTING 2-2: Setting the Session Object to Use the StateServer Option

```
<sessionState
    mode="StateServer"
    stateConnectionString="tcpip=127.0.0.1:42424"
    sqlConnectionString="data source=127.0.0.1;user id=sa;password="
    cookieless="false"
    timeout="20" />
```

Now the user can turn off IIS and then on again, and his or her sessions will remain intact, although doing this is a little more resource-intensive than running the sessions in-process.

If the mode is set to `StateServer`, the server looks to the `stateConnectionString` property to assign the sessions to a specified server and port. In this case, it is set to the local server (which is the default setting). You can easily change this so that the sessions are stored on a completely separate server.

Running sessions out of process provides a great advantage with ASP.NET. This is a great tool when running web applications in a web farm where you are unsure to which server the user will be directed. This gives you the capability to move users from one server to another, and yet maintain their states.

Maintaining Sessions on SQL Server

Another option to run sessions out of process is to employ SQL Server to store the user sessions. Storing sessions in SQL Server also enables users to move from one server to another and maintain their states. It is the same as the `StateServer` mode, but instead stores the sessions in SQL Server.

If you installed the .NET Framework, you also installed a mini-version of SQL Server on your computer. This SQL Server-lite version enables you to store your sessions to use for state management. However, it is recommended that you use a full-blown version of SQL Server, such as SQL Server 2008. This is a more dependable solution.

The first thing to do to use SQL Server as a repository for your sessions is to create the database within SQL that ASP.NET can use. Included in the version folder of ASP.NET (found at `C:\WINDOWS\Microsoft.NET\Framework\v4.0.30319`) are two scripts that work with SQL Server session management. The first is the install script, `InstallSqlState.sql`. This script tells SQL Server which database tables and procedures to create. You can look at the script instructions, which are quite readable, by opening the script in Notepad.

If you ever wish to remove these tables and stored procedures from SQL Server, use the uninstall script, `UninstallSqlState.sql`.

If you wish to use SQL Server to manage your sessions, run the install script. To do this, open up the command prompt again and navigate to the version folder of ASP.NET that you are running. On the command line, enter the following:

```
OSQL -S localhost -U sa -P -I InstallSqlState.sql
```

The OSQL utility enables you to enter Transact-SQL statements, system procedures, and script files. This utility uses Open Database Connectivity (ODBC) to communicate with the server. Running this command creates the tables and procedures needed to run the SQL Server session management option. The notation -S in the command line is specifying the location of the server that is to be used. In this case, you are using localhost, meaning your local server.

The notation -U refers to the SQL server's assigned username to gain access. In this case, it is just the typical sa.

The notation -P is for the SQL server's password, if required. In this case, it is not required. Therefore, you leave it blank.

Following the SQL server's setting specifications, you then specify the script that you wish to install, InstallSqlState.sql. This installs what is necessary to run SQL Server session management.

After you have created the necessary tables and procedures, change the <sessionState> node of the web.config file as shown in Listing 2-3.

LISTING 2-3: Using SQL Server as a StateServer

```
<sessionState
    mode="SQLServer"
    stateConnectionString="tcpip=127.0.0.1:42424"
    cookieless="false"
    timeout="20" />
```

To use SQL Server to manage sessions, the mode of the <sessionState> node must be set to SQLServer. After the mode is set to SQLServer, ASP.NET then looks to the sqlConnectionString property to find the SQL server to connect to when storing state. The value of this property should be set so that the data source is the server where SQL and any needed login information are located.

Deciding on the State of Sessions

The mode you choose for running sessions within your web application makes a considerable difference in the performance, functionality, and reliability of your web application.

Which mode should you choose? Following are the best conditions for each option:

- ➤ InProc — The session is run in the same process as the ASP.NET worker process. Therefore, this option should be used when the maintaining of sessions is not mission-critical to the application. This option has the best performance possible out of all the choices.

- ➤ StateServer — This Windows Service option runs the sessions out of process and is, therefore, best when used on multiple servers, or when sessions must be maintained if IIS is stopped and then restarted. This option provides better performance than the other out-of-process option, SQLServer.

- ➤ SQLServer — This out-of-process option is the most reliable choice because the sessions are stored directly in SQL Server. Even though this is the most reliable choice, this option ranks worst in performance.

To get the best performance from your use of sessions, you are able to declare on each page how you want to deal with the `Session` object using the `EnableSessionState` attribute within the `Page` directive. Following is an example of using this attribute:

```
<%@ Page Language="C#" EnableSessionState="True" CodeFile="Default.aspx.cs"
    Inherits="_Default" %>
```

The `EnableSessionState` is set to `True` by default (as shown in bold). This attribute has the following three options:

➤　`EnableSessionState="True"` — This is the default setting, and means that the ASP.NET page will make use of the `Session` object. The page will also use read/write access to the `Session` object for only the session ID that is being used.

➤　`EnableSessionState="False"` — Changing the value to `False` means that the page will not require access to the `Session` object. If your page is not using the `Session` object at all, it is best to set the value of this attribute to `False`, which will cause ASP.NET to schedule this particular page ahead of other pages that require the use of the `Session` object. This will help with the overall scalability of your ASP.NET application.

➤　`EnableSessionState="ReadOnly"` — Setting the value to `ReadOnly` means that your ASP.NET page will require only read access to the `Session` object. All pages that are only going to be reading from the `Session` object will benefit from this setting.

If your application is not going to make use of the `Session` object, the best thing to do with regard to performance is to then turn off session state. You can do this via the `web.config` or the `machine.config` file. In the `<sessionState>` element, you set the `mode` attribute to `Off`.

Working with Output Caching

Still focusing on the state management and caching strategies that can be employed on the server, another option at your disposal is caching. *Caching* is the process of storing frequently used data on the server to fulfill subsequent requests. It is tremendously better to grab objects to use in code from memory rather than repeatedly calling a data store. Caching will improve the overall performance, scalability, and availability of your ASP.NET applications.

Output caching is a way to keep the dynamically generated page content in the server's memory or disk for later retrieval. This type of cache saves post-rendered content so that it will not have to be regenerated again the next time it is requested. After a page is cached, it can be served up again when any subsequent requests are made to the server.

You apply output caching by inserting an `OutputCache` page directive at the top of an `.aspx` page, as follows:

```
<%@ OutputCache Duration="60" VaryByParam="None" %>
```

The `Duration` attribute defines the number of seconds a page is stored in the cache. The `VaryByParam` attribute determines which versions of the page output are actually cached. You can also generate different responses based on whether an HTTP-POST or HTTP-GET response is required by using the `VaryByHeader` attribute. Other than the `VaryByParam` attribute for the `OutputCache` directive, ASP.NET includes the `VaryByHeader`, `VaryByCustom`, `VaryByControl`, and `Location` attributes. Additionally, the `Shared` attribute can affect `UserControls`, as you will see later.

Caching in ASP.NET is implemented as an `HttpModule` that listens to all `HttpRequests` that come through the ASP.NET worker process. The `OutputCacheModule` listens to the application's `ResolveRequestCache` and `UpdateRequestCache` events, handles cache hits and misses, and returns the cached HTML, bypassing the Page Handler if need be.

VaryByParam

The `VaryByParam` attribute can specify which `QueryString` parameters cause a new version of the page to be cached, as shown here:

```
<%@ OutputCache Duration="90" VaryByParam="pageId;subPageId" %>
```

For example, if you have a page called `navigation.aspx` that includes navigation information in the `QueryString` (such as `pageId` and `subPageId`), the `OutputCache` directive shown here caches the page for every different value of `pageId` and `subPageId`. In this example, the number of pages is best expressed with an equation, as shown here:

```
cacheItems = (num of pageIds) * (num of subPageIds)
```

In this equation, `cacheItems` is the number of rendered HTML pages that would be stored in the cache. Pages are cached only after they are requested and pass through the `OutputCacheModule`. The maximum amount of cache memory in this case is used only after every possible combination is visited at least once. Although these are just *potential* maximums, creating an equation that represents your system's potential maximum is an important exercise.

If you want to cache a new version of the page based on any differences in the `QueryString` parameters, use `VaryByParam = "*"`, as in the following code:

```
<%@ OutputCache Duration="90" VaryByParam="*" %>
```

VaryByHeader

The `VaryByHeader` attribute works off of the different HTTP headers of the requests that come to the server.

It is important to "do the math" when using the `VaryBy` attributes. For example, you could add the `VaryByHeader` attribute and cache a different version of the page based on the browser's reported `User-Agent` HTTP header.

```
<%@ OutputCache Duration="90" VaryByParam="*" VaryByHeader="User-Agent"%>
```

The `User-Agent` identifies the user's browser type. ASP.NET can automatically generate different renderings of a given page that are customized to specific browsers, so it makes sense in many cases to save these various renderings in the cache. A Firefox user might have slightly different HTML than an Internet Explorer (IE) user, so you do not want to send all users the exact same post-rendered HTML. Literally dozens (if not hundreds) of `User-Agent` strings exist in the wild because they identify more than just the browser type. This `OutputCache` directive could multiply into thousands of different versions of this page being cached, depending on server load. In this case, you should measure the cost of the caching against the cost of re-creating the page dynamically.

Always cache what will give you the biggest performance gain, and prove that assumption with testing. Don't "cache by coincidence" using attributes like `VaryByParam = "*"`. *A common rule of thumb is to cache the least possible amount of data at first, and add more caching later if you determine a need for it. Remember that the server memory is a limited resource, so you may want to configure the use of disk caching in some cases. Be sure to balance your limited resources with security as a primary concern; do not put sensitive data on the disk.*

VaryByControl

`VaryByControl` can be a very easy way to get some serious performance gains from complicated `UserControls` that render a lot of HTML that does not change often. For example, imagine a `UserControl` that renders a `ComboBox` showing the names of all the countries in the world. Perhaps those names are retrieved from a database and rendered in the combo box as follows:

```
<%@ OutputCache Duration="2592000" VaryByControl="comboBoxOfCountries" %>
```

Certainly, the names of the world's countries do not change that often, so the `Duration` might be set to a month (in seconds). This example makes use of a server control called `comboBoxOfCountries` and works with its cached output. The rendered output of the `UserControl` is cached, allowing a page using that control to reap performance benefits of caching the control while the page itself remains dynamic.

VaryByCustom

Although the `VaryBy` attributes offer a great deal of power, sometimes you need more flexibility. If you want to take the `OutputCache` directive from the previous navigation example and cache by a value stored in a cookie, you can add `VaryByCustom`. The value of `VaryByCustom` is passed into the `GetVaryByCustomString` method that can be added to the `Global.asax.cs`. This method is called every time the page is requested, and it is the function's responsibility to return a value.

A different version of the page is cached for each unique value returned. For example, say your users have a cookie called `Language` that has three potential values: `en`, `es`, and `fr`. You want to allow users to specify their preferred language, regardless of their language reported by their browser. `Language` also has a fourth potential value — it may not exist! Therefore, the `OutputCache` directive in the following example caches many versions of the page, as described in this equation:

```
cacheItems = (num of pageIds) * (num of subPageIds) * (4 possible Language values)
```

To summarize, suppose there were ten potential values for `pageId`, five potential `subPageId` values for each `pageId`, and four possible values for `Language`. That adds up to 200 different potential cached versions of this single navigation page. This math is not meant to scare you away from caching, but you should realize that with great (caching) power comes great responsibility.

Caching in ASP.NET involves a trade-off between CPU and memory — how hard is it to make this page, versus whether you can afford to hold 200 versions of it. If it is only 5KB of HTML, a potential megabyte of memory could pay off handsomely, versus thousands and thousands of database accesses. Since most pages will hit the database at least once during a page cycle, every page request served from the cache saves you a trip to the database. Efficient use of caching can translate into cost savings if fewer database servers and licenses are needed.

The following `OutputCache` directive includes `pageId` and `subPageId` as values for `VaryByParam`, and `VaryByCustom` passes in the value of `"prefs"` to the `GetVaryByCustomString` callback function in Listing 2-4 (shown shortly):

```
<%@ OutputCache Duration="90" VaryByParam="pageId;subPageId" VaryByCustom="prefs"%>
```

The code shown in Listing 2-4 returns the value stored in the `Language` cookie. The `arg` parameter to the `GetVaryByCustomString` method contains the string `"prefs"`, as specified in `VaryByCustom`.

LISTING 2-4: GetVaryByCustomString Callback Method in the HttpApplication

```
public override string GetVaryByCustomString(HttpContext context, string arg)
{
    if(arg.ToLower() == "prefs")
    {
      HttpCookie cookie = context.Request.Cookies["Language"];
      if(cookie != null)
      {
          return cookie.Value;
      }
    }
    return base.GetVaryByCustomString(context, arg);
}
```

The `GetVaryByCustomString` method in Listing 2-4 is used by the `HttpApplication` in `Global.asax.cs`, and will be called for every page that uses the `VaryByCustom` `OutputCache` directive. If your application has many pages that use `VaryByCustom`, you can create a `switch` statement and a series of helper functions to retrieve whatever information you want from the user's `HttpContext` and to generate unique values for cache keys.

Extending <outputCache>

With the release of ASP.NET 4, you are now able to extend how the `OutputCache` directive works, and have it instead work off of your own custom means to caching. This means that you can wire the `OutputCache` directive to any type of caching means, including distributed caches, cloud caches, disc, XML, or anything else you can dream up.

To accomplish this, you are required to create a custom output-cache provider as a class, and this class will need to inherit from the new `System.Web.Caching.OutputCacheProvider` class. In order to inherit from `OutputCacheProvider`, you must override the `Add()`, `Get()`, `Remove()`, and `Set()` methods to implement your custom version of output caching.

Once you have your custom implementation in place, the next step is to configure this in a configuration file — the `machine.config` or the `web.config` file. There have been some changes made to the `<outputCache>` element in the configuration file to allow you to apply your custom cache extensions.

The `<outputCache>` element is found within the `<caching>` section of the configuration file, and it now includes a new `<providers>` sub-element.

```
<caching>
   <outputCache>
      <providers>
      </providers>
   </outputCache>
</caching>
```

Within the new `<providers>` element, you can nest an `<add>` element to make the appropriate references to your new output cache capability you built by deriving from the `OutputCacheProvider` class.

```
<caching>
   <outputCache defaultProvider="AspNetInternalProvider">
      <providers>
         <add name="myDistributedCacheExtension"
           type="Wrox.OutputCacheExtension.DistributedCacheProvider,
               DistributedCacheProvider" />
      </providers>
   </outputCache>
</caching>
```

With this new `<add>` element in place, your new extended output cache is available to use. One new addition here to also pay attention to is the new `defaultProvider` attribute within the `<outputCache>` element. In this case, it is set to `AspNetInternalProvider`, which is the default setting in the configuration file. This means that, by default, the output cache works as it always has done, and stores its cache in the memory of the computer that the program on which it is running.

With your own output cache provider in place, you can now point to this provider through the `OutputCache` directive on the page, as defined here:

```
<%@ OutputCache Duration="90" VaryByParam="*"
      providerName="myDistributedCacheExtension" %>
```

If the provider name isn't defined, then the provider that is defined in the configuration's `defaultProvider` attribute is utilized.

Partial Page (UserControl) Caching

Similar to output caching, *partial page caching* enables you to cache only specific blocks of a web page. For example, you can cache only the center of the page the user sees. Partial page caching is achieved with the caching of user controls, so you can build your ASP.NET pages to utilize numerous user controls, and then apply output caching to the selected user controls. This, in essence, caches only the parts of the page that you want, leaving other parts of the page outside the reach of caching.

This is a nice feature and, if done correctly, it can lead to pages that perform better. This requires a modular design to be planned up front so that you can partition the components of the page into logical units composed of user controls.

Typically, `UserControls` are designed to be placed on multiple pages to maximize reuse of common functionality. However, when these `UserControls` (`.ascx` files) are cached with the `@ OutputCache` directive's default attributes, they are cached on a per-page basis. That means that even if a `UserControl` outputs the identical HTML when placed on `pageA.aspx` (as it does when placed on `pageB.aspx`), its output is cached twice. By enabling the `Shared="true"` attribute, the `UserControl`'s output can be shared among multiple pages and on sites that make heavy use of shared `UserControls`:

```
<%@ OutputCache Duration="300" VaryByParam="*" Shared="true" %>
```

The resulting memory savings can be surprisingly large, since you only cache one copy of the post-rendered user control, instead of caching a copy for each page. As with all optimizations, you must test both for correctness of output, as well as memory usage.

> *If you have a* `UserControl` *using the* `OutputCache` *directive, remember that the* `UserControl` *exists only for the first request. If a* `UserControl` *has its HTML retrieved from the* `OutputCache`, *the control does not really exist on the* `.aspx` *page. Instead, a* `PartialCachingControl` *is created that acts as a proxy or ghost of that control.*

Any code in the `.aspx` page that requires a `UserControl` to be constantly available will fail if that control is reconstituted from the `OutputCache`. So, be sure to always check for this type of caching before using any control. The following code fragment illustrates the kind of logic required when accessing a potentially cached `UserControl`:

```
protected void Page_Load()
{
    if (PossiblyCachedUserControl != null)
    {
        // Place code manipulating PossiblyCachedUserControl here.
    }
}
```

Looking at .NET 4's New Object Caching Option

If you have ever worked with the `System.Web.Caching.Cache` object, you know that it is quite powerful, and that it allows for you to even create a custom cache. This extensibility and power has changed under the hood of the `Cache` object though.

Driving this is the `System.Runtime.Caching.dll`. What was in the `System.Web` version has been refactored out, and everything was rebuilt into the new namespace of `System.Runtime.Caching`.

The reason for this change wasn't so much for the ASP.NET developer, but instead it was for other application types such as Windows Forms, Windows Presentation Foundation (WPF) apps, and more. The reason for this is because the `System.Web.Caching.Cache` object was so useful that other application developers were bringing over the `System.Web` namespace into their projects to make use of this object. So, in order to get away from a Windows Forms developer needing to bring in the `System.Web.dll` into a project just to use the `Cache` object it provided, this was all extracted out and extended with the `System.Runtime.Caching` namespace.

As an ASP.NET developer, you can still make use of the `System.Web.Caching.Cache` object just as you did in all the prior versions of ASP.NET. It isn't going away. However, it is important to note that as the .NET Framework evolves, the .NET team will be making their investments into the `System.Runtime.Caching` namespace, rather than `System.Web.Caching`.

This means that, over time, you will most likely see additional enhancements in the `System.Runtime.Caching` version that don't appear in the `System.Web.Caching` namespace as you might expect. With that said, it doesn't also mean that you need to move everything over to the new `System.Runtime.Caching` namespace in order to make sure you are the strategic path of Microsoft, as the two caches are managed together under the covers.

Now, let's run through an example of using the cache from the `System.Runtime.Caching` namespace. For this example, the ASP.NET page will simply use a `Label` control that will show the name of a user that is stored in an XML file. The first step is to create an XML file and name the file `Username.xml`, as shown in Listing 2-5.

LISTING 2-5: The Contents of the Username.xml File

```xml
<?xml version="1.0" encoding="utf-8" ?>
<usernames>
  <user>Bill Evjen</user>
</usernames>
```

With this XML file sitting in the root of your drive, now turn your attention to the `Default.aspx` code-behind page to use the name in the file, and present it into a single `Label` control on the page. Listing 2-6 shows the code-behind for the `Default.aspx` page.

LISTING 2-6: Using the System.Runtime.Caching Namespace

```csharp
using System;
using System.Collections.Generic;
using System.Linq;
using System.Runtime.Caching;
using System.Xml.Linq;

namespace RuntimeCaching
```

```
    {
        public partial class Default : System.Web.UI.Page
        {
            protected void Page_Load(object sender, EventArgs e)
            {
                ObjectCache cache = MemoryCache.Default;

                string usernameFromXml = cache["userFromXml"] as string;

                if (usernameFromXml == null)
                {
                    List<string> userFilePath = new List<string>();
                    userFilePath.Add(@"C:\Username.xml");

                    CacheItemPolicy policy = new CacheItemPolicy();
                    policy.ChangeMonitors.Add(new
                        HostFileChangeMonitor(userFilePath));

                    XDocument xdoc = XDocument.Load(@"C:\Username.xml");
                    var query = from u in xdoc.Elements("usernames")
                                    select u.Value;

                    usernameFromXml = query.First().ToString();

                    cache.Set("userFromXml", usernameFromXml, policy);
                }

                Label1.Text = usernameFromXml;
            }
        }
    }
```

Listing 2-6 makes use of the new cache at `System.Runtime.Caching`. You are going to need to reference this namespace in your ASP.NET project in order for this to work.

To start, you create a default instance of the cache object.

```
ObjectCache cache = MemoryCache.Default;
```

You then can work with this cache as you would with the traditional ASP.NET cache object.

```
string usernameFromXml = cache["userFromXml"] as string;
```

To get the cache started, you must create an object that defines what type of cache you are dealing with. You can build a custom implementation, or you can use one of the default implementations that are provided with .NET 4.

```
CacheItemPolicy policy = new CacheItemPolicy();
policy.ChangeMonitors.Add(new HostFileChangeMonitor(userFilePath));
```

The `HostFileChangeMontior` is a means to look at directories and file paths, and to monitor for change. So, for example, when the XML file changes, then this will trigger an invalidation of the cache. Other implementations of the `ChangeMonitor` object include the `FileChangeMonitor` and the `SqlChangeMonitor`. The `HostFileChangeMontior` class implements the `FileChangeMonitor` class, and is a sealed class.

Running this example, you will notice that the text `Bill Evjen` is loaded into the cache on the first run, and this text will appear in the `Label1` control. Keep your application running, and then go back to the XML file to change the value. You will then notice that this will cause the cache to be invalidated on the page's refresh.

Nowadays, many developers make use of a service-oriented architecture and, therefore, work with a set of services to get what they need done. The next section takes an important and quick look at implementing caching for your services.

CACHING WEB SERVICES

Caching is an important feature in almost every application that you build with .NET. There are a lot of caching capabilities available to you in ASP.NET (as discussed in this chapter), but a certain feature of ASP.NET Web Services in .NET enables you to cache the Simple Object Access Protocol (SOAP) response sent to any of the service's consumers.

First, by way of review, remember that caching is the capability to maintain an in-memory store where data, objects, and various items are stored for reuse. This feature increases the responsiveness of the applications you build and manage. Sometimes, returning cached results can greatly affect performance.

XML web services use an attribute to control caching of SOAP responses — the `CacheDuration` property. Listing 2-7 shows its use.

LISTING 2-7: Utilizing the CacheDuration Property

```
[WebMethod(CacheDuration=60)]
public string GetServerTime() {
   return DateTime.Now.ToLongTimeString();
}
```

As you can see, `CacheDuration` is used within the `WebMethod` attribute much like the `Description` and `Name` properties. `CacheDuration` takes an `Integer` value that is equal to the number of seconds during which the SOAP response is cached.

When the first request comes in, the SOAP response is cached by the server, and the consumer gets the same timestamp in the SOAP response for the next minute. After that minute is up, the stored cache is discarded, and a new response is generated and stored in the cache again for servicing all other requests for the next minute.

Among the many benefits of caching your SOAP responses, you will find that the performance of your application is greatly improved when you have a response that is basically re-created again and again without any change.

Many developers stop at the software implementation of their solutions. Though, as a software developer, it is important to think about the hardware considerations as well. It is important to remember that how you establish your solution on the hardware, and how the hardware is configured, can have a dramatic impact on the overall performance. This next section takes a look at this topic.

HARDWARE CONSIDERATIONS

It is one thing to build an ASP.NET application that is coded to perform well, or works with caching to avoid subsequent calls to underlying data sources. Another consideration is to configure your application to take advantage of the hardware to which it is deployed. There are available resources that your ASP.NET takes advantage of as it runs.

Within the `<system.net>` element of your configuration file, you can control the maximum number of outbound HTTP connections that ASP.NET can perform. By default, it is set to 2, but you should readjust this number using the `maxconnection` attribute. Listing 2-8 shows the `maxconnection` attribute in use.

LISTING 2-8: Setting the maxconnection Attribute

```xml
<configuration>
   <system.net>
      <connectionManagement>
         <add name="www.swank.com" maxconnection="5" />
         <add name="*" maxconnection="4" />
      </connectionManagement>
   </system.net>
</configuration>
```

Using the `<connectionManagement>` element, you can manage either particular URLs, or even IP addresses. In this case, up to five connections will be allowed to `www.swank.com`, while everything else is allowed up to four connections (defined with the asterisk).

The question then is what should the number be? It really comes down to your CPU capabilities. Microsoft recommends that it should be set to 12 times the number of CPUs on your server. Therefore, if you are using a dual-processor server, this number should be set to 24.

Your ASP.NET application makes use of threads that are from the .NET thread pool to run. Instead of spinning up new threads, there is a set thread pool that loans threads out, and when your application is done with the thread, it is simply returned to this thread pool for later reuse.

The thread pool makes use of the available hardware resources for managing the number of threads. Most importantly, it makes use of the CPU and the CPU utilization to determine thread pool sizes. In addition, your application makes I/O operations when it works off files or makes any service calls.

There are settings in the `machine.config` file that determine some of the limits in how ASP.NET will manage the number of threads it can deal with. If you are putting your ASP.NET application on a multiprocessor server, then you have more to take advantage of, but you need to adjust the default settings in the `machine.config` file in order to do that.

Another area in the configuration files to pay attention to is the `<processModel>` section. Here you can set some values that deal with how your ASP.NET application deals with threading. The `<processModel>` element has a number of attributes to pay attention to here. The first one to note is the `maxIoThreads` attribute.

The `maxIoThreads` attribute allows you to specify the maximum number of I/O threads that exist within the .NET thread pool that is used by the ASP.NET worker process. The default value is 20. Instead of using this default value, change this value to 100. You do not have to worry about how this relates to the number of CPUs at your disposal, because it will automatically be multiplied by the number of CPUs detected. Therefore, if your application is on a dual-processor server, then the value used will be 200.

The `maxWorkerThreads` attribute allows you to specify the maximum number of threads that exist within the ASP.NET worker process thread pool. This attribute also has a default value of 20. Like the `maxIoThreads` attribute, you are going to want to set the `maxWorkerThreads` attribute to 100. Again, this is a value that will be assigned to the number of CPUs detected automatically.

Another attribute, the `minFreeThreads` attribute, is found with the `<httpRuntime>` element of the `machine.config` file. Because the ASP.NET runtime uses the free threads available in its thread pool to fulfill requests, the `minFreeThreads` specifies the number of threads that ASP.NET guarantees is available within the thread pool. The default number of threads is set to 8. For complex applications that require additional threads to complete processing, this attribute simply ensures that the threads are available, and that the application will not be locked while waiting for a free thread to schedule more work. Microsoft recommends that you set this number to 88 times the number of CPUs on your server. Therefore, if you are using a dual-processor server, this number should be set to 176.

The last attribute to pay attention to here is the `minLocalRequestFreeThreads` attribute, also found with the `<httpRuntime>` element. This attribute controls the number of free threads dedicated for local request processing. The default value of this attribute is set to 4. For this attribute, Microsoft recommends that you set it to 76 times the number of CPUs on your server. Therefore, if you are using a dual-processor server, this number should be set to 152.

Beyond what you can do from a software and hardware perspective, you will need to be able to benchmark the performance of your applications so that you can see where you can realize performance gains. The next section takes a look at the performance counters that are available for your use.

USING PERFORMANCE COUNTERS

Utilizing performance counters is important if you want to monitor your applications as they run. What exactly is monitored is up to you. A plethora of available performance counters are at your disposal in Windows, and you will find that there are more than 60 counters specific to ASP.NET.

Viewing Performance Counters Through an Administration Tool

You can see these performance counters by opening the Performance dialog found in the Control Panel, and then Administration Tools if you are using Windows XP. If you are using Windows 7, select Control Panel ⇨ System and Security ⇨ Performance Information and Tools ⇨ Advanced Tools ⇨ Open Performance Monitor. Figure 2-4 shows the dialog opened in Windows 7.

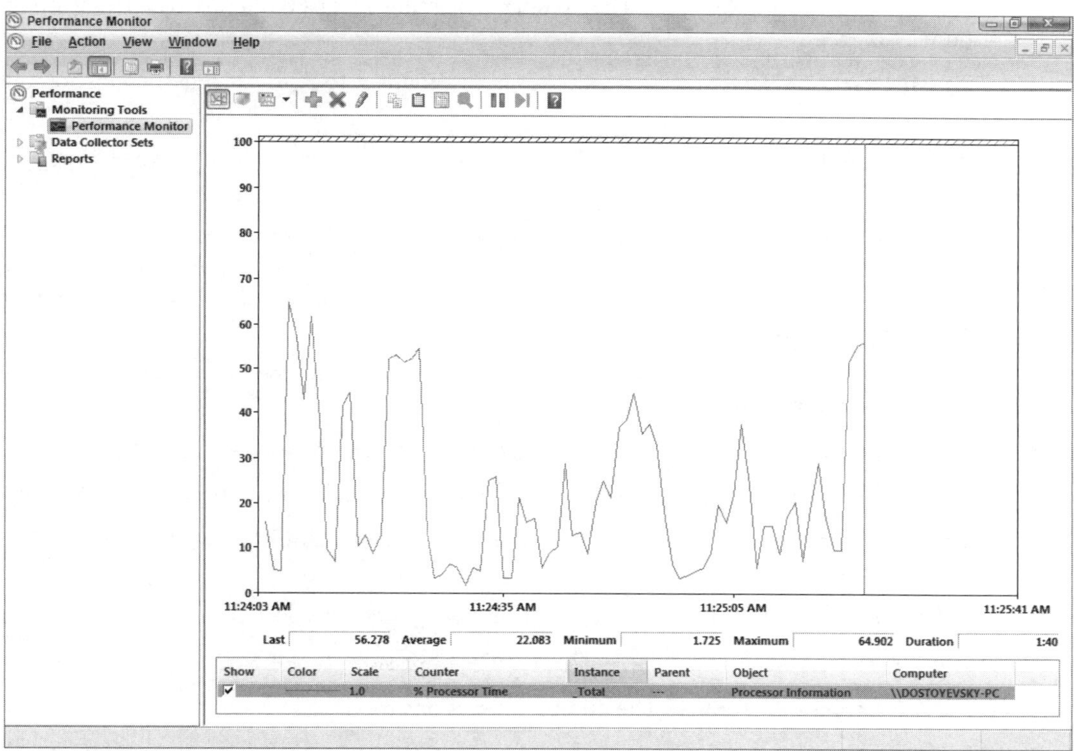

FIGURE 2-4: Performance dialog in Windows 7

Clicking the plus sign in the menu enables you to add more performance counters to the list. You will find a number of ASP.NET-specific counters in the list illustrated in Figure 2-5.

The following list details some of the ASP.NET-specific performance counters that are at your disposal, along with a definition of the counter (also available by checking the Show Description check box in Windows 7 from within the dialog):

➤ *Application Restarts* — The number of times the application has been restarted during the web server's lifetime.

➤ *Applications Running* — The number of currently running web applications.

➤ *Audit Failure Events Raised* — The number of audit failures in the application since it was started.

➤ *Audit Success Events Raised* — The number of audit successes in the application since it was started.

➤ *Error Events Raised* — The number of error events raised since the application was started.

➤ *Infrastructure Error Events Raised* — The number of HTTP error events raised since the application was started.

➤ *Request Error Events Raised* — The number of runtime error events raised since the application was started.

➤ *Request Execution Time* — The number of milliseconds it took to execute the most recent request.

➤ *Request Wait Time* — The number of milliseconds the most recent request was waiting in the queue.

➤ *Requests Current* — The current number of requests, including those that are queued, currently executing, or waiting to be written to the client. Under the ASP.NET process model, when this counter exceeds the `requestQueueLimit` defined in the `processModel` configuration section, ASP.NET begins rejecting requests.

➤ *Requests Disconnected* — The number of requests disconnected because of communication errors or user terminations.

➤ *Requests Queued* — The number of requests waiting to be processed.

➤ *Requests Rejected* — The number of requests rejected because the request queue was full.

➤ *State Server Sessions Abandoned* — The number of sessions that have been explicitly abandoned.

➤ *State Server Sessions Active* — The current number of sessions currently active.

➤ *State Server Sessions Timed Out* — The number of sessions timed out.

➤ *State Server Sessions Total* — The number of sessions total.

➤ *Worker Process Restarts* — The number of times a worker process has restarted on the machine.

➤ *Worker Processes Running* — The number of worker processes running on the machine.

These are the performance counters for just the ASP.NET v2.0.50727 category. You will also find categories for other ASP.NET-specific items such as the following:

➤ ASP.NET

➤ ASP.NET Applications

➤ ASP.NET Apps v4.0.30319

➤ ASP.NET State Service

➤ ASP.NET v4.0.30319

Performance counters can give you a pretty outstanding view of what is happening in your application. The data retrieved by a specific counter is not a continuous thing, because the counter is really taking a snapshot of the specified counter every 400 milliseconds. So, be sure to take that into account when analyzing the data produced.

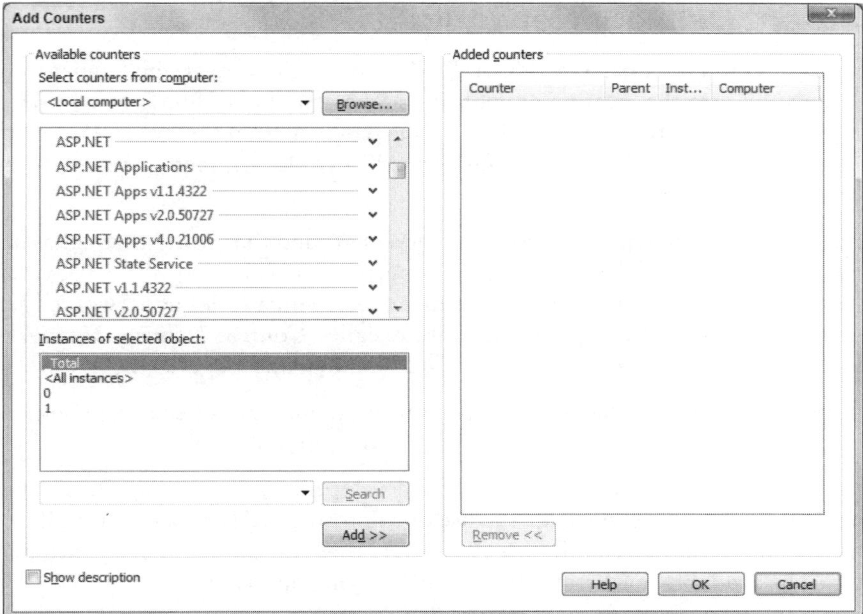

FIGURE 2-5: ASP.NET-specific counters

So far, this chapter has covered some of the more important topics when it comes to your application's performance. However, there are still a lot of little things that you can do to help the performance even more. The next section looks at some of these other items.

TIPS AND TRICKS

Of course, there are a bunch of random things you can do for your ASP.NET application to ensure that it runs and is processed by your users as fast as possible. Many of the tricks have to do with keeping the number of requests down, and making these requests as small as possible.

There are a couple of good tools that you should be using to grade your ASP.NET applications. Some favorites include Firebug (found as an add-on for Firefox) and Fiddler (found at `www.fiddlertool.com`). These allow you to see all the requests the client makes to the server where your application is hosted.

Keep Requests Down to a Minimum

You want to keep the number of requests down to a minimum. There are a couple of ways you can do this. One way is to limit the number of JavaScript and Cascading Style Sheet (CSS) calls by combining these files into single files. So, instead of two or more `.js` or `.css` files, all of which the client needs to make a singular request for, you combine those files into a single `.js` or `.css` file. Overall, this does make a difference.

Make Use of Content Delivery Networks

When an end user makes a request to a page in your ASP.NET application, invariably it goes through a number of hops to get to the location of your server. The number of hops an end user must take dramatically increases the further away the user's machine is from the server. For example, if your user is calling a server in St. Louis, Missouri, from Tokyo, Japan, then there will be more hops required than a user who already resides in St. Louis.

Companies like to put their larger content on a system of servers around that world that act as an *edge cache*. Therefore, instead of always having everyone come to your server to get the file, you can get that file closer to the end user by distributing the file to reside on a series of networked servers scattered throughout the world. These types of systems are called *Content Delivery Networks* (*CDNs*). Popular companies that do this type of work include Akamai and EdgeCast.

As an ASP.NET architect, you might be able to take advantage of these types of edge capabilities that will then dramatically increase the perceived performance of your applications.

Recently, Microsoft has provided a free CDN capability for developers who are using jQuery and Ajax. If you are using ASP.NET 4, you can enable the use of Microsoft's Ajax CDN very easily. Microsoft has put up a number of JavaScript libraries in a CDN that you can freely take advantage of in your applications. The available JavaScript libraries include the following:

- ➤ jQuery
- ➤ jQuery UI
- ➤ jQuery Validation
- ➤ jQuery Cycle
- ➤ Ajax Control Toolkit
- ➤ ASP.NET Ajax
- ➤ ASP.NET MVC JavaScript Files

To make use of one of these JavaScript files from a CDN, you simply need to just change the URL that is used in the `<script>` tag, as shown in Listing 2-9.

LISTING 2-9: Using the Microsoft Ajax CDN

```
<script src="http://ajax.aspnetcdn.com/ajax/jQuery/jquery-1.4.4.js"
 type="text/javascript"></script>
```

Here you can see that instead of calling your own server for the jQuery 1.4.4 library, this library is instead serviced from `ajax.aspnetcdn.com`. This means that when the end user invokes this call for this jQuery library, it will only come from the Microsoft CDN, and will never come from your server. This will be considerably faster for your end users, and will save you bandwidth in the end.

For a full list of supported JavaScript libraries and their associated URLs, visit `www.asp.net/ajaxlibrary/cdn.ashx`.

If your ASP.NET page is using Secure Sockets Layer (SSL), then you will want to call the Microsoft Ajax CDN using SSL as well, because this is supported. Listing 2-10 shows how to use the same jQuery call with SSL.

LISTING 2-10: Using the Microsoft Ajax CDN

```
<script src="https://ajax.aspnetcdn.com/ajax/jQuery/jquery-1.4.4.js"
 type="text/javascript"></script>
```

If you are using the `ScriptManager` server control in your ASP.NET Ajax applications, then you are going to want to use the new `EnableCdn` attribute that is now available in the control. Setting the value of this attribute to `true` will cause the Microsoft Ajax CDN to be utilized instead of your local server. This is shown in Listing 2-11. It should be noted that this only works in ASP.NET 4.

LISTING 2-11: Using the Microsoft Ajax CDN from the ScriptManager Control

```
<asp:ScriptManager ID="ScriptManager1" EnableCdn="true" runat="server" />
```

If you are using JavaScript libraries that are not found in the Microsoft Ajax CDN, Google offers a similar capability, and you can see if they are hosting what you are looking for. You can find the supported Google hosted libraries at `http://code.google.com/apis/libraries/devguide.html#AjaxLibraries`.

Enable the Browser to Cache Items Longer

There are elements to your ASP.NET page that do not change that often. For example, there are probably images that don't change that often, and it would be better to have these images stored in the end user's browser cache, rather than having that end user call for the same image over and over again as he or she comes to your pages. By default, all your page's artifacts are set to not be cached by the browser. You can change this behavior by setting an expiry date on the items you want cached.

A good approach is to put all of your JavaScript, CSS, and images in dedicated folders, and within those folders, control how long they are cached on the client. You can do this in a couple of different ways.

One way is to use the IIS Manager. Highlighting the folder you are working on within the IIS Manager, select the HTTP Response Headers icon in the available list of options, as shown in Figure 2-6.

Double-clicking the icon will give you a list of headers that are currently sent from IIS for each request. From here, you can click on the Set Common Headers link, and this will give you the dialog presented here in Figure 2-7.

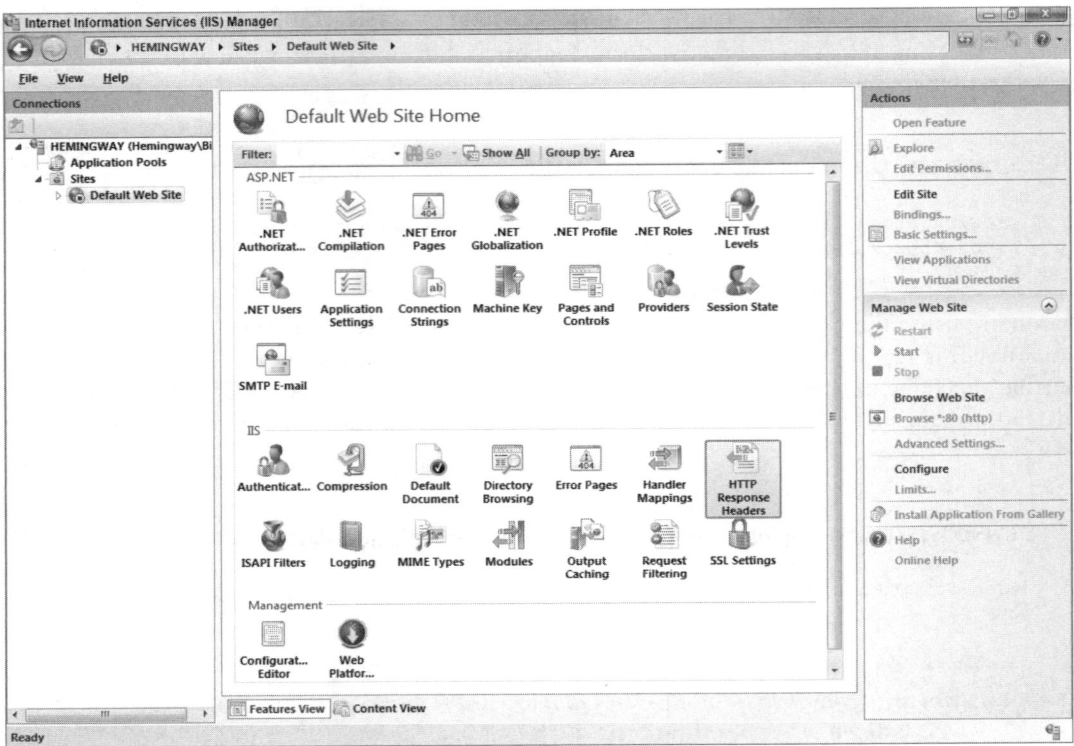

FIGURE 2-6: HTTP Response Headers icon in the available list of options

By selecting "Expire Web content," you have the option to expire the content immediately, after a set interval, or on a specific date. As shown in Figure 2-7, you can see that the folder is set to expire its contents after 7 days. After clicking the OK button, this will generate a `web.config` file within that folder with the content shown in Listing 2-12.

LISTING 2-12: The Generated web.config File

```xml
<?xml version="1.0" encoding="UTF-8"?>
<configuration>
    <system.webServer>
        <staticContent>
            <clientCache cacheControlMode="UseMaxAge"
              cacheControlMaxAge="7.00:00:00" />
        </staticContent>
    </system.webServer>
</configuration>
```

One thing to keep in mind is that if you set an image to be cached for some time, and the end user does indeed have this image cached, if you have made modifications to this image during this time, the end user will still see the one that is contained within his or her cache. One way around this is to simply have different names for your images as you change them. In this way, the end user will be calling an entirely new image, rather than using the one with the same name that resides in the cache.

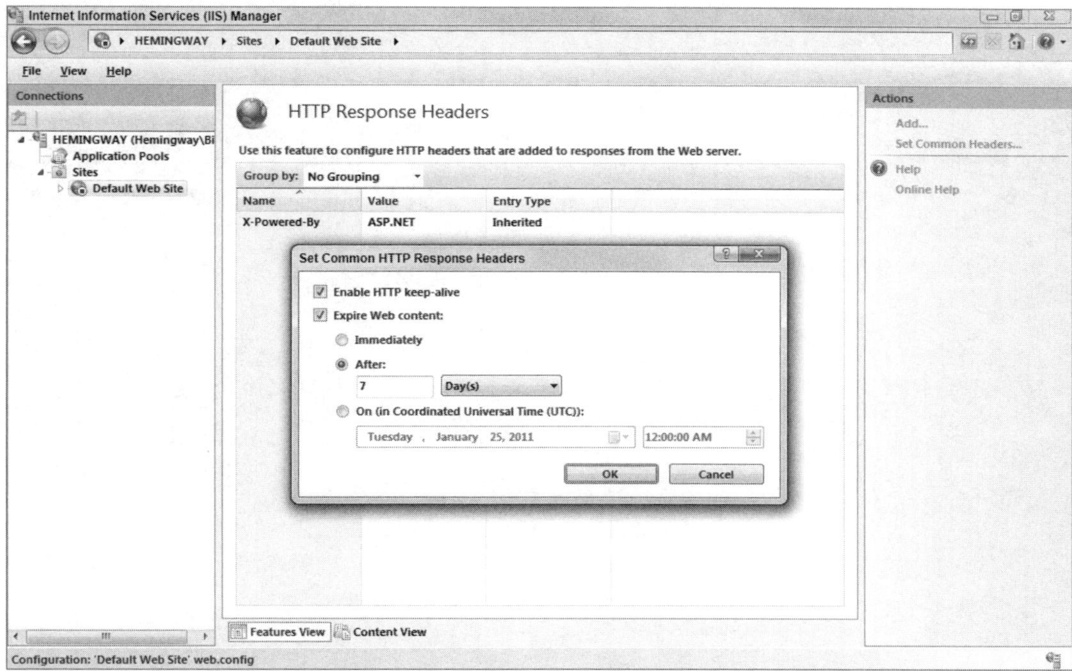

FIGURE 2-7: Set Common HTTP Response Headers dialog

Enabling Content Compression

When an end user makes a request to your web server, a header is sent in the request. Contained within the header is a declaration of whether the end user's browser can support a compressed response. Listing 2-13 shows a sample header that supports compression.

LISTING 2-13: A Request Header that States the Client Supports Compression

```
GET http://www.swank.com/ HTTP/1.1
Accept: text/html, application/xhtml+xml, */*
Accept-Language: en-US
User-Agent: Mozilla/5.0 (compatible; MSIE 9.0; Windows NT 6.1; WOW64;
    Trident/5.0)
Accept-Encoding: gzip, deflate
Connection: Keep-Alive
Host: www.swank.com
```

The important part of this header is the line `Accept-Encoding: gzip, deflate`. This tells the server that the client can support a compressed response. Sending back your responses compressed obviously helps with bandwidth.

IIS 7 enables you to easily compress your static or dynamic content. From the IIS Manager, highlight your site and select the Compression icon in the list of available options. You are provided with two options (if they are both installed) on the server. One is to enable dynamic content compression, and the other is to enable static content compression. You can see these options in Figure 2-8.

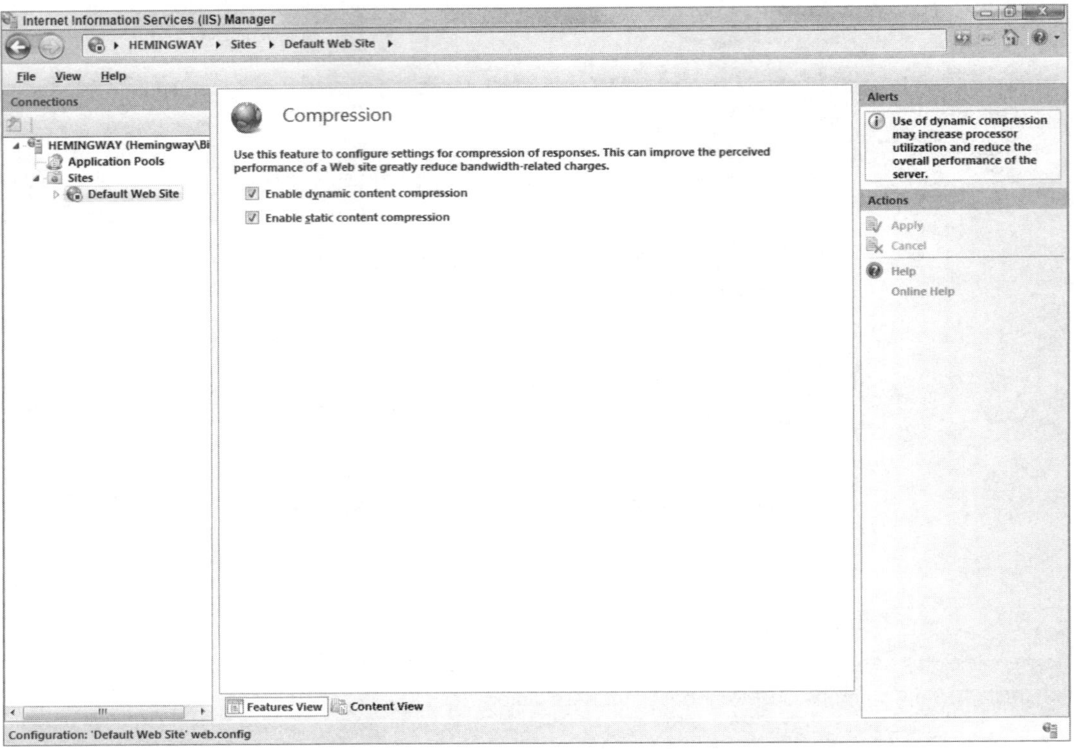

FIGURE 2-8: Compression options in IIS Manager

One thing to make note of is that if you enable dynamic compression, it takes work on the CPU to compress these responses on-the-fly, so monitor your CPU with this enabled to see if it makes sense for your application.

Location of Content in Your Pages

You might not think this would have an effect, but the placement of your auxiliary items on your page make a difference for the performance of your pages. The recommendation is to put all your CSS references at the top of your pages, and all the JavaScript references at the bottom of your page.

When dealing with CSS, you are going to want to put the CSS file in the `<head>` element of the ASP.NET page. This allows the page to load as items are downloaded to the client. As items start appearing on the page, it gives the end user the feeling that the page is loading fast.

Having your JavaScript `<script>` tags at the bottom of the page will not lock the download of the other page content, again, giving the appearance that the page is loading faster.

Make JavaScript and CSS External

In ASP.NET, it is possible to put your JavaScript and CSS code within the ASP.NET page itself. It is actually better to put all your JavaScript and CSS in external files (for example, `MyJavaScript.`

js). The reason for this is that if the JavaScript and CSS code is contained within external files, you can easily allow caching of this content. If it is contained within the ASP.NET page, it is not cached so easily.

In addition, if you are using this JavaScript or CSS in more than one place in your application, you will not have to download the code multiple times. The idea would be to cache it once, and then reuse it multiple times.

SUMMARY

The Internet has produced some great applications, but it has also made the development of these applications difficult. Because the Internet is a disconnected environment, (meaning that the only real time you are connected to an application or remote server is when you are making a request or getting a response), it is quite difficult at times to maintain state on it. However, ASP.NET has answered this difficulty with a number of solutions that, if used properly, can quickly make you forget about the disconnected world in which you work and play.

This chapter took a look at a lot of different things you can do to get your ASP.NET applications to perform. This chapter looked at how state works in your web applications, and the use of caching along with the Session object. This chapter also looked at how to configure your ASP.NET applications to take advantage of the hardware in which it is deployed. In addition to discussing performance counters for monitoring performance, this chapter also provided a set of tips and tricks to get the most from your applications.

ABOUT THE AUTHOR

Bill Evjen is an active proponent of .NET technologies and community-based learning initiatives for .NET. In 2000, he founded the St. Louis .NET User Group (www.stlnet.org). He is also the founder and former executive director of the International .NET Association (www.ineta.org), which represents more than 500,000 members worldwide. He has authored or co-authored more than 20 books, and also works closely with Microsoft as a Microsoft Regional Director and an MVP. Evjen is the CIO for Swank Motion Pictures (www.swank.com). Swank Motion Pictures provides both public performance licensing rights and licensed movies to numerous non-theatrical markets, including worldwide cruise lines, U.S. colleges and universities, K-12 public schools and libraries, American civilian and military hospitals, motor coaches, Amtrak trains, correctional facilities, and other markets such as parks, art museums and businesses. Evjen graduated from Western Washington University in Bellingham, Washington, with a Russian language degree. When he isn't tinkering on the computer, he can usually be found at his summer house in Toivakka, Finland.

3

Ethical Hacking of ASP.NET

by György Balássy

Web applications have at least three important characteristics that are absolutely independent of the technology they are built on: They must be user-friendly, fast, and secure. As a web developer, you are probably sensitive to these aspects, and keep them on high priority, because you know that they heavily determine the success of your website.

When you design the user interface and the architecture of your application, you can constantly focus on these three facets. You can try to find the best arrangement of the user interface (UI) elements, and try to fit the components to get the best performance results. However, even with your best efforts, you have an important component in your system that can help you to reach (or keep you from reaching) your goals: the web platform.

If you have an inherently slow base technology, you cannot boost it and make it fast, not even with your hardest work. Your application can be profoundly optimized for performance, but if the underlying platform is inherently slow, you are doomed — the speed of the underlying platform is the key to your success. You can have a cheetah, but if it travels on the back of a turtle, it takes a long time to reach its destination.

The same is also (or even more) true for security. Web applications today do not handle web protocols at the low level because the programming frameworks provide a high level of abstraction that increases developer productivity. This abstraction also means that the security aspects of a website are tightly coupled with the security features of the programming platform. When you build your web application, you no longer must find out how to implement authentication, or you do not have to invent a way to manage sessions, because they are provided out-of-the-box by the framework. Because these solutions are standard parts of the framework, it is expected that your application uses these standard solutions instead of a custom approach.

Your website and the developer framework you use are tightly chained together. And the old saying is still true: "A chain is only as strong as its weakest link."

You most likely have written code for the web for a while, and you already know much about SQL injection, cross-site scripting (XSS), and buffer overflows. They are dangerous threats, and it is mostly up to the application developer to prevent them. A single website that is vulnerable to SQL injection can lead to a compromised database, or even to a compromised server. A website that has a single XSS vulnerability can transform a client computer into a zombie member of a botnet. Application developers learned these lessons, and you most likely also know how to write code to protect your site, your server, and your visitors against these attacks.

But what about the code that was not written by you? Or what about the code that you utilize as a basis to build your own code on top of it? Can you be absolutely sure that the framework you use is secure? Of course, you naturally trust it because most frameworks are usually provided by big vendors and have a long history. But should you *really* trust them?

You can have a house, a castle, or even a well-protected fortress, but if you build it on a swamp, sooner or later it will go down. That's a serious risk you have to deal with. You must know the strengths and the weaknesses of your favorite developer platform, and you must eliminate the threats that the platform brings into your application. You build not only an independent application, but also a complete solution, and the platform is an integral part of it. If the built-in features are not secure enough, it is your responsibility to enhance them to provide a rock-hard solution to your customers.

This chapter guides you through the built-in security-related features of the ASP.NET platform. You see how they work, what threats they can handle, and what their weak spots are. You also see solutions that you can use in your own code to further enhance the security of your ASP.NET web application.

ETHICAL HACKING — IS THAT AN OXYMORON?

Online news sites and traditional newspapers like screamers because the big thrilling headlines attract the readers. The word *hacking* often appears in those headlines (did you notice the title of this chapter?) because it has some mysterious meaning almost as alluring as the magic world of Harry Potter.

Contrary to the expectations of most people, *The Jargon File* (which is the online glossary of hacker slang and an authoritative source) defines *hacker* in a positive way:

> *hacker /n./ [...] 1. A person who enjoys exploring the details of programmable systems and how to stretch their capabilities, as opposed to most users, who prefer to learn only the minimum necessary. 2. One who programs enthusiastically (even obsessively) or who enjoys programming rather than just theorizing about programming. [...] 4. A person who is good at programming quickly....*

> — THE JARGON FILE

This definition says nothing more than hackers are computer and network gurus. It does not say anything about evil intent to rule the world. The expression "ethical hacking" (or "white hat hacking") pushes this positive side further. *Ethical hackers* are security experts who specialize in penetration testing to ensure that IT systems are secure. Ethical hackers are the good guys who attack systems on behalf of their owners, seeking vulnerabilities that a malicious user could exploit.

It was almost certainly Sir Arthur Conan Doyle who first stated in his Sherlock Holmes stories that a detective must know the criminal's way of thinking and the criminal's tools to effectively hunt crime. The same is also true for cybercrime. You must be aware of the latest attacks and use the latest tools to find out how to protect your information systems against them.

In this chapter, you learn about many of those attacks, and about some useful tools that you should use to test your *own* applications. Did you notice the emphasis on the word "own"? It is important that these are *real* attacks and *real* tools, and they can be used for good or can be used for bad. I trust that you will use them only with good intent, to produce better applications and make our online world more secure.

FILLING YOUR TOOLBOX

To be an effective ethical hacker, you need two things: knowledge and tools. The first one is about theory, and the second one is about practice. Although there is nothing more practical than a good theory, to try out the concepts discussed in this chapter, you need some tools. This part of the chapter introduces you to some of the most useful web developer tools, and tools that you should definitely try. They can be used not only for security testing, but also for other tasks during web application development — such as fixing Cascading Style Sheet (CSS) code or debugging JavaScript code.

Fiddler

First, you need a *web debugging* proxy, which is an application that stands between *your* browser and *your* website. I emphasized the words "debugging" and "your" because this is not a network sniffing tool and does not provide you with access to someone else's network traffic. It can intercept the communication between an application (typically a browser) on your computer and a remote server, acting as a network proxy.

Several web debugging proxy tools are available on the Internet. I prefer to use Eric Lawrence's *Fiddler,* which is freeware you can download from `http://fiddler2.com`. With it, you can log all HTTP(S) traffic between your computer and the Internet. You can use Fiddler to inspect the communication, set breakpoints, and modify the outgoing HTTP requests or the incoming responses. It has an event-based scripting subsystem, but the most unique feature is that Fiddler can be extended using any .NET language.

After you install and start Fiddler, it tries to register itself in the operating system as a network proxy that runs on `127.0.0.1:8888`. As a consequence, applications that rely on the operating system's proxy settings automatically forward their traffic to Fiddler, and it logs the communication. For this reason, Microsoft Internet Explorer and Google Chrome require no additional configuration, but for Firefox, you may need to manually set the proxy.

Follow these steps to peek into the communication between the browser and the server:

1. Start Fiddler from the Windows Start menu.

2. Start Internet Explorer and open the `http://fiddler2.com` website.

3. Fiddler automatically captures the traffic as it is indicated on the first pane of the status bar (see Figure 3-1), so you can inspect the communication straight away.

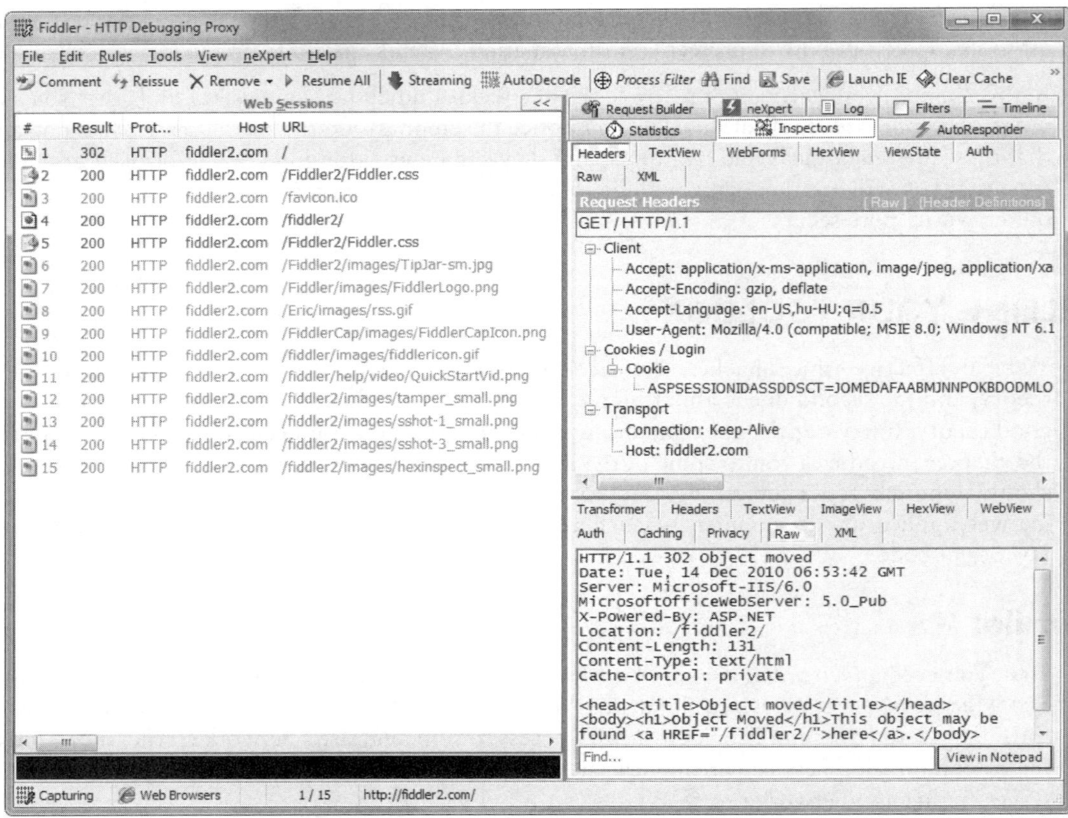

FIGURE 3-1: Browser traffic inspection with Fiddler

4. On the left pane, you can see the various sessions (HTTP request-response pairs) sent by your browser, and on the right pane, you can find the tool windows. Select a session on the left and the Inspectors tab on the right to display the details of the selected session.

5. The upper part of the Inspectors tab details the HTTP request, and the lower part displays the HTTP response. Both the upper and lower panes enable you to view the traffic in different modes. For example, you can click the Headers button to view only the header fields in logically grouped sections, or you can click the Raw button to examine the full traffic byte by byte.

Usually, a single web page involves multiple sessions to download the full content because separate requests are required for every single image and script file the page links to. This characteristic of the HTTP traffic can quickly lead to a long list of sessions on the left pane that hides the important details. Because of this, it is a good practice to filter the traffic using the features in the Rules menu and the Filters tab. When you finish logging the sessions you want to inspect, stop capturing with the Capture Traffic menu item in the File menu to avoid getting flooded with the additional requests.

To modify the network traffic, you can set breakpoints using the Automatic Breakpoints menu item in the Rules menu. You can set Before Requests and After Responses type breakpoints, which pause the execution before the request is sent to the server, or after the response is received by the proxy, but before it is forwarded to the browser. When these breakpoints are reached, Fiddler pauses, and you can manipulate the traffic in the Inspectors tab.

If you want to construct an HTTP request from scratch and examine how the server processes that request, you can use the Request Builder tab on the right pane.

Fortunately, the most frequently used features of Fiddler are also accessible with hotkeys, as shown in Table 3-1.

TABLE 3-1: Frequently Used Hotkeys of Fiddler

HOTKEY	FUNCTION
F12	Start or stop capturing.
F11	Set a Before Requests breakpoint.
ALT+F11	Set an After Responses breakpoint.
Shift+F11	Disable breakpoints.
F6	Open or close the session list pane.
F8	Jump to the Inspector tab.
CTRL+A	Select all sessions.
DEL	Remove the selected session.
CTRL+X	Remove all sessions.

Firebug

Another widely used tool for monitoring HTTP traffic is *Firebug*, which is an Open Source and free add-on for Firefox that you can download from `http://getfirebug.com`. Firebug fully integrates with Firefox, as you can see in Figure 3-2.

After you install Firebug, you can press F12 to open the tool window in the lower pane. To monitor the HTTP traffic, hover over the Net tab, click the down arrow, and then click Enabled to turn on capturing. From now on, all communication produced by the page you currently visit in the main browser window is automatically logged, and you can inspect it in the lower pane. If you do not need to monitor all types of traffic, you can apply a content type filter by clicking the buttons for HTML, CSS, JS, XHR, and so on below the Net tab.

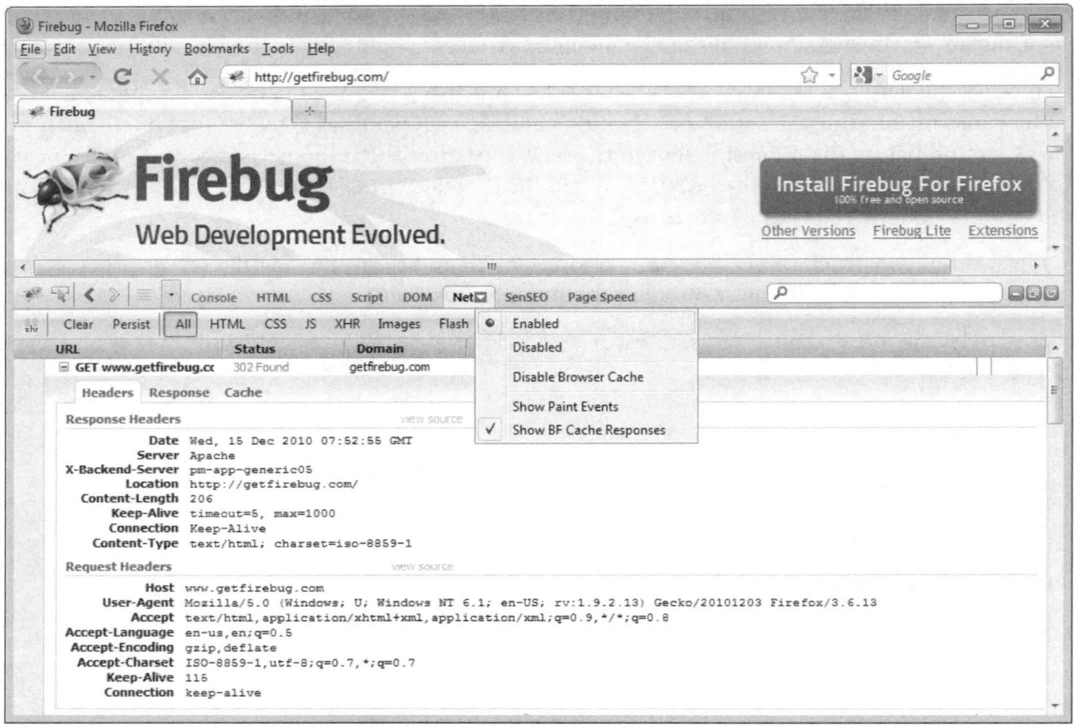

FIGURE 3-2: The Firebug add-on for Firefox

You can click the + sign in the row header to scrutinize the details of a single request and its corresponding response. The expanding pane shows the query string parameters, the request and response headers, the response body, and cache statistics. You can also add a Cookies tab here by installing the Firecookie add-on from the add-on gallery that further extends the capabilities of Firebug.

Firebug is a powerful tool with many hidden treasures. I strongly recommend that you visit its online documentation page and experiment using it in your daily work.

Internet Explorer 9 Developer Toolbar

Although, as a web developer, you probably already have Firefox installed on your machine, if you still prefer to use Internet Explorer, you can perform the same network monitoring tasks in your favorite browser, too. Internet Explorer 7 introduced the Developer Toolbar feature that incorporates similar features that Firebug provides, with the only major exception being the previously mentioned features of the Net tab. However, with Internet Explorer 9 (IE9), you do not have to miss this feature any more because Microsoft added a new Network tab to the Developer Toolbar, as shown in Figure 3-3.

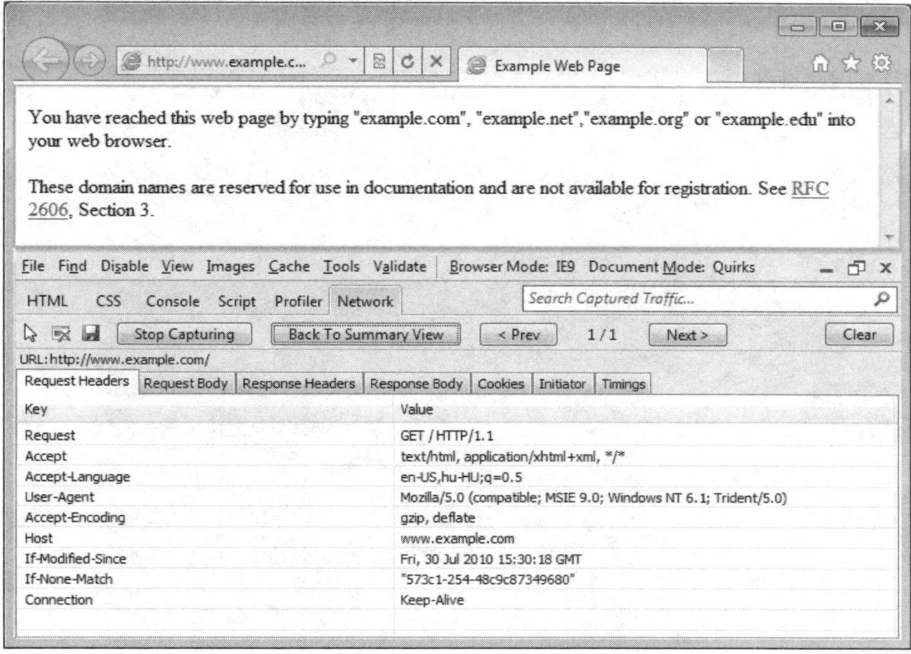

FIGURE 3-3: Network monitoring with the IE9 Developer Toolbar

The new Network tab in IE9 provides similar functionality that Firebug provides, with the only major difference being the UI layout.

Lens

The tools that you have learned about thus far provide general traffic-monitoring features that you can use to inspect any website independently from the technology they are built on. However, every technology has specialties, and you need special tools to test them. With its custom authentication, session, and state management, ASP.NET is no exception.

Lens is a free tool you can download from `http://ethicalhackingaspnet.codeplex.com` that you can use to test only ASP.NET applications. Lens is not only a penetration-testing tool, but it was also written with educational and demonstrational purposes in mind. For this reason, it contains links to additional online learning resources.

You can see the main (and only) window of Lens in Figure 3-4. To test a website, enter its URL into the Target URL textbox, and then choose a tab that corresponds to the feature you want to test. For example, in the ViewState tab, you can download, extract, and decode the `ViewState` of the given page (as you will see in more detail later in this chapter).

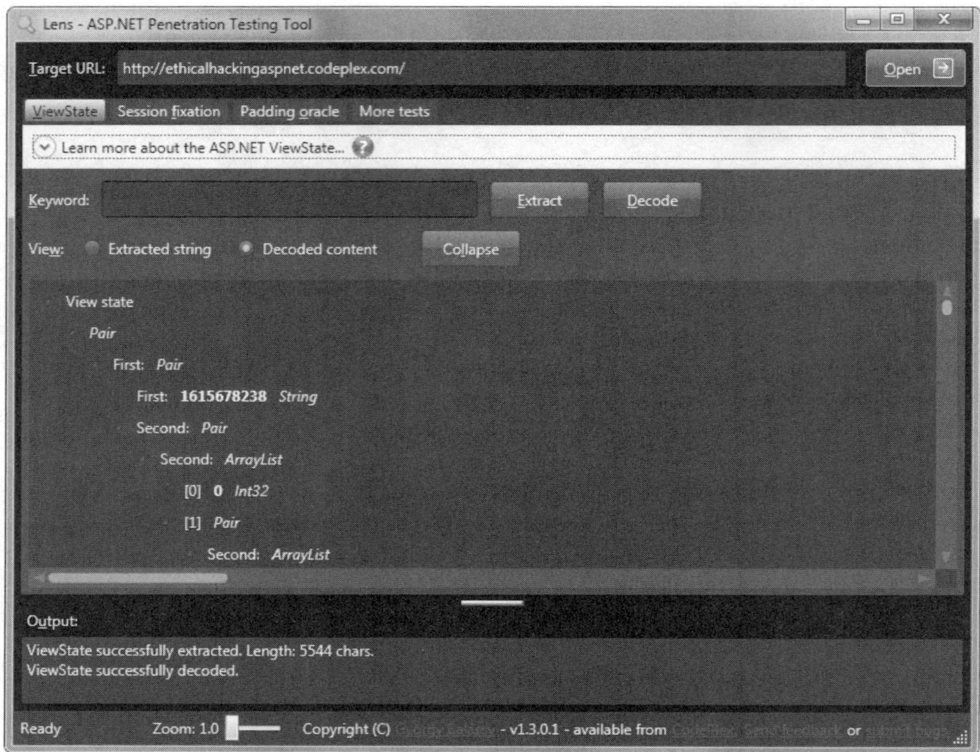

FIGURE 3-4: Lens, the ASP.NET penetration-testing tool

In addition to being a free tool, Lens is also Open Source, so you can download the full source code from the CodePlex site. It is written in .NET 4 with a Windows Presentation Foundation (WPF) graphical user interface (GUI) and a modular architecture, which enables quick extensibility.

UNDERSTANDING SESSION MANAGEMENT

Now that you have a handful of tools in your toolbox that you can use to test your solution, you need to understand how things work to know what and how you should test.

One of the most important parts of a web application is session management. The basic problem is that web pages have no memories, so when you visit a page on a website, the site always treats you as a completely new visitor. Accordingly, it doesn't know anything about your previous actions, even if you logged in before, or put something into your shopping basket a minute ago. The underlying protocol provides no solution for this problem, so from the HTTP perspective, with every new request, you are a brand new guest of the site, who just entered the front door.

But, of course, visitors need this kind of functionality, so they don't get asked again and again for the same information. In other words, they need a *session* that connects their movements from page to page, and because HTTP is *stateless*, it is implemented in a higher abstraction level, mostly by cookies.

Session Management in HTTP

Cookies are small pieces of data transmitted with the HTTP requests and responses. They are created on the server and sent to the client with an HTTP response. The browser stores them, and when the next request goes to the same server, the browser adds the same cookies to the request and sends its data back to the server. When the same cookie value is received with two separate requests by the server, the server treats them as part of the same session.

Cookies travel in the header section of the HTTP traffic. As a result, they have a limited size. As a consequence, most web applications do not store the full user state in the cookie, but instead they store it on the server side, give this property bag a session ID, and then store this small session ID in the session cookie, as shown in Figure 3-5.

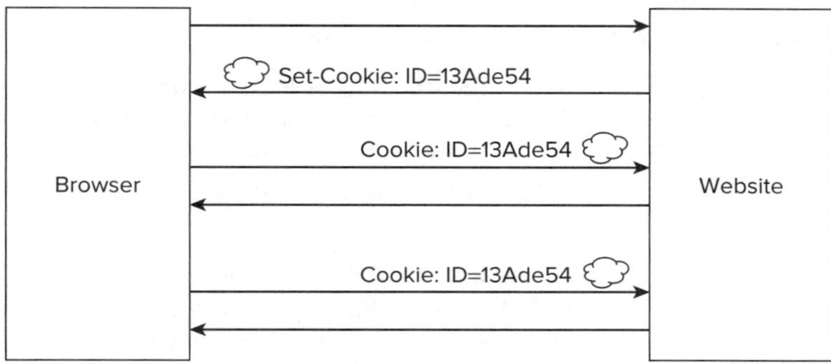

FIGURE 3-5: How cookies travel in HTTP headers

This cookie exchange can be perfectly caught on the act by Fiddler. Just visit a website (for example, `http://codeplex.com`) and look for a `Set-Cookie` header in the first response, as shown in Figure 3-6.

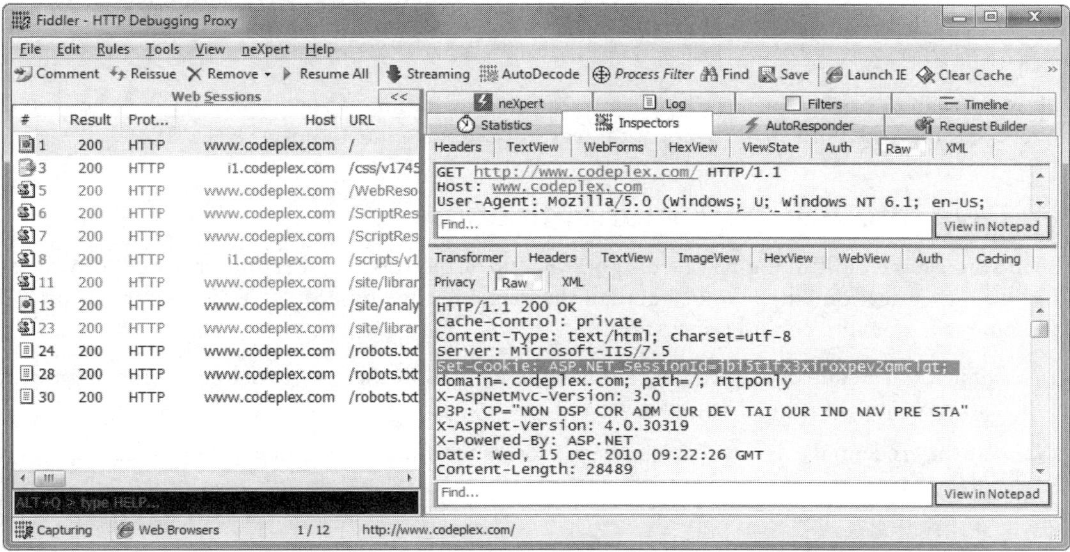

FIGURE 3-6: Inspecting the Set-Cookie header in Fiddler

Then, select a subsequent HTTP request that targets the same domain, and you see a `Cookie` header in the request that contains the same value.

Session Management in ASP.NET

In ASP.NET, you have two kinds of sessions: *simple sessions* and *login sessions*. The first one is mostly called just "session." (I added the "simple" prefix to it to help you to differentiate it from the second one.)

Simple sessions have nothing to do with authentication. When you use them, it does not matter whether your user is logged in. These types of sessions are just there to solve the problem detailed earlier in this chapter, and you use simple sessions to connect HTTP request and response pairs together that originate from the same client. You can use the `Session` object in ASP.NET to create a multipage form, or to implement a web shopping basket that does not require authentication.

On the other hand, login sessions are closely related to authentication. A login session starts when a user signs in and lasts until the same user signs out from your application. The main purpose of a login session is to track *who* exactly sends the requests to your application and to relay authorization decisions on that information. The login controls and the membership providers implement login sessions in ASP.NET.

Although there are these two kinds of sessions, both lead back to the same problem. There is no connection between the request-response pairs at the HTTP level. Both types of sessions are implemented using the same cookie-based concept; although, they use different cookies and have different strengths and weaknesses.

ATTACKING THE ASP.NET AUTHENTICATION

The most attractive target for a hacker in a website is the authentication. If the authentication fails and enables an unauthorized user to log in to the application, that can have unforeseeable consequences.

Before you can perform a penetration test on the authentication of your ASP.NET website, you must understand how the built-in authentication features are implemented in ASP.NET.

Deep Dive into ASP.NET Authentication

When you use the built-in login controls and the out-of-the-box membership provider, all you see is that the authentication "just works," and all the magic is done by ASP.NET in the background. The following is happening behind the curtains:

1. The `Login` control calls the `ValidateUser` method of the configured `MembershipProvider` that checks the user's login credentials.

2. If the credentials are invalid, the login process terminates, and an error message displays for the user.

3. If the credentials are valid, the `Login` control calls the `SetAuthCookie` method of the `FormsAuthentication` class that reads the settings from the `web.config` file and then creates the authentication cookie and attaches it to the `HttpResponse`.

4. The user is redirected with a HTTP 302 status code to the original page. The response contains the `Set-Cookie` HTTP header with a default cookie name, `.ASPXAUTH` (the name starts with a dot).

5. The cookie is received by the browser and stored in its cookie store. When the browser must send a request later to the same domain, the cookie is attached to the `Cookie` header of the request.

6. The cookie is received by the `FormsAuthenticationModule` on the server. This HTTP module checks the cookie and, if the cookie is valid, it creates a new `FormsIdentity` and a `GenericPrincipal` object and assigns them to the current `HttpContext`.

The most important part is no doubt how the authentication cookie is created and what it contains. The `SetAuthCookie` method is responsible for creating the authentication cookie, and it puts a `FormsAuthenticationTicket` object into it. Figure 3-7 shows the structure of the `FormsAuthenticationTicket` class.

The ticket contains the following property values:

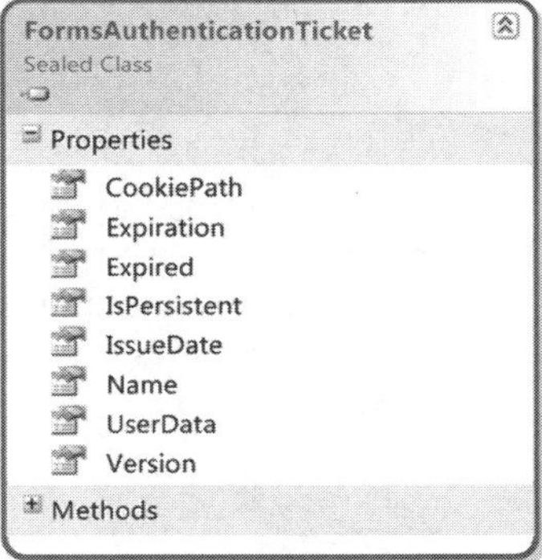

FIGURE 3-7: The FormsAuthenticationTicket class

➤ `CookiePath` — The directory where the cookie is active. So, if you want the cookie to be only sent to pages in the `Members` directory, set the `CookiePath` to `/Members`.

➤ `Expiration` — The expiration date and time of the ticket.

➤ `Expired` — A Boolean value that indicates whether the ticket is expired.

➤ `IsPersistent` — A Boolean value that indicates whether the authentication cookie is persistent.

➤ `IssueDate` — The date and time when the ticket is issued.

➤ `Name` — The login name of the user.

➤ `Version` — A numeric constant that defines the algorithms used by the framework to build the cookie. This version number is 2 in ASP.NET 4 (since ASP.NET 2.0).

The `UserData` property is empty by default and can be used for custom purposes.

By default (you can configure it in the `web.config` file), the ticket is protected with a *hash* then it is *encrypted* and converted to a hex string before it is added to the authentication cookie.

Stealing the Ticket

As you saw earlier in this chapter, the heart of the authentication is not the user's password, but the ticket that sits inside the cookie. If you can get a valid ticket, you no longer need the original password of the user because it is the ticket that is validated at every single request, and it directly contains the unique login name of the user. If malicious users can successfully attack the ticket, they can reach that goal.

One method for the attacker to get the ticket is to use XSS. As you probably know, the possibilities of XSS extend much further than just capturing a cookie. XSS can even help an attacker take total control of the victim's computer. However, it is still a classic and widely used way to steal your cookie with your login ticket in it. Fortunately, ASP.NET, by default, creates `HttpOnly` cookies, and that greatly reduces the risk of this attack.

`HttpOnly` is a single flag in the cookie, which signals to the browser that the cookie should not be accessed by any script code on the page, and that it can be used only for HTTP transfers. If you do not want to access the cookie value in JavaScript, it is recommended that you set this flag to mitigate script-based attacks against the cookie.

The ticket is transmitted in the header of the HTTP traffic so that it travels in clear text on the wire, (refer to Figure 3-6). Although the ticket itself is encrypted, as you see later, the attacker does not need to decrypt it to maliciously use it. Having the ticket is enough for the attacker to act on your behalf. For this reason, it is crucial that you protect the ticket in transmit at least as seriously as the password, and you have to use Secure Sockets Layer (SSL) for that.

You have probably heard many times that encryption is extremely CPU-intensive, and that you must minimize HTTPS to free up resources on your server. That was probably true once, but not today. In January 2010, Gmail switched to using HTTPS for everything by default. Of course, the more-secure protocol had its overhead, but guess how much? Less than 1 percent! You should read the case study about it at www.imperialviolet.org/2010/06/25/overclocking-ssl.html.

By default, ASP.NET authentication does not force you to use HTTPS, but it is recommended that you change this setting in the `web.config` file by setting the `requireSSL` attribute of the `forms` tag to `true`, as shown here:

```
<authentication mode="Forms">
  <forms requireSSL="true" ... />
</authentication>
```

With this change, you can force ASP.NET to set the `Secure` flag of the cookie to `true`, which mandates that the browser transmits the cookie only over HTTPS and never on plain HTTP.

You can test your configuration with Fiddler. By default, Fiddler does not decrypt HTTPS traffic, so you see what an attacker could see from your encrypted traffic. If you turn on the Decrypt HTTPS Traffic option in the Fiddler Options dialog, Fiddler creates self-signed certificates to intercept the encrypted traffic. If you can read the traffic without turning on this option, that means it goes on HTTP and not on HTTPS. If you allow Fiddler to decrypt HTTPS traffic, but you don't see any change in the browser (not even a warning dialog for self-signed certificates), then you are not ready yet.

Do not use self-signed certificates in production. They are open doors for man-in-the-middle attacks because the attacker can easily replace them and then sniff the network traffic between the browser and the server.

Tampering with the Ticket

After stealing your authentication cookie, the attacker will try to see what you have in it. Fortunately, by default, the ticket is encrypted with the *machine key*, so the attacker cannot read the values in the cookie.

The next question is whether the attacker can alter the cookie. The structure of the cookie is public, and a finite number of encryption algorithms are used by the .NET Framework. Can attackers modify the cookie, or can they create a nice-looking cookie from scratch? Fortunately, ASP.NET also protects your application against this kind of attack by adding a server-side secret value to the ticket hash. Even if the attackers know all values and algorithms, they can't bake a fresh cookie without knowing this server-side secret.

So, by default, you are safe from these two types of cookie-manipulation attacks. However, you can turn off these protections (but you should *never* do so) in the `protection` attribute of the `forms` tag in the `web.config` file. This setting is inherited from the machine-wide settings. Hence, if you want to ensure that your application uses encryption and validation independently from other applications on the server, you should set this explicitly in your local `web.config` file, as shown here:

```
<authentication mode="Forms">
  <forms protection="All" ... />
</authentication>
```

I recommend using this setting explicitly in your `web.config` *file because it makes your application independent from server-level settings, and it is easy to check during a code review.*

Hijacking the Login Session

Earlier in this chapter, you saw that the key to a successful authentication is not the user's password, but the authentication ticket. If attackers can get a valid authentication cookie that contains the ticket, and can send it back to the server, and the application accepts it, they can act on behalf of the original user. In other words, attackers can take control of the login session, and, for this reason, this kind of attack is called the *login session hijacking*.

Unfortunately, the built-in forms authentication mechanism in ASP.NET is vulnerable to this type of session hijacking. You can test it by following these steps:

1. Start Fiddler to capture all traffic that runs between your browser and the website.

2. Open your favorite browser, and sign in to an ASP.NET website you want to test.

3. Inspect the `HTTP 302 Redirect` response in Fiddler that contains a `Set-Cookie` HTTP header. If the name of the cookie is `.ASPXAUTH`, the site most likely uses the default forms authentication implementation.

4. Copy the value of the cookie (the long unreadable numbers after the = sign) to the clipboard. Now you have the authentication cookie that you have just captured from your own traffic. Malicious attackers must sniff the network to get this cookie, but finally they have the same data you have just copied to the clipboard. In the following steps, you test whether the application accepts this cookie if it is sent back from a different client.

5. Start Lens and enter the URL of the website in the Target URL textbox.

6. Switch to the Session Fixation tab that provides various session-related tests. Enter the name of the cookie (most likely `.ASPXAUTH`) into the Cookie Name textbox, and paste the value from the clipboard in the Cookie Value field, as shown in Figure 3-8.

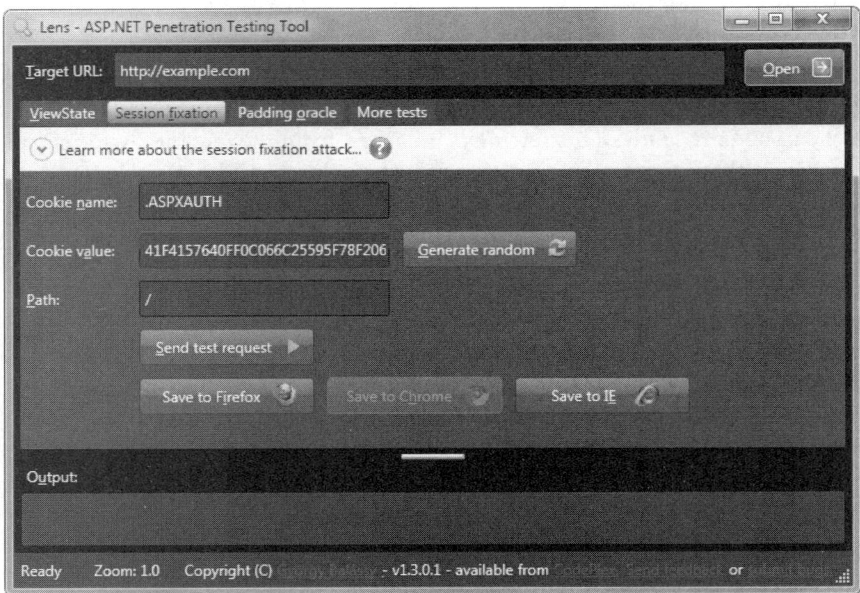

FIGURE 3-8: Creating an authentication cookie in Lens

7. Click any of the enabled Save To buttons to create a session cookie with the given value directly in the local cookie store of the browser you selected. This cookie attaches to the request the next time you open the website in that browser. To successfully test your

application against session hijacking, you must select a different browser than what you used in Step 2. In this way, you can simulate that the cookie is sent back from a different location.

> *The term* location *at this point means a different browser, and it is a valid test scenario because the cookie stores of the browsers are fully isolated. If you want to test for a different client IP address, you can start Lens on a different computer and follow the same steps to create the authentication cookie on that machine.*

8. Open the browser that you chose in Step 7, and simply visit the website you are testing. The browser automatically attaches the previously stored cookie to the request, and, if the website accepts it, you will be immediately signed in as the original user you used in Step 2. That means that your application is vulnerable to login session hijacking. If the website does not treat you as a signed-in user, or displays an error message, your website is safe from session hijacking.

By default, all ASP.NET applications that use the built-in authentication implementation with the default configuration are vulnerable to this attack.

Protecting Your Application Against Login Session Hijacking

Unfortunately, ASP.NET does not provide a configuration setting or any built-in magic switch to protect your application against login session hijacking. Although you can mitigate the risk using HTTPS encrypting, the traffic does not solve the original problem. You must write some code to strengthen your application.

The original problem is that the cookie is not bound to a single client. If the website can detect that the cookie is sent back from a different client, the site is safe. Standard cookies do not provide any way to check the original owner of them, so the only option is to add some additional information to the content of the cookie.

First, you must determine what data can fulfill your needs. For example, you can use the `User-Agent` header that identifies the browser, and also the IP address of the client for this purpose.

> *Both the* `User-Agent` *header and the IP address can help you raise the barrier that attackers meet when they attack your application. However, you should know that, unfortunately, none of these solutions are perfect in all circumstances. The* `User-Agent` *header can change if the users mask their browser for compatibility reasons. (This happens quite often among advanced Opera users.) The IP address of the client may also change, if it has a dynamic address, or switches networks — for example, a mobile computer, virtual private network (VPN), or wireless network. Even so, I still recommend that you use these values, but be prepared with a friendly error message to the users because there can be valid actions that modify these values.*

As you saw in the "Deep Dive into ASP.NET Authentication" section earlier in this chapter, the cookie contains an encrypted ticket, and you also learned about the structure of the ticket. Luckily, the `FormsAuthenticationTicket` class provides a standard way to add additional information to it in the `UserData` property. This is a simple string property, and you can store anything in it because it is not used by the ASP.NET runtime. Just like any other property value of the ticket, it will be encrypted, and also be protected from tampering.

First, you must override the default cookie-creation mechanism of ASP.NET, and that requires you to add some custom code to the `Login` control, and omit the `RedirectFromLoginPage` method of the `FormsAuthentication` class.

To create a custom cookie, start by asking ASP.NET to create a standard one on your login page, just after you validate the user's credentials:

```
HttpCookie cookie = FormsAuthentication.GetAuthCookie
   ( userName, chkRememberMe.Checked );
```


Code file [Authentication\Login.aspx.cs] available for download at Wrox.com.

This cookie contains the ticket that you can access by decrypting the cookie value:

```
FormsAuthenticationTicket oldTicket = FormsAuthentication.Decrypt( cookie.Value );
```


Code file [Authentication\Login.aspx.cs] available for download at Wrox.com.

With the properties of the original ticket, you can create a new one, with the only difference being that you set the `UserData` property this time:

```
FormsAuthenticationTicket newTicket = new FormsAuthenticationTicket(
   oldTicket.Version, oldTicket.Name, oldTicket.IssueDate,
   oldTicket.Expiration, oldTicket.IsPersistent, userData );
```


Code file [Authentication\Login.aspx.cs] available for download at Wrox.com.

The `userData` variable can contain any additional information you want to embed into the ticket, such as the `User-Agent` and the IP address of the client. Besides the values you add for security reasons, you can embed additional values you need for every request, but for performance reasons you do not want to store or look up on the server every time. For example, the following code adds the user's role, unique identifier, and e-mail address to the cookie:

```
string userAgent = HttpContext.Current.Request.UserAgent;
string clientIP = HttpContext.Current.Request.UserHostAddress;
string userData = String.Format( CultureInfo.InvariantCulture,
     "{0}|{1}|{2}|{3}|{4}", clientIP, userAgent, role, userId, email );
```


Code file [Authentication\Login.aspx.cs] available for download at Wrox.com.

In the next step, you encrypt the new ticket:

```
cookie.Value = FormsAuthentication.Encrypt( newTicket );
```

And, finally, you add the new encrypted ticket to the HTTP response:

```
Response.Cookies.Add( cookie );
```

Code file [Authentication\Login.aspx.cs] available for download at Wrox.com.

To redirect the user to the original page, do not call the `RedirectFromLoginPage` method because it always creates the standard authentication cookie. You should do that in two steps:

```
string redirectUrl = FormsAuthentication.GetRedirectUrl( userName, false );
Response.Redirect( redirectUrl );
```

Code file [Authentication\Login.aspx.cs] available for download at Wrox.com.

With these steps, you have created a standard authentication cookie that behaves just like the original one, but it contains additional information about the client. The next step is to validate this information when the cookie is sent back by a client with the next HTTP request.

The best place to check the `UserData` is the `Application_PostAuthenticateRequest` event in the `global.asax` file. This event handler is called right after the `FormsAuthenticationModule` validated the other fields of the ticket, and here you can access its results. You can start by getting the identity of the user if the user was successfully authenticated by the forms authentication module:

```
IPrincipal user = HttpContext.Current.User;

if( user.Identity.IsAuthenticated &&
    user.Identity.AuthenticationType.Equals( "Forms",
    StringComparison.OrdinalIgnoreCase ) )
{
  FormsIdentity formsIdentity = HttpContext.Current.User.Identity as FormsIdentity;

  // Next code lines come here…
}
```

Code file [Authentication\Global.asax] available for download at Wrox.com.

The `FormsIdentity` class enables you access the ticket and the `UserData` value submitted by the client:

```
string userData = formsIdentity.Ticket.UserData;
```

Code file [Authentication\Global.asax] available for download at Wrox.com.

The `userData` field contains the IP address and the `User-Agent` of the client who originally requested the cookie. All you must do now is to compare these values with the values of the current client:

```
string[] userDataParts = userData.Split( '|' );
string clientIP = userDataParts[ 0 ];
string userAgent = userDataParts[ 1 ];
PortalRole role = (PortalRole) Enum.Parse( typeof( PortalRole ),
    userDataParts[ 2 ] );
```

```
int userId = Int32.Parse( userDataParts[ 3 ] );
string email = userDataParts[ 4 ];

HttpRequest req = HttpContext.Current.Request;

if( !req.UserHostAddress.Equals( clientIP, StringComparison.OrdinalIgnoreCase ) )
  throw new SecurityException();

if( !req.UserAgent.Equals( userAgent, StringComparison.OrdinalIgnoreCase ) )
  throw new SecurityException();
```

Code file [Authentication\Global.asax] available for download at Wrox.com.

For simplicity, the previous code snippet just throws a `SecurityException`, *but you have to be sure that these events are logged and a friendly error message is displayed to the user. But be careful not to provide too much information about the error that can help the attacker.*

The previous code snippet demonstrates how you can store any value in the login cookie. For example, because ASP.NET gives you access only to the login name of the current user, it can be also useful to cache the user's internal ID in the cookie to simplify database operations. You can also create custom identity and principal classes that implement the `IIdentity` and the `IPrincipal` interfaces, and you can make these values available to every part of your website by assigning them to the current HTTP context and the current thread:

```
MyPortalIdentity portalIdentity = new MyPortalIdentity( user.Identity.Name,
      userId, role, email );
MyPortalPrincipal portalPrincipal = new MyPortalPrincipal( portalIdentity );
HttpContext.Current.User = portalPrincipal;
Thread.CurrentPrincipal = portalPrincipal;
```

Code file [Authentication\Global.asax] available for download at Wrox.com.

After you add this workaround to your code, do not forget to retest your solution with Fiddler and Lens, as described in detail earlier in this chapter.

Cross-Site Request Forgery

As a security-conscious web developer, you already know about XSS attacks that rely on the user's trust for the website. In this section, you learn about another type of attack, which is the inverse of XSS, which exploits that the website trusts the user.

Most websites protect sensitive operations by requiring authentication. For example, if you have an online banking site, it can provide the following URL that enables the transferring of money:

```
http://bank.example.com/Transfer?To=111-222-333&Amount=1000
```

As you can see, the query string contains the target bank account number (the `To` field) and the amount of money to transfer (the `Amount` field). You can send an HTTP GET request to this URL, but, of course, the website checks that you have logged in before and processes the request only if you are successfully authenticated.

But how does the website know that you are already signed in? It checks if the request contains a login cookie. Therefore, if you send an HTTP GET request to this URL *and* attach a valid login cookie to the request, the bank completes the transfer. Accordingly, if *attackers* can send an HTTP GET request to a similar URL that contains *their* bank account number as the target and attach *your* login cookie to the request, your money will be stolen by the bad guys.

If you read the previous sections of this chapter, you already know how to protect your login cookie from being stolen and sent back from another location. So, the only option left for the attacker is to force you to send a request to a maliciously crafted URL and attach your login cookie to it. You would be shocked at how easy it is. All the attackers need is a webpage where they she can embed a simple image tag:

```
<img src="http://bank.example.com/Transfer?To=666-666-666&Amount=9999" />
```

This forces your browser to send an HTTP GET request to the bank's website asking for a transfer to the attacker's bank account. And here comes the best part — if your browser has a cookie for `bank.example.com`, the browser will be more than happy to attach it to the request, and the website sees it as an authenticated request from you.

You probably noticed the Remember Me check box on the login page of many websites. If you check this option, it asks the website to create a *persistent cookie*. This type of cookie is stored not only in the browser's memory, but also on disk, so it survives browser or system restarts. The website remembers you because the browser remembers the cookie. So, if you logged in to your bank site a week ago and checked the Remember Me check box, your authentication cookie still sits on your disk and will be sent with your request to save you from re-authenticating yourself.

If you have a previously stored persistent login cookie and visit a website that contains the image tag just described, you will be the victim of this attack without even noticing it. A single click can be enough, and that's why this kind of attack is often called a *one-click attack*, or, more formally, *cross-site request forgery (CSRF)*.

> *There are two things to consider here. Firstly, although the name* one-click attack *is widely used for CSRF attacks, using them as synonyms is technically not absolutely correct. One-click attacks are actually a subset of CSRF. Secondly, this example used an HTTP* GET *target, but the attack does not bound to* GET *requests.* POST *requests are also vulnerable; although, they require a bit more coding to exploit.*

Protecting Against CSRF Attacks

As you saw earlier, persistent cookies facilitate CSRF, so your first idea could be to completely disable persistent cookies to protect your application. Although it actually mitigates this attack, my experience is that users like and use this feature, especially in websites they frequently access.

The root problem with CSRF is that the website trusts the user. If a valid request is received from the client, the website treats it as if it were intentionally sent by the user. The question is how the website can differentiate between intentional requests and requests sent by the browser without the user's consent. That's a difficult problem, because, from the server's standpoint, an intentional and a malicious request look absolutely the same.

The other characteristic of CSRF is that the attacker can build a fully valid request beforehand, which means that the attacker formerly knows every single value that the server expects in a request. By making all requests a bit different with values that the attacker can't find out, you can mitigate this attack.

One common part of every POST request in an ASP.NET website is the view state. ASP.NET provides a built-in mechanism, the ViewStateUserKey property, to add additional protection to the view state by adding any arbitrary value to it that is checked when the integrity of the view state is validated by the runtime. If you add an extra value that ties the view state to the current user or to the current session, you can raise the barrier for a successful CSRF attack.

The ViewStateUserKey property can be set only in the Page_Init phase of the page life cycle, as you can see in the following code snippet:

```
protected override void OnInit( EventArgs e )
{
  base.OnInit( e );

  if( this.User.Identity.IsAuthenticated )
  {
    this.ViewStateUserKey = this.Session.SessionID;
  }
}
```

Although this setting raises the barrier for CSRF attacks, it does not protect you in all situations:

➤ The ViewStateUserKey protects only pages that have view state enabled.

➤ The ViewStateUserKey is not checked when view state Method Authentication Code (MAC) validation is turned off.

➤ The view state MAC (and the ViewStateUserKey with it) is checked only for POST requests. Therefore, you must ensure that all your GET requests are idempotent.

➤ Unfortunately, ASP.NET ignores HTTP verbs when processing form values, so the ViewState can be posted back also in a query string parameter to completely bypass the MAC validation.

What's more, when the user's session times out, the runtime throws a view state MAC validation error that you must gracefully handle.

Additional Protection Against CSRF

The anti-CSRF solution you learned earlier heavily relies on the ASP.NET view state with its advantages and disadvantages. However, there are situations in which you do not want to use view state, or you cannot use view state.

For example, there is no view state in the ASP.NET Model-View-Controller (MVC). Fortunately, the MVC library out-of-the-box provides a mechanism to protect your application against CSRF via the `AntiForgeryToken` *helper.*

In this case, you can use any other parts of the HTTP traffic to make your requests and responses unique. For example, you can add a random value to a hidden field on the page and store the same value in the session on the server side. Later, when a request comes in, you can check that these two values are equal. This approach is implemented as a free downloadable `HttpModule` in the .NET CSRF Guard project of Open Web Application Security Project (OWASP) from `www.owasp.org/index.php/.Net_CSRF_Guard`.

However, if your application does not rely on sessions, turning it on only for anti-CSRF is a big overhead. The `AntiCSRF` module (also downloadable for free from `http://anticsrf.codeplex.com`) solves this problem by storing the session-specific secret in a form field and in a session cookie, and mandating that the two values be the same for every request.

If you implement a secret-based protection like the .NET CSRF Guard or the `AntiCSRF` module, ensure that your application is free from XSS vulnerabilities, and that your `GET` requests are idempotent.

ATTACKING THE ASP.NET SESSION

At the beginning of this chapter, you learned about the two kinds of sessions ASP.NET supports: the classic session and the login session. After learning about the login session, it's now time to learn about various attacks against the simple session.

ASP.NET Session Under the Covers

The ASP.NET session is managed by an HTTP module (called the `SessionStateModule`) that works independently from the authentication modules. When a new client connects to your website, this module generates a new session identifier, and stores this ID in an HTTP cookie or in the URL, related to the `cookieless` attribute of the `sessionState` tag in the `web.config` file. This section focuses on the default cookie-based sessions.

In contrast to the login sessions, the value stored in the cookie is not encrypted and not protected with a hash. It is just the raw session ID. ASP.NET first generates a 15-byte random ID and then encodes it to a 24-character string that can be used directly as a cookie value.

Besides this, there are many similarities between the authentication and the session, and, therefore, similar attacks can target them.

Guessing the Session ID

As you have seen, the heart of the session is the session ID. If the attackers can get the session ID, they can build a session cookie and can send it to the website to steal the session. In most web platforms, the session ID is an integer number. If the session ID numbers are created sequentially or with a simple random-number generator, the attackers can look up their own session ID and have a fairly good guess about the IDs currently used by other users of the website.

Fortunately, ASP.NET does not use incremental session numbers but generates the ID with the .NET Framework's built-in `RNGCryptoServiceProvider`. This class produces cryptographically strong random numbers that are really, really difficult to guess. The number is 15-bytes long, so it would also take a long time to find an existing session ID by probing.

Stealing the Session Cookie

If attackers can't guess your session ID, they must steal your session cookie to access the ID. Just like with the login cookie, a classic method to grab it is XSS. Fortunately (again, just like with the login cookie), ASP.NET by default adds the `HttpOnly` attribute to the cookie. Therefore, it cannot be accessed by the webpage, which makes it difficult to steal via XSS.

Another way the attacker can access your session cookie is by sniffing the network. If you connect to the website through nonsecure HTTP, the requests and the responses are sent in clear text, so any access to the communication can reveal your session cookie.

> *If you use sessions in your ASP.NET application, the first response after you store any value in the* `Session` *dictionary contains your session cookie. From that time, your browser attaches the cookie to every HTTP request it sends to the server. Because the cookie is almost always on the wire, the attackers can capture it even if they have access to the HTTP traffic for a limited time.*

Unfortunately, ASP.NET does not provide any built-in configuration feature to force the browser to transmit the session cookie only through HTTPS, and never on HTTP. It is up to you, the developer, to architect your application to secure the session cookie because out-of-the-box, every ASP.NET application is vulnerable to session hijacking.

Testing Your Application Against Session Hijacking

As you have learned, neither the cookie nor the server stores any additional information about the client. The session ID alone is enough to get access to anyone's session. So, if attackers possess the cookie, they can send it back to the website from any other computer because the session is not bound to any particular client.

Follow these steps to test your web application against session hijacking:

1. Start Fiddler to capture all traffic that runs between your browser and the website. Do some actions on the site that store some value in the session (for example, put an item in your shopping basket if the site is for web shopping).

2. Study the communication log, and look for a `Set-Cookie` HTTP header in the response, or `Cookie` header in the request that has the name `ASP.NET_SessionId`.

3. Copy the 24-character value of the cookie to the clipboard.

4. Start Lens, and enter the URL of the website in the Target URL textbox.

5. Switch to the Session Fixation tab that provides various session-related tests. By default, the Cookie Name textbox contains `ASP.NET_SessionId`, so most likely, you won't have to change it. Paste the value from the clipboard to the Cookie Value field

6. Click any of the enabled Save To buttons to create a session cookie with the given value directly in the local cookie store of the browser you selected. This cookie will be attached to the request the next time you open the website in that browser. To simulate that you submit the session cookie from a different location, select a different browser from the one you used in Step 1 to generate the traffic.

7. Open the browser that you have chosen in the previous step, and simply visit the website you're testing. The browser automatically attaches the previously stored cookie to the request. If the website accepts it, you see the same state you created in the first browser. (For example, the item will be in your basket.) This means your application is vulnerable to session hijacking. If the website does not show your original state, or displays an error message, your website is safe from session hijacking.

Protecting Your Website Against Session Hijacking

The root problem of session hijacking is that the cookie is not bound to a particular client. This was also the root problem for the login session hijacking, and you have already learned how you can add additional protection by storing the IP address and the `User-Agent` of the client in the cookie. The same method works here, too. However, the implementation is completely different because the built-in `SessionStateModule` does not provide the level of extensibility you have with the `FormsAuthenticationModule`.

To fix the session management, you can create a new HTTP module that sits in the ASP.NET pipeline in front of the `SessionStateModule`. When the website first generates the session cookie, this new module modifies the session cookie and attaches some additional information to it, just before the cookie is sent to the client. When the browser submits the cookie back to the website, it is first examined by the new module, and the additional information is checked. If the extra data is valid, it is removed, and the original session cookie value is passed to the `SessionStateModule`. If the validation fails, the new front-end module terminates the execution. The additional data can be any information that identifies the original client. (I recommend that you to use the IP address and the `User-Agent` of the browser.)

Figure 3-9 shows the architecture of the solution with the custom module highlighted:

To implement this solution, first you must create a new class that implements the `IHttpModule` interface. In the `Init` phase of the execution, you must subscribe to the `BeginRequest` and `EndRequest` events to tamper with the request and the response.

```
public class SecureSessionModule : IHttpModule
{
    public void Init( HttpApplication context )
    {
        context.BeginRequest += new EventHandler( this.OnBeginRequest );
```

```
        context.EndRequest += new EventHandler( this.OnEndRequest );
    }
}
```

Code file [Session\SecureSessionModule.cs] available for download at Wrox.com.

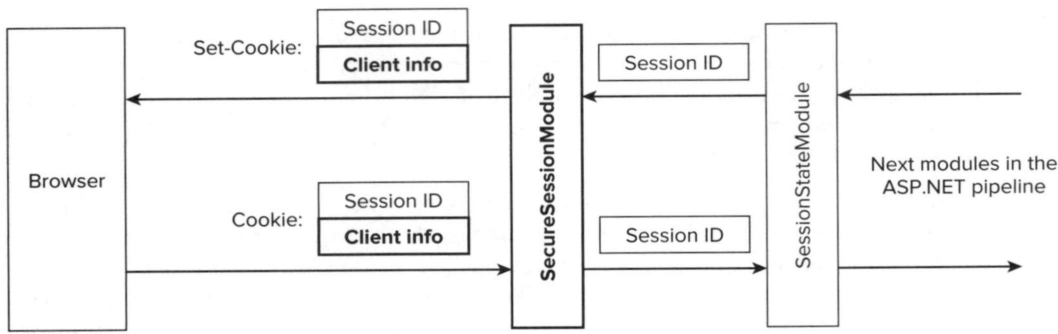

FIGURE 3-9: The custom SecureSessionModule in the ASP.NET pipeline

The first time the website creates a session cookie, it will be sent to the browser in a HTTP response. In the `OnEndRequest` handler, you can access this cookie and add a MAC to it:

```
public void OnEndRequest( object sender, EventArgs e )
{
    HttpCookie cookie = this.GetCookie( HttpContext.Current.Response.Cookies );

    if( cookie != null )
    {
        string mac = this.GenerateMac( cookie.Value, HttpContext.Current.Request );
        cookie.Value += mac;
    }
}
```

Code file [Session\SecureSessionModule.cs] available for download at Wrox.com.

The previous code uses two helper methods. The first one is `GetCookie` that is used to find the ASP.NET session cookie in the HTTP response:

```
private HttpCookie GetCookie( HttpCookieCollection cookies )
{
    for( int i = 0; i < cookies.Count; i++ )
    {
        HttpCookie cookie = cookies[ i ];
        if( cookie.Name.Equals( "ASP.NET_SessionId",
            StringComparison.OrdinalIgnoreCase ) )
        {
            return cookie;
        }
    }
```

```
    return null;
  }
```


At first, it may seem to be a bit lengthy, but believe me, it is necessary. In this phase of the execution, using the indexer of the `HttpCookieCollection` may have side effects, and using a `foreach` loop instead of the `for` loop may throw exceptions.

The second helper function is the `GenerateMac` private method. This method is responsible for generating a *Hash-based Message Authentication Code (HMAC)* that contains the sensitive properties of the client. Because, unlike the authentication ticket, the session cookie is not encrypted and not signed, it is up to you to ensure that the values cannot be tampered with by the attacker. An HMAC is a kind of hash, which uses a server-side secret to protect the data from regeneration by a malicious user. The `GenerateMac` method utilizes the built-in `System.Security.Cryptography.HMACSHA512` class of the .NET Framework to calculate the HMAC.

```
private string GenerateMac( string sessionID, HttpRequest request )
{
  string content = String.Format( CultureInfo.InvariantCulture, "{0}|{1}",
    request.UserHostAddress, request.UserAgent );

  byte[] key = Encoding.UTF8.GetBytes( "Any server side secret..." );

  using( HMACSHA512 hmac = new HMACSHA512( key ) )
  {
    byte[] hash = hmac.ComputeHash( Encoding.UTF8.GetBytes( content ) );
    return Convert.ToBase64String( hash );
  }
}
```


After the HMAC containing the IP address and the `User-Agent` of the client is calculated, it is concatenated to the original cookie value in the `OnEndRequest` handler. This new value is sent to the client and is sent back to the server with the next HTTP request.

When a new request comes in, the `OnBeginRequest` handler is executed. This handler examines the request, and if it contains a session cookie, it validates the HMAC by generating a new HMAC, and comparing it with the values passed by the client. If the values differ, it may indicate a session-hijacking attack. Finally, if the HMAC is valid, the HMAC is removed from the cookie before the ASP.NET session module uses it. The implementation of the `OnBeginRequest` method is shown in the following code snippet:

```
public void OnBeginRequest(object sender, EventArgs e)
{
  HttpRequest request = HttpContext.Current.Request;
  HttpCookie cookie = this.GetCookie(request.Cookies);

  if( cookie != null )
```

```csharp
  {
    string value = cookie.Value;

    if(!String.IsNullOrEmpty(value))
    {
      string sessionID = value.Substring(0, 24);
      string clientMac = value.Substring(24);

      string serverMac = this.GenerateMac(sessionID, request);

      if( !clientMac.Equals(serverMac, StringComparison.OrdinalIgnoreCase) )
      {
        throw new SecurityException("Hack!");
      }

      // Remove the MAC from the cookie before ASP.NET uses it.
      cookie.Value = sessionID;
    }
  }
}
```

Code file [Session\SecureSessionModule.cs] available for download at Wrox.com.

After you create the new `SecureSessionModule`, open your `web.config` file, and add it to the ASP. NET request-processing pipeline:

```xml
<configuration>
  <system.web>
    <httpModules>
      <add name="SecureSessionModule" type="SecureSessionModule"/>
    </httpModules>
  </system.web>
</configuration>
```

As mentioned during the discussion of the login session hijacking, using the IP address and the `User-Agent` header can help to raise the security barrier, but they are not perfect solutions in all circumstances.

Session Fixation

If attackers can't discover your session ID after you first have it, they still have the option to discover the session ID even before you use it. In other words, if attackers can force a user's browser to use a pre-set session ID determined by the attackers, the attackers have no need to steal the session cookie anymore — they already knows what is in it!

This kind if attack is called *session fixation*, and Figure 3-10 shows how it works:

1. A malicious user, Mallory, finds a way (for example, through a browser vulner-ability or external application) to store a new cookie for a website in the cookie store of Alice's browser, with the name of `ASP.NET_SessionId` and with the value of `123451234513245123451234`.

2. The next time Alice visits the website, the browser attaches the cookie from the cookie store.

3. Mallory stores the same session cookie in her own browser, and when she visits the website, she can connect to the same session that Alice uses.

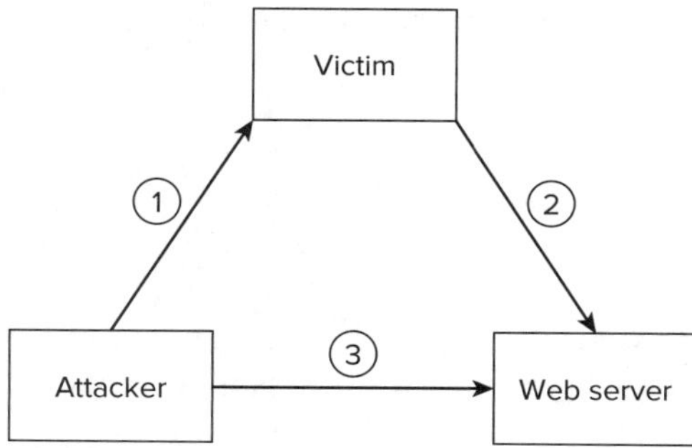

FIGURE 3-10: Session fixation

Unfortunately, by default, ASP.NET is vulnerable to session-fixation attacks. But examining what makes the platform susceptible to this kind of attack can help you to mitigate it.

Protecting Your Application Against Session Fixation Attacks

The first problem is that the attacker knows everything about the cookie: its name and the format of the value it should contain. The first step to raise the barrier is to change the name of the cookie from the default `ASP.NET_SessionId` to something unique in the `web.config` file:

```
<sessionState cookieName="MyCookieName" />
```

The second step is to generate a custom cookie value. By default, ASP.NET accepts any 24-character-length cookie value that contains characters from "a" to "z" and "0" to "5." If you want to generate a custom cookie value, you can do it by creating a new session ID manager that implements the `System.Web.SessionState.ISessionIDManager` interface.

The built-in implementation is the `SessionIDManager` class that takes care of even the cookieless operation. Therefore, if you want to change only the way the session ID is created, you can derive directly from the `SessionIDManager` base class and override the `CreateSessionID` method:

```
public class MySessionIdManager : System.Web.SessionState.SessionIDManager
{
  public override string CreateSessionID( System.Web.HttpContext context )
  {
    // Custom session ID creating goes here...
  }

  public override bool Validate( string id )
  {
    // Validation logic goes here...
  }
}
```

Obviously, if you change how you generate the session ID, you must change how the incoming values are validated. In the previous code, you can see the `Validate` method, which can also be overridden to serve this purpose. The platform implementation of the `Validate` method checks only the format of the session cookie value. But if you want to protect your application against session fixation, you must add an additional layer of security. You must check that the session ID submitted by the client was previously created by the `CreateSessionID` method for the current client.

After you have your custom session ID manager implementation, you must configure it in the `web.config` file:

```
<configuration>
  <system.web>
    <sessionState sessionIDManagerType="MySessionIdManager" />
  </system.web>
</configuration>
```

So far, you were dealing with only cookie-based sessions, but ASP.NET also supports cookieless sessions. The support for cookieless sessions was added to the platform to support clients that disable cookies, or cannot manage cookies at all (for example, early mobile browsers), but thankfully that era has ended. Because cookieless sessions store the session identifier in the URL (and that makes the attacker's job easier), I strongly recommend that you to work only with cookie-based sessions and completely disable the cookieless fallback in the `web.config` file:

```
<sessionState cookieless="UseCookies" />
```

To protect your application against session fixation and session hijacking, you can combine the methods described in the "Protecting Your Website Against Session Hijacking" section earlier in this chapter with a custom session ID manager.

HACKING THE VIEW STATE

One of the biggest advantages of ASP.NET over other web platforms is that web controls automatically preserve their state across postbacks. This feature, which gives tremendous productivity for developers, is provided by the view state. As an ASP.NET developer, you have probably already learned that the view state is actually a property bag that stores the state of the controls on the page, which is later serialized by the runtime into the hidden __VIEWSTATE field. You also probably know what impact the view state has on the page life cycle. In this section, you learn about the security-related side effects of using the view state.

Peeking into the View State

The view state is automatically maintained by the ASP.NET runtime. Web controls and web pages, by default, store arbitrary values in the `ViewState` and `ControlState` properties, and the runtime takes care of serializing and deserializing these properties to the hidden __VIEWSTATE field during the page life cycle. Because the values are stored in a form field (which travels to the client as part of the HTML code of the page), you must treat the field as public information for your visitors. Because ASP.NET developers store and retrieve values from the `ViewState` property conveniently in server-side code, they tend to forget that any data placed in the view state is actually publicly visible on the client.

When you look into the generated HTML markup of your page, you can see that the serialized view state looks something like this:

```
<input type="hidden" name="__VIEWSTATE" id="__VIEWSTATE" value=
"/wEPDwUKLTkzNjEzMDI5NA9kFgJmD2QWAmYPZBYEZg9kFgICAQ8WAh4EaHJlZgU4
aHR0cDovL2kxLmNvGVwbGV4LmNvbS9jc3MvdjE3NDUwL2k5NDIxMS9TdHlsZVNoZ
WV0LmFzaHhkAgEPZBYIAgEPZBYCZg8PFgIeCEltYWdlVXJsBTJodHRwOi8vaTEuY2
9kZXBsZXguY29tL0ltYWdlcy92MTc0NTAvbG9nby1ob211LnBuZ2RkAgIPFgIeBFR
leHQFSjxzY3JpcHQgc3JjPSIvc2l0ZS9saWJyYXJ5L3N2eS9icm9rZXIuanMiIHR5
cGU9InRleHQVamF2YXNjcmlwdCI+PC9zY3JpcHQ+ZAIDDw8WAh8BBS5odHRwOi8va
TMuY29kZXBsZXguY29tL0ltYWdlcy92MTc0NTAvYmxhbnsucG5nFgIeBm9ubG9hZA
UZc2VsZi5sb2dvSW1hZ2VMb2FkZWQ9dHJ1ZWQCBA8WAh4HVmlzaWJsZWdkZNaxicg
/ZsYrWPagVP35MS3HEdiV" />
```

Although it looks cryptic, it is not encrypted at all. To serialize the objects in the `ViewState` property, ASP.NET uses the `LosFormatter` (Limited Object Serialization) class, which is designed for highly compact, ASCII format serialization. Internally, it uses the `ObjectStateFormatter` class that is capable of serializing any object graph. However, by default, it does not encrypt the output, but only converts it to Base64 to make it suitable for storing in a HTML form field. Because these serializer classes are public, a malicious user can deserialize and decode your view state and peek into its content. If you (or any control you use) store some sensitive data in the view state or in the control state, it may lead to information disclosure, which is an often underestimated but dangerous threat.

> *You can set the* `EnableViewState` *attribute of the* `@Page` *directive or the* `<pages>` *tag in the* `web.config` *file, or any single control to* `false` *to completely turn off view state. Turning off the view state is a good idea if you don't need it, but if you do, you must ensure you use it securely. You can also use the* `ViewStateMode` *property in conjunction with* `EnableViewState` *to accomplish the same.*

Testing Your View State Against Information Disclosure

You can use Lens to test your pages against information disclosure in the view state by following these steps:

1. Start Lens, and enter the full URL of the page you want to test into the Target URL textbox. You can click the Open button to verify the URL you entered.

2. Go to the ViewState tab, and click the Extract button to download the page. Snip out the content of the `__VIEWSTATE` hidden field. The Output pane shows the length of the extracted value, as shown in Figure 3-11.

3. Click the Decode button to decode the downloaded content. This changes the lower pane to a tree view that displays the decoded content. However, you can always switch between the original and the decoded view by clicking the Extracted String and the Decoded Content radio buttons.

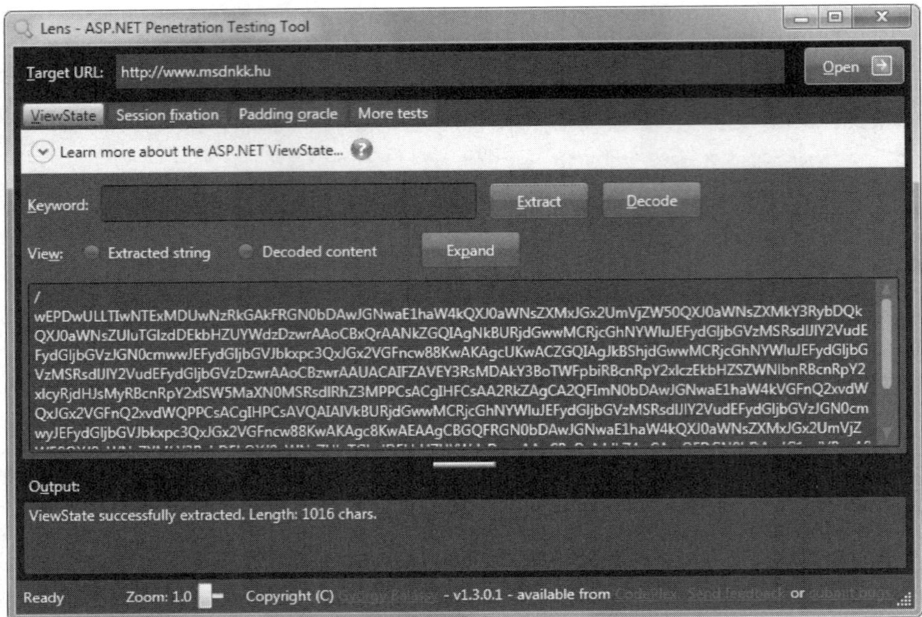

FIGURE 3-11: Using Lens to extract the ViewState from a page

4. If you are just looking for a particular string in the view state, you can enter it into the Keyword field, and Lens automatically highlights the tree node that contains the text with red as you type. Figure 3-12 shows the tree view and the keyword highlighting.

The view state you downloaded corresponds with the current state of the current page. You must test every page of your website independently for information disclosure. To test every page state, you can also directly paste the serialized view state value into the "Extracted String view of Lens," and then click the Decode button to decode it.

Encrypting Your View State

Fortunately, ASP.NET provides a built-in mechanism to encrypt the content of the `ViewState` property via the `ViewStateEncryptionMode` property of the `Page`. This property can have one of the following three values:

➤ `Auto` — The view state is encrypted only if a control requests encryption by calling the `RegisterRequiresViewStateEncryption` method of the `Page` class. This is the default value. That also implies that if you develop a control that stores sensitive information in the `ViewState` property, you can call this method to encrypt the value.

➤ `Always` — The view state information is always encrypted, regardless of the sensitivity of its content. If you utilize third-party controls that may have access to sensitive object values, you should use this option.

➤ `Never` — The view state information is never encrypted, even if a control requests encryption.

You can enable view state encryption in the `@Page` directive or in the `<pages>` section of the `web.config` file.

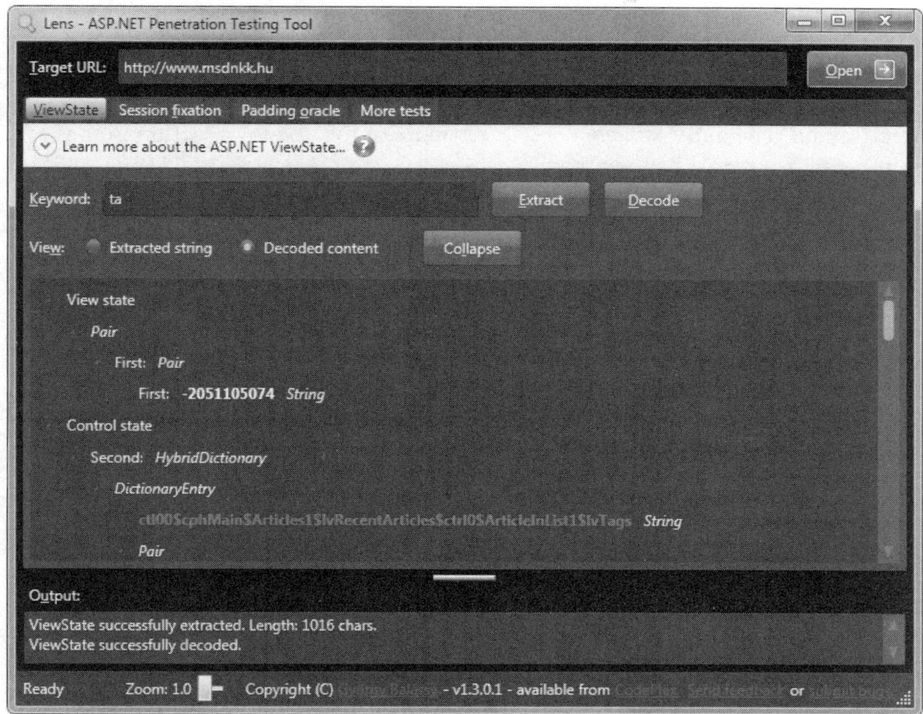

FIGURE 3-12: The decoded ViewState and keyword search in Lens

Some built-in web controls, by default, may request the page to encrypt the `ViewState`. If you have a `FormView`, a `ListView`, a `GridView`, or a `DetailsView` on the page, and you set the `DataKeyNames` property to a non-null value, it asks the page for view state encryption. The reason for this is that these controls store the key field values in the control state, which is being serialized with the view state to the same hidden field.

You can use Lens to test if the view state is encrypted on the page. After extracting the `__VIEWSTATE` value, when you click the Decode button, an error message in the Output pane displays if the view state cannot be decoded because it is encrypted.

Tampering with the View State

View state has an important role not only in persisting control state, but also in event processing. Change events (for example, the `TextChanged` event of the `TextBox` control) don't cause immediate postback, but instead their event handlers are executed later when the form is submitted to the server, based on the content of the view state. If attackers can maliciously tamper with the view state data, they can not only change the state of the controls on the page, but can also even influence which event handlers are executed on the server.

Fortunately, by default, ASP.NET protects the view state against client-side modification with an HMAC. The method is similar to one you saw in the "Protecting Your Website Against Session Hijacking" section earlier in this chapter, using the keys configured in the `validationKey` attribute of the `machineKey` section of the `web.config` file.

Although view state MAC protection can be turned off, I strongly recommend you never do so because it can have serious security consequences. Ensure that the `EnableViewStateMac` property of the `@Page` directive and the `enableViewStateMac` attribute of the <pages> section in the `web.config` is always set to `true`, as shown here:

```
<pages enableViewStateMac="true" ... />
```

MAC validation is enforced only on HTTP `POST` requests, so if the request is not a postback, the `ViewState` MAC is never checked.

Reposting the View State

When the ASP.NET runtime processes the object graph in the `ViewState` property, it serializes the type and value of the objects. However, it does not store two additional, important properties of the view state:

➤ The timestamp when the view state is created or any expiration date to it

➤ The identifier of the session or the user who visits the page

Because of the lack of this information, an attacker can capture another user's valid view state and can post it back to the server at any later time. In this way, a malicious user can attack your website or abuse the victim's data in the view state. To mitigate this threat, you can use the `ViewStateUserKey` property of the page, which you already learned about in the "Cross-Site Request Forgery" section earlier in this chapter.

However, if you enable `ViewStateUserKey`, be aware that the number of view state MAC validation errors may increase on your site, and the following exception will be thrown several times:

```
HttpException (0x80004005): Validation of viewstate MAC failed. If this
    application is hosted by a Web Farm or cluster, ensure that
    <machineKey> configuration specifies the same validationKey and
    validation algorithm. AutoGenerate cannot be used in a cluster.
```

In my experience, the most common reason for this exception is that users tend to submit pages after session timeout or login session timeout. In these cases, the view state is encrypted with a key based on the user's session ID that expires by the time the postback occurs, and the runtime throws the exception. Two workarounds may help you to handle this problem:

➤ Apply the *Post/Redirect/Get (PRG) pattern* to avoid re-posts when the user refreshes the page in the browser.

➤ Maintain a JavaScript timer on the client that notifies the user before the session times out to avoid posting back to an expired session.

You must also be sure that view state MAC exceptions are gracefully handled, and a friendly error page is displayed to the visitors of your site. Unfortunately, this error is a general `HttpException`, but the inner exception is a `ViewStateException`, and you can check for that type in the `Application_Error` event handler in the `global.asax` file of your application:

```
private void Application_Error( object sender, EventArgs e )
{
  Exception ex = this.Server.GetLastError();

  if( ex is HttpException && ex.InnerException != null &&
    ex.InnerException is ViewStateException )
  {
    // TODO: Log the error here...

    // Clear the error.
    this.Server.ClearError();

    // TODO: Redirect the user to a friendly error page here...
  }
}
```

TRICKING EVENT HANDLERS

Earlier in this chapter, you learned how a malicious attacker can exploit the weaknesses of the ASP. NET authentication, session, and view state mechanisms. The last part of this chapter discusses another feature of ASP.NET used on almost every single web page: event handling.

Web controls and event-based programming are probably the most important features of ASP.NET that promoted the success of this platform, by hiding the low-level protocol details, and making web development as simple as desktop application development. To provide this level of abstraction, ASP. NET creates one big hidden form on the page, which is submitted to the server when a postback event occurs on the client. The way the form is submitted depends on the control that causes the postback:

➤ If the control is a `Button` or an `ImageButton`, the form is submitted by the browser when the button is activated. These controls, by default (when the `UseSubmitBehavior` property is `true`), generate standard `input` elements with `type="submit"` or `type="image"` attributes.

➤ If the control that triggers the postback is a `LinkButton`, a `CheckBox`, or a `RadioButton` with `AutoPostBack="true"` attribute, the form is submitted by a tiny client-side JavaScript generated by the ASP.NET runtime. This JavaScript function (called `__doPostBack`) fills two hidden form fields (the `__EVENTTARGET` and the `__EVENTARGUMENT` fields) with the ID of the control that caused the postback, and with any additional event parameters, respectively.

If you capture the HTTP POST request generated by the browser, you can clearly see these values in the HTTP body (irrelevant header lines omitted):

```
POST http://localhost:1124/Default.aspx HTTP/1.1
Host: localhost:1124

__EVENTTARGET=LinkButton1&__EVENTARGUMENT=&__VIEWSTATE=%2FwEPDwUKMTQ1OTQ0MTY
yOWRknEdK5e5oeG%2BwlkzU3XqnsLvH%2FZSyW6p6j%2FcIsjMRJMo%3D&__EVENTVALIDATION=
%2FwEWAgKT14CuCgLM9PumD6UtsOk9JGNhr%2FHBC0YgaY3a5ZVBFa5QvTO1fI%2BOTzKp
```

Because a client-side script is responsible for filling these form fields, the values can be manipulated by a malicious user before they are sent to the server. Luckily, ASP.NET provides a built-in mechanism, called *event validation,* that provides some level of protection against this type of modification.

Event Validation Internals

When a web control is rendered, it may call the `RegisterForEventValidation` method of the `ClientScriptManager` class. This method computes the hash code of the client ID of the control and the hash code for the event argument, and then XORs these values. The resulting hash is added to an internal `ArrayList` that is serialized to the hidden __EVENTVALIDATION form field on the page when the page is rendered. The serialization is performed by the `ObjectStateFormatter` class, the same class used by the `ViewState` serialization. This also means that the event-validation data is also protected with an HMAC, and when the `ViewState` is encrypted, the __EVENTVALIDATION field also gets encrypted.

When the form data is posted back to the server, the runtime calls the `ValidateEvent` method of the `ClientScriptManager` that decodes the __EVENTVALIDATION field content and ensures that the postback was triggered by a valid control with a valid argument value.

> **TURNING OFF EVENT VALIDATION**
>
> A common scenario for developers confronted with event validation is client-side scripting. For example, if you create an empty `DropDownList` control, and then load the items with JavaScript, the server may throw an "Invalid postback or callback argument" exception, because the items added on the client side are missing from the __EVENTVALIDATION field.
>
> An easy workaround is to turn off event validation, but, unfortunately, this cannot be done on the control level, but only on the page level. Because this is an open call for hackers, I strongly do not recommend doing so, and because of that, I won't even show you how to do it. Although there are perfectly valid times when it is okay to turn it off, you should think twice before you even search for the corresponding property.
>
> On the other hand, you can also call the `Page.ClientScript.RegisterForEvent Validation` method to register your dynamically created controls or values.

Hacking Event Validation

The algorithm described earlier looks practical, and it helps to protect your application against malformed POST attacks. Unfortunately, there are two problems with the implementation:

➤ The implementation is not consistent across the various controls. For example, the `Button` control enables postback even when it is disabled.

➤ Just like the __VIEWSTATE, the __EVENTVALIDATION state is not bound to a particular page state.

Both of these problems can have serious consequences.

Pushing the Disabled Button

If you look into the source code of the `AddAttributesToRender` method of the `Button` class, you can see that the `RegisterForEventValidation` method is called independently from the value of the `Enabled` property of the control. That means the `__EVENTVALIDATION` field contains a valid reference even for disabled buttons. Therefore, a malicious user can create a request that triggers the `Click` event handler, even if the button is disabled.

You can try this behavior for yourself by following these steps:

1. Create an `ASPX` page with a disabled `Button` and a `Label`:

```
<asp:Button ID="Button1" runat="server" Enabled="False"
  onclick="Button1_Click" Text="Button" />
<asp:Label ID="Label1" runat="server" Text="Label" />
```

2. Create an event handler for the `Button1` to indicate that the `Click` event is triggered:

```
protected void Button1_Click( object sender, EventArgs e )
{
  this.Label1.Text = "It works!";
}
```

3. Start Fiddler, and click the Request Builder tab. Create the following `POST` request that triggers a postback on the `Button1` control:

```
POST http://localhost:11124/Default.aspx HTTP/1.1
Host: localhost:1124
Content-Length: 196
Content-Type: application/x-www-form-urlencoded

__VIEWSTATE=%2FwEPDwULLTE0MDUxNTAzOTRkZJN4%2FA8LlvP81wb0Bq7KNKVhfUIP3arRKvj7
WYWbp7H1&__EVENTVALIDATION=%2FwEWAwLM68mpDAKM54rGBgK7q7GGCNCQWa9IGCZDaMDYCo2
BAx%2BtsDa1ROsmqXSp7AVvc%2FX4&Button1=Button
```

 *The values of the `__VIEWSTATE` and `__EVENTVALIDATION` fields in the `POST` body may be different in your environment, but you can get those values by visiting the page and inspecting the generated HTML markup.*

4. Click the Execute button in Fiddler. Then select the newly created session on the left, and switch to the Inspectors tab. If the "It Works!" text displays in the HTTP result, then you successfully pushed a disabled button!

This scenario is simple, but you can use the same method to test your pages against this `POST` attack. Naturally, fully populated pages produce much more complex `POST` requests, but you don't have to build them from scratch. You can capture them, and then use the Replay function of Fiddler.

Pushing the Invisible Button

Contrary to the `Enabled` property, web controls handle the `Visible` property correctly when they register for event validation. However, there are scenarios in which a malicious user can still trigger invisible controls.

As you learned earlier, event validation is based on the content of the __EVENTVALIDATION hidden form field, which, in turn, is bound to the current page, but not to the current rendered HTML markup. Because of this, a malicious user can capture a generated __EVENTVALIDATION value and post it back with another HTTP POST request.

For example, you can have a `Product.aspx` page on your website that displays the details of a single product based on an `id` value in the query string. There is a Discount Order button on your page, but it is visible only for certain products. Because the same page is displayed for all products, attackers can take the __EVENTVALIDATION field from a discounted product, and send it back with a POST request that points to the URL of a full-priced item, and they can order it at the lower price.

Another example of when an attacker can circumvent event validation occurs when the same page is displayed for the user once with controls visible and at other times with controls hidden. Because event validation does not contain any timestamp, a malicious user can save the value of the __EVENTVALIDATION field when the button is visible and post it back later when the button is hidden to trigger the `Click` event handler of the button.

Both examples are based on the internal behavior of the event-handling and event-validation features in ASP.NET. Because they work the same way in all ASP.NET web pages, an attacker can have a fairly good chance of successfully exploiting them.

Protecting Your Site Against POST Attacks

The farthest a POST attack can get is executing an event handler on the server. It cannot do anything wrong in itself; it can just run code you do not want to execute. Therefore, if you want to protect your web pages against POST attacks, you must add additional layers of protection between the UI and the sensitive code.

If you see some code like this, you should be suspicious of the page being vulnerable to POST attacks:

```
// If the user is not admin, disable a feature.
if( !this.User.IsInRole( "Admin" ) )
{
  this.MyButton.Enabled = false;
}
```

To strengthen this code, you can not only disable the button, but you can also unsubscribe from the `Click` event handler using the `-=` operator:

```
// If the user is not admin, disable a feature.
if( !this.User.IsInRole( "Admin" ) )
{
  this.MyButton.Enabled = false;
  this.MyButton.Click -= this.MyButton_Click;
}
```

To add further protection, you can insert additional checks at later phases of the execution. For example, in addition to disabling the UI, you can run similar validation (in this case, an authorization check) within the event handler:

```
protected void MyButton_Click( object sender, EventArgs e )
{
```

```
    if( this.User.IsInRole( "Admin" ) )
    {
      // Do something serious here...
    }
  }
```

If the code in the event handler executes a stored procedure, you can perform a validation check there, too, just before the data is updated in the database.

This kind of approach is called the *defense in depth* strategy, in which multiple layers of countermeasures protect the integrity of the data on your website.

SUMMARY

In this chapter, you learned about various attacks that can target your website. Even if you write the most secure code on the planet, because your application is built on top of a particular web platform, your site inherits its security strengths and weaknesses.

Just like any other web platform, ASP.NET also has effective built-in protection against the most common web-based attacks. However, ASP.NET is also susceptible to weaknesses because it cannot cover the full range of attacks. Although the ASP.NET platform is robust, malicious users can find ways to exploit its weaknesses. As an ASP.NET developer, you must know about these threats and the appropriate countermeasures to protect your application.

This chapter examined attacks against the ASP.NET authentication, session, `ViewState`, and event handlers. This chapter has not presented the full picture. These are only the most important pieces of the puzzle. The ASP.NET platform gains new features in every release, and those features may come with their own secure and unsecure parts.

While you have been reading these chapter, security experts around the world are working hard to find new vulnerabilities to exploit your website, or to find ways to protect against them. Remember, security is not a state or a product, but rather a constant process you can repeat over and over.

ABOUT THE AUTHOR

György Balássy teaches web portal development as a lecturer at the Budapest University of Technology and Economics. He is a founding member of the local MSDN Competence Center (MSDNCC), having an important role in evangelizing the .NET platform as a speaker, book author, and consultant. Balássy provided leadership in the foundation of the Hungarian .NET community as a key evangelist on Microsoft events and technical forums, and as the head of the Portal Technology Group in the MSDNCC. He is a regular speaker on academic and industrial events, presenting in-depth technical sessions on .NET, ASP.NET, Microsoft Office development, and ethical hacking, with which he won the Best Speaker and the Most Valuable Professional (MVP) awards in SharePoint and ASP.NET multiple times, and was selected to be a member of the ASPInsiders group. Since 2005, Balássy has been the Microsoft Regional Director in Hungary. You can visit his blog at `http://gyorgybalassy.wordpress.com`, or reach him at `balassy@aut.bme.hu`.

How to Build a Real World Silverlight 5 Application

by Gill Cleeren

With the introduction of Silverlight, Microsoft made its entry in the Rich Internet Applications (RIA) space. Previously, this market segment was dominated by technologies such as Adobe Flash. After being announced in 2007, Silverlight quickly evolved from a pure JavaScript-oriented development model in version 1, over a .NET-based model since version 2, into a rich platform ready for line-of-business (LOB) application development in versions 3 to 5. Today, Silverlight is installed on more than 70 percent (according to www.riastats.com) of all PCs, and this adoption keeps climbing. Not only is it a framework to build RIAs, it also has become the de facto framework for building applications for Windows Phone 7.

As mentioned, since version 2, Silverlight applications can be built using .NET. Both C# and VB.NET can be used as development language. On the other hand, XAML is used to create (in a declarative manner) the user interface. The XAML language was introduced with WPF at the time of .NET 3.0. Therefore, the learning curve for Silverlight for most .NET developers is not steep — you can leverage a lot of your knowledge.

Although you can fall back on many things you already know from "regular" .NET, Silverlight applications have their peculiarities. This chapter provides an overview of some issues you'll face when you leave the paved road of "demoware" (although this is not a real word, it is used here to reference applications in which you use just the standard things, and nothing more) and get your hands dirty in real-world applications. Of course, each issue is provided with a solution as well.

This chapter starts with the design phase. In this context, "design" refers to creating a proto-type of the application. You see how this can be done in a clean way (and in Silverlight!) using SketchFlow.

The next issue addressed is data. Microsoft has several focus domains with Silverlight, and one of them (probably the most important one) is LOB development. An LOB app without data is probably nonexistent, so you need a solid way to get your data into your Silverlight applications. You'll learn about Windows Communication Foundation (WCF) RIA Services for this. When you have the data, Silverlight offers a well-designed data-binding framework. You'll learn about some concepts of the data-binding engine in Silverlight as well.

Just like a solid building needs a good foundation, a good Silverlight application needs a good architecture as well. The community has put its efforts behind the Model-View-ViewModel (MVVM) pattern. You learn how you can easily implement this pattern, and how it can help you to build your application in a more testable and maintainable fashion.

To finish this chapter, you learn how to customize controls to fit the needs of your application.

SETTING THE SCENE FOR THE APPLICATION

A chapter on building a real-world Silverlight application requires...a real-world application. Before continuing, explore the scenario for the application you'll build.

Recently, a local cinema chain, "At The Movies," began looking for a system to enable visitors to book their seats upfront. With this system, they wanted to avoid people rushing into the theater when the doors opened. For people like me, such a system is a blessing because I'm often too late to get one of the good seats.

The system must fulfill the following requirements:

➤ Enable the users to enter their personal data (first name, last name, and e-mail). No accounts are to be created, but the information must be stored in a database. Therefore, the user does not need a password.

➤ Enable the user to make a selection out of the currently playing movies and consult the details about the movie (such as duration, rating, and website).

➤ Enable the user to select a show time for the selected movie, and for this selection, indicate the number of seats.

➤ Enable the user to enter payment information.

➤ Show the user the confirmation about the reservation.

For the application, the database schema shown in Figure 4-1 is used throughout this chapter.

You can find the application with all the code and a sample database on this book's companion website at www.wrox.com.

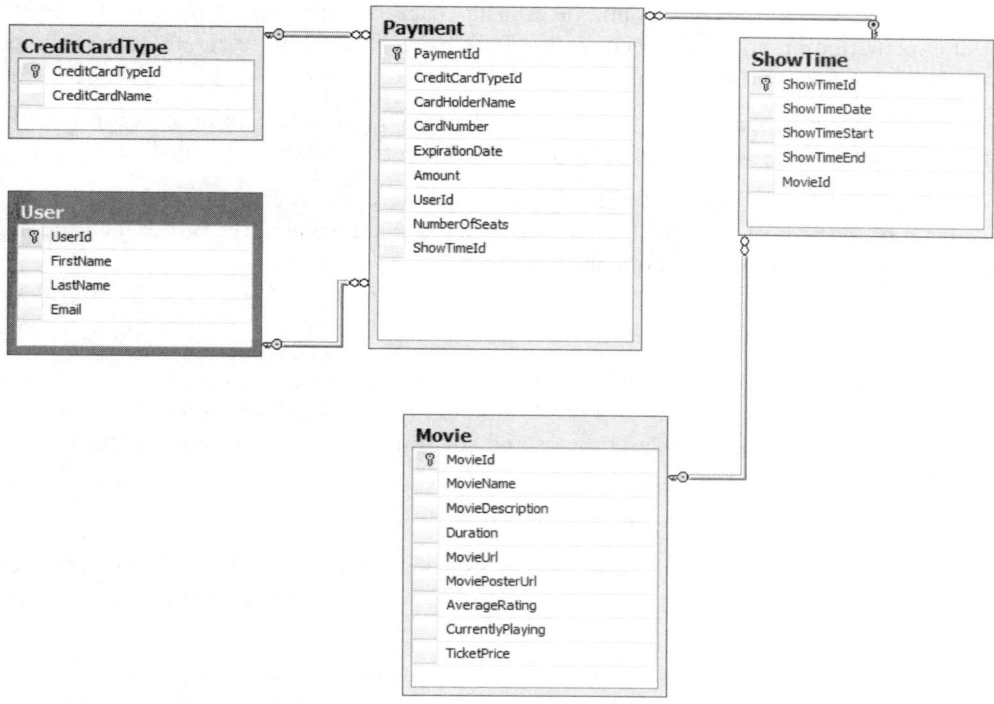

FIGURE 4-1: Application database schema

PROTOTYPE FIRST, CODE LATER — USING SKETCHFLOW

In my daily life as an application architect, I'm often involved in the startup phase of a project. One of the most crucial tasks in this phase is gathering the requirements of the system to-be, often done by an analyst. This is not an easy task. In many situations, the involved stakeholders have a different vision of the new system.

Nonetheless, based on the feedback and basic information, a rough prototype of the system can be created, mostly in the form of sketches. It's vital for the project that the requirements are captured in the best way possible in the early stages of the project. The later a change must be implemented, the more expensive this change will be.

The analyst often refers to tools such as Visio and PowerPoint to create the sketches of the proto-type. Although these are great tools, they aren't perfect for prototyping. For starters, neither Visio nor PowerPoint has the capability to create a prototype that's interactive. You can't create a Visio prototype in which you can click some button and arrive in another sheet, reflecting the real naviga-tion of the final application.

What the analyst delivers in the end is a bundle of printed sheets, containing mockups of screens and a lot of explanation on how the screen works. This makes it difficult for the stakeholder to envision what the final system will look like.

Also, neither of the tools is built to be a prototype designer. They lack the common controls with which an application can be constructed. (Specific stencil sheets can be downloaded for Visio.)

Finally, there's no easy way to give feedback. The development of a prototype should be done iteratively. A version of the prototype is created, new feedback is gathered, and the prototype is updated accordingly — and all this should be possible quite easily.

Introducing SketchFlow

With the introduction of Expression Blend 3 came a new tool called *SketchFlow*. This new tool enables building interactive prototypes for both Windows Presentation Foundation (WPF) and Silverlight, supporting an iterative design process and containing the most common controls in Silverlight applications.

Looking at the name SketchFlow actually reveals two other words:

➤ The "Sketch" part refers to the fact that the designs you create with SketchFlow are sketchy, as if they were drawn with a pencil. This emphasizes that the prototype is just a prototype, not a working application.

➤ The "Flow" part of the name explains that, within the prototypes you create with SketchFlow, a flow can be constructed, enabling you to interact and navigate throughout the application as if it were a finished application.

Come to think of it, it's actually a good thing Microsoft made the applications look sketchy. What would your customer say if he saw your "working prototype" after just 2 days, days after you estimated that the entire project would take about 100 days? When building a prototype with SketchFlow, you are actually building a Silverlight application. The outcome is nothing but a plain Silverlight application. This means that, if desired, you can even write some C# code behind the prototype screens!

The application won't run by itself. It is hosted in the so-called SketchFlow Player you learn about later. This effectively means that the prototype can be uploaded to a server and accessed by all stakeholders so that they get a feeling of the application. Within the SketchFlow Player, you can give feedback, which can then be captured inside SketchFlow again afterward. This enables the iterative design of the prototype.

A common question about SketchFlow prototypes is whether it's a good idea to take the SketchFlow application as the base for the "real" application. The answer is generally "No." The reason is that, in an iterative design process, you don't want to spend time on designing the UI as it should be done. Think of things such as user controls, reuse of components, and so on. These aren't things you want to be bothered with during a phase in which you want to get the flow of the application finalized. Moreover, if the prototype is created by an analyst, it won't be designed with the final code in mind.

Finding Your Way Around SketchFlow

Learning SketchFlow is easy. The only thing that may take some time, certainly if you aren't experienced with Expression Blend yet, is finding your way around the interface. What better way to learn than trying it out, right?

Start SketchFlow by starting Expression Blend. Within Blend, select File ➪ New Project, and, in the New Project dialog, under the Silverlight node, select Silverlight SketchFlow application. When Blend is ready, you can see that, apart from some SketchFlow-specific panels, the interface is similar to Blend. The following panels, specific for SketchFlow, can be identified:

➤ *SketchFlow Map* — In this panel, you can see the screens and their connections. Think of this as a "mind map" for your application.

➤ *SketchFlow Feedback* — You can import feedback gathered from stakeholders directly into SketchFlow and see it in the designer. You learn more about this a bit later.

➤ *SketchFlow Animation* — Use this panel to create SketchFlow-specific animations. SketchFlow animations are not used in this overview.

Apart from these panels, under the Assets ➪ SketchFlow node, you can find the sketch-version of the controls to be used in the prototype, as shown in Figure 4.2.

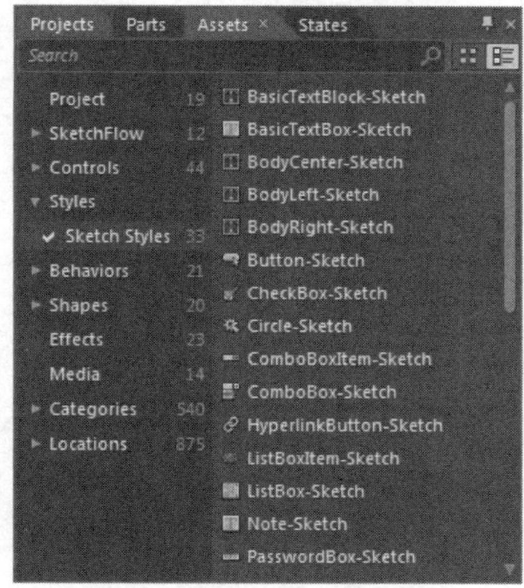

FIGURE 4-2: The SketchFlow controls

Creating the Application's Prototype

Now that you know about SketchFlow, you can use this knowledge to create a prototype for your own application. Luckily for you, the people of "At The Movies" did their homework and summed up the requirements of the application nicely. You can start creating the prototype based on these requirements.

The Map of the Application

Judging from the requirements, you could implement the application as a wizard, so the navigation would be straightforward, consisting out of five screens, starting with the user data entry and finishing with the confirmation of the reservation. You can build this out in the Map panel inside SketchFlow as follows:

1. When starting a new SketchFlow application, a first screen is created automatically named Screen 1. Start by renaming this to **Login** by double-clicking the name of the screen. Figure 4-3 shows the screen block item.

FIGURE 4-3: Screen block item

2. To add a second, connected screen, you have two options. The easiest one is to place the mouse over the Login screen and wait a few seconds until a menu pops out underneath the screen (as shown in Figure 4-4). The first button generates a connected screen. The second option is to simply right-click the screen and select "Create a Connected Screen."

FIGURE 4-4: Menu underneath the screen

3. When created, you can drag around the newly generated screen. Rename this screen to **MovieSelection**. Figure 4-5 shows the result.

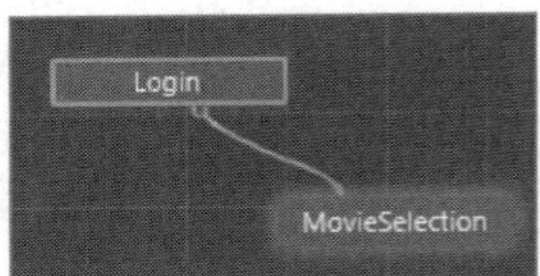

FIGURE 4-5: The newly created MovieSelection screen

4. Continue to create the entire screen map. The requested, wizard-like application has a flat navigation structure, as shown in Figure 4-6.

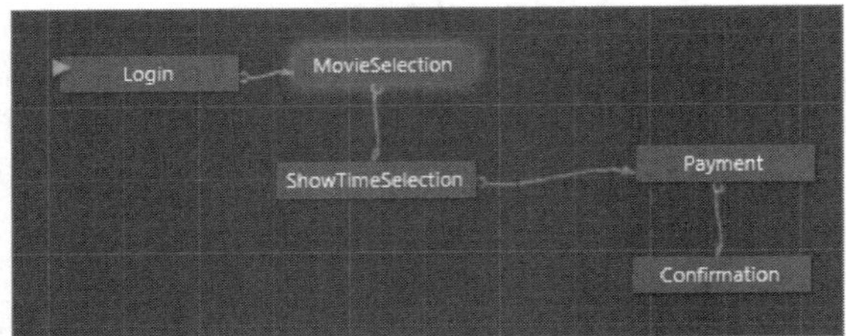

FIGURE 4-6: Screen map

Now that the structure of the application is in a format that corresponds to the requirements of "At the Movies," you can start designing the screens.

Screen Mockup

The application you have at this point contains nothing more than a few empty screens. Showing this to the customer may not yield the expected results — on the contrary! Screen by screen, you can start adding SketchFlow controls to create mockups of the screens. For spacing reasons, now look at how to create only the MovieSelection screen. (The other screens are similar.) Follow these steps:

1. You can find all controls available to use in SketchFlow (in other words, those having a "sketchy" style) under the Assets Panel ⇨ Styles ⇨ Sketch Styles. Not all controls,

including the `DataGrid`, have a sketchy asset, so if a `DataGrid` is needed, you must use the default one.

2. Start by adding a `TextBlock` sketch by dragging it onto the designer. Set the text to **Select the movie you want to see!**.

3. Select the `Button` sketch asset, and add it to create the Next button at the bottom.

4. Add a `ListBox`-sketch and a `ComboBox`-sketch control.

Figure 4-7 shows how the screen looks at this point.

SketchFlow enables more than just static controls. One of these extras is adding a data source containing sample data. You can customize this data source to mimic the real data. The capability to add a sample data source is actually inherited from Expression Blend. It's helpful when designing an application because you can visualize how the screen will look with data filled in.

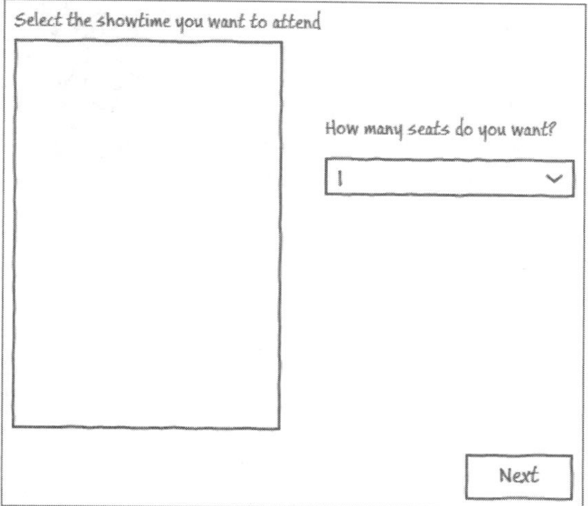

FIGURE 4-7: The MovieSelection screen so far

Create such a data source by following these steps:

1. In the Data Panel, click the Create Sample Data button, and select New Sample Data. Give the data source a name such as **MovieDataSource**.

2. The generated data source contains a collection in which each item has two properties (`Property1` of type `String` and `Property2` of type `Boolean`). You can change existing properties or add new ones. To generate the items as shown in Figure 4-6, you need two properties — the first one of type `Image`, the second one of type `String`.

3. To generate the `Image` property, rename `Property1` to **MovieImage** and change its type to `Image`. By default, Blend adds images of chairs. You can override this by pointing to a folder containing more relevant images (in this case, containing movie posters).

4. Rename the second property, `Property2`, to **MovieName**. In the Properties window of the property, you can change what the generated string looks like (for example, the length).

5. To generate the `ListBox` with the sample data automatically, drag the Collection (not the individual fields) onto the design surface.

6. Because the prototype should resemble (as much as possible) the final application, you must make it possible for the user to click an item and see the details. To generate the detail fields, change the mode to Details Mode. Now, select both the `MovieImage` and the `MovieName` fields and drag them onto the design surface. While dragging, you see that the cursor indicates you are about to create a details view.

Figure 4-8 shows the screen with this sample data added.

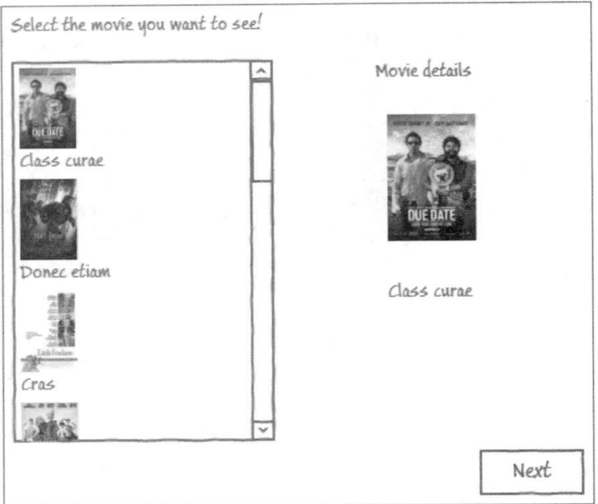

FIGURE 4-8: Sample data added

With the data now in place, you need to enable the navigation. To show in the mockup that the user can navigate from this screen to the ShowTimeSelection screen, right-click the previously created Next button. In the context menu that appears, select Navigate To ⇨ ShowTimeSelection, as shown in Figure 4-9. The other screens are similar.

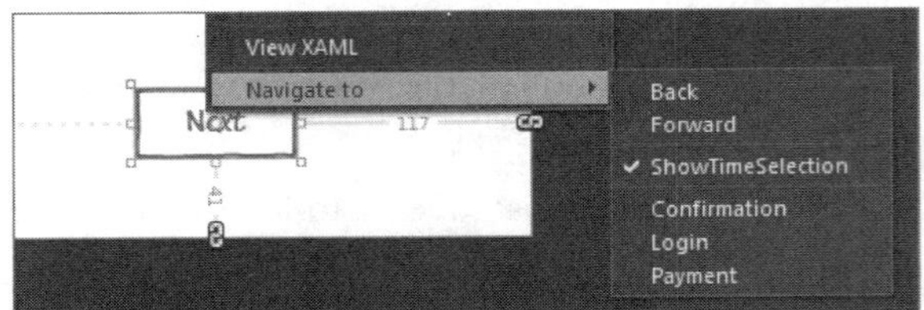

FIGURE 4-9: Enabling navigation

> *You can find the complete mockup on the companion website for this book at* `www.wrox.com.`

Testing the Prototype and Gathering Feedback

Now that the mockup screens have been created, the prototype is ready for prime time! As mentioned earlier, any application you build in SketchFlow this way is nothing more (or less) than a regular Silverlight application. (Hence, you could have added some C#/VB.NET code if you wanted.) You can test the application simply by pressing F5. Blend builds the application as usual.

Upon opening the browser, you can see that the application gets hosted in the Silverlight Player, which is also a Silverlight application. In the Player, you can see the prototype application, the map, and a feedback panel. The application is fully functional. You can click the Next button you created to arrive on the ShowTimeSelection screen.

You can upload the application to any server. To do so, Blend contains a Package SketchFlow function, available via File ⇨ Package SketchFlow Project. This opens Windows Explorer, showing the files that need to be copied to a server. Automatically, this also generates a new revision.

You can now allow the customer to test the application and provide feedback on what you have already built. Follow these steps:

1. From the My Feedback panel, select Enable Ink Feedback. The cursor changes into a paintbrush.

2. Draw a circle around the Next button in the Designer, as shown in Figure 4-10.

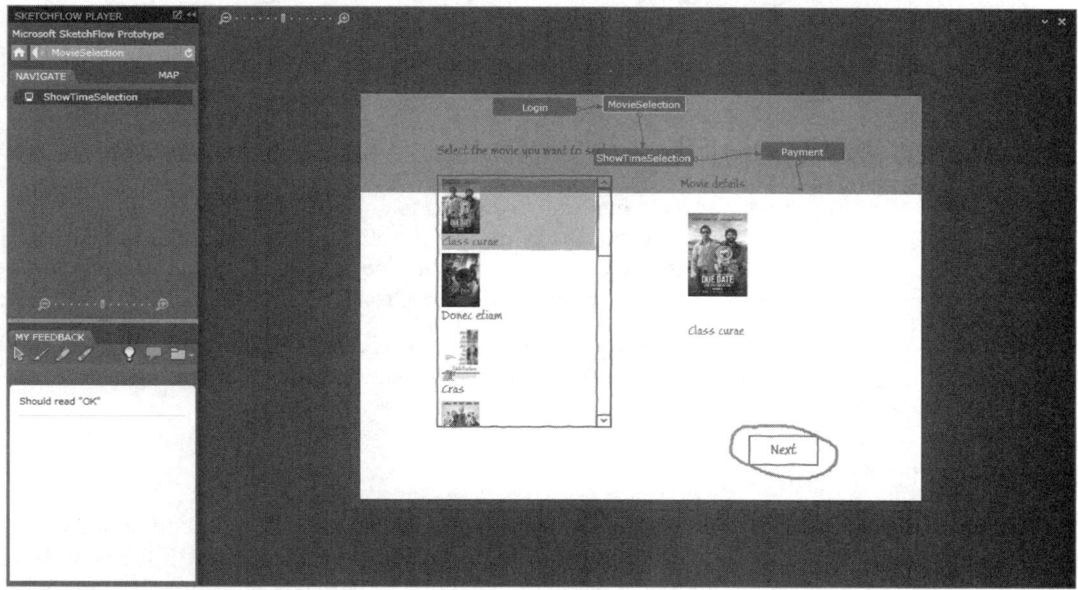

FIGURE 4-10: Circling the Next button

3. Again, in the feedback panel, type some feedback about the Next button.

4. The feedback can now be saved by clicking the Folder icon and selecting Export Feedback. A `*.feedback` file can be saved locally containing the entered feedback.

You can import the gathered feedback into SketchFlow again. By default, the feedback appears under the revision for which it was made, making it easy to see in which iteration a change or a remark was made.

1. In SketchFlow, open the SketchFlow Feedback panel, and click Add. Select the previously generated `*.feedback` file.

2. In the Design surface, the ink displays, and the relevant comment is shown in the Feedback panel. This way, the creator of the prototype can easily make changes to incorporate the remarks of the users. This is shown in Figure 4-11.

After several iterations, the prototype you have created will be what the customer is looking for. This agreed-upon prototype makes it easy to know what all involved stakeholders are talking about because all requirements should be possible to map to a function or screen in the prototype.

Now that the prototype is ready, you can (finally) start with the real coder's job.

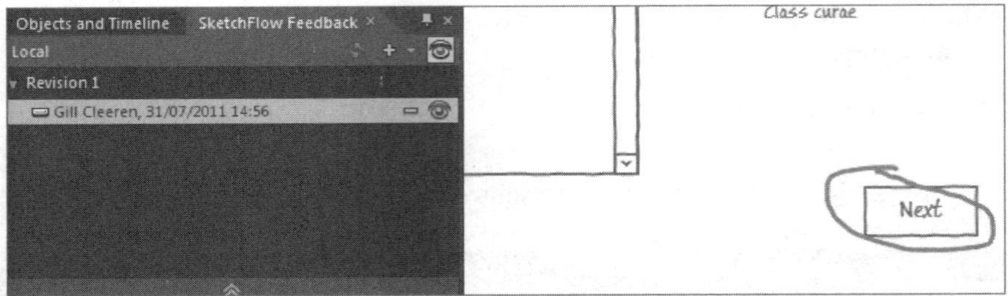

FIGURE 4-11: Circling the Next button to show changes

DATA-BINDING PRIMER

In my opinion, one of (if not *the*) most important concepts to grasp in Silverlight is *data binding*. In most (perhaps all) LOB applications, data forms the heart of the application. Simplifying tasks such as displaying, editing, sorting, and filtering shortens the development time of applications quite a lot and gives developers more time to focus on the real business problems. Data binding does exactly that — and more!

Later in this chapter, you learn how data binding also forms the foundation on which the MVVM pattern is built. In this part, you learn what you need to know about data binding to understand other, more advanced concepts.

Hello, Data Binding

Before looking at data bindings in action, you need to know what the engine can do for you. The data-binding engine in Silverlight enables you to bind data to controls in the UI. It has nothing to do with data access. The data with which data binding works is data coming from objects — in-memory data, so to speak.

The concept of data binding is nothing new. It already exists in ASP.NET and in Windows Forms. But the binding engine was not as sophisticated as the one included with Silverlight. Silverlight actually inherited the data-binding capabilities from its big brother, WPF. The latter has some extra options in its binding engine, but Silverlight supports most commonly used features, so you are definitely not short of functions in Silverlight!

 *With every new version of Silverlight (including Silverlight 5), more features are added to the data-binding engine, making the difference between WPF and Silverlight in the data-binding area smaller with every release.*

Binding Syntax

A data binding is always defined by four items:

➤ *The data object you are binding to* — This object is often referred to as the *source object* for the data binding.

> ➤ *A property on this object* — This property is referred to as the *source property*.

> ➤ *A control in the UI* — This is referred to as the *target control* because this is the target of the data. The target object must derive from `DependencyObject`.

> ➤ *A property on this control* — This property (referred to as the *target property*) must be a dependency property. Don't worry, though, because most properties (`FontSize`, `Background`, and so on) are dependency properties, so you are in no way limited here.

Because these four items make up the binding, it's logical that they appear when you create a data binding via code, both in XAML and C#. Most of the time, a binding will be created using XAML. Bindings from code-behind are mostly used when they are dynamically created.

Assume you want to bind the `Text` property of a `TextBlock` to the `FirstName` property of a `Person` instance. The XAML syntax looks like the following:

```
<TextBlock Text="{Binding FirstName}">
```

If you look at the elements you find in this binding, it seems that one has gone missing. The `TextBlock` is the target control, and its `Text` property is the target property. Using a markup extension (which can be recognized by the curly braces), you bind the value of the `Text` property to the source property, `FirstName`. So, the source object seems to be missing.

The reason for this is that, most of the time, the `DataContext` is used. Because of the hierarchical XAML structure (which is XML), you can define the source for the binding on a higher level in the XAML tree so that all controls within that common parent get access to that source. This is exactly what the `DataContext` enables you to do. You define the `DataContext` on a common parent (for example, a `Grid`), and all controls within that `Grid`, if they don't have a source specified for their data binding, look up in the XAML tree for a non-null `DataContext`. When found, the control uses the referenced object as its source for the data binding. The `DataContext` can be set from XAML code, or from code-behind.

The nice thing about the `DataContext` is that is takes away the need to define on each control what the source for the binding actually is (which would actually make the code much less readable). `DataContext` will be used quite a bit in this chapter's sample application.

Although the `DataContext` is most commonly used, you can define the source object for the data binding in other ways:

> ➤ *Using the* `Source` *property of the data binding* — You can refer to an object stored in resources (at the page, `UserControl`, or even application level).

> ➤ *Using the* `ElementName` *property* — You can create a binding between two controls. Both the source and the target of the data binding are, in this case, a control. To define such a binding, you can use the `ElementName` property within the binding declaration, referring to the element name that should be used as the source for the binding.

> ➤ *Using the* `RelativeSource` *property* — Although this is not often used, it enables you to create a binding to an element relative to the current element.

Binding Modes

You can use data binding both for data display and data entry. You can indicate how you want the data to *flow*. The default is from the source to the target, but even there, you have two options. Table 4-shows a list of the options you have in Silverlight 4.

TABLE 4-1: Binding Modes in Silverlight 5

MODE	ACTION
OneWay	OneWay is the default. Data initially flows from the source to the target. However, if the source object implements the INotifyPropertyChanged interface, and the value of one of its properties changes, this changed value displays in the UI as well. Silverlight's data-binding engine takes care of the automatic synchronization for you.
OneTime	Similar to OneWay, the data flows from the source to the target. However, if the source changes (even if it implements the INotifyPropertyChanged interface), the target will not be updated.
TwoWay	In a TwoWay binding, the data flows in two directions. If the user enters a value (in a TextBox, for example), this data will be pushed back to the original object. This mode enables capturing user input.

INotifyPropertyChanged Interface

The INotifyPropertyChanged interface was mentioned in Table 4-1. This interface makes it possible to synchronize the value of the properties of controls if the source values have changed. The interface itself is simple, as you can see in Listing 4-1.

LISTING 4-1: The INotifyPropertyChanged Interface

```
namespace System.ComponentModel
{
    // Summary:
    //     Notifies clients that a property value has changed.
    public interface INotifyPropertyChanged
    {
        // Summary:
        //     Occurs when a property value changes.
        event PropertyChangedEventHandler PropertyChanged;
    }
}
```

The interface defines just one event, the PropertyChanged event. This event is to be raised whenever the value of a property changes in the source object. When Silverlight notices that you are binding to a source object that implements this interface, it automatically listens for this event being raised from the source object. When it is raised, Silverlight updates the UI to reflect the changes in the property.

This will be the case only if the binding has been defined with either a `OneWay` or `TwoWay` mode. For collections, a similar interface exists, namely `INotifyCollectionChanged`. Because this interface is more complex to implement, a specific collection is available that already implements this interface: the `ObservableCollection<T>`. The `ObservableCollection` notifies when items are added or removed from the interface. It won't notify if individual items are changing.

Converters

Before discussing how to use data binding to build your application, take a brief look at converters. A *converter* can be seen as a hook in the data-binding process. It enables you to do an action on the value coming from source or target in a data-binding scenario, such as converting or formatting. Basically, it's nothing more than a class that implements the `IValueConverter` interface. Listing 4-2 shows the definition of this interface.

LISTING 4-2: The IValueConverter Interface

```
namespace System.Windows.Data
{
    public interface IValueConverter
    {
        object Convert(object value, Type targetType, object parameter,
            CultureInfo culture);

        object ConvertBack(object value, Type targetType, object parameter,
            CultureInfo culture);
    }
}
```

The `Convert()` method is automatically invoked by Silverlight when a converter is used on a data-binding expression when the data flows from the source to the target. As an example, let's say you are working with an account balance, which obviously can be positive or negative. A converter can be used to "convert" the value to a green color if positive, or red if negative. A converter can (but is not obliged to) return the same data type. (Here, the converter receives a numeric value and returns a `SolidColorBrush`.)

Converters are handy and, in any application, you'll find them to be useful in several scenarios.

Creating a Data Bound Screen

The application that the people of "At the Movies" asked to create relies on data quite a lot. You'll soon see how to get the data to the application, but first focus first on displaying and capturing the data based on data-binding concepts. If you think back to the prototype you created in SketchFlow, it's obvious that each screen will be binding to data in some way.

For example, consider the user data-entry screen, where the user must enter his or her first name, last name, and e-mail. The to-be-entered data can be captured in a data class called `Person`. This class implements the `INotifyPropertyChanged` interface, as shown in Listing 4-3.

LISTING 4-3: Person Class

```csharp
public class Person: INotifyPropertyChanged
{

    public event PropertyChangedEventHandler PropertyChanged;

    private string _firstName;
    private string _lastName;
    private string _email;

    public int UserId { get; set; }

    public string FirstName
    {
        get
        {
            return _firstName;
        }
        set
        {
            if (_firstName != value)
            {
                _firstName = value;
                RaisePropertyChanged();
            }
        }
    }

    private void RaisePropertyChanged(string propertyName)
    {
        if (PropertyChanged != null)
        {
            PropertyChanged
                (this, new PropertyChangedEventArgs(propertyName));
        }
    }

    //LastName and Email are similar
}
```

Code file [Snowball.AtTheMovies.Silverlight.UI/Model/Person.cs] available for download at Wrox.com.

As shown partially in Listing 4-4, in the XAML code called `UserDataEntryView`, you can create some `TextBox` controls. Each of these is bound to a public property of the `Person` class. The bindings have been marked as a `TwoWay` binding, so all entered data goes from the target control (the `TextBox`) to the source object (the `Person` instance). Note here, though, that no source is defined for the binding.

LISTING 4-4: XAML Code (Partial) for UserDataEntryView


```
<TextBox x:Name="FirstNameTextBox"
    Text="{Binding FirstName, Mode=TwoWay}"></TextBox>
<TextBox x:Name="LastNameTextBox"
    Text="{Binding LastName, Mode=TwoWay}"></TextBox>
<TextBox x:Name="EmailTextBox
    Text="{Binding Email, Mode=TwoWay}"></TextBox>
```

Code file [Snowball.AtTheMovies.Silverlight.UI/View/UserDataEntryView.xaml] available for download at Wrox.com.

In the code-behind for this view shown in Listing 4-5, you can now instantiate the `Person` class and set this instance as the `DataContext` for a common parent. This can be a containing `Grid` or even the `UserControl` itself.

LISTING 4-5: Code-Behind for the UserDataEntryView


```
public partial class UserDataEntryView : Page
{
    public UserDataEntryView()
    {
        InitializeComponent();

        Person person = new Person();
        this.DataContext = person;
    }
}
```

Code file [Snowball.AtTheMovies.Silverlight.UI/View/UserDataEntryView.xaml.cs] available for download at Wrox.com.

At this point, you should have a deep enough understanding of the concepts of data binding. You'll use data binding a lot more when exploring the following topics. Now focus on getting the real data from the server into the Silverlight application, and vice versa, using *WCF RIA Services.*

WCF RIA SERVICES IN ACTION

By now, everyone knows that Silverlight is a client-side framework. Being client-side brings some questions to the table about accessing data. Data resides in a database on the server side. How can you access that data from Silverlight applications?

Looking at the assemblies and namespaces available in Silverlight, it lacks all ADO.NET classes, and it has no LINQ-To-SQL or Entity Framework (EF) capabilities. This means that it won't be possible to get a Silverlight application to connect with a server-side database just by using a connection string.

Actually, this would be anything but secure. Silverlight code runs on the user's machine, and you know that all code there is insecure by default. Each user would get access to that connection string in no time. Sadly, not all users have good intentions with your data.

Also, at this point, there's no out-of-the box support for a client-side database in Silverlight. A client-side database would not be a solution for many problems. No developer would write code that downloads an entire product database to the client. (At least I hope not!)

That being said, there's no reason to panic. A solution exists in the form of services. Services can provide an access point to a database, in most cases, not directly, but probably through a business layer and a data access layer (DAL). Microsoft did provide Silverlight with support for many types of services, so accessing data over any kind of service should not be an issue for the business application developer.

Table 4-2 contains an overview of supported service types in Silverlight.

TABLE 4-2: Supported Service Types in Silverlight 5

TYPE	DESCRIPTION
ASMX Web services	These are regular web services used mostly to support legacy systems still using this type of services.
WCF Services	These provide the richest support in Silverlight and should be your default for service access. They provide the fastest data transfer with binary encoding, support for security, and duplex communication.
RSS/POX (Plain Old XML)	Silverlight can read out XML returned from a service. LINQ-To-XML, `XmlReader/XmlWriter`, is supported. In the case of RSS, `Syndication` classes provide a typed way of reading out the XML.
REST	Representational State Transfer (REST) is a protocol used by many large web applications to expose their functionality (for example, Flickr, Twitter, and so on). Data is exchanged in XML, JavaScript Object Notation (JSON), or ATOM.
Sockets	Although WCF supports duplex communication in Silverlight, sockets provide real duplex communication. Because this is restricted to specific port numbers, it is usable only in an intranet environment.
WCF Data Services	These expose an entity model over a service in XML. Using the WCF Data Services Client Library, an abstraction layer is added that takes away the need to perform XML parsing and URL creation. WCF Data Services can be used from regular .NET and ASP.NET as well.
WCF RIA Services	Specifically designed for Silverlight, WCF RIA Services provides developers with an end-to-end way to handle data inside Silverlight applications.

Choosing the Service-Layer Technology

With the variety of options shown in Table 4-2 available, you may wonder what to use. As with many things, the best answer is, "It depends."

For example, assume you already have an existing service architecture in place based on ASMX Web Services. It's probably not beneficial (or, perhaps, not even possible) to upgrade the entire service façade just because you're adding a Silverlight interface. ASMX Web Services work just as well.

If, however, you must start from scratch, WCF is a better choice. It's the default framework for building services since .NET 3.0. Plain WCF services have the advantage of being usable from other platforms such as ASP.NET. It should also be your default choice if you must perform duplex communication over the Internet. If you need duplex communication that goes over an intranet environment, sockets (or WCF using `net.tcp`) might be a better choice.

REST services, on the other hand, are great to use if you need your services to use standards-based methods because it uses XML by default.

As you can see, it does depend on the situation.

With the introduction of WCF RIA Services (often referred to as RIA Services), the choice became even more difficult. Microsoft added a framework specifically for working with data in n-tier Silverlight applications. Although built for Silverlight, RIA Services are, at their core, WCF services, and, therefore, also accessible from other technologies.

Hello to You, WCF RIA Services

Before examining why RIA Services will be used for accessing the data for the "At The Movies" application, let's be clear on what exactly all this actually means.

One of the "issues" when using regular WCF services for accessing data from a Silverlight application is that for all actions you must do, you must write a new method. Reading out all movies requires a new method. Reading out all movies ordered by release date requires another one. Filtering movies by genre requires yet another one. You get the picture. In many cases, although you try to reuse these service methods over different applications, it often is not that simple. You end up with a bunch of methods that are specific for the application at hand.

A "traditional" n-tier Silverlight application architecture has another "issue" in terms of validation. Although data must be validated within the service code on the server-side, to keep the responsiveness on the client as good as possible, you must validate on the client as well. As you may have guessed, this often results in creating duplicate code. And if there's one thing that most developers hate, it's duplicate code — or that they ran out of coffee!

With WCF RIA Services, Microsoft attempts to make working with data in n-tier solutions easier. It's not easy to describe RIA Services in just one definition because it is more than just one thing:

➤ It's a framework.

➤ It contains assemblies added both on the server side and on the client side. These assemblies make it easy to have an end-to-end solution to work with data.

➤ It's also tooling. When RIA Services are installed, code will automatically be generated on the client based on the code from the service, avoiding your having to write the same code twice. This is, among others, the case for validation logic. Validation attributes applied on the entities on the service will be copied to the client side. Also, for the entities you must work with, CRUD (Create, Read, Update and Delete) methods are generated automatically.

➤ It also integrates with ASP.NET security. If you have an existing ASP.NET membership infra-structure already in place, this can be reused.

Code-generation and many things happening behind the scenes might make some developers scared, thinking that what you can build with RIA Services is nothing more than some demo-ware. This is absolutely not the case.

You can use RIA Services to create scalable and architectural well-designed applications, in which the amount of code that must be written, and the issues of dealing with asynchronous develop-ment, are reduced to a minimum. This, however, does not tie you into an architecture you may not be comfortable with. Although it can be used to use data end-to-end, you can bend it just like you want. Indeed, RIA Services makes building n-tier RIA applications a lot easier!

Why WCF RIA Services?

Now that you understand what RIA Services is, you may be thinking why RIA Services is chosen over another technology for the "At The Movies" application (or any other small or medium-size application). The previously mentioned code-generation is handy. For example, when you have annotations on your server-side entities (mostly for validation), the framework automatically copies them to the client, so you must write your code only once — that is, on the server-side.

It can even be said that RIA Services hides that you are sending data back and forth asynchronously. It hides the details of making asynchronous calls. Not having to write code for all CRUD operations is certainly another plus.

RIA Services is optimized for working with EF. However, it is data access layer (DAL) neutral. This means that it can work with others, but it'll cost you some more work. Tying to RIA Services, there-fore, doesn't bind you to a specific DAL technology.

Architecture and Concepts of RIA Services

Architecturally, Silverlight applications that use RIA Services are not that different from applica-tions that use other services, as shown in Figure 4-12.

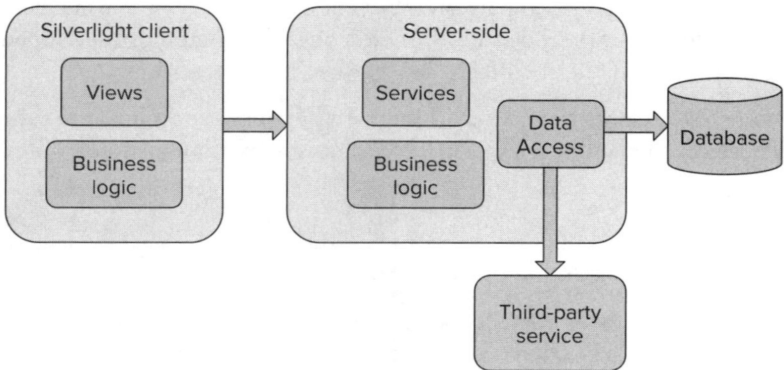

FIGURE 4-12: Using RIA Services versus other services

When creating an RIA Service, within the client project, code gets generated. With a WCF or an ASMX service, there's also code generated in the form of a proxy. The proxy generated here, however, is much, let's say, "smarter." You'll learn shortly how it differs from another proxy. The entities used in the service methods are generated on the client as well, including validation logic, resulting in your not having to create and maintain duplicated code.

Creating the Server-Side

When learning about data binding, you worked with a self-created `Person` class. In most situations, that's not how you'll work. You won't have your business objects as classes just in the Silverlight application. This section follows the end-to-end path of data, coming from the database all the way to the UI, of course, passing by RIA Services. Before delving into that, take a look at how you can organize the solution.

Setting Up the Solution

Ensuring that the solution structure is well-organized is a first and important step to an understandable development project. Follow these steps to set up the solution structure:

1. The solution for this project is called `Snowball.AtTheMovies`. (`Snowball.be` is the name of my blog, hence the prefix in my code.) The solution is a Silverlight navigation application. Visual Studio creates both a web project and a Silverlight application.

2. RIA Services can be placed in a web project. They can be part of the website that gets created with a new Silverlight project. Although this is fine for small projects, perhaps, in a real-world solution, this should not be the place where you put them. Instead, there is a project template available that helps you out here — the WCF RIA Services Class Library. When adding such a project to the solution, a server project for the services and a client project for the client-side generated code are created. Add an instance of this project template and rename the two projects to match the naming convention: `Snowball.AtTheMovies.Services.Web` for the server-side project and `Snowball.AtTheMovies.Services` for the Silverlight project.

3. Add a class library (`Snowball.AtTheMovies.Model`) where you'll add the Entity Model.

4. Create the following references:

   ➤ The RIA Services (`Snowball.AtTheMovies.Services.Web`) project must reference the model project (`Snowball.AtTheMovies.Model`).

   ➤ The web project must reference the services project.

   ➤ The Silverlight project must reference the client-side services project (`Snowball.AtTheMovies.Services`).

5. You must enable RIA Services in the web project because they will be hosted from that URL. To get this to work, add the following references in the web project:

   ➤ `System.ServiceModel.DomainServices.EntityFramework`

   ➤ `System.ServiceModel.DomainServices.Hosting`

   ➤ `System.ServiceModel.DomainServices.Server`

6.   In the `web.config` file of the web project, configuration code must be added to enable RIA Services. You can also find this code, shown in Listing 4-6, on this book's companion website at www.wrox.com.

LISTING 4-6: Web.config

```xml
<?xml version="1.0"?>

<configuration>
    <system.web>
        <authentication mode="Forms"/>
        <httpModules>
          <add name="DomainServiceModule"
               type="System.ServiceModel.DomainServices.
               Hosting.DomainServiceHttpModule,
               System.ServiceModel.DomainServices.Hosting,
               Version=4.0.0.0, Culture=neutral,
               PublicKeyToken=31bf3856ad364e35" />
        </httpModules>
        <compilation debug="true" targetFramework="4.0">
          <assemblies>
            <add assembly="System.Data.Entity, Version=4.0.0.0,
                 Culture=neutral, PublicKeyToken=b77a5c561934e089" />
          </assemblies>
        </compilation>
    </system.web>

  ...

  <system.webServer>
    <modules runAllManagedModulesForAllRequests="true">
      <add name="DomainServiceModule"
           preCondition="managedHandler"
    type="System.ServiceModel.DomainServices.
        Hosting.DomainServiceHttpModule,
        System.ServiceModel.DomainServices.Hosting,
        Version=4.0.0.0, Culture=neutral,
        PublicKeyToken=31bf3856ad364e35" />
    </modules>
    <validation validateIntegratedModeConfiguration="false" />
  </system.webServer>
  <system.serviceModel>
    <serviceHostingEnvironment aspNetCompatibilityEnabled="true"
        multipleSiteBindingsEnabled="true" />
  </system.serviceModel>

</configuration>
```

Code file [Snowball.AtTheMovies.Web/Web.config] available for download at Wrox.com.

Figure 4-13 shows the final solution structure. For organizational purposes, a few solution folders (`Client`, `Server` and `Assemblies`) have been added, which will be used later.

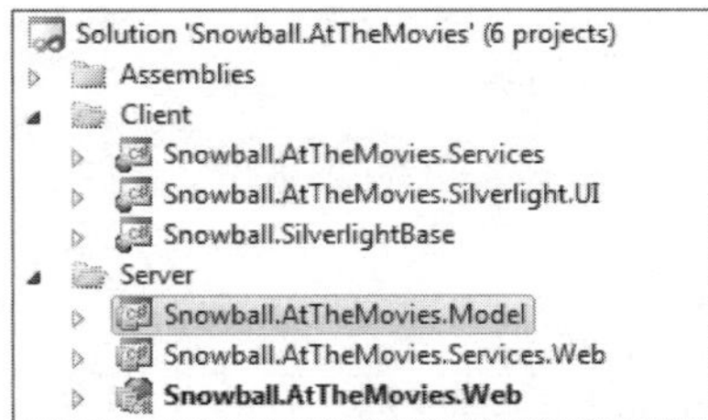

FIGURE 4-13: Final solution architecture

Data Access Using Entity Framework

RIA Services is optimized to work with Entity Framework (EF), which is why it is recommended that you use EF when choosing RIA Services. If you are forced to use another data access technology such as `nHibernate`, RIA Services will still be usable. However, it will require more manual work to get things up and running. Because "At The Movies" has not put any specific technology requirements on the project, you're free as a bird to select what you want. Therefore, the choice is made to use EF for this particular project.

In the `Snowball.AtTheMovies.Model` project, you add the Entity Model, `AtTheMovies.edmx`, here. Because the application is quite simple still, you can do a one-on-one mapping to the tables in the database. EF is an Object-Relational Mapper (ORM) and supports changing the entities. It can take care of the mappings that must be created to the database tables for you. Figure 4-14 shows the model, which is similar to the database model shown at the beginning of the chapter.

In the `AtTheMoviesModel.Designer.cs` file, a context is generated, as well as the entities of the model. This code is generated and regenerated after a change in the model, so it should not be altered by you. In case you must add code to the generated entities, you can do so using partial classes. This even includes adding annotations (for validation purposes) on properties.

Assume you want to add a validation rule that the `Amount` property on the `Payment` class should always be smaller than `200`. You can apply this using the `RangeAttribute`. A second rule might be that the `CardNumber` is required; this can be applied using the `RequiredAttribute`. However, there's no such thing as a partial property to add this attribute on. Instead, you must add a second class, in this case, called `PaymentMetaData`, which contains the metadata for the `Payment` class. This class is linked to the first one using the `MetadataTypeAttribute`. The attributes on the properties are merged with the attributes on the `Payment` class (generated by EF), based on their names. Listing 4-7 shows the creation of this partial class.

LISTING 4-7: Payment Class

```
[MetadataType(typeof(PaymentMetaData))]
public partial class Payment
{
    internal sealed class PaymentMetaData
    {
        [Required]
        public string CardNumber { get; set; }
```

continues

LISTING 4-7 *(continued)*

```
        [Range(1, 200)]
        public Decimal Amount { get; set; }
    }
}
```

Code file [Snowball.AtTheMovies.Model/Payment.cs] available for download at Wrox.com.

Later, you see that this attribute returns in the generated code on the client.

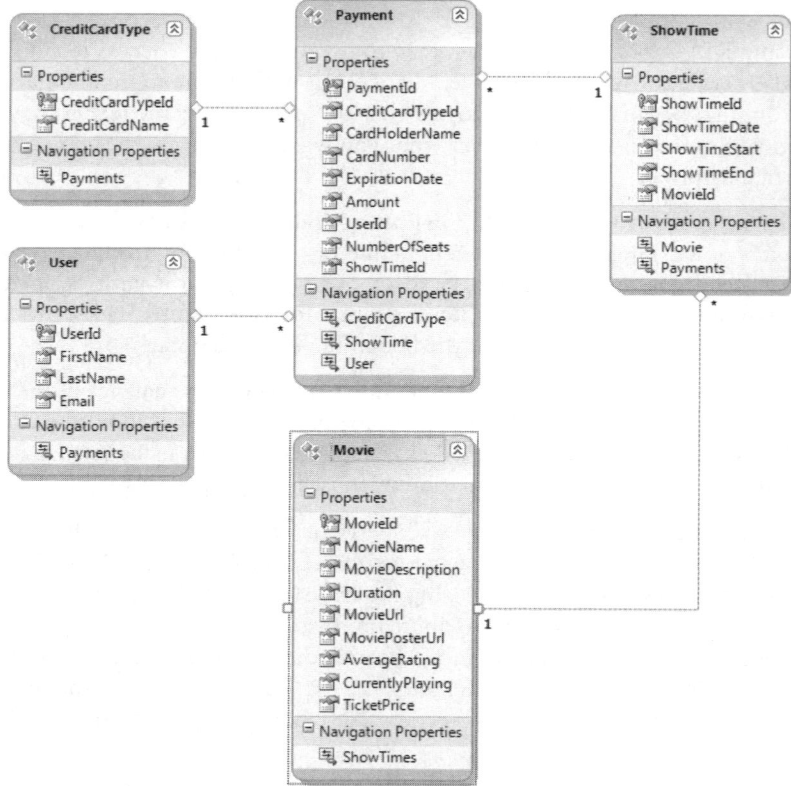

FIGURE 4-14: The Entity Model

Creating the Actual Services

With the model and data access ready, you can turn your attention to the services. Let's start building the services for the MovieSelection screen. As explained previously, the tooling that comes with RIA Services takes away some tiresome work. If wanted, you can have it create some default CRUD operations for the desired entities.

To create the services, start by adding a domain service class to the `Snowball.AtTheMovies.Services.Web` project. A service within RIA services is referred to as a `DomainService`. It is the access point for your Silverlight application to get data, either coming from a database or another service.

The tooling requires that the build is up-to-date so that it can find the entities in your code. Initiate a build if not performed yet, and then add a domain service class to the project called `MovieService`. Immediately, a dialog pops up, enabling you to configure the service, as shown in Figure 4-15.

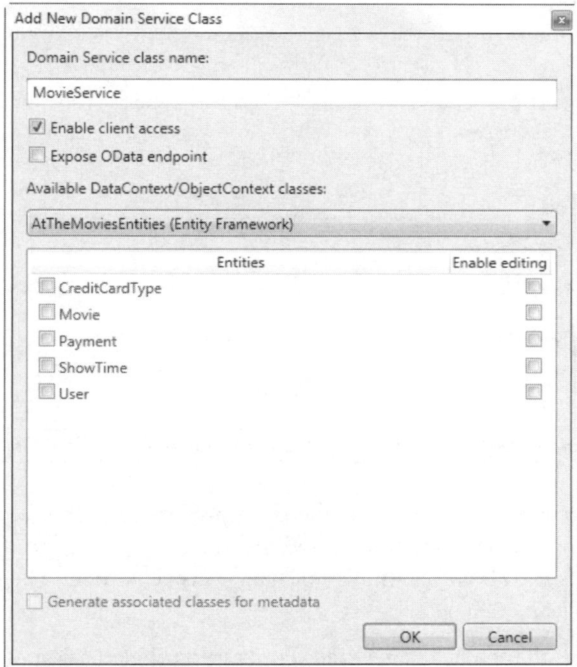

FIGURE 4-15: Dialog for configuring the service

The "Enable Client Access" check box indicates whether you want the service code to be generated on the client as well. Selecting this box results in the `EnableClientAccess` attribute to be applied on the class. The second check box, "Expose OData Endpoint," enables exposing data from the `DomainService` as OData, facilitating data sharing. This way, you can access the data from the service (for example, from Excel).

As previously mentioned, the tooling works best with EF, which is clearly visible here. The available `DataContexts` are listed and the entities for them are shown. You have the option to select which entities are needed for the service you are creating. Optionally, you can also have the tooling to generate the basic CRUD operations.

In version 1 of RIA Services, you could not share an entity over multiple services. This meant that if you had two services (for example `PaymentService` and `MovieService`), you could have only the `User` entity in one of the two. In real-world systems, this caused problems. No real system is designed so that all entities are clearly separated. (It's probably not even a good idea to try doing so!) As of this writing, version 1.0, Service Pack 1 Beta is the latest version, which adds support for shared entities, making it possible to segment the `DomainServices` more like you want.

In `MovieService`, all the logic resides that has to do with `Movie` and `ShowTime`. Therefore, click both the `Movie` and the `ShowTime` entities because these will be needed in the implementation of the service. You won't be adding or updating these entities in this application, so leave the "Enable Editing" check box unchecked. Listing 4-8 shows the code that is generated.

LISTING 4-8: Generated DomainService Class Code


```
// [RequiresAuthentication]
[EnableClientAccess()]
public class MovieService : LinqToEntitiesDomainService<AtTheMoviesEntities>
{
    public IQueryable<Movie> GetMovies()
    {
        return this.ObjectContext.Movies;
    }

    public IQueryable<ShowTime> GetShowTimes()
    {
        return this.ObjectContext.ShowTimes;
    }
}
```

Code file [Snowball.AtTheMovies.Services.Web/PaymentService.cs] available for download at Wrox.com.

For the movie selection screen (refer to the screen mockup section where the prototype of this screen was shown), you need a list of currently playing movies. (It's not a good idea to allow the user to select a movie that's not playing anymore, is it?) However, that's not what was generated. The `GetMovies()` method returns a list of all movies.

Although this code is generated, you can freely change it. It's generated only upon the creation of the service. So, you can either change the `GetMovies()` method or add a new one. Let's go for the second option, as shown in the Listing 4-9, which uses the `GetAllCurrentMovies()`.

LISTING 4-9: GetAllCurrentMovies() Method

```
public IQueryable<Movie> GetAllCurrentMovies()
{
    return this.ObjectContext.Movies.Where(m =>
        m.CurrentlyPlaying == true);
}
```

For now, you have enough logic within the service, so you should now look at what all this work on the server results in on the client.

But wait just a minute. How can the client code know to use this `GetAllCurrentMovies()` method to retrieve a list of movies?

Convention Is the Rule

As you may have noticed, the generated methods (so-called *query methods*) start with `Get` and return an `IQueryable<Entity>`. For RIA Services, the latter is a sign that this method can be used for retrieving movies. Similarly, starting a method name with `Insert` and passing an entity as a parameter is enough for RIA Services to know that the specified method does an insert.

The rule here is *convention*. RIA Services expects this naming pattern, and the generated code on the client will be based on this naming schema. The principle of *convention-over-configuration* has been known for quite some time but has been somewhat lacking in Microsoft products. Seeing this principle applied here is a sign that you'll see this more and more in Microsoft products in the future as well.

That being said, it's not always possible to stick to these convention rules. I've dealt with customers where the code names need to be translated in the local language. To counter this, it's possible to use attributes, overruling the convention. Table 4-3 shows a summarized list of the conventions, attributes, and their usage.

TABLE 4-3: Conventions and Attributes Used by RIA Services

CONVENTION PREFIX	CONFIGURATION ATTRIBUTE	USAGE
`Insert, Add, Create`	`Insert`	Accepts an entity as a parameter and inserts this into the data source.
`Update, Change, Modify`	`Update`	Accepts an entity as a parameter and updates this entity in the data source.
`Remove, Delete`	`Delete`	Accepts an entity as a parameter and removes this entity from the data source.
`(Get), (Retrieve)`...	`Query`	Retrieves a single entity `T`, an `IQueryable<T>` or an `IEnumberable<T>`. It's common to prefix with `Get` or `Retrieve`; although, you're not obliged to do so. Any method name works just fine.

The `IQueryable<T>` return value of the retrieval methods is a special case. An `IQueryable` represents an expression tree, a concept in LINQ that enables evaluating a query against a specific data source. This means that you can build a query on the client, and it will be appended to the query on the server side.

On the data store, an optimal query will be executed, based on the provider. This effectively means that you can build a filtering query on the client. This query can then be combined with the server-side query, resulting in a query being fired on the data store, returning results back to the client.

Meanwhile, in the Silverlight Project

Upon building the solution, RIA Services' tooling works hard to generate the client-side code. In the `Snowball.AtTheMovies.Services` project (if you followed the same convention as used with this solution, this project is in the `Client` solution folder), set the Show All Files option to `true`. You see a folder called `Generated_Code`, as shown in Figure 4-16. Although not part of your project, this folder contains the *proxy code*, based on the `DomainService` you created earlier.

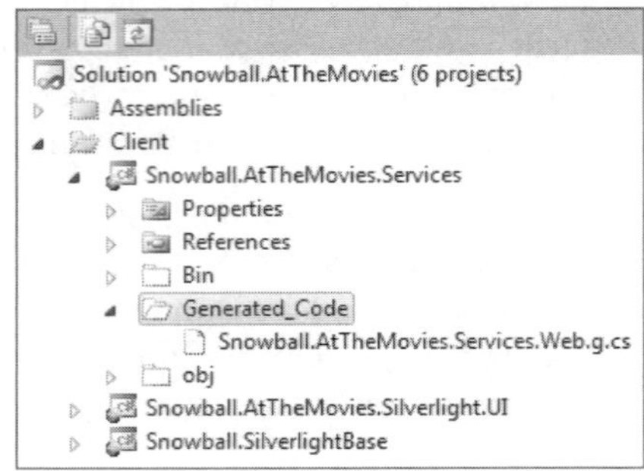

FIGURE 4-16: Generated_Code folder

In the generated code, you can find a client-side context of type `DomainContext` called `MovieContext`. For each domain service you create, a domain context generates. This context can be seen as the point of contact for the client code. It's a proxy to the service methods, but it's also responsible for things like change tracking for entities on the client. The latter is done using an `EntityContainer`, which contains an `EntitySet` for each entity. (In this case, you have an `EntitySet` for both the `Movie` and the `ShowTime` entities.) Listing 4-10 shows part of the generated code of the `Snowball.AtTheMovies.Services.Web.g.cs` file.

LISTING 4-10: EntityContainer with EntitySet

```
internal sealed class MovieContextEntityContainer : EntityContainer
{
    public MovieContextEntityContainer()
    {
        this.CreateEntitySet<Movie>(EntitySetOperations.None);
        this.CreateEntitySet<ShowTime>(EntitySetOperations.None);
    }
}
```

Code file [Snowball.AtTheMovies.Services/Generated_code/Snowball.AtTheMovies.Services.Web.g.cs] available for download at Wrox.com.

The domain context supports batching as well. If you change more than one entity on the client, you can save them in a batch to the service.

You can now use the generated code to fill the list of movies. Now take a look at building this screen.

Loading Data in the MovieSelection Screen

To make things easier to follow, Figure 4-17 shows the screen you are working toward. To save some space, the entire XAML is not included. Take a look at the solution on this book's companion website (`www.wrox.com`) for this.

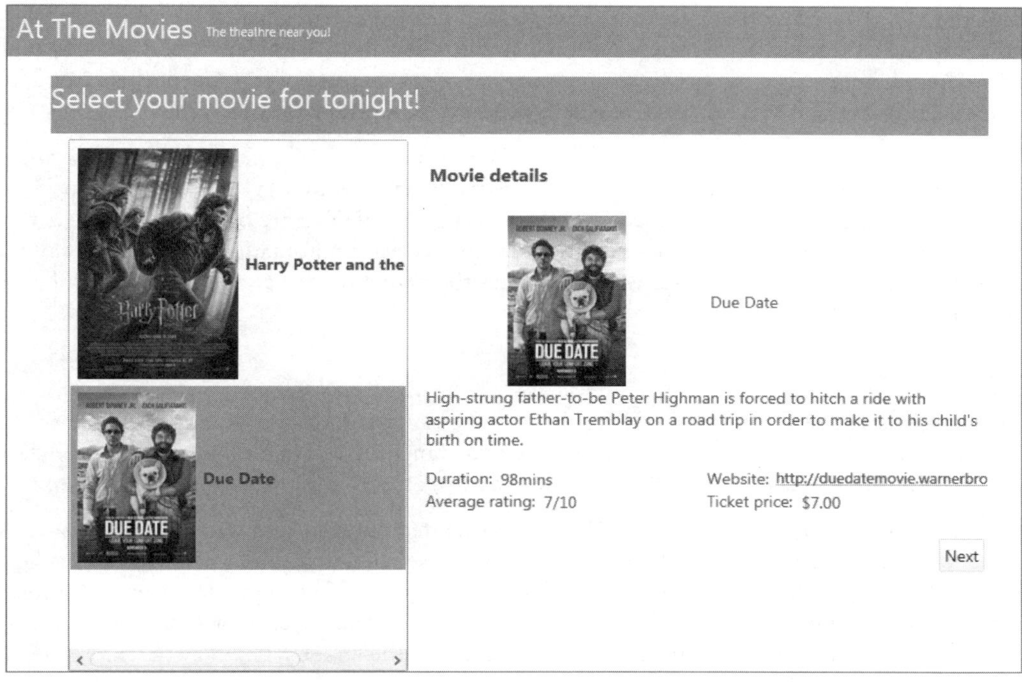

FIGURE 4-17: MovieSelection Screen

The first thing you must be concerned with is filling the list with all current movies. You have built this method within the `MovieService` already, so it's usable from the Silverlight application. Listing 4-11 shows how to do this.

LISTING 4-11: Loading Data from the DomainService


```
private MovieContext _context;

public MovieSelectionView()
{
    InitializeComponent();
    _context = new MovieContext();
}

// Executes when the user navigates to this page.
protected override void OnNavigatedTo(NavigationEventArgs e)
{
    EntityQuery<Movie> query = _context.GetAllCurrentMoviesQuery();
    _context.Load(query);
    CurrentMovieListBox.ItemsSource = _context.Movies;
}
```

Code file [Snowball.AtTheMovies.Silverlight.UI/View/MovieSelectionView.xaml.cs] available for download at Wrox.com.

The code in the `OnNavigatedTo()` method is what should interest you most. It is executed when using the navigation framework — you have navigated to the page. The context, `MovieContext`, is instantiated, and you use the `GetAllCurrentMoviesQuery()` method of it. Indeed, this resembles quite a lot working with a regular service, where you have a normal proxy as well.

You bind the `ItemsSource` property of the `ListBox` to a property `Movies` on the `MoviesDataContext`. When RIA Services notices that you have one or more methods on your service that return an `IQueryable<T>`, the previously mentioned `EntitySet` is generated. You are binding to this exact `EntitySet` here. However, the data does not arrive in this property automatically. You must call the `Load()` method explicitly. Although RIA Services hides the asynchronous coding, the data still is loaded in an asynchronous manner.

Polishing the Screen

If you ran the exact code as printed, your result won't be exactly the same. What you see in the `ListBox` is just the `ToString()` implementation, not the fancier UI with an image and a `TextBlock`. This is achieved using a custom `DataTemplate` for the `ItemTemplate` property of the `ListBox`.

This template can be seen as a piece of XAML that is generated for each item within the `ListBox`. The `DataContext` for each item is the bound object, so you can use regular data-binding expressions here as well. Listing 4-12 shows the XAML for this `DataTemplate`. Although you can place this code directly in the `App.xaml`, it's common to create one or more resource dictionaries and reference these from the `App.xaml`. That's exactly why this `DataTemplate` is located in the `Assets/CoreStyles.xaml` file.

LISTING 4-12: DataTemplate for the Movie Selection ListBox


```xml
<Style x:Key="MovieSelectionListBoxStyle" TargetType="ListBox">
    <Setter Property="Margin" Value="5"></Setter>
    <Setter Property="Width" Value="290"></Setter>
    <Setter Property="ItemTemplate">
        <Setter.Value>
            <DataTemplate>
                <StackPanel Orientation="Horizontal">
                    <Image Source="{Binding MoviePosterUrl,
                        Converter={StaticResource
                        localImageUrlConverter}}"
                        Margin="3"></Image>
                    <TextBlock Text="{Binding MovieName}"
                        TextWrapping="Wrap"
                        VerticalAlignment="Center"
                        Style="{StaticResource
                        MovieSelectionTextBlockStyle}">
                        </TextBlock>
                </StackPanel>
            </DataTemplate>
        </Setter.Value>
    </Setter>
</Style>
```

Code file [Snowball.AtTheMovies.Silverlight.UI/Assets/CoreStyles.xaml] available for download at Wrox.com.

A good coding practice in Silverlight is to place this inside a style, as shown. This style then is applied using the code from Listing 4-13.

LISTING 4-13: Applying the Style on the ListBox


```
<ListBox x:Name="CurrentMovieListBox"
    Grid.Row="1" Grid.Column="0"
    Style="{StaticResource MovieSelectionListBoxStyle}">
</ListBox>
```

Code file [Snowball.AtTheMovies.Silverlight.UI/View/MovieSelectionView.xaml] available for download at Wrox.com.

Finally, when a selection is made in the `ListBox`, you must ensure that the `Grid` containing the details of the movie knows where its children should get their data from. Whenever the selection changes, this must update as well.

This can be achieved by changing the `DataContext` of this `Grid` to the selected item in the `ListBox` (each item is a `Movie` anyway). Listing 4-14 shows just this.

LISTING 4-14: XAML Code for the Detail Grid (Partly)


```
<Grid DataContext="{Binding ElementName=CurrentMovieListBox, Path=SelectedItem}">
            ...
    <Image Source="{Binding MoviePosterUrl,
                Converter={StaticResource localImageUrlConverter}}" >
    </Image>
    <TextBlock Text="Movie details"
            Style="{StaticResource SubTitleTextBlockStyle}">
    </TextBlock>
    <TextBlock x:Name="MovieNameTextBlock"
            Text="{Binding MovieName}"
            Style="{StaticResource LabelTextBlockStyle}">
    </TextBlock>
    <TextBlock x:Name="MovieDescriptionTextBlock"
            Text="{Binding MovieDescription}"
            Style="{StaticResource DefaultTextBlockStyle}">
    </TextBlock>
    ...
</Grid>
```

Code file [Snowball.AtTheMovies.Silverlight.UI/View/MovieSelectionView.xaml] available for download at Wrox.com.

The other screens can be re-created in a similar fashion. To save space, they aren't presented here.

APPLYING THE MVVM PATTERN

When you look back at the code you just wrote, you see that there's nothing actually wrong with it. There isn't, certainly not. If you keep working on the other screens the way you started, things will work out fine, and the application for "At The Movies" will turn out just fine. You wrote some

XAML code and most of the code in the Silverlight application arrives in the code-behind. Figure 4-18 shows a graphical overview of the code so far.

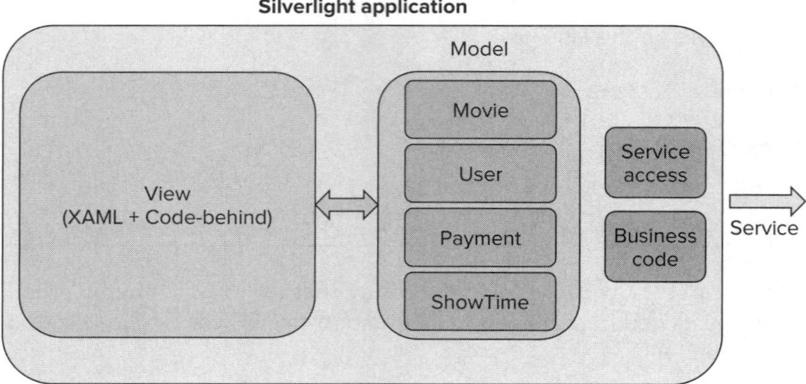

FIGURE 4-18: Application code thus far

As you can see, the bulk lies in the View, consisting of the XAML and code-behind. The code also directly accesses the model, and services are directly invoked from the View code as well. Although there's not anything wrong with this approach, it's not easy to test. The code in the code-behind is difficult to test in isolation because it's closely linked to the View objects.

A better approach exists in the *Model-View-ViewModel* (*MVVM*) approach. Take a look at what the schema for my application evolves into, as shown in Figure 4-19.

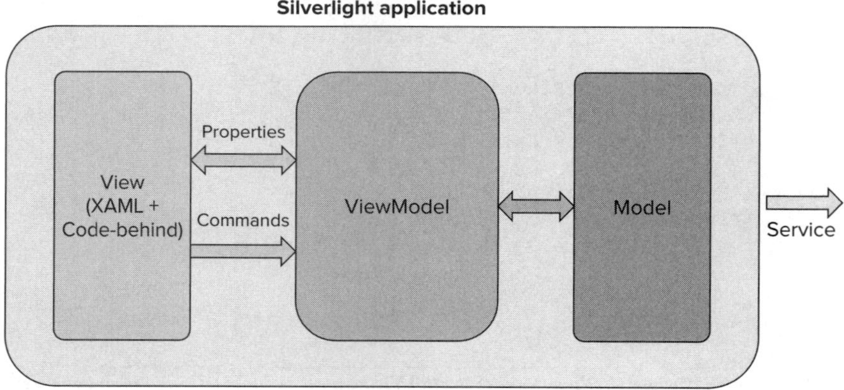

FIGURE 4-19: Evolution of the application

The View has been on a serious diet! Although the amount of XAML is still roughly the same, the code-behind part is a lot smaller. There's almost no more code left in the code-behind (more on that later). The bulk of the code has now moved into the ViewModel, an abstraction of the View. This ViewModel exposes state and operations. *State* means properties, to be used by the View. *Operations* are commands. The ViewModel is set as the `DataContext` for the View, so in the View, bindings can be created to properties and commands of the ViewModel.

No direct link exists between the View and the Model anymore. The ViewModel sits in between.

Different Parts, Different Roles

Before you start refactoring your code to include the MVVM pattern, take a look in a bit more detail at the different building blocks.

The View

The View should contain mostly XAML. Although there is some code in the code-behind, it should be minimal. All code that should be tested should not be in the code-behind. The View binds to the ViewModel, which exposes data in the form of properties. Event handlers should not be used to handle events (such as clicking on a button). Instead, commands can be used, which are exposed from the ViewModel as well.

Silverlight 4 contains limited support for commanding, in that it's supported only on the `ButtonBase` class. Using a simple workaround with a behavior, other controls can bind any event to a command as well. In the end, the View is the area of the designer!

The ViewModel

The ViewModel contains the state and the operations available for the View — in other words, the View can bind to them. The ViewModel can be seen as an abstraction of the View. Properties represent the state. For example, a list of movies can be a property of the ViewModel, to which the View can bind.

Commands represent the operations available to the View. All the code to be tested should live in the ViewModel. It can be tested in isolation, without interference of, for example, a UI element. The ViewModel does not know in which View it's used. Sometimes, different views are bound to one ViewModel.

The Model

The Model is any data model you want to use in the application. This can be a proxy, generated from adding a service reference. There should be no direct access from the View to the Model. Instead, the ViewModel gets the data from the Model and prepares it for the UI to use. The Model does not know the ViewModels using it.

Choosing the MVVM Approach

Whether to build your application based on an MVVM architecture may be a question that pops into your mind. One of the main advantages is, of course, the better *separation of concerns* (SOC) within your code. (And everyone knows this is a good thing.)

Making your View thin so that it becomes entirely the area of the designer on your team is a good principle. Your logic can automatically become more testable and maintainable. As mentioned, testing View code is difficult. On the other hand, testing the ViewModel is much easier. Also, through the better SOC, for example, when the View changes, there's a big chance that no change is needed to the ViewModel, thus improving the maintainability.

On the other hand, as you'll soon see, there's still more manual work to be done (that is, more code to be written) when using MVVM. Several great frameworks are out there that can take on part of that work for you. This can be a bit confusing because there are quite a few implementations available. Of course, MVVM remains a pattern, and everyone gives his or her own implementation to the pattern.

Picking a Little Helper — MVVM Light

As mentioned, using MVVM can be a bit more work because there's more manual code to be written. One of the frameworks that can help with this is MVVM Light, written by Laurent Bugnion. As the name implies, it is a lightweight framework, available as Open Source, so you can make changes where you want.

The code for the project can be downloaded from the CodePlex site via `http://mvvmlight. codeplex.com`. For refactoring purposes here, use just the binaries, which can also be downloaded from the CodePlex site.

In the solution, add a `Solution` folder and place in it the `GalaSoft.MvvmLight.SL4.dll` assembly. Create a reference to the assembly from the Silverlight project. You're now ready to start refactoring to MVVM.

Refactoring to MVVM

In this section, you refactor your code to use the MVVM pattern. First prepare the project to accommodate the changes you want to make.

Add in the Silverlight project `View`, `ViewModel`, and `Model` folders. In these folders, you can place the classes of the respective roles.

The Model

The code that communicates with the `DomainService` no longer can be in the code-behind; place it in a Model class. For the `MovieSelectionView` discussed earlier, you must work with `Movie` entities. You create a class `MovieModel` in the `Model` folder. In this class, you need a method that retrieves all currently playing movies. Listing 4-15 shows the code for this class.

LISTING 4-15: MovieModel Class

```
public class MovieModel
{
    private MovieContext _context;
    private LoadOperation<Movie> _movieLoadOperation;
    private Action<ObservableCollection<Movie>> getAllCurrentMoviesCallback;

    public MovieModel()
    {
```

```
        _context = new MovieContext();
    }

    public void GetAllCurrentMovies
        (Action<ObservableCollection<Movie>> GetAllCurrentMoviesCallback)
    {
        _getAllCurrentMoviesCallback = GetAllCurrentMoviesCallback;

        var query = _context.GetAllCurrentMoviesQuery();
        _movieLoadOperation = _context.Load(query);
        _movieLoadOperation.Completed +=
            new EventHandler(OnGetAllCurrentMoviesCompleted);
    }

    private void OnGetAllCurrentMoviesCompleted(object sender, EventArgs e)
    {
        _movieLoadOperation.Completed -= OnGetAllCurrentMoviesCompleted;
        var movies = new EntityList<Movie>
            (_context.Movies, _movieLoadOperation.Entities);
        _getAllCurrentMoviesCallback(movies);
    }
}
```

Code file [Snowball.AtTheMovies.Silverlight.UI/Model/MovieModel.cs] available for download at Wrox.com.

The `GetAllCurrentMovies()` method takes `Action<ObservableCollection<Movie>>` as a parameter. This shows once again that the data retrieval from the `DomainService` is asynchronous. This `Action` points to the method (part of the ViewModel, as you'll see soon) that you'll call from the callback (`OnGetAllCurrentMoviesCompleted`) when the data has been received. Accessing the service is similar to what you saw earlier.

The ViewModel

The ViewModel for the movie selection screen is a class located in the `ViewModel` folder called `MovieSelectionViewModel`. This class must notify the View about changes happening to its properties to ensure that the data-binding engine keeps the View in sync. Therefore, this class should implement the `INotifyPropertyChanged` interface. However, you can benefit from MVVM Light here and have the class inherit from `ViewModelBase`. The latter already implements `INotifyPropertyChanged` and has a method, `RaisePropertyChanged`, that you can use to raise the event of a changing property.

Looking back at what the screen needs, you see that it needs a list of movies. When clicking a movie, you display the details of the movie. Previously, you did the latter by setting the `DataContext` of the `Grid` to the `SelectedItem` within the `ListBox`. Although that's fine, in the MVVM approach, you must know which movie was selected by the user (to save it later back to the service). Therefore, you also expose a `SelectedMovie` property on the ViewModel, to which the View can bind. Listing 4-16 shows the code for the ViewModel. Only the relevant parts are shown here for spacing reasons.

LISTING 4-16: MovieSelectionViewModel Class (Partial)

```csharp
public class MovieSelectionViewModel : ViewModelBase
{
    private MovieModel _movieModel;
    private Movie _selectedMovie;
    private ObservableCollection<Movie> _currentMovies;

    public MovieSelectionViewModel()
    {
        _movieModel = new MovieModel();

        LoadAllCurrentMovies();
    }

    private void LoadAllCurrentMovies()
    {
        _movieModel.GetAllCurrentMovies(GetAllCurrentMoviesCallback);
    }

    public void GetAllCurrentMoviesCallback
        (ObservableCollection<Movie> movies)
    {
        if (movies != null)
        {
            CurrentMovies = movies;
        }
    }

    public ObservableCollection<Movie> CurrentMovies
    {
        get
        {
            return _currentMovies;
        }
        set
            {
                _currentMovies = value;
                RaisePropertyChanged("CurrentMovies");
            }
    }

    public Movie SelectedMovie
    {
        get
        {
            return _selectedMovie;
        }
        set
        {
            _selectedMovie = value;
            MovieSelectedCommand.RaiseCanExecuteChanged();
            RaisePropertyChanged("SelectedMovie");
        }
```

```
        }
    }
```

Code file [Snowball.AtTheMovies.Silverlight.UI/ViewModel/MovieSelectionViewModel.cs] available for download at Wrox.com.

As you can see, the ViewModel knows the Model and asks it to load the `Movies` in the `LoadCurrentMovies()` method. The `GetAllCurrentMoviesCallback()` gets called from the mode when the asynchronous loading of the data is complete.

The View

The View is a `Page` or a `UserControl`, located in the `View` folder. The View for the movie selection is `MovieSelectionView.xaml`. The code-behind should be as clean as possible. By all means, it should not contain any code that is to be tested. The code in Listing 4-17 is all there is in the code-behind.

LISTING 4-17: Code-Behind for the MovieSelectionView

```
public partial class MovieSelectionView : Page
{
    public MovieSelectionView()
    {
        InitializeComponent();
    }
}
```

Code file [Snowball.AtTheMovies.Silverlight.UI/View/MovieSelectionView.xaml.cs] available for download at Wrox.com.

That seems clean, doesn't it? The XAML is bound to an instance of the ViewModel. The latter exposes a `CurrentMovies` and a `SelectedMovie` property, as shown in Listing 4-18.

LISTING 4-18: MovieSelectionView.xaml Bound to the ViewModel

```
<ListBox x:Name="CurrentMovieListBox"
        ItemsSource="{Binding CurrentMovies}"
        SelectedItem="{Binding SelectedMovie, Mode=TwoWay}">
</ListBox>
...
<TextBlock x:Name="MovieNameTextBlock"
        Text="{Binding SelectedMovie.MovieName}" >
</TextBlock>
<TextBlock x:Name="MovieDescriptionTextBlock"
        Text="{Binding SelectedMovie.MovieDescription}">
</TextBlock>
...
```

Code file [Snowball.AtTheMovies.Silverlight.UI/View/MovieSelectionView.xaml] available for download at Wrox.com.

Hold on. How does the View know which ViewModel to take? There are different answers to this question. A possible solution is to use *Managed Extensibility Framework (MEF)*. However, you won't use MEF here. Another solution is to use a locator. A *locator* is a class that contains a property for each ViewModel. The code in Listing 4-19 shows the relevant part of the `ViewModelLocator` class, part of the solution.

LISTING 4-19: ViewModelLocator.cs (Partial)


```
public class ViewModelLocator
{
    private MovieSelectionViewModel _movieSelectionViewModel;
    private UserDataEntryViewModel _userDataEntryViewModel;

    public ViewModelLocator()
    {
        _userDataEntryViewModel = new UserDataEntryViewModel();
        _movieSelectionViewModel = new MovieSelectionViewModel();
    }

    public  MovieSelectionViewModel MovieSelectionViewModel
    {
        get
        {
            return _movieSelectionViewModel;
        }
    }

    public UserDataEntryViewModel UserDataEntryViewModel
    {
        get
        {
            return _userDataEntryViewModel;
        }
    }
}
```

Code file [Snowball.AtTheMovies.Silverlight.UI/ViewModelLocator.cs] available for download at Wrox.com.

Once the locator code has been written, we need to instantiate it. A specific resource dictionary, `MVVMDictionary.xaml`, was created to place this instance in. Listing 4-20 shows the code for this file.

LISTING 4-20: Setting the DataContext to a ViewModelLocator Property


```
<ResourceDictionary
    xmlns="http://schemas.microsoft.com/winfx/2006/xaml/presentation"
    xmlns:x="http://schemas.microsoft.com/winfx/2006/xaml"
```

```
     xmlns:vm="clr-namespace:Snowball.AtTheMovies.Silverlight.UI">
     <vm:ViewModelLocator x:Key="Locator" />
</ResourceDictionary>
```

Code file [Snowball.AtTheMovies.Silverlight.UI/Assets/MVVMDictionary.xaml] available for download at Wrox.com.

In the XAML for the UI, you can now set the `DataContext` of the `Page` (or `UserControl`, depending on what you use) to the public property of the related ViewModel, as shown in Listing 4-21.

LISTING 4-21: Setting the DataContext to a ViewModelLocator Property

```
<navigation:Page x:Class=
    "Snowball.AtTheMovies.Silverlight.UI.View.MovieSelectionView"
        ...
        DataContext="{Binding MovieSelectionViewModel,
                    Source={StaticResource Locator}}">
```

Code file [Snowball.AtTheMovies.Silverlight.UI/View/MovieSelectionView.xaml] available for download at Wrox.com.

You have now successfully refactored to MVVM. Now take a look at what must happen when the user interacts with a control.

At Your Command

Because you must keep the code-behind as clean as possible, you can't start adding event handlers to it. Instead, you can use commands. Using a command, you can link an action in the ViewModel to an event in the View, such as clicking a button. Since version 4, Silverlight has support for the `ICommand` interface, which is shown in Listing 4-22.

LISTING 4-22: The ICommand Interface

```
public interface ICommand
{
    event EventHandler CanExecuteChanged;
    bool CanExecute(object parameter);
    void Execute(object parameter);
}
```

To use a command, you must write a class that implements the `ICommand` interface, expose an instance of this class on the ViewModel, and finally bind the `Command` property of a control to this property.

Although that works fine, you can fall back on MVVM Light again, which provides the `RelayCommand`. This class already implements the `ICommand` interface, so you can skip the step of writing your own implementation. In the MovieSelection screen, you must perform an action when the user clicks the Next button. You can do so by creating a `RelayCommand` instance in the ViewModel called `MovieSelectedCommand`, as shown in Listing 4-23.

LISTING 4-23: Initializing the MovieSelectedCommand


```
public MovieSelectionViewModel()
{
    _movieModel = new MovieModel();

    LoadCommands();
    LoadAllCurrentMovies();
}

public RelayCommand MovieSelectedCommand { get; set; }

private void LoadCommands()
{
    MovieSelectedCommand = new RelayCommand(OnMovieSelected,
                OnCanMovieSelected);
}

public void OnMovieSelected()
{
    //do some action
}

public bool OnCanMovieSelected()
{
    return _selectedMovie != null;
}
```

Code file [Snowball.AtTheMovies.Silverlight.UI/ViewModel/MovieSelectionViewModel.cs] available for download at Wrox.com.

In the `LoadCommands()` method, you initialize the `RelayCommand`. The first parameter is an `Action`, which is executed when the command fires. The second parameter is a `Func<bool>`, which returns whether the command can execute. Based on this Boolean value, a command can be enabled or disabled. When `false` is returned, if bound to a button, the button will be disabled.

You now need to link the command on the ViewModel with the `Command` property of the button. This can be done using the code shown in Listing 4-24.

LISTING 4.24: Binding the Command Property


```
<Button Content="Next" Command="{Binding MovieSelectedCommand}">
</Button>
```

Code file [Snowball.AtTheMovies.Silverlight.UI/View/MovieSelectionView.xaml] available for download at Wrox.com.

When the button is clicked, the code in the `Command` (in the `Execute()` of the `ICommand` interface) is executed.

Messaging

Using the MVVM pattern, you achieve loose coupling. However, between the different ViewModels, communication must take place.

For example, in the "At The Movies" application, when going from one screen to the next, you must pass on the entered data. (The show time screen must know what movie was selected to search for the show times for the selected movie.) Solving this by creating references between ViewModels may end up in spaghetti code of references between ViewModels, and this would take away the advantage of the ease of testability.

To solve this, a mediator/messenger can be used. Using a pub/sub model, a ViewModel registers with the messenger, saying that it will publish messages of a certain type. Another ViewModel can register with that same messenger to receive messages of a certain type. When the messenger receives a message, it sends that message to all registered classes. This way, the two ViewModel classes can communicate without a hard reference between them.

MVVM Light has a `Messenger` class on board that you can use for this purpose. You can create instances of this `Messenger`, or you can use the default `Messenger` instance, available in the `ViewModelBase`. Use the latter option here. To send data from one ViewModel to another, a base or a custom type can be used. Let's use `UserDataModelMessage`. The definition for this class is shown in Listing 4-25. The `UserDataPresentationModel` type used here is just a data transfer object (DTO) class containing the user's selections to pass between screens.

LISTING 4-25: UserDataModelMessage Class

```
public class UserDataModelMessage: MessageBase
{
    public UserDataPresentationModel CurrentUserDataModel { get; set; }
}
```

Code file [Snowball.AtTheMovies.Silverlight.UI/Messages/UserDataModelMessage.cs] available for download at Wrox.com.

The code in Listing 4-26 contains the completed `OnMovieSelected`, part of the `MovieSelectionViewModel`. In this method, you register with the `Messenger` to send a message of the type shown in Listing 4-25. The `ShowTimeSelectionViewModel` parameter points to the target type. You can indicate which type must receive the message in order not to send the message to too many recipients, as shown in Listing 4-26.

LISTING 4-26: Registering to Send a Message to the Default Messenger

```
public void OnMovieSelected()
{
    Messenger.Default.Send<UserDataModelMessage, ShowTimeSelectionViewModel>
        (new UserDataModelMessage()
```

continues

LISTING 4-26 *(continued)*

```
            { CurrentUserDataModel = _currentUserDataModel });
   }
```

Code file [Snowball.AtTheMovies.Silverlight.UI/ViewModel/MovieSelectionViewModel.cs] available for download at Wrox.com.

In the `ShowTimeSelectionViewModel`, you can register to accept this message, as shown in Listing 4-27.

LISTING 4-27: Registering to Receive a Message from the Default Messenger

```
private void InitializeMessenger()
{
        Messenger.Default.Register<UserDataModelMessage>
           (this, OnUserDataModelMessageReceived);
}
```

Code file [Snowball.AtTheMovies.Silverlight.UI/ViewModel/MovieSelectionViewModel.cs] available for download at Wrox.com.

The ViewModels can now communicate without a reference between them.

CREATING CUSTOMIZED CONTROLS

So far, the controls you have been using are nothing more than the standard controls such as a `TextBox` or a button. Silverlight wouldn't be Silverlight if it could not support a way to customize these controls. To finish the sample application, let's incorporate some customized controls.

Control Templates

With standard styling, you can change only values of properties such as `FontSize`, `Width`, or `HorizontalAlignment`. In many cases, this is more than enough. When you want to completely redesign the control's looks, however, you won't get there. In this case, changing the control's template can help out.

Templating is the technique in which you remove the standard look for the control and replace it with a new look. The behavior is still the same. If you re-template a button, you remove the gray rectangle, including gradients, and things like the hover effect, but it still works like a button. When you click it, it still triggers an event that you can catch (either with an event handler or a `Command`).

To create a new template for an existing control, you can do everything manually. This includes creating a new template from scratch, linking template values with values of the control instantiation using a `TemplateBinding`, specifying where the content goes using a `ContentPresenter`, and so on. In the code in Listing 4-28, a control template is defined inside a style to create a red circular button.

LISTING 4-28: Control Template Code

```xml
<Style x:Key="ButtonStyle" TargetType="Button">
    <Setter Property="Template">
        <Setter.Value>
            <ControlTemplate>
                <Grid>
                    <Ellipse Stroke="Gray" StrokeThickness="5"
                             Fill="Red"
                             Height="{TemplateBinding Height}"
                             Width="{TemplateBinding Width}" >
                    </Ellipse>
                    <ContentPresenter HorizontalAlignment="Center"
                            VerticalAlignment="Center">
                    </ContentPresenter>
                </Grid>
            </ControlTemplate>
        </Setter.Value>
    </Setter>
</Style>
```

Code file [Snowball.AtTheMovies.Silverlight.UI/Assets/SDKStyles.xaml] available for download at Wrox.com.

Although this creates a new, round button, some issues exist with this approach. For example, there's no feedback on when you are clicking or hovering. This can all be re-created, but it takes quite some work.

A better approach is to use the *Visual State Manager* (VSM) and the *Parts & States* model. This model specifies that a control can be in a specific state and can have one or more parts with which the user can interact. The states define in what situations the control can be. For a button, this can be `Pressed`, `MouseOver`, and so on. The VSM takes care of bringing the control from one state to the other when needed, and also manages the transitions that must happen between the states. With the VSM, templating a control merely comes down to defining how the control should look in the various states.

This model dramatically improves how easy it is to create custom controls. If you want to do all this manually, it's possible. However, Expression Blend supports the VSM as well, making it much easier to create custom control templates.

Now look at how you can create a more movie-themed button by changing the standard gray Next button into a movie clapper with some text on it. Follow these steps:

1. As mentioned, to make things easier, work from Expression Blend. You can open the solution you already have entirely in Blend without there being any need to change anything.

2. In the `MovieSelectionView.xaml`, right-click the Next button, and, under Edit Template, select Create Empty. In the Resource creation dialog, set the name to **MovieClapperButtonTemplate** and select Application as the scope for the template.

3. In the "Objects and Timeline" panel, the `ControlTemplate` displays, containing just an empty `Grid` as its root container.

4. From the files provided on this book's companion website (`www.wrox.com`), download and add the `action.png` Movie Clapper icon to the project (preferably under the `Assets` folder).

5. Drag the image onto the Designer, and position it in the center of the `Grid`.

6. Add a `ContentPresenter` and center this horizontally as well. The `ContentPresenter` represents a placeholder for the actual content of the control. In this case, the button contained just some text (Next), so when dragged on, the Designer displays the text as well. If your control contains other content (such as nested controls), these would become the new content.

7. To ensure that the image sizes along with the size of the control, you can use a `TemplateBinding`. Such a binding links a value within the control template with a value on the control initialization. You must create such a binding between the `Width` and `Height` of the image and `Width` and `Height` of the control. In the Properties window, navigate to the property (`Width` and `Height`) and click the options rectangle at the far right. From the menu, select Template Binding ⇨ Width (or Height).

FIGURE 4-20: The new button

At this point, the control looks like Figure 4.20.

If you run the application now, the button looks as expected but doesn't give feedback on events such as `MouseOver` or being `Pressed`. To add these, open the States panel in Blend. In this panel, the states supported by the control are shown in two groups, the `VisualStateGroups`. A control can't be in more than one state from a group at the same time. However, it can be in a combination of states belonging to several groups.

You can now define some visuals for the states. Follow these steps:

1. Select the `MouseOver` state. Automatically, the Designer starts recording the state changes. Make a small change, such as rotating the image slightly.

2. Now, select the `Pressed` state. In the Designer, apply another change, such as resizing the image slightly to create the effect of clicking the button.

3. If you move from state X to state Y, by default, the change happens immediately, causing the transition to be unsmooth. To solve this, you can use a `VisualTransition`. Using `VisualTransition`, you can specify how long the state change should take. You can use the easy route by letting Silverlight do the interpolation, or define a custom animation for this. For most occasions, letting Silverlight perform the transition is just fine. To add it, you change the Default Transition for the entire state group, or apply a more specific transition when going or moving away from a specific state. For example, set the Default Transition to 0.2 seconds. Then, select in the `MouseOver` state the Add Transition button, and select the * ⇨ `MouseOver`. Set this to 0.5 seconds. All transitions, except the last added one, take 0.2 seconds.

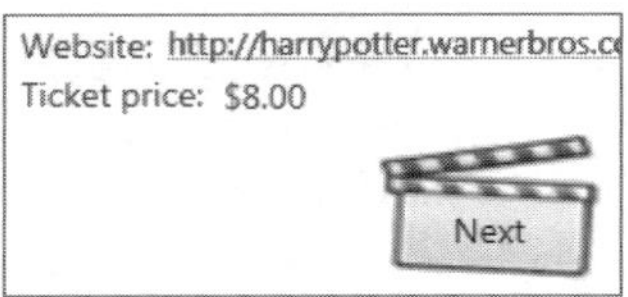

FIGURE 4-21: Slightly rotated button

With the state and transition information ready, you can test your control again. In Figure 4-21, it's slightly rotated when the mouse hovers over.

SUMMARY

There's no doubt that building LOB applications with Silverlight is easy. You can fully leverage your knowledge of .NET. Most concepts apply in Silverlight in the exact same way. On the other hand, some specifics require some more investigation, and after reading this chapter, you have learned about quite a few of them.

By taking a step back before starting the actual development and using a tool such as SketchFlow, you can create prototypes of your application with ease. Because it's based entirely on Silverlight, the prototypes you create this way reflect the real situation, and can help in building what the customer needs.

The data platform in Silverlight is extremely well thought-out. You learned about the data-binding capabilities of Silverlight, which also form the foundation for the MVVM pattern. This rich engine dramatically brings down the amount of code that must be written for a data-driven application. Getting in the data is no problem either. You used RIA Services to get to the data. Other types of services are available as well, so that won't hold you back in getting data into your apps.

The MVVM pattern makes the applications you build in Silverlight more testable and more maintainable. You used MVVM Light here to help you out in some areas.

ABOUT THE AUTHOR

Gill Cleeren is Microsoft Regional Director (`www.theregion.com`), Silverlight Most Valuable Professional (MVP) (former ASP.NET MVP), and Telerik MVP. He lives in Belgium, where he works as a .NET architect at Ordina (`www.ordina.be/`). Passionate about .NET, he's always playing with the newest bits. In his role as Regional Director, Cleeren has given many sessions, webcasts, and trainings on new as well as existing technologies (such as Silverlight, ASP.NET, and WPF) at conferences including TechEd Berlin 2010, TechDays Belgium — Switzerland — Sweden, DevDays NL, NDC Oslo Norway, SQL Server Saturday Switzerland, Spring Conference UK, Silverlight Roadshow in Sweden, Telerik RoadShow UK, and so on. He's also the author of many articles in various developer magazines and for `www.silverlightshow.net`. He organizes the yearly Community Day event in Belgium. Cleeren also leads Visug (`www.visug.be`), the largest .NET user group in Belgium. He is also the co-author of *Microsoft Silverlight 4 Data and Services Cookbook* (Birmingham, United Kingdom: Packt Publishing, 2010). You can reach Gill via his blog (`www.snowball.be`) and via his Twitter account (`@gillcleeren`).

5

Silverlight — The Silver Lining for Line-of-Business Applications

by Jeremy Likness

Archeologists claim that humans mastered fire approximately 400,000 years ago. Controlled blazes warmed early tribes as they moved into cooler regions and used their flames to hold predators at bay. Generations later, I would smile at the irony that I was investing most of my time putting out fires. I was the development manager of a team that wrote software to help companies manage their mobile devices. It seemed that the browsers were managing *us* as we spent more and more time testing, writing, and reworking code to achieve the holy grail of cross-browser compatibility.

The aptly named "Acid" tests allude to the corrosive and loose interpretation of standards intended to drive the consistent rendering of Hypertext Markup Language (HTML) documents on any platform or browser. You can visit the `www.acidtests.org` site to run the tests that can mercilessly pound your computer with standards-based tags and JavaScript to produce a smiling face that happily declares, "This browser is compliant."

Most browsers failed these tests miserably when they were first released, while line-of-business (LOB) application developers independently discovered that building a rich online experience involved more than just quality code and smart design. Too many honest ASP.NET developers were unwillingly dragged into the realm of Cascading Style Sheet (CSS) and JavaScript "hacks." They were left worn, haggard, and irritated at the effort it required to make a seemingly simple user interface (UI) behavior work across the full spectrum of target platforms and browsers.

I knew there had to be a better way.

Meanwhile, Microsoft had already released two versions of a product with the "Jolt core" code-named "Windows Presentation Foundation/Everywhere" that finally morphed to the identity we are familiar with today: Silverlight. The first version of Silverlight provided a JavaScript API with some rich graphics controls that would support only JavaScript Object Notation (JSON) and XML-based data. Developers bemoaned the lack of basic features needed for rich web applications, and the world at large scratched their heads wondering why the world needed another video player to compete with Flash.

The development community began to take notice when Silverlight 2 hit the web with a new engine, this time a streamlined version of the full .NET core Common Language Runtime (CLR). This created a plethora of options that included the capability to write code using familiar languages such as C# and Visual Basic, the use of complex types, and a data-binding engine reminiscent of the mature Windows Presentation Foundation (WPF) platform. Silverlight 3 and 4 later provided capabilities ranging from network detection and isolated storage, to offline mode and printing.

There was a better way!

The proof of concept I developed took 2 weeks to build from start to finish, and convinced management that Silverlight was something worth looking into. Just a month after that, we had strategic portions of the application moved to Silverlight. We completely eliminated any need to code for browsers because it would run as-is on any platform that supported the plug-in. The UI was far more advanced than what was possible using HTML markup, and the entire project was written using the C# language our team was familiar with.

I estimate that the switch to Silverlight enabled the team to produce four times more code in a sprint using Silverlight compared to ASP.NET. In a recent Microsoft-run Silverlight Firestarter event, the company Global Pay shared similar statistics, adding that the client footprint makes it possible to deploy an enterprise-scale application at 1/31th the cost of traditional methods because of savings on data center iron. (The work is offloaded to the customer.)

To truly appreciate the power of Silverlight for building LOB applications, it makes sense to start at the beginning. In this chapter, you build a simple "Hello, World" application and learn how to go from a clean slate to a fully functional, cross-platform and browser solution in just a few minutes.

GETTING STARTED

To follow the steps in this chapter, you must prepare your environment for Silverlight development. The easiest way to do this is to visit the Silverlight website and follow the instructions available at `www.silverlight.net/getstarted/`.

Hello, Business World!

It's time to start with your first application!

Open Visual Studio 2010, and choose Silverlight Application on the New Project page, as shown in Figure 5-1. Name your application **HelloBizWorld**.

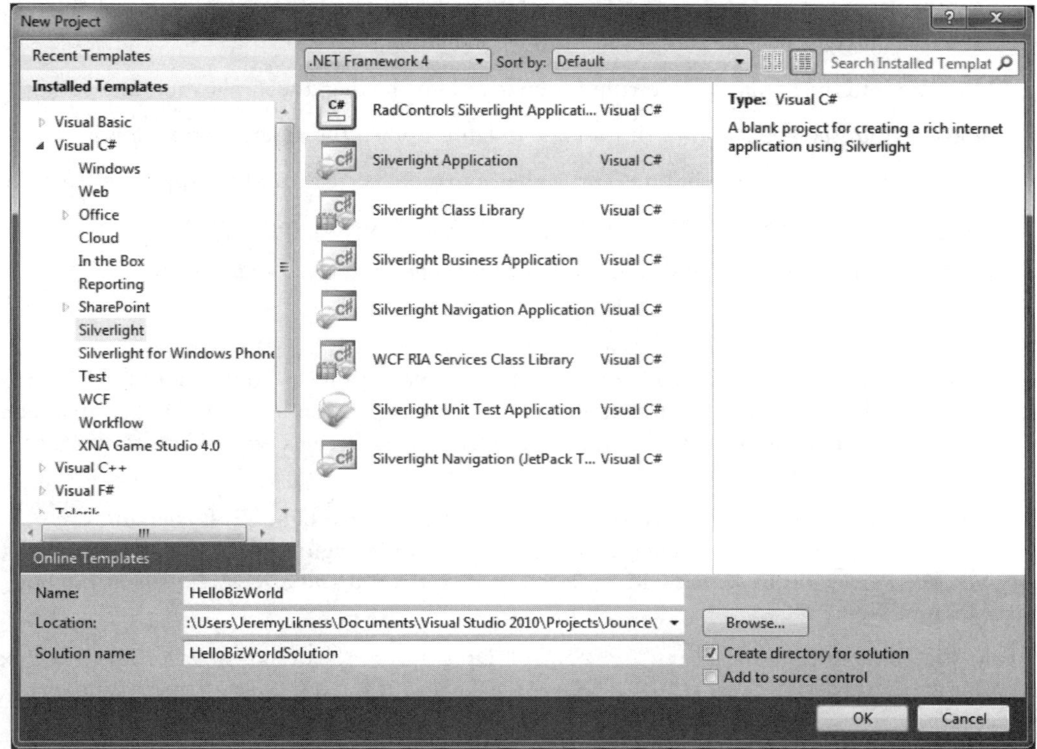

FIGURE 5-1: Creating a new project

When the New Silverlight Application dialog appears, simply click OK. Visual Studio creates two projects, as shown in Figure 5-2.

The `HelloBizWorld.Web` project is a typical ASP. NET web project to host the Silverlight application. `HelloBizWorld` is the Silverlight solution. Following are two main parts to the solution you can see:

➤   `Application` class

➤   `UserControl` class

The Application Class

The `Application` class inherits from `Application` and is the root type that drives the Silverlight program. Two files exist for this class: `App.Xaml` and `App.Xaml.cs`. The Extensible Application Markup Language (XAML) is a declarative XML-based language used for initializing types and objects. You learn more about XAML later in this chapter.

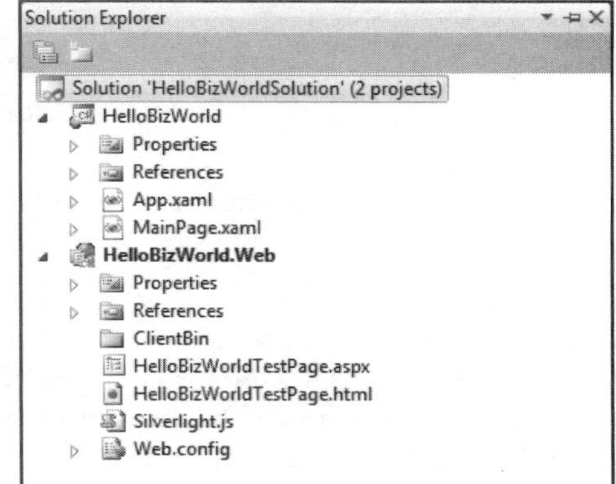

FIGURE 5-2: Automatically created projects

The other file is the C# *code-behind* file. This partial class declaration extends the class defined in XAML. The default code-behind does several things, including the following:

➤ Hooking into the application startup for code to launch when the application first runs

➤ Hooking into the application exit for code to launch when the application is closed

➤ Wiring the unhandled exception event so that unhandled errors can be trapped and dealt with

➤ Assigning the *root visual,* which is the top-level "view" for the application

The application can also host global resources that other types and classes can consume.

The UserControl Class

The `UserControl` class is a user-defined control that is visible within the application. By default, a `UserControl` called `MainPage.xaml` is created. This `UserControl` also has code-behind, just like the application class. This is the control that the application class creates and assigns to the root visual when the application first starts.

This is also where you can perform most of your work with the Silverlight UI. By default, the designer opens on the main page. Depending on how you have configured your Visual Studio 2010 settings, you should see a split screen with a *design view* at the top and a *XAML view* at the bottom, as shown in Figure 5-3.

Open your toolbox and click the `TextBlock` control. Drag it onto the design surface. The text box outline appears in the design area, while the XAML element for the text box is inserted into the XAML area.

Edit this element and update the XAML so that it looks like Listing 5-1.

LISTING 5-1: TextBox for the Hello, Business World Application


```
<TextBlock HorizontalAlignment="Center" VerticalAlignment=
    "Center" Text="Hello, Business World" />
```

Code file [021965 CH05 code for download.zip] available for download at Wrox.com.

Press CTRL+F5. Your application will compile, and you should see a web browser window open with the text, "Hello, Business World."

Congratulations! You've just written your first Silverlight application. Behind the scenes, the Visual Studio compiler generated a dynamic link library (DLL) for your project and packaged it into a special file known as a XAP (pronounced "Zap"). This file contains a manifest listing the content and all the resources needed by your Silverlight application (such as DLLs, embedded images and fonts, and resource files). This file is actually a compressed ZIP file.

A XAP file is nothing more than a ZIP file with a different extension. To see the contents of the XAP file, simply rename it to have a `ZIP` extension, and open it with Windows Explorer.

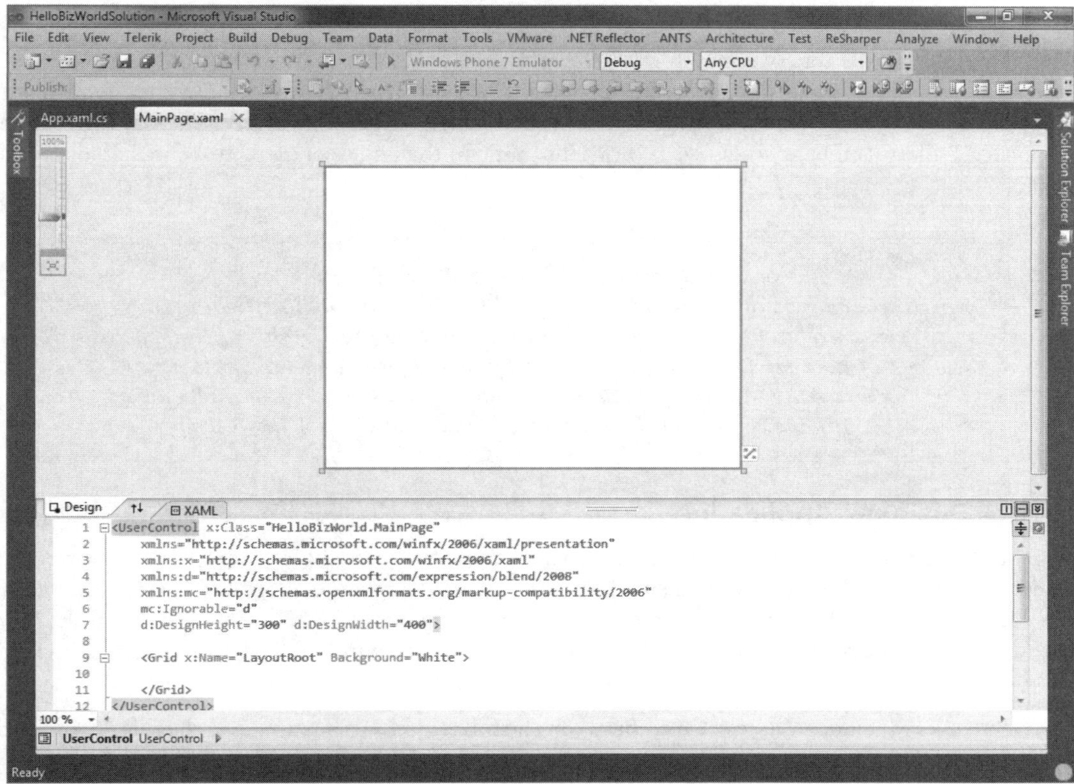

FIGURE 5-3: Two views in the Silverlight UI

The XAP file is automatically copied to a special folder in the web project called `ClientBin`. The Silverlight plug-in understands how to download the XAP file and extract the contents to run your application.

Project Templates

When you created the Silverlight project, you may have noticed several different project templates. Each template can help structure a new application based on your specific goals. You need to be familiar with the various project types so that you know which template to use when starting a new project.

Silverlight Application

You have already used the Silverlight Application template, which is the most common template. This template can create a sample web project to host your Silverlight application and a basic template for the application. It can also create a default page to start with. This should be the starting point for any of your Silverlight applications, unless you have a more specific need addressed by the other templates.

Silverlight Class Library

The Silverlight Class Library template creates an independent DLL that can be linked into other Silverlight projects. It is similar to the standard C# Class Library. Use this template to create a set of types, methods, and properties that will be shared across different projects. Class libraries do not output XAP files. Rather, a single DLL is output that can then be referenced to be included in other projects.

Silverlight uses a special subset of the core CLR that drives the full .NET Framework. You cannot reference a DLL created for .NET from Silverlight because it may contain references to namespaces not supported by Silverlight. However, you can build a DLL in Silverlight and reference it from a .NET application. Therefore, when you want to create a common DLL shared between Silverlight and .NET applications, you should create it as a Silverlight Class Library.

Silverlight Business Application

Silverlight Business Application is a comprehensive template that includes examples of functionality needed in typical LOB software. A theme (for skinning, or setting the application style and colors) is provided, along with the built-in navigation framework that enables you to jump between the Home page and the About page. A Login button introduces a pop-up window (in Silverlight, this is created using the `ChildWindow` control) to enable a login and a registration.

The web project includes classes shared between the Silverlight application and the .NET application on the server. This project also introduces the concept of web services, and provides sample service endpoints for registering a user and logging in.

In addition, various controls, helper classes, and utilities are commonly used in applications. This is an advanced template that should be used only after you are familiar and comfortable with developing Silverlight applications.

Silverlight Navigation Application

Like the Silverlight Business Application template, the Silverlight Navigation template provides a default theme and uses the built-in navigation framework to create a multipage application. Unlike the Silverlight Business Application template, this template does not include the sample login and registration processes, shared libraries, or services. This template is lightweight and is often used as the starting point for applications that require URL-based navigation.

Other Application Templates

Other application templates may be downloaded from the web or installed with other packages. For example, the Silverlight Unit Testing Framework enables you to write and run unit tests in the browser. This package introduces the Silverlight Unit Test Application template used to create a new project for unit tests.

With any application, you are given the option to enable Windows Communication Foundation (WCF) Rich Internet Application (RIA) Services. WCF RIA Services is a special feature of Silverlight that makes it easier to interact with data on the server. It uses a technique known as *projection* to make working with data look and feel like you are accessing the data directly inside of the Silverlight application. Behind the scenes, the technology generates web service endpoints and coordinates the activity on the client with the server to provide a seamless data experience.

Table 5-1 compares the various Silverlight templates you can use for a new project.

TABLE 5-1: Silverlight Application Templates

YOU NEED	APPLICATION	SHARED LIBRARY	NAVIGATION FRAMEWORK	WCF SERVICE EXAMPLE
Silverlight Application	X			
Silverlight Business Application	X		X	X
Silverlight Class Library		X		
Silverlight Navigation Application	X		X	

XAML Is Object XML

Earlier in the chapter, you were introduced to a concept known as XAML. When I ask developers to define what XAML is, I often hear answers related specifically to Silverlight and the UI, such as the following:

➤ "XAML is a UI markup language."

➤ "XAML is something special in Silverlight for designing screens."

➤ "XAML is used to lay out controls in Silverlight."

XAML is simply the XML representation of an object graph. The XAML interpreter can use the markup to create and initialize various types. The "X" in XAML refers to the extensibility and flexibility of the language. Although XAML is often used to provide layout instructions for controls, any object with a parameterless constructor can be instantiated through XAML.

To help you better understand XAML, Listing 5-2 shows the markup for `MainPage.xaml` in the application you wrote earlier.

LISTING 5-2: MainPage.xaml

```
<UserControl x:Class="HelloBizWorld.MainPage"
    xmlns="http://schemas.microsoft.com/winfx/2006/xaml/presentation"
    xmlns:x="http://schemas.microsoft.com/winfx/2006/xaml"
    xmlns:d="http://schemas.microsoft.com/expression/blend/2008"
    xmlns:mc="http://schemas.openxmlformats.org/markup-compatibility/2006"
    mc:Ignorable="d"
    d:DesignHeight="300" d:DesignWidth="400">
```

```
    <Grid x:Name="LayoutRoot" Background="White">
        <TextBlock HorizontalAlignment="Center" VerticalAlignment=
            "Center" Text="Hello, Business World" />
    </Grid>
</UserControl>
```

Code file [021965 CH05 code for download.zip] available for download at Wrox.com.

The XAML interpreter can read the code and interpret it like this:

1. Create an instance of the `MainPage` type.

2. In the `Content` of `MainPage`, create an instance of a `Grid` type.

3. Set the name of the grid to `LayoutRoot`.

4. Set the background of the grid to the color white.

5. Create an instance of the `TextBlock` type.

6. Set various properties on the text block.

Anything possible through XAML is also possible through code. The XAML in Listing 5-2 is equivalent to the C# code shown in Listing 5-3.

LISTING 5-3: C# equivalent for the MainPage.xaml

```
var control = new MainPage();
var grid = new Grid();
grid.SetValue(NameProperty, "LayoutRoot");
grid.Background = new SolidColorBrush(Colors.White);
var textBlock = new TextBlock
                {
                    HorizontalAlignment = HorizontalAlignment.Center,
                    VerticalAlignment = VerticalAlignment.Center,
                    Text = "Hello, Business World."
                };
grid.Children.Add(textBlock);
control.Content = grid;
```

Understanding that XAML is actually a set of instructions to initialize types and set properties can help you build better Silverlight LOB applications, and troubleshoot them more easily.

Hosting Silverlight Applications

One powerful feature of Silverlight is that it can be hosted on virtually any server. Silverlight is simply a special type of file downloaded from the web server. It is the browser's job to recognize the file and interpret it as a Silverlight application. When it is downloaded to a browser with the Silverlight plug-in installed, the plug-in takes over to open the XAP file and execute the Silverlight program.

So, what's the secret to hosting the Silverlight application? It's simple. Using the web server of your choice, you need to perform only two steps:

1. Place the XAP file in the hosted site.

2. Configure the Multipurpose Internet Mail Extensions (MIME) type for the XAP file.

MIME is not just used in e-mail. MIME types are also used by web servers to determine how to process and deliver content. With Silverlight XAP files, the server simply needs to map the `.xap` file extension to the MIME type `application/x-silverlight-app`. That's all that is needed to instruct the browser to execute the Silverlight plug-in.

Providing Excellent IApplicationService

Bad habits are tough to break, so it's always good to start with best practices. One thing you'll notice as you begin to work with Silverlight is that the majority of examples on the web, and the templates provided in Visual Studio, all tend to follow a pattern of hooking into start-up, shut-down, and exception-handling events in the code-behind for the `App.xaml` file. Although this practice certainly makes sense for smaller, standalone applications, LOB applications can use a better approach.

For example, consider a module that helps serialize objects to isolated storage so that it may be used in different applications. The module reads some configuration data from the initialization parameters passed into the Silverlight application by the web control. Parsing these parameters in the `App.xaml` code-behind would mean modifying the code for every application that uses the module. This is not only inconvenient to the developer, but also introduces risk by creating another step, and a potential area to introduce bugs.

A cleaner approach is to implement the two interfaces provided by Silverlight for these types of modules: `IApplicationService` and `IApplicationLifetimeAware`.

The `IApplicationService` interface provides two simple methods: `StartService` and `StopService`. The `StartService` method is called when the application first starts up. It is passed an `ApplicationServiceContext` object that contains all the initialization parameters. This is the perfect place to parse configuration information and store it for later use. When the application exits, the `StopService` method is called. This enables the module to clean up data and store any necessary information before the application exits.

If you require even more control, consider implementing `IApplicationLifetimeAware` in addition to `IApplicationService`. This introduces the methods `Starting`, `Started`, `Exiting`, and `Exited`. These methods provide more fine-grained control. For example, `Starting` is called before the `Application.Startup` event is fired, whereas `Started` is called after. The former may provide configuration information, whereas the latter can interact with views that have been initialized, or other modules.

Listing 5-4 shows an example snippet of code to configure a logging framework using the `IApplicationService` interface.

LISTING 5-4: Example IApplicationService

```
public class LoggerService : IApplicationService
{
    const string TRACE_LEVEL_KEY = "TraceLevel";

    public LoggerService()
    {
        _traceLevel = TraceLevel.Warning; // default
    }

    private TraceLevel _traceLevel;

    public ILogger Logger { get; private set; }

    public static LoggerService Current { get; private set; }

    public void StartService(ApplicationServiceContext context)
    {
        Current = this;
        if (context.ApplicationInitParams.ContainsKey(TRACE_LEVEL_KEY))
        {
            _traceLevel = (TraceLevel)Enum.Parse(typeof (TraceLevel),
                context.ApplicationInitParams[TRACE_LEVEL_KEY], true);
        }

        Logger = new CustomLogger(TraceLevel);
        Logger.WriteLine(TraceLevel.Information, "Logger service started.");
    }

    public void StopService()
    {
        Logger.WriteLine(TraceLevel.Information, "Logger service stopped.");
    }
}
```

Classes that implement these interfaces are easy to integrate into other applications. When you have
a reference to the project that implements the interfaces, you can include the type in the `App.xaml`
using the special `ApplicationLifetimeObjects` collection, as shown in Listing 5-5.

LISTING 5-5: Using a Class that Implements IApplicationService

```
<Application.ApplicationLifetimeObjects>
    <MySilverlightApp:LoggerService/>
</Application.ApplicationLifetimeObjects>
```

This is another example of how Silverlight provides the right tools for LOB applications, making it
easy for you to produce modules that can be integrated across your product lines.

CHOOSING THE RIGHT SILVERLIGHT FRAMEWORK

LOB applications are often composed of multiple modules that can be shared across product lines, and that may be developed by separate teams within the enterprise. Often, there is a design team independent of the development team. Writing quality software that accommodates this type of environment can be challenging. Fortunately, Silverlight has well-established patterns and best practices that facilitate enterprise development.

One reason it is important to understand the patterns and practices for Silverlight is to facilitate "developer-designer workflow." Although it is less impactful on smaller projects, larger projects typically have separate design and development teams. The traditional workflow in this scenario is to receive the requirements for the application, wait for the design team to produce the wireframes, and finally, turn it all over to the development team to build. Often, developers would then return the code to the design team to "clean up" and finish the product.

With Silverlight and the clean separation provided by XAML and the data-binding engine, this workflow can be streamlined in a major way. After the functionality of the application has been determined, development and design may begin immediately. The design team can work completely independently of the development team when the right architecture is used because both efforts are integrated using a special type of class called a *ViewModel*. ViewModels are examined in more detail later in this chapter, but for now, think of them as a "contract" agreed upon between the design team and the development team, enabling both to build their parts of the project independently, and glue them together at the end.

So, how do you create the right framework to handle the optimal development workflow? The good news is that you don't need to reinvent the wheel. There are several out-of-the-box frameworks available to help you construct your applications. These frameworks provide shortcuts, commonly used functions and utilities, and guidance for how to implement common concerns. The bad news is that sometimes it can be a challenge choosing the right framework.

Getting SOLID: MVC, MVP, and MVVM

Most Silverlight articles and blog posts address Model-View-ViewModel (MVVM) in some form or another. The pattern is almost synonymous with both Windows Presentation Foundation (WPF) and Silverlight development. You might be asking yourself, "Why do I need to learn a new pattern? What's wrong with the patterns I'm used to, like MVC?"

The answer lies in the S.O.L.I.D. principles of software design:

- *Single Responsibility* — A class should focus only on one specific task.

- *Open/Closed Principle* — A class should be open for extensibility and closed for modification.

- *Liskov Substitution Principle* — A derived class should behave the same if it is cast to its base class.

➤ *Interface Segregation* — Interfaces should be fine-tuned to address specific concerns.

➤ *Dependency Injection* — Dependencies should be based on abstract contracts, not concrete implementations.

The principles collectively are considered by many to be the cornerstones of object-oriented design. Silverlight is typically written using C# or VB.NET, which are both object-oriented languages. Most design patterns, including Model-View-Controller (MVC), Model-View-Presenter (MVP), and MVVM, provide guidance to help applications adhere to these principles.

The MVC pattern addresses the concern of separating the view from the business logic that drives the view. As shown in Figure 5-4, the controller manages the view directly, while the view exposes events to send information back up to the controller. The model is the rest of the application infrastructure used to communicate with the back-end processes and business logic, and typically surfaces information interesting to the view through properties that the view can inspect and display.

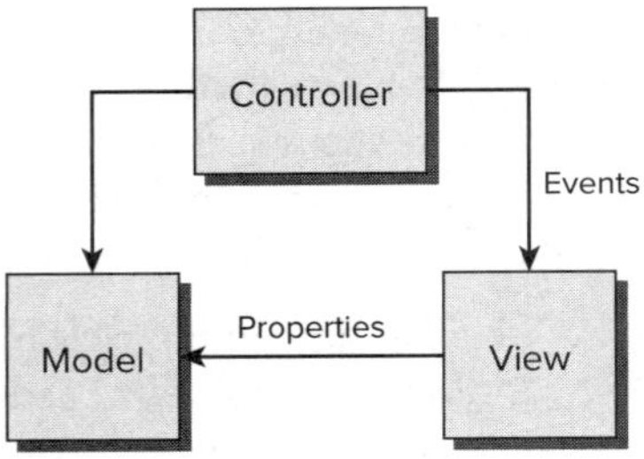

FIGURE 5-4: The MVC pattern

In MVP, the view is often created first (unlike MVC, where the controller returns the view). To separate the concerns of the view from the business logic, the view always raises events that the presenter listens to. The presenter then interacts with the view via an interface, as shown in Figure 5-5. The interface enables the view to be mocked during testing, and allows multiple views to be managed by the same presenter.

MVVM is similar to these patterns. All the patterns contain a View (which is the UI component) and a Model (which is typically data), but can also encapsulate behavior and business logic in the system. The ViewModel is a special structure that is more like a controller than a presenter. The ViewModel maintains the View's state but is not directly aware of the View. There is no interface it uses to communicate with the View. Instead, MVVM specifically addresses a feature of the Silverlight Framework known as *data binding*.

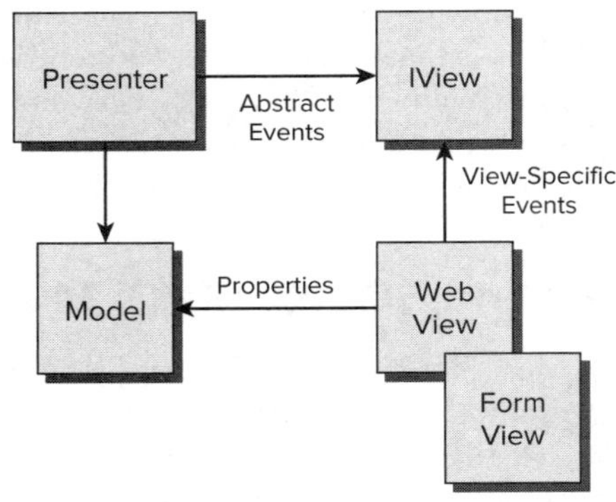

FIGURE 5-5: The MVP pattern

As shown in Figure 5-6, *data binding* is the process that connects the UI to the ViewModel. In that View, certain elements may specify a binding. (This is most often done in XAML.) The binding is like a contract that prescribes how a View should obtain its data, and how it can publish events and inputs from the user. The binding is tied to a special property on the View known as the `DataContext`. The data context is most often the ViewModel itself. It exposes properties that the bindings refer to.

The ViewModel is the link between the View and the rest of the application. It may communicate with interfaces to obtain configuration information, or call services to retrieve data. The information is then exposed via properties on the ViewModel that can be bound to the View itself. Figure 5-6 shows several examples, such as a "busy" property to indicate when work is being performed, a command to submit a form, a collection of items, and a "current item" based on user selection.

The ViewModel contains the properties that are data-bound to the View. The ViewModel does not have specific knowledge of the View. For example, the ViewModel may contain a Boolean property that determines whether a panel is displayed. The ViewModel will not directly reference the View or refer to a `Panel` object. Instead, the View contains a data-binding directive that correlates the visibility of the panel with the value of the property.

In this way, ViewModels can be designed to hold the data and commands that a View requires. They can be independently tested without the presence of a View, and even be attached to different Views. Conversely, Views can be designed with special design-time ViewModels that satisfy the data-binding directives with sample data. This enables a clean separation of concerns while taking advantage of the data-binding system built into both Silverlight and WPF.

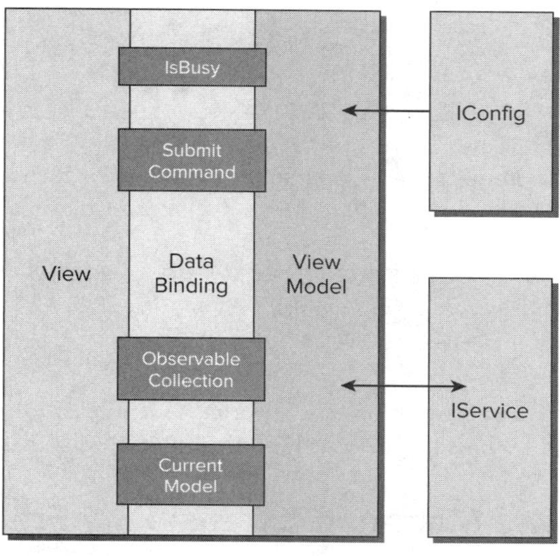

FIGURE 5-6: The MVVM pattern

Dependency Injection and Inversion of Control

Dependency injection and *inversion of control* refer to the design practice of allowing an external object to determine the concrete implementation to use for a dependency. It is a useful principle because it enables the class to focus on a single concern (what the class was designed for, in alignment with the Single Responsibility Principle) and delegates external concerns elsewhere. This layer of abstraction often uses interfaces to decouple the class from the dependency. The dependency is injected by another mechanism, and the control is inverted from the class to an external mechanism.

The traditional problem is that a particular implementation always has its own dependencies. A module that generates PDF reports might need to also reference a third-party PDF tool. Any module requiring report generation then must also reference the same tool. This can lead to complex relationships and dependencies within the application.

A cleaner way would be for the modules to rely on a contract for reporting, and leave the details of how the report is generated to the report module itself, without having to carry additional dependencies.

The practices described previously can enable you to write decoupled code that is easy to test, maintain, and extend. With any decoupled system, there must be some point of resolution, in which interfaces and abstract classes are resolved to concrete types. (The module may reference a report interface, but eventually a real report module must be invoked to implement the interface.) Although a variety of patterns address this concern (for example, using a factory to retrieve an instance), several Silverlight Frameworks were built to specifically solve the problem.

Microsoft offers a product called Unity from the Patterns & Practices team. Unity was originally targeted to the Core CLR but was extended to support the latest versions of Silverlight. Unity provides attributed and fluent configuration.

 *Visit the Unity site online at* `http://msdn.microsoft.com/en-us/library/ff678312.aspx`.

Ninject is an Open Source solution for dependency injection known for being lightweight, fast, and easy to use. Ninject also uses an attribute-based system, along with fluent configuration.

 *You can download Ninject online at* `http://ninject.org/`.

Other solutions for Silverlight include AutoFac (`http://code.google.com/p/autofac/`) and Castle Windsor (`www.castleproject.org/container/index.html`).

The Managed Extensibility Framework

Although third-party tools do exist to address the problem of inversion of control, there is a solution provided within the .NET Framework that satisfies most dependency injection requirements in Silverlight. The framework also provides some powerful functionality to facilitate extensibility of applications, including a built-in way to modularize your Silverlight applications and dynamically load code at runtime. The problems of extensibility, discovery, and metadata (tagging modules with information) are addressed by the *Managed Extensibility Framework (MEF)*.

Most inversion of control frameworks deal with what you know. At runtime (or during your tests), you can configure the framework to map a known concrete type to an interface. This is often done in a class referred to as a *bootstrapper* (a term that comes from the idea of "pulling yourself up by your boot straps"). Whenever a piece of code requests that interface, the concrete type is provided. In modular applications, the implementation for a particular interface might exist in a separate assembly (or in the case of Silverlight, XAP file). How can you connect that type to your interface when the type is not "known" to the CLR?

With MEF, the solution is simple. MEF introduces the concept of a `ComposablePart`. A part includes a contract, imports, and exports.

The *contract* defines what the part should address. A contract is a combination of an identifier and a type. The *type* might be an interface, an abstract class, or a concrete type. The *identifier* can default to the type name, or any arbitrary value used to further categorize the part. For example, an "error" identifier might be appended to a string type to specify a part that contains strings for errors.

The *imports* are all of the types that require the part. (Think of a retail store that must import products.) Whenever you require a part, you specify a property to hold the part, and then tag it with an attribute that indicates MEF should supply an implementation.

The *exports* are the implementations (like a manufacturer that provides product). Whenever you implement the contract for a part, you may export that implementation to make it available to MEF, which performs a task referred to as *composition* that matches exports to imports and makes the parts available to your application.

To illustrate how MEF works, create a new Silverlight application using the Silverlight Application template, as described earlier in this chapter. Name your project **HelloMEF**. After the projects have been created, right-click the References under your Silverlight project in the Solution Explorer, and add references from the .NET tab to `System.ComponentModel.Composition` and `System.ComponentModel.Composition.Initialization`. These are the DLLs used by MEF.

In the XAML file, simply place a `TextBlock` control so that your XAML looks like Listing 5-6.

LISTING 5-6: MainPage.xaml for the Hello, MEF Example


```xml
<UserControl x:Class="HelloMEF.MainPage"
    xmlns="http://schemas.microsoft.com/winfx/2006/xaml/presentation"
    xmlns:x="http://schemas.microsoft.com/winfx/2006/xaml"
    xmlns:d="http://schemas.microsoft.com/expression/blend/2008"
    xmlns:mc="http://schemas.openxmlformats.org/markup-compatibility/2006"
    mc:Ignorable="d"
    d:DesignHeight="300" d:DesignWidth="400">

    <Grid x:Name="LayoutRoot" Background="White">
        <TextBlock x:Name="tbText"/>
    </Grid>
</UserControl>
```

Code file [021965 CH05 code for download.zip] available for download at Wrox.com.

In the code-behind for the main page, add the code shown in Listing 5-7.

LISTING 5-7: MainPage.xaml.cs for the Hello, MEF Example


```csharp
namespace HelloMEF
{
    public partial class MainPage
    {
        [Import]
        public string Text { get; set; }

        public MainPage()
        {
            InitializeComponent();
            CompositionInitializer.SatisfyImports(this);
            tbText.Text = Text;
        }
    }
}
```

Code file [021965 CH05 code for download.zip] available for download at Wrox.com.

This code helps define a part. The contract for the part is a string. (This is implicitly derived from the tagged property.) In the constructor for the main page, the `CompositionInitializer` is called. This is a special class that MEF provides for Silverlight projects that examines the Silverlight application for parts and satisfies any requests. In this case, it sees the request for a string part and looks to satisfy it.

If you run the code now, you receive an error because the part is not complete. You haven't added an export yet.

To provide an export and "complete" the part, simply add a new class and name it `Exports.cs`, as shown in Listing 5-8. The class isn't used by the application, except to provide the exports that MEF needs. The exports can just as easily be provided in other classes, including the main page.

Available for download on Wrox.com

LISTING 5-8: Exports.cs for the Hello, MEF Example

```
namespace HelloMEF
{
    public class Exports
    {
        [Export]
        public string HelloMef
        {
            get { return "Hello, MEF!"; }
        }
    }
}
```

Code file [021965 CH05 code for download.zip] available for download at Wrox.com.

Now, when you run the application, you should see the text, "Hello, MEF!" appear.

The `Import` and `Export` tags both create a part. The contract for that part is the string type. The import is provided by the main page (it requires the part to show the text) and the export is provided by the `Exports` class. (It supplies the implementation.)

The `CompositionInitializer` is a helper class specifically for Silverlight. Underneath the covers, MEF operates using a container. The container is simply a place to hold parts. Within the container are several catalogs. A *catalog* is a way of instructing MEF where to look for parts.

An `AssemblyCatalog` scans the assembly passed to it for imports and exports. A `TypeCatalog` can simply have types passed to it and scans the type definition for imports and exports. In Silverlight, a special `DeploymentCatalog` handles parts in a deployment, or XAP file. A container may have only one catalog. The special `AggregateCatalog` enables a collection of catalogs to be used.

The code in Listing 5-9 shows an example of this.

LISTING 5-9: Containers and Catalogs with MEF

```
var mainCatalog = new AggregateCatalog(new DeploymentCatalog());
var container = new CompositionContainer(mainCatalog);
CompositionHost.Initialize(container);
CompositionInitializer.SatisfyImports(this);
```

An aggregate catalog is created, and a deployment catalog is passed to it. This instructs MEF to scan the current XAP file for parts. The `Initialize` method is called to tell MEF to "use this container" instead of the default one MEF would otherwise use. Finally, when the container and catalogs are specified, MEF is instructed to perform the composition by satisfying any import requests in the current class.

This was just a simple example to show how MEF works. MEF provides many more rich features that you may want to explore. For example, MEF can enable you to import multiple implementations for a contract and tag those with attributes to enable filtering and sorting. Through a feature called *recomposition*, MEF can also enable you to dynamically load new XAP files that also contain exports and can automatically merge those exports into your existing classes at runtime.

These features make it more than an inversion of control container and highlight the power of MEF as an extensibility framework. By using imports, you can not only defer implementation of functionality, but also allow it to be extended at runtime through concepts such as modules and plug-ins. Finally, MEF truly shines because it is part of the .NET Framework, so there is no need to download a third-party control or sort through licensing issues. If you have the Silverlight Framework installed, you can take advantage of MEF.

MVVM Frameworks

Now that you've explored some fundamentals for best coding practices in Silverlight LOB applications, you can find that existing frameworks help to address the majority of your basic concerns. In MVVM LOB applications, following are the common concerns:

- Managing `INotifyPropertyChanged`
- Connecting view models to views
- Providing infrastructure for `ICommand` implementation
- Enabling manipulation of visual states from the ViewModel
- Messaging between ViewModels
- Enabling modularity

`ICommand` *is an interface that exists in both WPF and Silverlight. The command pattern is a useful way to separate the trigger (that is, a button or mouse click) for an action from the action itself, and the rules concerning whether the action may be performed. Although Silverlight provides no native implementation of* `ICommand`, *many of the MVVM frameworks described in this chapter provide an implementation for you.*

Several frameworks exist to help solve these problems. Choosing the right framework can help you save time by supplying the fundamentals your LOB applications need. Selecting the right framework is a question of what you are comfortable with, whether you have a preference over how the inversion of control concerns are addressed, which features are important, and whether the license is compatible with your company's requirements.

Now take a look at a few popular frameworks to help you start. All these frameworks are Open Source projects hosted at CodePlex.

Prism

Prism is a framework provided by the Microsoft Patterns & Practices team. As of this writing, it is in Version 4.0. Prism is a large application with thorough documentation. It includes a library that can be used in your project, a reference application, and several quick-starts to target specific areas.

Prism enables you to choose which dependency injection framework you use, with built-in support for both Unity and MEF. It contains a command implementation, messaging via the event aggregator pattern, and a set of tools for modules and navigation. It is perhaps one of the most well-known frameworks, having started on the WPF platform, as evidenced by the hundreds of thousands of downloads on the site.

Prism can be accessed online at `http://compositewpf.codeplex.com/`.

MVVM Light

MVVM Light is one of the most popular frameworks for Silverlight, and is used in many commercial Silverlight and Windows Phone 7 projects. It provides explicit support for design-time modeling of data, a ViewModel locator pattern for helping bind ViewModels to Views, and lightweight messaging service.

One reason why MVVM Light may be so popular is that it also includes several project templates and code snippets to make it easy to start new projects. Common code constructs such as raising a property change notification are tackled by convenient code snippets. There is a large user community that supports and is familiar with the toolkit, and it is a great starting point for anyone looking to build Silverlight LOB applications.

MVVM Light is, as the name implies, far more lightweight than many other frameworks, including Prism. This makes it easier to grasp and understand for beginners to the MVVM pattern.

Download MVVM Light online at `http://mvvmlight.codeplex.com/`.

nRoute

Another popular MVVM framework is nRoute. This framework is well known for supporting several different asynchronous patterns and for working closely with Reactive Extensions (Rx). Rx enables asynchronous operations to be handled as "push streams" that drive events as they happen.

One notable feature of nRoute is the "reverse `ICommand`." This enables binding events in the View to the ViewModel, while keeping the two decoupled. The framework has extensive documentation and several sample projects.

nRoute is available online at `http://nroute.codeplex.com/`.

Calburn.Micro

Calburn.Micro is an extremely small (only a few thousand lines of code) framework that packs a powerful punch. It is well known for its convention-based data-binding model. (View elements are bound to the ViewModel based on naming conventions and element types, rather than explicit binding commands.) The framework also takes a "ViewModel first" approach, which means that ViewModels are created and then spin up the Views, instead of the more common practice of having a View request to or bind to a ViewModel.

Another interesting feature of Calburn.Micro is the use of co-routines. *Co-routines* are state engines that help developers manage asynchronous code. Using co-routines, you can aggregate several asynchronous processes into a set of sequential code blocks that are easy to understand and follow. It is a great way to bridge the gap between existing functionality and what will be released in the next version of C# with the `await` keyword.

Caliburn.Micro is available online at `http://caliburnmicro.codeplex.com/`.

Jounce

Jounce is a tool that I developed less as a framework and more as guidance. The idea behind Jounce is to provide common patterns and best practices for developing large LOB applications in Silverlight using MEF and the MVVM pattern. Jounce relies heavily on MEF to help connect ViewModels and Views, and for routing modules. It provides *region management* (handling how and where Views are generated), an event aggregator, a versatile navigation framework, and easy logging facilities.

Jounce also includes several quick-starts that demonstrate different ways to manage patterns in Silverlight applications. One example is the use of a special "entity ViewModel" that facilitates tracking changes and firing validations for Create/Read/Edit/Update (CRUD) operations. Another example shows how to integrate with the Silverlight Navigation Framework.

Jounce is available online at `http://jounce.codeplex.com/`.

Table 5-2 provides a high-level overview of the various frameworks, based on statistics taken from CodePlex and feedback from users about the required learning curves.

TABLE 5-2: MVVM Frameworks

FRAMEWORK	IOC CONTAINER	SIZE	COMPLEXITY
Prism	MEF, Unity, other	Large	Difficult
MVVM Light	SimpleIoC	Medium	Easy
nRoute	Native	Medium/Large	Intermediate
Caliburn.Micro	MEF, Unity, other	Small	Intermediate
Jounce	MEF	Small	Intermediate

TAKING SILVERLIGHT OUT-OF-THE-BOX

Silverlight provides a set of powerful features for enterprise applications. Earlier in this chapter, you learned about some of the core frameworks that power Silverlight applications. Now it's time to learn about some advanced features that make Silverlight shine. From dynamic loading to desktop installs, local databases, and inter-application communication, you can find there are plenty of powerful features to meet the demands of your software product.

Dynamic Loading

Silverlight runs on the client browser. This can be extremely beneficial but also introduces some risk. From an enterprise perspective, distributing workload to the client by running business logic and validations locally can benefit the entire system by easing the strain on the central server. As a developer, however, you must take care not to overtax the client's system. Sending too much information can create unwanted delays, and allocating memory for various features and functions may degrade performance.

Dynamic loading helps solve these problems by enabling you to divide your application into logical units that load independently. The initial application is small and results in a faster load time over the network, and a smaller memory footprint on the client. Areas of functionality are loaded on demand as the user requests them. Typically, users launch an application to work in a particular area. Although the entire application may span dozens of areas of functionality, only the ones currently used are loaded into memory and onto the client system.

The easiest way to handle dynamic loading "out-of-the-box" in Silverlight is to take advantage of the MEF. As you learned earlier, MEF contains a special deployment catalog. By default, the deployment catalog simply references the current XAP. You can pass a URI to the deployment catalog and instruct MEF to download a separate XAP file.

To create a dynamic module using MEF, you first create a project using the Silverlight Application template (not the Silverlight Class Library template). The Silverlight Application template is required to compile the code into a XAP file and generate the necessary manifest, while the Silverlight Class Library template generates a standalone assembly. You can delete the `App.xaml` and `MainPage.xaml` files because these won't be needed in the dynamic module. In the new project, you can then create classes, types, and controls, and either specific imports or exports as required by your application.

Listing 5-10 shows all the code required to download a dynamic XAP file named `Plugin.XAP`. After the XAP file is loaded, MEF automatically recomposes the parts and integrates the additional exports into the application. (The deployment catalog must be added to the main container, so this example assumes an aggregate catalog is available that has already been loaded into the main container.)

LISTING 5-10: Example of Loading a Dynamic XAP File

```
var deploymentCatalog = new DeploymentCatalog("Plugin.XAP");
mainAggregateCatalog.Catalogs.Add(deploymentCatalog);
deploymentCatalog.DownloadAsync();
```

The deployment catalog has additional methods to enable you to track the progress of the download, receive a notification when the download has completed, and respond to any errors.

Out-of-Browser Applications

Silverlight is a special type of application that is easily delivered over the web. The default place for Silverlight to run is in a trusted sandbox within the browser. Silverlight does not need to be confined to this space, however. Silverlight enables for a special mode called *Out of Browser (OOB)* that enables your application to run standalone.

There are two important reasons why you might want to consider an OOB application. The first is offline execution. The main limitation of web applications is that they require an active Internet connection to function. For agents in the field using an LOB application to collect information, this can be problematic because they are not always guaranteed connectivity at their customer locations.

By allowing the application to run offline, your users can run the application even when an Internet application doesn't exist. With the use of isolated storage (which will be discussed shortly), you can even store information and forward it when the Internet becomes available. The default mode for OOB works across any platform that Silverlight runs on, including both Windows and OS X.

The second compelling reason to write OOB applications is when you require elevated trust. By default, Silverlight applications (even OOB ones) run in a "security sandbox." To avoid disruption to the client computer, access to various features such as communication ports, USB, or even disk storage outside of isolated storage is prohibited. There are some applications that require access to these sensitive resources. For example, an application that scans barcodes would need access to the communication and USB ports that connect to the scanning device.

By specifying "elevated trust" for your Silverlight OOB application, you can gain access to these resources. The user is asked to "opt-in" and allow the application access to sensitive data. When this happens, you can do things such as performing COM inter-op and accessing areas in the file system that are normally restricted. Silverlight 5 can also offer direct access to USB ports and provide a facility to p/Invoke or directly call unmanaged code.

Isolated Storage

In many cases you may want to store information locally on the client machine running the Silverlight application. Although Silverlight does not come with an embedded database, it does provide access to a specialized file system known as *isolated storage*. Isolated storage is not specific to Silverlight and exists as part of the core .NET Framework as an "information sandbox" for applications to store data without requesting elevated trust.

Isolated storage in Silverlight is unique because it provides some control over quotas for storage space and specialized partitions for your data. You can choose to scope data specific to a domain (so that any applications from the same domain may access the data), or to an application. Both modes are specific to the user, so a different user signed on to the same machine cannot directly access the same data.

Isolated storage enables for value/key combinations to be stored in special collections known as *site settings* (specific to the domain) and *application settings* (specific to the application). In addition, you can access the file system directly to store and retrieve files. This creates a great opportunity for caching information and storing local data by serializing it to disk.

In an OOB application, you have the opportunity to store local data and allow the application to run offline and disconnected from the Internet. The local data can drive the application and store changes made by the user. When the application comes online, the data can then be transmitted and synchronized with the server.

Several local database options also exist that create databases on top of isolated storage. Many of these are licensed/commercial databases, and a few provide full relational database capabilities including transactions.

For an Open Source option, consider the Open Source Sterling project that I maintain. Sterling is an object-oriented database that automatically serializes most classes and complex object graphs. It supports keys (including foreign keys) and indexes to enable fast in-memory queries that then lazy-load the full objects from disk.

You can read more about Sterling and download it online at `http://sterling.codeplex.com/.`

Communication

Silverlight has a robust communication stack that offers several modes of transmitting data between client and server, web services, and other applications. In addition to out-of-the-box support for standards-based web services, Silverlight can open direct sockets for communication and handle custom protocols.

Silverlight has powerful interoperability with the host HTML Document Object Model (DOM). Silverlight can call JavaScript methods and expose methods for JavaScript to call. This enables integration with traditional ASP.NET Ajax applications and hooks into postback and callback functionality.

The Silverlight `WebClient` can open any network-based URL and retrieve the data asynchronously. This enables parsing remote web pages, downloading RSS feeds, and even communicating with traditional Plain Old XML (POX)-based solutions. A common technique is to expose data using Representational State Transfer (REST) and JavaScript Object Notation (JSON). The Silverlight web client can access REST resources, retrieve the JSON data, and cast it to a strongly typed object for processing.

One powerful and unique feature in Silverlight is the Local Communication API. This API facilitates communication between different Silverlight applications running on the same computer. This is true regardless of what domain the applications were served from, or whether they run OOB.

To create a communication channel, one application simply instantiates a named sender, and the other creates a receiver with the same name. The creation of channels can include information to restrict the channel to other instances of the same application, to the same domain, or to enable any type of cross-channel communication. After a channel is created, you can simply register for events. And when the sender sends a message, the receiver can fire the event and pass the message.

A practical use for this is for authentication scenarios. The OAuth protocol, for example, requires opening a new window so that the user may authenticate with a separate web page. Although there is a URL for the user to return to, this forces the user to leave the currently running Silverlight application. By using local communication, a separate Silverlight application can receive the completed OAuth request and then communicate with the original application to pass credentials. This enables a seamless login experience without having to restart the Silverlight application.

THE FUTURE OF SILVERLIGHT

Silverlight was formally released in 2007 as a sort of "super JavaScript" interface and has evolved as of the version 5 beta in 2011 to a robust in-browser subset of the full core CLR, with support for offline and out-of-browser modes. Although you've been introduced to a few of the important LOB concepts and features, there is far more functionality available in Silverlight for LOB applications. Following are a few of the key features available as of version 5:

➤ Multicolumn text modes

➤ PostScript vector printing

➤ WS-Trust support (a security standard for web services)

➤ Support for 64-bit operating systems

➤ GPU-accelerated three-dimensional (3D) graphics API

➤ Embedded HTML content (a "web browser" within your Silverlight application)

➤ Interoperability with Microsoft Office

➤ Interface with USB and COM ports

➤ Run unmanaged code using p/Invoke

➤ Full profiling and test support

Perhaps two of the most powerful and compelling benefits of Silverlight are that it is easily delivered via the web, and it is available on multiple platforms and browsers. This means that your team can focus on building one robust application, rather than a different application for Windows and OS X environments, all without wasting precious cycles on browser-incompatibility issues.

SUMMARY

Silverlight powered the back-end health monitoring system used by Microsoft during the 2010 Vancouver Winter Olympics. It has been used by major cities to provide consumer interfaces for monitoring traffic, and even to provide feedback to the city about issues such as the locations of potholes. The medical community has embraced the rich UI and uses Silverlight for advanced imaging. Financial institutions use it within their SharePoint applications to provide rich, interactive dashboards and drilldowns.

In this chapter, you learned how Silverlight enables you to leverage existing languages and the familiar Visual Studio environment to build LOB applications. The availability of XAML enables powerful workflows with parallel design and development. Silverlight provides hooks and interfaces to build modular applications that are extensible through the use of the Managed Extensibility Framework (MEF).

A special design pattern called MVVM has evolved to take advantage of the unique qualities of data binding provided by the Silverlight framework. Several implementations of the pattern have evolved as Open Source frameworks you can leverage to start building LOB applications right away.

Features like isolated storage and out-of-browser applications make it an ideal platform to build offline solutions that target multiple platforms. Silverlight's communication stack enables you to connect directly to existing SOAP, Plain Old XML (POX), and JavaScript Object Notation (JSON) web services. These features continue to evolve with each successive release, with Silverlight 5 introducing some of the most important LOB features to date.

If you haven't tapped into the power of the Silverlight framework, you'll want to start exploring right away. It just might be the silver lining you've been looking for.

ABOUT THE AUTHOR

Jeremy Likness is a Silverlight-focused developer/architect and technical project manager with sales and entrepreneurial experience, a passion for mentoring and public speaking, and a strong social media presence. In July 2010, he received the Microsoft Most Valuable Professional (MVP) award for his work with Silverlight. Backed by 15 years of experience developing enterprise applications, he currently serves as a senior consultant and project manager for Wintellect. He has worked with software in multiple vertical industries, including insurance, health and wellness, supply-chain management, and mobility. His primary focus for the past decade has been building highly scalable web-based solutions using the Microsoft technology stack with a recent focus on Silverlight and WCF.

Tips and Tricks for Designers and Developers

by Daron Yöndem

Building high-quality software is getting more and more complex every day. The customer expectations are rising as available tools and technologies evolve. Providing the best set of features or functionalities is just a starting point on the way to building premium quality software. Customers want to see a visually appealing interface, and they want to get in touch with the software in a sensational way.

With these requirements, where functionality meets beautifully designed interfaces, development teams face another design aspect called *user experience (UX) design.* It's not only about having the best set of colors or shapes on the screen. It's also about how you want your customers to use your software, or how you want them to *feel* using your software.

In this complex world, it is crucial to incorporate a different set of skills into one project. Creating stunning visuals, building animations, designing user interface (UI) controls, organizing the content, and integrating functionalities with back-end systems are just some of the tasks that should be successfully accomplished to create the best quality software.

The job is too much to be a one-man show. Different roles and people should be involved in the making of a great application. At the highest level, these roles are often defined as *developers* and *designers.*

The success of an end product developed by a group of people is mostly based on the collaboration skills of each member of the team. Developers and designers must work together seamlessly. The need for collaboration has always been there, but the available tools or technologies did not offer an efficient way to fulfill the promise. This is where Microsoft's UI platforms, Silverlight and Windows Presentation Foundation (WPF), take the stage.

UNDERSTANDING THE DIFFERENCES BETWEEN SILVERLIGHT AND WPF

The Extensible Application Markup Language (XAML) is the key for all collaboration features of both Silverlight and WPF. You need to understand the relationship between XAML and the back-end platform that can help to connect the design surface with the code written by a developer.

First, XAML is a markup language. That means it is both human-readable and computer-readable. Being human-readable is extremely important because the learning curve for a markup language is much smoother compared to the other programming languages. Many designers have no programming background but can write and manipulate markup languages such as HTML.

Second, it is not obligatory to learn the syntax of the markup because there is always a What-You-See-Is-What-You-Get (WYSIWYG) editor that can help designers or developers easily produce the XAML needed, and without errors.

Choosing XAML over Other Markups

XAML is not just a markup language representing visual elements. It's also a way to define behaviors, styles, triggers, control templates, data templates, data binding, and animation. All these features are easily accessible through WYSIWYG editors such as Microsoft Expression Blend. From a developer's perspective, you could consider XAML a declarative language, where it is possible to define custom controls developed separately.

Understanding the Separation of Concerns

I remember saying in a conference, "The only way you can have a designer and developer working together on a project is to let them work separately." I think this is still true. Thanks to XAML, both Silverlight and WPF can offer an environment in which a developer can write code without tampering with the design, or a designer can create UIs that include animations and even simple data binding.

TIPS AND TRICKS FOR DESIGNERS

With tools such as Expression Blend, whatever you design is a part of the real application! No one needs to transform, transport, or do any kind of additional process to get the visuals or the interface you create into the real application. You directly work on the real application, which runs when you press the F5 button within Expression Blend. With this in mind, to create developer-friendly designs, you should be aware of the tips and tricks presented here.

Naming Your Objects

Every time you start to create a UI in Microsoft Expression Blend, such as the one shown in Figure 6-1, you should remember that whatever objects you put on screen, there is a big chance that developers on your team will use and access them. To let them access the visual objects you put on the screen, you must name the objects.

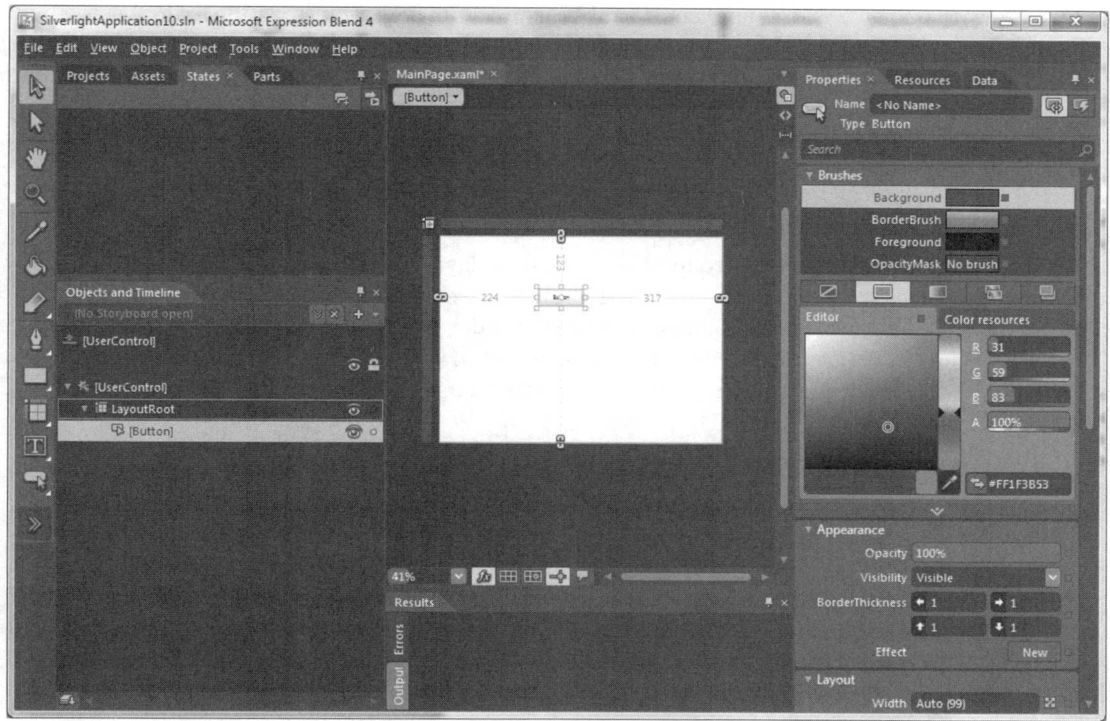

FIGURE 6-1: Naming objects on a screen interface

Check to see if your company has documentation about the naming conventions used by developers. Implement those conventions in Expression Blend while naming UI objects. If you don't have such documentation, it is time to create it so that you can be in sync with your team when starting to name your objects at this level of the development process.

Do not name everything you have on screen. First, if you start naming every object you use in your design, your developer will have a difficult time finding the right object name in a long list within Visual Studio. It is likely that you will have thousands of UI elements on screen, including every shape, rectangle, and line you used while creating the artwork.

If you are sure about an element that developers will never need to access or manipulate, don't name that element. This will also affect the performance of your application. There will be performance differences between having 1,000 UI elements with only 100 of them named and 1,000 elements with all of them named.

Designing in Photoshop

Microsoft Expression Studio has all the tools you need to design a UI. If you want a tool to create assets and vector artwork, Expression Design can help you with the support of XAML export, so you can use the assets in Expression Blend while creating the final user experience and the interactivity.

However, if you feel you are more comfortable using Photoshop, you can still create the design in that environment and then later import the design into Expression Blend. Keep in mind, however, that the design you create in Photoshop will still be used by developers on your team directly without any major changes or transformation.

You should definitely be familiar with and use layers in Photoshop. All the layers and folders you create in Photoshop will be UI elements in Silverlight/WPF, and developers can access the objects by calling the names you assign in Photoshop.

Moreover, the logic you use to group objects or create layers in Photoshop is far more important than simply being a design aspect. Creating a folder named `Buttons` and including an irrelevant image or design element in the folder can confuse the developers on your team. You can use the layers and folders in Photoshop as containers in Silverlight/WPF, which you can sometimes use to move objects or make them transparent from the end user's perspective.

Importing Assets from Photoshop

As mentioned earlier, Expression Blend supports importing whole designs from Photoshop. During this import process, you face critical choices.

The first choice concerns the text elements. During the import process, the text elements you have in Photoshop can be converted to bitmap files, or kept as dynamic `TextBlocks`. The difference is that a bitmap is static with its content (in other words, it will just be an image), whereas a `TextBlock` is dynamic content (meaning that developers can change the text).

So, you might be wondering, why not make everything dynamic? Text in a dynamic `TextBlock` is rendered with a font file. You can include your font file inside your application, or use generic fonts accessible on all systems. However, if you use a custom font, and never plan to change the text, why would you carry that huge font file with you inside your application? A better choice is to just convert the text to an image, as shown in Figure 6-2, and keep it there as long as you need.

Using Sample Data for a Better Design Experience

Expression Blend supports providing sample data without any help from the developer, so you can build your design seeing the end-product in a real-life fashion. To create a sample data source, you must go to the Data tab inside Expression Blend, as shown on the right side of Figure 6-3.

Inside the Data tab, click Create Sample Data ➪ New Sample Data menu. Be sure to keep the Enable Sample Data When Application Is Running check box checked.

Now create a sample collection of items you need to give life to your design. For example, you can rename the collection you have to **Products** and start defining what a product is by specifying different properties. For this example, say that a product should have a name, perhaps a photo, and a price, as shown on the right side of Figure 6-4. The name should be a text string. The price should be a number, and the photo should be an image. All these implementations are already inside Expression Blend.

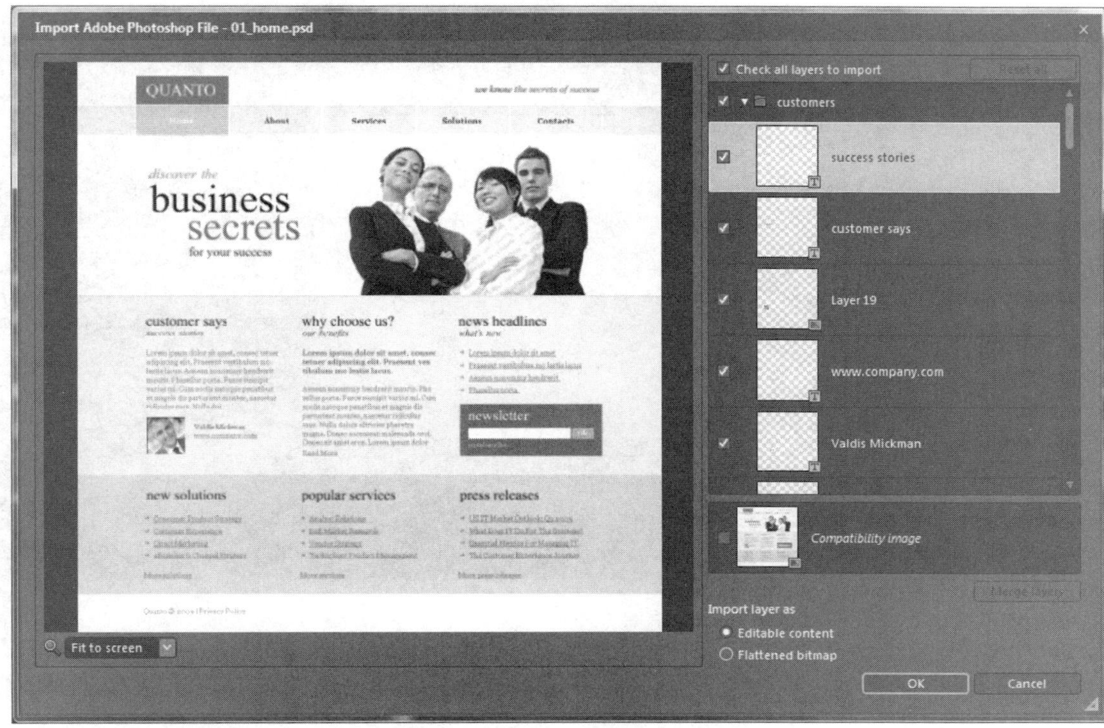

FIGURE 6-2: Converting text to an image for display

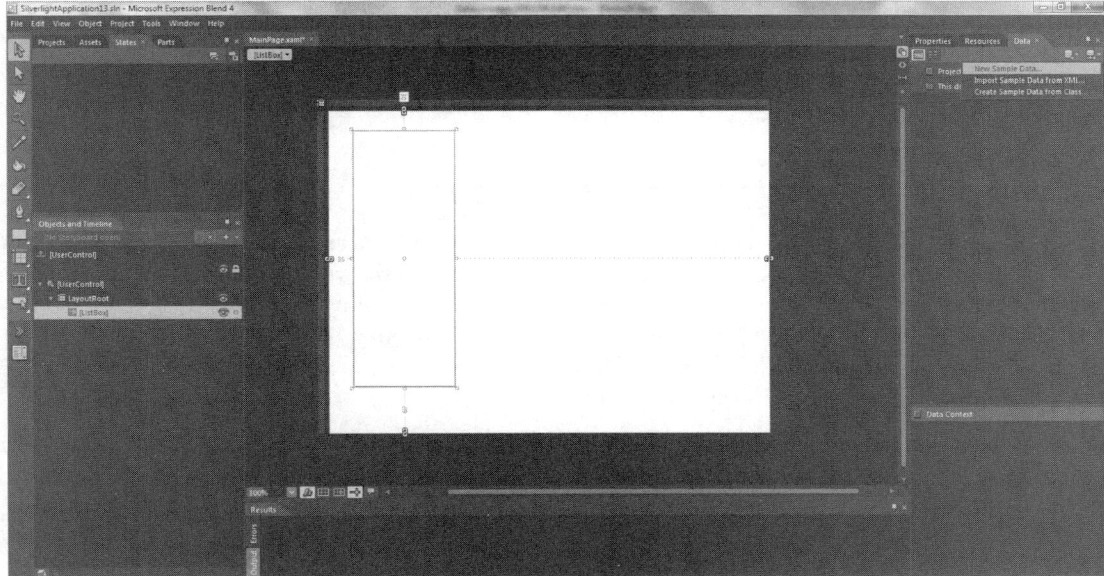

FIGURE 6-3: Accessing the Data tab in Expression Blend

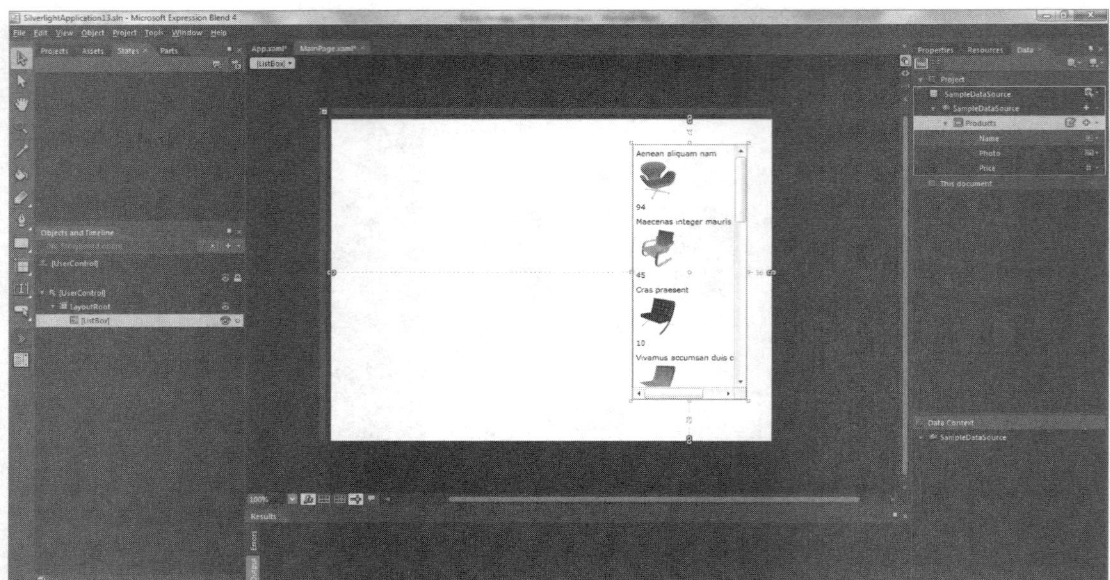

FIGURE 6-4: Collection of items in Expression Blend

The final step is to drag and drop the collection onto a UI element that can show a list of items. A `listbox`, `combobox`, or a `datagrid` are just some of the controls you can use.

TIPS AND TRICKS FOR DEVELOPERS

What distinguishes Silverlight and WPF from all the other platforms where you can write C# code are the UI engine (the XAML) and the data-binding mechanism that enables you to separate the design and the development. Now take a look at some tips and tricks you can implement to be a designer-friendly developer.

Showing Sample Data in Design Mode

Say that you are writing full data-access or business logic code, or maybe developing some custom controls implementing visual elements as well. If your control shows some kind of data, the data most likely will be fetched from the source, and bound to the control when the project or application runs. This means that designers on your team cannot see that data while working in Expression Blend. They need to design the interface without seeing the content and then run the application to see everything filled in. Obviously, this is not good.

To improve the designer's experience, you can include some sample data in your project, or maybe change the way data access works when the project runs in Design mode. When a user control is opened inside Expression Blend, the state you are inside is called Design mode. If you can detect when the code runs in Design mode, you can simply fill in some sample data, as shown here:

```
if (System.ComponentModel.DesignerProperties.GetIsInDesignMode(this))
{
```

```
//This code runs in design mode (Blend)
    }
```

In this code, you simply call the `GetIsInDesignMode` method providing a `UIElement` that you want to check to see whether it is running inside Expression Blend's design surface.

Using Behaviors to Make Things Easier

As a developer, perhaps you will never use a behavior. This is a feature that designers can use inside Expression Blend, which is exactly why developers should know what a behavior is.

A behavior is like a function in your code. You can specify parameters and give it a job to do. The difference is that this time the function you write will be used by designers on your team. You can delegate a lot of repetitive work to designers, and they can work independently from your code, without knocking on your door for millions of tiny coding requests.

A behavior encapsulates a functionality that can be triggered through another event. For example, you could create a simple `MessageBox` behavior that would show the regular `MessageBox` windows, but this time, a designer would do that inside of Expression Blend without writing one line of code.

To create a behavior, you must add the `System.Windows.Interactivity` reference to your project. The following code helps you inherit from a `System.Windows.Interactivity.TriggerAction` generic class:

```
public class MsgBoxTrigger :
    System.Windows.Interactivity.TriggerAction<UIElement>
{
    protected override void Invoke(object parameter)
    {

    }

}
```

You must create a new class by inheriting the `System.Windows.Interactivity.TriggerAction` generic class. To implement the new functionality you need, you override the `Invoke` method. However, in this example, you need some content or text to show with the `MessageBox`. To get that input from the designer, add a property to the `MsgBoxTrigger` class, as shown here:

```
public class MsgBoxTrigger :
    System.Windows.Interactivity.TriggerAction<UIElement>
{
    protected override void Invoke(object parameter)
    {

    }

    public string MessageText { get; set; }
}
```

Finally, you must implement the functionality, which, in this case, is the following simple `MessageBox` code:

```
public class MsgBoxTrigger :
    System.Windows.Interactivity.TriggerAction<UIElement>
{
    protected override void Invoke(object parameter)
    {
        MessageBox.Show(MessageText);
    }

    public string MessageText { get; set; }
}
```

Now you are ready to deliver this code to your designer, or add it inside your project so that your designer can use the behavior in Expression Blend, as shown in Figure 6-5.

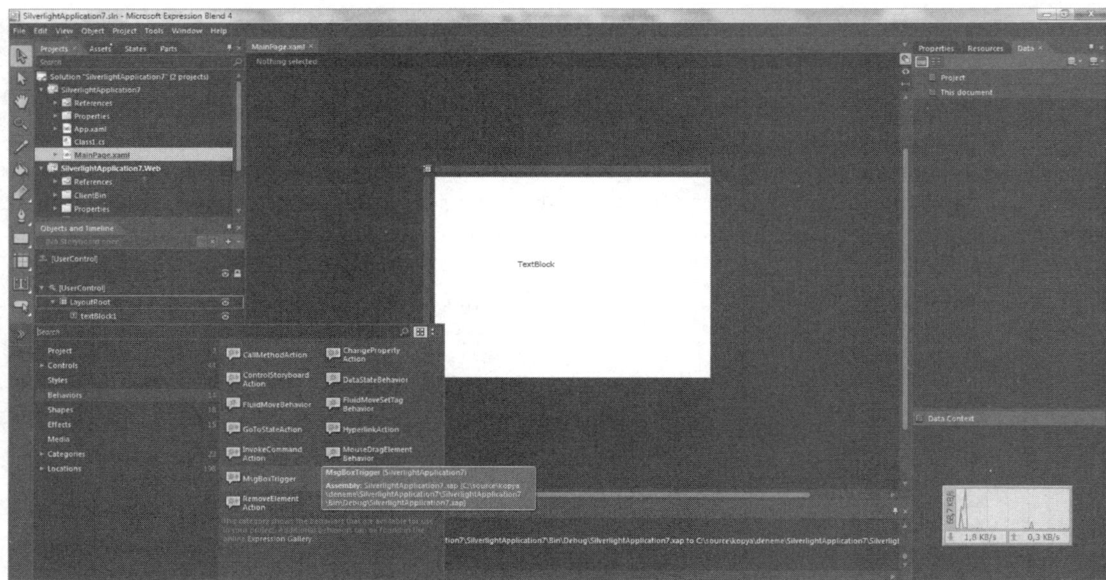

FIGURE 6-5: Using a behavior in Expression Blend

If you open the project in Expression Blend, you see your new behavior in the Assets Library under the Behaviors section, as shown on the left side of Figure 6-6. From now on, designers can drag and drop the behavior onto any `UIElement`, specify with which event they want to fire the `MessageBox`, and specify what text shows as the message.

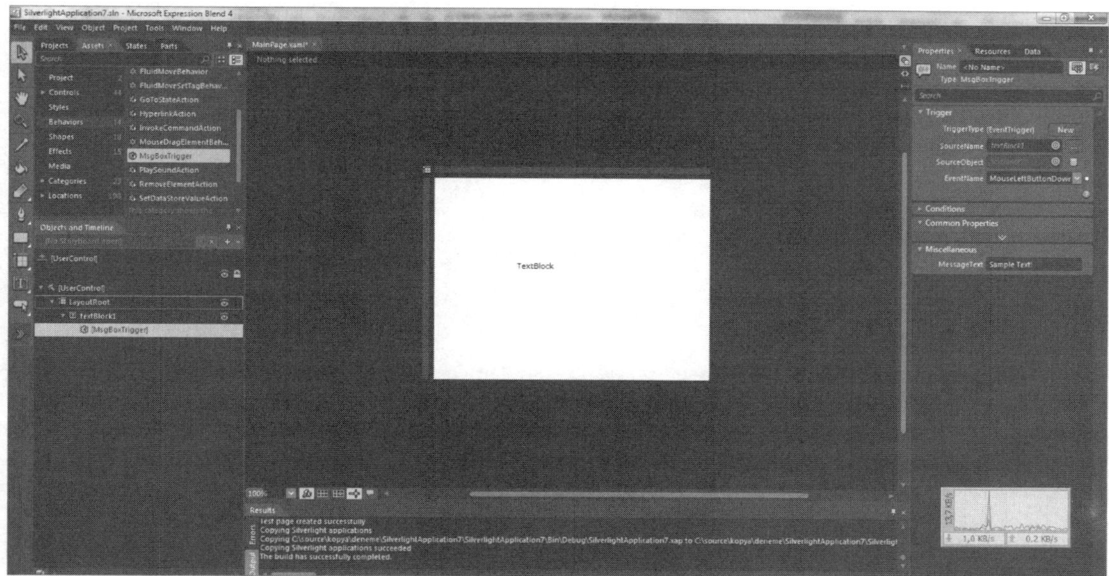

FIGURE 6-6: Assets Library in the Behaviors section

SUMMARY

Both WPF and Silverlight have the tools you need to collaborate and work together as a team with designers and developers. The rules you can follow as a team or individually can be different, and the tips and tricks are endless. In this chapter, you saw some of the major challenges and how to beat them.

ABOUT THE AUTHOR

Daron Yöndem is the founder of Deveload Software, a UX company based in Turkey. He is a Microsoft Regional Director and received a Gold Global Impact Award in 2009 and 2010. As an international speaker, Yöndem has hosted sessions in conferences including TechEd, MSDays, DevReach, PDC, and OpenDoor. He is the INETA MEA President, a Silverlight MVP, author of two books on ASP.NET AJAX, and a book on HTML5. He is passionate about UX, and can host sessions everywhere, anytime. He hosted more than 180 sessions in 2010, including a full night of free Silverlight community training called SilverNight! You can follow his thoughts at `http://daron.yondem.com`.

7

MVVM Patterns in Silverlight 4

by Kevin Grossnicklaus

As developers working with either the Silverlight or Windows Presentation Foundation (WPF) platforms, it is a safe bet that you have already heard about the Model-View-ViewModel (MVVM) pattern for developing user interfaces (UIs). Numerous books, magazine articles, and blogs enthusiastically explain the benefits of MVVM and demonstrate the advantages of leveraging this new development pattern. The unfortunate reality when working with MVVM is that, although the primary concepts of the pattern provide definite benefits to developers, there is no universally accepted implementation.

Because the core libraries for Silverlight and WPF development do not ship with any reusable MVVM-specific constructs for developers to utilize when developing an MVVM-based architecture, it is up to individual developers to "roll their own" framework components, or adopt one of the numerous third-party frameworks that have sprung up to fill this void. Much of the MVVM knowledge out there (whether in print or on the Internet) originates from bright developers who realize innovative and effective ways to utilize new technologies such as Silverlight and XAML to streamline how patterns such as MVVM are implemented.

Although this innovation is one of the great things about our industry, developers new to MVVM who look for guidance on "best practices" are often overwhelmed with all the differing MVVM solutions and architectures being promoted. Many of these recommendations and concepts contain great ideas, and most are only slightly different solutions to the same fundamental MVVM patterns. This is not necessarily a bad thing but does force new developers to have a deeper fundamental understanding of the problems these frameworks try to solve prior to deciding which framework or implementation pattern is best for them.

This chapter explains some of these fundamental choices and walks you through the development of a set of MVVM framework components for use in Silverlight line-of-business (LOB) applications. To focus solely on the MVVM components that make up this framework, this discussion generally assumes that you are proficient in Silverlight development, and that you have an understanding of XAML and data binding. Other chapters in this book focus on specific implementation concepts related to building Silverlight applications, many of which are complementary to the MVVM-based architecture you build here.

DEVELOPING YOUR OWN FRAMEWORK

Before beginning a review of the MVVM pattern itself and designing a UI architecture to support it, let's first discuss the reason you are developing your own framework.

You can choose to build upon many existing options that can give your applications an out-of-the-box MVVM architecture, and near the end of this chapter, you learn about a few of the most common options available, as well as their capabilities. For many projects and teams, selecting one of these prewritten frameworks is the best choice for a solid foundation. For other teams, a custom-developed framework for implementing MVVM concepts is definitely preferable, given the particular needs and capabilities of the teams.

Even when choosing to use a prewritten framework, properly determining which one best suits a project's needs is critical. Although they all fundamentally exist to solve similar problems, they all do so via different implementations that each come with different limitations and benefits.

You should become as familiar as possible with the full capabilities of any platform, and study as many different solutions to the same problem as possible, before deciding which solution or framework is the best fit for your environment. Thus, the purpose of this chapter is to familiarize you with the concepts of MVVM through the exercise of putting together a small framework to support this pattern. In doing so, you can not only gain an understanding of basic MVVM concepts, but you can also better evaluate all the available options, as well as recognize their strengths and weaknesses.

GETTING TO KNOW MVVM

Before diving too far into the development of a whole MVVM framework, it is worth taking a minute to review the general reasons why this pattern exists, and why it has gained such popularity within the WPF and Silverlight development spaces.

At its simplest, the MVVM pattern is a recommended practice for the separation of concerns for UI components and the data in which they are intended to display. Developers looking to implement this pattern are asked to separate their UI logic into three distinct components:

➤ *Model* — These are the data structures that represent objects within a particular application's target domain. The MVVM pattern requires that these classes be contained within a distinct tier, and, to the extent possible, that they encapsulate all their own business rules and validation logic. Beyond a few implementation details you learn about later in this chapter, the MVVM pattern doesn't care where these Model objects come from, or how they are written.

➤ *View* — The View component of an MVVM-based interface is simply the visual representation of a particular screen or a component. All code within the View tier (whether declarative via XAML or written in a .NET language such as C# or VB.NET) should be 100 percent related to UI concerns. As you quickly can realize, because of the power of XAML and Silverlight data binding, it is common for a View to be declared 100 percent in XAML, and to have no code-behind beyond the default initialization code provided by your integrated development environment (IDE).

➤ *ViewModel* — The ViewModel tier is represented by a nonvisual .NET class that encapsulates all the logic necessary to load or save any model data, and to expose it to the View for display or interaction. The ViewModel should also react to any actions taken by a user via the View (such as button-click events).

Although these brief descriptions provide the 50,000-foot overview of the parts of an MVVM UI, in practice, there is obviously more that goes into making all the moving parts work. Many of these details become apparent as you develop an actual MVVM framework.

Also, these descriptions focus solely on the "what" aspect of the primary MVVM components, and don't explain why they are important, or what benefit all this provides to the general .NET developer.

One of the primary reasons the .NET industry has begun to heavily adopt these types of patterns is generally related to testability. As the concept of a Test-Driven Development (TDD) process has become more mainstream (and as unit testing has become less shocking to most developers and more of a common, day-to-day practice), it became necessary to revisit how and where you put the majority of your code to simplify this process. Mixing critical business logic into the code-behind of your UIs made it less possible to include unit tests for these areas, hampering the whole development process.

A solution in which your logic was separated from your interfaces was necessary. Although the concept of this type of separation had existed for years, it was only recently that .NET developers married these patterns with the current capabilities of the .NET platform to develop frameworks such as ASP.NET Model-View-Controller (MVC) and Silverlight MVVM. In both ASP.NET MVC and MVVM, the goal is to create a clean separation of logic into a layer outside of the UI. The reason for two different patterns is directly related to the differences in platform capabilities between Silverlight and ASP.NET. In the request-and-response model that the web imposes on ASP.NET, the MVC framework is a perfect fit, whereas the data-binding capabilities of Silverlight make the MVVM pattern much more suitable.

Many developers who are new to MVVM and attempting to implement this pattern for the first time not only become confused with all the implementation details and possibilities, but also often come to a point in which they question the value of the pattern versus the complexity of the implementation. They often point to examples where tasks that traditionally took a few lines of code in the code-behind of a Silverlight `UserControl` now take much more code to cleanly adhere to the separation of logic and UI.

This is often the case when developers opt to adhere to a pattern such as MVVM for the consistency and benefits that it provides, and to do things "right," versus the ability to quickly throw something together. Ultimately, many of the benefits of consistently adhering to a pattern such as MVVM are not immediately recognizable, but rather are earned with lower cost of maintenance and the delivery of higher-quality software.

To achieve goals such as these does, at times, require you to implement more code. That said, when correctly used, the data-binding interaction between Views and ViewModels should generally lead to much less of the traditional "spaghetti" code developers commonly write for complex UIs.

Finally, before putting all the pieces in place, you need to know that the MVVM concepts discussed in this chapter apply not only to Silverlight applications, but also to those written using WPF, or even those written for the Windows Phone 7 platform. Although there may be minor implementation tweaks because of platform differences, the core concepts remain the same, and MVVM frameworks exist for all three platforms.

CREATING AN MVVM FRAMEWORK

Now comes the point where you can begin to put the wheels in motion, developing an MVVM architecture that you can use in your projects. The framework you develop follows many of the same patterns as those available for download on this book's companion website (www.wrox.com). Working through the development on your own framework can definitely jump-start your understanding of MVVM frameworks in general and hopefully help you better appreciate the components of other frameworks.

This will be a reusable framework, and, although there is absolutely no reason you couldn't take the resulting components and incorporate them directly into your existing or upcoming projects, you should also take the knowledge you gain through the development of this framework and use it to better evaluate all your MVVM options. If it turns out that the implementation you develop here suits your needs, then, by all means, build on top of it, and extend it as required. If it does nothing more than clarify some of the MVVM concepts that you've already been evaluating in other frameworks (thus helping you better adopt those products), then that is acceptable as well.

Remember, there is no "right way" to develop a framework such as this. Instead, you should employ generally accepted patterns and some implementation details that are found to be common among multiple frameworks. For this reason, I am always fascinated to review the implementations of others to help glean good ideas on where to go with my next projects and frameworks. I hope the framework you build here gives you some of those same ideas.

If nothing else, I hope to stir discussion to make you realize that, even if you wouldn't implement things exactly as you would here, forming your own opinions on the code of others is a great way to learn.

Framework Goals

As mentioned, the primary goal for this sample framework is to demonstrate some of the key concepts required for a usable MVVM-based application. However, prior to starting, it is also worth pointing out some of the specific items you should focus on during its development.

➤ *Model development best practices* — This discussion does not focus on any particular data-access technology but instead focuses on characteristics of a good model layer that makes these classes more usable within your framework.

➤ *Common ViewModel infrastructure* — Most MVVM frameworks have some standardization for the capabilities of a ViewModel, and the one presented here can do the same. Already built-in components and patterns exist for implementing Models and Views, but the ViewModel concept has no such standardization, and, thus, you will develop some core classes on which new ViewModels will be created.

➤ *Registration of Views and ViewModels* — Keeping track of which Views should be used to display and visualize each of the ViewModel classes is critical to easy management of your

MVVM components. You will want to develop a means to easily make this association and use it throughout your infrastructure.

➤ *Displaying Views to the user* — Developers should be able to easily display a new View as the content of another control, or as a modal dialog window. The framework developed here can provide this capability and manage all the setup of the correct associations between Views and ViewModels.

➤ *Managing visible Views* — With LOB applications of any complexity, developers usually need to manage multiple open Views at once. In an MVVM framework, managing Views and providing the capability to access open Views is critical.

➤ *Building composite UIs from multiple Views* — Rarely are complex UIs the result of a single View and are instead made up of many smaller Views that make up a single UI. You learn how a framework such as the one developed here can help support this composition of Views.

The entire source code for the resulting framework is provided with the downloads for this book on the companion website (www.wrox.com). It is included with a small sample Silverlight 4 application demonstrating its capabilities by providing a UI like the one shown in Figure 7-1.

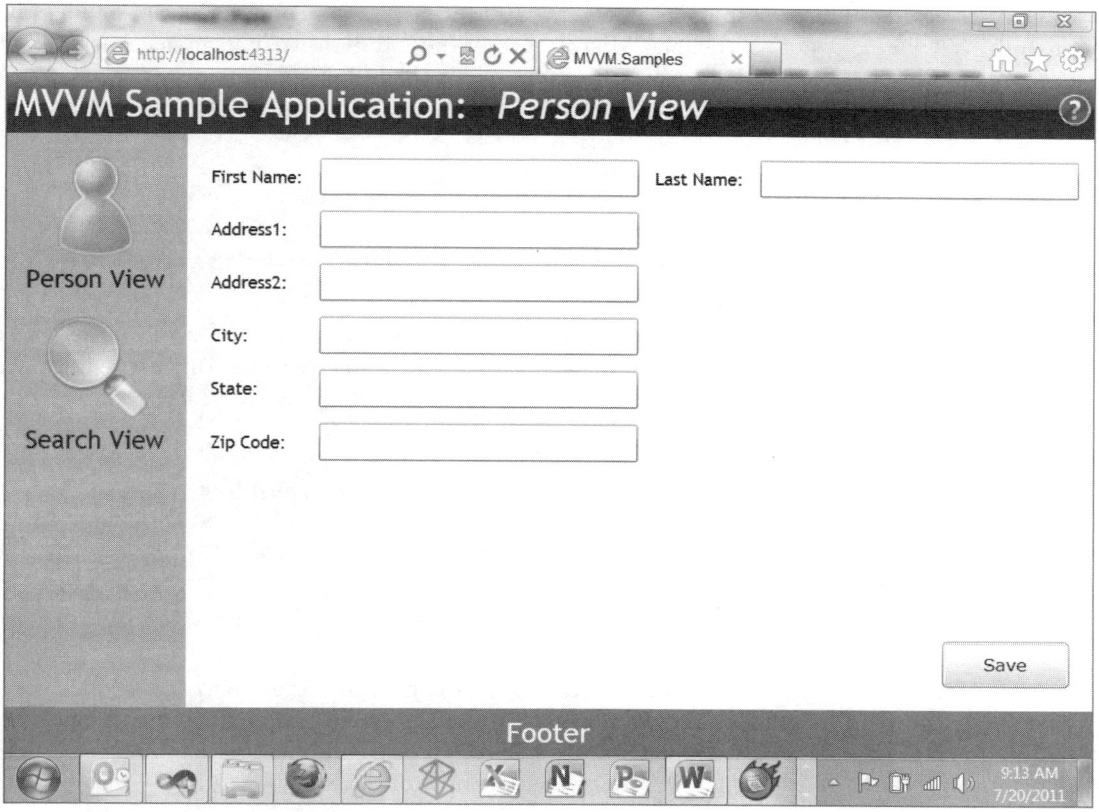

FIGURE 7-1: Example UI

If you prefer not to enter all the code as it is found in the following sections, you can download the completed solution and just follow along.

Framework Technologies

For purposes of this chapter, you perform all framework development using the following technologies:

- ➤ Visual Studio 2010 Express (available at www.microsoft.com/express/web)

- ➤ C# 4.0 programming language

- ➤ Silverlight 4 SDK (installed via the Microsoft Web Platform Installer found at//www .microsoft.com/web/downloads/platform.aspx)

- ➤ Silverlight 4 Control Toolkit (available at http://silverlight.codeplex.com)

- ➤ Microsoft's Unity Container (available at http://unity.codeplex.com)

If you do not already have Visual Studio 2010 installed, you can download the Express version of this tool from the link shown in the previous list. The Silverlight Control Toolkit is a collection of rich Silverlight controls that Microsoft provides for download from the CodePlex website. These controls are available at no cost under an Open Source license and are updated out-of-band with the full .NET Framework. This enables Microsoft to be more responsive in its management, and to release new additions much more frequently than it would the full .NET Framework.

> *It is important to note that there are multiple versions of Visual Studio 2010 Express. For the Silverlight development required for this chapter, you can use Visual Web Developer 2010 Express.*

For extensibility, the framework developed here uses the Unity Inversion of Control (IoC) container. Many other options for IoC containers provide great value. The choice to use Unity here is arbitrary because any IoC container you are comfortable with could be utilized as necessary.

> *If you are new to the concept of IoC containers, you should consult the Unity documentation at* http://unity.codeplex.com *or spend some time researching the concept online for one of the many online blog posts or articles describing the subject.*

An additional point about the usage of an IoC container in general is that many MVVM frameworks today are also starting to take advantage of Microsoft's Managed Extensibility Framework (MEF). MEF provides a robust foundation for such frameworks, and the choice of IoC versus MEF is again an arbitrary decision made by you or the developer of the framework upon which you are

building. I encourage you to spend some time researching both options and to make your own edu-
cated decision about which technology you feel more comfortable using.

*In my own experience, I have used both MEF and IoC containers as the core
of my architectures, and both are powerful. I do not drastically change my
approach regardless of the technology, but there are times I do bend a little this
way or that to better utilize what I am given from the tool.*

Beyond the technologies listed here, many other technologies are complementary to an MVVM
architecture and, without which, a real-world Silverlight LOB application would not be possible.
The following list shows some of these technologies presented here for information purposes but are
considered to be outside the scope of this chapter:

➤ Windows Communication Foundation (WCF)

➤ WCF Rich Internet Application (RIA) Services

➤ ADO.NET Entity Framework (EF)

*Some of these technologies are covered in somewhat greater detail elsewhere in
this book, and the reason they are called out here is to demonstrate that it takes
a lot of technologies to provide the foundation for a robust application. Those
required for the MVVM framework developed in this chapter are but a small
sampling of what you will ultimately need to use.*

Getting Started

The first step in the creation of a usable MVVM framework is to create the Visual Studio solutions
and projects you will utilize for the rest of the framework. For purposes of this discussion, this is
nothing more than a single Visual Studio solution containing the following three projects:

➤ `MVVM.Shell` — This is a standard Silverlight 4 application.

➤ `MVVM.HostSite` — This is an ASP.NET application that hosts the `MVVM.Shell` Silverlight
application and serves as the start-up project for the solution.

➤ `MVVM.Framework` — This is a Silverlight 4 class library that contains all the reusable MVVM
components and services and makes them available for use on many projects outside of just
this sample.

After these three projects have been created in Visual Studio, you must create a project reference
between the `MVVM.Shell` application and the `MVVM.Framework` application. You can do this via the

Add Reference dialog box, which is necessary so that the primary Silverlight application can have access to the reusable MVVM components.

Whenever I start up a new project such as this, I spend a lot of time verifying my project setup. This includes my default namespace settings, my project references, the folder structure in which these projects exist on my hard disk and, ultimately, in my source control repository using tools such as Microsoft's Team Foundation Server or SubVersion (SVN).

In addition to these three projects, you must ensure that you have access to the Microsoft Unity IoC container and the Silverlight Control Toolkit controls. You can install references to these components either by manually downloading them from the previously listed links, or by using NuGet to add references to the necessary packages to your project. As with all source code from this chapter, the necessary dynamic link libraries (DLLs) can be found in a `Binaries` folder alongside the completed solutions to the sample MVVM framework with the source code that accompanies this book.

While many developers have their own preferences for how to add and manage references to external DLLs, there is a strong industry movement toward the use of the NuGet Visual Studio extension for managing references to Open Source libraries and tools. You can easily install NuGet from the Visual Studio 2010 Extension manager, or by downloading it directly from `http://nuget.org/`.

When developing a solution that has external dependencies — for example, Unity and the Silverlight Control Toolkit — you need to efficiently manage the required DLLs and to treat them as part of source control for versioning purposes. This simplifies the setup for all developers collaborating on the same project.

I traditionally create a `Binaries` folder on my hard disk alongside my Visual Studio project folders. I then copy all required dependent DLLs into this folder, and when adding binary references to my project files, I add them to the files in this folder, thus making them relative references, and available to all new developers attempting to build my source code. Figure 7-2 shows how the solution for this framework looks on disk.

After all the base projects and references are configured to your liking, you can build and run your solution to see the default (and empty) Silverlight control display in a browser.

Defining ViewModels

The first of many moving parts in this framework development process will be developing a common infrastructure for defining ViewModels.

As mentioned earlier, a ViewModel is intended to be a nonvisual class that encapsulates all interaction between a Model and a View. If the Model describes the data, and the View describes the UI itself, then the ViewModel could be thought of as containing the glue that loads all the right pieces of data and exposes them in such a way that the View can easily display them.

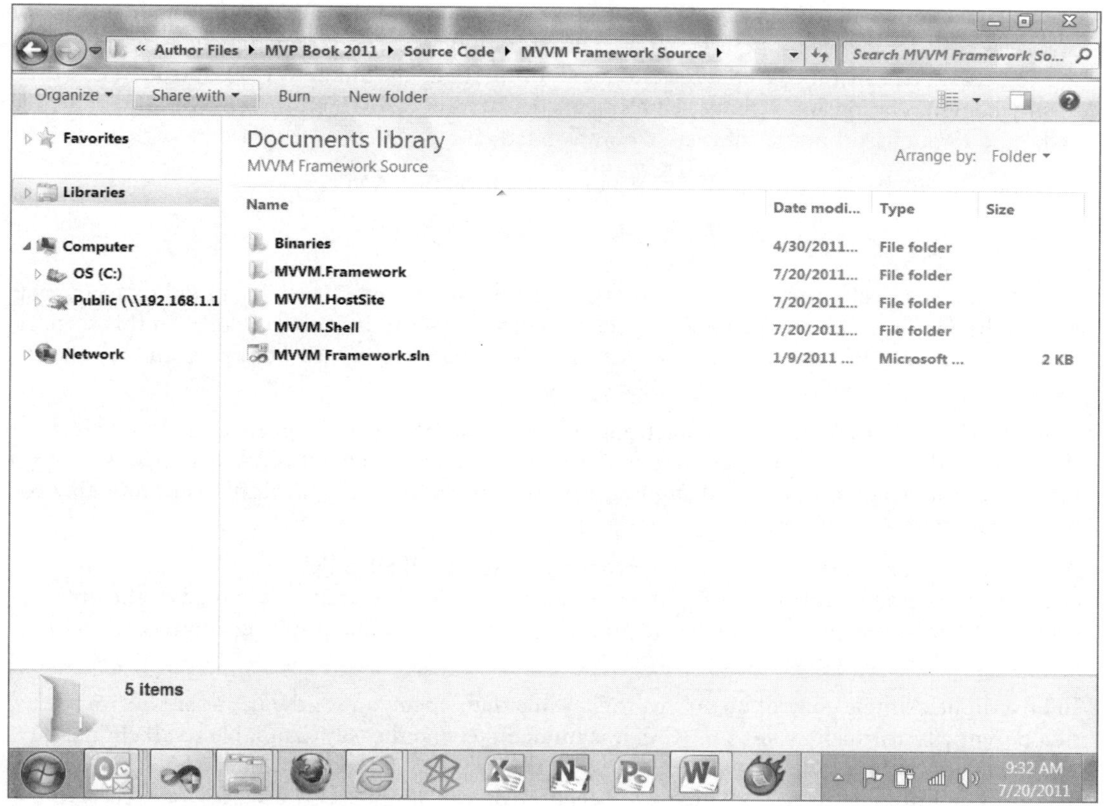

FIGURE 7-2: Files and folders for sample framework

Additionally, the ViewModel class must receive and handle notifications when a user performs specific interactions through the View, such as pressing a button or changing the value of a textbox. Obviously, this is an oversimplification of what can and should be done in a View, but, for now, the important thing you should start focusing on is defining what a ViewModel is and how it gets tied to a View.

First, an important (and yet simple) concept new MVVM developers must understand is the basic premise behind Silverlight and WPF data binding. All Silverlight controls contain a dependency property called `DataContext`. The `DataContext` property can be set to any object, and, through a XAML concept called *markup extensions*, properties of the control in the View can be easily "bound" to public properties of the class that has been assigned to the `DataContext` of that control.

Consider the following snippet of code:

```
var _view = new PersonView();

var _viewModel = new PersonViewModel();

_view.DataContext = _viewModel;
```

In this code, you instantiate a new instance of a user control called `PersonView` and a new instance of a class called `PersonViewModel`. After creating both objects, you immediately assign the `PersonViewModel` instance to the `DataContext` property of the `PersonView` control. When this seemly benign relationship is made, UI elements declared in XAML on the `PersonView` control can be bound to public properties of the `PersonViewModel`.

Consider the following example of a `TextBox` declaration in XAML:

```
<TextBlock Text="{Binding Title}"/>
```

This `TextBlock` declaration uses the XAML `{Binding}` markup extension to bind its `Text` property to the `Title` property of whatever object is currently set to its `DataContext`. In this scenario, although it cannot be seen, you can assume that the `PersonViewModel` object assigned to the View's `DataContext` has a public property called `Title`.

The astute observer might notice something strange about the these snippets of code — you assigned the ViewModel to be the `DataContext` of the View class itself, but this XAML snippet showing the binding to the `Title` property is demonstrated using a `TextBlock` control that is presumably sitting somewhere within the `PersonView` user control.

As mentioned earlier, the `DataContext` property exists on all Silverlight controls but is unique because if a current control's `DataContext` is `null` and someone attempts to read it, the property accessor (that is, the `get{}` block of the property) returns the value resulting from a call to the `Parent.DataContext` property.

In Silverlight's simple control hierarchy, this means that when you set the `DataContext` property of a parent control such as `PersonView`, it is immediately (and easily) available to all child controls who have not had their direct `DataContext` properties set to a different value. This is especially useful when utilizing the MVVM pattern because you can simply set the ViewModel class to the `DataContext` property of the View, and all child controls of that specific view can be bound to properties of the ViewModel.

Because any object can be assigned to the `DataContext` property of any control or View, there are technically no limitations relating to the types or structure of a ViewModel. That said, in real-world situations in which a single project or solution might contain dozens of different ViewModels, it is generally preferable to maintain consistency among all ViewModels. It is also highly desirable to develop reusable code that works on any or all ViewModels, regardless of which developer created them. For this to work, all ViewModels must implement common interfaces or inherit from common base classes that contain these standard members.

Before proceeding, be sure you understand one additional data-binding concept: *change notification*. When utilizing the `{Binding}` markup extension to synchronize the properties of the ViewModel with the control values of the View, you must consider when a change to the control updates the ViewModel property, and also when and how a programmatic change to a ViewModel property results in the control being visually updated.

When a data-bound Silverlight control is initially displayed, the data-binding infrastructure queries the value of the `DataContext` property to which the control is bound, and assigns the correct values to the data-bound property of the control. Then, when a user interacts with a Silverlight control via the keyboard or the mouse, the data-binding infrastructure is notified, and the appropriate change can be made to the bound property of the ViewModel. This is fairly straightforward because the act of a user making a change to a control is an easily triggered event.

For a user's action upon a control (such as entering text into a textbox or checking a check box) to be propagated back to the value of a bound property, the data binding must be configured to be in a mode of TwoWay. *This is discussed later in this chapter.*

On the other hand, in the example snippet presented earlier in which a `TextBlock` control's `Text` property was bound to the `Title` property of a ViewModel, you must ask what would happen if, in code, you updated the ViewModel's `Title` property at some point after the control was initially displayed. Would the `TextBlock` control immediately change to reflect this change?

The short answer is "No." Unfortunately, in Silverlight data binding, the controls do not natively listen for changes to the objects to which they are bound unless certain conditions are met. The first of these conditions is that the `DataContext` object (the ViewModel) must notify others of changes to its state by implementing one of a specific set of interfaces. These interfaces are simple and expose a specific event that others can listen to when needing to be notified of changes.

Following are the interfaces used for change notification:

➤ `System.ComponentModel.INotifyPropertyChanged` — This is used when a single class must raise an event indicating that one of its properties has been changed.

➤ `System.Collections.Specialized.INotifyCollectionChanged` — This is used when creating a custom collection that needs to notify others that an item has been either added or removed.

When creating a large set of classes to represent a complex domain, it often gets tedious to repeatedly implement the `INotifyPropertyChanged` interface. For this reason, it is common to create an abstract base class for use by domain classes that need it.

Beyond binding to a class that supports one of the described interfaces, the second condition to support this advanced level of data binding is that the `{Binding}` markup extension must be configured to listen for changes made to the user interface controls.

By default, Silverlight data binding is initialized in a mode called `OneWay`, which indicates that changes are propagated from the bound property to the control, but not from the control back to the bound property. With controls that accept user input such as textboxes, check boxes, combo boxes, and others, it is usually the developer's intent to have actions made by a user upon these controls to also affect the underlying property to which these controls are bound. This is done by specifying a value of `TwoWay` for the data-binding `Mode`, as follows:

```
<TextBlock Text="{Binding Title, Mode=TwoWay}"/>
```

When working with Silverlight data binding, there are three different possible values for a specific binding's `Mode`:

➤ `OneWay` — One-way data binding means that changes to the underlying object are reflected in the bound controls, but that a user's changes to the control via mouse or keyboard are not reflected in the underlying object. This is the default value.

➤ `OneTime` — One-time data binding indicates that the binding is used to assign the initial value to the control property, but beyond that point, the binding goes away, and there is no automatic synchronization of the two properties.

➤ `TwoWay` — Two-way data binding means that programmatic changes to the property are reflected visually on any bound properties of the control, and that a user's changes to the control are reflected in the underlying bound property. This mode is only successful if the target object of the binding implements one of the previously mentioned change notification interfaces (that is, `INotifyPropertyChanged`), and if the control itself allows changes to be made by the user. For example, a `TextBox` would benefit from a binding mode of `TwoWay` because a user can modify the text, whereas a `TextBlock` control wouldn't be able to take advantage of this mode, since a user cannot interact with its properties.

So, how do you start the example framework so that it can quickly and easily provide this change notification capability to your framework objects? For purposes of this discussion, add a new class to the root of the `MVVM.Framework` project called `BaseObservableObject`. This class can provide a common implementation of this interface, and many other classes within the framework will simply inherit this interface.

```csharp
using System.ComponentModel;

namespace MVVM.Framework
{
    public abstract class BaseObservableObject : INotifyPropertyChanged
    {
    public abstract class BaseObservableObject : INotifyPropertyChanged
    {
        public event PropertyChangedEventHandler PropertyChanged;

        protected void OnPropertyChanged(string propertyName)
        {
            var handlers = PropertyChanged;

            if (handlers != null)
            {
                handlers(this, new PropertyChangedEventArgs(propertyName));
            }
        }
    }
}
```

Like any event or interface implementation, you need to realize that it takes two sides to make a successful implementation. First, your ViewModel objects must implement the interface and correctly raise the `PropertyChanged` event when data actually changes. On the other hand, Views and other listeners must correctly recognize that a class implements this interface, and must react accordingly when notified of changes to data.

Fortunately, the Silverlight data-binding infrastructure is inherently familiar with this interface and automatically keeps any dependency property in sync with a data-bound property of a class implementing `INotifyPropertyChanged`. This is especially important when a developer wants to implement two-way binding.

THE "MAGIC-STRING" ISSUE

The `BaseObservableObject` is a basic means to provide common code to implement the `INotifyPropertyChanged` interface. As you become aware of the common need for such an `INotifyPropertyChanged` implementation, you can begin to recognize the wide variety of solutions available to serve the same purpose.

Although almost all frameworks achieve this goal through a commonly adopted base class, some of these classes expose methods that utilize generics, whereas others utilize lambda expressions to specify the property that is currently being changed. Still others use .NET reflection as the means to determine which property is currently being modified.

The basic difference between all such implementations comes down to how much code can be abstracted into the base class, versus how much knowledge of the change notification is required of the calling developer.

A primary concern of developers implementing such a base class is the embedding of "magic strings" for the `PropertyName` parameter of the event. In the example provided in the section, "Defining ViewModels," it was left to the calling code to specify the "name" of the property that is changing when calling `OnPropertyChanged`. This string is critical in notifying listeners which property has changed and, as is typical with C# and .NET, the string is case-sensitive. If the `NameLast` property were changing, and a developer inadvertently called `OnPropertyChanged` and passed `"Namelast"` as the parameter, any UI component bound to this property would not be aware a change had occurred and would now reflect out-of-date data.

The number and variety of proposed solutions to this magic-string issue are part of the reason that there is no industry-accepted base class for providing change notifications. The base class utilized in the sample provided in this chapter simply relies on the calling developer to be aware of the case-sensitivity and specify the correct property name.

When working with collections of data, the `INotifyCollectionChanged` interface should be implemented to enable UI elements such as grids or list boxes to be notified when items are added or deleted from the underlying collection. Fortunately, the .NET Framework provides an enhanced version of the commonly used generic `List<>` that implements this interface. This collection, called `System.Collections.ObjectModel.ObservableCollection<>`, provides a plug-and-play replacement for the generic `List<>` class with the added benefit of implementing `INotifyCollectionChanged`.

Now that you understand some of the specifics of Silverlight data binding and change notification, move on with the creation of the ViewModel infrastructure. For this framework, you develop both a common ViewModel interface and an abstract class to simplify the implementation of new ViewModels.

Begin by adding a new interface class called `IViewModel` to the root of the `MVVM.Framework` project. The following code should be added to that class:

```
using System.ComponentModel;

namespace MVVM.Framework
{
    public interface IViewModel : INotifyPropertyChanged
    {
        string Title { get; set; }

        void Initialize(object parameters);

        bool IsBusy { get; }

        bool IsDirty { get; }

        void Save();

        void Refresh();
    }
}
```

Through this interface, you specify that (for consistency and to be used elsewhere in the framework) each of the ViewModel classes contain at least the six specified members. The signatures of the remaining components of the framework enforce the usage of this interface to ensure compliance with the MVVM pattern.

In the previously specified `IViewModel` interface, you declare the following members:

➤   `Title` — This simple string property will be utilized when needing to display the name of a particular View.

➤   `Initialize(object parameters)` — It is within this common method that developers can place any custom loading code specific to a particular ViewModel.

➤   `IsBusy` — Because of the asynchronous nature of Silverlight development, it is frequently necessary to know if a particular screen is waiting on a long-running operation. This property enables you to track that state at a ViewModel level.

➤   `IsDirty` — On screens where a user is actively modifying data, the `IsDirty` property enables you to keep track of whether pending changes have been made to a particular screen.

➤   `Save` — This method contains any custom persistence code.

➤   `Refresh` — Because Silverlight is a stateful UI technology, it is common that users of LOB applications may find themselves looking at stale data. Providing them with the means to refresh the data on a particular screen can ultimately be where you incorporate the `Refresh` method of a particular ViewModel.

These members suit the purposes of the discussion in this chapter and are meant to cover many common MVVM scenarios. If your scenario would benefit from additional common members across all ViewModels, then the `IViewModel` interface would be the location where you could enforce that globally.

Unfortunately, you cannot see a demonstration of the full capability of each of these ViewModel properties and methods within this chapter. But, as you add additional functionality, you can see how the consistency of the `IViewModel` interface opens a number of doors to more reusable code and services within a common framework.

When developing functionality in the MVVM framework, the creation of ViewModel classes is extremely common, and, as a result, so is the implementation of the `IViewModel` interface. For this reason, you create an abstract base class that developers can inherit from to take advantage of a pre-written implementation of much of the common ViewModel code.

To do this, add a new class to the root of the MVVM framework project, and name this class `BaseViewModel.cs`:

```csharp
namespace MVVM.Framework
{
    public abstract class BaseViewModel : BaseObservableObject, IViewModel
    {
        public abstract void Initialize(object parameters);

        public virtual void Save()
        {

        }

        public virtual void Refresh()
        {

        }

        private string title = string.Empty;

        public string Title
        {
            get
            {
                return title;
            }
            set
            {
                if (title!=value)
                {
                    title=value;
```

```
                        OnPropertyChanged("Title");
                }
            }
        }

        private bool isBusy = false;

        public bool IsBusy
        {
            get
            {
                return isBusy;
            }
            protected set
            {
                if (isBusy!=value)
                {
                    isBusy=value;
                    OnPropertyChanged("IsBusy");
                }
            }
        }

        private bool isDirty = false;

        public bool IsDirty
        {
            get
            {
                return isDirty;
            }
            protected set
            {
                if (isDirty!=value)
                {
                    isDirty=value;
                    OnPropertyChanged("IsDirty");
                }
            }
        }
    }
}
```

Some key aspects of the `BaseViewModel` implementation are worth pointing out:

➤ The class itself is flagged as `abstract`, which disallows direct instantiation of `BaseViewModel` objects, and instead requires developers to derive its functionality through inheritance.

➤ The class itself inherits from the previously implemented `BaseObservableObject`, which provides it with the `INotifyPropertyChanged` interface and access to the protected `OnPropertyChanged` method for raising change events.

➤ The `Initialize` method is flagged as `abstract`, forcing any class inheriting from `BaseViewModel` to provide its own `Initialize` implementation. Alternatively, the `Save` and `Refresh` methods are both flagged as `virtual`, which dictates that derived classes are not required to provide their own implementation but may override and do so if they want.

➤ Each property of declaration raises the `PropertyChanged` event when a value actually changes. Following this pattern is a bit more verbose and tedious than would be possible if you could use the C# 3.0 auto-generated properties, but this is a requirement for the best possible MVVM experience.

Now that you have a common ViewModel interface (`IViewModel`) and a base implementation of this interface (`BaseViewModel`), you can continue on with the example framework by putting these components to use to create and display Views.

Creating New Views and ViewModels

The next logical step in the creation of the MVVM framework is to create the first View and ViewModel pair.

Based upon the work you performed in the previous section, creating a new ViewModel is fairly straightforward and, at its simplest, constitutes nothing more than creating a new class and inheriting all the base functionality from `BaseViewModel`.

Do this by first creating a folder within the `MVVM.Shell` project called `Views` and, within that new folder, creating a new class called `HeaderViewModel.cs`. Within that new class file, add the following code:

```csharp
using MVVM.Framework;

namespace MVVM.Shell.Views
{
    public class HeaderViewModel : BaseViewModel
    {
        public override void Initialize(object parameters)
        {
            Title = "MVVM Sample Application";

        }
    }
}
```

The `HeaderViewModel` example contains possibly the most basic of ViewModels and does not perform any real work, other than assigning its own `Title` property. It is worth noting that — because of the inheritance from `BaseViewModel` — the `HeaderViewModel` class already implements `IViewModel` and `INotifyPropertyChanged`, which can greatly simplify your upcoming work and enable it to be easily managed via the framework.

Now that you have a ViewModel declared, the next step is to create a View for this ViewModel. This View needs to contain the visual elements that are actually visible by the end user (whereas the ViewModel contains the logic that makes the View work).

To create this View, add a new Silverlight `UserControl` called `HeaderView.xaml` to the `Views` folder of the `MVVM.Shell` project. After this View has been created and the design surface for `HeaderView.xaml` is visible, add a single `TextBlock` control to the View to get you started, as shown in the following XAML:

```xml
<UserControl x:Class="MVVM.Shell.Views.HeaderView"
    xmlns="http://schemas.microsoft.com/winfx/2006/xaml/presentation"
    xmlns:x="http://schemas.microsoft.com/winfx/2006/xaml"
    xmlns:d="http://schemas.microsoft.com/expression/blend/2008"
    xmlns:mc="http://schemas.openxmlformats.org/markup-compatibility/2006"
    mc:Ignorable="d"
    d:DesignHeight="300" d:DesignWidth="400">

    <Grid x:Name="LayoutRoot" Background="White">
        <TextBlock Text="{Binding Title}"/>
    </Grid>
</UserControl>
```

Here, note that the `TextBlock` control's `Text` property is bound to the `Title` property of its `DataContext`. This data binding won't be apparent in the UI until you get farther in your framework and reach a point where you can associate Views and ViewModels. If you review the code provided with this chapter on this book's companion website (www.wrox.com), you can find a more aesthetically pleasing ViewModel and a more sophisticated implementation.

Before getting into the intricacies of associating your Views and ViewModels, and actually getting something to display to the user, it is worth taking a moment to discuss the naming and organizing of your Views and ViewModels.

You created a folder called `Views` and, in it, created two files: `HeaderViewModel.cs` and `HeaderView.xaml` (which does include a code-behind file, so you could say you created three files).

First, notice that the ViewModel class contains the word `ViewModel` as a suffix to its name, and the View contains the word `View`. This is not a requirement and is just a common naming convention utilized to help make the various components easy to find. Because both the View and ViewModel files are specific to a `Header` View, they contain that name. Unlike ASP.NET MVC, in this MVVM framework, the naming of these items has no direct impact on their usage in your framework and is simply a boon to maintainability.

Beyond the naming convention, you included both the View and the ViewModel in the same folder where the files sit side-by-side. This, too, is a matter of preference and differs from the ASP.NET MVC pattern to include special folders for controllers (similar to your ViewModels) and Views.

Become familiar enough with the MVVM pattern and standardize on your own naming and organizational best practices that help you best organize your projects. In an MVVM environment, you ultimately create more files than you may be used to, and, when something goes wrong, you want to easily find the necessary files to troubleshoot. This is the primary reason you should care about naming and organization at this point.

Registering Views and ViewModels

Now that you have created a simple View and ViewModel pair, you have reached a critical point in which you must decide how best to make the association between them. Earlier, you learned how this concept was critical to any MVVM framework and is one of the areas in which they differ the most.

The most basic means of associating them is to leave the responsibility of knowing which Views and ViewModels go together up to developers. This can be seen in the following code snippet:

```
var viewModel = new HeaderViewModel();

var view = new HeaderView();

view.DataContext = viewModel;
```

In the scenario in which developers want to display a header, they would need to be aware that the `HeaderView` user control was the intended view for the `HeaderViewModel` ViewModel and would be required to directly make the `DataContext` association.

Although this solution is functional, it is also highly error-prone and not as flexible as you might like. With a View such as a header (which may be displayed only once in an application), this might not be a huge issue. However, with other Views that may appear multiple times in an application, you might end up with the previous code existing multiple times throughout a project. In this scenario, if you decide to change the View you were using for the header, you would wind up searching for every single place throughout the solution in which a new `HeaderView` was created.

While a number of solutions to this problem exist, the framework described in this chapter solves this problem by keeping a centralized list of the available Views and ViewModels.

Before implementing the infrastructure to make this association, add a class to centrally control the data. You do this by adding a class called `ViewService` to the `MVVM.Framework` project. The `ViewService` class will be the central location within your framework where you implement the majority of your most reusable MVVM code. This primarily includes the means to associate Views and ViewModels, as well as the capability to show a View within a content control.

The `ViewService` class is the first (and primary) class within your MVVM framework that makes use of the Microsoft Unity IoC container. You need an instance of a Unity container exposed as a simple property directly off of the `ViewService` class. You can see this in the following code for the base `ViewService` implementation:

```
using System;
using Microsoft.Practices.Unity;

namespace MVVM.Framework
{
    public class ViewService
    {
        public IUnityContainer Container
        {
            Get;
          set;
        }
    }
}
```

Again, if you are unfamiliar with the concepts of IoC containers, take the time to familiarize yourself with their capabilities. For the purposes of this framework, you will simply be utilizing the Unity container to create new instances of the specified Views and ViewModels as needed. You see how this is accomplished in the next section.

For now, the first capability you add to the `ViewService` class is the capability to maintain a list of Views and ViewModels in a "registry." This registry can be nothing more than a generic dictionary of types used to look up types. The following line of code needs to be added to the `ViewService` class to provide storage for the registry:

```
private Dictionary<Type, Type> viewModelRegistry = new
        Dictionary<Type, Type>();
```

Within this dictionary, you utilize the "key" to store the type of ViewModel, and the "value" stores the type of View associated. The concept of using the dictionary can inherently enforce a one-view-per-one-ViewModel limitation with the framework.

The MVVM framework developed in this chapter keeps track of a View-ViewModel registry that is keyed on the ViewModel and not the View. The primary implication of this choice is that it makes this framework very ViewModel-centric. When developers want to display a particular View, they indicate this by providing the ViewService with the type of the corresponding ViewModel. Then the framework uses the registry to look up the appropriate type of View, and handles the creation of an instance of both, assigning the data context, and displaying the View. Many MVVM frameworks are also keyed on the View and, although they work in fundamentally the same way, developers specify the type of View they want, and the type of ViewModel is inferred through various means.

So, how do you leverage this ViewModel registry and provide access to developers to make the association between Views and ViewModels? The first means to provide this association can be to add a single method to the `ViewService` class called `RegisterView`, as shown here:

```
public void RegisterView(Type viewModelType, Type viewType)
{
    if (!typeof(IViewModel).IsAssignableFrom(viewModelType))
    {
        throw new ArgumentOutOfRangeException("ViewModelType does
            not implement IViewModel");
    }

    _viewModelRegistry[viewModelType] = viewType;
}
```

The `RegisterView` method accepts both a type of View and a type of ViewModel, and after validating that the provided View implements `IViewModel`, it simply adds the values to the dictionary.

What might seem unusual at first is that this registry works with types, and not with explicit instances of a View or a ViewModel. Instead of accepting objects of type `IViewModel` and `UserControl`, you accept two instances of `System.Type`.

The reason for this is that, when configuring this registry, you do not want to create a new ViewModel but are instead preparing for some point later in the overall process when a developer wants to actually show something. At this point, the correct View and ViewModel will be created in memory.

Also, the same type of View and ViewModel pair might be created and shown many times simultaneously. (Think Visual Studio tabs displaying multiple instances of the C# code editor in different tabs.) Your registry must enforce only one entry per ViewModel, and this is achieved through the simple use of the generic `Dictionary<K, V>` class as the in-memory storage.

If you deal with types and not instances, how would a developer make the association between a View and a ViewModel? The following code provides an example of how this is done using the C# `typeof` keyword:

```
viewService.RegisterView(typeof(PersonViewModel), typeof
    (PersonView));
```

In this code snippet, you simply tell the `ViewService` class that, whenever a developer wants to create and utilize a ViewModel called `PersonViewModel`, you will use and display a new instance of the `PersonView` class as the visual representation for the UI.

When would a call to `RegisterView` be executed within your project? A call to `RegisterView` would need to occur only once and would generally occur during the startup or initialization phase of your application. As a developer, you must make a single call to `RegisterView` for every View/ViewModel pair within your application, which could be dozens or even hundreds in large applications. Unfortunately, this again could become error-prone (and cumbersome) and requires that you remember to add these lines of code to your startup every time you create a new View and ViewModel pair.

A better approach would be to implement a means to programmatically tag a view with the type of ViewModel to which it should be associated. You can achieve this through the use of .NET attributes. You can create a fairly basic .NET attribute and then decorate each View class with this attribute to specify its associated ViewModel class.

In addition, to achieve the desired effect, you must add a bit more functionality to the `ViewService` class to scan a provided .NET assembly for all Views tagged with this attribute and add them accordingly to the ViewModel registry. This can provide a more automated means to maintain the registry and can be less error-prone in production. This is generally the route most MVVM frameworks that are built upon MEF use. This implementation can be coded with a similar architecture but will not rely on MEF to import your associations.

For those who are unfamiliar with the concept to develop custom attributes in .NET, this is an excellent example of their use and how simple and powerful they can be both to create and to search for and utilize.

The first step in this new enhancement is to create a new class called `ViewAttribute` within the root of the `MVVM.Framework` project. After the class is created, add the following code:

```
using System;

namespace MVVM.Framework
{
    [AttributeUsage(AttributeTargets.Class)]
    public class ViewAttribute : Attribute
    {
        public ViewAttribute(Type viewModelType)
        {
            ViewModelType = viewModelType;
        }

        private Type viewModelType = null;

        public Type ViewModelType
        {
            get
            {
                return viewModelType;
            }
            set
            {
                if (value == null || !typeof(IViewModel).IsAssignableFrom(value))
                {
                    throw new ArgumentException("Cannot associate view with a
                        class which does not implement IViewModel");
                }

                viewModelType = value;
            }
        }

    }
}
```

Take a moment to review the `ViewAttribute` class to see a few key things:

➤ It inherits from `System.Attribute`, which, by definition, makes it available to use as a custom attribute.

➤ The name of the class (`ViewAttribute`) ends with the word `Attribute`. Although this is not a requirement, this does enable you to shorten the name of the attribute when applying it to its targets. In essence, instead of specifying the full name `[ViewAttribute]` you can simply use `[View]`. You see this in action shortly.

➤ The custom `ViewAttribute` has a single parameter of type `System.Type`, with which you require anyone creating an instance of `ViewAttribute` to specify an `IViewModel` type with which you make your association.

So, what does all this actually mean? It means that if you open up the `HeaderView.xaml.cs` class (that is, the code-behind class for the previously created `HeaderView.xaml` user control), you can now decorate this class with the View attribute, as shown here:

```
[View(typeof(HeaderViewModel))]
public partial class HeaderView : UserControl
{
```

This addition of the `ViewAttribute` to the `HeaderView` class declaration did not require you to utilize the full `ViewAttribute` name. You can use the shortened version because, when using .NET attributes, the suffix `Attribute` is inferred.

At this point, you have a custom attribute you can utilize to decorate View classes, but other than existing in code and being attached to the `HeaderView` class, it is not used for anything. For the `ViewAttribute` to truly be useful to you, you must add another method to the `ViewService` class that looks for classes that have this attribute attached and then registers them accordingly.

To add this functionality, add the following method to the `ViewService` class in the MVVM `.Framework` project:

```
public void RegisterViews(Assembly assembly)
{
    //Get all types in assembly that have the [View] attribute
    var viewTypes =
assembly.GetTypes().Where(t => t.GetCustomAttributes(true).Any(x => x is
    ViewAttribute));

    //Register each found view/viewmodel type
    foreach (var viewType in viewTypes)
    {
        var attribute =
            (ViewAttribute)viewType.GetCustomAttributes(true).Where(x
                => x is ViewAttribute).FirstOrDefault();

        RegisterView(attribute.ViewModelType, viewType);
    }
}
```

Although relatively short, the `RegisterViews` method is one of the more complex methods in the entire example framework. It first accepts a single parameter of type `assembly`. This enables you to actually scan for View and ViewModel pairs across multiple assemblies. This proves to be especially useful in modular architectures such as Microsoft's Prism framework, where an application is broken into multiple module assemblies, each of which may or may not be loaded at runtime.

After you provide the method with an assembly, the first line of code in the `RegisterViews` method utilizes reflection, LINQ, and C# lambda expressions to perform a search through all classes defined in that assembly for any that have the `ViewAttribute` attached to them. When a list of all resulting types is found, you simply loop through the results and register them via the previously provided `RegisterView` method of the `ViewService` class.

With the addition of the `RegisterView` and `RegisterViews` methods to the `ViewService`, you can now utilize a single line of code like the following to automatically find all Views and their associated ViewModels within any .NET assembly:

```
viewService.RegisterViews(Assembly.GetExecutingAssembly());
```

This line of code searches for Views only in the currently executing assembly.

Having the ability to automatically detect any new Views within an assembly is much easier than being forced to add a new line of code to manually associate each View with its respective ViewModel. Also, when the need arises to remove a View from its association with a ViewModel, you can either delete the View entirely, or simply remove the `[View]` attribute from that View, and add it to another View. The `RegisterViews` method can handle the rest the next time you run the application.

Displaying Views

Now look at the pieces you have put in place thus far:

➤ A common ViewModel infrastructure via `IViewModel` and `BaseViewModel`

➤ An initial View and ViewModel called `HeaderView` and `HeaderViewModel`

➤ A custom attribute called `ViewAttribute` you can use to decorate Views to loosely associate them with ViewModels

➤ A location for common MVVM functionality called `ViewService`, including the capability to search for and maintain a registry of View/ViewModel pairs

Thus far, you have quite a bit of the "behind the scenes" infrastructure, and have yet to get to the point where you can make something visible and start to see interaction between a View and a ViewModel. Now, you will start to see where all your hard work begins to pay off.

This section discusses the addition of a single method to the `ViewService` class to display Views, while also configuring the `MVVM.Shell` project to better host the MVVM framework, and to be in a position to display Views.

Because you have already performed much of the legwork, and you now understand a number of the concepts, dive right in by adding the following method to the `ViewService` class:

```
public IViewModel ShowView(ContentControl host, Type viewModelType,
    object parameters)
    {
        if (Container == null)
        {
            throw new ArgumentNullException("Container is null");
        }

        if (host == null)
```

```
    {
        throw new ArgumentNullException("Host");
    }

    if (viewModelType == null)
    {
        throw new ArgumentNullException("ViewModelType");
    }

    if (!typeof(IViewModel).IsAssignableFrom(viewModelType))
    {
        throw new ArgumentOutOfRangeException("Type specified by
            ViewModelType does not implement IViewModel");
    }

    //verify that we have a registered view for this view model
    if (!viewModelRegistry.ContainsKey(viewModelType))
    {
        throw new Exception("No registered view found for specified
            view model");
    }

    //get the type of view we will create from our registry
    Type viewType = viewModelRegistry[viewModelType];

    if (!typeof(UserControl).IsAssignableFrom(viewType))
    {
        throw new ArgumentOutOfRangeException("Type specified by
            ViewType does not inherit from UserControl");
    }

    //use the Unity container to create a new instance of our view
    var view = (UserControl)Container.Resolve(viewType);

    //use the Unity container to create a new instance of our view model
    var viewModel = (IViewModel)Container.Resolve(viewModelType);

    //call any custom initialization code for this view model
    viewModel.Initialize(parameters);

    //make the DataContext property of the view our association between
    //the view and view model
    view.DataContext = viewModel;

    //display the resulting view in the host
    host.Content = view;

    return viewModel;
}
```

The `ShowView` method here might seem to contain the most code for anything you have written thus far, but it is surprisingly simple. It accepts three parameters: an instance of a `ContentControl`, a `System.Type` instance representing the type of ViewModel you want to use, and a parameter called `Parameters` that represents some arbitrary data you want to pass to the resulting ViewModel.

The bulk of the code in the ShowView method is actually code checking the validity of the parameters and verifying they are what you expect. Although this type of defensive programming can be done a number of ways and is valuable in most (if not all) methods that you write, more of this type of code is included here to emphasize that, in an MVVM framework such as you develop here, a method such as ShowView will be one of the most utilized. ShowView will be called more than any other method throughout the entire application and, thus, will make it the most prone to errors in which the calling developer inadvertently passes in parameters specifying incorrect values.

If you take out all the parameter validation found in the ShowView method just to review what remains, you are left with the following few lines of code:

```
//use the Unity container to create a new instance of our view
var view = (UserControl)Container.Resolve(viewType);

//use the Unity container to create a new instance of our view model
var viewModel = (IViewModel)Container.Resolve(viewModelType);

//call any custom initialization code for this view model
viewModel.Initialize(parameters);

//make the DataContext property of the view our association between the view
//and view model
view.DataContext = viewModel;

//display the resulting view in the host
host.Content = view;

return viewModel;
```

The first thing you do is use your View/ViewModel registry to find the View associated with the requested ViewModel. When you have this type, you utilize the Unity IoC container to resolve (or create) a new instance of this View. The use of the IoC container here offers some nice benefits because you can have a container that has "dependencies" via constructor parameters or public properties that are resolved (or "injected") via Unity. When you have a new instance of your View, you again use the Unity container, and this time instantiate a new instance of your ViewModel (again relying on the IoC concept to resolve all dependencies).

The next thing you do is call the Initialize method of the new ViewModel, thus giving the specific ViewModel the opportunity to begin loading its data, or to perform any other initialization work. When the Initialize method has been called, you immediately make the DataContext assignment discussed earlier so that the elements within the View can easily be data-bound to properties of the ViewModel.

You then assign the View (which is a visible UserControl) to be the Content property of the ContentControl provided as a parameter. This results in your View now displaying within the UI area assigned to the ContentControl (specified by the Host parameter).

The final step is to return the IViewModel instance back to the caller. This is useful in scenarios in which a developer making a call to ShowView wants to retain a reference to the created

ViewModel to be notified of changes, or to otherwise maintain a connection to the data being displayed. It is worth noting that the ViewModel never has a reference to the View that is being used to display it.

One thing you may have noticed about the approach being followed here is that it is heavily ViewModel-centric. You created common functionality for ViewModels, and your interfaces tend to expose things as ViewModels and, more specifically, classes implementing the `IViewModel` interface. When using this type of framework, developers are forced to think in terms of ViewModels and let the framework determine which View is appropriate. This is by design and focuses on getting developers to adhere to the MVVM pattern by considering all interfaces by the ViewModels first. Different MVVM frameworks available today are either ViewModel-centric or View-centric in how they force developers to deal with these concepts.

The next step is to put together a shell to "host" your Views and ViewModels so that you can actually see one displayed. One of the key things to consider in any architecture is how all the moving pieces fit together at runtime. In this case, you have some setup that must occur upon application startup to help get the right components in place. This setup includes such things as the creation and tracking of your View service, as well as the registering of your Views and ViewModels via calls to `RegisterViews`.

With IoC components such as Unity, or with the use of an extensibility framework like MEF, there are many common patterns for registering and locating key services or functionality. To keep this chapter focused on MVVM framework, the primary concern here is the capability to track a single instance of `ViewService` so that you can maximize the use of a single View/ViewModel registry.

An easy way to make this possible is simply to make your `ViewService` class a singleton. Another possibility would be to make it a simple static class. For the purposes of this discussion, make the `ViewService` a singleton.

You can make the `ViewService` a singleton by adding the following code:

```
private static ViewService currentInstance = null;

private ViewService()
{
    //This code exists to make the ViewService constructor private
}

public static ViewService Current
{
    get
    {
        if (currentInstance == null)
        {
            currentInstance = new ViewService();
        }
        return currentInstance;
    }
}
```

After it is added inside the `ViewService` class, this code converts your class into a singleton through two steps:

1. The constructor of the `ViewService` class is declared as `private`. This disallows developers from directly instantiating new instances of `ViewService` from their own code (thus creating multiple copies of this class, which is what you do not want).

2. It adds a private `static` field that will be used to maintain a reference to the only instance of `ViewService` within your application. This static field is retrieved via a read-only property called `Current`.

To take advantage of this singleton pattern, and to demonstrate its use, add some initialization code to the example application. A common place to put this is in the `App.Xaml.cs` file of the `MVVM.Shell` project. This is the code file for the primary Silverlight project and will have events that fire during application startup. First, add the following `using` statements to the top of this file:

```
using System.Reflection;
using Microsoft.Practices.Unity;
using MVVM.Framework;
```

Next, add the following few initialization lines to the `Application_Startup` event of the `App` class:

```
private void Application_Startup(object sender, StartupEventArgs e)
{

    ViewService.Current.Container = new UnityContainer();
    ViewService.Current.RegisterViews(Assembly.GetExecutingAssembly());


    this.RootVisual = new MainPage();
}
```

The initialization code demonstrates that the `ViewService` class can be accessed via the static `ViewService.Current` method. Because you do not need to instantiate a new instance here, you can simply assign a new instance of the Unity container to the `Container` property and then utilize the previously implemented `RegisterViews` method to scan the current assembly for all Views tagged with `ViewAttribute`. After this code is executed, you are ready to utilize `ViewService` throughout the rest of the application.

The next step is hooking up your Views to organize the `MainPage.xaml` file into a set of containers to hold them. To do so, you configure the currently empty XAML file to host a grid that provides the general layout of the UI. Each cell of your grid contains a `ContentControl` that you utilize as hosts for the Views in your MVVM architecture.

Add the following XAML to the `MainPage.XAML` file within the `MVVM.Shell` project:

```
<Grid x:Name="LayoutRoot">
    <Grid.ColumnDefinitions>
        <ColumnDefinition Width="*" />
        <ColumnDefinition Width="5*" />
```

```
        </Grid.ColumnDefinitions>
        <Grid.RowDefinitions>
            <RowDefinition Height="Auto" />
            <RowDefinition Height="*" />
            <RowDefinition Height="Auto" />
        </Grid.RowDefinitions>
        <ContentControl x:Name="HeaderContent" Grid.Row="0" Grid.Column="0"
            Grid.ColumnSpan="2" HorizontalContentAlignment="Stretch"
            VerticalContentAlignment="Stretch"/>
        <ContentControl x:Name="FooterContent" Grid.Row="2" Grid.Column="0"
            Grid.ColumnSpan="2" HorizontalContentAlignment="Stretch"
            VerticalContentAlignment="Stretch" />
        <ContentControl x:Name="NavigationContent" Grid.Row="1" Grid.Column="0"
            HorizontalContentAlignment="Stretch"
            VerticalContentAlignment="Stretch"/>
        <ContentControl x:Name="MainContent" Grid.Row="1" Grid.Column="1"
            HorizontalContentAlignment="Stretch"
            VerticalContentAlignment="Stretch"/>
    </Grid>
```

This layout is nothing overtly fancy and instead simply provides a header, a footer, a navigation column on the left, and a main content area in the center of the screen. The `HorizontalContentAlignment` and `VerticalContentAlignment` of all `ContentControl`s are set to `Stretch`. In this particular layout, this can help with some of your aesthetic issues by stretching your Views to fill the cells accordingly.

To begin to put Views into your layout, simply add the following boldfaced line of code to the constructor of the `MainPage.xaml.cs` file:

```
public MainPage()
{
    InitializeComponent();

    ViewService.Current.ShowView(HeaderContent, typeof
        (HeaderViewModel), null);

}
```

With the single call to the `ViewService.ShowView` method, you have effectively utilized your entire MVVM framework. The first parameter passed into this method is the `HeaderContent` control, which is declared in the `MainPage.Xaml` file. The second parameter is the type of ViewModel you want to display. It is critical to understand that you are not passing an instance of the ViewModel, but rather the `System.Type` instance that represents a type of ViewModel. Within the `ShowView` method, you use the Unity container to create a new instance of this type and then utilize your previously initialized registry of Views and ViewModels to find the appropriate View. After all the build-up code has executed, you set the resulting View to be content of the specified host (in this case, `HeaderControl`).

You can now add additional UI components to the `HeaderView` and take advantage of the MVVM infrastructure you've built to bind controls back to the properties of the `HeaderViewModel`.

At this stage, when developers want to add a new screen anywhere within an application, they need to perform the following steps:

1. Create a new ViewModel class that implements `IViewModel` or inherits from `BaseViewModel`.

2. Create a new Silverlight `UserControl` class, and place the `ViewAttribute` on the class declaration.

3. Use the `ViewService.ShowView` method to display the current View into the appropriate user control.

As shown previously in Figure 7-1, you can see the primary "sections" of the screen that make up the header, footer, left navigation, and main content area. Although not all UIs do (or should) follow this pattern, it does demonstrate how even the simplest of interfaces can be broken up into various areas (or "regions") that can be treated as distinct components. In the next section, you develop a more robust way to manage these regions that provide better communication and control for the application as a whole.

Building Composite Screens

It is rare that an application consists of a single View area or that even a single screen is made up of a single View. Take a look at Figure 7-3, which shows a screen shot of a Silverlight application composed of multiple Views (and corresponding ViewModels).

In your framework thus far, you have developed the capability to create Views and ViewModels, and display the results in a single content control. Although this capability is critical, another major hurdle you will soon face is the need to display specific Views in specific regions of the UI, or even display other Views as pop-up windows.

Keeping track of which content control is responsible for displaying the content for a particular region of the UI is key, and you must provide the capability to easily locate these "region" controls. To accomplish this, enhance `ViewService` to enable the tracking of a new set of classes for managing these regions.

In the example framework (and in others such as Microsoft's Prism framework for building composite Silverlight and WPF applications), the term *region* indicates an area of your screen that hosts different Views. For each region in a UI, you create and register a new instance of a class called a *region manager*. The region manager class manages the current View or Views visible within a current region. It also enables you to show or hide Views in a region and get access to the View currently displayed or selected within a region.

To accomplish this, let's define exactly what a region manager is by creating a new interface within the `MVVM.Framework` project called `IRegionManager`. Following is the code for this interface:

```
using System;
using System.Collections.ObjectModel;
using System.Windows.Controls;

namespace MVVM.Framework
{
    public interface IRegionManager
```

```
    {
        IViewModel CurrentView { get; }

        ObservableCollection<IViewModel> OpenViews { get; }

        Control HostControl { get; }

        IViewModel ShowView(Type viewModelType, object parameters);

        void CloseView(IViewModel viewModel);
    }
}
```

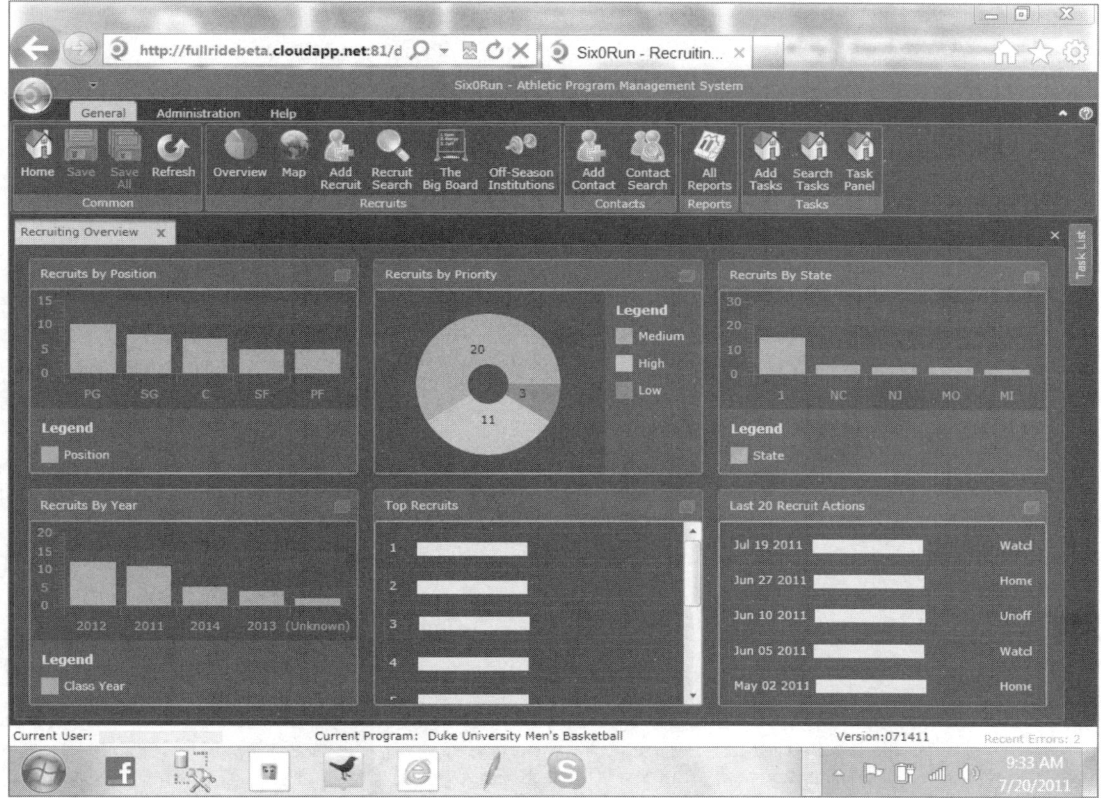

FIGURE 7-3: Silverlight application that is composed of multiple Views

This interface provides a peek at the functionality you will ultimately add to a region manager class. Again, notice that the region manager deals primarily with the `IViewModel` interface. Developers are again asked to utilize ViewModels when working with UIs and to let the framework determine which View is appropriate.

As you can see, the `IRegionManager` class exposes a `CurrentView` property and an `OpenViews` property, both of which are intended to expose information about which ViewModels are currently visible within a particular region. The `HostControl` property of the `IRegionManager` provides access directly to the actual Silverlight control that is currently hosting the region. The ShowView and CloseView methods provide developers with the means to manage the Views within the particular region.

Much like the process followed earlier by providing an abstract BaseViewModel implementation for the IViewModel interface, you again create an abstract class for the IRegionManager class. This can help in creating new region managers by providing a common implementation of specific functionality. Following is the code for the BaseRegionManager implementation:

```
using System;
using System.Collections.ObjectModel;
using System.Windows.Controls;

namespace MVVM.Framework
{
    public abstract class BaseRegionManager : BaseObservableObject, IRegionManager
    {
        private readonly ObservableCollection<IViewModel> openViews = new
            ObservableCollection<IViewModel>();
        private IViewModel currentViewModel;
        private Control hostControl;

        public IViewModel CurrentView
        {
            get { return currentViewModel; }
            protected set
            {
                currentViewModel = value;
                OnPropertyChanged("CurrentView");
            }
        }

        public ObservableCollection<IViewModel> OpenViews
        {
            get { return openViews; }
        }

        public Control HostControl
        {
            get { return hostControl; }
            protected set
            {
                hostControl = value;
                OnPropertyChanged("HostControl");
            }
        }

        public abstract IViewModel ShowView(Type viewModelType, object parameters);

        public abstract void CloseView(IViewModel viewModel);
    }
}
```

The `BaseRegionManager` implementation provides a simple implementation of the `IRegionManager` properties but specifies both `ShowView` and the `CloseView` as being abstract methods. This forces any developers implementing the `BaseRegionManager` to provide their own implementation of these methods. `BaseRegionManager` is nothing more than an abstract "middle layer" intended to simplify the implementation of a set of region managers for specific types of regions.

The first implementation of a region manager will be one called `SingleViewRegionManager`. As the name implies, `SingleViewRegionManager` is meant to handle the interaction with a basic `ContentControl` region that hosts a single View/ViewModel UI at a time. The `CurrentView` property provides access to the single View being displayed, and the `OpenViews` collection always exposes only a single ViewModel (or none, if no View is currently being displayed).

You must add the `SingleViewRegionManager` class to the root of the `MVVM.Framework` project. The full implementation of a `SingleViewRegionManager` is as follows:

```csharp
using System;
using System.Windows.Controls;

namespace MVVM.Framework
{
    public class SingleViewRegionManager : BaseRegionManager
    {
        public SingleViewRegionManager(ContentControl contentHost)
        {
            if (contentHost == null)
            {
                throw new ArgumentNullException("ContentHost");
            }

            HostControl = contentHost;
        }

        public override IViewModel ShowView(Type viewModelType, object parameters)
        {
            if (CurrentView != null)
            {
                CloseView(CurrentView);
            }

            IViewModel viewModel =
                ViewService.Current.ShowView((ContentControl)
                HostControl, viewModelType, parameters);

            CurrentView = viewModel;

            OpenViews.Add(viewModel);

            return viewModel;
        }

        public override void CloseView(IViewModel viewModel)
```

```
        {
            if (CurrentView.Equals(viewModel))
            {
                CurrentView = null;
                OpenViews.Clear();
                ((ContentControl)HostControl).Content = null;
            }
        }
    }
}
```

As you can see, this implementation is fairly simple and leans heavily on the `BaseRegionManager` implementation from which it inherits. There are some significant points to make about the `SingleViewRegionManager`.

The constructor for this class accepts a single parameter of type `ContentControl` and validates that this control is passed in correctly. With this constructor in place, every `SingleViewRegionManager` control must be directly associated with a single `ContentControl`. At this stage, your framework does nothing to limit multiple region managers from attempting to manage the content for the same `ContentControl`, but this is something that is definitely possible.

The `ShowView` method of the `SingleViewRegionManager` utilizes the previously written `ViewService.ShowView` method to perform the actual work of creating and associating the Views and ViewModels after correctly closing any View that is already visible.

The `CloseView` method clears out any visible content and cleans up the `CurrentView` property and `OpenViews` collection.

Because this particular region manager is meant for scenarios in which only a single View is visible at a time, the implementation is relatively straightforward.

So, now that you have invested some time to create a region manager interface, a base class, and a single implementation, you must begin to hook up this infrastructure to see it in action.

First, find some way to globally keep track of your region managers in a central location available to any areas of your application. Again, you utilize the `ViewService` class as the central location and add the following to `ViewService` to help keep track of your region managers:

```
private readonly Dictionary<string, IRegionManager> regionManagers =
    new Dictionary<string, IRegionManager>();

public void RegisterRegionManager(string regionName,
            IRegionManager regionManager)
{
    if (regionManager == null || string.IsNullOrEmpty(regionName))
    {
        throw new ArgumentException("Invalid arguments");
    }

    regionManagers[regionName] = regionManager;
}
```

```
public IRegionManager GetRegionManager(string regionName)
{
    return regionManagers[regionName];
}
```

In the code above, we use another generic dictionary class to keep track of your region managers. Each region manager will be assigned a string name to help you globally locate it. The `RegisterRegionManager` and `GetRegionManager` methods simply provide controlled access to this central registry.

Next, you must put the entire region manager infrastructure to use and hook it into your `MainPage` class (which is the location being utilized for this initialization code). To do this requires rewriting the code you had previously in the constructor of your `MainPage` class in the `MVVM.Shell` to look like the following:

```
public MainPage()
{
    InitializeComponent();

    //register our dialog region manager...
    ViewService.Current.RegisterRegionManager("Dialog",
        new DialogRegionManager());

    var headerRegion = new SingleViewRegionManager(HeaderContent);
    var navigationRegion =
  new SingleViewRegionManager(NavigationContent);

    var footerRegion = new SingleViewRegionManager(FooterContent);
    var mainRegion = new SingleViewRegionManager(MainContent);

    ViewService.Current.RegisterRegionManager("Header", headerRegion);
    ViewService.Current.RegisterRegionManager("Footer", footerRegion);
    ViewService.Current.RegisterRegionManager("Navigation",
                    navigationRegion);
    ViewService.Current.RegisterRegionManager("Main", mainRegion);

    headerRegion.ShowView(typeof(HeaderViewModel), null);
    navigationRegion.ShowView(typeof(NavigationViewModel), null);
    footerRegion.ShowView(typeof(FooterViewModel), null);
    mainRegion.ShowView(typeof(PersonViewModel), null);
}
```

This configuration is broken into three sections for readability:

> ➤ The first section creates four `SingleViewRegionManager` instances related to the header, footer, navigation, and main content controls.

> ➤ Next, using the previously discussed `RegisterRegionManager` method of the `ViewService`, you register each of these View managers with a simple string name for future identification and retrieval.

> ➤ Finally, you use the `ShowView` method of each region manager to provide an initial display.

This sample references three ViewModels for which you have no implementation. If you download and review the sample code provided with this chapter (from this book's companion website at www.wrox.com*), you can see a full implementation of the framework that includes Views and ViewModels for the footer and navigation, and an edit screen for a fictitious "Person" object. If you enter the preceding code without the navigation, footer, and person ViewModels, just do not enter the last three lines of code.*

With the appropriate region managers registered during your initialization phase, you can (from anywhere within your application) show a View in the main View area with a single line such as the following:

```
ViewService.Current.GetRegionManager("Main").ShowView(typeof(PersonViewModel),
    null);
```

With every View you have displayed thus far, you pass in a null *value for your parameters. If necessary, you could pass any object for your parameters, and this value would be passed to the* IViewModel.Initialize *method.*

Displaying Dialogs

To demonstrate the flexibility of the region manager infrastructure, take a look at one more region manager implementation that you can use to display Views as pop-up windows using the Silverlight Control Toolkit. To do this, you create a `DialogRegionManager` class in the `MVVM.Framework` project. Following is the code for this class:

```
using System;
using System.Collections.Generic;
using System.Linq;
using System.Windows;
using System.Windows.Controls;
using System.Windows.Data;

namespace MVVM.Framework
{
    public class DialogRegionManager : BaseRegionManager
    {
        private readonly Dictionary<IViewModel, ChildWindow> openWindows =
                new Dictionary<IViewModel, ChildWindow>();

        public override IViewModel ShowView(Type viewModelType,
                        object parameters)
        {
            var childWindow = new ChildWindow();
```

```csharp
            IViewModel viewModel = ViewService.Current.ShowView(childWindow,
                        viewModelType, parameters);

        AddBinding(viewModel, "Title", childWindow,
                    ChildWindow.TitleProperty);
        AddBinding(viewModel, "Height", childWindow,
                    ChildWindow.HeightProperty);
        AddBinding(viewModel, "Width", childWindow,
                    ChildWindow.WidthProperty);

        openWindows[viewModel] = childWindow;
        childWindow.Closed += childWindowClosed;

        childWindow.Show();
        return viewModel;
    }

    private void childWindowClosed(object sender, EventArgs e)
    {
        KeyValuePair<IViewModel, ChildWindow> item =
            openWindows.Where(x =>
          x.Value.Equals(sender)).FirstOrDefault();

        item.Value.Closed -= childWindowClosed;

        openWindows.Remove(item.Key);
    }

    public override void CloseView(IViewModel viewModel)
    {
        if (openWindows.ContainsKey(viewModel))
        {
            openWindows[viewModel].Close();
        }
    }

    private static void AddBinding(object sourceObject, string sourcePath,
                        DependencyObject destinationObject,
                        DependencyProperty destinationProperty)
    {
        var sourceBinding = new Binding(sourcePath);
        sourceBinding.Source = sourceObject;
        sourceBinding.Mode = BindingMode.TwoWay;

        BindingOperations.SetBinding(destinationObject,
                destinationProperty, sourceBinding);
    }
    }
}
```

Without examining every line of the `DialogRegionManager` implementation, a few points are worth noting. First, this region manager requires a reference to the `System.Windows.Controls.dll` found in the Silverlight Control Toolkit. Within this assembly is an infrastructure to display a Silverlight

`ChildWindow` control. The dialog region manager provided here does not support displaying the dialog modally, and execution of code continues immediately upon a call to `ShowView`.

For `DialogRegionManager` to be made available throughout your application, you must register it upon startup of the application by adding the following line to the constructor of the `MainPage` class in the `MVVM.Shell` project:

```
ViewService.Current.RegisterRegionManager("Dialog", new
        DialogRegionManager());
```

After this code has been added to your initialization, you can now display any ViewModel and View as a dialog window with code similar to the following:

```
ViewService.Current.GetRegionManager("Dialog").ShowView(typeof
        (AboutViewModel), null);
```

Although the `DialogRegionManager` does not manage a particular region of a specific UI, it does demonstrate the flexibility of the architecture in that various types of region managers can be developed to manage the same View/ViewModel pairs within the context of different types of hosts, or even as dialogs. Registering these various region managers and making them available from a central location allows them to be utilized globally within an application and provides all components the capability to access the currently displayed ViewModel classes in any particular region.

A major missing piece so far is the lack of more types of region managers. At this point, you have a region manager for working with areas of an interface that can have only one View open at a time, and a region manager that displays Views as dialog windows.

In a more production-oriented framework, you would incorporate region managers for regions that allow for multiple Views (such as tabbed View managers or list View managers). These are fairly straightforward, and plugging such region managers into the flexible region manager infrastructure is left as an exercise for you to do. You now have the foundation for such implementations by including a collection of `OpenViews` on your `IRegionManager` interface. The two provided region managers do not take full advantage of this collection, but more robust region managers would do so.

Communicating Between Views

Now that you have the capability to conceptualize your entire UI as a set of distinct regions (albeit with a limited number of region managers), you are faced with the frequent need to communicate from one ViewModel to another. A good example of this would be if you would like the title of the currently visible ViewModel being displayed in the "Main" region to be displayed in the `HeaderViewModel`. This is a common need in applications and will be the first time you take advantage of the `Title` property of your ViewModels.

To get access to the current ViewModel displayed in any particular region, you can now utilize code such as the following:

```
var _currentMainView = ViewService.Current.GetRegionManager("Main").CurrentView;
```

If you evaluate the source code for the `HeaderView` and `HeaderViewModel` in the provided sample application, you can see an example of how one ViewModel (`HeaderViewModel`) can listen for changes to a property of another ViewModel to display the title of the main view. The implementation provided in the code for download accompanying this book keeps the title of the current main view visible within the UI of the header.

Another key means of communication between Views is the concept of a messaging infrastructure that utilizes a centralized system for raising and reacting to message. Neither the `ViewService` class nor the region manager classes you have implemented within this sample framework expose any type of messaging infrastructure to notify others when key actions related to Views occur. Adding such messages to triggers such as opening a new View or closing a View is left for you to do on your own, which can add significant value to this type of framework. Many of the more robust MVVM frameworks discussed later in this chapter support some type of loosely coupled messaging capability to help provide a more complete MVVM solution.

Putting the MVVM Framework to Use

You have reached a point in the development of this example framework in which you have created a number of useful classes and services you could utilize across a wide array of Silverlight applications. By isolating all framework-specific components into the `MVVM.Framework` class library, you can easily reuse this library on multiple projects.

To achieve the most consistency, you should also standardize on some of the initialization infrastructure and add some additional region managers for more complex scenarios. But, given the code provided, it is reasonable to assume that a new Silverlight project could be started, and the new framework incorporated with little work. The components provided are small enough and flexible enough to also be easily incorporated into an existing application.

It should be obvious that there are a number of key components missing from this example framework that would be critical to any common LOB application. These would include reusable components for such things as logging, caching, data access, security, and other core services. Other chapters in this book touch on some of these topics, whereas solutions to others are frequently discussed on blogs or articles throughout the Internet.

EXISTING MVVM FRAMEWORKS

The previous sections of this chapter focused on the development of a custom framework for managing the complexity of an MVVM project. This framework was developed from scratch with little dependencies on external components beyond Microsoft's Unity container and some components from the Silverlight 4 Toolkit. Although you accomplished the goal to provide core MVVM functionality, the true question is what is the goal of this framework?

As discussed at the beginning of this endeavor, you should have gained some value from working through the provided code and grown the provided framework into something that provides direct value to you and your team. Some of you may evaluate the provided implementation and use it to increase your knowledge of such frameworks to a point in which you can better evaluate and select from one of the many existing MVVM frameworks.

There is no right answer or "silver bullet" for which framework best suits the needs of a particular team. I like various aspects of many frameworks, and dislike others. I try to choose the right tool for the job and then absorb the better ideas and incorporate those into my own designs and platforms.

To help give you some initial guidance on your search for an appropriate MVVM framework, the following sections provide some guidance on various frameworks you might consider as the foundation for your own MVVM platform.

Prism

Although not directly an MVVM framework, Microsoft Prism is a great foundation on which to consider building your MVVM applications. The newest version of the Prism framework, version 4, provides a reference MVVM application that includes a large amount of documentation and sample applications.

Prism provides a complete bootstrap infrastructure to standardize your application startup, an extremely useful composite UI infrastructure to manage your screen regions, a loosely coupled event aggregator, and a nice system for modularizing your applications into separate projects that can be loaded into a common shell at runtime.

In addition, Prism provides a common framework that shares a significant amount of code between Silverlight, WPF, and Windows 7 applications. This means that the concepts and patterns you learn for developing a Prism application for one technology are immediately applicable to other technologies.

Although the Prism framework provides a significant amount of great functionality, its lack of a standard MVVM implementation is a slight drawback. The reference implementation serves as more of a demonstration than a foundation of reusable components. To make up for this, there are many great articles and blog posts on building more MVVM capabilities into the standard Prism framework.

Prism does come with a significant amount of documentation to help get developers started, and the CodePlex community is a great resource for those with questions on specific features or capabilities.

Prism is Open Source and available from Microsoft at `http://compositewpf` `.codeplex.com,` *and can also be installed via NuGet.*

MVVM Light

The MVVM Light framework is a framework focused more on providing a common set of MVVM components for Silverlight, WPF, and Windows 7 Phone developers. In this way, it is similar to the basic framework you put together in this chapter (although significantly more feature-rich and documented).

Some of the highlights of the MVVM Light framework are that it provides a large amount of nice services for developers to build upon or use directly out-of-the-box. MVVM Light also ships with

Visual Studio project templates and code snippets that greatly simplify many common MVVM tasks and the setup of new projects built on the MVVM Light framework.

MVVM Light also has a significant amount of documentation and guidance available and has a great user community to go to for support as necessary.

The MVVM Light framework is, like Prism, provided as an Open Source solution and is also hosted on CodePlex at `http://mvvmlight.codeplex.com`. *MVVM Light is also available via NuGet.*

Caliburn.Micro

Caliburn.Micro is another popular foundation for building MVVM applications. Caliburn.Micro has a significant amount of infrastructure to support both MVVM and other UI patterns such as Model-View-Controller (MVC) and Model-View-Presenter (MVP). Caliburn provides a solid foundation for using commands and messaging and an extensible application model. Caliburn.Micro is extremely lightweight and provides some great convention-based patterns for automatically binding action controls such as buttons to ViewModel methods, but also to easily configure data binding. Caliburn.Micro also features the capability for developers to work in a View-centric or ViewModel-centric mode.

Like the two previously mentioned frameworks, Caliburn.Micro is full-featured, as well as heavily supported and documented. In some ways, Caliburn.Micro offers a significantly more full-featured framework than either Prism or MVVM Light.

Caliburn.Micro is also hosted on CodePlex and can be found at `http://cali-` `burnmicro.codeplex.com/`.

Other Frameworks

Beyond the three frameworks highlighted here, a quick Internet search can point you to dozens of other Silverlight, WPF, or Windows 7 MVVM frameworks. Some of these frameworks are innovative solutions to the common problems discussed throughout this chapter, whereas others are creative ways to build upon other platforms, such as Prism or MVVM Light.

Different frameworks are going to provide different solutions to the same problems, and each uses a mixture of the same common components (such as IoC containers or MEF) to achieve its specific goals. You should review any frameworks you can before making the decision that any one is a better platform for your application.

In addition to evaluating a framework for specific features, some developers simply "get" certain frameworks more than others that they may struggle to comprehend. This understanding is key to the successful adoption of any framework, so it is worth weighing that before making your final decision.

ADDITIONAL CONSIDERATIONS

Now that you have put a fairly substantial amount of MVVM "plumbing" in place for use in streamlining the usage of Views and ViewModels, spend a little time examining some of the addition items you must consider as a developer moving into this type of framework.

At this point, your code has been focused on managing the complexity surrounding keeping track of Views and ViewModels, associating them with each other, and displaying them within the appropriate areas of a UI. Although managing the Views and ViewModels is important, it is only one part of a much bigger picture when considering your standard LOB applications. Unfortunately, as a developer, you must have a thorough understanding of a wide array of concepts to be truly effective at building great Silverlight applications.

This section points out a few of those areas as a means to provide guidance on which areas can be useful for developers to perform additional research.

Data Binding

To be efficient in this type of environment, you must be fluent in the data binding and various patterns for keeping properties of the ViewModel in sync with the visually represented state of the user controls displayed in the View. The framework developed in this chapter (as well as any other MVVM framework you might use) can assist with the management of the components, but typically do little to provide assistance with the actual interaction between the Views and the Models.

Although this chapter has emphasized the advantages of MVVM, end users do not care about such low-level implementation details, and they simply see the application as a means for them to interact with some data or other UI elements. From this standpoint, a thorough understanding of the user experience is important, and it would benefit any Silverlight developer to become as knowledgeable as possible on the syntax and capabilities of this.

Commands

One key area of complexity many developers struggle with in working with MVVM is the capability to react to button clicks or other action events on the View and to execute code that interacts with the ViewModel. This is easily achieved through the use of the `ICommand` infrastructure built into Silverlight.

The `ICommand` interface enables developers to encapsulate the actions triggered by action controls into a set of reusable "command" classes. In Silverlight, action controls such as the button each have a property called `Command` that can be set or bound to any class that supports the `ICommand` interface. A number of efficient patterns exist for implementing your own `ICommand` classes and managing this interaction. Many developers have their own standards they follow in this regard.

The sample framework provided with the source code for this chapter provides an implementation of a `DelegateCommand` class that utilizes lambda expressions to propagate the execution of actions back to methods of the ViewModel. The use of some type of command delegate is common in many Silverlight and WPF frameworks and eliminates the need to create many small command objects that provide little value.

Data Access

This chapter has intentionally stayed away from discussions on the possible means of data access available to Silverlight developers. Any LOB application (whether written utilizing MVVM) will have the need to query some source of data, and to possibly submit changes to this data back to a persistent data store.

Because Silverlight is a client-side technology that runs in the browser, direct access to a database is not allowed, and instead communication must pass through the server. Silverlight provides a few powerful options for communicating back to the server, and they all rely solely on WCF as the means to make asynchronous calls from the Silverlight client to an appropriate endpoint to query or submit data.

When on the server, any existing .NET data access technology can be used to query the appropriate relational data (if that type of access is required). EF is a great option for many modern data-access scenarios.

Another great option for data access from Silverlight is the use of the WCF RIA Services infrastructure. Utilizing this framework for data access provides numerous capabilities that are extremely useful in an MVVM architecture. Not only are most of the complexities of WCF abstracted away from the developers, but the generated domain objects are a great fit as the model portion of your framework. These domain classes natively implement the `INotifyPropertyChanged` interface and support the data annotation means of validating data and incorporating business rules. RIA Services is discussed elsewhere in this book, and a review of its capabilities is highly recommended for those looking to build robust Silverlight LOB applications, whether utilizing MVVM.

SUMMARY

This chapter focused on the concepts required to build a basic MVVM framework in Silverlight 4. You have learned about some related concepts and technologies that are worth researching prior to deciding on what direction to take with your own MVVM needs.

This chapter started off by pointing out that the MVVM space does not enjoy a single solution that is widely adopted, but is instead filled with dozens of great solutions that are as different as they are similar. When working with frameworks such as these, what works for one team might be tedious and not a good fit for another, so you should work through the framework provided in this chapter as a means of enhancing your understanding of what most of these frameworks are trying to accomplish. Then, when drawing comparisons to what has been done here to the framework options available to you, you will be in a better position to make a smart decision.

ABOUT THE AUTHOR

Kevin Grossnicklaus founded ArchitectNow, LLC, in 2009, after spending ten years as the .NET Practice Lead and Chief Architect at SSE, a St. Louis-based technology firm. While at SSE, he oversaw the design, implementation, and delivery of mission-critical software applications to dozens of local and national firms. In 2000, while at SSE, Grossnicklaus was as an early adopter of the Microsoft .NET platform (then called the Next Generation of Web Services, or NGWS), and became active in the local development community, sharing his knowledge and experience with these tools and technologies with any developers willing to learn. Since then, he has worked with developers throughout the world on many projects around the newest .NET technologies. In 2004, Grossnicklaus became an instructor at Washington University's Center for the Application of Information Technology (CAIT) program, where he continues to teach all of the .NET-related topics in both C# and VB.NET. Today, through ArchitectNow (`www.architectnow.net`), he is sharing his knowledge of technology with teams around the world.

8

Windows Phone "Mango" for Silverlight Developers

by Alex Golesh

Microsoft Windows Phone 7 brought great opportunities to the mobile developers' community by introducing two familiar development frameworks to the mobile world — Silverlight and XNA. However, the first version of Windows Phone left developers with some unsupported scenarios, and the platform did not support some wanted features. The next version of the Windows Phone operating system, codenamed "Mango," addresses the most popular requests, and even some completely new scenarios, while improving the developer experience.

This chapter familiarizes you with Windows Phone, codenamed Mango (referred to simply as Mango throughout this chapter), by examining the hardware foundation, the software foundation, the application model, and the integration service.

HARDWARE FOUNDATION

As announced by Microsoft, all Windows Phone 7 devices will be supported by Mango. Also, the newer generation of Windows Phone devices will support additional hardware components, such as the gyroscope sensor and a new system on chip (SoC). To support the new hardware components and improve usage scenarios for existing components, the Mango release adds several new APIs.

Let's take a closer look at two important new APIs: the Camera API and the Sensors API.

Camera API

With the Mango release, developers can access a live camera feed, which enables some interesting scenarios (such as augmented reality applications, live image processing, and others).

Mango provides two alternatives for using the on-board camera: Silverlight's 4 Webcamera APIs and the completely new `PhotoCamera` class. Let's take a closer look at these APIs so that you can understand the differences between them.

The Silverlight 4 Webcamera approach should be familiar to Silverlight developers. It can be shared (both in terms of XAML and code-behind) with desktop applications. It uses the `CaptureSource` class from `System.Windows.Media` namespace and supports the capturing of video, still images, and audio. `CaptureSource` is used as a source for `VideoBrush` instances to show a live camera preview.

Consider the following simple user interface (UI):

```
<Rectangle Width="780" Height="460" Margin="10">
    <Rectangle.Fill>
        <VideoBrush x:Name="previewVideo"/>
    </Rectangle.Fill>
</Rectangle>
```

This XAML code snippet defines a rectangle that is filled with a `VideoBrush` named `"previewVideo"`.

The following code snippet initializes a `CaptureSource` instance and assigns it as a source to the `VideoBrush`:

```
captureSource = new CaptureSource();
captureSource.VideoCaptureDevice =
    CaptureDeviceConfiguration.GetDefaultVideoCaptureDevice();

previewVideo.SetSource(captureSource);

captureSource.Start();
```

This simple technique enables a live camera feed onscreen. In addition, you can use `CaptureSource` to capture still images.

To capture the image, `CaptureSource` provides an asynchronous method (`CaptureImageAsync`) and two events that handle successful and unsuccessful capture attempts. It is up to the developer to subscribe to these events, call the method, and handle the results, as shown here:

```
captureSource.CaptureImageCompleted += new
    EventHandler<CaptureImageCompletedEventArgs>
    (captureSource_CaptureImageCompleted);
captureSource.CaptureFailed += new
    EventHandler<ExceptionRoutedEventArgs>
    (captureSource_CaptureFailed);

//...
captureSource.CaptureImageAsync();

//...
void captureSource_CaptureFailed(object sender, ExceptionRoutedEventArgs e)
{
    //Error processing goes here...
}
```

```
//...
void captureSource_CaptureImageCompleted(object sender,
    CaptureImageCompletedEventArgs e)
{
    if (null == e.Error)
    {
    //Capture successful. Captures image is
    //WriteableBitmap in e.Result

    //Images processing goes here…
    }
}
```

As you can see, capturing and previewing the image is a simple process; although, developers have no access to the phone's hardware Camera button, no access to the camera's flash, and no control over the camera's auto-focus. These issues do not exist when using the new `PhotoCamera` class from the `Microsoft.Devices` namespace.

`PhotoCamera` initialization takes time, so if your application page uses this device, you should start initialization at the earliest possible time after `PhotoCamera` class initializations are complete. Override the `OnNavigatedTo` function, and create a new instance of the `PhotoCamera` class, as shown here:

```
protected override void OnNavigatedTo(System.Windows.Navigation.
    NavigationEventArgs e)
{
    photoCamera = new PhotoCamera();
    photoCamera.Initialized +=
        new EventHandler<CameraOperationCompletedEventArgs>
            (photoCamera_Initialized);

    previewVideo.SetSource(photoCamera);

    base.OnNavigatedTo(e);
}
```

The `PhotoCamera` class can be used as a source for `VideoBrush` instances as well. The events of the `PhotoCamera` class can be consumed only after the camera is initialized. Subscribe to camera events in the `Initialized` event handler, as shown here:

```
void photoCamera_Initialized(object sender,
CameraOperationCompletedEventArgs e)
{
    if (photoCamera.IsFlashModeSupported(FlashMode.Auto))
        photoCamera.FlashMode = FlashMode.Auto;

    //Select the lowest available resolution
    photoCamera.Resolution = photoCamera.AvailableResolutions.ElementAt(0);

    photoCamera.AutoFocusCompleted += new
        EventHandler<CameraOperationCompletedEventArgs>
        (photoCamera_AutoFocusCompleted);
```

```
        CameraButtons.ShutterKeyPressed += new
            EventHandler(photoCamera_ButtonFullPress);
        CameraButtons.ShutterKeyHalfPressed += new
            EventHandler(photoCamera_ButtonHalfPress);
        CameraButtons.ShutterKeyReleased += new
            EventHandler(photoCamera_ButtonRelease);
        photoCamera.CaptureCompleted += new
            EventHandler<CameraOperationCompletedEventArgs>
              (photoCamera_CaptureCompleted);
        photoCamera.CaptureImageAvailable += new
            EventHandler<ContentReadyEventArgs>
            (photoCamera_CaptureImageAvailable);
    }
```

The `CameraButtons` class is a `static` class that enables subscribing to the hardware's Camera button events. Because this class is `static`, you must release the event subscription as soon as possible to prevent getting false events, and to release camera-related variables:

```
    protected override void OnNavigatedFrom
        (System.Windows.Navigation.NavigationEventArgs e)
    {
        photoCamera.Initialized -= photoCamera_Initialized;
        photoCamera.AutoFocusCompleted -= photoCamera_AutoFocusCompleted;
        CameraButtons.ShutterKeyPressed -= photoCamera_ButtonFullPress;
        CameraButtons.ShutterKeyHalfPressed -= photoCamera_ButtonHalfPress;
        CameraButtons.ShutterKeyReleased -= photoCamera_ButtonRelease;
        photoCamera.CaptureCompleted -= photoCamera_CaptureCompleted;
        photoCamera.CaptureImageAvailable -= photoCamera_CaptureImageAvailable;

        photoCamera.Dispose();
        photoCamera = null;

        base.OnNavigatedFrom(e);
    }
```

After the camera is initialized and working, you can issue `Focus()` commands (for example, at the `ShutterKeyHalfPressed` event handler) and `CaptureImage()` commands (at the `ShutterKeyPressed` event handler):

```
    void photoCamera_ButtonHalfPress(object sender, EventArgs e)
    {
        photoCamera.Focus();
    }

    void photoCamera_ButtonFullPress(object sender, EventArgs e)
    {
        photoCamera.CaptureImage();
    }
```

Another feature of the `PhotoCamera` class available to developers is the capability to preview buffers in different formats. The `GetPreviewBuffer_XXXX` functions copy the current viewfinder frame into an array to enable frame processing:

```
    int[] pixelData = new int[(int)(photoCamera.PreviewResolution.Width *
        photoCamera.PreviewResolution.Height)];
    photoCamera.GetPreviewBufferArgb32(pixelData);
```

This feature enables applying live effects on the viewfinder's image.

Camera Best Practices

Keep in mind the following when writing code for the Camera APIs:

➤ Use the Webcamera API for simple scenarios and compatibility with desktop solutions.

➤ Use the PhotoCamera API when fine control over the image capturing is needed, or image processing is needed.

➤ Use the lowest possible resolution when processing a live video stream.

➤ Release camera devices as soon as they are no longer needed.

➤ Use `VideoBrush` to present live previews on screen.

Sensors API

The initial release of Windows Phone supported the accelerometer sensor. Mango adds support for three additional sensors:

➤ Gyroscope

➤ Compass (magnetometer)

➤ Motion sensor

All the sensor classes are located in the `Microsoft.Devices.Sensors` namespace and derive from the `SensorBase<T>` abstract class. This means that all sensors have a common usage pattern, and differ only by additional methods and internal implementation. Figure 8-1 shows the general sensor interaction pattern.

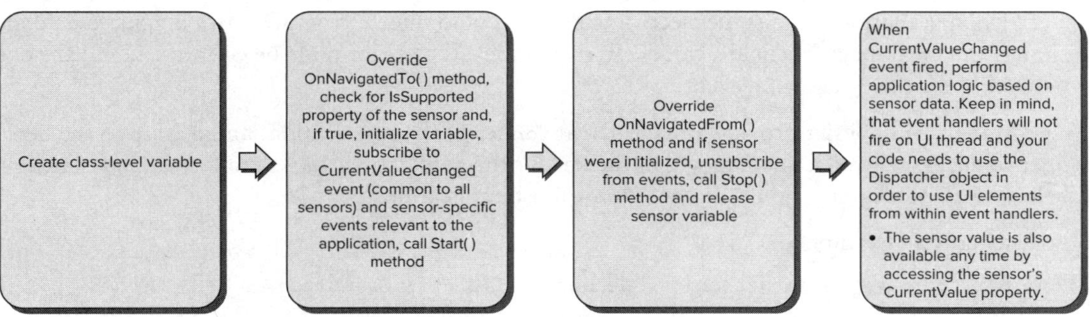

FIGURE 8-1: General sensor interaction pattern

Gyroscope

A *gyroscope* is a device for measuring or maintaining orientation, based on the principles of conservation of angular momentum. In Mango, the Gyroscope API provides the rotational velocity around each one of three axes (X, Y, and Z) of the device in radians per second. This sensor is a new addition to the Windows Phone 7 sensors family. It is optional and exists only on a small number of new devices, and not on original Windows Phone devices.

The `GyroscopeReading` class (exposed via `CurrentValue` property) provides the gyroscope's `RotationRate` (which is the rotational velocities around each one of three axes of the device) and a `Timestamp` (which indicates when the reading was taken).

The gyroscope sensor readings are subject to significant drift.

Compass

The *compass* sensor (also known as the *magnetometer* sensor) provides the following data in its `CurrentValue` property:

➤ `HeadingAccuracy` — This is the accuracy of compass heading readings in degrees. You use this value for compass calibration.

➤ `MagneticHeading` — This is the compass heading relative to Earth's magnetic north (provided in degrees).

➤ `TrueHeading` — This is the compass heading relative to Earth's geographic north (provided in degrees).

➤ `MagnetometerReading` — This is the raw magnetometer reading values in microteslas (that is, values provided in XNA's `Vector3` type). To use these readings, you must add a reference to the `Microsoft.Xna.Framework` assembly.

In addition, the compass sensor enables applications to subscribe to the `Calibrate` event. When this event is fired, the application must present instructions for performing sensor calibration. Sensor calibration is performed by waving the device in a figure-eight pattern. This calibration is required because the magnetometer sensor is subject to external interference. Metal obstacles, high-voltage electrical installations, and some electronic devices could interfere with Earth's magnetic field and change the local magnetic field's values. In these cases, the sensor must be calibrated, and the compass API fires the `Calibrate` event.

The Mango API doesn't provide any `CalibrationComplete` notification, and it is up to the developer to decide when data accuracy is sufficient for the application. In general, `HeadingAccuracy` below 10 to 15 degrees should be enough for most applications.

Following is an example:

```
void compass_Calibrate(object sender, CalibrationEventArgs e)
{
    //Show calibration instructions
    stkCalibration.Visibility = Visibility.Visible;
    //Hide compass sensor related UI
    imgRose.Visibility = Visibility.Collapsed;
    //Set "Is Calibrating" flag to consume it later
    compassCalibrating = true;
}

void compass_CurrentValueChanged(object sender,
    SensorReadingEventArgs<CompassReading> e)
```

```
    {
        //Check if compass is calibrating
        if (compassCalibrating)
        {
            //Check if current HeadingAccuracy below threshold value
            if (e.SensorReading.HeadingAccuracy < 10)
            {
                //Compass calibrated, restore the compass UI
                compassCalibrating = false;

                //...
            }
        }

        if (!compassCalibrating)
        //Compass calibrated, use the data
        //...
    }
```

Motion

The *motion* sensor is a virtual sensor that combines the gyroscope, compass, and accelerometer sensors. The motion sensor performs math calculations to combine data from all sensors. The data is combined using an algorithm that compensates for the inaccuracies of each independent sensor, making the motion sensor the most accurate sensor.

The motion sensor should be used when available, and should be preferable over each independent sensor. The availability of this sensor depends on the physical sensors available on the device. Table 8-1 summarizes the availability of the motion sensor.

TABLE 8-1: Motion Sensor Availability

ACCELEROMETER	COMPASS	GYROSCOPE	MOTION
Yes	Yes	Yes	Yes (full quality)
Yes	Yes	No	Yes (degraded quality)
Yes	No	Yes	No
Yes	No	No	No

In Table 8-1, "degraded quality" means that sensor data is still available, but the values are subject to some approximations. If the `IsSupported` property of the motion sensor is `false`, applications should use the accelerometer (which is always available because it is required by basic hardware specification for all Windows Phone 7 devices) and other input and control mechanisms.

The motion sensor requires calibration over time because it uses compass sensor data. The calibration process is similar to compass calibration.

Sensors Best Practices

Keep the following in mind when working with sensors:

- ➤ Always use the `Motion` sensor when available.

- ➤ Always check the `IsSupported` property for any sensor before initializing/using it in your application.

- ➤ Initialize sensors only when needed, and release them as soon as possible (when they are no longer needed).

- ➤ Always prepare backup input and control mechanisms if certain sensors are not available on the device.

- ➤ Those changes in the hardware platform benefit most when combined with changes made in the software foundation.

SOFTWARE FOUNDATION

In this section, you will learn about what's new in Mango with regard to the runtime and tools.

Runtime Improvements

From a developer's standpoint, the biggest improvement in Mango is Silverlight 4 integration. Although the initial release of Windows Phone enabled Silverlight 3 development with some phone-specific additions, Mango brings the capability to use the full Silverlight 4 development environment with powerful features such as implicit styles, `RichTextBox` control, `ViewBox` control, touch-event support (such as tap, double-tap, and so on) and languages support (for example, for Register Transfer Languages, or RTLs).

In addition, Mango brings many performance improvements over previous versions of Windows Phone, such as a generational Garbage Collector (GC), separate input thread, and profiler support.

Tools Enhancements

Mango introduces many enhancements in Visual Studio 2010 to help developers create better applications. Mango tools provide better developer support for developing sensor-enabled applications.

In the previous release, developing an accelerometer-enabled or a GPS-enabled (location-aware) application required a developer-unlocked phone device, or some community solution to emulate sensor input. With the Mango release, sensor emulation is supported by the Windows Phone Emulator. To emulate accelerometer or location readings, open the Additional Tools window in the Emulator, as shown in Figure 8-2.

FIGURE 8-2: Additional Tools window in the Emulator

The opened Additional Tools window enables accelerometer and location-change emulation. To simulate the accelerometer data, move the pink ball using the mouse, as shown in Figure 8-3.

The Location tab (shown in Figure 8-4) enables you not only to send the current location to the Windows Phone Emulator, but also to record a virtual path through specified geographical points, and send them at given time intervals to emulate the device's movement.

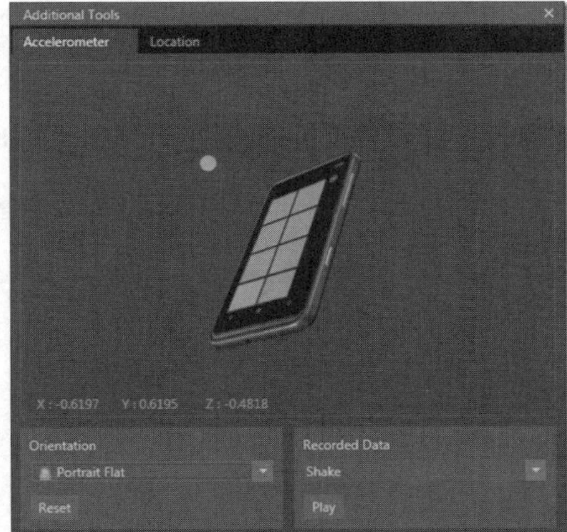

FIGURE 8-3: Simulating accelerometer data

FIGURE 8-4: Location tab

Although the Windows Phone Emulator provides you with a way to simulate the accelerometer and GPS location data, you are advised to check your application on a real device as well because real sensor data is subject to environmental influence, network availability, magnetic fields, and so on. Always check your application on a real device to see how it behaves under real-world conditions.

Some additional new features in Mango include a local database engine based on SQL CE, an improved network stack with TCP and UDP sockets support, an enhanced web browser based on Internet Explorer 9 (IE9) with HTML5 support, and the `VideoBrush` object. Mango introduces a new type of application as well: hybrid Silverlight and XNA applications.

Network Sockets

Mango introduces support for TCP and UDP sockets. UDP sockets support both unicast and multicast communication (on Wi-Fi). In addition, Mango introduces a Connection Manager component that manages connections on the phone. It is responsible for connecting the application with a data source, as well as providing information about the type of data network the phone uses (for example, Wi-Fi, 3G, EDGE, and so on).

The socket APIs are compatible with Silverlight on the desktop (where applicable). Table 8-2 compares Silverlight 4 and Mango sockets.

TABLE 8-2: Socket Comparison

AREA	SILVERLIGHT 4 (DESKTOP)	SILVERLIGHT 4 (MANGO)
TCP sockets	Sockets	Socket
UDP sockets	UdpAnySourceMulticastClient	UdpSingleSourceMulticastClient
	UdpAnySourceMulticastClient	
	UdpSingleSourceMulticastClient	
Addressing	SocketAddress	SocketAddress
	IPAddress	IPAddress
	IPEndPoint	IPEndPoint
Name Resolution	DnsEndPoint	DnsEndPoint

The following code snippet demonstrates how to create a TCP socket connection:

```
_endPoint = new DnsEndPoint("192.168.0.2", 5000);
_socket = new Socket(AddressFamily.InterNetwork, SocketType.Stream,
     ProtocolType.Tcp);

SocketAsyncEventArgs args = new SocketAsyncEventArgs();
args.UserToken = _socket;
args.RemoteEndPoint = _endPoint;
args.Completed += new
     EventHandler<SocketAsyncEventArgs>(OnSocketConnectCompleted);
_socket.ConnectAsync(args);
```

The following code snippet demonstrates how to join UDP casting:

```
Client = new UdpAnySourceMulticastClient(address, port);
Client.BeginJoinGroup(
               result =>
               {
                    Client.EndJoinGroup(result);
                    Dispatcher.BeginInvoke(
                      delegate
                      {
                         OnAfterOpen();
```

```
                          Receive();
                      });
              }, null);
```

Silverlight/XNA Hybrid Applications

Mango introduces a new model of hybrid applications. These applications enable XNA content inside Silverlight applications, which introduces a completely different level of graphics inside those applications.

XNA is a game framework used to create games for the Xbox360, PC, and Windows Phone. It provides a game engine and a lot of boilerplate code that helps developers create two-dimensional (2D) and three-dimensional (3D) games. XNA's 2D graphics are based on image sprites (textures), and its 3D graphics are based on real 3D models created in professional 3D-design tools. The framework provides APIs to display these graphics using an immediate graphics mode (the developer has full control over each single frame displayed by the application), as well as a set of comprehensive math libraries to help with game development logic.

In Mango, Silverlight/XNA integration is done at the page level, which means XNA content is part of a Silverlight page. The XNA rendering mechanism takes over the Silverlight one using the `SharedGraphicsDeviceManager` class, as shown here:

```
SharedGraphicsDeviceManager.Current.GraphicsDevice.SetSharingMode(true);
```

This way, the XNA graphics take over the whole page with the Silverlight rendering engine not running at all. To present in the Silverlight UI, Mango provides a new class, `UIElementRenderer`, from the `Microsoft.Xna.Framework.Graphics` namespace. This class is responsible for rendering the Silverlight `UIElement` (and its siblings) into textures that can be used for rendering in XNA, along with other game graphics.

The following code snippet demonstrates how to initialize the `UIElementRenderer` instance to render a whole Silverlight page into a texture:

```
uiRenderer = new UIElementRenderer(LayoutRoot, (int)LayoutRoot.ActualWidth,
    (int)LayoutRoot.ActualHeight);
```

At XNA's `Draw()` time, simply render the `UIElement` and paint it on screen, as shown here:

```
// Update the Silverlight UI
uiRenderer.Render();

// Draw the sprite
spriteBatch.Begin();
spriteBatch.Draw(uiRenderer.Texture, Vector2.Zero, Color.White);
spriteBatch.End();
```

The result is an application that mixes Silverlight and XNA graphics (with real hardware-accelerated 3D graphics). These applications can look like what is shown in Figure 8-5.

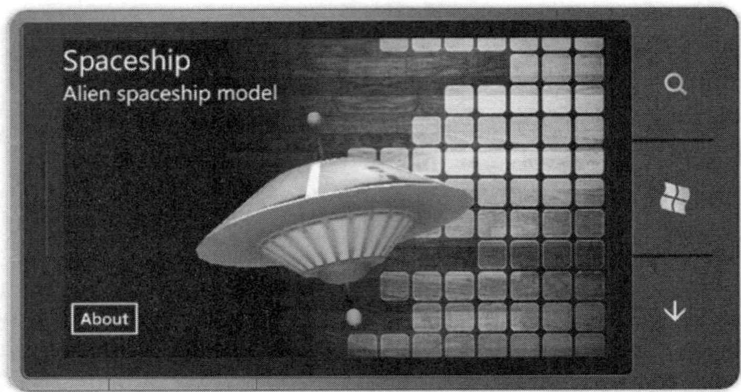

FIGURE 8-5: Application mixing Silverlight and XNA graphics

Local Database

Mango adds a local database engine to the device. The database engine on the phone is based on the SQL CE engine. Mango applications use LINQ-to-SQL for all database operations. LINQ-to-SQL provides an object-oriented approach to working with data and is composed of an object model and a runtime. The database files are stored in isolated storage on the phone and available to the application only (which means multiple applications cannot share the same database).

Following are some suggested scenarios for local database usage in applications:

- ➤ "Shopping list"-style applications
- ➤ Complex schema databases, which usually include a few tables (five to seven), hundreds of records, along with numerous relations, constraints, and foreign keys
- ➤ "Dictionary"-style applications
- ➤ Reference data that usually has a huge amount of static reference data with few tables (two to three) and constraints, with one or two of the tables holding huge amounts of data (500,000 to 1 million records)
- ➤ "Local cache" for applications

The database serves as a local cache for data fetched from the cloud, sometimes in combination with application-specific data. Usually, such cache data contains very few tables with relatively simple data. Those tables usually hold up to hundreds of records for a defined period of time (until application logic defines the data there as expired).

LINQ-to-SQL provides Object-Relational Mapping (ORM) capabilities that enable your managed application to use Language Integrated Queries (LINQ) to communicate with a relational database. LINQ-to-SQL maps the object model (which you express with .NET-managed code) to a relational database.

When your application runs, LINQ-to-SQL translates language-integrated queries into database "language" and then sends them to the database for execution. When the database returns the results, LINQ-to-SQL translates them back to objects that you can work with in your own programming language.

LINQ-to-SQL works with the `DataContext` object, which defines the object model of the data. Usually, `DataContext` defines the data using plain old CLR objects (POCO) and attributes conventions.

 *The current version of Windows Phone developer tools doesn't provide any visual designer to assist in creating the `DataContext` and entity classes. You can create those classes manually as described here.*

To create your own `DataContext` classes, derive them from the `DataContext` base class. A `DataContext` derived class is a managed class that defines table structure and a mapping between the object model and the database schema. The mapping is created by decorating objects with mapping attributes. These attributes specify database-specific features (such as tables, columns, primary keys, indexes, and so on).

The `DataContext` class (with mapped properties) is used to create a local database on the phone. The code-first approach (which uses managed code to define the schema and create the database) is the preferred approach for Windows Phone applications.

Following are some key points about local databases created by applications:

➤ A local database exists only for parent application.

➤ The database is not shared across different applications on the device and is accessible only by the parent application.

➤ Only the LINQ-to-SQL query mechanism is supported. T-SQL is not supported.

APPLICATION MODEL

In this section, you will learn about application model changes, and will see how those changes lead to more responsive applications, and enable very interesting user scenarios.

Fast Application Switching (FAS)

The initial version of the Windows Phone operating system supported only one active application. When applications were sent to the background, their state was serialized and kept in isolated storage. This process is called *tombstoning,* and an application that had undergone it was considered *tombstoned.* When users returned to a tombstoned application, they would have to wait a while as the application deserialized its state. Developers had to take care of saving the application's state and resuming it.

With Mango, that is no longer the case. There is only one active (foreground) application. When an application is sent to the background, the operating system keeps its image (variables, execution state, and so on) alive in memory for as long as possible without impairing the performance of the currently active application.

This new state of the application is called *dormant.* When a user reactivates the dormant application, the experience is virtually instantaneous because restoring the application's in-memory image is a fast operation. In cases when the dormant application's memory must be released to ensure active application performance is not impaired, Mango tombstones the dormant application, and the user must wait to get back to the application (as was the case in the previous Windows Phone release). This new mechanism is called *Fast Application Switching* (*FAS*).

Mango application developers must be aware of this new behavior and respond accordingly when the application is resuming. When an application is activated, `ActivatedEventArgs` has a new property, `IsApplicationInstancePreserved`, which indicates the latest state of resumed application. If `IsApplicationInstancePreserved` is `true`, then all application memory is intact, and virtually nothing should be done. If `IsApplicationInstancePreserved` is `false`, you must perform an "old-styled" tombstoning resume operation, as shown here:

```
private void Application_Activated(object sender, ActivatedEventArgs e)
{
// Ensure that application state is restored appropriately
if (!e.IsApplicationInstancePreserved)
{
WasTombstoned = true;

//Your code to resume from tombstoning ...
}
else
{
WasTombstoned = false;
}
}
```

The default behavior of the Mango application life-cycle manager is to preserve application images in memory as long as possible. The tombstoning process can take place automatically by the phone's operating system when it is needed.

To enable debugging of tombstoned applications, you can use the new version of the developer tools to force an application to forego FAS in favor of tombstoning. To force tombstoning, open the project's properties, and navigate to the Debug tab, as shown in Figure 8-6.

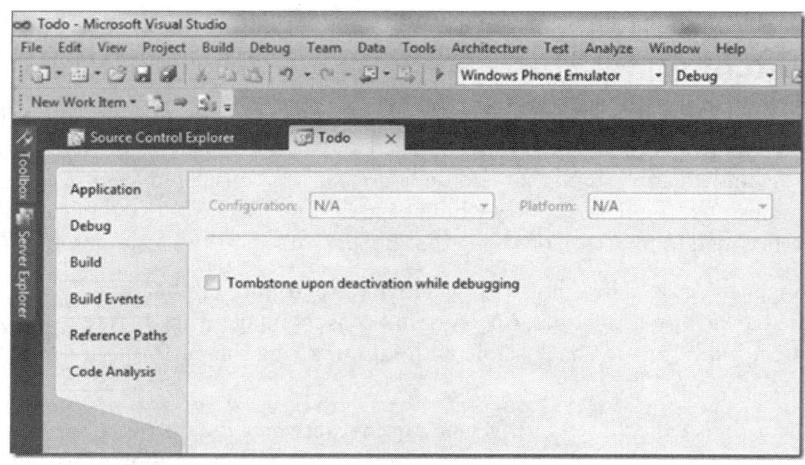

FIGURE 8-6: The Debug tab

Clicking the check box that says Tombstone upon Deactivation While Debugging forces your application to consistently perform tombstoning upon deactivation while the debugger is attached. Clear the check box to have the application use FAS again.

Multitasking

One of most requested and discussed features of the Mango release is multitasking. In Mango, the multitasking term has slightly different meaning than standard (PC) multitasking. *Multitasking* for Mango phones means the capability to execute an application's code while the application in not active, and to play audio started by the application in the background. This is achieved by *background agents*.

In addition to background agents, Mango also introduces APIs to download and upload files while an application is in the background, as well as to add reminders and alarms to get the user's attention. You learn about these features later in the chapter.

Background Agents

The background agents are class libraries that are "manifested" within the application. They can perform periodic tasks (or resource-intensive tasks), and play audio from a local file or audio stream. As shown in Figure 8-7, the developer tools provide a starting point for creating agents.

Audio background agents enable continued play of sounds, even if the application is closed. These sounds integrate into the universal volume control on the phone to ensure the consistency of the user experience on the device. An audio agent can start playing from a provided URL or stream and notify the application of file/buffer completion, user actions from the universal volume control (like skip to next/previous track), as well as provide the application with playback status, progress, and metadata.

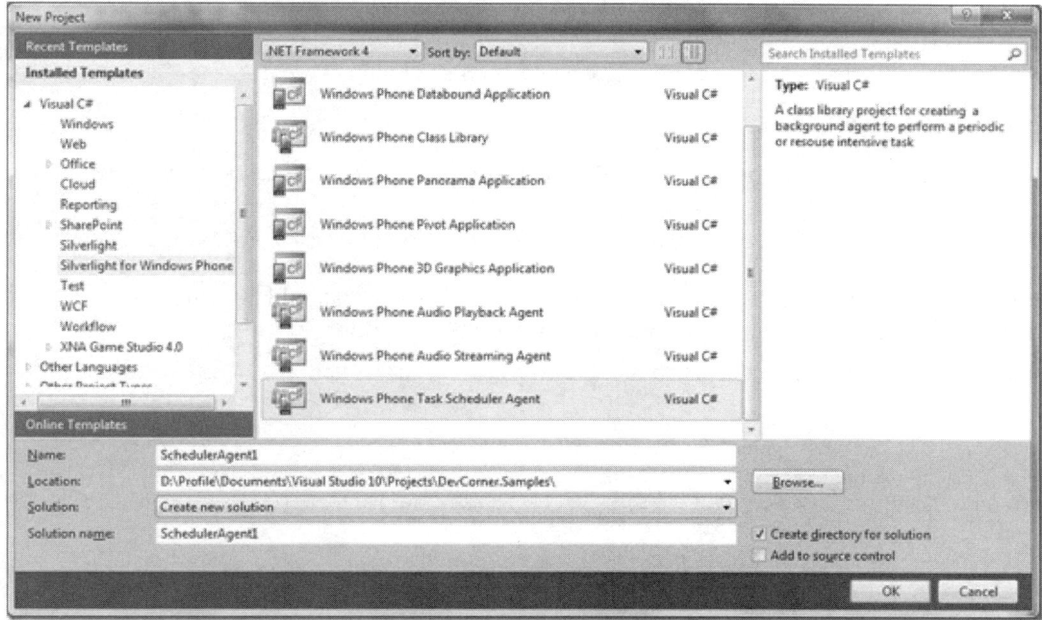

FIGURE 8-7: The Windows Phone agent templates

Audio playback agents help to create scenarios in which an application provides the URL (or URL list) to play and provide some custom logic for skipping forward and backward, and to pause/resume/stop.

Audio streaming agents provide the raw audio buffers. These are used to enable scenarios that require custom logic to decrypt (and sometimes decompress) the stream before playback.

Task scheduler agents enable applications to run some business logic when the application is in the background, or even when it is tombstoned.

Applications can create a `PeriodicTask` or `ResourceIntensiveTask` (both from `Microsoft.Phone.Scheduler` namespace). These tasks must be initialized while the application is active, but can run while the application is in the background. Applications may have only one such task from each type.

➤ `PeriodicTasks` run once every 30 minutes for a duration of about 15 seconds and are constrained to consume no more than 10 percent of the CPU resources and 6MB of memory.

➤ `ResourceIntensiveTasks` run only when the system is in an idle state, connected to an external powers source, and with a noncellular network available. It can run for the duration of 10 minutes and be constrained to use no more than 6MB of memory.

Additionally, both tasks are limited to a set of APIs that can be executed. Table 8-3 helps to demonstrate that limitation.

TABLE 8-3: Task Limitations

ALLOWED	RESTRICTED
Update tiles.	Display UI.
Show toast notification.	Use XNA libraries.
Use location services.	Use microphone or camera.
Most framework APIs use network.	Use sensors.
Read/write to isolated storage.	Play audio (may only use background audio APIs).
Use sockets.	

The new task (either `PeriodicTask` or `ResourceIntensiveTask`) should be registered using `ScheduledActionService` and removed when not needed anymore.

```
private void btnStartStopBgTask_Click(object sender, RoutedEventArgs e)
{
    if (!isBackgroundTaskEnabled)
    {
        PeriodicTask periodicTask = new PeriodicTask("TheWorker");
        periodicTask.Description = "The worker task";
        periodicTask.ExpirationTime = DateTime.Now.AddDays(1);
```

```
        ScheduledActionService.Add(periodicTask);
        isBackgroundTaskEnabled = true;
    }
    else
    {
        ScheduledActionService.Remove("TheWorker");
        isBackgroundTaskEnabled = false;
    }
}
```

Keep the following in mind when working with agents:

➤ Agents run for up to 14 days and should then be renewed, or they will be removed by the system.

➤ Agents are persisted across reboots.

➤ The user can control agents through the system's control panel.

➤ The total amount of periodic agents (systemwide) is 18.

Notifications

Mango provides a new API to create time-based, on-phone notifications. These notifications can be from one of two types: alarms or reminders.

Figure 8-8 shows the alarm type, which has the following characteristics:

➤ Modal

➤ Buttons for "snooze" and "dismiss"

➤ Sound customization enabled

➤ No application deep-link invocation (that is, getting back to a specific navigation page) allowed

➤ No stacking

The following code snippet is used to create the alarm shown in Figure 8-8:

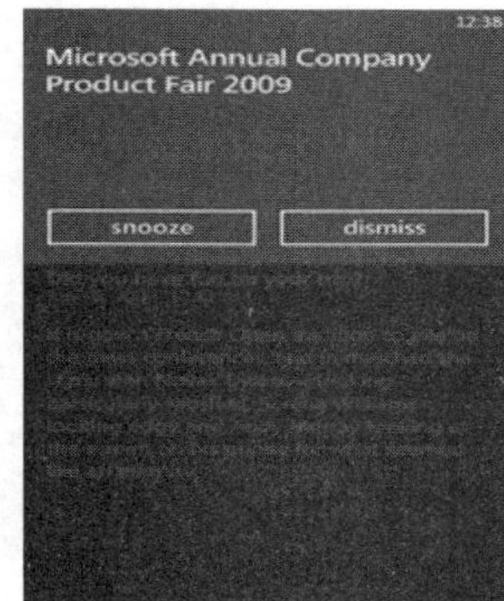

FIGURE 8-8: Alarm notification

```
using Microsoft.Phone.Scheduler;

private void AddAlarm(object sender, RoutedEventArgs e)
{
    Alarm alarm = new Alarm("Long Day");
    alarm.BeginTime = DateTime.Now.AddSeconds(15);
    alarm.Content = "Microsoft Annual Company Product Fair 2009";
    ScheduledActionService.Add(alarm);
}
```

Figure 8-9 shows a reminder notification, which has the following characteristics:

➤ Rich information provided

➤ Other reminders can be integrated

➤ Buttons for "snooze" and "dismiss"

➤ Deep linking into the application allowed

➤ Global settings for the phone followed

The following code snippet is used to create the reminder shown in Figure 8-9:

```
using Microsoft.Phone.Scheduler;

private void AddReminder(object sender, RoutedEventArgs e)
{
    Reminder reminder = new Reminder("CompanyMeeting");
    reminder.BeginTime = DateTime.Now.AddSeconds(15);
    reminder.Content = "Soccer Fields by The Commons";
    reminder.Title = "Microsoft Annual Company Product Fair 2009";
    reminder.RecurrenceType = RecurrenceInterval.Yearly;
    reminder.NavigationUri = new Uri("/Reminder.xaml", UriKind.Relative);
    ScheduledActionService.Add(reminder);
}
```

FIGURE 8-9: Reminder notification

The `NavigationUri` property enables you to deep link into the application when the user taps the reminder.

Background Transfer Service

An additional exciting feature in Mango is *background file transfer*, which enables the transfer of files (in both directions — upload and download) even when the application is dormant or is tombstoned. You may start a file transfer while the application is in the foreground and complete the transfer in the background. The file transfer will be preserved across device reboots. After the application is started after one or more background transfers have been completed, it receives all events from corresponding background transfers upon reactivation.

Every application can queue up to five background transfer requests. All the requests are queued into the phone's service and served in first in, first out (FIFO) order. Transferred files can be served from the `/shared/Transfers` folder only. This means that files for upload should be copied into this folder before scheduling the upload request, and the downloaded file will be placed into this folder upon completion. Files should be moved to their final locations by the application. By default, big files (that is, more than 20MB) will be downloaded only when the device has Wi-Fi connectivity.

Transfers (both ways) are started by creating a `BackgroundTransferRequest` instance and adding it to the `BackgroundTransferService` queue, as shown here:

```
void StartDownload()
{
    btr = new BackgroundTransferRequest(remoteVideoUri, localDownloadUri);
```

```
        btr.TransferPreferences = TransferPreferences.AllowCellularAndBattery;

        BackgroundTransferService.Add(btr);
        btr.TransferProgressChanged += new
            EventHandler<BackgroundTransferEventArgs>
            (btr_TransferProgressChanged);
        btr.TransferStatusChanged += new
            EventHandler<BackgroundTransferEventArgs>
            (btr_TransferStatusChanged);
    }
```

The following event enables control over the transfer flow:

```
    void btr_TransferProgressChanged(object sender, BackgroundTransferEventArgs e)
    {
        double progress = e.Request.BytesReceived * 100 /
            e.Request.TotalBytesToReceive;
        //Your code here...
    }
```

When the transfer finishes, it is up to application to remove it from the `BackgroundTransferService` queue, as shown here:

```
    void btr_TransferStatusChanged(object sender, BackgroundTransferEventArgs e)
    {
        if (btr.TransferStatus == TransferStatus.Completed)
        {
            btr.TransferProgressChanged -= btr_TransferProgressChanged;
            btr.TransferStatusChanged -= btr_TransferStatusChanged;
            BackgroundTransferService.Remove(btr);

            //Your code here...
        }
    }
```

As mentioned, big files use Wi-Fi by default to download, like the Marketplace application does. Also, in some cases, big files can download only when the device is connected to a power source. To override this default behavior, change the `TransferPrefereneces` property of `BackgroundTransferRequest` instance to the following:

```
    btr.TransferPreferences = TransferPreferences.AllowCellularAndBattery;
```

INTEGRATION SERVICE

The changes in Mango enable very interesting scenarios and improvements for the end user, while still preserving the phone health. This can provide even more benefits by using improvements in integration features.

Secondary Tiles

The Mango release enables multiple main screen tiles for applications.

In the initial Windows Phone release, the user could pin an application to the main screen, and the push notification mechanism was used to update this tile.

With the Mango release, in addition to the old mechanism, developers can programmatically pin additional application tiles (*secondary tiles*) to the main screen. These secondary tiles can be updated using the push notification mechanism, enable deep linking (navigation to a specific application page when the user taps the tile), and provides two interchangeable surfaces. If both tile surfaces contain data (at creation), the tile flips randomly to expose both sides.

The following snippet shows how to create a two-sided tile:

```
StandardTileData initialData = new StandardTileData
{
    BackgroundImage = new Uri("images/DEFAULT.png", UriKind.Relative),
    Title = "Mood",
    BackContent = "No updates yet",
    BackTitle = "More info",
};
ShellTile.Create(new Uri("/MoodInfo.xaml?Name=Alex", UriKind.Relative),
    initialData);
```

The URI provided at creation time serves as the tile's unique identifier and as a link to an application page.

Push Notifications

All Windows Phone applications are capable of subscribing to push notification events. The notifications are provided by the Microsoft Push Notification Service (MPNS), which identifies the device by a unique URI. This URI is generated when the device subscribes to the push notifications and opens a push notification channel.

Push notifications can be from three types:

➤ *Raw notifications* — These notifications will be delivered to the application and are processed while the application is running in the foreground.

➤ *Toast notifications* — These notifications will be delivered to the application when it is in the background, and are displayed in the system notification area (that is, the upper part of the device).

➤ *Tile notifications* — These notifications will be delivered when the application is in the background and will change the application's tiles (main or secondary).

Figure 8-10 shows both types of background notifications (toast and secondary tiles).

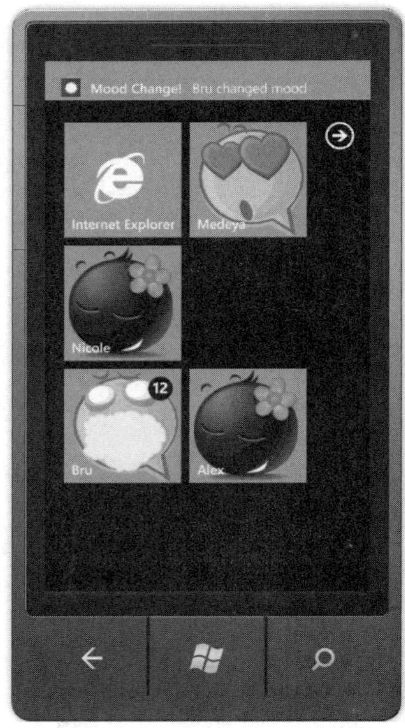

FIGURE 8-10: Background notifications

Push notifications are received as an XML payload sent through MPNS to the device. The sender is usually some kind of server, which attempts to update relevant client applications with new information.

To send tile push notifications to specific clients, you must prepare and send the following XML payload:

```
<?xmlversion="1.0"encoding="utf-8"?>
<wp:Notification xmlns:wp="WPNotification">
  <wp:Tile Id="THE URL">
    <wp:BackgroundImage><background image="" path=""></wp:BackgroundImage>
    <wp:Count><count></wp:Count>
    <wp:Title><title></wp:Title>
    <wp:BackTitle><back side="" title=""></wp:BackTitle>
    <wp:BackContent><back side="" content=""></wp:BackContent>
    <wp:BackBackgroundImage><back side="" background="" image=""
        path=""></wp:BackBackgroundImage>
  </wp:Tile>
</wp:Notification>
```

In this case, the `Id` attribute value identifies the tile. A primary tile has the value of /, and secondary tiles have a value leading to an actual application page. For example, the secondary tile from the mood application shown in Figure 8-10 has `"/MoodInfo.xaml?Name=Alex"` as a value.

To send toast notifications to a specific client, you must prepare and send the following XML payload:

```
<?xmlversion="1.0"encoding="utf-8"?>
<wp:Notification xmlns:wp="WPNotification">
  <wp:Toast>
    <wp:Text1><string></wp:Text1>
    <wp:Text2><string></wp:Text2>
    <wp:Param><THE URL=""></wp:Param>
  </wp:Toast>
</wp:Notification>
```

The `<The URL>` parameter enables deep linking to a specific application page when the user taps the notification.

Contacts/Appointments Data Access

Mango provides an API to take advantage of the user's contacts and appointments. To search for appointments and contacts, use the `Appointments` and `Contacts` classes located under `Microsoft.Phone.UserData` namespace.

The `Contacts` class contains information that indicates the accounts used to provide the information. The information is provided via an `Accounts` property. It holds a collection of accounts with an account kind (of `StorageKind` type) and account name.

`Contacts` can be searched using the `SearchAsyc` method. The result is returned as a `Contact SearchEventArgs` class instance. It has a collection of `Results`, and each item in the `Results` collection holds an instance of `Contact` class from `Microsoft.Phone.UserData` namespace. It has all the information about the contact (such as `PhoneNumbers`, `DisplayName`, `EmailAddresses`,

`Companies`) the `Accounts` associated with this contact, and indicates whether the contact is pinned to the start screen (`IsPinnedToStart`).

The following code snippet shows how to search for contacts and group the results by the first letter in their display names:

```
contacts = new Contacts();
contacts.SearchCompleted += contacts_SearchCompleted;
contacts.SearchAsync(String.Empty, FilterKind.None, null);

void contacts_SearchCompleted(object sender, ContactsSearchEventArgs e)
{
// Group all contacts according to the first letter in their display name
var itemsSource = e.Results.GroupBy(c => c.DisplayName.First()).
OrderBy(group => group.Key).
Select(group => new ContactsGroup(group));
// ...
}
```

Similarly to the `Contacts` class, the Windows Phone APIs provide the `Appointments` class under the `Microsoft.Phone.UserData` namespace to search through the user's appointments. The `Appointments` class is initialized similarly to the `Contacts` class, as shown here:

```
appointments = new Microsoft.Phone.UserData.Appointments();
appointments.SearchCompleted += new
        EventHandler<AppointmentsSearchEventArgs>
        (appointments_SearchCompleted);
```

To start the search, invoke the `SearchAsyc` method, which asynchronously searches for appointments that occur between the specified start date and time, and end date and time. The following code snippet searches for all appointments in all accounts in the next 5 days:

```
appointments.SearchAsync(DateTime.Now, DateTime.Now.AddDays(5), null);
```

The `SearchCompleted` event handler returns the `Start` and `End` date/time used to search for the current result set. Each item in the `Results` collection holds an instance of `Appointment` class from the `Microsoft.Phone.UserData` namespace. It has all the information about the appointment (such as `Location`, `Organizer`, `Attendees` list, `Subject`, and so on).

SUMMARY

The Mango release of Windows Phone 7 provides developers with many new features and enables many new interesting scenarios. Combined with features from the original Windows Phone release, it exposes a powerful (yet easy) mechanism to create modern mobile applications and leverage the full power of modern devices. It introduces very interesting end-user scenarios that range from controlling the application with built-in sensors and executing background activities, to having multiple application tiles on the main screen and updating them via push notifications.

ABOUT THE AUTHOR

Alex Golesh is a senior architect at Sela Group and a Silverlight division manager. He is an international expert who specializes in Silverlight, Windows Presentation Foundation (WPF), Windows Phone 7, and XNA. Golesh is currently consulting for various enterprises in Israel and worldwide, architecting and developing Rich Internet Application (RIA) and Smart Client-based solutions. He has been developing training samples and courses for various product groups at Microsoft (Redmond, WA). He conducts lectures and workshops, and leads projects worldwide in the fields of RIA, Smart Client, and Windows Phone 7. He has conducted WPF and Silverlight training in India, Sweden, and Poland as a part of the Metro Program Microsoft Early Adoption program. He has received recognition as a Microsoft Most Valuable Professional (MVP) in Silverlight.

9

Pragmatic Services Communication with WCF

by Christian Weyer

Windows Communication Foundation (WCF) has been around for quite a few years. Its first incarnation showed up with .NET 3.0 in 2006. But still I meet a lot of people out there in the wilderness of software projects that do not know about it, let alone use and embrace it. Whenever you need to think about designing and implementing distributed applications in .NET, WCF is one of the major choices at hand — whether you have colleagues who hate it, or friends who love it.

This chapter presents some practical and pragmatic approaches and implementations to service-oriented communication based on WCF. This chapter goes beyond the prototypical introduction, and beyond common sense you can read in other books or publications. The facts and opinions presented here have been gathered in countless real-world client projects since the first beta versions of Indigo, as WCF was called once upon a time.

Keep in mind that this chapter is neither a beginner's introduction to WCF, nor a fully embracing, "everything WCF" reference — but rather something in between, actually.

You may read a few ideas and approaches in this chapter that surely go beyond common opinions and contradict statements in other publications about service orientation in general, and especially about WCF. According to the most often heard answer by software consultants when asked how to tackle and solve a certain problem — "Oh, that depends." — and the best approach is to shed a case-minded light on WCF. This is what I call "pragmatic" versus "dogmatic." And this is also the reason why people should talk only about best practices if they put these "best practices" into context. Without any project- or use-case-bound context, there is no such thing as best practice. Therefore, a lot of the things presented and argued about in this chapter are the way they are because the scenario and (sample) application in question presents a certain set of requirements — and it always depends on the client project's requirements and circumstances.

SAMPLE PROJECT

To present some pragmatic solutions to various problems in the realm of distributed service-oriented applications, let's use a sample project for illustrating both requirements and strategies for design implementation.

The sample scenario is a system for managing a collection of movies. End users can browse their movie data, see movie posters, and stream a trailer of their favorite movies. The sample project in this chapter uses a classic modeling and implementation approach to realize the application architecture — which is also known as *operation-based service orientation* (more on that later).

You can download the entire source code for the movie database application system, and the `Thinktecture.ServiceModel` library as part of the download package for this book located on this book's companion website (`www.wrox.com`).

The sample application scenario used in the chapter can surely create some discussion among readers. This is because it sounds and smells like a typical candidate for a more resource-oriented modeling. (Some may want to call it REST-ish.) Nevertheless, I chose it for two reasons: it provides a plethora of typical requirements to realize, and it is a good vehicle to demonstrate a pragmatic way to use several WCF features with a mix of the more traditional Simple Object Access Protocol (SOAP)-based and a more refreshing web-based modeling approach.

> **AIN'T NO SECURITY HERE!**
>
> One important and essential aspect of building distributed applications is obviously security. The various shades of security — authentication and authorization being the most obvious — must be planned from the start. Okay, sometimes there are situations in which you can "just pour" security over an application, but usually it is not possible.
>
> For this chapter and for the demo application, security has been completely left out. However, Chapter 10, "Securing WCF Services Using the Windows Identity Foundation (WIF)," does a fantastic job of explaining why you should use the new security model introduced by Windows Identity Foundation (WIF), and how you can implement it with your WCF-based consumers and services.

SERVICE ORIENTATION REVISITED

Before getting your hands dirty with WCF, I should paint my picture of designing and building distributed applications. It is the picture I paint in maybe 80 percent to 90 percent of all cases in which I must solve a problem and provide a solution with distributed pieces of a software system. That means there are other cases. But it does not mean that there are exceptions to the rule because there is no such rule. It means there is an additional (but different) way to do things, which you learn about later in this chapter when I use that different approach to complement the demo application with additional features that demand certain requirements.

Distributed Means Communication

Building distributed applications is different. Sorry to be so bold, but that is the simple truth. I still meet developers who try to build applications that reside on different machines, maybe in different networks, the same way they used to write object-oriented systems over the past, say, 10 years. An increasingly high demand for realizing software systems in a nonlocal manner has emerged. The cloud is just the cherry on the top. But to be frank, this is all not new, but still it seems to be forgotten and played down.

Many of you know and remember the famous nine fallacies of distributed computing:

1. The network is reliable.

2. Latency is zero.

3. Bandwidth is infinite.

4. The network is secure.

5. Topology doesn't change.

6. There is one administrator.

7. Transport cost is zero.

8. The network is homogeneous.

9. Location is irrelevant.

 *The original seven fallacies were introduced by L. Peter Deutsch (a fellow for the Association for Computing Machinery) in 1994.*

Classic, isn't it? You must obey a few of these fallacies a bit more, namely "the network is reliable," "latency is zero," "transport cost is zero," "bandwidth is infinite," "the network is secure," and "location is irrelevant."

Some (if not all) of the programming models over the past several years that tried to help developers build distributed applications disregarded or even violated these facts — or, put another way, they proved the fallacies. Any inherently object-oriented approach led to developers into thinking that they were doing good old object orientation — modeling objects with state and behavior, simply putting them across the wire, and all would be good.

The object-oriented approach (like DCOM or .NET Remoting) pretends everything is just as before, as if everything happens locally — no network, nothing. But experience has shown that this is usually going to fail. I am not going to blame .NET Remoting. You can build good distributed systems (to a certain extent) that are not falling into the traps of the fallacies with .NET Remoting. But in the end it is — sorry, it was — just too object oriented.

Developers need a way to think more explicitly about distribution. Inevitably, distribution means communication. And communication means that you must think about and deal with things that you may not have had to deal with up until now.

 *Software architects and developers these days are forced to rethink if they have never built nonlocal software before. Even if you do not plan to distribute now, you must design with distribution in mind for later.*

So, it seems obvious that WCF is here to solve all these problems and help developers, right? Well, yes and no. Just like other frameworks (or foundations), WCF is a piece of infrastructure that eases some distributed pains. But, usually, WCF is not enough. You must build an ecosystem around (or on top of) it to finally build distributed systems. In addition, WCF does not always make your life easier. It is both too easy (to get it wrong, and still think in objects and act locally) and too complex.

(If you have already dealt with it, you may still have a bad stomach from the plethora of features, its configuration hell, or, often, impractical default settings.)

But, as you learn in this chapter, WCF is here — it is in the .NET Framework with full product support — and won't go away any time soon. (Cross your fingers.) As a solution architect or developer, you need a sane view of distributed applications, and a solid knowledge about WCF, to build pragmatic solutions with it.

So, what makes WCF tick? Why is it a good choice for building distributed applications? It provides a basic idea of how you think about and how you model your applications.

Service Orientation

WCF was built on top of a concrete and simple idea: services.

A *service* is a conceptual means to model functionality (something your application must provide, based on the business problem at hand) that fits together in a way so that this functionality can be easily designed, implemented, tested, and accessed. Perhaps you could think of services as an abstraction on top of objects and components. If you think about services as yet another abstraction, they are not actually anything new; they are just a logical advancement in software design.

Designing in a services way means to focus on the business side of your software (but with communication always in mind) for better encapsulation of functionality and decoupling from other parts in your overall architecture.

That said, services and service orientation do not have anything to do with XML or Web Services or even the well-known client-server idea of distributed applications.

> ### WHAT'S IN A SERVICE? A SIMPLE DEFINITION
>
> A *service* is a means to design associated business functionality by expressing explicit boundaries. A *consumer* talks to a service by sending and receiving messages that hold the relevant data to fulfill the business needs.
>
> This implies that, in a services world, you usually do not think about technical platforms. You do not think in Java or .NET programming constructs and data types. What you should care about in the first phase is the architectural base, not the technology to implement.

If you look around, two ways to realize the idea of services centers on the following design methods:

➤ *Operation oriented* — This means that you model a service with an explicit interface. This service (as already outlined) can receive messages and send messages. Now, as shown in Figure 9-1, operations group together the data, the messages, and the message exchange pattern used for communicating between the service consumer and the service itself via endpoints. This might be in line with a more traditional thinking and does not cause too much friction. (Cross your fingers!)

➤ *Resource oriented* — This way to do services takes a completely different approach. It aligns with the ideas and concepts of the web, HTTP, and hypertext. You model your service as an explicitly exposed and visible state machine (Representational State Transfer [REST], anyone?) that will be accessed and triggered via a universal interface. This approach is powerful, but honestly, creates severe friction for most developers and architects.

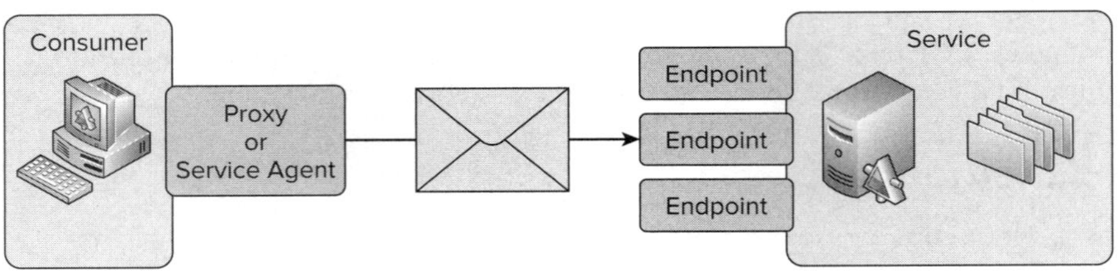

FIGURE 9-1: Operations-oriented approach

Taking a pragmatic approach to designing services can lead to the best result you can expect. And a good dose of pragmatism means that you must be aware of both service styles, and know what you can realize with a given framework.

WCF in .NET Framework 4.0 supports the classical operation-based design method and a web-coined way to model services. But rather than calling this REST, let's call it the web programming model. *(This is what Microsoft actually refers to.) In WCF, these are two mutually complementary approaches and conflate in the WCF programming and hosting model — whether that's good or bad.*

WCF BASICS 101

After this quick introduction into the services world, now start a journey through WCF land. Because WCF is about communication, start by laying some common ground to help understand the underpinnings of this application communication foundation. But do not fear — this is not an introduction to WCF. This is a quick recap, with a strong focus on the essential parts of WCF.

You must know the basic ideas and concepts of WCF to have fun with this chapter.

Basic Toolset

Over the past few years, you surely have heard about the Microsoft marketing "child's play" analogy of WCF — it's as easy as A-B-C! Well, it turns out that this is kind of a misleading message.

Let's immediately take a look at how WCF thinks about services, consumers, messages, and endpoints, as shown in Figure 9-2.

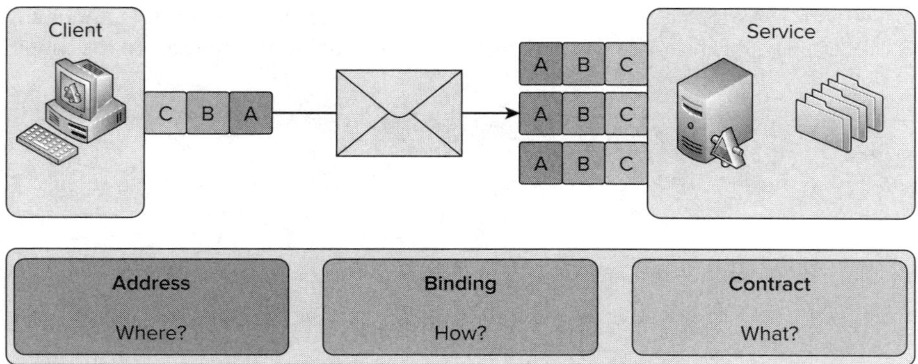

FIGURE 9-2: How WCF views consumers, messages, and endpoints

A WCF service exposes endpoints. An endpoint consists of *A*, *B*, and *C*. So easy! But, for me, one essential piece is missing. Figure 9-3 shows a different version of this illustration.

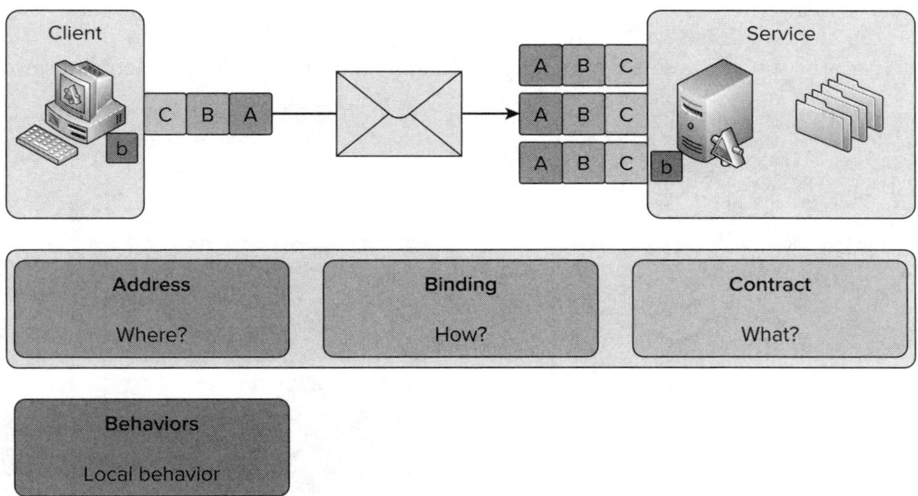

FIGURE 9-3: WCF properties defining success and failure

With WCF, you must know about the *A*, the *B*, the *C*, and the *b*. As explained here, these are the properties that decide success and failure.

➤ *Address* — Obviously, a consumer must know where to send messages to. This is what the address of an endpoint is all about.

➤ *Binding* — This one is hard to grok in the first place. Let's postpone it for a while. It is discussed in deeper detail later in this chapter.

➤ *Contract* — The contract is the agreement of the parties exchanging the message on how the data, the messages, and the message exchange patterns will look.

➤ *Behaviors* — With behaviors, a developer can inject local functionality into an endpoint or an entire service. Usually, this behavior (like instancing or threading) is not exposed on the endpoints.

 *Oh, but the Law of Leaky Abstractions (LOLA) is everywhere! See* `www.joelonsoftware.com/articles/LeakyAbstractions.html`.

To get a lot out of WCF beyond the standard configuration, you must understand the *B* — the binding — and its power.

The Power of the B

A number of people have tried to explain the word *binding*. Simply put, it is the binding of the communication contract to the underlying physical communication environment, along with protocols (including application-level protocols). The actual important "thingy" is not the binding itself, but rather the *binding element*. A binding consists of a stack of binding elements.

Figure 9-4 shows the mental model of a binding where binding elements are chosen from basically three families (transport protocols, message encoders, and application-level protocols and features).

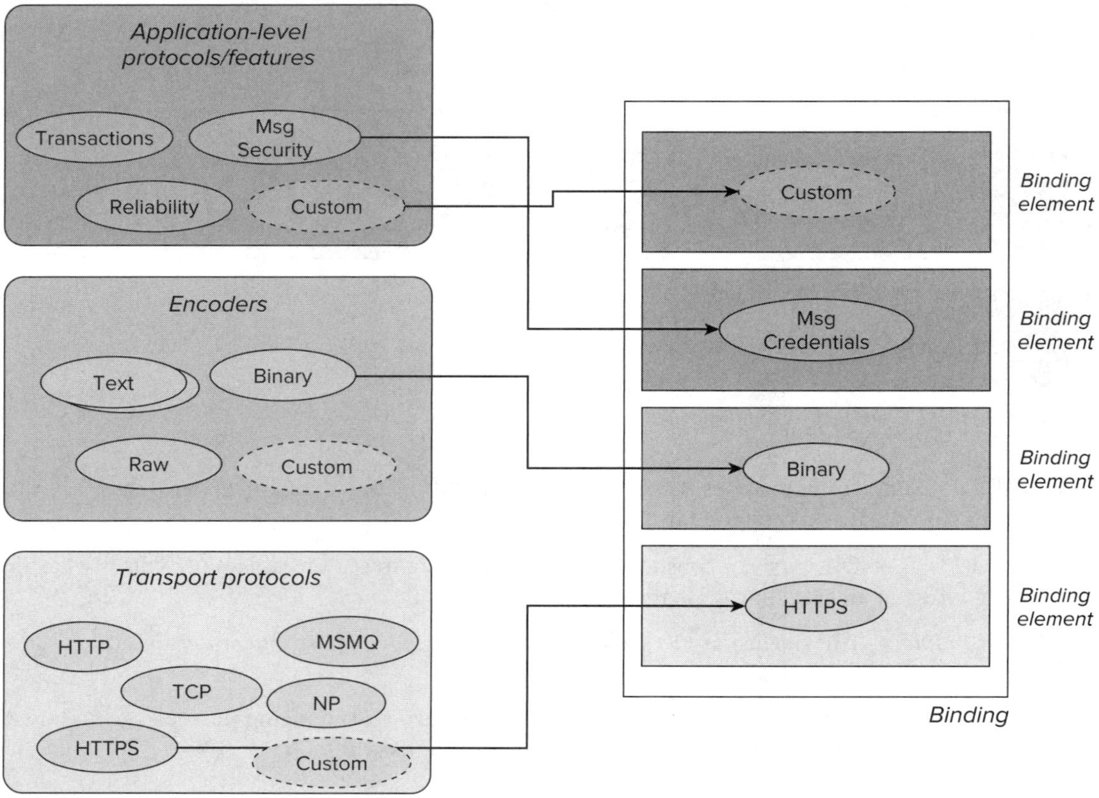

FIGURE 9-4: A stack of elements in a binding

Figure 9-4 shows a custom binding that looks like this in stack notation:

➤ Custom protocol feature (for example, some custom-baked correlation infrastructure)

➤ Message credentials

➤ Binary message encoder (with SOAP 1.2)

➤ HTTPS

On the other hand, if you look at the binding elements of the well-known `basicHttpBinding`, this resolves to the following binding elements stack:

➤ Text message encoder (with SOAP 1.1)

➤ HTTP

You can look at the elements of any binding by using this simple code snippet:

```
var binding = new BasicHttpBinding();
BindingElementCollection bindingElements =
    binding.CreateBindingElements();
```

As shown in Figure 9-5, you can look in the debugger to prove the claim.

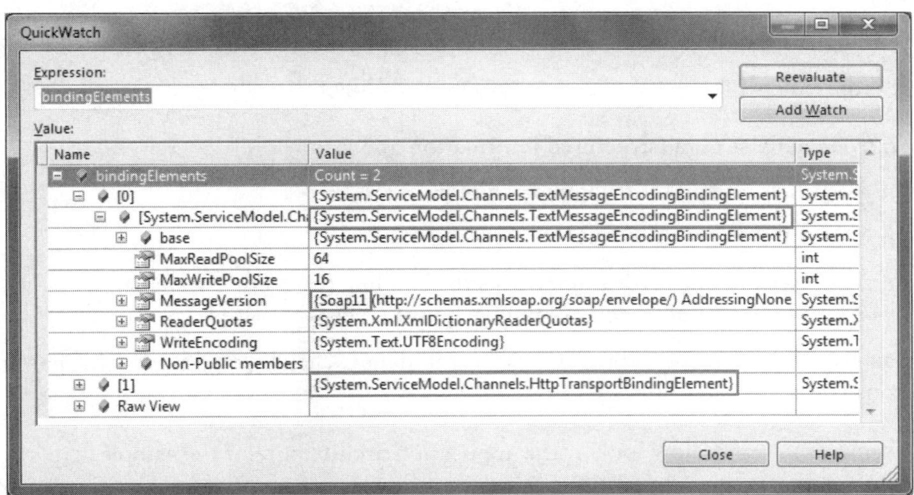

FIGURE 9-5: Proving the claim through the debugger

The more you get to know the setup and configuration of the standard bindings, and the more you learn about custom bindings and the available set of binding elements, the more you can get from WCF — and learn to love it (or at least learn to value it). Combine the power of the binding and the flexibility achieved through behaviors, and you are the master of WCF.

If you wanted to encapsulate and package a custom binding with some pre-defined configurations, you could create a user-defined binding by deriving a class from `Binding`.

Less Is More

Last, but not least, let's clarify something you may already have read between the lines in this chapter so far: WCF is powerful. Actually, WCF is "feature-ful." WCF is complex — if you use it the wrong way.

The rule for success with WCF is that "less is often really more." Do not let the sheer mass of features and potential XML configuration of WCF dazzle your brain. If you know your toolset well, it will play along your lines.

Now, jump into the big pond of communication.

APPLICATION SCENARIO

As mentioned, this chapter utilizes a concrete sample application scenario. Take a look at the requirements of the application, how it is designed, and what the structure of the involved software artifacts looks like. After this section, you should be up and running, and ready to tackle some of the real-world-proven tips and tricks promised earlier in this chapter.

Requirements

Let's begin by defining the requirements and context of the application discussed here.

The major list of requirements for the application system reads like this:

➤ Browse movie database data (structured information about movies)

➤ Stream movie posters (small unstructured arbitrary data)

➤ Stream movie trailers (large unstructured arbitrary data)

➤ Different client user interface (UI) frameworks for building consuming applications (Windows-based smart clients, but also mobile apps, maybe web-based)

➤ As-easy-as-possible application communication and data exchange for service providers and service consumers

With these requirements in mind, now look at the application architecture of the sample.

Application Architecture

Figure 9-6 shows a high-level view of the overall application architecture for the simple movie database sample.

Indeed, this is a not-too-complex distributed architecture. In reality, you will quite likely deal with much more complex situations. Anyway, for the purpose of this chapter, this architecture will suffice.

In the sample code that you can find on the companion website for this book (www.wrox.com), there is only one custom-built client application. This client was built with Windows Forms. The second consuming application in the game here is a media streaming player of your choice. The Windows client is talking to two services: the movie and the media service.

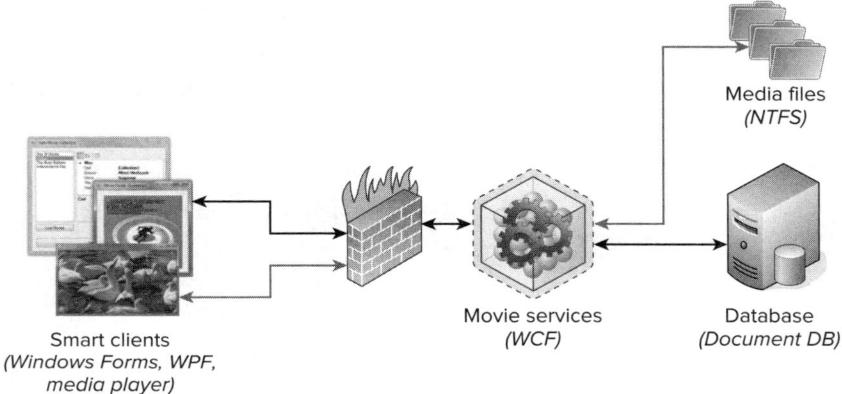

FIGURE 9-6: High-level view of sample application architecture

The first service offers structured data about the movies stored in the back-end database. It was decided that a document database rather than a relational database will be used to remove the unnecessary need of the object-relational mismatch. (Also, the system defines a heavy-read and low-write scenario, so a document database should make sense here.)

The second service is responsible for delivering the raw data for the movie posters as images (in `JPEG` format) and the movie trailers as video snippets (in `AVI` format). Although the path to these files is stored in the database, the actual files reside on the file system of the server. As you can see, the major communication pattern at hand is pure request and response.

Oh yes: I am still building — at least test and demo — applications with Windows Forms. If you want to learn how to build good extensible WPF application these days, just hop over (after you have read this chapter!) to Chapter 13, "Practical WPF Data Binding."

You are probably aware that WCF supports a plethora of communication patterns, such as request-response, one-way, and duplex. Using a one-way communication style all over your architecture can greatly increase the loose coupling and overall scalability but usually turns out to be quite a big undertaking (for example, in terms of complexity).

The next step is to look at the final Visual Studio 2010 solution structure used to design and develop this application.

Application Structure

Usually, the samples shown in books are just that — samples. And therefore, they miss some of the more interesting things you normally need to think about and realize in a real project. One of these interesting things is the solution and project structure in Visual Studio.

For some time, I have developed a common way of slicing various parts of my service-oriented distributed applications. Maybe you'll like this way, and, therefore, let's look at it a little bit.

Figure 9-7 shows the Visual Studio 2010 solution structure for the sample movie database.

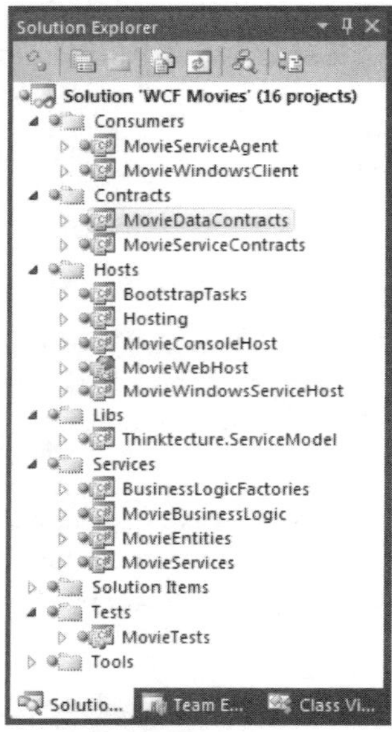

FIGURE 9-7: Visual Studio 2010 solution structure

Let's walk through it by looking at the various solution folders.

> `Consumers` — The Windows Forms client application uses a service agent dynamic link library (DLL), which encapsulates the communication details and exposes a communication-free and WCF-agnostic interface to the consuming applications.

> `Contracts` — This folder holds two DLL projects, one for the service contracts and one for the data contracts. You learn more about this later in this chapter, and you learn about the way to model services by choosing the "right" contract modeling approach.

> `Hosts` — The `Hosting` folder houses three different host projects: the Console host for testing, the Windows Service host for self-hosting, and the web host for hosting in Internet Information Server (IIS)/Windows Process Activation Service (WAS). Furthermore, two helper libraries have common hosting requirements and functionality factored out of the hosts.

➤ `Libs` — Some of the interesting features and tips presented in this chapter have been located in a helper class library called `Thinktecture.ServiceModel`.

➤ `Services` — Think of this as the heart of the entire system. Here you can find the implementation of the service façades, together with the service-internal business entities used to get and save data from the database to eventually perform some logic. These entities are used by the actual business logic (which, in this application, is thin).

➤ `Tests` — There is one single test project for the movies application that holds different integration and a few unit tests.

I should also mention the database used in the movies application. One goal was to not start a war over object-relational mapping (ORM) and which ORM technology to use. So, I basically had two choices: Write the data to disk and get it again from there, or use a document-like database. I decided for the latter (and hope to not start a war on that battlefield), and the choice fell on `RavenDB`. The choice was made because it can run in an embedded mode, and the simple API it provides made it a good candidate for this chapter's sample.

 `RavenDB` *is powerful and can run as a service itself inside IIS — but none of its database server/service features are used here.*

Let's now dive into the architectural basis of doing distributed application programming with WCF — modeling services.

MODELING SERVICES

Every service-oriented application should be started by designing the explicit boundaries for the application parts called services.

 *Obviously, the first step is to identify the services you need, as well as which data they offer and accept. This is part of the business-related analysis and design. It has barely anything to do with technology (or even software architecture). It is a process that differs a lot from customer to customer, from project to project, from use case to use case. And yes, it may be influenced by some technical constraints and requirements. To reconcile everything is the task of a good distributed application architect.*

In a WCF-minded services world, the contracts are the most important piece that you must think about first.

Contracts

With WCF, you have two approaches to modeling contracts. One approach is to use XML Schema Definition (XSD) and Web Service Definition Language (WSDL) first, and then have WCF-specific code generated for you through tools. Another approach is to start by thinking about a service's contract shape and needs, and then denoting it with WCF's attribute-based syntax.

Both ways can lead to the same result. However, it has been proven that the latter can mislead developers into thinking too much about object-oriented programming (that is, in terms of objects). Developers then tend to deduce that this magic runtime called WCF can do everything for them, and it always does it right. The remainder of this chapter focuses on exactly this approach (using attributes) to explicitly decide that you are talking about data and services, and not about objects and pointers.

Following are several artifacts to use when modeling WCF contracts:

> *Service contracts* — This is essentially the shell for the semantic description of the service and denotes the interface definition.

> *Operations* — Operations form the message exchange pattern to use.

> *Messages* — You can have a raw message type in your operation to work with.

> *Message contracts* — There is a way to influence how a message looks like on the wire with headers and body (according to SOAP) by using a message contract type.

> *Data contracts* — Usually, the data traveling between services and consumers is modeled by a data contract (often referred to as *data transfer objects*, or *DTOs*).

> *Fault contracts* — You can explicitly model fault data that expresses erroneous situations and carries just enough data for the consumer to deal with it.

Now look at some of these artifacts and examine the options you have, as well as the options you need.

Service Contracts

If taken literally, the service contract is the only contract that you need in WCF to model a service. When following the WCF metadata-driven modeling approach, you annotate your interface types with the `[ServiceContract]` attribute.

I also see people annotating classes with `ServiceContractAttribute`, *but I do not like this. A service contract mimics a (.NET) interface, and if I want to use the contract in a shared contracts assembly (as illustrated later in this chapter), I can just do so when annotating the interface, not the service class.*

The `ServiceContractAttribute` class has several parameters to set. Table 9-1 helps you focus on the important ones (that is, the ones that you should set at minimum).

TABLE 9-1: Essential ServiceContractAttribute Properties

PROPERTY NAME	DESCRIPTION
Name	The name of the service contract. This will be projected into the XML-centric metadata (WSDL port names, in this case). If this is not set, it will default to be derived from the .NET type name.
Namespace	The XML namespace of the service contract. This will be projected into the XML metadata (WSDL). If this is not set, it will be derived from the .NET namespace the annotated types lives in.
ConfigurationName	A shortcut name. If this is set, you can use this alias value to specify the contract in an endpoint definition in the configuration.

With this in mind, you can then start modeling the contract of the movie service like this:

```
namespace MovieServiceContracts
{
    [ServiceContract(Name = "MovieService",
        Namespace = MovieServiceConstants.ServiceNamespace,
        ConfigurationName = "IMovieService")]
    public interface IMovieService
    {
    }
}
```

Code file [from Contracts/MovieServiceContracts/IMovieService.cs] available for download at Wrox.com.

Of course, a service without any operation, without any functionality, does not make a lot of sense.

Operation Contracts

With services in general, and WCF in particular, you can choose from several *message-exchange patterns* (*MEPs*):

- ➤ One-way
- ➤ Request-response
- ➤ Solicit response
- ➤ Duplex

The most common one is request-response. This is a blocking call that optionally sends data in a request message, and optionally receives data in a response message. I say "optionally" because the data can actually be empty. The target of the message is described not by the data traveling in the message payload, but rather by metadata of the message (for example, a message header).

You can implement all kinds of MEPs with WCF, but following is a completed service contract with request-response operation contracts mimicking the semantics of the movie service:

```
namespace MovieServiceContracts
{
    [ServiceContract(Name = "MovieService",
        Namespace = MovieServiceConstants.ServiceNamespace,
        ConfigurationName = "IMovieService")]
    public interface IMovieService
    {
        [OperationContract(Name="AddMovie",
            Action = "AddMovie", ReplyAction = "AddMovieReply")]
        void AddMovie(MovieDetailsData movie);

        // Update...
        // Delete...

        [OperationContract(Name = "ListMovies",
            Action = "ListMovies", ReplyAction = "ListMovies")]
        List<MovieData> ListMovies(PagedDataRequest request);

        [OperationContract(Name = "GetMovie",
            Action = "GetMovie", ReplyAction = "GetMovie")]
        [FaultContract(typeof(NoSuchMovieFault))]
        MovieDetailsData GetMovie(string movieId);
    }
}
```

Code file [Contracts/MovieServiceContracts/IMovieService.cs] available for download at Wrox.com.

Again, similar to the service contract, the operations of the service (which are denoted as methods of the .NET interface) are annotated with an `[OperationContract]` attribute. This attribute also has some properties worth looking at, as shown in Table 9-2.

TABLE 9-2: Essential Properties of OperationContractAttribute

PROPERTY NAME	DESCRIPTION
Action	The SOAP operation action and the operation input message action. This will be projected into the XML metadata (WSDL). If it is not set, it will be derived from the .NET method name.
Name	The name of the operation. This will be projected into the XML-centric metadata (WSDL operation name, in this case). If it is not set, it will default to be derived from the .NET method name.
ReplyAction	The operation output message action. This will be projected into the XML metadata (WSDL). If it is not set, it will be derived from the .NET method name.

Now, I can hear a lot of you shouting, "What? Synchronous? What? Blocking?" Understandably, there is a wish for decoupling the processing of the operation execution from the main thread. You can achieve this on both sides — the service and client. WCF offers an asynchronous programming model for this.

This asynchronous programming model can be used on the service side if you happen to have heavily I/O-bound services (for example, services that talk to external resources a lot, such as other services or databases). The same goes for the consumer part. If you want to easily put the operation calls into a background and decouple it from your UI thread, then this programming model can help you out.

Following is a simple asynchronous version of the former created service and operation contract:

```csharp
namespace MovieServiceContracts
{
    [ServiceContract]
    public interface IMovieServiceAsync :
        IMovieService
    {
        [OperationContract(
            Name="AddMovie",
            Action = "AddMovie", ReplyAction = "AddMovieReply",
            AsyncPattern = true)]
        IAsyncResult BeginAddMovie(MovieDataContracts.MovieDetailsData movie,
            AsyncCallback callback, object asyncState);

        void EndAddMovie(IAsyncResult result);

        [OperationContract(
            Name = "ListMovies",
            Action = "ListMovies", ReplyAction = "ListMoviesReply",
            AsyncPattern = true)]
        IAsyncResult BeginListMovies(MovieDataContracts.PagedDataRequest
            request, AsyncCallback callback, object asyncState);

        System.Collections.Generic.List<MovieDataContracts.MovieData>
            EndListMovies(IAsyncResult result);

        [OperationContract(
            Name = "GetMovie",
            Action = "GetMovie", ReplyAction = "GetMovieReply",
            AsyncPattern = true)]
        IAsyncResult BeginGetMovie(string movieId, AsyncCallback callback,
            object asyncState);

        MovieDataContracts.MovieDetailsData EndGetMovie(IAsyncResult result);
    }
}
```

Code file [Contracts/MovieServiceContracts/IMovieServiceAsync.cs] available for download at Wrox.com.

There are multiple variants possible for the WCF asynchronous programming model. You can find an overview and explanation at `http://msdn.microsoft` `.com/en-us/library/ms734701.aspx`. *By the way, the story will get much better with the upcoming* `await` *pattern in C# 5.*

The important piece is the `AsyncPattern` property of the `[OperationContract]` attribute. This indicates to WCF that this operation should be treated differently. It informs the runtime that a `Begin` method has a matched `End` method that conforms to the .NET Framework asynchronous method design pattern. Note that `OperationContract` is applied to the `BeginXYZ` method — the resulting operation that shows up in metadata like WSDL will be just `XYZ`.

So, should you always write this lengthy and error-prone asynchronous code? I don't. I am lazy. Because you already have all the necessary information in the synchronous version of the contract, you can apply some automatic code-generation magic to spit out the asynchronous shape of it. In most cases, I use Microsoft's Text Template Transformation Toolkit (T4) for this. The downloadable code for this book has the full template available, but following is the central piece of T4 code that generates the asynchronous version from the synchronous contract:

```
...
using System;
using System.ServiceModel;

namespace <#= codeNamespace.Name #>
{
    [ServiceContract]
    public interface <#= codeInterface.Name #>Async :
        <#= codeInterface.Name#>
    {
        <#
            PushIndent("            ");

            int methodCount = 0;

            foreach (CodeFunction method in codeFunctions)
            {
                if(methodCount > 0)
                {
                    WriteLine(String.Empty);
                    WriteLine(String.Empty);
                }

                WriteAsyncOperationContract(method);
                WriteLine(string.Empty);

                methodCount ++;
            }

            ClearIndent();
        #>
    }
}
...
```

Code file [Contracts/MovieServiceContracts/IMovieServiceAsync.tt] available for download at Wrox.com.

T4 is built into Visual Studio. See `http://msdn.microsoft.com/en-us/library/bb126445.aspx` *for an introduction to the topic.*

T4 is powerful. It is free, and the ecosystem of templates grows steadily.

Now that you have your operations defined, what should travel into and out of your services? One option is to specify a raw message that you can work with.

Messages

Raw is good. But what do I mean by "raw"? A *raw message* in an operation represented by the `System.ServiceModel.Channels.Message` type in WCF. `Message` represents a programming model for the idea of a SOAP InfoSet-based message. You use a `Message` type usually in these situations:

- ➤ For full control over the message processing

- ➤ In a universal interface approach

- ➤ With streaming data in or out of a service

SOAP InfoSet is defined in the SOAP1.2 specification (`www.w3.org/TR/soap12-part0/`*).*

Sometimes your requirements may be that you do not want a strongly typed message or data description in your operation contract. If you must have the serializer out of the way and implement a general-purpose processing operation in your service, then a raw message can help you. This is surely the simplest shape of an operation using `Message`:

```
[OperationContract(Name = "Process",
    Action = "*", ReplyAction = "*")]
Message Process(Message message);
```

You learn more about streaming later in this chapter.

Message Contracts

WCF offers yet another way to deal more closely with the actual underlying message. With the `[MessageContract]` attribute, you can annotate your classes to mimic a SOAP message. I have found that I barely use `MessageContract` these days. If I want real interoperability, I tend to go for the schema-based contract-first approach. A situation in which I may end up using a message contract is (again) streaming. You learn more about this later.

In the end, on the wire, everything is a message. And in the WCF pipeline as well, everything is a message in the shape of the Message *type. It just depends on the flavor of contract you choose in your operations as to whether the raw message shows up, or the serializer kicks in to give you a strongly typed view on the message and data.*

And now, for the most common way to define data traveling in a services world, meet the data contract.

Data Contracts

By far, the most common way to model data in a WCF services world is the *data contract*. Often, a data contract is described as the WCF incarnation of the DTO pattern. Although this is technically true, I have an issue here. I do not like the word "object" in this context. When developers think about objects, they usually think about a full-blown, real object with state and behavior.

For more information on the DTO pattern, see "Data Transfer Object" by Martin Fowler at `http://martinfowler.com/eaaCatalog/dataTransfer Object.html`*.*

In this case, you are dealing with data, just data. These data types are meant to be used to transfer data (wrapped in messages) across the wire. This has absolutely nothing to do with classical notion of objects — au contraire!

Therefore, refer to this pattern as the *Data Transfer Structure (DTS)*. For the movie sample application, you can define a data contract that carries essential and basic movie data like this:

```csharp
[DataContract(Name = "Movie", Namespace = MovieDataConstants.DataNamespace)]
public class MovieData
{
    [DataMember(Name = "Id", IsRequired = true)]
    public string Id { get; set; }
    [DataMember(Name = "Title", IsRequired = true)]
    public string Title { get; set; }
}
```

Code file [Contracts/MovieDataContracts/MovieData.cs] available for download at Wrox.com.

As you can see, the attribute-based annotation pattern in WCF just continues here. You use the `[DataContract]` attribute to explicitly model data that is intended for your service's contract, and to be used to exchange data over a service boundary. These types reside in the `System.Runtime .Serialization` assembly because they can be used independently from WCF.

Yes, since .NET 3.5, it is also possible to completely omit the data contract attributes on the DTO types. But this is not what I do. I want to ensure that everyone involved in designing and implementing a distributed system understands that this is a special data type targeted at a special purpose.

Table 9-3 shows the two important properties of `DataContract`, the `Name` and `Namespace` properties.

TABLE 9-3: Essential Properties of DataContractAttribute

PROPERTY NAME	DESCRIPTION
Namespace	The XML namespace of the data contract. This will be projected into the XML-centric metadata (XSD). If it is not set, it will default to be derived from the .NET namespace the class lives in.
Name	The name of the data contract. This will be projected into the XML-centric metadata (XSD). If it is not set, it will default to be derived from the .NET class name.

You must explicitly state which of the data members of your data contract type should be exposed by WCF to the outside world. This is achieved by using the `[DataMember]` attribute. Now, it's important to emphasize that the default serializer used by WCF is the `DataContractSerializer`.

The behavior of this serializer is a well-known one in the world of XML. In a lax way, it does not require the defined data fields to be in place when looking at a piece of XML to serialize it into an object. This means that when your data contract contains a field `Title`, and the incoming XML does not contain it, then the serializer emits a default value. If you want to force that a given version of your data contract must have all the data present, then you can instruct the serializer to require certain fields to be present in the XML to parse.

As shown in Table 9-4, together with this `Required` attribute, you again have the `Name` attribute to make up the two essential properties for `[DataMember]`.

TABLE 9-4: Essential Properties of DataMemberAttribute

PROPERTY NAME	DESCRIPTION
Name	The name of the data member/field. This will be projected into the XML-centric metadata (XSD). If it is not set, it will default to be derived from the .NET field or property name.
Required	Forces the serializer to ensure that the annotated field is present in the XML to deserialize.

With the necessary (essential) things to obey when using data contracts now out of the way, you can move on to some advice from the real world.

Keep your data contracts lean and mean. Do not try to apply object-oriented programming (OOP) techniques such as crazy inheritance hierarchies or even polymorphism on your data contracts. This is not about OOP; this is about data. It is common to have redundant data in two different (but semantically related) data contracts. This makes working with different versions easier.

For example, there is a `MovieDetailsData` data contract in addition to the `MovieData` data contract in the sample application. This DTO contains more information about a movie, but is intentionally not derived from `MovieData` to have a loose coupling, also on the DTO layer.

```
[DataContract(Name = "MovieDetails", Namespace = MovieDataConstants.DataNamespace)]
public class MovieDetailsData
{
    [DataMember(Name = "Title", IsRequired = true)]
    public string Title { get; set; }
    [DataMember(Name = "Year", IsRequired = true)]
    public int Year { get; set; }
    [DataMember(Name = "Director", IsRequired = true)]
    public string Director { get; set; }
    [DataMember(Name = "Cast", IsRequired = true)]
    public List<ActorData> Cast { get; set; }
    [DataMember(Name = "Genre", IsRequired = true)]
    public string Genre { get; set; }
}
```

Code file [Contracts/MovieDataContracts/MovieDetailsData.cs] available for download at Wrox.com.

If you are wondering where the value for the `Namespace` property comes from, this is just a constant string value collected in a common class for constants, as shown here:

```
public static class MovieDataConstants
{
    public const string DataNamespace = "http://tt.com/movies/data/";
}
```

Code file [Contracts/MovieDataContracts/Constants.cs] available for download at Wrox.com.

This is basically what you need to know about data contracts. And, yes, the Microsoft Development Network (MSDN) documentation and other books have tons more of information on this. But when using the pragmatic approach to keep things simple, and following a certain mindset of service orientation, you will most likely not need more than what is outlined here.

Fault Contracts

Another important piece of information in a service description is what kind of error can occur, and which data an error can carry. For this, the SOAP-minded services world has the capability to describe fault data in a service's metadata. This feature is also available in WCF via the fault contract.

To express which fault or faults can occur when invoking an operation, you simply annotate (you guessed it!) the operation with a `[FaultContract]` attribute, like this:

```
[OperationContract(Name = "GetMovie",
    Action = "GetMovie", ReplyAction = "GetMovieReply")]
[FaultContract(typeof(NoSuchMovieFault))]
MovieDetailsData GetMovie(string movieId);
```

The fault contract is described as a data contract just like the other data contracts you've already learned about:

```
[DataContract(Name = "NoSuchMovieFault", Namespace =
    MovieDataConstants.DataNamespace)]
public class NoSuchMovieFault
{
    [DataMember(Name = "MovieId", IsRequired = true)]
    public string MovieId { get; set; }
}
```

This fault contract information on the operation is projected into the WSDL of a service, and the fault data contract is projected into the XSD used by the WSDL.

In the service façade implementation, you can throw a `FaultException` of the defined fault contract type and provide the necessary fault data:

```
throw new FaultException<NoSuchMovieFault>(
    new NoSuchMovieFault { MovieId = movieId });
```

> *To use good WCF metadata and, therefore, provide good interoperability, you should always respect and think about the essential properties of service, operation, data, and fault contracts discussed here. It can pay dividends in the future.*

Paging Data

I cannot tell you how many times I've seen an operation modeled like this in a real software project:

```
[OperationContract(Name = "ListMovies",
    Action = "ListMovies", ReplyAction = "ListMovies")]
List<MovieData> ListMovies();
```

It looks innocent, right? Just give me that movie data list and I am fine. Give me 10 movies. Good. Give me 100 movies. Okay. Give me 10,000 movies. Well…now everything seems to be slow and tends to break down.

An essential piece to keep in mind when modeling operations is to think about limiting the data that goes into and travels out of a service. First, when a service is serving client applications to display and work with data, it surely does not make sense to request more than maybe 100 or a few hundred data items. Second, the more data you send across the wire, the more work the serializer has (on two sides), and the more it depends on which network your application is running over. It is just good style to model the *paging of data* into your operations.

One possible approach is illustrated here:

```
[OperationContract(Name = "ListMovies",
   Action = "ListMovies", ReplyAction = "ListMovies")]
List<MovieData> ListMovies(PagedDataRequest request);
```

This is passing in a page data DTO that carries the information from the client — which data and how much it wants to request from the service.

Available for download on Wrox.com

```
[DataContract(Name = "PagedDataRequest", Namespace =
      MovieDataConstants.DataNamespace)]
public partial class PagedDataRequest
{
    [DataMember((Name = "PageCount")]
    public int PageCount { get; set; }

    [DataMember(Name = "PageSize")]
    public int PageSize { get; set; }
}
```

Code file [Contracts/MovieDataContracts/PageData.cs] available for download at Wrox.com.

Obviously, not every consuming application is a good citizen. Therefore, the service should always apply an upper boundary of data it returns. This means that the data coming back out of the service may then also indicate how many data records have been returned.

Metadata

Let's talk a bit about some tips for exposing metadata to your service's consumers.

One of the most often heard desires is to completely get rid of the infamous `http://tempuri.org` namespace in a WCF WSDL. This is an easy one. Ensure that you set your namespace value on three things:

➤   The `Namespace` property on the `ServiceContract`, as shown here:

```
[ServiceContract(Name = "MovieService",
    Namespace = MovieServiceConstants.ServiceNamespace,
    ConfigurationName = "IMovieService")]
public interface IMovieService
```

➤   The `Namespace` property on the `ServiceBehavior` (which denotes a service behavior as mentioned before through a .NET attribute), as shown here:

```
[ServiceBehavior(Namespace = MovieServiceConstants.ServiceNamespace,
    ConfigurationName = "MovieService")]
public class MovieService : IMovieService
```

➤ The `bindingNamespace` property of the endpoint (in `config`) or `Namespace` property of the binding used on the endpoint (in code), as shown here:

```
var binding = new BasicHttpBinding();
binding.Namespace = MovieServiceConstants.ServiceNamespace;

host.AddServiceEndpoint(
    typeof(IMovieService),
    new BasicHttpBinding(),
    "basic");
```

In past years, a couple more issues have shown up. Let's look at them one by one.

Flat WSDL

When exposing WCF services to other platforms such as Java or PHP, you may find that the Web Service toolkits and stacks used on those platforms cannot understand the WSDL that WCF exposes. This is most likely because WCF factors the WSDL into different physical files. This manifests itself in `wsdl:import` and `xsd:import` statements inside the main WSDL. And this is exactly the reason why a number of foreign stacks (especially older versions) cannot process WCF's WSDLs.

There is a solution. A few years back, I wrote an extension for the WCF pipeline that enables flattening out of the WSDL description into a single file without any imports. This extension is an endpoint behavior for WCF and implements the `IWsdlExportExtension` interface. The full source code is available, but what follows is the essential piece of the `FlatWsdl` class:

```
public class FlatWsdl : IWsdlExportExtension, IEndpointBehavior
{
    ...

    public void ExportEndpoint(WsdlExporter exporter,
      WsdlEndpointConversionContext context)
    {

      if (exporter.GeneratedWsdlDocuments.Count > 1)
      {
        Trace.TraceError(Resources.ExInconsistantXmlNamespaces);
        throw new InvalidOperationException(Resources.ExInconsistantXmlNamespaces);
      }

      ServiceDescription wsdl =
        exporter.GeneratedWsdlDocuments[0];
```

```csharp
XmlSchemaSet schemaSet =
  exporter.GeneratedXmlSchemas;
Collection<XmlSchema> importsList = new Collection<XmlSchema>();

for (int i = 0; i < wsdl.Types.Schemas.Count; i++)
{
  XmlSchema schema = wsdl.Types.Schemas[i];
  ResolveImportedSchemas(schema, schemaSet, importsList);

  if (schema.Includes.Count == 0 && schema.Items.Count == 0)
  {
    wsdl.Types.Schemas.RemoveAt(i--);
  }
}

while(importsList.Count != 0)
{
  int l = importsList.Count - 1;
  wsdl.Types.Schemas.Add(importsList[l]);
  importsList.RemoveAt(l);
}
}

private void ResolveImportedSchemas(XmlSchema schema,
  XmlSchemaSet schemaSet, Collection<XmlSchema> importsList)
{
  for (int i = 0; i < schema.Includes.Count; i++)
  {
    XmlSchemaImport import = schema.Includes[i] as XmlSchemaImport;

    if (import != null)
    {
      ICollection realSchemas = schemaSet.Schemas(import.Namespace);

      foreach (XmlSchema ixsd in realSchemas)
      {
        if (!importsList.Contains(ixsd))
        {
          importsList.Add(ixsd);

          ResolveImportedSchemas(ixsd, schemaSet, importsList);
        }
      }

      schema.Includes.RemoveAt(i--);
    }
}
```

```
            }
        }
    }
```

<hr>

Code file [Thinktecture.ServiceModel\Wsdl\FlatWsdl.cs] available for download at Wrox.com.

<hr>

What you now need to do is add this behavior to your endpoint in question. This can be done centrally on your `ServiceHost` object. The `Thinktecture.ServiceModel` library contains a custom service host that does the dirty work for you:

```
private void AddFlatWsdl()
{
    foreach (ServiceEndpoint endpoint in Description.Endpoints)
    {
        endpoint.Behaviors.Add(new FlatWsdl());
    }
}
```

<hr>

Code file [from Thinktecture.ServiceModel\ServiceHost.cs] available for download at Wrox.com.

<hr>

Take this extension together with the previously mentioned way to set your service's XML namespace in three different places, and you are good to have a flattened WSDL, as shown in Figure 9-8 (using a different service, not the movie service).

```
<?xml version="1.0" encoding="utf-8" ?>
- <wsdl:definitions name="ProductCatalog" targetNamespace="http://www.thinktecture.com/samples/services/productcatalog"
    xmlns:wsdl="http://schemas.xmlsoap.org/wsdl/" xmlns:wsx="http://schemas.xmlsoap.org/ws/2004/09/mex"
    xmlns:wsa10="http://www.w3.org/2005/08/addressing" xmlns:tns="http://www.thinktecture.com/samples/services/productcatalog"
    xmlns:soap12="http://schemas.xmlsoap.org/wsdl/soap12/" xmlns:wsu="http://docs.oasis-open.org/wss/2004/01/oasis-200401-wss-
    wssecurity-utility-1.0.xsd" xmlns:wsp="http://schemas.xmlsoap.org/ws/2004/09/policy"
    xmlns:wsap="http://schemas.xmlsoap.org/ws/2004/08/addressing/policy"
    xmlns:msc="http://schemas.microsoft.com/ws/2005/12/wsdl/contract"
    xmlns:wsa="http://schemas.xmlsoap.org/ws/2004/08/addressing" xmlns:wsam="http://www.w3.org/2007/05/addressing/metadata"
    xmlns:wsaw="http://www.w3.org/2006/05/addressing/wsdl" xmlns:soap="http://schemas.xmlsoap.org/wsdl/soap/"
    xmlns:xsd="http://www.w3.org/2001/XMLSchema" xmlns:soapenc="http://schemas.xmlsoap.org/soap/encoding/">
  - <wsdl:types>
    - <xs:schema attributeFormDefault="qualified" elementFormDefault="qualified"
        targetNamespace="http://schemas.microsoft.com/2003/10/Serialization/" xmlns:xs="http://www.w3.org/2001/XMLSchema"
        xmlns:tns="http://schemas.microsoft.com/2003/10/Serialization/">
        <xs:element name="anyType" nillable="true" type="xs:anyType" />
        <xs:element name="anyURI" nillable="true" type="xs:anyURI" />
        <xs:element name="base64Binary" nillable="true" type="xs:base64Binary" />
```

FIGURE 9-8: Using the extension to flatten WSDL

Metadata URLs

When hosting a WCF service behind a load balancer, the WSDL description contains the URLs for the machine on which the actual WCF service servicing the metadata request resides. This is a well-known bug in WCF and has been fixed in .NET 4.0. You can force WCF to use the server address from the request and insert this into the metadata simply by adding a service behavior to your services:

```
<serviceBehaviors>
  <behavior name="metadata">
    <useRequestHeadersForMetadataAddress>
      <!--
      <defaultPorts>
        <add scheme="http" port="81" />
        <add scheme="https" port="444" />
      </defaultPorts>
      -->
    </useRequestHeadersForMetadataAddress>
  </behavior>
</serviceBehaviors>
```

A fix for .NET 3.5 SP1 is also available at `http://support.microsoft.com/kb/971842` *and* `http://support.microsoft.com/kb/981002`.

This behavior fixes the issue so that load-balanced environments and WCF can live happily together.

SCHEMA-BASED CONTRACT-FIRST MODELING

In cases in which you strive for high interoperability scenarios, you may need to change your mind. An approach that has proven successful over the years is called *schema-based contract-first*.

When developing web services, the following are the usual steps:

1. Design your contract's data, messages, and interface.

2. Generate code from the contract.

This first step can be done either in code, or with XML and XSD. As it turns out, a number of enterprise-scale projects prefer to take the option to start with XML and XSD. For many integration and application-development scenarios (not only at the enterprise level), it is customary to negotiate a WSDL/XSD-based specification for the web services, and then to embark on the actual development of the code that implements that specification.

However, dealing with raw XML and WSDL can be error-prone. In particular, with WSDL, it is nontrivial to handle because the original WSDL specification enables room for some complicated constructs and contracts to be defined. You need tools that enable you to work at this level consistently and reliably.

There are some Open Source tools called `WSCF.blue` (`http://wscfblue.codeplex.com/`) that address this need.

The following shows the main steps involved in schema-first web service development.

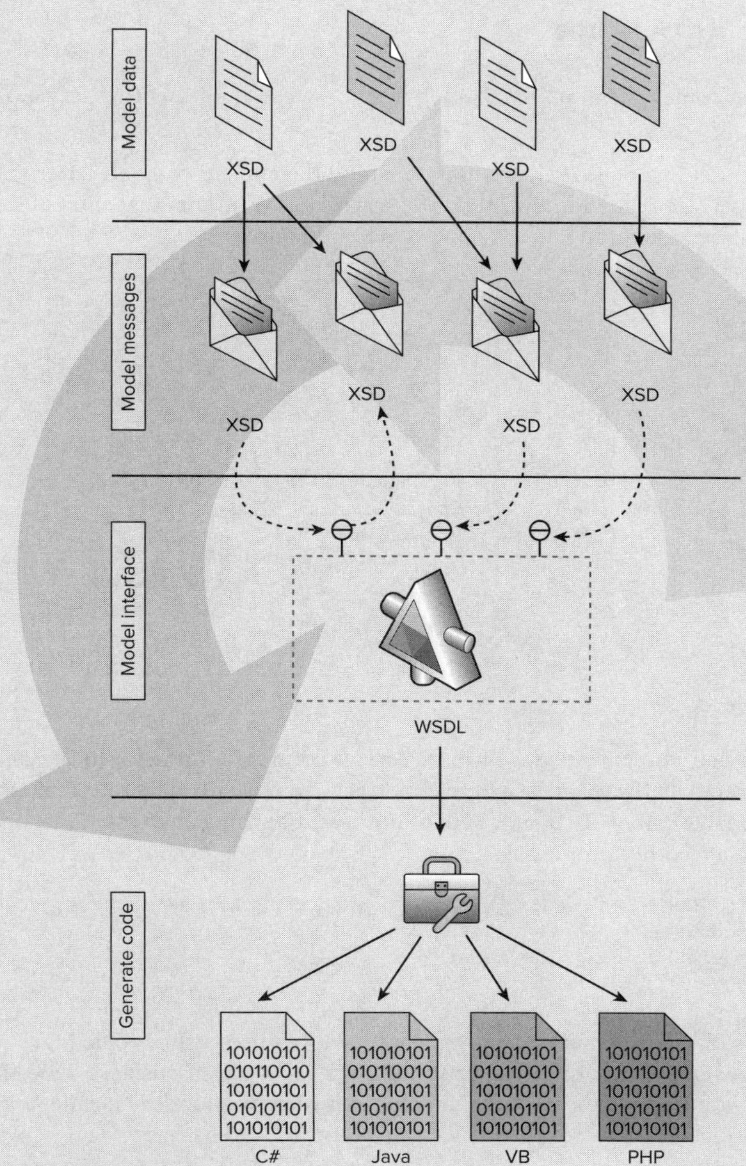

Source: MSDN Magazine article "Schema-based Development with Windows Communication Foundation" (http://msdn.microsoft.com/en-us/magazine/ee335699.aspx)

This discussion does not go into any more detail on this topic. Feel free to download the tool and try it out.

That's it then for the modeling, designing, and contracts part of this chapter. Now move on to see how to actually bring some life to your services.

IMPLEMENTING SERVICES

This section examines some central points to keep in mind when implementing services in a WCF-minded world.

Before diving into the details, be sure that you understand the current context. After you have modeled your contracts, you are ready to implement the services. This means that, first and foremost, you must implement a service façade like the one shown in Figure 9-9.

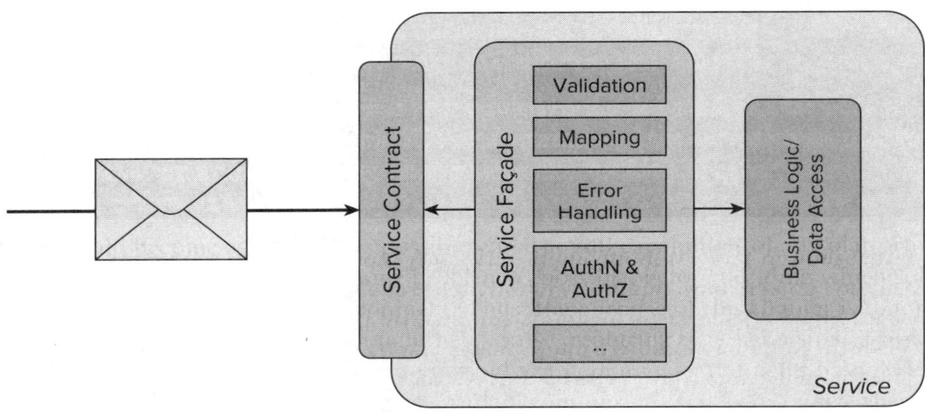

FIGURE 9-9: Service façade

This façade is a class that implements one or more service contract interfaces. In the case of the movie sample, it implements the `IMovieService` contract. You usually decorate a service façade class with a `ServiceBahaviorAttribute` to configure essential things like the name or the namespace, in addition to other properties.

```
[ServiceBehavior(Namespace = MovieServiceConstants.ServiceNamespace,
    ConfigurationName = "MovieService")]
public class MovieService : IMovieService
...
```

Inside of the methods of this class, you usually do not have any use-case-specific logic or even data-access code. As it turns out, this is quite a slim shim if you think about business logic. The idea is that the actual inner workings of the application logic can work without the façade, without WCF, and without distribution at all.

The façade is the service-communication-specific entry point into your service implementation. Typical tasks include the following:

➤   Authentication and authorization

➤   Input validation

> ➤ Mapping of DTOs and internal entities
>
> ➤ Error handling
>
> ➤ Caching (such as output caching)

The remainder of this section examines some of the more important tasks. (As mentioned previously, security is handled in Chapter 10.)

Validation

You surely remember your younger days when you went out to visit a dance club with your friends. There was this tall big guy at the entrance checking IDs and faces (and clothes, and shoes…).

You should always have such a "doorman" in your services. You should always validate incoming data. The service façade is the central entry point from the outside world, and before you do anything with the data being sent, you must ensure that it is in the shape you expect, and the values within the boundaries are what you expect. (Service façade validation may collide with business-level validation rules in some cases.)

Part of the validation is already handled by the serializers. But you want to add business-level validation to it. Either do it manually by checking every parameter coming in to your service façade operation, or use a metadata-driven approach. One idea here is to leverage an aspect-oriented framework such as PostSharp (`www.sharpcrafters.com/`) to encapsulate the validation logic and rules into a central implementation.

Of course, you can always roll your own in WCF — this is what a lot of people love WCF for — and maybe as many people hate it for this exact same reason. In this case, you would implement an `IParameterInspector` or `IDispatchMessageInspector` on the service side, and hook it up into the WCF pipeline.

> *For more information, see the MSDN article, "How to: Perform Input Validation in WCF" at* `http://msdn.microsoft.com/en-us/library/ff647875.aspx`.

Mapping

It has been stated more than once in this chapter that the service contract contains data-transfer structures to exchange data between the callers and the callee. This immediately implies that you do not want to see full-fledged business entities on the service edge. These entities live inside of the service boundary, are usually more eloquent, and have more features than what you want to expose through the service façade.

What this mean is that you must map the incoming data in the shape of data contracts to the internal representations — and vice versa.

Not only with WCF, but also in applications built with ASP.NET Model-View-Controller (MVC), or even on the client side in programs built with WPF or Silverlight, you see the need to map one shape of object to another shape of object. So, you are actually looking at object-to-object mapping. And this problem has been solved for you.

There are tools and libraries to make your life easier. I usually end up with using AutoMapper (`http://automapper.codeplex.com/`), but EmitMapper (`http://emitmapper.codeplex.com/`) is also a good choice. These folks are convention-based mappers. If your object representations conform to their conventions, then mapping is actually more or less a one-liner.

Oh yeah, I can hear you shouting out that this must be a slow operation — to map objects at runtime, maybe by using reflection emit. Yes, there is some overhead, and you must decide (by including tests) whether this overhead causes you pain. But believe me, in most distributed applications I have come across, the overhead of a mapper is the least overhead you will worry about.

For AutoMapper, the first step is to set up the map for a destination and target type, such as shown here:

```
Mapper.CreateMap<Movie, MovieData>();
Mapper.CreateMap<Movie, MovieDetailsData>();
```

Code file [from BootstrapTasks\EntityMapperBootstrapTask.cs] available for download at Wrox.com.

Available for download on Wrox.com

This tells the static `Mapper` class from AutoMapper that you want to map from `Movie` to `MovieData`, and from `Movie` to `MovieDetailsData`. `Movie` is the internal business entity and looks like this:

Available for download on Wrox.com

```
public class Movie
{
    private List<Actor> cast;
    private Media mediaFiles;

    public string Id { get; set; }
    public string Title { get; set; }
    public int Year { get; set; }
    public string Director { get; set; }
    public string Genre { get; set; }
    public List<Actor> Cast
    {
        get
        {
            if (cast == null)
                cast = new List<Actor>();

            return cast;
        }
        set
        {
            cast = value;
        }
    }
```

```csharp
public Media MediaFiles
{
    get
    {
        if (mediaFiles == null)
            mediaFiles = new Media();

        return mediaFiles;
    }
    set
    {
        mediaFiles = value;
    }
}
```

Code file [Entities\Movie.cs] available for download at Wrox.com.

Setting up the route in this direction is straightforward — but what about the reverse case where you want to map `MovieData` to `Movie`? `MovieData` has considerably less data fields than the `Movie` entity. Here you must tell AutoMapper to ignore those fields, as shown here:

```csharp
Mapper.CreateMap<MovieData, Movie>()
        .ForMember(dest => dest.Cast, opt => opt.Ignore())
        .ForMember(dest => dest.Director, opt => opt.Ignore())
        .ForMember(dest => dest.Genre, opt => opt.Ignore())
        .ForMember(dest => dest.Year, opt => opt.Ignore())
        .ForMember(dest => dest.MediaFiles, opt => opt.Ignore());
```

Code file [from BootstrapTasks\EntityMapperBootstrapTask.cs] available for download at Wrox.com.

After you have set up the maps, you can simply call the `Map` method on the `Mapper` class whenever you want to map from one object to another. In the movie sample, a helper class has been created that has a couple of extension methods on the source types. This makes mapping super easy.

```csharp
public static class EntityMapper
{
    public static MovieData Map(this Movie movie)
    {
        return Mapper.Map<Movie, MovieData>(movie);
    }

    public static Movie Map(this MovieDetailsData movie)
    {
        return Mapper.Map<MovieDetailsData, Movie>(movie);
    }

    public static Movie Map(this MovieData movie)
    {
        return Mapper.Map<MovieData, Movie>(movie);
    }

    public static MovieDetailsData MapAll(this Movie movie)
```

```csharp
    {
        return Mapper.Map<Movie, MovieDetailsData>(movie);
    }

    public static List<MovieData> Map(this List<Movie> movie)
    {
        return Mapper.Map<List<Movie>, List<MovieData>>(movie);
    }
}
```

Code file [MovieServices\EntityMapper.cs] available for download at Wrox.com.

AutoMapper can be a real saver, but you should use it wisely.

Tracing

The tracing feature can and will save your life — one day. When an application goes well, and errors and exceptions occur, then everything is fine. But when unexpected things happen, you will be lucky if you have information on what went wrong and why. In a service-based application, this is usually a difficult task. The essential pieces of the architecture are "headless" — there is no UI, there is no place to pop up a message box, or display an error page.

WCF has tracing built in, which builds on top of the tracing infrastructure in the .NET Framework. Whenever I get a call or an e-mail from clients and a WCF-based application does not behave as expected, I suggest that they turn on tracing — and indeed, maybe 80 percent of all problems get solved immediately by looking at the traces.

Therefore, the first thing is to have a configuration snippet to turn on tracing in WCF. (This will be done in the hosting project. You learn more about hosting later in this chapter.)

```xml
<system.diagnostics>
  <sources>
    <source name="System.ServiceModel"
            switchValue="Warning, ActivityTracing"
            propagateActivity="true">
      <listeners>
        <add type="System.Diagnostics.DefaultTraceListener"
             name="Default"/>
        <add name="ServiceModelTraceListener"/>
      </listeners>
    </source>
  </sources>
  <sharedListeners>
    <add initializeData="moviehost.svclog"
         type="System.Diagnostics.XmlWriterTraceListener, System,
             Version=4.0.0.0, Culture=neutral,
             PublicKeyToken=b77a5c561934e089"
         name="ServiceModelTraceListener"
         traceOutputOptions="Timestamp"/>
```

```
    </sharedListeners>
    <trace autoflush="true" />
  </system.diagnostics>
```

Code file [MovieConsoleHost\app.config] available for download at Wrox.com.

What is important is the `switchValue` attribute of the `System.ServiceModel` source. With this value, you indicate the level of verbosity with which WCF should emit tracing data into the trace file. Now you have WCF emitting tracing data, and you can inspect the trace files with the service trace viewer tool from the Windows SDK. This tool can be found at `C:\Program Files\Microsoft SDKs\Windows\v6.0A\Bin\SvcTraceViewer.exe`. (Again, this can save your life! I promise.)

 *Be sure that the process in which your WCF service is running has write access to the location where you want to save the trace file.*

A not-so-nice fact about tracing is that you must specify it in your configuration file, and if you want to turn it on or off, it may considerably slow down the processing inside of your services (especially if you use a trace level of `Verbose`). You must restart the hosting process. There is help, though. I will show you a way to switch tracing on or off at runtime.

The key feature you must enable in WCF is the built-in Windows Management Instrumentation (WMI) provider. Using WMI, you can then enable and disable tracing at runtime.

```
<system.serviceModel>
  <diagnostics wmiProviderEnabled="true"/>
```

 *A strange bug is in the WMI feature of WCF. See the README file and the updated .mof file in the sample code available on this book's companion website to understand what it means, and how to fix it.*

When WMI is on, you can either use WMI in a .NET-based program via the `System.Management` namespace from the `System.Management` assembly, or simply hack up a small Windows PowerShell script.

Following is a script to enable tracing:

```
$ms = get-wmiobject -class "AppDomainInfo" -namespace "root\servicemodel" -
    computername "." | where {$_.Name -eq "MovieConsoleHost.exe"}
$ms.TraceLevel = "Warning, ActivityTracing"
$ms.Put()
```

And the following is the equivalent to turn it off:

```
$ms = get-wmiobject -class "AppDomainInfo" -namespace "root\servicemodel" -
    computername "." | where {$_.Name -eq "MovieConsoleHost.exe"}
$ms.TraceLevel = "Off"
$ms.Put()
```

Needless to say, the process executing these scripts (or the APIs in .NET) must run at elevated context.

That is it — again, brief and concise, but powerful.

The last tip for tracing and implementing services is to not just use WCF's intrinsic tracing, but also leverage `System.Diagnostics` in your code. The easiest is to use `TraceSources` for your service implementation, and use the trace source to trace information, warnings, or error messages. With the .NET diagnostics architecture in place, you can then define and hook up trace listeners to listen on the trace sources.

Although there are a number of third-party and Open Source libraries out there for tracing (such as log4net or NLog), in this discussion, I focus on the features built into .NET Framework where possible, and where it makes sense.

Defining and using a trace source is straightforward:

```csharp
[ServiceBehavior(Namespace = MovieServiceConstants.ServiceNamespace,
    ConfigurationName = "MovieService")]
public class MovieService : IMovieService
{
        private IMovieManager movieManager;
        private TraceSource trace;

        public MovieService()
        {
            trace = new TraceSource("mdb.Movies");
            trace.TraceInformation("MovieService ctor...");
...
```

Code file [from MovieServices\MovieService.cs] available for download at Wrox.com.

In the configuration file, you then hook up the listeners, such as the following Windows event log listener:

```xml
<system.diagnostics>
  <sources>
    <source name="mdb.Movies"
            switchValue="Verbose" >
      <listeners>
        <add name="EventLogTraceListener" />
      </listeners>
```

```
        </source>
      </sources>
      <sharedListeners>
        <add name="EventLogTraceListener"
             type="System.Diagnostics.EventLogTraceListener"
             initializeData="mdb Movies" />
      </sharedListeners>
    </system.diagnostics>
```

Code file [from MovieWindowsServiceHost\app.config] available for download at Wrox.com.

Now your code is emitting trace data. If you take the next step and combine the traces from your services and the traces from WCF, you can even view everything inside of the WCF service trace viewer tool, and use its features like filtering or searching.

Did I already tell you that tracing can save your life?

All the nice contracts and façades are pretty much useless if you are not actually offering your services for consumption. So, let's hop over to hosting them.

HOSTING SERVICES

Admittedly, the discussion in the previous section already hinted at and used hosting features. Thus, it is finally the time to cover hosting options for your WCF services. Several options exist in WCF to host applications, and it is good to know about what to use when, and where to hook into the hosting logic to get the most out of WCF.

Customizing Hosting

Independent from the hosting method you are using (which is covered in this section), at one point, you will face the need to hook up into the process of spawning up a WCF service. What you will end up with is a custom implementation of a *service host factory* by deriving `ServiceHostFactory` or `ServiceHostFactoryBase`.

With a service host factory, you can intercept the startup phase of your services, in both self-hosted and web-hosted environments. Usually, a service host factory goes hand-in-hand with a custom service host that implements the actual customizations.

```
public class MoviesServiceHostFactory : ServiceHostFactory
{
    public override ServiceHostBase CreateServiceHost(
      string constructorString, Uri[] baseAddresses)
    {
        var host = base.CreateServiceHost(constructorString, baseAddresses);

        // apply your logic here...

        return host;
    }
}
```

```
protected override ServiceHost CreateServiceHost(
  Type serviceType, Uri[] baseAddresses)
{
    var host = base.CreateServiceHost(serviceType, baseAddresses);

    // apply your logic here...

    return host;
}
}
```

Code file [from Hosting\MoviesServiceHostFactory.cs] available for download at Wrox.com.

Customizations may include the following:

➤ Adding some standard endpoints or endpoint configurations

➤ Hooking up orthogonal features that your service does not need to be aware of

➤ Adding some startup or bootstrap logic (examined later in this section)

➤ Providing entry points for dependency injection containers

Now, with the service host factory tool in your tool belt, it is time to examine the hosting options.

Testing with Console Hosts

Some of you may think I am going crazy now — but this is a true story. A client called us and said that his server application is no longer available, and the client applications throw countless exceptions. After going through several possible error causes, we found that he was using a console host to run the services. And yes, it turned out that he did not minimize the console window, but closed it and did not realize it.

Console hosts are only meant for demonstrating and simple testing — nothing more. When I use a console host in this book, it's probably because I can show some things a bit easier. But in real life, WCF services that are meant as server functionality should be hosted in robust environments as outlined in this discussion.

Self-Hosting with a Windows Service

There are situations in a service-based distributed application in which you want to completely control the hosting environment. Furthermore, there are services that are encapsulating and exposing long-running business processes that are not compatible with a short-lived request-response style of communication. If you are in this camp, then hosting your WCF services in a Windows Service is the way to go.

The movie database sample also contains a Windows Service project, including an installer to install the Windows Service with the well-known Windows tools, as shown in Figure 9-10.

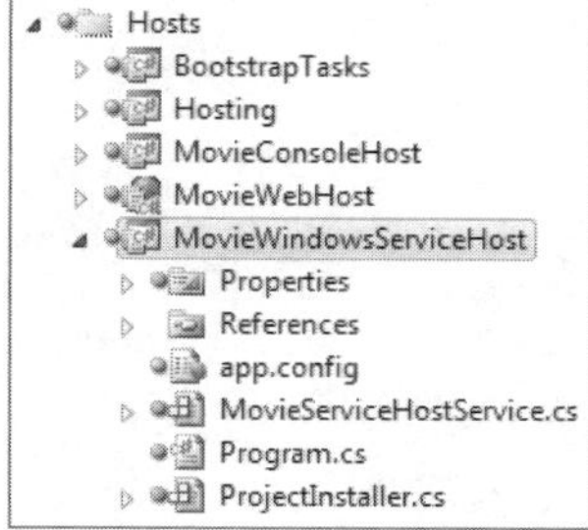

FIGURE 9-10: Windows Service project

Whereas a console host is for testing and showing things to other developers, the Windows Service host must be robust in its behavior. When opening the `ServiceHost` instances, you should catch all exceptions and trace them — you know, a Windows Service is even more "headless." The same goes for stopping services. Additionally, it is wise to handle the event for unhandled exceptions on the `AppDomain` hosting the Windows Service.

All this is implemented in the Windows Service host for the movie database sample.

```csharp
public partial class MovieServiceHostService : ServiceBase
{
    tt.ServiceHost host;
    tt.ServiceHost streamingHost;

    public MovieServiceHostService()
    {
        InitializeComponent();

        AppDomain.CurrentDomain.UnhandledException +=
            new UnhandledExceptionEventHandler(CurrentDomain_UnhandledException);
    }

    protected override void OnStart(string[] args)
    {
        Directory.SetCurrentDirectory(AppDomain.CurrentDomain.BaseDirectory);

        try
        {
            var host = MoviesServiceFactory.GetDefault();
            host.SetupMoviesServiceHost();
            host.Open();

            var streamingHost = MediaServiceFactory.GetDefault();
            streamingHost.SetupMediaServiceHost();
            streamingHost.Open();
        }
        catch (Exception ex)
        {
            Trace.TraceError("Error while stopping mdb hosts: {0}", ex.Message);
```

```csharp
                throw;
            }
        }

        protected override void OnStop()
        {
            try
            {
                if (host != null)
                    host.Close();

                if (streamingHost != null)
                    streamingHost.Close();
            }
            catch (Exception ex)
            {
                Trace.TraceError("Error while starting mdb hosts: {0}", ex.Message);
                throw;
            }
        }

        private void CurrentDomain_UnhandledException(object sender,
            UnhandledExceptionEventArgs e)
        {
            Trace.TraceError("Error in mdb hosts: {0}", (e.ExceptionObject as
                Exception).Message);
        }
    }
```

Code file [from MovieWindowsServiceHost\MovieServiceHostService.cs] available for download at Wrox.com.

There is even another layer of error handling that you can hook into. The `ServiceHost` base class defines several events that may be needed for handling errors, such as the following:

```
Faulted
UnknownMessageReceived
```

When hosting in a Windows Service, it is a recommended security practice to use a least-privileged user account to run the process. This user must have rights to do several things, including the following:

➤ Listening on HTTP-based ports via `http.sys`

> *For development environments, a recommended tool to use to set up permission for HTTP on Windows can be found at* `www.stevestechspot.com/downloads/httpconfig.zip`.

➤ Permissions to read to or write from Microsoft Message Queuing (MSMQ) queues if needed

➤ Access to the file system (for example, for writing trace files)

➤ Permissions to custom event log sources

➤ Allowing access to involved data sources (for example, when using SQL Server with integrated security)

These requirements are usually handled by an installing application you must build that sets up all the necessary configuration and permissions.

When you have followed all the important steps, you are good to run your service inside of a Windows Service, as shown in Figure 9-11.

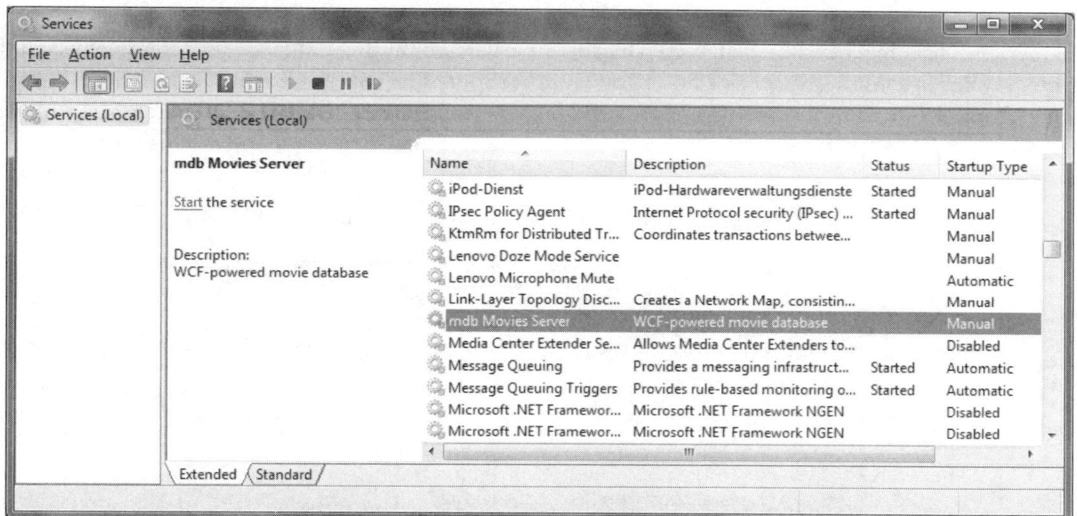

FIGURE 9-11: Running a service inside of a Windows Service

Web-Hosting with WAS

Probably the most commonly used hosting method is running WCF services inside of IIS. Since IIS7, this actually means running WCF services in Windows Activation Services (WAS).

Although WAS provides the capability to host WCF with endpoints based not only on HTTP or HTTPS, but also on named pipes (TCP or MSMQ), I would probably not take this route. The problem is that IIS is still a web server, and you still do not have the full control over the life cycle of both the worker process (you could manage that though) and the .NET application domain the WCF service is running in.

There are several partly undocumented situations in which you may just lose your `AppDomain`, including maybe data that was currently processed. Because `net.tcp`-based services are especially run in per-session mode in most cases, this may have some unwanted and not anticipated side effects (such as loss of session and data).

A list of possible causes can be found at `http://blogs.msdn.com/tess/archive/2006/08/02/asp-net-case-study-lost-session-variables-and-appdomain-recycles.aspx.`

Again, if you must host some services in a non-HTTP-like, nonshort-lived style, you should strive for Windows Services.

When hosting in IIS/WAS, there are three ways to do this:

➤ Using physical `.svc` files for each service

➤ Specifying virtual paths to `.svc` services in `web.config`

➤ Using a `ServiceRoute` object to integrate with the `System.Web.Routing` feature

Using `.svc` files has been part of WCF since its first version, and means that you create physical files for every service (actually, service host) you want to offer. The routing feature has been available since .NET 4.0, and as a prerequisite for using it, you must enable the ASP.NET integration mode for WCF.

A `.svc` file contains a declaration hinting at what service class and which service host factory (optional) you want to bootstrap. For the example movie service, it looks like this:

```
<%@ ServiceHost Language="C#" Service="MovieServices.MovieService"
    Factory="Hosting.MoviesServiceHostFactory" %>
```

If you do not want to have a plethora of files in your web hosting project, then you can use virtual paths in `web.config`, as shown here:

```
<system.serviceModel>
  <serviceHostingEnvironment>
    <serviceActivations>
      <add service="MovieServices.MovieService"
           factory="Hosting.MoviesServiceHostFactory"
           relativeAddress="service.svc" />
    </serviceActivations>
  </serviceHostingEnvironment>
```

The strange thing is that the relative address literally needs to end with `.svc`.

On the other hand, when using the routing approach, you no longer need a `.svc` file (physical or logical), and you hook up your routes in `global.asax`:

```
public class global : System.Web.HttpApplication
{

    protected void Application_Start(object sender, EventArgs e)
    {
        RouteTable.Routes.Add(
            new ServiceRoute(
                "service", new MoviesServiceHostFactory(),
                typeof(MovieService)));
    }
    ...
```

The `ServiceRoute` class can be found in the `System.ServiceModel.Activation` assembly, which was introduced with .NET 4.0. For this feature to work, though, you must enable ASP.NET compatibility mode. This is done by adding it on the service host environment:

```
<system.serviceModel>
  <serviceHostingEnvironment aspNetCompatibilityEnabled="true">
```

The routing feature is implemented as an HTTP module. To use it, you must instruct IIS to offer it to your requests:

```
<system.webServer>
  <modules runAllManagedModulesForAllRequests="true"/>
</system.webServer>
```

And, finally, you must add a setting to the service host implementation indicating that you are actually willing to opt-in to compatibility mode:

```
[AspNetCompatibilityRequirements(RequirementsMode=
    AspNetCompatibilityRequirementsMode.Allowed)]
[ServiceBehavior(Namespace = MovieServiceConstants.ServiceNamespace,
    ConfigurationName = "MovieService")]
public class MovieService : IMovieService
```

After these changes, you are good to go, and the movie service is available with a `.svc` file, as shown in Figure 9-12.

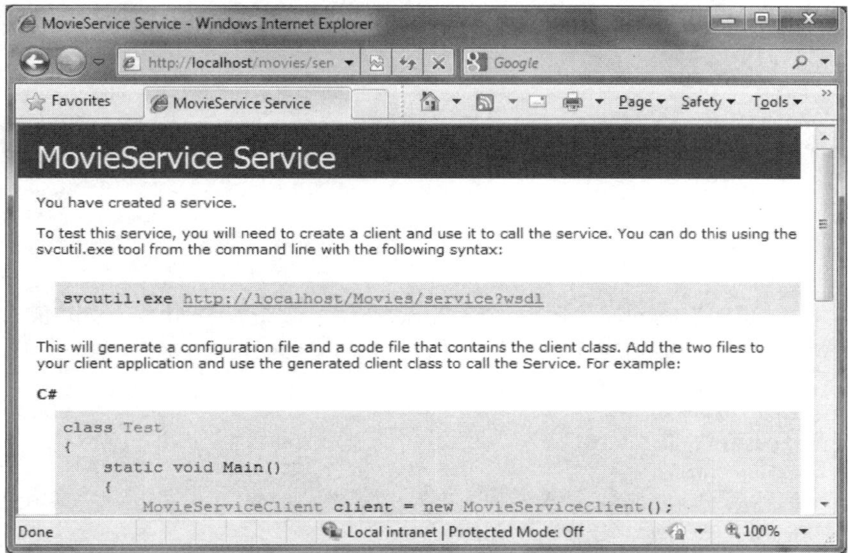

FIGURE 9-12: The movie service available with a .svc file

There is actually another way to host WCF. You can host WCF services in the Windows Server `AppFabric`, an extension to the IIS/WAS-based hosting model. The scope of this book, however, does not enable coverage of `AppFabric`. And, to be honest, for pure WCF services, there are not a whole lot of existing features in it.

Bootstrapping

The service host and service host factory infrastructure offered by WCF is already a good means to inject custom code for the startup phase. But, in practice, a number of situations show up in which you want to have an easy way to plug into the startup of your services without worrying too much about extending the WCF pipeline every time.

For this purpose, you can doggy-bag a bootstrap tasks collection on your custom service host. A *bootstrap task* is a simple interface with just one method. (You can optionally also have teardown or shutdown methods.)

```
public interface IBootstrapTask
{
    void Execute();
}
```

On your service host, you then have a collection of bootstrap tasks:

```
public class MyServiceHost : System.ServiceModel.ServiceHost
{
    private IList<IBootstrapTask> bootstrapTasks;

    public IList<IBootstrapTask> BootstrapTasks
    {
        get
        {
            if (bootstrapTasks == null)
            {
                bootstrapTasks = new List<IBootstrapTask>();
            }

            return bootstrapTasks;
        }
    }
```

And, for the registered tasks to be executed upon service host start, you simply call them in the service host's `InitializeRuntime` method:

```
protected override void InitializeRuntime()
{
    ExecuteBootstrapTasks();
    base.InitializeRuntime();
}

private void ExecuteBootstrapTasks()
{
    foreach (var task in BootstrapTasks)
    {
        if (task != null)
        {
            task.Execute();
        }
    }
}
```

Now, you may be wondering what a typical bootstrap could be and look like. Actually, you have already seen a perfect example of it in this chapter. Think about setting up the maps for an object-to-object map such as AutoMapper. There's no better place to do this stuff than in a bootstrap task:

```csharp
public class EntityMapperBootstrapTask : IBootstrapTask
{
    public void Execute()
    {
        Mapper.CreateMap<MovieData, Movie>()
                .ForMember(dest => dest.Cast, opt => opt.Ignore())
                .ForMember(dest => dest.Director, opt => opt.Ignore())
                .ForMember(dest => dest.Genre, opt => opt.Ignore())
                .ForMember(dest => dest.Year, opt => opt.Ignore())
                .ForMember(dest => dest.MediaFiles, opt => opt.Ignore());
        Mapper.CreateMap<MovieDetailsData, Movie>()
            .ForMember(dest => dest.Id, opt => opt.Ignore())
            .ForMember(dest => dest.MediaFiles, opt => opt.Ignore());

        Mapper.CreateMap<Movie, MovieData>();
        Mapper.CreateMap<Movie, MovieDetailsData>();

        Mapper.CreateMap<Actor, ActorData>();
        Mapper.CreateMap<ActorData, Actor>();

        Mapper.AssertConfigurationIsValid();
    }
}
```

Code file [BootstrapTasks\EntityMapperBootstrapTask.cs] available for download at Wrox.com.

The actual registration of your bootstrap tasks can then happen either explicitly in your code, or by using an IoC container, which loads all known types based on the `IBootstrapTask` interface.

```csharp
host.BootstrapTasks.Add(new EntityMapperBootstrapTask());
```

This is a convenient and powerful piece of infrastructure.

As with many other implementation tips in this chapter, you can find a customized `ServiceHost` *with bootstrap task support in* `Thinktecture` `.ServiceModel.dll`.

What is left for a full end-to-end communication is the consuming side. So, let's take a look at how to build consuming (or simply "client") applications.

CONSUMING SERVICES

Up until now, you have read a lot about how to design and implement services. It's now time to talk about consuming services.

Shared Contracts

When you are used to the concept of Web Services, it seems natural for service-based communication to need some kind of XML-based metadata to start building your client applications. Usually, you get told to point your development tool of choice to that WSDL and XSD metadata over there, and WCF performs some magic and generates .NET code and a configuration file for you to work with. But why would you want to follow this path if you have all communication parties under your control, and even more, all code is implemented on the .NET platform?

For these cases — and these are by far the most I have run into so far — you can use the shared contracts assembly approach. You surely remember the solution structure of the sample application shown in Figure 9-13.

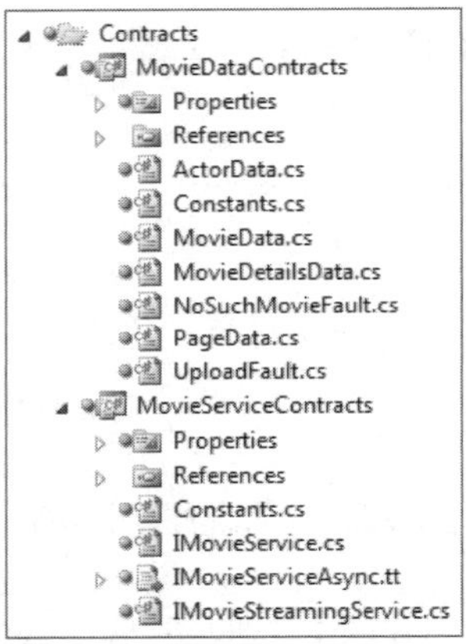

FIGURE 9-13: Solution structure of the sample application

All the necessary information, especially the contract metadata, is encapsulated in the data and service contracts assemblies. If you can share these assemblies, you can use WCF helper classes to work against these contracts without having to take the round trip with WSDL and so on.

This central class is `ChannelFactory<T>` from the `System.ServiceModel` namespace. This tiny helper can provide a configured transparent proxy to your service endpoint:

```
var cf = new ChannelFactory<IMovieServiceChannel>(
    "non-default");
IMovieService movieServiceClient = cf.CreateChannel();
```

The string parameter to the constructor hints at the endpoint configuration to pick up from the configuration file for the client application. You learn more about endpoint-specific settings, tweaking for bindings, and other things later. But this brings up one obvious downside of the pure shared contracts approach. You must care for the `app.config` file on your own, and ensure that it is up to date.

Other than that, this is already it. With `IMovieService` in hand, you can do the service class. A small tweak can bring even more joy, though. Just derive an interface definition from the original service contract and from `IClientChannel` (from the `System.ServiceModel` namespace):

```
public interface IMovieServiceChannel : IMovieService, IClientChannel
{}
```

Now you have the full power of the client channel and can, for example, subscribe to the channel events, as shown in Figure 9-14.

```
var cf = new ChannelFactory<IMovieServiceChannel>(
    "default");
movieServiceClient = cf.CreateChannel();
movieServiceClient.Clo
```


FIGURE 9-14: Realizing the full power of the client channel

One last thing to consider is that the expensive part is creating the channel factory. It may be a good idea to cache this channel factory, especially in high-traffic and high-load environments.

Asynchronous Calls

Because this topic has been touched on previously in this chapter, at this point, just recall that it is essential to know that synchronous request/response calls from consuming applications into services are blocking the calling thread. Earlier in this chapter, you learned how to automatically get an asynchronous version of a WCF service contract by applying a T4 template for code generation.

Another simple and pragmatic way is to use the `ThreadPool` and put the call onto a background thread with the synchronous version of the contract, and handle the response in the appropriate callback.

Whatever way you choose, you must know how to keep your client applications responsive.

Service Agent Pattern

Beyond the pure technicalities discussed previously, I use the *service agent* pattern over and over on the consuming side. If you want to visually materialize a service agent, then Figure 9-15 may help.

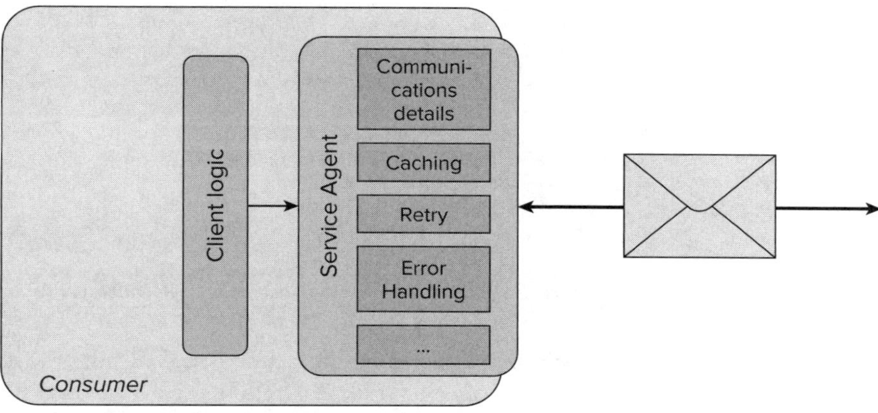

FIGURE 9-15: Materializing a service agent

In Figure 9-15, the Service Agent is kind of the counterpart of the service façade. It takes over especially the communication details with one or several WCF (or other) services and provides a business-specific view to the client application. The following discussion examines some of the typical tasks a service agent performs, including the following:

➤ Communication details

➤ Error handling

➤ Retry logic

➤ Caching data

The sample solution for the example movie service application splits the service agent into its own DLL, which is then used by the client application (in this case, a Windows Forms application), as shown in Figure 9-16.

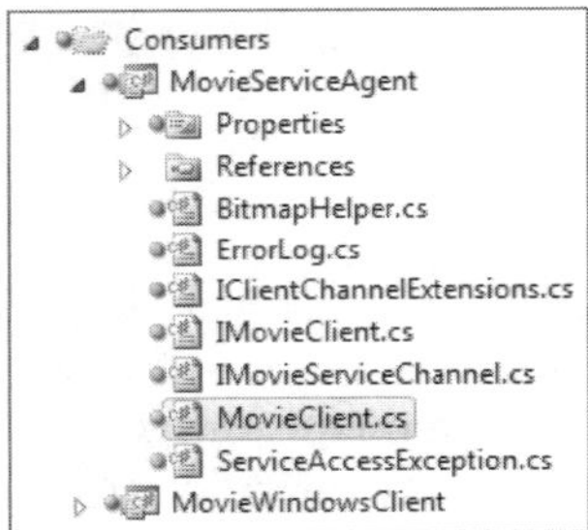

FIGURE 9-16: Splitting the service agent into its own DLL

So, what do I mean by "communication details" then? At the beginning of this chapter, you learned that in a real project, you probably end up with several styles of service orientation combined — operation- and resource-based. Your client applications — the UI part, at least — usually does not care about those details.

Take a look at the interface that the client application uses to talk to the service agent:

```csharp
public interface IMovieClient
{
    void AddMovie(MovieDetailsData movie);
    // Update...
    // Delete...
    List<MovieData> ListMovies(PagedDataRequest request);
    MovieDetailsData GetMovie(string movieId);
    byte[] GetMoviePoster(string movieId);
    Uri GetMovieStreamUrl(string movieId);
}
```

Code file [MovieServiceAgent\IMovieClient.cs] available for download at Wrox.com.

This interface tries to focus on the business aspects, not the communication details. Under the hood, the implementation of this interface uses some WCF-specific tricks for calling the movie service, and also uses a plain, pure HTTP-based class to get data for the media (screenshots and trailers) available for a given movie.

> *Frankly, there are communication details in the interface in the shape of the data contracts. To completely decouple the client from the communication layer, you would introduce client- and view-specific entities, which would then map onto the data contracts (for example, with AutoMapper).*

Another task related to the previous one is to perform proper error and exception handling for WCF calls. There is quite verbose documentation on MSDN (`http://msdn.microsoft.com/en-us/library/aa354510.aspx` and `http://msdn.microsoft.com/en-us/library/aa355056.aspx`) telling you how to behave when calling WCF services. There are quite a lot of things to adhere to and to write for every call you do. I thought it would be nice to have some helper that makes the code a bit easier to read, maybe like this:

```csharp
public MovieDetailsData GetMovie(string movieId)
{
    var movieData = new MovieDetailsData();

    movieServiceClient.HandleExceptions(() =>
    {
            movieData =
            movieServiceClient.GetMovie(movieId);
    });

    return movieData;
}
```

Code file [from MovieServiceAgent\MovieClient.cs] available for download at Wrox.com.

The `HandleExceptions` method is an extension method on the `IClientChannel` interface introduced earlier. The full implementation follows the best practices for calling WCF services from MSDN:

```csharp
public static void HandleExceptions(this IClientChannel channel, Action action)
{
    try
    {
        action();
    }
    catch (TimeoutException timeout)
    {
        ErrorLog.WriteError(timeout);
        channel.Abort();
        throw new ServiceAccessException("Timeout");
    }
    catch (FaultException<NoSuchMovieFault> noMovieFault)
    {
```

```
        ErrorLog.WriteError(noMovieFault);
        channel.Abort();
        throw new ServiceAccessException(noMovieFault.Message);
    }
    catch (FaultException unknown)
    {
        ErrorLog.WriteError(unknown);
        channel.Abort();
        throw new ServiceAccessException("Unknown fault");
    }
    catch (CommunicationException communication)
    {
        ErrorLog.WriteError(communication);
        channel.Abort();
        throw new ServiceAccessException("Communication");
    }
    catch (Exception e)
    {
        ErrorLog.WriteError(e);
        channel.Abort();
        throw;
    }
}
```

Code file [from MovieServiceAgent\IClientChannelExtensions.cs] available for download at Wrox.com.

The `ServiceAccessException` is a custom exception that is caught in the calling application code — the only exception the programmer has to deal with.

But what happens if exceptions (or certain types of exceptions) occur? Simply throw? Or is there any chance to retry the call until you think that it makes no sense to try further? With the exact same idea as for error handling, you can make your life easier when retrying calls. Following is an implementation in which you can specify how many times to retry, and how long to wait between the calls:

```
public static void RetryCall(this IClientChannel channel, int retries,
    int timeToWait, Action action)
{
    var currentRetry = 0;
    var success = false;
    var firstCall = true;
    Exception exception = null;

    while (!success && !(currentRetry == retries))
    {
        try
        {
            if (timeToWait > 0)
            {
                if (firstCall == false)
                    Thread.Sleep(timeToWait);
            }
```

```
                firstCall = false;

                action();

                success = true;
            }
        catch (ServiceAccessException sax)
        {
            currentRetry++;
            exception = sax;
        }
        catch (TimeoutException tex)
        {
            currentRetry++;
            exception = tex;
        }
        catch (CommunicationException cex)
        {
            currentRetry++;
            exception = cex;
        }
    }

    if (currentRetry == retries)
    {
        if (exception != null)
            throw exception;
    }
}
```

Code file [from MovieServiceAgent\IClientChannelExtensions.cs] available for download at Wrox.com.

This is simplified code. Usually, you end up with some exponential backoff strategy for the timeouts when retrying.

Consuming services is not only meant for GUI-based applications, but also for a services-to-services communication. No matter what kind of client application you are building, you should be sure to hide them from the intrinsics of the communication platform and techniques used.

COMPLEMENTING SERVICE APPROACH

All the samples until now have been in an operation-oriented service style. If you refer back to the beginning of the chapter, you can recall another approach, the resource-oriented approach for service orientation. Now take a look at this way to define services for your pragmatic view of services and WCF.

And again — as already stated at the beginning of this chapter — I won't go anywhere near REST and discuss the principles of it. First, there is an entire chapter in this book talking about REST, and second, I want to be pragmatic and demonstrate based on the requirements outlined for the sample application that certain scenarios are better implemented by a resource-oriented way.

This scenario is to give back data to calling clients based on an HTTP/HTTPS URL. This data could be structured data such as the movie data, but, in this case, it is raw data for the movie poster and trailer.

Web Programming Model

Since .NET 3.5, it is possible in WCF to map URLs to service operations. This is possibly the easiest way to solve the problems outlined if you completely want to stick to WCF. The idea is to define a fragment of a URI, and map that to the signature of a service contract operation. Microsoft calls this the *web programming model* of WCF (to ensure that this is not about REST in the first place).

If you are an ASP.NET developer, and have experience with HTTP handlers or ASP.NET MVC, then you may be addicted to sticking with this platform. If you need easy self-hosting, however, WCF can still be a good option.

A simple example to illustrate this would be an operation that delivers movie information on a given defined URL, as shown here:

```
[ServiceContract]
public interface IMovieServiceWeb
{
    [WebGet(UriTemplate = "movies/{movieId}")]
    MovieData GetMoviePoster(string movieId);
}
```

This operation returns the well-known `MovieData` data contract and accepts a string for the movie ID. The magic pieces here are the `WebGet` (indicating an HTTP `GET` call) attribute and `UriTemplate` property (which maps incoming URL parts and query string to operation contract parameters). If you have a base URL for the service of `http://tt.com/mdb/`, then you can get details for the movie with ID 42 at `http://tt.com/mdb/movies/42`.

You need a reference to the `System.ServiceModel.Web` *assembly, by the way.*

This call can happen by simply pointing your browser to this URL.

By default, the serialization format is XML using the `DataContractSerializer`, but you can easily change this behavior to be JavaScript Object Notation (JSON). This can happen in three ways:

➤ Use `ResponseFormat` of `WebGet` attribute, as shown here:

```
[WebGet(UriTemplate = "movies/{movieId}",
    ResponseFormat=WebMessageFormat.Json)]
MovieData GetMoviePoster(string movieId);
```

➤ Set the default format in the configuration file (via a behavior or on the standard endpoint), as shown here:

```
<behaviors>
  <endpointBehaviors>
    <behavior>
      <webHttp defaultOutgoingResponseFormat="Json"/>
    </behavior>
```

➤ Enable automatic format selection, based on the incoming `Accepts` HTTP header in configuration, as shown here:

```
<behaviors>
  <endpointBehaviors>
    <behavior>
      <webHttp automaticFormatSelectionEnabled="true"/>
    </behavior>
  </endpointBehaviors>
```

A fact worth noting is that, with the web programming model, you no longer need to set all those attributes for names, namespace, and so on because there is no such thing as a metadata description in this world.

The way the WCF web programming model is actually used in the movie sample application is to return arbitrary, nonstructured, binary data to the caller. For this purpose, you do not use any strongly typed data contract, but rather use the `Message` or even a `Stream` type, as can be seen for the `IMovieStreamingService` contract:

```
[ServiceContract]
public interface IMovieStreamingService
{
    [WebGet(UriTemplate="posters/{movieId}")]
    Stream GetMoviePoster(string movieId);

    [WebGet(UriTemplate = "streams/{movieId}")]
    Stream GetTrailerStream(string movieId);

    [WebInvoke(Method = "POST", UriTemplate = "posters/{movieId}")]
    void UploadMoviePoster(string movieId, Stream poster);

    [WebInvoke(Method = "POST", UriTemplate = "streams/{movieId}")]
    void UploadTrailerStream(string movieId, Stream trailer);
}
```

Code file [MovieServiceContracts\IMovieStreamingService.cs] available for download at Wrox.com.

This means that WCF can support XML, JSON, and raw data out-of-the-box for the web programming features. For the details about how this is actually used to efficiently stream data to the callers, you must be patient, as this is covered in the following section.

Hosting and Consuming

After you define your contracts, you must implement them. You can do so by just deriving a service class from the interface as usual, and not thinking about the web at all. Or you could enhance and optimize your service implementation by playing with the rules of the web. If you choose the latter, then there is the `WebOperationContext` static class available to work on the HTTP request and response properties the way you need to.

After designing and implementing the service, you again need to host it. An endpoint suitable for the web programming model must have a binding of type `WebHttpBinding`. In addition, you must swap the operation invoker inside the WCF pipeline. This is done by adding a `WebHttpBehavior` to the configured endpoint. The latter can be achieved manually, or you just use the `WebServiceHost` class instead of `ServiceHost`. `WebServiceHost` to automatically attach the correct behavior.

```
public static void SetupMediaServiceHost(this WebServiceHost host)
{
    host.BootstrapTasks.Add(new EntityMapperBootstrapTask());
    host.BootstrapTasks.Add(new RavenDBEmbeddedBootstrapTask());

    host.AddServiceEndpoint(
        typeof(IMovieStreamingService),
        new WebHttpBinding("media"),
        "media");
}
```

Code file [from Hosting\MediaServiceHostFactory.cs] available for download at Wrox.com.

Now move over to the other side and call this service URL. Because this is playing by the rules of HTTP, you can choose whatever programming API you like, including `HttpWebRequest` and `WebClient`. For the sake of completeness, there is also a `WebChannelFactory<T>` in `System.ServiceModel.Web`, but using a channel factory way of talking to web/REST services somehow seems to defeat the original idea.

Some more advanced and streamlined APIs for web and REST client are DynamicRest (`https://github.com/NikhilK/dynamicrest`) or Hammock (`https://github.com/danielcrenna/hammock`).

The far more interesting aspect for clients is that, based on the service agent pattern discussed earlier, you can now combine both the operation and the resource way of doing services in the `MovieClient` class.

```
public class MovieClient : IMovieClient, IDisposable
{
    private IMovieServiceChannel movieServiceClient;
```

```
private WebClient webClient;
private string baseWebUri =
    ConfigurationManager.AppSettings["baseStreamingUri"];
private const string postersResource = "posters/";
private const string moviesResource = "streams/";

public MovieClient()
{
    var cf = new ChannelFactory<IMovieServiceChannel>("default");
    movieServiceClient = cf.CreateChannel();

    webClient = new WebClient();
}
```

Code file [from MovieServiceAgent\MovieClient.cs] available for download at Wrox.com.

To get the full picture, look at how you can request a poster image for a given movie — just getting it back as a byte array.

```
public byte[] GetMoviePoster(string movieId)
{
    var url = new Uri(new Uri(baseWebUri + postersResource), movieId);

    return webClient.DownloadData(url);
}
```

Code file [from MovieServiceAgent\MovieClient.cs] available for download at Wrox.com.

The helper methods to get an `Image` *object from a byte array are included in the sample code for the book.*

And finally, how can you get the actual movie trailer stream? Well, it turns out that playing the trailer is not the task of the Windows Forms application because it will be delegated to a media player application. (Or in WPF or Silverlight, you could just hand it over to the `MediaElement`.) Therefore, all you need is the full URL to the movie trailer:

```
public Uri GetMovieStreamUrl(string movieId)
{
    var url = new Uri(new Uri(baseWebUri + moviesResource), movieId);

    return url;
}
```

Code file [from MovieServiceAgent\MovieClient.cs] available for download at Wrox.com.

What is left to cover is how to efficiently transfer the binary data from the WCF service to the consumers. This topic is part of the next section, where you learn about optimization strategies in services-based systems.

OPTIMIZATION STRATEGIES

One of the central ideas in this section is that service orientation has nothing to do with XML or angle brackets, and it is not limited to structured or even strongly typed data and messages. This seems to be a myth. Now see how you can get more out of services, and especially WCF.

Tweaking

WCF is easy as A-B-C, as you recall from earlier in this chapter. Especially, the B defines the power in your hands when using WCF. Over the past few years, I have learned that using different bindings is surely sexy and interesting, but it is not the case that I am using for transport based on HTTP on Mondays, TCP on Tuesdays, and MSMQ on Wednesdays.

In practice, it turns out that the system my client and I were building ended up in a high percentage of all cases using HTTP or HTTPS. Sure, `net.tcp` can be extremely good at performing binding when the use case fits well. Other than that, HTTP-based communication has a number of benefits, including the following:

➤ It fits perfectly into a stateless communication pattern.

➤ Client-side channels are easier to handle (because of the "stateless-ness").

All the strange exception handling needed for checking that a channel is faulted or not is not necessary when using stateless HTTP-based bindings.

➤ It is easy to load balance.

➤ When using `WebGet`, it fits into existing caching infrastructures.

If I must choose a transport for a binding, and do not actually know the exact requirements for such things as throughput and latency, I always try HTTP (or HTTPS for that matter) first. This plays into my general thinking to try to keep services stateless as much as possible.

Okay — so I say that HTTP is the king! How then do I get the most out WCF with HTTP? Easy!

The secret is to leave the default standard bindings alone, and look at creating your own binding. The easiest way to do this is to use a custom binding — the more advanced and easier-to-reuse approach is building a user-defined binding (by deriving from `Binding` or a derived class). And one of my favorite bindings is putting the binary message encoder on top of HTTP/HTTPS.

A custom binding for binary-over-HTTP can be easily defined in the configuration file:

```xml
<bindings>
  <customBinding>
    <binding name="binaryHttp">
      <binaryMessageEncoding />
      <httpTransport />
    </binding>
  </customBinding>
...
```

You now must reference the custom binding in your endpoint definition like this:

```xml
<endpoint name="binary"
          address="http://thinkpadcw:8889/binary"
          binding="customBinding"
          bindingConfiguration="binaryHttp"
          contract="IMovieService" />
```

Voilá! How complicated was that? Feel free to use this binding now on the service and the client side, and see the original angel-brackets-pregnant communication payload go away, now replaced with a binary representation. (This binary format is, by the way, also specified and open. Check it out at `http://msdn.microsoft.com/en-us/library/cc216513(v=PROT.10).aspx`.)

You are now ready to take a look at the binding on the endpoint in the debugger on the client side, as shown in Figure 9-17.

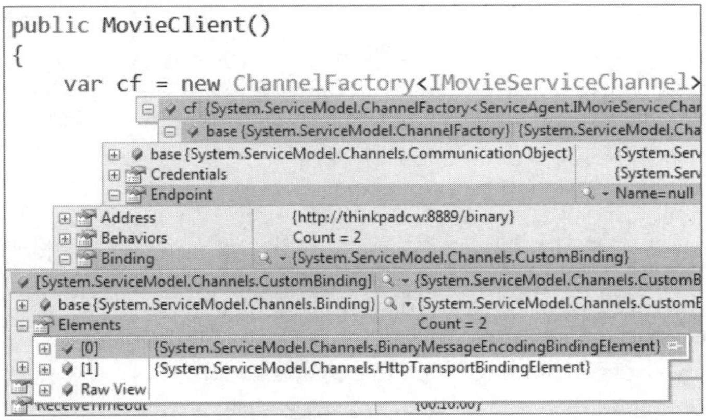

FIGURE 9-17: Binding on the endpoint in the debugger on the client side

An even further proof on the wire (watch out for the `application/soap+msbin1` content-type) can be seen by routing the traffic through Fiddler, as shown in Figure 9-18.

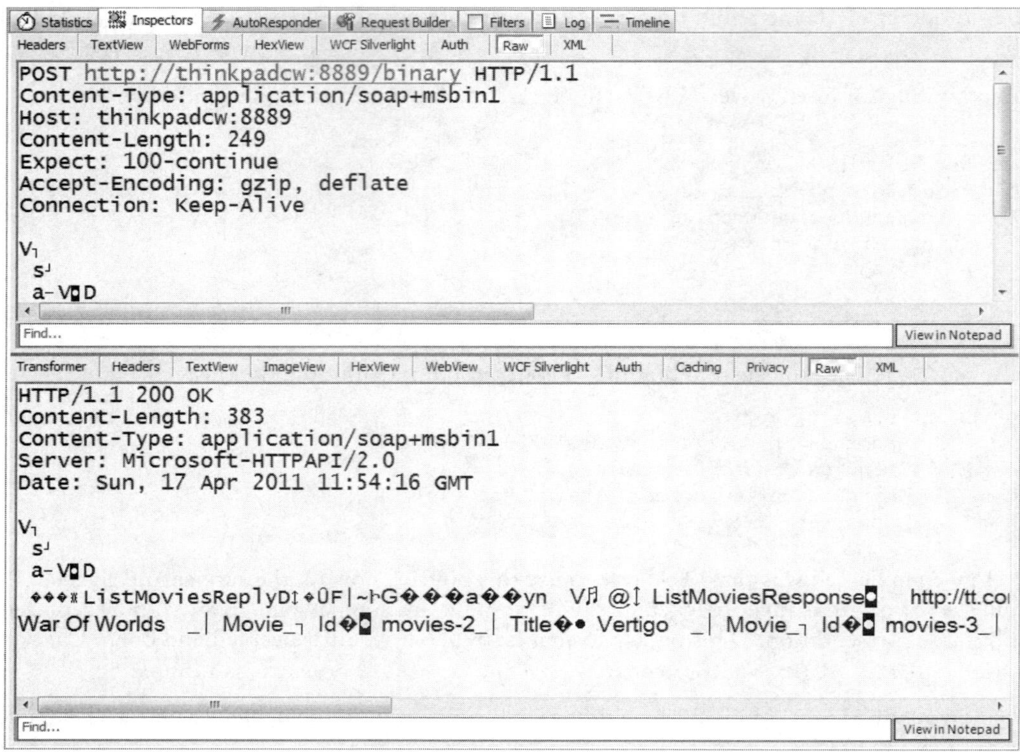

FIGURE 9-18: Routing the traffic through Fiddler

> *Fiddler is a web debugging proxy available at* `www.fiddler2.com/fiddler2/`.

DEFAULT VALUES ON BINDING ELEMENTS

As you read this chapter, I suppose you have come across those neat default settings in WCF, like the settings on the bindings (or to be precise, on the inner binding elements). To fully leverage the power of the binding, you must tweak a lot of these defaults, such as `maxReceivedMessageSize` and friends. Only if you tweak these settings for your scenario can you get the best out of the B.

Again, you can take this idea one step further and encapsulate the functionality (plus some more like advanced security settings) into a user-defined binding I like to call `NetHttpBinding`.

```
public class NetHttpBinding : Binding
```

This custom binding class should be accompanied by configuration classes to use `NetHttpBinding` not only in code, but also via WCF's configuration system. (See the `Thinktecture.ServiceModel` library where `NetHttpBinding` is implemented.) In this chapter's movie sample application, I have used both bindings for you to see how to configure and apply them.

> ### HTTP OUTGOING CONNECTION LIMIT
>
> Be aware of the default HTTP limit for outgoing HTTP calls. When you write code that consumes an HTTP service or resource, there is a maximum of two connections per domain by default. This includes `HttpWebRequest`, `WebClient`, and WCF channels/proxies with an HTTP-based binding.
>
> Luckily, you can override this behavior, either globally for all connections, or just for a certain host, in the configuration file:
>
> ```
> <system.net>
>   <connectionManagement>
>     <add address="*"
>           maxconnection="10"/>
>   </connectionManagement>
> </system.net>
> ```
>
> This small setting can be a life-saver, especially in middle-tier scenarios in which an application or service calls another service via HTTP(S).

Another large area of tweaking possibilities is the various behaviors you can have in your WCF stack. Maybe the most prominent one is the service throttling behavior.

```
<serviceBehaviors>
  <behavior>
    <serviceThrottling
      maxConcurrentCalls="32"
      maxConcurrentSessions="200"
      maxConcurrentInstances="232" />
  </behavior>
</serviceBehaviors>
```

The default values are as follows:

➤ `MaxConcurrentCalls` — 16 times `ProcessorCount`.

➤ `MaxConcurrentSessions` — 100 times `ProcessorCount`.

➤ `MaxConcurrentInstances` — The total of the previous two.

The settings and values are there to prevent denial-of-service (DoS) attacks and similar service degradation causes.

In large-scale, short-lived services scenarios, you may quickly run into the default's limits, and you must severely tweak the settings.

You can trust me that there is still a lot more to do to tweak WCF even more. But some of these measurements depend on the exact requirements, and usually trade-offs must be decided and performed. Following are just a couple (without priority or order):

➤ Optimizing serialization (with `NetDataContractSerializer`, or a prefix-optimizing serializer, or using third-party serializers)

➤ Applying dynamic compression, especially on HTTP channels

When hosting is IIS, you get dynamic content compression for your content types for free.

➤ Using service instance pooling optimization if you have expensive-to-instantiate services

➤ Using a caching mechanism in your services architecture

Of course, you all know that doing performance, throughput, and scalability testing makes sense only when you have built into Release mode and turned off all "Debug-iness."

But there is one special item for further optimizing your services communication — and this is streaming.

Streaming

The default communication mode in WCF is buffered transfer. This means that all the data is loaded in memory and then put through the WCF pipeline onto the wire. For large and especially arbitrary data, this is suboptimal. Enter streaming.

Streamed transfer mode can be an efficient means to exchange data over WCF. Following are two defining entities:

➤ Shape of contracts

➤ Transfer mode setting on binding

Contracts must follow certain rules to work with streamed transfer:

➤ Use of `Message` type only as operation parameters

➤ Use of `Stream` type only as operation parameters

➤ Use of the `[MessageContract]` type as operation parameters (where headers are always buffered)

➤ Use of the `IXmlSerializable` type in a data contract

So, coming back to the movie sample, this is the contract you use to stream in and out data for the movie posters and trailers. (You already saw this interface earlier.)

```
[ServiceContract]
public interface IMovieStreamingService
{
    [WebGet(UriTemplate="posters/{movieId}")]
    Stream GetMoviePoster(string movieId);

    [WebGet(UriTemplate = "streams/{movieId}")]
    Stream GetTrailerStream(string movieId);

    [WebInvoke(Method = "POST", UriTemplate = "posters/{movieId}")]
    void UploadMoviePoster(string movieId, Stream poster);

    [WebInvoke(Method = "POST", UriTemplate = "streams/{movieId}")]
    void UploadTrailerStream(string movieId, Stream trailer);
}
```

Code file [MovieServiceContracts\IMovieStreamingService.cs] available for download at Wrox.com.

On the bindings you use to expose the contract via endpoints, you must set the `transferMode` property accordingly:

➤ `Streamed` — Enables streaming communication in both directions

➤ `StreamedRequest` — Enables streaming the request only

➤ `StreamedResponse` — Enables streaming the response only

This works on all bindings except `netMsmqBinding` *and* `msmqIntegrationBinding`.

The movie service host looks like this:

```
host.AddServiceEndpoint(
    typeof(IMovieStreamingService),
    new WebHttpBinding("mediaStreaming") { TransferMode = TransferMode.Streamed },
    "media");
```

Now, think about the power of using the web programming model, `WebGet`, `WebHttpBinding`, and `transferMode` as streamed...yes, you got it!

Figure 9-19 shows the movie service host in action (that is, memory and CPU percentage used by the process) while streaming an HD video snippet.

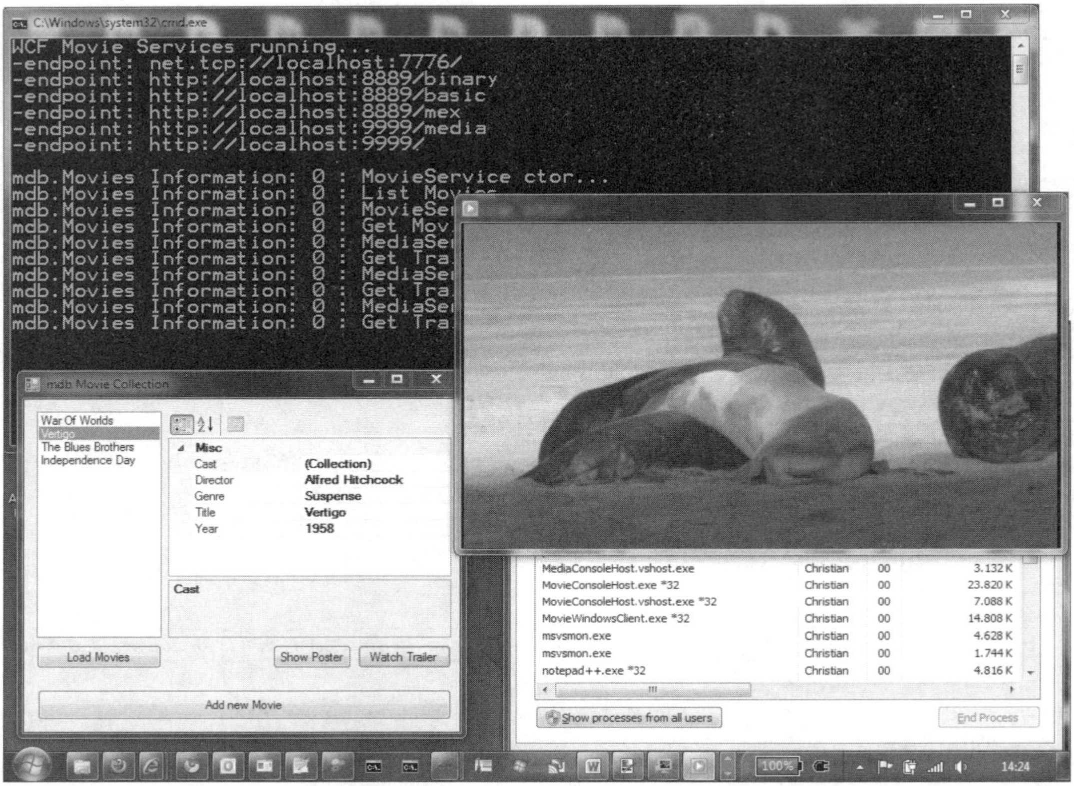

FIGURE 9-19: Movie service host in action

For copyright reasons, this is not a real trailer for the "Vertigo" movie.

One last thing is that streamed transfer has issues when hosting WCF services in IIS. When a WCF service using streaming is hosted in IIS, then ASP.NET buffers the request at its layer. The request does not come up to WCF until ASP.NET is done with it.

SUMMARY

Throughout this chapter, you have seen several approaches that have been successfully applied in real-world projects. Some of them fit only if the scenario of your project is similar to the requirements of the scenario presented here. Others are general tips and code snippets that you can use in every WCF-based project.

The "C" in WCF is for *communication*. And you can build quite sophisticated and powerful application based on WCF. You just need to know the power and the strengths of WCF, and how to navigate around the traps.

There is a lot more in WCF, especially for pragmatic solutions based on WCF.

ABOUT THE AUTHOR

Christian Weyer is co-founder of and solution architect at thinktecture, a company providing in-depth technical consulting and training services for software architects and developers. Weyer has been focusing on the ideas and concepts of service orientation and their practical translation in customer projects over the past few years, with Windows Communication Foundation (WCF), Windows Workflow Foundation (WF), and Cloud Computing (with platforms like the Windows Azure platform) being the main areas and technologies applied recently. He tries to focus on the end-to-end aspects of distributed application architecture, design, and implementation. Weyer's views on end-to-end architecture and distributed solutions are considered both mature and innovating. A number of customers have put confidence into his experience when it comes to applying .NET, WCF, and WF to real problems, and dealing with ideas like "Software plus Services." In addition, he is an instructor and course author for DevelopMentor. The national and international developer and architect community knows Weyer from his weblog, webcasts, forums activities, user group talks, and conference performances. He was selected as one of the Microsoft MVPs for Windows Azure (Architecture), and is an independent Microsoft Regional Director for Germany. Get in touch with him at `christian.weyer@thinktecture.com`.

10
Securing WCF Services Using the Windows Identity Foundation (WIF)

by Dominick Baier

If you are a software security geek like me, the world of distributed applications is one of the most exciting places to be. You can encounter a multitude of client types, network and authentication protocols, credential types, and requirements. In other words, you have just the complexity you need to feel like a real expert — or a little lost.

Although, in theory, the Windows Communication Foundation (WCF) has all the features you need to build even the most complex distributed systems, as always, complexity is the biggest enemy of security. That's the reason why Microsoft gave WCF security (and .NET security, in general — but more on that later) a refresh that enables you to build these systems with better abstraction layers and less error-prone code. This refresh is called the Windows Identity Foundation (WIF), and this chapter examines how to use this technology with WCF Simple Object Access Protocol (SOAP) and Representational State Transfer (REST) services.

> *The sample code used in this chapter, as well as the* `Thinktecture.IdentityModel` *library, is part of the code available for download on this book's companion website (*`www.wrox.com`*). Parts of the code are based on the movie database service described in Chapter 9.*

IDENTITY IN .NET APPLICATIONS

Since the first release of the .NET Framework, Microsoft wanted to give developers a standard and unified way to represent identity and access control in applications.

This section provides a brief history of the approaches Microsoft took, and how WCF changed the game. It concludes with a description of the concepts that WIF adds, and, more important, why WIF is the new (and preferred) way to model identity in your applications.

Especially when it comes to concepts such as claims, tokens, and federation, this chapter cannot provide a full introduction. Look at the free guide to identity and access control from Microsoft's Patterns & Practices group at `http://tinyurl.com/claimsguide`*. For a more WIF API-centric book, check out* Programming Windows Identity *Foundation by Vittorio Bertocci (Redmond, Washington: Microsoft Press, 2010).*

Identity in the Base Class Library

The `System.Security.Principal.IPrincipal` interface provides a standard way to do role-based access checks and, in turn, wrap an instance of the `IIdentity` interface that holds the username and information about the authentication method. In addition, there is a per-thread storage "slot" to store that principal on `Thread.CurrentPrincipal`. Listing 10-1 shows this interface.

LISTING 10-1: IPrincipal and IIdentity

```
interface IPrincipal
{
  IIdentity Identity { get; }
  bool IsInRole(string roleName);
}

interface IIdentity
{
  bool IsAuthenticated { get; }
  string AuthenticationType { get; }
  string Name { get; }
}
```

This enables writing standard plumbing to query authentication and authorization information for the current user. (Because the principal is stored on a thread-static property, it enables scenarios in which multiple concurrent clients use the application — such as WCF or ASP.NET.) Examples of such standard plumbing would be Base Class Library (BCL) classes such as `PrincipalPermission`, or ASP.NET's `URL Authorization`.

These interfaces are deliberately minimal to provide common ground, and are meant for customization to adapt to different authentication types and application scenarios. The framework itself includes a number of implementations for such common scenarios as the following:

➤ `WindowsPrincipal/WindowsIdentity` — Represents a Windows user and groups

➤ `GenericPrincipal/GenericIdentity` — Represents a generic user (for example, backed by a custom user database)

> ➤ `FormsIdentity` — Represents an ASP.NET Forms Authentication user and information in the corresponding cookie

Other common credential types such as an X.509 certificate, unfortunately, don't have an `IPrincipal` representation.

On the other hand, because so many different implementations exist (and each comes with its own optimization for the concrete authentication type to make it more useful), it was difficult to write applications that should support multiple authentication and credential types. This could be especially challenging for independent software vendors (ISVs) who must write generic software without *a priori* knowledge of the security and authentication system of their customers.

Another consequence of the `IPrincipal` interface design is the focus on role-based security for authorization. This is not a bad thing because roles are extremely useful for coarse-grained authorization. But when you want to do more fine-grained security decisions (or maybe even just personalization), you must come up with your own custom implementations (which not always helps the greater good).

Identity in WCF

WCF was designed a few years later than the BCL. While retaining some backward compatibility with the original `IPrincipal` idea, WCF also featured a brand new security system to cater for the vast amount of scenarios it was built for.

WCF security was built around the notion of security tokens and claims. The WCF team created a completely new object model centered on the `ServiceSecurityContext` type for that purpose.

SECURITY TOKENS AND CLAIMS

WCF introduced important security concepts into the .NET Framework. One is the notion of a *security token*. A token is the outcome of an authentication process and describes a credential. WCF comes with a number of implementations of security tokens (all derived from the abstract base class called `SecurityToken`), such as for Kerberos, usernames and passwords, X.509 certificates, and Security Assertion Markup Language (SAML). One interesting aspect of security tokens is that they can be serialized and transferred between services (even across traditional security boundaries). This is important when it comes to security token services, SAML, and federation.

In a nutshell, a *claim* is a statement about an entity, typically a user in your system. A claim consists of three pieces of information: the type of the statement, the statement itself, and the issuer of that statement. When translated into the role mindset, this is a claim, such as "dominick is a domain administrator (says the domain controller)." But claims go further than roles because they enable more than just simple yes/no decisions, such as, "dominick's e-mail address is `dominick.baier@thinktecture.com` (says our directory service)." Claims can be hydrated from the contents of a security token, or you have application local logic that adds claims to the client's security context.

Both tokens and claims can be accessed in WCF via `ServiceSecurityContext.Current` (WCF's version of `Thread.CurrentPrincipal`).

This new system was more powerful and flexible compared to the standard .NET facilities — but this came with a price. First, programming against and extending the new system was more difficult and often required an intimate knowledge of the inner workings of WCF to succeed. But even worse, this new system broke backward compatibility to the BCL system in a lot of areas. (`Thread.CurrentPrincipal` is only available in certain situations in WCF.) When you were in a situation in which you needed to maintain both ASP.NET and WCF code, you often ended up duplicating security-related code to work against both security systems. Again, this could lead to errors and complexity.

Windows Identity Foundation

The purpose of the WIF library is to combine the power of the WCF security concepts with the simplicity and pervasiveness of the BCL `IPrinpical` approach.

This is achieved by introducing a class called `Claim` (and a corresponding `ClaimCollection`):

```
public class Claim
{
    public virtual string ClaimType { get; }
    public virtual string Value { get; }
    public virtual string Issuer { get; }

    // rest omitted
}
```

This enables packaging an arbitrary number of statements about the current user. To attach these statements to the current thread of execution in your application, claims-aware versions of `IPrincipal` and `IIdentity` have been created. They are called `IClaimsPrincipal` and `IClaimsIdentity`, and enable coupling a collection of claims with the current principal:

```
interface IClaimsPrincipal : IPrincipal
{
    ClaimsIdentityCollection Identities { get; }

    // rest omitted
}

interface IClaimsIdentity : IIdentity
{
    ClaimCollection Claims { get; }

    // rest omitted
}
```

Deriving from `IPrincipal` and `IIdentity` has the handy side effects that you can start using `Thread.CurrentPrincipal` again (regardless of ASP.NET or WCF), and that "legacy" code won't break when enabling WIF (because this code can simply see the standard BCL versions of the interfaces, which behave the same for backward-compatibility reasons). Also, because the `IClaimsIdentity` is generic and can hold arbitrary information, there is less (to no) need to provide custom implementations of the principal and identity.

Layering WIF on top of the WCF (and ASP.NET) security system has several benefits:

➤ Claims become a first-class citizen in every .NET application. Although WIF provides the plumbing to "claim-enable" arbitrary applications, you can find out-of-the-box support for WCF and ASP.NET.

➤ A number of new easy-to-use extensibility points are included. And, even more important, the same extensibility exists for ASP.NET and WCF, which means that you must write that code only once, and it works the same in both environments.

➤ The handling of credentials types and security tokens has been dramatically simplified (especially when compared to WCF's native programming model).

➤ By providing a single abstraction (the claims collection) over arbitrary authentication protocols and credential types, your code becomes agnostic to these low-level details. That effectively means that you can decouple your application logic from the low-level security details, which is huge.

In addition to replacing the principal/identity with a claims-aware version, WIF adds three other important concepts: *security token handlers*, *claims transformation*, and *claims-based authorization*. The following sections provide a brief description of the mechanisms. You use them later in the sample so that you can see them in action.

 *WIF is a single assembly called* `Microsoft.IdentityModel`. *When installed, it is serviced by Windows Update. You can also redistribute the assembly yourself if you like.*

Security Token Handlers

Security token handlers are the glue between claims and security tokens. They have two purposes:

➤ Serialize and deserialize tokens (`ReadToken` and `WriteToken`)

➤ Turn a token into an `IClaimsIdentity`, and vice versa (`CreateToken` and `ValidateToken`)

When a token arrives in WCF, the first thing that WIF does is hand it over to the token handler for claims validation and claims extraction. WIF already ships with a number of token handlers to handle common token types, including the following:

➤ Kerberos service tickets

➤ Username/password

➤ X.509 certificates

➤ SAML 1.1 and 2.0

You can find them in the `Microsoft.IdentityModel.Tokens` namespace.

If you need to add support for a new token type, you have to write "only" a token handler for that specific token. WIF takes care of integrating that into the WCF runtime (more on that later). This might still not be a trivial task, but it is much easier compared to WCF's native extensibility points.

More common is that you might want to customize how an existing token handler handles a token. In this case, you can simply derive from that existing token-handler, and override an existing method, or inject your own logic. The whole token-handler design explicitly enables such customization. (Kudos to the WIF team!)

THE SAML 1.1 TOKEN HANDLER

A nice example of the customizability of the built-in token handlers is the handler for SAML 1.1 tokens. The `CreateToken` method is part of the `SecurityTokenHandler` base class and is used by WIF plumbing (or by yourself when you write your own WIF plumbing). The `CreateToken` method itself uses a pipeline of virtual methods that actually creates the security token. You are free to override every aspect of this pipeline. It looks as follows:

➤ `CreateStatements` — Creates the SAML subject, attribute, and authentication statements. This method calls out to the following:

   ➤ `CreateSamlSubject` — Looks for a name identifier claim and uses this to create the SAML subject. Additionally, if this claim has properties that describe the name format and qualifier, these values will be added to the subject. The last step is to set the proof key identifier and subject confirmation method (holder of key/bearer).

   ➤ `CreateAttributeStatement` — Creates the attribute statement based on the supplied claims.

   ➤ `CreateAuthenticationStatementFromAuthentication Information` — Creates the authentication statement based on the authentication information.

➤ `CreateConditions` — Sets the token lifetime and audience URIs restrictions.

➤ `CreateAdvice` — Creates the SAML advice. By default, no advice is created.

➤ `CreateAssertion` — Creates the SAML assertion based on the statements, the conditions, and the advice.

➤ `GetSigningCredentials` — Returns the credential used to sign the token.

➤ `GetEncryptingCredentials` — Returns the credential used to encrypt the token. If this method returns `null`, the token will not be encrypted.

Claims Transformation

An important concept of claims-based systems is transformation. By default, WIF turns incoming security tokens into claims (or an `IClaimsPrincipal`, to be exact). This is the job of the token handler.

The information inside the security token may or may not be directly usable by the application (typically not). So, for example, a Windows token contains the Windows account name and the security identifiers (SIDs) of the groups this account is a member of. An X.509 security token contains things such as public keys or serial numbers. This is typically not the information your application cares about. Rather, it cares about things such as authorization or personalization information such as a shopping cart limit, or trivial things such as the first name of the user.

This is where claims transformation comes in. The outcome of the security token handler's work is passed to a `ClaimsAuthenticationManager`. WIF passes the `IClaimsPrincipal` into the `Authenticate` method. In there, you can now do whatever modification to that principal you want to do (or even create a new one). You then return that modified principal back to WIF so that it can travel further toward application code.

Listing 10-2 shows an example of claims transformation.

LISTING 10-2: Claims Transformation with ClaimsAuthenticationManager

```
class ClaimsTransformer : ClaimsAuthenticationManager
{
    public override IClaimsPrincipal Authenticate(string resourceName,
      IClaimsPrincipal incomingPrincipal)
    {
        // extract some unique identifier from the incoming token
        var user = incomingPrincipal.Identities.Single().Name;

        // build claims principal and return to WIF
        return CreatePrincipal(user);
    }
}
```

Claims-Based Authorization

Earlier, you learned that .NET's `IPrincipal` interface was designed for role-based security via the `IsInRole` method. This often led to code like what is shown in Listing 10-3.

LISTING 10-3: Role-based Authorization with IsInRole

```
public void AddCustomer(Customer customer)
{
    if (Thread.CurrentPrincipal.IsInRole("Sales"))
    {
        // add customer
    }
}
```

This code has a fundamental flaw — it mixes business logic with (security) infrastructure, which is a clear violation of separation of concerns. Practically speaking, this can lead to two issues:

➤　Whenever the security requirements change (like another role should have access, too), you must recompile, retest, and reship the whole application (or business logic).

➤   These `IsInRole` calls (or `PrincipalPermission/Attribute`) are sprinkled all over your code base. Whenever changes occur, you must ensure that you don't miss a call while updating the application.

WIF advocates a slightly different approach that helps to keep both concerns separate. As opposed to embedding security-related information directly in your business code, you describe only what the current code tries to do (via a resource/operation pair), and hand it off to a separate component to make the security decision, as shown in Listing 10-4.

LISTING 10-4: Claims-Based Authorization

```
// coarse grained and declarative
[ClaimsPrincipalPermission(SecurityAction.Demand,
    Resource = "Customer", Operation = "Add")]
public void AddCustomer(Customer customer)
{
    // fine grained and imperative
    ClaimsPrincipalPermission.CheckAccess(
      "AddCustomerInRegion",
      Customer.Region);

    // add customer

}
```

This triggers a call to the `ClaimsAuthorizationManager`. The `CheckAccess` method has a single argument of type `AuthorizationContext`. The context, in turn, holds the supplied resource and action, as well as the `IClaimsPrincipal` of the user. It is now the job of the authorization manager to check these values against some authorization policy, as shown in Listing 10-5.

LISTING 10-5: ClaimsAuthorizationManager

```
public class AuthorizationManager : ClaimsAuthorizationManager
{
    public override bool CheckAccess(AuthorizationContext context)
    {
        // extract required values from context
        var action = context.Action.First().Value;
        var resource = context.Resource.First().Value;
        var client = context.Principal.Identities.First();

        // evaluate against authorization policy
        return CheckAuthorizationPolicy(action, resource, client);
    }
}
```

An interesting detail about `AuthorizationContext` is that the resource and operation is modeled as a collection of claims. This enables describing these two "values" in an arbitrarily complex way — for example, "the user tries to print on a printer (but this printer is a color laser printer with 50 pages/minute on floor 3)."

In addition to invoking the authorization manager imperatively, WCF (or, rather, the WIF extensions to WCF) also calls the `CheckAccess` method for every incoming request. This time, the endpoint address and SOAP action (or HTTP verb for REST services) is passed in. This serves as a replacement for the "old" WCF `ServiceAuthorizationManager`.

This generic authorization extensibility also enables third parties to plug in authorization systems that operate at a higher abstraction layer. Think of graphical designers or digital simulation languages (DSLs).

Recapping the Building Blocks

You just learned about the three basic building blocks of WIF — token handlers, claims transformation, and authorization. Strictly speaking, these are three independent mechanisms — but typically, WIF combines them to a pipeline that plugs into a hosting platform such as WCF and ASP.NET:

➤   Turn an incoming security token into claims using a token handler.

➤   Transform those token-based claims into application claims.

➤   Do per-request (or explicit) authorization.

➤   Set `IClaimsPrincipal` on `Thread.CurrentPrincipal`.

The actual WIF pipeline is more complex, and a lot of extensibility points have not been mentioned. Look at the WIF SDK under "Building Relying Party Applications" for more information.

WCF AND WIF

Now that you know why WIF exists, and what its fundamental building blocks are, start using it in a simple WCF service.

The following sections are based on the `SimpleDemo` sample from code available for download on this book's companion website (`www.wrox.com`). If you want to follow along, there is a "before" solution (which is plain WCF) and an "after" solution (which uses WIF and the extensibility points discussed here).

Prerequisites

The first thing you should do is download WIF and the SDK. Although WIF contains the library, the SDK gives you additional tools such as IntelliSense for the configuration file, as well as some wizards.

After downloading these packages, you can start using WIF by adding a reference to `Microsoft.IdentityModel` and `System.IdentityModel` (in addition to the typical WCF libraries like `System.ServiceModel`).

You must also register a new configuration section. Add the following to your `app.config`/`web.config` file:

```
<configSections>
  <section name="microsoft.identityModel"
          type="Microsoft.IdentityModel.Configuration.
```

```
MicrosoftIdentityModelSection, Microsoft.IdentityModel,
Version=3.5.0.0, Culture=neutral,
PublicKeyToken=31bf3856ad364e35"/>
</configSections>
```

Now you are ready to start configuring and enabling WIF in the WCF service.

Configuring and Enabling WIF

When you enable WIF in a WCF service, the following things change:

➤   WCF's native `ServiceSecurityContext` is disabled. All client identity information can now be consistently found on `Thread.CurrentPrincipal` (as an `IClaimsPrincipal`).

➤   All token processing now is done by WIF's internal pipeline and the security token handlers.

➤   As a consequence of the previous point, `ClaimsAuthenticationManager` and `ClaimsAuthorizationManager` are invoked as part of the request processing.

You enable WIF by calling `FederatedServiceCredentials.ConfigureServiceHost` and passing in your WCF service host. This is the easiest option for situations like self-hosting or for a service host factory.

You can also enable WIF using the WCF configuration. In this case, add the `<federatedService-HostConfiguration />` behavior to the service behavior section. You get this new behavior by registering the following behavior extension in the `<system.serviceModel>` configuration section:

```
<extensions>
  <behaviorExtensions>
    <add name="federatedServiceHostConfiguration"
         type="Microsoft.IdentityModel.Configuration.
             ConfigureServiceHostBehaviorExtensionElement,
             Microsoft.IdentityModel, Version=3.5.0.0,
             Culture=neutral, PublicKeyToken=31bf3856ad364e35"/>
  </behaviorExtensions>
</extensions>
```

> ### WIF INTERNALS: FEDERATEDSERVICECREDENTIALS.CONFIGURESERVICEHOST
>
> WIF is built on top of public WCF extensibility points. When you do some WCF customization, it might be interesting to see how WIF manages to add its own processing pipeline and `IClaimsPrincipal` into the WCF runtime.
>
> When you call `ConfigureServiceHost` (or use the behavior in configuration), the following things happen under the cover:
>
> ➤   WIF replaces the standard WCF `ServiceCredential` with its own `FederatedServiceCredential`. This replaces WCF's internal security token processing with the WIF pipeline.

> ➤ `FederatedSecurityTokenManager` replaces the standard
> `SecurityTokenManager`.
>
> ➤ The security token handler collection replaces the internal WCF secu-
> rity token provisioning, serialization, and authentication mechanisms.
>
> ➤ WIF also replaces the WCF internal claims generation by replacing the stan-
> dard service authorization manager with the `IdentityModelService`
> `AuthorizationManager`.
>
> ➤ By setting the WCF `PrincipalPermissionMode` to `Custom`, this new ser-
> vice authorization manager is allowed to set `Thread.CurrentPrincipal`.
> This is how the claims coming from the security token handler make their
> way onto the thread static property, and into the WCF service code.

The following sections describe some typical WCF and WIF configuration settings for common
scenarios.

Windows Authentication

Because Windows authentication is always the default in WCF, no special configuration is necessary
for WIF as well. The token handler for Windows authentication produces three claim types: `name`
(the Windows account name of the client); `primarysid` (the SID of the user); and `groupsid` (the SID
of the groups the user is member of).

If you must translate SIDs to display names (such as group names), you can use the `SecurityIdentifier`
and `NTAccount` classes from the BCL. The following code translates all `groupsid` claims to strings containing the Windows group names:

```
var id = Thread.CurrentPrincipal.Identity as IClaimsIdentity;

Console.WriteLine("\nWindows groups:");
id.Claims.Where(claim => claim.ClaimType ==
    ClaimTypes.GroupSid).ToList().ForEach(c =>
{
    var sid = new SecurityIdentifier(c.Value);
    var acc = sid.Translate(typeof(NTAccount)) as NTAccount;
    Console.WriteLine(acc);
});
```

Another specialty with Windows authentication is that you get a more specialized version of
`IClaimsPrincipal` and `IClaimsIdentity`. They are called `WindowsClaimsPrincipal` and
`WindowsClaimsIdentity`, and derive from the standard `WindowsPrincipal` and `WindowsIdentity`.
The benefit is that you also get the Windows-centric functionality of the base classes like the Win32
token handle or the capability to impersonate the account.

WIF also includes a special service called the Claims to Windows Token Service (C2WTS). This
service enables creating a `WindowsIdentity` without having to know the actual password of the
account. This is useful in multihop scenarios in which you must access a Windows-secured resource

(such as SQL Server) somewhere in the call chain. This is a highly privileged service (as you can imagine), and thus, is disabled by default. Consult the WIF documentation for more information.

Username/Password Authentication

WIF includes standard security token handlers for username- and password-based authentication when the credential validation is based either on Windows accounts or a membership provider.

Windows authentication is the standard for `Username` endpoints in WCF, but in case you need to do some custom validation and happen to have a membership provider, you must simply replace the standard token handler, as shown here:

```xml
<microsoft.identityModel>
  <service>
    <securityTokenHandlers>
      <!-- use the membership provider to authentication UserName tokens -->
      <remove type="Microsoft.IdentityModel.Tokens.
          WindowsUserNameSecurityTokenHandler, Microsoft.IdentityModel,
          Version=3.5.0.0, Culture=neutral,
          PublicKeyToken=31BF3856AD364E35" />
      <add type="Microsoft.IdentityModel.Tokens.
          MembershipUserNameSecurityTokenHandler, Microsoft.IdentityModel,
          Version=3.5.0.0, Culture=neutral,
          PublicKeyToken=31BF3856AD364E35">
        <userNameSecurityTokenHandlerRequirement
            membershipProviderName="MembershipProviderName" />
      </add>
    </service>
</microsoft.identityModel>
```

When you already have an existing (nonmembership) password validation library, or want to do some customization, you can write your own (specialized) username security token handler. This is easier than it sounds and is mostly boilerplate code.

You basically start by deriving from `UserNameSecurityTokenHandler` and implementing the `ValidateToken` method. To be a "good" token handler, you must behave in a certain way (like checking configuration, checking for replay detection, or bootstrap tokens). You end up writing standard code where only the password validation logic is application-specific, as shown in Listing 10-6.

LISTING 10-6: Generic UserName Security Token Handler


```csharp
public class GenericUserNameSecurityTokenHandler : UserNameSecurityTokenHandler
{
    public override ClaimsIdentityCollection ValidateToken(SecurityToken token)
    {
        if (token == null)
        {
            throw new ArgumentNullException("token");
        }

        if (base.Configuration == null)
```

```csharp
    {
        throw new InvalidOperationException("No Configuration set");
    }

    UserNameSecurityToken unToken = token as UserNameSecurityToken;
    if (unToken == null)
    {
        throw new ArgumentException("The SecurityToken is not
                a UserNameSecurityToken", token);
    }

    // ValidateUserNameCredential is app specific logic
    if (!ValidateUserNameCredential(unToken.UserName, unToken.Password))
    {
        throw new SecurityTokenValidationException(unToken.UserName);
    }

    var claims = new List<Claim>
    {
        new Claim(ClaimTypes.Name, unToken.UserName),
        new Claim(ClaimTypes.AuthenticationMethod,
            AuthenticationMethods.Password),
        AuthenticationInstantClaim.Now
    };

    var identity = new ClaimsIdentity(claims);

    if (base.Configuration.SaveBootstrapTokens)
    {
        if (this.RetainPassword)
        {
            identity.BootstrapToken = unToken;
        }
        else
        {
            identity.BootstrapToken = new UserNameSecurityToken(
                unToken.UserName, null);
        }
    }

    return new ClaimsIdentityCollection(new IClaimsIdentity[] { identity });
}

public override bool CanValidateToken
{
    get
    {
        return true;
    }
}
}
```

<hr>

Code file [GenericUserNameSecurityTokenHandler.cs] available for download at Wrox.com.

You would then implement the `ValidateUserNameCredential` method and replace the built-in token handler with this custom one. Typically, username token handlers produce only a single username claim (besides the standard authentication method and instant claims).

You can also configure and add token handlers programmatically. The following code snippet adds the custom token handler and opens the service host:

```
ServiceHost host = new ServiceHost(typeof(ClaimsService));

// retrieves configuration
var wifConfiguration = new ServiceConfiguration();

// replace built-in username token handler
wifConfiguration.SecurityTokenHandlers.AddOrReplace(
    new GenericUserNameSecurityTokenHandler();

// add WIF to service host and open
FederatedServiceCredentials.ConfigureServiceHost(host, wifConfiguration);
host.Open();
```

X.509 Certificate Authentication

In the case of X.509 client certificate authentication, the standard `X509SecurityTokenHandler` is used. This handler produces a number of standard claims such as the thumbprint, distinguished name, public key, or serial number.

Certificate validation is a two-step process in WIF. First, the token handler uses the standard WCF certificate validation mechanism. You have the choice between chain trust, peer trust, and no validation. You can specify the validation mode in the `<microsoft.identityModel>` configuration section (either at the global level, or the handler level). You can also write a custom validator by deriving from `X509CertificateValidator`.

After successful validation, the WIF token handler also uses the *issuer name registry* to determine if the issuer of that certificate is trusted in your service. WIF ships with one standard implementation of such a registry called the `ConfigurationBasedIssuerNameRegistry`. As the name implies, this enables adding trusted certificate authorities (CAs) by registering the certificate thumbprint through configuration. The value of the `name` attribute is then used by the token handler to set the `Issuer` property on the `Claim` class.

```
<microsoft.identityModel>
  <service>
    <!-- that's the default setting -->
    <certificateValidation certificateValidationMode="ChainTrust" />

    <!-- registers trusted CAs -->
    <issuerNameRegistry type="Microsoft.IdentityModel.Tokens.
        ConfigurationBasedIssuerNameRegistry, Microsoft.IdentityModel,
        Version=3.5.0.0, Culture=neutral,
        PublicKeyToken=31bf3856ad364e35">
      <trustedIssuers>
        <add thumbprint="xyz"
            name="Internal CA" />
      </trustedIssuers>
```

```
      </issuerNameRegistry>
    </service>
  </microsoft.identityModel>
```

The combination of both facilities enables an easy implementation of the typical pattern where you first check the validity of an incoming certificate using chain validation, and then narrow down your trusted certificates by providing a registry list.

Because you can provide your own issuer name registry implementation, you have total freedom to determine what is "trusted" in your service. Listing 10-7 shows a sample issuer name registry that does no checking against a list, but simply returns the thumbprint of the issuer certificate. This is sometimes useful for testing — but don't use it in production environments.

Available for download on Wrox.com

LISTING 10-7: Test Issuer Name Registry

```csharp
public class TestIssuerNameRegistry : IssuerNameRegistry
{
    public override string GetIssuerName(SecurityToken securityToken)
    {
        if (securityToken == null)
        {
            throw new ArgumentNullException("securityToken");
        }

        X509SecurityToken token = securityToken as X509SecurityToken;
        if (token != null)
        {
            return token.Certificate.Thumbprint;
        }

        throw new SecurityTokenException(
          securityToken.GetType().FullName);
    }
}
```

Code file [TestIssuerNameRegistry.cs] available for download at Wrox.com.

SAML Token Authentication

WIF has built-in support for SAML 1.1 and 2.0 tokens. The token handlers decrypt and validate incoming SAML tokens, and turn the various statements into claims. But you must supply various configuration values to make this happen:

➤   The decryption key (private key) to decrypt incoming tokens

➤   A list of trusted token issuers

➤   A list of accepted audience URIs

This is typically done using the `<microsoft.identityModel />` configuration section, but, as always, you can also supply the configuration via code. It's a little confusing that you can also configure some aspects using the standard WCF configuration, and `ConfigureServiceHost` has some intelligence to parse both configuration sections and merge them. However, in general, I would recommend moving everything into the WIF configuration section.

Listing 10-8 shows a sample WIF configuration for SAML tokens.

LISTING 10-8: Sample WIF Configuration for SAML Tokens

```
<microsoft.identityModel>
  <service>

    <!-- list of accepted audience uris -->
    <audienceUris>
      <add value="https://server/service.svc" />
    </audienceUris>

    <!-- specifies how the issuer certificates get validated -->
    <certificateValidation certificateValidationMode="ChainTrust" />

    <!-- key used to decrypt incoming tokens -->
    <serviceCertificate>
      <certificateReference findValue="CN=Service"
                            x509FindType="FindBySubjectDistinguishedName"
                            storeLocation="LocalMachine"
                            storeName="My" />
    </serviceCertificate>

    <!-- registers trusted token issuers
         similar to x.509 certificate authentication,
         the certificate used to sign the token
         gets passed into the registry -->
    <issuerNameRegistry type="Microsoft.IdentityModel.Tokens.
        ConfigurationBasedIssuerNameRegistry, ...">
      <trustedIssuers>
        <add thumbprint="xyz"
            name="Internal Identity Provider" />
      </trustedIssuers>
    </issuerNameRegistry>

  </service>
</microsoft.identityModel>
```

Sessions

WIF builds on top of the WCF session feature (or, more specifically, the `WS-SecureConversation` support). When `WS-SecureConversation` is turned on (that's the `establishSecurityContext` attribute on the binding configuration), the outcome of the claims transformation process on the first request gets cached on the server, and a unique identifier gets round-tripped using a SOAP header. On subsequent requests, this identifier is used to rehydrate the cached `IClaimsPrincipal`. The SAML security token handler and the `ClaimsAuthenticationManager` don't get called anymore. Because claims transformation is potentially expensive (for example, making round trips to data stores), sessions can improve performance.

But sessions also have downsides:

➤ Introducing state at the protocol level makes the client programming model more difficult. You must deal with things such as timeouts, faulted channels, and re-creating proxies.

➤ Sessions are, by default, incompatible with load balancing.

In the case in which you want to use WIF's session management in a load-balanced environment, you must put WIF into "cookie mode." This means that the complete `IClaimsPrincipal` from `ClaimsAuthenticationManager` is serialized and round-tripped (as opposed to keeping the principal on the server side, and round-tripping an identifier). In this mode, the WCF client proxy sends the complete principal on each request, and the receiving node can rehydrate the principal from the `SecureConversation` header.

Unfortunately, the standard bindings don't expose that option directly — you need a custom binding for that. The "trick" here is to set `requireSecurityContextCancellation` to `false` — which is just a fancy way to say "serialize the session token (also known as the principal) into the message." The following custom binding mimics the `WS2007FederationHttpBinding` in `TransportWithMessageCredential` security mode:

```xml
<customBinding>
  <binding name="federation_cookie">
    <security authenticationMode="SecureConversation"
            messageSecurityVersion="WSSecurity11
                                    WSTrust13
                                    WSSecureConversation13
                                    WSSecurityPolicy12
                                    BasicSecurityProfile10"
            requireSecurityContextCancellation="false">
      <secureConversationBootstrap authenticationMode="IssuedTokenOverTransport"
                                messageSecurityVersion="WSSecurity11
                                    WSTrust13
WSSecureConversation13
                                    WSSecurityPolicy12
BasicSecurityProfile10">
        <issuedTokenParameters>
          <issuerMetadata address="https://…" />
        </issuedTokenParameters>
      </secureConversationBootstrap>
    </security>

    <textMessageEncoding />
    <httpsTransport />
  </binding>
</customBinding>
```

But that's not the complete story. When you round-trip the principal back to the user, it must be protected. Otherwise, the client could simply change the claims and resubmit the modified session token.

The standard WIF behavior is to use the DPAPI user key to protect the principal. This key cannot easily be shared between nodes in a cluster. Another more explicit (and practical) option is to use an RSA key. Most typically, you would use your SSL certificate, or the certificate used to decrypt incoming tokens, to protect the serialized principal.

Fortunately, WIF makes it easy to customize such low-level details. You must derive from `SessionSecurityTokenHandler` and modify the *transforms*. (Think of transforms as a mini pipe-line for serializing the session token that contains the principal.) Listing 10-9 shows an example.

LISTING 10-9: Session Security Token Handler for Load-Balanced Scenarios

```
public class LoadBalancedSessionSecurityTokenHandler : SessionSecurityTokenHandler
{
    public LoadBalancedSessionSecurityTokenHandler(X509Certificate2
            protectionCertificate)
        : base(CreateRsaTransforms(protectionCertificate))
    { }

    private static ReadOnlyCollection<CookieTransform> CreateRsaTransforms
      (X509Certificate2 protectionCertificate)
    {
        var transforms = new List<CookieTransform>()
                        {
                            new DeflateCookieTransform(),
                            new RsaEncryptionCookieTransform
                                (protectionCertificate),
                            new RsaSignatureCookieTransform
                                (protectionCertificate),
                        };

        return transforms.AsReadOnly();
    }
}
```

You would then replace the built-in session token handler with this new one:

```
ServiceHost host = new ServiceHost(typeof(ClaimsService));

// retrieves configuration
var wifConfiguration = new ServiceConfiguration();

// replace built-in username token handler
wifConfiguration.SecurityTokenHandlers.AddOrReplace(
    new LoadBalancedSessionSecurityTokenHandler
        (wifConfiguration.ServiceCertificate);

// add WIF to service host and open
FederatedServiceCredentials.ConfigureServiceHost(host, wifConfiguration);
host.Open();
```

You can see that there is a lot of custom code and configuration necessary to get sessions up and running for nonsingle-server scenarios. Regardless of clustering, I personally prefer to turn off sessions altogether and do my own server-side caching in `ClaimsAuthenticationManager`. *Using products such as AppFabric Caching or* `memcached`, *you can also do distributed caching across multiple cluster nodes.*

Recapping Configuring and Enabling

WIF supports a lot of scenarios and configuration options out-of-the-box. Generally, you start by creating your normal WCF endpoints and binding configuration, and then you call `ConfigureServiceHost` before opening the WCF service host. Typically, the WIF runtime can take care of the rest, and your service code calls the `IClaimsPrincipal` on `Thread.CurrentPrincipal`.

In general, you should keep your WCF endpoint configuration as simple as possible. Use mixed-mode security (that's the `TransportWithMessageCredential` security mode) whenever possible because it can give you the best performance combined with the expressiveness of `WS-Security` tokens. Also, try to avoid sessions.

Furthermore, have a look at the following three blog entries to learn more about the WIF configuration system in general, as well as its extensibility:

> ➤ www.leastprivilege.com/WIFConfigurationNdashPart1ServiceConfiguration.aspx

> ➤ www.leastprivilege.com/
>   WIFConfigurationNdashPart2SecurityTokenHandlerConfiguration.aspx

> ➤ www.leastprivilege.com/WIFConfigurationNdashPart3Extensibility.aspx

Transforming and Accessing Claims

Adding claims transformation to a WCF service is a matter of deriving from `ClaimsAuthenticationManager` and implementing the `Authenticate` method. (See the previous explanation of claims transformation.)

After that, you can register the authentication manager using configuration (or code):

```
<microsoft.identityModel>
  <service>

    <claimsAuthenticationManager type="MyAuthenticationManager, Assembly" />

  </service>
</microsoft.identityModel>
```

CLAIMS TRANSFORMATION

I typically start by defining what the client identity should "look like" — in other words, on which claims the service or business logic can rely. I then make sure that the `ClaimsAuthenticationManager` can provide exactly these claims; otherwise, the request should fail.

This also involves removing claims that are not needed (or even better, creating a new principal with exactly the required claims that you have defined earlier).

Also, try to keep the claim set as minimal as possible — just enough claims so that the service can do its work. Remember that you also have the `ClaimsAuthorizationManager` abstraction that provides a lot of flexibility to couple authorization information with a principal.

The claims collection on `IClaimsIdentity` was explicitly designed to be LINQ-friendly. This enables you to use the query syntax or the extensions methods to query claims, and provides a lot of expressiveness.

I prefer the extensions methods because it is easy to clearly state your expectations. For example, the following query demands an e-mail claim to be present:

```
var email = id.Claims.First(c => c.ClaimType == ClaimTypes.Email);
```

You can even go one step further and demand that a claim exists only once in the claims collection. Being that explicit might reveal bugs in complex transformation scenarios in early stages:

```
var dob = id.Claims.Single(c => c.ClaimType == ClaimTypes.DateOfBirth);
```

You can also build convenience wrappers around the LINQ queries. When you have a look at the `Thinktecture.IdentityModel` library that is part of the code available for download from this book's website (`www.wrox.com`), you can see a couple of extension methods for `IClaimsPrincipal` and `IClaimsIdentity` that give you methods such as `FindClaims`, `GetClaimValue`, `DemandClaim`, and so on.

> ### ACCESSING CLAIMS
>
> It's okay for low-level code like transformation or authorization (and sometimes façades) to work directly on the `IClaimsPrincipal`.
>
> Business code should use an abstraction like a `User` class with properties that, in turn, queries the claims collection. This way, the technical details don't blur into your business logic, and you can also change the underlying implementation independently of the business code (and vice versa).
>
> Also, keep in mind that you might want to inject principals in your code to make unit testing easier.

Authorization

You have already learned about the concept of claims-based authorization in WIF. You add an authorization manager either via code or configuration, as shown here:

```
<microsoft.identityModel>
  <service>

    <claimsAuthorizationManager type="MyAuthorizationManager, Assembly" />

  </service>
</microsoft.identityModel>
```

From that point on, your authorization manager will be automatically called on a per-request basis. The authorization context will be populated with the SOAP action as the action, and the endpoint address as the resource. For REST services, it will be the HTTP verb as the action, and the resource URL as the resource. In all cases, these are represented as single-name claims.

This enables doing coarse-grained authorization based on the endpoint and operation the client tries to call. When you return `false` from the `CheckAccess` method, a `SecurityException` is triggered. WCF automatically translates security exceptions into an access-denied fault message. On the WCF client side, these types of fault messages are turned into a `SecurityAccessDeniedException` that the client can explicitly catch.

Those who know about the underlying native WCF `ServiceAuthorizationManager`, *also know that this mechanism enables inspecting the contents of the incoming message during per-request authorization. This feature was rarely used and didn't make it in the WIF authorization abstraction. If you need this feature, have a look at the* `Thinktecture.IdentityModel` *library, which contains a sample of how to resurface message inspection.*

For triggering the authorization manager from within your code, WIF has the `ClaimsPrincipalPermission` class (and a corresponding attribute as well). The attribute is similar to per-request authorization — the authorization manager is called automatically when the client invokes the operation. But you have control over the values for action and resource.

If you need more fine-grained control over resources and actions, you can use `ClaimsPrincipal Permission.CheckAccess`. This method wraps the resource and action into name claims, and passes them on as an authorization context to the registered authorization manager. In the case of a negative outcome, a `SecurityException` fires.

The built-in WIF API for authorization has two shortcomings:

➤ Because per-request authorization and calls to `ClaimsPrincipalPermission` both generate name claims, it is tedious to distinguish between them in your authorization manager code.

➤ `CheckAccess` always triggers a `SecurityException` when authorization fails. A way to branch code using a Boolean return value is missing.

You can work around both issues thanks to the WIF extensibility model.

The key to all customizations and domain-specific additions you want to make to authorization is grabbing the registered authorization manager and calling the `CheckAccess` method yourself. This enables you to create your own `AuthorizationContext` object, which, in turn, gives you full control over shape and form of your action and resource claims.

WIF puts an instance of the current configuration onto a message property called `ServiceConfiguration`. From there, you can reach into the `ClaimsAuthorizationManager`. Listing 10-10 shows an example.

LISTING 10-10: Accessing WIF Configuration (Works in Both WCF and ASP.NET)

```
public static class IdentityModelConfiguration
{
    /// <summary>
    /// Gets the current WIF service configuration.
    /// </summary>
    /// <value>The service configuration.</value>
    public static ServiceConfiguration ServiceConfiguration
    {
        get
        {
            if (OperationContext.Current == null)
            {
                // no WCF
                return FederatedAuthentication.ServiceConfiguration;
            }

            // search message property
            if (OperationContext.Current.IncomingMessageProperties
              .ContainsKey("ServiceConfiguration"))
            {
                var configuration = OperationContext.Current
                  .IncomingMessageProperties["ServiceConfiguration"]
                    as ServiceConfiguration;
                if (configuration != null)
                {
                    return configuration;
                }
            }

            // return configuration from configuration file
            return new ServiceConfiguration();
        }
    }
}
```

Code file [IdentityModelConfiguration.cs] available for download at Wrox.com.

Invoking `CheckAccess` is now a matter of the following:

```
var authZ =
  IdentityModelConfiguration.ServiceConfiguration.ClaimsAuthorizationManager;

if (authZ.CheckAccess(…))
{
  // code
}
```

The `Thinktecture.IdentityModel` library contains code to further customize authorization based on this sample. This makes it easy to use claim types from namespaces that you control, thus making them easy to spot inside the authorization manager.

A well-hidden feature of WIF is that some parts of the configuration system can be extended. This also applies to claims authorization. It is possible to append an arbitrary XML fragment to the `<claimsAuthorizationManager />` *section. This way, you can declaratively pass in a hint to an authorization policy file, or add some other configuration entries. The WIF SDK has a sample that shows how to append an authorization policy that can be parsed at startup time (see* `Samples\Extensibility\Claims Based Authorization`*).*

Tracing

Tracing in WCF is essential for troubleshooting. WIF adds a new trace source that you should absolutely enable during development and for testing.

You can register for the trace source using the following configuration snippet:

```
<system.diagnostics>
    <source name="Microsoft.IdentityModel"
            switchValue="Verbose" >
      <listeners>
        <add name="IdentityModelTraceListener" />
      </listeners>
    </source>
  </sources>

  <sharedListeners>
    <add initializeData="wif.svclog"
        type="System.Diagnostics.XmlWriterTraceListener, System,
            Version=4.0.0.0,
            Culture=neutral,
            PublicKeyToken=b77a5c561934e089"
        name="IdentityModelTraceListener"
        traceOutputOptions="Timestamp">
    </add>
  </sharedListeners>

  <trace autoflush="true" />

</system.diagnostics>
```

POSSIBLE SOLUTIONS FOR SECURING THE MOVIE DATABASE SOAP SERVICE

To see WIF in action, use the movies WCF service from Chapter 9 to add some security features. Start with an intranet-based scenario and later add federation.

The movie service has three types of clients:

➤   A website that uses the back-end services to provide read-only content to browser-based users.

➤ Internal users who must view, review, update, and create new content.

➤ At a time, certain movie genres will be outsourced to external content providers. These external providers can directly add content to the system using the WCF services.

The first two client types use Windows authentication to access the movie services. The external providers get access via a federation gateway using SAML tokens.

Internal Users

For enabling internal users, the course of events is as follows:

1. Add a service endpoint that does Windows authentication.

2. Enable and configure WIF.

3. Establish an identity via claims transformation.

4. Add authorization instrumentation and policy.

Adding Windows Authentication

The first step is to add a Windows authenticated endpoint to the movies service. Use mixed-mode security with a disabled session for that. That means you must first enable SSL. Exactly how this works depends on the hosting environment. You either have to bind SSL to an endpoint using IIS, or use the `netsh` command-line tool for self-hosting. In the case of self-hosting, you must also add a new base address to the WCF configuration:

```
<service name="MovieService" behaviorConfiguration="soapBehavior">
  <host>
    <baseAddresses>
      <add baseAddress="net.tcp://localhost:7776"/>
      <add baseAddress="http://localhost:8888"/>
      <add baseAddress="https://localhost:8889"/>
    </baseAddresses>
  </host>
</service>
```

To add the actual endpoint, you must add code to the `MoviesServiceFactory` in the `SetupMoviesServiceHost` method:

```
var secureIntranetBinding = new WS2007HttpBinding(SecurityMode.
    TransportWithMessageCredential);
secureIntranetBinding.Security.Message.ClientCredentialType =
    MessageCredentialType.Windows;
secureIntranetBinding.Security.Message.EstablishSecurityContext = false;

host.AddServiceEndpoint(
    typeof(IMovieService),
    secureIntranetBinding,
    "binary");
```

To see if the client is actually authenticated, add a bit of tracing code to `MovieService` in the `ListMovies` method:

```
public List<MovieData> ListMovies(PagedDataRequest request)
{
    trace.TraceEvent(TraceEventType.Information, 0, "List Movies...");

    if (Thread.CurrentPrincipal.Identity.IsAuthenticated)
    {
        var info = string.Format("{0} ({1})",
            Thread.CurrentPrincipal.Identity.Name,
            Thread.CurrentPrincipal.Identity.GetType().Name);

        trace.TraceInformation(info);
    }
    else
    {
        trace.TraceInformation("Anonymous request");
    }

    // rest omitted
}
```

The next step is to change the Windows client to use the authenticated endpoint. This means that you must add the same binding to the client configuration, as well as change the endpoint address the client uses:

```
<client>
  <endpoint name="default"
            address="https://localhost:8889/binary"
            binding="ws2007HttpBinding"
            bindingConfiguration="IntranetSecure"
            contract="MovieServiceContracts.IMovieService" />
</client>

...

<ws2007HttpBinding>
  <binding name="IntranetSecure">
    <security mode="TransportWithMessageCredential">
      <message clientCredentialType="Windows"
               establishSecurityContext="false" />
    </security>
  </binding>
</ws2007HttpBinding>
```

That's it! When you now run the client, the service can trace the client's Windows account name in the `ListMovies` call. But when you have a closer look at the Common Language Runtime (CLR) type of the client identity, you see `WindowsIdentity`.

To get claims, the last step is to enable WIF. Insert a call to `FederatedServiceCredentials.ConfigureServiceHost(host)` into the host (or the host factory for IIS hosting). When you rerun the client, the identity is now of type `WindowsClaimsIdentity` (which means WIF is doing its work).

Claims Transformation

The next step is to establish an identity for the client that the service can rely on. This is done in the claims authentication manager. For this scenario, the identity of the clients should have the claims shown in Table 10-1.

TABLE 10-1: Client Identity

CLAIM	DESCRIPTION
Name	Name of the client.
Company	Identifier for an external content provider. "Internal" refers to internal users.
Role	A user can have the following roles: Viewer, Reviewer, and Author.
Genre	Optionally, a user can be restricted to work only on specific genres (only relevant for reviewers and authors). Internal users have access to all genres by default.

In the case of Windows users, you expect certain groups in Active Directory (AD) to be in place. The claims transformation process then parses these group memberships and turns them into application roles.

As shown in Listing 10-11, the implementation of `ClaimsAuthenticationManager` distinguishes between internal users and external ones. You add the logic for external users in a later step.

LISTING 10-11: ClaimsAuthenticationManager

```
public class ClaimsTransformer : ClaimsAuthenticationManager
{
    public override IClaimsPrincipal Authenticate(string resourceName,
        IClaimsPrincipal incomingPrincipal)
    {
        // internal user
        var windowsUser = incomingPrincipal.Identity as WindowsClaimsIdentity;
        if (windowsUser != null)
        {
            return CreatePrincipalForWindowsUser(windowsUser);
        }

        return base.Authenticate(resourceName, incomingPrincipal);
    }

    private IClaimsPrincipal
        CreatePrincipalForWindowsUser(WindowsClaimsIdentity windowsUser)
    {
        var claims = new List<Claim>
        {
```

```
            new Claim(ClaimTypes.Name, windowsUser.Name),
            new Claim(MovieClaimTypes.Company, "Internal")
        };

        using (var principal = new WindowsClaimsPrincipal(windowsUser))
        {
            // check Windows groups and turn them into roles
            if (principal.IsInRole("Users"))
            {
                claims.Add(new Claim(ClaimTypes.Role, "Viewer"));
            }
            if (principal.IsInRole("MovieAuthors"))
            {
                claims.Add(new Claim(ClaimTypes.Role, "Author"));
            }
            if (principal.IsInRole("MovieReviewers"))
            {
                claims.Add(new Claim(ClaimTypes.Role, "Reviewer"));
            }
        }

        // internal users have access to all genres
        claims.Add(new Claim(MovieClaimTypes.Genre, "All"));

        return ClaimsPrincipal.CreateFromIdentity(new ClaimsIdentity(claims));
    }
}
```

Because all information is extracted directly from the Windows token and no database round trips are necessary here, there is no need for a caching layer.

Authorization

After you establish a security context and identity for the current user, you can annotate your code with authorization requirements.

At a coarse-grained level, you can either use the per-request authorization or add authorization attributes to the service façade — this gives you "is the user allowed to call this operation" semantics. Use the imperative approach described earlier when you need more detailed information before you call the authorization manager. Listing 10-12 shows an example.

LISTING 10-12: Service Façade with Authorization Annotations

```
[ApplicationClaimPermission(SecurityAction.Demand,
    Operation = "Add",
    Resource = "Movie")]
public void AddMovie(MovieDetailsData movie)
{ ... }

[ApplicationClaimPermission(SecurityAction.Demand,
    Operation = "List",
    Resource = "Movie")]
```

continues

LISTING 10-12 *(continued)*

```
public List<MovieData> ListMovies(PagedDataRequest request)
{ … }

[ApplicationClaimPermission(SecurityAction.Demand,
    Operation = "GetDetails",
    Resource = "Movie")]
public MovieDetailsData GetMovie(string movieId)
{ … }
```

The access control for genres is an example for an authorization decision that needs more knowledge than that the user is invoking a certain operation. In this case, the `ListMovies` operation would probably use the genre's claims to construct a query. The `GetMovie` and `AddMovie` operations, in turn, would return an Access Denied message when users try to request or add a movie that they are not authorized for. Listing 10-13 shows how to do this.

LISTING 10-13: Sample Imperative Authorization

```
[ApplicationClaimPermission(SecurityAction.Demand,
    Operation = "GetDetails",
    Resource = "Movie")]
public MovieDetailsData GetMovie(string movieId)
{
    trace.TraceEvent(TraceEventType.Information, 0, "Get Movie...");

    try
    {
        var movie = movieManager.GetMovie(movieId).MapAll();

        // check if user is allowed
        var genreClaim = new Claim(
          Constants.ClaimTypes.Genre, movie.Genre);

        if (ApplicationClaimPermission.CheckAccess(
          Constants.Actions.GetDetails,
          Constants.Resources.Genre, genreClaim))
        {
            return movie;
        }

        trace.TraceEvent(TraceEventType.Error, 401, string.Format(
            "Authorization failed for user: {0} / genre: {1}",
              Thread.CurrentPrincipal.Identity.Name,
              movie.Genre));

        throw new SecurityException();
    }
    catch (MovieNotFoundException mnfex)
    {
        trace.TraceEvent(TraceEventType.Error, 0, mnfex.Message);
```

```
        throw new FaultException<NoSuchMovieFault>(
            new NoSuchMovieFault { MovieId = movieId });
    }
  }
```

Listing 10-14 shows a simple implementation of an authorization manager that enforces the access policy.

LISTING 10-14: Authorization Manager

```
public class AuthorizationManager : ClaimsAuthorizationManager
{
    public override bool CheckAccess(AuthorizationContext context)
    {
        // distinguish between per-request authZ and app authZ
        if (!IsApplicationAuthorization(context))
        {
            return base.CheckAccess(context);
        }

        // check which resource the client tries to access
        var resource = context.Resource.First().Value;
        switch (resource)
        {
            case Constants.Resources.Movies:
                return AuthorizeMovieAccess(
                    context.Action, context.Principal);
            case Constants.Resources.Genre:
                var genre = context.Resource.First(c =>
                    c.ClaimType == Constants.ClaimTypes.Genre).Value;
                return AuthorizeGenreAccess(genre, context.Principal);
        }

        return false;
    }

    private bool IsApplicationAuthorization(
      AuthorizationContext context)
    {
        return (context.Action.FirstOrDefault(claim =>
            claim.ClaimType == ApplicationClaimPermission.ActionType)
              != null);
    }

    private bool AuthorizeMovieAccess(
      Collection<Claim> actions, IClaimsPrincipal principal)
    {
        var action = actions.First().Value;

        switch (action)
        {
            case Constants.Actions.List:
                return principal.IsInRole(Constants.Roles.Viewer);
```

continues

LISTING 10-14 *(continued)*

```
            case Constants.Actions.GetDetails:
                return principal.IsInRole(Constants.Roles.Viewer);
            case Constants.Actions.Add:
                return principal.IsInRole(Constants.Roles.Author);
        }

        return false;
    }

    private bool AuthorizeGenreAccess(
      string genre, IClaimsPrincipal principal)
    {
        if (principal.ClaimExists(Constants.ClaimTypes.Genre, "All"))
        {
            return true;
        }

        return principal.ClaimExists(
          Constants.ClaimTypes.Genre, genre);
    }
}
```

Adding an External Content Provider

Because WCF and WIF also support SAML tokens, it is easy to grant external users access to the movie service. This is typically accomplished by providing a *federation gateway* that the external parties can use to request a token for the services they want to access. In a Microsoft-oriented environment, the Active Directory Federation Services 2 (ADFS 2) product would be such a federation gateway.

The setup and configuration of ADFS 2 is out of scope of this book, and actually not relevant. But some interesting points affect the service design:

➤ External partners use the federation gateway to request a token for the service.

➤ The federation gateway knows who the external partner is and has rules for how to transform the incoming claims to claims that the service can process.

➤ The gateway can generate a token with the following claims:

  ➤ A claim containing the unique username of the external client

  ➤ A claim containing the company name (or identifier)

➤ The service transforms these incoming claims to the client identity the service code expects. This can, for example, involve querying a database to query the roles and to find out which genres the external user has access to.

This way, you can provision external users with minimal effort. As you'll see, you'll have to slightly modify only the claims transformation logic. All the service and authorization code can stay the same. Compared to "traditional" approaches, this is a huge simplification.

Adding the Service Endpoint for External Users

For accepting issued tokens, you must add a new endpoint in the service host factory. This endpoint advertises the address of the federation gateway in its metadata so that the external clients know how to request tokens for the service:

```
// endpoint for external users
var fedEndpoint = new
EndpointAddress("https://gateway/adfs/services/trust/mex");

var externalBinding = new WS2007FederationHttpBinding(
  WSFederationHttpSecurityMode.TransportWithMessageCredential);
externalBinding.Security.Message.EstablishSecurityContext = false;
externalBinding.Security.Message.IssuerMetadataAddress = fedEndpoint;

host.AddServiceEndpoint(
    typeof(IMovieService),
    externalBinding,
    "issuedtokens");
```

Next, you must configure WIF so that it can process the issued tokens. This involves the following:

➤ Registering the federation gateway as a trusted issuer of tokens. This is accomplished using the issuer name registry mechanism of WIF.

➤ Specifying a certificate for decrypting incoming tokens. For example, this could be the SSL certificate.

➤ Specifying allowed audience URIs. This is a value that must be coordinated between the federation gateway, the service, and the client. Think of it as a logical (sometimes also physical) name for the service.

Consider the following example:

```
<microsoft.identityModel>
  <service>
    <claimsAuthenticationManager type="Security.ClaimsTransformer,
        SecurityPlumbing"/>
    <claimsAuthorizationManager type="Security.AuthorizationManager,
        SecurityPlumbing"/>

    <!-- audience URI of movie service application -->
    <audienceUris>
      <add value="https://moviedb/" />
    </audienceUris>

    <!-- certificate for token decryption -->
    <serviceCertificate>
      <certificateReference storeLocation="LocalMachine"
                            storeName="My"
                            x509FindType="FindBySubjectDistinguishedName"
                            findValue="CN=Service" />
    </serviceCertificate>

    <!-- registers the federation gateway as a trusted token issuer -->
```

```
<issuerNameRegistry type="Microsoft.IdentityModel.Tokens.
    ConfigurationBasedIssuerNameRegistry,
    Microsoft.IdentityModel, Version=3.5.0.0,
    Culture=neutral, PublicKeyToken=31bf3856ad364e35">
  <trustedIssuers>
    <add thumbprint="d1 c5 b1 25 97 d0 36 94 65 1c e2 64 fe 48 06
        01 35 f7 bd db"
          name="FederationGateway" />
  </trustedIssuers>
</issuerNameRegistry>

<!-- only federation gateway allowed anyways, so no extra certificate
    validation -->
<certificateValidation certificateValidationMode="None" />
  </service>
</microsoft.identityModel>
```

Adjusting Claims Transformation

The only code modification you must make is in the claims authentication manager. Two things
need to happen here:

➤   It is mandatory that external users have a username and a company claim.

➤   Role information and allowed genres for external users are stored in a database. This infor-
    mation must be turned into claims.

From a service and business logic point of view, there is no difference between internal and external
users now.

The new authentication manager looks like this (with parts removed):

```
public class ClaimsTransformer : ClaimsAuthenticationManager
{
    TraceSource trace = new TraceSource("mdb.Movies");

    public override IClaimsPrincipal Authenticate(
      string resourceName, IClaimsPrincipal incomingPrincipal)
    {
        trace.TraceInformation("Client: " + incomingPrincipal.Identity.Name);
        // internal user
        var windowsUser = incomingPrincipal.Identity as WindowsClaimsIdentity;
        if (windowsUser != null)
        {
            trace.TraceInformation("internal user");
            return CreatePrincipalForWindowsUser(windowsUser);
        }

        trace.TraceInformation("external user");
        return CreatePrincipalForExternalUser(resourceName, incomingPrincipal);
    }

    private IClaimsPrincipal CreatePrincipalForExternalUser(
      string resourceName, IClaimsPrincipal incomingPrincipal)
```

```
    {
        // make sure required claims exist
        var name = incomingPrincipal.GetClaimValue(ClaimTypes.Name);
        var company = incomingPrincipal.GetClaimValue
            (Constants.ClaimTypes.Company);

        var claims = new List<Claim>
        {
            new Claim(ClaimTypes.Name, name),
            new Claim(Constants.ClaimTypes.Company, company)
        };

        GetRolesForUser(name, company).ForEach(
            role => claims.Add(new Claim(ClaimTypes.Role, role)));
        GetGenresForUser(name, company).ForEach(
            genre => claims.Add(new Claim(Constants.ClaimTypes.Genre, genre)));

        return ClaimsPrincipal.CreateFromIdentity(new ClaimsIdentity(claims));
    }
}
```

The Client

Because of the design of the movie service client, all WCF specifics are encapsulated in the service agent library. This is where you add the code for token-based authentication.

The logic for setting up the communication channel to the service is as follows:

1. The client authenticates with its local identity provider and requests a token. This is done using Windows authentication.

2. The client then uses its identity token to request a service token from the federation gateway.

3. The service token is attached to the service channel factory, which, in turn, generates the client proxy.

WIF includes the necessary plumbing to request tokens from token services. It is implemented as a specialized WCF channel factory called `WSTrustChannelFactory`. For attaching tokens to service channels, WIF also includes extension methods that make this operation simple. The initialization could look as follows:

```
public class MovieClient : IMovieClient, IDisposable
{
    public MovieClient()
    {
        // request token from idp (windows authentication)
        var idpToken = GetIdPToken();

        // request token from federation gateway (using idp token)
        var serviceToken = GetServiceToken(idpToken);

        // setting up channel factory
        var movieServiceClientFactory = new
          ChannelFactory<IMovieServiceChannel>("default");
```

```csharp
        movieServiceClientFactory.ConfigureChannelFactory();
        movieServiceClientFactory.Credentials.SupportInteractive = false;

        movieServiceClient = movieServiceClientFactory
           .CreateChannelWithIssuedToken<IMovieServiceChannel>(serviceToken);
    }

    private SecurityToken GetIdPToken()
    {
        var factory = new WSTrustChannelFactory(
            new WindowsWSTrustBinding(SecurityMode.TransportWithMessageCredential),
            new EndpointAddress(idpUrl));
        factory.TrustVersion = TrustVersion.WSTrust13;

        var rst = new RequestSecurityToken
        {
            RequestType = RequestTypes.Issue,
            AppliesTo = new EndpointAddress(fedGwUrl),
            KeyType = KeyTypes.Symmetric
        };

        var channel = factory.CreateChannel();
        return channel.Issue(rst);
    }

    private static SecurityToken GetServiceToken(SecurityToken idpToken)
    {
        var binding = new IssuedTokenWSTrustBinding();
        binding.SecurityMode = SecurityMode.TransportWithMessageCredential;

        var factory = new WSTrustChannelFactory(
            binding,
            fedGwUrl);
        factory.TrustVersion = TrustVersion.WSTrust13;
        factory.Credentials.SupportInteractive = false;

        var rst = new RequestSecurityToken
        {
            RequestType = RequestTypes.Issue,
            AppliesTo = new EndpointAddress(realm),
            KeyType = KeyTypes.Symmetric
        };

        factory.ConfigureChannelFactory();
        var channel = factory.CreateChannelWithIssuedToken(idpToken);
        return channel.Issue(rst);
    }
}
```

Assessing the Solution

You have just seen that you can add claims-based identity to an existing service without having
to do major surgery on the architecture or code structure. This provides the benefit of having a

more expressive representation of identity, as well as the decoupling of authorization from business logic flow.

As a "side effect," it was easy adding support for external users and third-party authentication.

POSSIBLE SOLUTIONS FOR SECURING THE MOVIE DATABASE REST SERVICE

The (security) situation is a little different in the REST world (and I use this term in a fuzzy way) compared to SOAP. SOAP has `WS-Security`, which is a powerful (sometimes too powerful) protocol for authentication and message protection. On the other hand, REST has no standard mechanisms that go beyond standard HTTP-based authentication (for example, basic authentication — maybe Windows authentication for certain scenarios). Still, you can use WIF to move your REST services to the claims-based model.

In the spirit of the last section, start with securing the REST service using Windows authentication. Then move to custom authentication methods (such as SAML), which is a great opportunity to show you how to use the WIF core API to claims-enable service scenarios not supported out-of-the-box.

Internal Users

The good news is that WIF supports WCF REST services with HTTP authentication out-of-the-box. That means that you can reuse all the code and infrastructure you created earlier.

All you must do is enable Windows authentication on the binding and `WebClient`, and enable WIF in the web service host. From that point, your claims transformation code for Windows clients will be called, and the same authorization manager will be invoked. Job done!

If you don't like to share these components between your services, you don't have to, of course. In this case, you can use the `<service />` element in the WIF configuration to create several named independent configuration settings. The call to `ConfigureServiceHost` has an overload that accepts the name of such a named configuration.

Token-Based Authentication

As stated earlier, there are no real standards around token-based authentication and REST services. But most authentication schemes out in the wild have one thing in common. The authentication information (from simple username/password to tokens) is typically transmitted using the HTTP authorization header.

The exact layout of that header (such as token format or encoding) is often simply defined by the service provider. Because there are no clear standards at the moment, WIF does not include direct support for these "homegrown" authentication handshakes, but the WIF API can be used to implement the support yourself. For the purpose of this example, add support for a SAML bearer token.

 *A number of emerging standards exist for token-based authentication for REST services. The most promising and complete seems to be OAuth 2, which is currently under development. As soon as the specifications are finalized, it is expected that WIF will also directly support these new protocols.*

In a nutshell, following are the necessary steps to add your own SAML support to a WCF web service host:

1. Parse the incoming HTTP request, and extract the authorization header.

2. Extract the SAML token from the header, and validate it.

3. Turn the token into an `IClaimsPrincipal`, and set `Thread.CurrentPrincipal`.

4. Wrap this functionality in a WCF `ServiceAuthorizationManager`.

5. Wrap the authorization manager in a service host and factory.

This sounds like a lot of work, but luckily most of the heavy lifting is done by WIF. You need to provide only the header parsing code and the plumbing; WIF takes care of all token-related processing. Again, you can also share your claims transformation and authorization code.

A (shortened) version of such an `ServiceAuthorizationManager` could look like this:

```
public class FederatedWebServiceAuthorizationManager
  : ServiceAuthorizationManager
{
    protected override bool CheckAccessCore(OperationContext operationContext)
    {
        var properties = operationContext.ServiceSecurityContext
          .AuthorizationContext.Properties;
        var to = operationContext.IncomingMessageHeaders.To.AbsoluteUri;

        // parse HTTP header and turn SAML token into IClaimsPrincipal
        IClaimsIdentity identity;
        if (TryGetIdentity(out identity))
        {
            // call claims transformation and set the IClaimsPrincipal
            var principal = _configuration.ClaimsAuthenticationManager
              .Authenticate(
                to,
                ClaimsPrincipal.CreateFromIdentity(identity));
            properties["Principal"] = principal;

            // call claims authorization manager
            return CallClaimsAuthorization(principal, operationContext);
        }
        else
```

```
            {
                SetUnauthorizedResponse();
                return false;
            }
        }
```

Turning the SAML token string into an `IClaimsPrincipal` is accomplished with the help of WIF's security token handlers:

```
    private IClaimsIdentity GetSamlIdentityFromHeader(string header)
    {
        var token = header.Substring("SAML access_token=".Length);

        var samlToken = _configuration.SecurityTokenHandlers.ReadToken(
          new XmlTextReader(new StringReader(token)));
        return _configuration.SecurityTokenHandlers.ValidateToken(samlToken).First();
    }
```

On the client side, you can reuse the code for requesting tokens for the SOAP service. The only difference is that you must request a bearer token (see the movie sample client). This token then must be placed on the authorization header so that the service-side plumbing can pick it up.

Also, look at the samples called "REST" and "OData" in the `Thinktecture.IdentityModel` library.

SUMMARY

This chapter was a whirlwind tour through several important security topics: WCF security, claims-based identity, and federation.

WCF is the foundation for everything here. It provides the runtime and messaging system, as well as the hooks to extract security information from incoming messages. WCF also has the federation functionality already built in, but it isn't accessible and easy to use all the time.

WIF sits on top of WCF and makes claims a first-class citizen via the `IClaimsPrincipal` abstraction. It furthermore streamlines the WCF security stack by providing more easy-to-use hooks in the form of security token handlers. And, finally, WIF adds the concepts of claims transformation and claims-based authorization.

As you have seen, when used in combination, this allows building logic on a nice abstraction layer so that even onboarding the external users could be accomplished with minimal code changes (and zero code changes to the actual business logic).

You should always use WIF when building distributed systems — federated or not. The claims-based model provides more expressiveness and better abstractions than the native WCF security system. It also makes you ready for whatever security scenarios you might have to implement in the future.

ABOUT THE AUTHOR

Dominick Baier is an internationally recognized expert on security of .NET and Windows applications. He supports companies worldwide with design and implementation of security features in their software as a security consultant at thinktecture (www.thinktecture.com). As one of the few "Developer Security" Microsoft MVPs, he works directly with various security teams in Redmond, Washington. Offshoots of this cooperation are the books *Developing More Secure Microsoft ASP. NET 2.0 Applications* (Redmond, Washington: Microsoft Press, 2006) and *Guide to Claims-based Identity & Access Control* (Redmond, Washington: Microsoft Press, 2010). Baier also leads the security, WCF, and Azure curriculum at DevelopMentor (www.develop.com). You can find a wealth of security-related resources, as well as conference slide decks and tools/sample code, at his blog at www.leastprivilege.com.

11

Applied .NET Task Parallel Library

by Jeffrey Juday

It has become a multicore world, and parallel programming must be embraced for a developer to capitalize on all the burgeoning multicore potential. Embracing parallel programming in .NET means a developer must learn about the Task Parallel Library (TPL).

Although .NET has always had features often associated with concurrency and parallel algorithms such as threading and mutexes, the goal of the aTPL is to make concurrency and parallel construction even easier. Borrowing from academia, commercial best practices, and incorporating some unique innovations, the TPL has been assembled to simplify .NET parallel programming. The TPL introduces some new constructs and sports an improved `ThreadPooling` mechanism.

Parallel programming is often divided into *data parallelism* and *task parallelism*. Data parallelism in .NET is encapsulated into parallel loops and parallel LINQ. Underpinning parallel loops and parallel LINQ are all the TPL task parallelism classes. Although a developer could leverage parallel loops and parallel LINQ without delving into all TPL classes, diverging from some simple scenarios requires some deeper understanding. A deeper data parallelism understanding actually entails learning how to work with a core set of TPL classes.

That same reasoning goes for learning task parallelism. A developer can leverage task parallelism with a few TPL classes. Again, though, diverging from well-defined scenarios requires understanding some core TPL classes.

By demonstrating class usage and common operations, this chapter introduces the core TPL classes.

Like all new .NET features, the TPL has a learning curve. An introduction using the core classes to solve a common problem can flatten the TPL learning curve. Developers reading the discussions and studying the sample code presented here will learn about the following concepts:

➤ `Task` class

➤ Concurrent collections

➤ TPL approaches to exception handling

➤ Approaches to canceling parallel operations

➤ Implementing the actor/agent design pattern

➤ Continuations

➤ Configuring a parallel workload

PROBLEMS AND SOLUTIONS

A good way to learn how to apply new components is to solve a common problem. Often, it helps to start with a common solution to a common problem, and then move to the new approaches to the problem. Recursively walking a directory hierarchy and totaling all the bytes occupied by a particular file type is a common problem most developers are already familiar with. Code based on a recursive algorithm is a common solution to the problem.

Typically, the algorithm walks a tree resembling the shape shown in Figure 11-1.

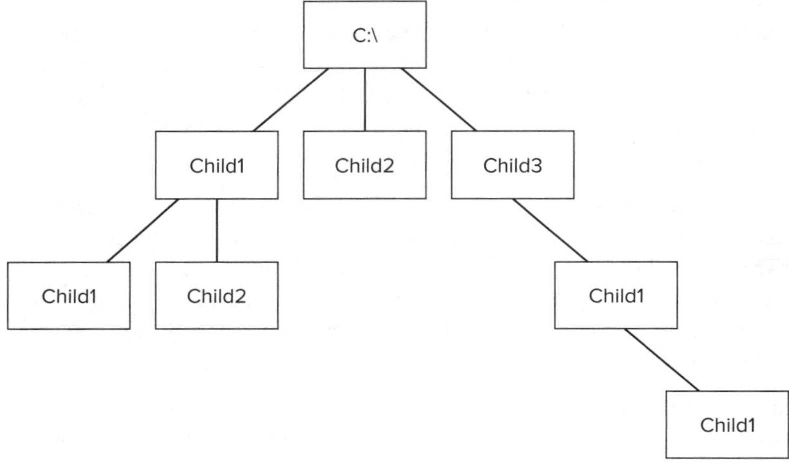

FIGURE 11-1: Typical directory structure

Recursing a directory tree takes a divide-and-conquer approach. It starts at the root, chooses a path, walks down each branch, and reverses, doing the same thing down another path. The following snippet shows recursive code serially traversing a directory tree and totaling the number of bytes occupied by `.docx` files:

```
public void Run()
{
    var totalBytes = Visit(_root);

    Console.WriteLine("Total bytes == " + totalBytes );
}

private long Visit(string subDir)
{
    long totalBytes = 0;

    try
    {
        var dir = new DirectoryInfo(subDir);
        var children = dir.EnumerateDirectories().Select(info =>
            { return info.FullName; });
        long bytes = 0;

        bytes = dir.EnumerateFiles("*." + _extension).Sum(f =>
            { return f.Length; });

        totalBytes = totalBytes + bytes;

        foreach (var directory in children)
        {
            totalBytes = totalBytes + Visit(directory);
        }
    }
    catch (Exception ex)
    {
        Console.WriteLine("EXCEPTION: " + ex.Message +
            " skipping to next folder");
    }

    return totalBytes;
}
```

Code file [Ch11_Code_Samples.zip] available for download at Wrox.com

The `DirectoryInfo` class includes methods and properties from the directory associated with the path supplied in the `DirectoryInfo` constructor. `EnumerateDirectories` returns an `IEnumerable` of child `DirectoryInfo` classes. `EnumerateFiles` returns a collection of `FileInfo` classes contained in the directory. A filter parameter returns only the `FileInfo` classes with the particular extension (`.docx`). `Sum` is a LINQ aggregate function that operates on any numeric property or function. Notice the tail recursion call to `Visit`. The whole process terminates when the root `Visit` completes.

The solution works fine. However, the solution is slow, and doesn't utilize all the resources of a modern personal computer. The solution runs on a single thread, and will occupy only one processor. Modern systems have more than one processor. An ideal solution would spread the work across all available processors.

So, now you understand this common problem. The remainder of this chapter solves the problem applying two different TPL solutions. Each approach to the problem introduces a new set of core TPL classes. One example, called `TPLParentChild`, closely mimics the recursive execution in the directory recursion example just discussed. A second example, called `TPLContinuation`, exhibits a completely different style altogether.

Each example is a conceptual leap from the original recursive example presented earlier. It's difficult to see a need for a data structure without seeing a legitimate need for the component. So, all solutions are fully working applications. Emphasis is placed on how to apply the TPL, rather than simply an explanation of the various classes.

Although totaling the bytes occupied by `.docx` files may seem trivial, the patterns and approaches to the problem mimic common patterns and approaches to other TPL solutions. TPL solutions often have a recursive nature to them by applying a similar divide-and-conquer approach that the following solutions describe.

Often, a TPL solution performs an operation on a tree or hierarchical data structure like, for example, a *Directed Acyclic Graph (DAG)*. A directory structure is a data structure that most developers are familiar with. A directory structure also happens to be based on a DAG. Each directory is a vertex, and edges are the parent-to-subdirectory relationship. In other words, these approaches and patterns apply to real-world problems.

USING TASKS

To leverage the TPL, developers must partition the parallel portions of an application into *tasks*. Tasks are a sort of sheath for a class method, lambda expression, `Func<T>`, `Action`, or the result of an operation. Tasks represent a workload, and the result of the executed workload.

To envision a need for a task, consider what happens when a method executes. Internally, the method may declare variables and do some computation. A method may or may not return a value. It may also generate an exception.

Now, consider what would be important to know if a developer wants to ship off a method to be executed in some other part of the application. Aside from the result (exception or value), a developer may want to know the method's current status. Has the method started running? Is the method waiting to run? What if a developer wants to wait on the completion of a method? What if a developer has more than one method? How can a developer wait on the result of more than one method?

All this functionality is encapsulated in the `Task` class.

Task Class

Tasks come in two flavors: a `Task` class and a generic `Task<TResult>` class. A developer can find the `Task` and generic `Task<TResult>` class in the `System.Threading.Tasks` namespace. Following are some of the methods and properties of the `Task` and `Task<TResult>` classes:

```csharp
public class Task : IThreadPoolWorkItem, IAsyncResult, IDisposable
{
        public Task(Action action);
        public Task(Action<object> action, object state);
        public Task(Action action, CancellationToken cancellationToken);
        public Task(Action action, TaskCreationOptions creationOptions);
        public Task(Action<object> action, object state, CancellationToken
    cancellationToken, TaskCreationOptions creationOptions);

        public bool IsCanceled { get; }
        public bool IsCompleted { get; }
        public bool IsFaulted { get; }
        public TaskStatus Status { get; }

        public Task ContinueWith(Action<Task> continuationAction);
        public void RunSynchronously();
        public void Start();

        public void Wait();
        public static void WaitAll(params Task[] tasks);
        public static int WaitAny(params Task[] tasks);
}

public class Task<TResult> : Task
{

        public Task(Func<TResult> function);
        public TResult Result { get; internal set; }
        public Task ContinueWith(Action<Task<TResult>> continuationAction);

}
```

These methods and properties comprise basic task functionality. There are additional task methods that will be dealt with later in this chapter. `Task<TResult>` inherits from `Task`. An astute developer may notice that `Task` implements `IAsyncResult`. The .NET Asynchronous Programming Model (APM) uses `IAsyncResult` to coordinate an asynchronous invocation. Though a full discussion of APM is beyond the scope of this chapter, you need to realize that tasks have usefulness that go beyond task parallelism.

Tasks require an `Action`. `Task<TResult>` (a generic `Task`) includes a `Result` property and, therefore, `Task<TResult>` requires a `Func<T>`. A `Func<T>` and `Action` delegate can be created from a class method or lambda expression.

Following are code examples of `Task` and `Task<TResult>` classes constructed with variations matching `Func<T>` and `Action`:

```
Task task = new Task(() =>
{
Console.WriteLine("The Task Ran"); }
);

Task<string> taskWithResult = new Task<string>(() =>
    {
        return "This task has a result";
    }
);

var f = new Func<string>(() =>
    {
        return "In a func";
    }
);

Task<string> taskWithFunc = new Task<string>(f);

Task taskWithClassMethod = new Task(Program.SampleMethod);
```

Code file [Ch11_Code_Samples.zip] available for download at Wrox.com

Almost everything in the TPL revolves around `Tasks` and `Task<TResult>`. `Task` and `Task<TResult>` are referred to as *tasks* for the remainder of the chapter. After a task is created, it must be started for the TPL to schedule the task to run. Typically, a developer starts a task and, somewhere in the code, waits for the task to complete. Following are some variations on starting and waiting:

```
task.Start();
task.Wait();

taskWithResult.Start();
taskWithResult.Wait();
Console.WriteLine(taskWithResult.Result);

taskWithFunc.Start();
taskWithFunc.Wait();
Console.WriteLine(taskWithFunc.Result);

taskWithClassMethod.Start();
taskWithClassMethod.Wait();
```

Code file [Ch11_Code_Samples.zip] available for download at Wrox.com

Later in this chapter, you learn more about variations on waiting and actions that a developer can take in response to a completed task.

A separate class called a `TaskScheduler` handles and executes tasks. Tasks may be executed on the thread pool, or from within the `TaskScheduler`. Figure 11-2 shows a task's execution path.

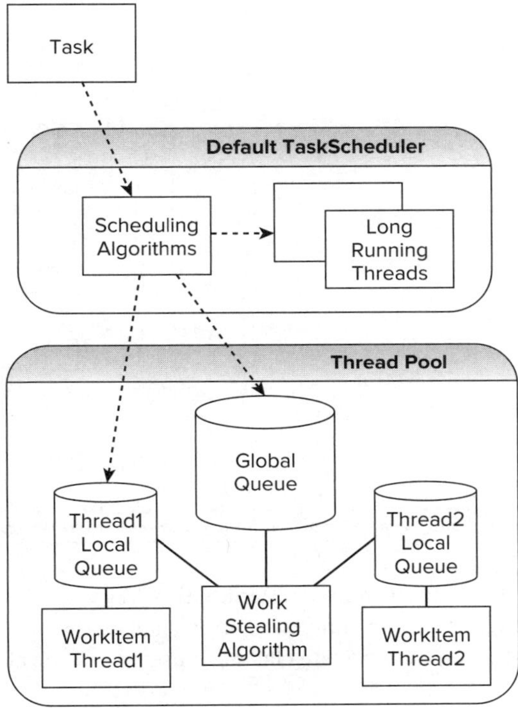

FIGURE 11-2: Executing a task (with dotted lines depicting the path of a task)

A task can specify a custom `TaskScheduler` (if one is available), or utilize the default `TaskScheduler`. The default `TaskScheduler` maintains a pool of threads and works with the `ThreadPool`.

Depending on `TaskCreationOptions` and other conditions, a task can be queued to run a number of ways. Idle threads can search for work in the global `ThreadPool` queue, or steal work from another thread's local queue.

Closures

Lambda expressions are a common way to compose tasks. Lambda expressions are often used to implement a `Closure`. The following code demonstrates a `Closure`:

```
static Action RunClosure(int whichOneToRun)
{
    var messagePrefix = "You ran ";
    Action act = null;
```

```
        switch (whichOneToRun)
        {
            case 1:
                act = new Action(() =>
                    {
                        var msg = messagePrefix + "1";
                        Console.WriteLine(msg);
                    }
                );
                break;
            case 2:
                act = new Action(() =>
                    {
                        var msg = messagePrefix + "2";
                        Console.WriteLine(msg);
                    }
                );
                break;
        }

        return act;
    }
```

Code file [Ch11_Code_Samples.zip] available for download at Wrox.com

Notice how the local variable `messagePrefix` is utilized by the `Action`. Although a `Closure` and lambda expression are not necessary for building tasks, in a simple situation such as the one shown here, a `Closure` eliminates the need to create a separate private class and use one of the class instance methods.

Although a `Closure` can make code more readable, care must be exercised with `Closures`. In the following example, when the `Action` is invoked, the loop has exited, and the looping variable is not the expected value:

```
static Action RunClosureBad()
{
    Action act = null;

    for (int n = 0; n <= 5; ++n)
    {
        if (n == 2)
        {
            act = new Action(() =>
                {
                    Console.WriteLine("This should be a 2 but it is
                        a " + n.ToString());
                    Console.WriteLine("This should say Some value
                        is here but it says " + obj.MyVal);
                }
            );
        }
    }
}
```

```
        return act;
    }
```


Because the outer method continues to execute after the `Action` variable is assigned, the `n` retains the last assignment value. In this situation, the value becomes the value that terminates the loop.

A better approach is to restructure the code so that it looks similar to the following sample:

```
Action act = null;

for (int n = 0; n <= 5; ++n)
{
    if (n == 2)
    {
        var nMoreLocal = n;

        act = new Action(() =>
        {
                Console.WriteLine("This should be a 2 and it is a "
                    + nMoreLocal.ToString());
        }
        );
    }
}
return act;
```


Notice how the `nMoreLocal` variable "caches" the value for the expression to use when it executes.

When implementing a `Closure`, developers must also beware of `using` statements, which invoke the `Dispose` method after a variable breaks the confines of the `using` block. Executing beyond the block and generating an exception are two ways code leaves a `using` block.

So, in the following example, although the `obj` variable is still technically "in scope," it is essentially useless because its `Dispose` method has been called before the variable is used:

```
class SampleDisposed : IDisposable
{
    public string MyVal { get; set; }

    public SampleDisposed(string myVal) { this.MyVal = myVal; }

    public void Dispose()
    {
        this.MyVal = "Dispose has been called";
    }
}
```

```
static Action RunClosureBad()
{
    Action act = null;

    using (var obj = new SampleDisposed("Some value is here"))
    {
        for (int n = 0; n <= 5; ++n)
        {
            if (n == 2)
            {
                act = new Action(() =>
                    {

                        Console.WriteLine("This should say Some value
                            is here but it says " + obj.MyVal);
                    }
                );
            }
        }
    }
    return act;
}
```

Code file [Ch11_Code_Samples.zip] available for download at Wrox.com

This example is trivial, but had the `using` statement been for one of the many more complex classes in the .NET Framework that implement `IDisposable`, the expression would have undoubtedly generated an exception.

The following code fixes the `using` statement issues:

```
Action act = null;

for (int n = 0; n <= 5; ++n)
{
    if (n == 2)
    {
        var nMoreLocal = n;

        act = new Action(() =>
        {
            using (var obj = new
              SampleDisposed("Some value is here"))
            {
                Console.WriteLine("This should be a 2 and it is a "
                    + nMoreLocal.ToString());
                Console.WriteLine("This should say Some value is
                    here and it does say " + obj.MyVal);
            }
        }
        );
    }
```

```
    }
    return act;
```


The `using` statement was moved inside of the lambda expression and the result better aligns with the developer's intent.

Applying Tasks

Putting tasks to work starts with thinking about a task's workload. Tasks can be short bursts of work, or can execute for the lifetime of a process. As discussed earlier, a separate TPL class called `TaskScheduler` handles scheduling and executing a task on a thread pool. A developer injects `TaskScheduler` "hints" when creating a task. Taking the hints into account, along with the resources available on the machine, `TaskScheduler` adjusts the thread pool.

A default `TaskScheduler` is included in the TPL. Building a custom `TaskScheduler` is beyond the scope of this chapter. Following was the original recursive example from earlier in this chapter:

```
public void Run()
{
    var totalBytes = Visit(_root);

    Console.WriteLine("Total bytes == " + totalBytes );
}

private long Visit(string subDir)
{
    long totalBytes = 0;

    try
    {
        var dir = new DirectoryInfo(subDir);
        var children = dir.EnumerateDirectories().Select(info => {
            return info.FullName; });
        long bytes = 0;

        bytes = dir.EnumerateFiles("*." + _extension).Sum(f => { return
            f.Length; });

        totalBytes = totalBytes + bytes;

        foreach (var directory in children)
        {
            totalBytes = totalBytes + Visit(directory);
        }
    }
    catch (Exception ex)
    {
        Console.WriteLine("EXCEPTION: " + ex.Message + " skipping to
            next folder");
```

```
        }
        return totalBytes;
    }
```


Following is part of a parallel programming solution to the recursive computation discussed earlier in this chapter:

```
public void Run()
{

    StartGettingInput();

    var totalBytes = Visit(_root,TaskCreationOptions.LongRunning);
        //Root is long running

    Console.WriteLine("Total bytes == " + totalBytes );
}

private long Visit(string subDir, TaskCreationOptions opts)
{
    CancellationTokenSource cancelLocal =
     new CancellationTokenSource();

    var cancelJoinedToken =
        CancellationTokenSource.CreateLinkedTokenSource
        (_cancelGlobal.Token, cancelLocal.Token).Token;

    var task = new Task<long> ( new Func<long> (() =>
        {

            long bytes = 0;
            long bytesChildren = 0;

            cancelJoinedToken.ThrowIfCancellationRequested();

            var dir = new DirectoryInfo(subDir);
            var children = dir.EnumerateDirectories().Select(info => {
                return info.FullName; });
            bytes = dir.EnumerateFiles("*." + _extension).Sum(f => {
                return f.Length; });
            List<Task<long>> childTasks = new List<Task<long>>();

            //Run children
            foreach (var directory in children)
            {
                var localDir = directory;

                var tNew = Task.Factory.StartNew<long>(obj =>
                {
                    return Visit(localDir,
                        TaskCreationOptions.AttachedToParent);
                }
```

```
                    , cancelJoinedToken,
                TaskCreationOptions.AttachedToParent);
                    childTasks.Add(tNew);
                }

                //Get the child results
                if (childTasks.Count > 0)
                {
                    Task.WaitAll(childTasks.ToArray());

                    //If you get a cancel or exception the line below is
                    //never executed.
                    bytesChildren = childTasks.Sum(t => { return t.Result; });
                }
                else { bytesChildren = 0; }

                return bytes + bytesChildren;
            }
        )
        , cancelJoinedToken, opts);

        return this.RunVisit(task,cancelLocal);
    }
```

Code file [Ch11_Code_Samples.zip] available for download at Wrox.com

---

Some of this code should look familiar. The computation is the same, and the directory query is the same. The new parts are the task creation, task waiting, and a concept called *cancellations* that is examined later in this chapter. StartNew (a method on the default TaskScheduler) creates and immediately starts a task.

Figure 11-3 shows what conceptually happens when the code runs.

The code walks the directory tree just like the original recursive example. The main difference is that, instead of moving down one path, backing upward, and then down another path, the code simultaneously fans out down all paths. Each visit to child directories blocks a parent task until all child tasks return a result. Consider what the number of blocked parent tasks means to the TPL when it must schedule hundreds of tasks to run on a much smaller pool of threads. How does the TPL decide what to run first? The TPL is not aware of the underlying nature of the directory tree.

This is where the task creation "hints" come into play. The following code snippet shows some of the TaskCreationOptions (hints) available to a developer.

```
public enum TaskCreationOptions
{
None = 0,
PreferFairness = 1,
LongRunning = 2,
AttachedToParent = 4,
}
```

TaskCreationOptions provide execution guidelines to the TPL. Being guidelines, the options are not guaranteed. Rather, options should be considered TPL suggestions. Other TPL execution semantics may override the options. You learn more about why the TPL may want to override the guidelines later in this chapter.

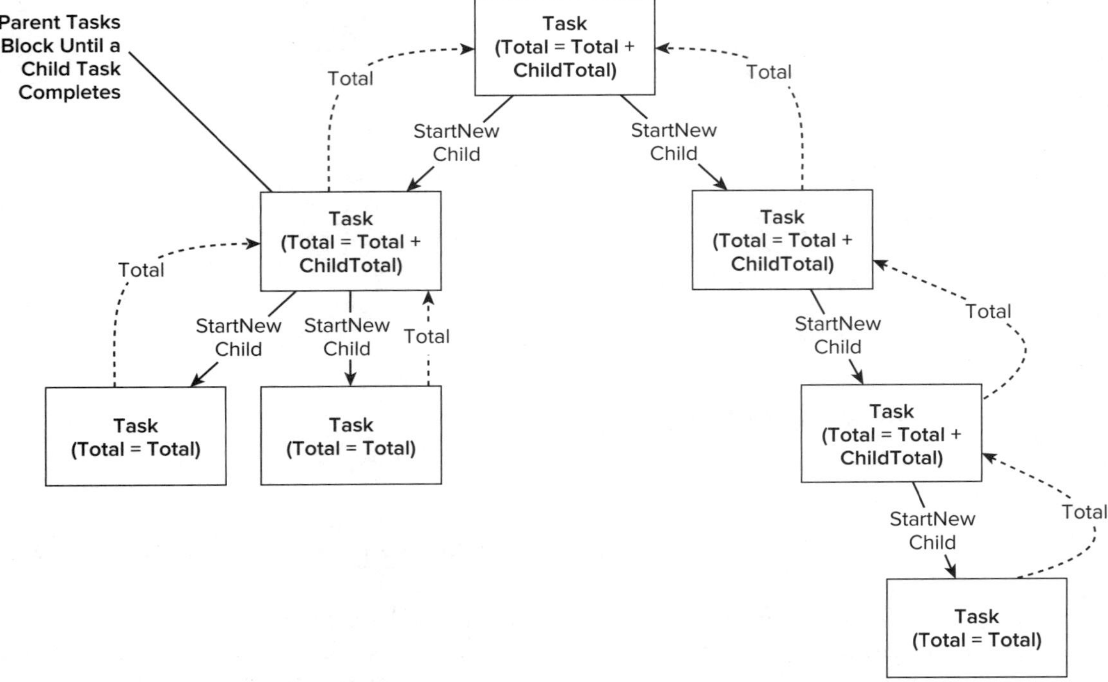

FIGURE 11-3: Running TPLParent sample

In the sample, `AttachedToParent` suggests to the TPL that the result of the parent task is based on the result of the created task. Creating the linkage means that the TPL could execute a child task on the same thread as the parent task.

So, for example, child tasks and the child tasks of a child task may all execute on the same thread. Because the solution may create hundreds of tasks, running a child on the same thread eliminates the need to occupy multiple blocking threads all waiting on their child tasks to complete. The TPL documentation refers to this behavior as *inlining* a task.

As stated earlier, a parent task blocks until its children complete. In the sample, `childTasks` stores the children. `WaitAll` does just what its name would have you believe. It blocks on the `WaitAll` call until all of the tasks complete. After all tasks in the `childTasks` variable each execute the function that returns the total number of bytes occupied by files with the `.docx` extension, the value can be retrieved from the `Result` property.

The root parent task is created with the `LongRunning TaskCreationOption`. This hint indicates to the TPL that this task may need its own thread. Because values are totaled at each child, the total of the root's children is the total for all subdirectories. When children of the parent root complete, execution is complete.

UNDERSTANDING TPL-STYLE EXCEPTION HANDLING

Although it's important to specify a task relationship for performance reasons, there are other reasons beyond performance that specifying a parent-child relationship can help — in particular, exception handling.

Understanding AggregateException

Parallel programming exception handling addresses unique challenges. Unlike a serially executing application where only one method may be executing at a time, a parallel application may have hundreds of simultaneously executing methods. That means that a parallel application could simultaneously generate hundreds of exceptions.

`AggregateException` is the TPL's answer to packaging all those exceptions. Some TPL methods act like collection points for `Try`/`Catch` blocks. For example, The `Wait` methods utilized earlier exhibit exception-collecting behavior.

Now take a quick look at `AggregateException`. Following are some methods of `AggregateException` class:

```
public class AggregateException : Exception
{
        public AggregateException(string message);
        public AggregateException(string message,
            params Exception[]innerExceptions);
        public AggregateException Flatten();
        public void Handle(Func<Exception, bool> predicate);
}
```

Like all exceptions, `AggregateException` inherits from the base `Exception` class. Also, `AggregateException` may include `InnerExceptions` and, therefore, stacks of exceptions. The `Flatten` and `Handle` methods are what sets `AggregateExceptions` apart. `Flatten` recurses through the `InnerExceptions`, finding all the other `AggregateExceptions`, and builds a new `AggregateException` composed of just the non-`AggregateExceptions`. `Handle` invokes the `Func<Exception, bool>` passed to it on each of the `Exceptions` contained in the class.

Like any exception, unhandled TPL exceptions can crash an application. The TPL imposes some lighter restrictions on how it interprets an unhandled exception.

TPL documentation uses the term *observed exception*. Observed exceptions are considered handled. When the `Exception` property of the task generating the exception is examined, the exception is considered "observed" and, therefore, handled. An exception is also considered "observed" when the `Handle` method on an `AggregateException` labels the exception as handled. (You learn more about this later in this chapter.)

Implementing Exception Handling

Following is some exception-handling code from the `TPLParentChild` sample:

```
private long RunVisit(Task<long> task, CancellationTokenSource cancelLocal)
{
    try
```

```
        {
            task.Start();

            this.ExecuteOnInput(cancelLocal);

            task.Wait();

            return task.Result;
        }
        catch (AggregateException agExp)
        {
            agExp.Flatten().Handle(this.HandleException);

            return 0;
        }
    }


    private bool HandleException(Exception ex)
    {
        if (ex is TaskCanceledException)
        { Console.WriteLine("Task was cancelled"); }
        else
        {
            Console.WriteLine("EXCEPTION: " + ex.Message);
        }

        return true;
    }
```

Code file [Ch11_Code_Samples.zip] available for download at Wrox.com

The TPL channels an executing task's exceptions back to a point in code by performing a `Wait` or `WaitAll` for a task or collection of tasks. `Task.WaitAny` does not exhibit the same behavior as `Wait` or `WaitAll`. Unlike `Wait` or `WaitAll`; `WaitAny` doesn't funnel exceptions to the `Catch` portion of the `Try/Catch` block. `Try/Catch` can be employed just like other .NET exception handling.

`Flatten` may at first seem odd. However, as alluded to earlier, specifying `TaskCreationOptions` `.AttachedToParent` tells the TPL that exceptions can be aggregated up to the parent task. Thinking about the directory `.docx` totaling sample, this means that `AggregateExceptions` with `InnerExceptions` of `AggregateExceptions` way down scores of layers deep could be created. Had the TPL aggregated each `AggregateException` into a new `AggregateException`, this would have meant building an `AggregateException`, whether it was important to examine the exception.

As seen in the previous example, `Handle` invokes a delegate on each `InnerException`. If the invoked delegate returns `true`, the exception is considered "observed" and, therefore, handled.

The TPL also includes a "last ditch" exception-handling event on the `TaskScheduler`. Any unobserved exception can generate a call to the event. The following code demonstrates how to hook this event:

```
TaskScheduler.UnobservedTaskException +=
    new EventHandler<UnobservedTaskExceptionEventArgs>
    (Program.UnobservedHandle);
```

Unobserved exceptions can crash an application. Although the TPL exception handling lowers the bar a bit, exceptions should still not be ignored.

UNDERSTANDING CANCELLATIONS

Stopping a parallel workload often means scores of tasks each in different stages of execution must somehow halt what is being done without destabilizing an application. Developers familiar with threads may notice the absence of an `Abort` equivalent on the `Task` class. Although the TPL can schedule a running task and decide whether it's safe to run a particular task before another task, the TPL is ignorant of the nature of the code it runs. Running code could entail modifying sensitive data structures, or even making physical changes to data on the hard drive.

Parallel programming requires some tools for making an "orderly exit," as well as some way to distinguish between a "local" exit (where, for example, a single task must be canceled) and a "global" exit (where the entire process is shutting down, and must "call-in" all running tasks).

Applying Cancellations — Basics

You can use the earlier `TPLParentChild` sample again to demonstrate a common way to do a cancellation. Here is the `TPLParentChild` sample code again:

```
public void Run()
{
    StartGettingInput();

    var totalBytes = Visit(_root,TaskCreationOptions.LongRunning);
        //Root is long running

    Console.WriteLine("Total bytes == " + totalBytes );
}

private long Visit(string subDir, TaskCreationOptions opts)
{
    CancellationTokenSource cancelLocal = new CancellationTokenSource();
    var cancelJoinedToken =
        CancellationTokenSource.CreateLinkedTokenSource
        (_cancelGlobal.Token, cancelLocal.Token).Token;

    var task = new Task<long> ( new Func<long> (() =>
        {

            long bytes = 0;
            long bytesChildren = 0;

            cancelJoinedToken.ThrowIfCancellationRequested();

            var dir = new DirectoryInfo(subDir);
            var children = dir.EnumerateDirectories().Select(info => {
                return info.FullName; });
            bytes = dir.EnumerateFiles("*." + _extension).Sum(f => {
```

```
                return f.Length; });
            List<Task<long>> childTasks = new List<Task<long>>();

            //Run children
            foreach (var directory in children)
            {
                var localDir = directory;

                var tNew = Task.Factory.StartNew<long>(obj =>
                {
                    return Visit(localDir,
                        TaskCreationOptions.AttachedToParent);

                    //
                }                                  , cancelJoinedToken,
                    TaskCreationOptions.AttachedToParent);
                childTasks.Add(tNew);
            }

            //Get the child results
            if (childTasks.Count > 0)
            {
                Task.WaitAll(childTasks.ToArray());

                //If you get a cancel or exception the line below is
                //never executed.
                    bytesChildren = childTasks.Sum(t =>
                        { return t.Result; });
            }
            else { bytesChildren = 0; }

            return bytes + bytesChildren;
        }
    )
    , cancelJoinedToken, opts);

    return this.RunVisit(task,cancelLocal);
}
```

<hr>

Code file [Ch11_Code_Samples.zip] available for download at Wrox.com

<hr>

Cancellations involve two classes: `CancellationTokenSource` and `CancellationToken`. Implementing a cancellation requires code that periodically checks the status on a `CancellationToken`.

Cancellations are handled through the exception infrastructure. Developers either throw an `OperationCancelledException`, or call the `ThrowIfCancellationRequested` method, which conditionally throws the `OperationCancelledException` when a cancellation is signaled. Calling `Cancel` on the `CancellationTokenSource` changes the `CancellationToken` status to canceled.

Like any other exception, a `TaskCancelException` bubbles up through an application until it is handled. Applications must catch a `TaskCancelException` to acknowledge the cancellation. Tasks have a canceled state if they are created with a `CancellationToken` parameter. When a cancellation is signaled, tasks associated with a canceled `CancellationToken` changes state to canceled. Task cancellation state can also be explicitly set using another class called `TaskCompletionSource`.

If the same behavior is executed for "local" as well as a "global" cancellation, tokens can be joined so only a single token can be monitored, or a single `CancellationTokenSource` can be invoked. The earlier sample demonstrated this behavior. A static function called `CreateLinkedTokenSource` on the `CancellationTokenSource` class accepts multiple `Tokens` and links the `Tokens` to a `CancellationTokenSource` class.

Various task-creation and `Wait` methods accept a `CancellationToken`. Following are some examples:

```
public Task(Action action, CancellationToken cancellationToken);

public Task ContinueWith(Action<Task> continuationAction, CancellationToken
    cancellationToken);

public bool Wait(int millisecondsTimeout, CancellationToken cancellationToken);

public static void WaitAll(Task[] tasks, CancellationToken cancellationToken);

public static int WaitAny(Task[] tasks, CancellationToken cancellationToken);
```

Exercise care when including a `CancellationToken` parameter, especially for the `Wait` methods. For example, the `WaitAll` call from the `ParentChild` sample earlier in the chapter could have just as easily included a `CancellationToken` parameter, rather than checking for a `CancellationToken` before executing. Here is the code again:

```
var task = new Task<long> ( new Func<long> (() =>
    {

        long bytes = 0;
        long bytesChildren = 0;

        cancelJoinedToken.ThrowIfCancellationRequested();

        var dir = new DirectoryInfo(subDir);
        var children = dir.EnumerateDirectories().Select(info => {
            return info.FullName; });
        bytes = dir.EnumerateFiles("*." + _extension).Sum(f => {
            return f.Length; });
        List<Task<long>> childTasks = new List<Task<long>>();

        //Run children
        foreach (var directory in children)
        {
            var localDir = directory;

            var tNew = Task.Factory.StartNew<long>(obj =>
            {
                return Visit(localDir,
                    TaskCreationOptions.AttachedToParent);
            }
            , cancelJoinedToken,
```

```
                TaskCreationOptions.AttachedToParent);
            childTasks.Add(tNew);
        }

        //Get the child results
        if (childTasks.Count > 0)
        {
            Task.WaitAll(childTasks.ToArray());

            //If you get a cancel or exception the line below is
            //never executed.
            bytesChildren = childTasks.Sum(t =>
                { return t.Result; });
        }
        else { bytesChildren = 0; }

        return bytes + bytesChildren;
    }
)
, cancelJoinedToken, opts);
```

Code file [Ch11_Code_Samples.zip] available for download at Wrox.com

Implementing `WaitAll` this way could have nullified the effect of the `AttachedToParent` `TaskCreationOption`, and negatively impacted performance. Monitoring creates overhead and can change the TPL's behavior. Passing the `CancellationToken` to a method instructs the TPL to monitor the cancellation. The TPL would have had to monitor the `CancellationToken` and, therefore, may not have opted to run the child task within the thread of the parent task.

As stated earlier, the TPL doesn't like to abort a thread. To monitor a cancellation on `WaitAll`, the TPL must periodically check for cancellation. Inlining attaches an additional task to the end of the completed parent task. On a solution like `TPLParentChild`, there may be hundreds of tasks. So, when doing something such as monitoring a cancellation, often it can favor approaches that minimize the long-running tasks and opt for standard task scheduling so that the TPL can monitor between executing tasks.

Applying Cancellations — Register Action, Interlocked

Cancellations can be configured to run code. A delegate, lambda, `Action`, or method can be registered to execute when a cancellation is activated. Following is code demonstrating the `Register` method:

```
int getInput = 0;

_collector.Cancellation.Register(() =>
    {
        Interlocked.Increment(ref getInput);
    }
);
```

Code file [Ch11_Code_Samples.zip] available for download at Wrox.com

Developers can call `Register` on the same token multiple times, thus registering multiple `Action`s. The registered `Action` is executed synchronously, so the recommendation is that a developer do something fast and simple, as shown in the previous example. `Register` is helpful when, for example, a developer wants to hide the `CancellationToken` from another part of the application. Instead of supplying a place to receive a `CancellationToken`, only the `Action` is required.

Other parts of the application modify the `getInput` variable. For example, in the sample code, user input-handling code may also transition the variable. Notice how the sample utilizes the `Interlocked` class rather than locking the variable, or declaring a volatile variable.

`Interlocked` is a more performant alternative to a lock, and a safer alternative to using a volatile variable. Like a lock, the `Interlocked` class ensures that only one thread modifies the value, only `Interlocked` is more efficient than a full lock. Unlike a volatile variable, `Interlocked` performs the read, change, and write-back all in one step. Although the previous example uses a primitive (`int`), `Interlocked` includes methods to handle reference types.

Following are some of the methods for the `Interlocked` class:

```
public static class Interlocked
{
    public static int Add(ref int location1, int value);
    public static long Add(ref long location1, long value);
    public static double CompareExchange(ref double location1,
        double value, double comparand);
    public static float CompareExchange(ref float location1, float value,
        float comparand);
    public static int CompareExchange(ref int location1, int value,
        int comparand);
    public static IntPtr CompareExchange(ref IntPtr location1,
        IntPtr value, IntPtr comparand);
    public static long CompareExchange(ref long location1, long value,
        long comparand);
    public static object CompareExchange(ref object location1,
        object value, object comparand);
    public static T CompareExchange<T>(ref T location1, T value,
        T comparand) where T : class;
    public static int Decrement(ref int location);
    public static long Decrement(ref long location);
    public static double Exchange(ref double location1, double value);
    public static float Exchange(ref float location1, float value);
    public static int Exchange(ref int location1, int value);
    public static IntPtr Exchange(ref IntPtr location1, IntPtr value);
    public static long Exchange(ref long location1, long value);
    public static object Exchange(ref object location1, object value);
    public static T Exchange<T>(ref T location1, T value) where T : class;
    public static int Increment(ref int location);
    public static long Increment(ref long location);
    public static long Read(ref long location);
}
```

Internally, assigning a variable is a two-step (or more) process. First, there is a read and then an assignment. A thread could be preempted just after the read but before the write. When the methods just described are invoked, the operation is treated atomically. So, the read-and-write operations are never separated.

USING CONCURRENT COLLECTIONS — CONCURRENTQUEUE

Concurrency often involves shared memory. Tasks may need to share read-and-write access to a collection. Because threads may run concurrently, locking the object in memory before writing was always the only way to ensure only one thread was writing at a time. Locking creates contention, and contention can slow performance.

Although achieving this through locking has always been possible in the .NET Framework, the TPL includes optimized collections for parallel operations. ConcurrentQueue is one of a handful of concurrent collections found in the System.Collections.Concurrent namespace. Following is the ConcurrentQueue class:

```
public class ConcurrentQueue<T> : IProducerConsumerCollection<T>,
    IEnumerable<T>, ICollection, IEnumerable
{
    public ConcurrentQueue();
    public ConcurrentQueue(IEnumerable<T> collection);
    public int Count { get; }
    public bool IsEmpty { get; }
    public void CopyTo(T[] array, int index);
    public void Enqueue(T item);
    public IEnumerator<T> GetEnumerator();
    public T[] ToArray();
    public bool TryDequeue(out T result);
    public bool TryPeek(out T result);
}
```

As would be expected, ConcurrentQueue includes all the usual queuing operations such as Peek, Enqueue, and Dequeue. The following code demonstrates using ConcurrentQueue to queue a keystroke so that the TPLParentChild sample can run a cancellation through user input:

```
private ConcurrentQueue<ConsoleKey> _cancelAllCommand = new
    ConcurrentQueue<ConsoleKey>();
private ConcurrentQueue<ConsoleKey> _cancelLocalCommand = new
    ConcurrentQueue<ConsoleKey>();

private void StartGettingInput()
{
    var task = new Task(() =>
    {
        var getInput = true;

        while (getInput)
        {
            var key = Console.ReadKey().Key;//Block here until a key is
                entered

            switch (key)
            {
                case ConsoleKey.C:
                    _cancelAllCommand.Enqueue(key);
                    break;
                case ConsoleKey.K:
                    _cancelLocalCommand.Enqueue(key);
```

```
                    break;
                case ConsoleKey.Enter:
                    getInput = false;
                    break;
            }
        }
    }
    , TaskCreationOptions.LongRunning);

    task.Start();
}
```


Part of the `RunVisit` method demonstrated earlier in this chapter scans the cancellation queues for input, and executes either a global or local cancellation, depending on the input key. Following is the code again:

```
private long RunVisit(Task<long> task, CancellationTokenSource cancelLocal)
{
    try
    {
        task.Start();

        this.ExecuteOnInput(cancelLocal);

        task.Wait();

        return task.Result;
    }
    catch (AggregateException agExp)
    {
        agExp.Flatten().Handle(this.HandleException);

        return 0;
    }
}

private void ExecuteOnInput(CancellationTokenSource cancelLocal)
{
    ConsoleKey key = default(ConsoleKey);

    if (_cancelAllCommand.TryDequeue(out key))
    {
        _cancelGlobal.Cancel();
    }

    if (_cancelLocalCommand.TryDequeue(out key))
    {
        cancelLocal.Cancel();
    }
}
```

Like many of the `Concurrent` collections, `ConcurrentQueue` implements the `IProducerConsumer Collection` interface. This becomes more important later in this chapter. The `IProducer ConsumerCollection` interface is implemented explicitly, so it does not appear in IntelliSense. The method is visible only when accessing the class through an `Interface` variable, as shown in the following example:

```
IProducerConsumerCollection<int> prod = new ConcurrentQueue<int>();
int val = -1;

prod.TryAdd(5);

prod.TryTake(out val);

Console.WriteLine("Here was the added value " + val.ToString());
```

Code file [Ch11_Code_Samples.zip] available for download at Wrox.com

UNDERSTANDING CONTINUATIONS

Making a task's execution contingent on the success or failure of another task is accomplished using a *continuation*. A continuation works a lot like an event callback or delegate. A continuation can be any type of code that is compatible with a task. Examples are `Action`, lambda expression, `Func<T>`, and so on.

When the TPL executes a continuation, it creates and schedules another task, or it runs the continuation `Action` within the thread of the completed task. The task on which continuation is contingent is often referred to as the continuation's *antecedent*.

Following are examples of continuations:

```
//Single Continuation
var actToRun = new Action<Task<string>>(antecedent =>
    {
        Console.WriteLine("Task result was " + antecedent.Result);
    }
);

var taskWithContinue = new Task<string>(() =>
    {
        return "yes it ran";
    }
);

taskWithContinue.ContinueWith(actToRun);
taskWithContinue.Start();
taskWithContinue.Wait();


//Multiple antecedents
var list = new List<Task<string>>();

list.Add(Task.Factory.StartNew<string>(() =>
```

```
    {
        Console.WriteLine("Run 1");
        return "task 1 ran"; }
    )
);

list.Add(Task.Factory.StartNew<string>(() =>
    {
        Console.WriteLine("Run 2");
        return "task 2 ran"; }
    )
);

list.Add(Task.Factory.StartNew<string>(() =>
    {
        Console.WriteLine("Run 3");
        return "task 3 ran";
    }
    )
);

var actAfterAll = new Action<Task<string>[]>(tasks =>
    {
        Console.WriteLine("Running AfterAll Continuation...");
        foreach(var t in tasks)
        {Console.WriteLine(t.Result); }
    }
);


        Task.Factory.ContinueWhenAll(list.ToArray(), actAfterAll);
```


As demonstrated in these samples, a continuation can be joined to a task or the default `TaskScheduler`. Continuations can execute contingent on the completion, success, or failure of a task, or the completion of an array of tasks. Often, a continuation needs to examine the `Result` of the antecedent. So, a continuation must be configured to accept the antecedent task. Multiple `ContinueWith` invocations can register a continuation `Action` for each invocation. The following sample code demonstrates this:

```
var task = new TaskCompletionSource<string>(new
    List<Action<Task<string>>>());
var acts = new Action<Task<string>>[3]
{
t =>
{
    Thread.Sleep(2000);
    Console.WriteLine("0 ran..." + t.Result + " " +
        Thread.CurrentThread.ManagedThreadId.ToString());
}
, t =>
{
    Thread.Sleep(2000);
```

```
        Console.WriteLine("1 ran..." + t.Result + " " +
            Thread.CurrentThread.ManagedThreadId.ToString());
    }
    , t =>
    {
        Thread.Sleep(2000);
        Console.WriteLine("2 ran..." + t.Result + " " +
            Thread.CurrentThread.ManagedThreadId.ToString());
    }

    };//end of array

    //Starts separate Task for each
    task.Task.ContinueWith(acts[0]);
    task.Task.ContinueWith(acts[1]);
    task.Task.ContinueWith(acts[2]);

    task.SetResult("Task result here");
```

Code file [Ch11_Code_Samples.zip] available for download at Wrox.com

Like a task, a continuation has `TaskContinuationOptions` such as `LongRunning`, `AttachedToParent`, and `PreferFairness`. Continuations also work with `CancellationTokens`. For example, continuations that have not fired, but are configured with a `CancellationToken` that has been signaled, can move to the canceled state.

Continuations can fulfill multiple execution requirements. For example, a continuation can be configured to handle only exceptions. Continuations can be arranged into a dependency graph so that downstream `Actions` won't start until one or more upstream antecedents have completed.

TaskCompletionSource

Earlier in this chapter, you learned that a running task must execute on a thread somewhere within the TPL. That means that running a task not only occupies a thread for the duration of the task, but it also takes time to queue and schedule. Situations arise when a developer may want to, for example, activate a continuation without incurring the overhead to execute a task.

The following code demonstrates such a situation. In the code, a timer performs a delayed task execution.

```
var timerTime = new TimeSpan(0, 0, 5);
TaskCompletionSource<DateTime> comp = null;
Timer timer = null;

comp = new TaskCompletionSource<DateTime>();

timer = new System.Threading.Timer(obj =>
{
    comp.SetResult(DateTime.Now);
    timer.Dispose();
}
```

```
, null, timerTime, TimeSpan.FromMilliseconds(Timeout.Infinite));

comp.Task.Wait();
```

Code file [Ch11_Code_Samples.zip] available for download at Wrox.com

`System.Threading.Timer` handles the execution. So, a blocked or running task would be redundant and would be wasting a thread. According to the .NET documentation, `Dispose` must be run when the timer is no longer needed. `TaskCompletionSource` has a `Task` property. The code executes a `Wait` on the `Task` property. `TaskCompletionSource` could have been a useful place to hang a continuation without scheduling a task and tying up a blocking thread that is waiting for a timer to fire.

The example called the `SetResult` method, but there are other methods for changing to a canceled or exception state. Like a `Task` class, the `TaskCompletionSource` constructor also supports `TaskCreationOptions` and a `state` parameter that is demonstrated later in this chapter.

Implementing Continuations

The following sample code is part of another solution to the `.docx` totaling problem introduced at the beginning of this chapter. Instead of relying on the parent-child `AttachToParent` options in the TPL, the code explicitly defines the parent-child relationship using continuations.

```
private class TaskVisitorFactory : ITaskVisitorFactory
{
    private CancellationToken _cancelGlobal;
    private IProcessorResults _results = null;

    public TaskVisitorFactory(CancellationToken cancelGlobal,
        IProcessorResults results)
    {
        _cancelGlobal = cancelGlobal;
        _results = results;
    }

    public void Create(TaskCompletionSource<string> allChildCompletion,
        string directoryPath, IEnumerable<string> children, string
        extension)
    {
        List<Task> tasks = new List<Task>();

        if (!(_cancelGlobal.IsCancellationRequested))
        {
            foreach (var child in children)
            {
                var curChild = child;
                var visitor = new DirectoryVisitor(_results, this,
                    curChild, extension);
                var task = new Task(visitor.Visit, _cancelGlobal);

                //Handle cancellation at the individual task level
                //Continue when all have been cancelled; some may
```

```
            //have run;
            //this allows everything to happen in natural flow
            task.ContinueWith(tCont => { visitor.CancelVisit(); }
                , TaskContinuationOptions.OnlyOnCanceled
                | TaskContinuationOptions.ExecuteSynchronously);

            //The task is completed when the Action completes
            //and all of its children signal complete
            tasks.Add(task); //Child
            tasks.Add(visitor.TaskVisitAllChildren); //Child's children

            task.Start();
        }
    }

    //When all the children and children's children complete signal
    //Parent children complete
    if (tasks.Count > 0)
    {
        Task.Factory.ContinueWhenAll(tasks.ToArray(), t =>
        {
            foreach (var cur in t)
            {
                if (cur.Exception != null)
                {
                    cur.Exception.Handle(e =>
                    {
                        Console.WriteLine("EXCEPTION Observed: " +
                            e.Message);
                        return true;
                    });
                }

            }

            allChildCompletion.SetResult(directoryPath);

        });
    }
    else
    { allChildCompletion.SetResult(directoryPath); }
    }
}
```

Code file [Ch11_Code_Samples.zip] available for download at Wrox.com

Figure 11-4 shows the assembled relationships.

You create multiple antecedent continuations on the `Task.Factory` property. Multiple task antecedents are handled by the `TaskFactory` class. `ContinueWhenAll` includes the immediate child tasks and the task associated with the child's children. A task's children's children are represented by a `TaskCompletionSource`. A parent task registers a continuation that waits for all tasks it has created, as well as the `TaskCompletionSource` contained in the created child task. Also demonstrated

is configuring a continuation to handle only exceptions via the `TaskContinuationOptions`
`.OnlyOnCancelled`. `TaskContinuationOptions` support combinations of `TaskContinueOptions`.
However, care should be taken to ensure mutually exclusive options are not selected.

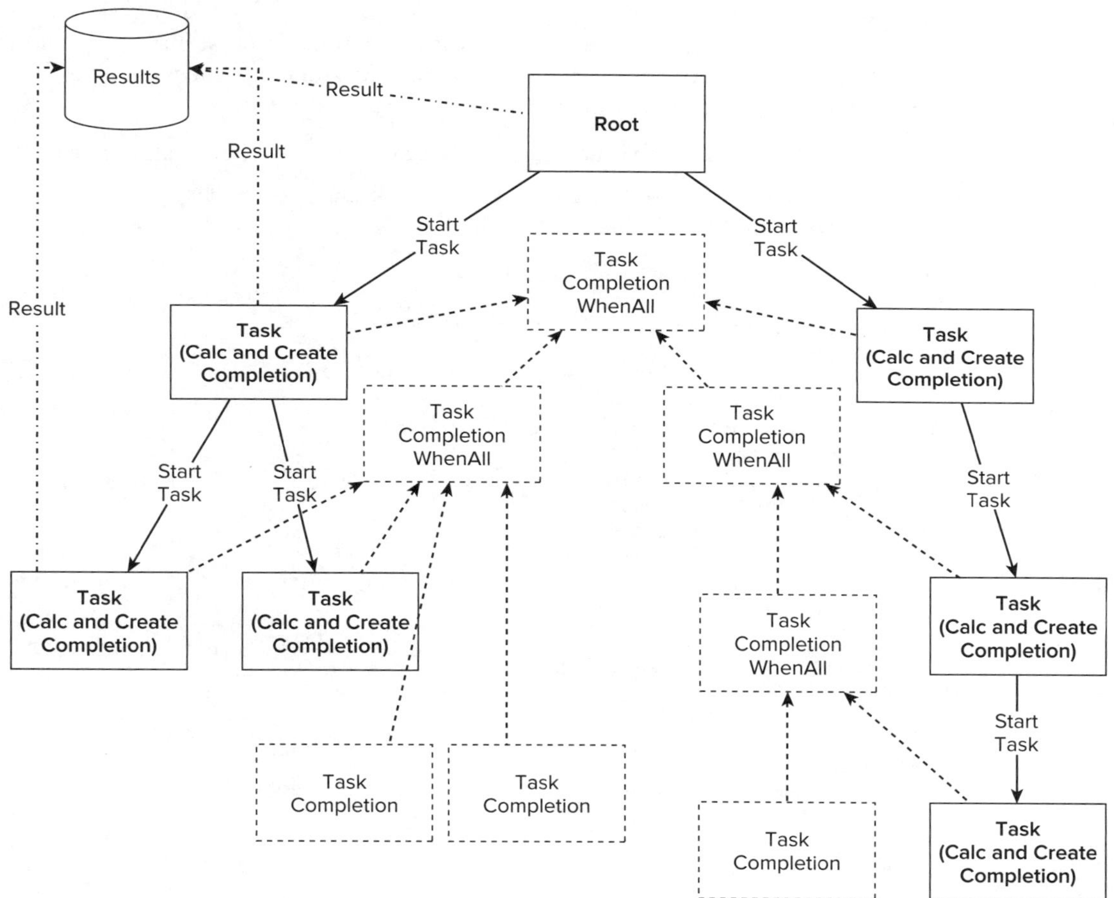

FIGURE 11-4: TPLContinuation sample layout

Although it is not as obvious, notice how this solution has a recursive feel to it. Just like the
`TPLParentChild` solution discussed earlier in the chapter, this solution takes a divide-and-conquer
approach. Each directory computation visit is allocated to a task. Marking completions is explicitly
dealt with by another class assembling the relationships with continuations.

The `TPLParentChild` and standard recursive examples earlier in the chapter implicitly relied on the
structure of the algorithm to mark completed directories. Essentially, the marking of completed and
visiting were coupled together.

Receiving a total from all children meant that the directory, its children, and children's children
were all processed. Completing the root directory meant the whole process was completed.

`TPLParentChild` was much simpler, but not as flexible. By coupling the computation to the completion, `TPLParentChild` could not, for example, fork off some additional calculations unrelated to the parent-child task relationship without making major changes to the algorithm.

Rather than allocating and running a blocking task (and thread), the child's children task is a `TaskCompletionSource`. Executing `ContinueWhenAll` runs a continuation that marks all children complete. The arrangement frees threads for doing directory visits and leaves the progress and ordering to relationships expressed in continuations.

Each task created in the previous code executes the following `DirectoryVisitor` class code:

Available for download on Wrox.com

```csharp
public Task<string> TaskVisitAllChildren { get { return
    _completionAllChildren.Task; } }

public void Visit()
{
    var comp = new ProgressMessage(_directoryPath);

    try
    {
        var dir = new DirectoryInfo(_directoryPath);
        long bytes = 0;
        IEnumerable<string> children =
            dir.EnumerateDirectories().Select(info =>
            { return info.FullName; });

        bytes = dir.EnumerateFiles("*." + _extension).Sum(f =>
            { return f.Length; });

        //Report results to Collector
        comp.SetMessagePayload(new DirectoryVisitComplete(bytes ));
        _results.PostResults(comp);

        //Spawn children
        _factory.Create(_completionAllChildren, _directoryPath,
            children, _extension);
    }
    catch (Exception ex)
    {
        comp.SetMessagePayload(new DirectoryVisitException(ex));
        _completionAllChildren.SetResult(_directoryPath); //No children
            to process
        _results.PostResults(comp);
    }
}
```

Code file [Ch11_Code_Samples.zip] available for download at Wrox.com

An exception is generated if a developer attempts to change a `TaskCompletionSource` status. Utilizing the `Try` methods is a safe way to change status if multiple places could also change status. In the example, a status change could be attempted in the `ContinueWhenAll` and in the task. Totaling is sent to a separate process that collects and summarizes the results. This process is examined later in this chapter.

AsyncState

As stated earlier in this chapter, tasks implement `IAsyncResult`. One of the `IAsyncResult` implementation requirements is `AsyncState`. Tasks participating in the asynchronous calls make use of this property. But for other tasks, the property is typically `null`. Though using `AsyncState` with other tasks is not required, its existence means a developer could attach other pieces of information to a task, and indirectly to a `TaskCompletionSource`. `AsyncState` would appear to be an empty piece of class real estate.

This section demonstrates how the property can be leveraged but focuses on what can be done, rather than what is recommended practice.

Extension functions enable a developer to add methods without creating subclasses or interfaces. They're ideal for tapping what was attached to `AsyncState`. The following example code demonstrates how classes can be attached to `AsyncState`, and how a couple of extension functions leverage `AsyncState`:

```csharp
static void RunAsyncState()
{
    var action = new Action(() =>
        {
            Console.WriteLine("Running the Async Action");
            Thread.Sleep(2000);
        }
    );

    var objs = new Tuple<string, Action>("I'm Tom", action);

    var comp = new TaskCompletionSource<object>(objs);

    comp.Task.ContinueWith(t => { Console.WriteLine("Continuation
        ran.."); });

    Console.WriteLine("Starting Async Action..");
    comp.GetAttachedAction()();

    Console.WriteLine("Do something else here...");
    Thread.Sleep(500);

    Console.WriteLine("Completed Async Action.. its message was " +
        comp.GetAttachedMessage());

    //Activate the continuation
    comp.SetResult(null);

}


static class TPLExts
{
    public static Action GetAttachedAction<T>(this TaskCompletionSource<T>
        taskComp)
    {
        return ((Tuple<string, Action>)taskComp.Task.AsyncState).Item2;
```

```
        }

        public static string GetAttachedMessage<T>(this TaskCompletionSource<T>
            taskComp)
        {
            return ((Tuple<string, Action>)taskComp.Task.AsyncState).Item1;
        }

    }
```

Code file [Ch11_Code_Samples.zip] available for download at Wrox.com

The attached tuple is composed of a string and an `Action`. Extension functions (`GetAttachedAction`, `GetAttachedMessage`) are implemented on the `TaskCompletionSource`. You learned about the significance of `TaskCompletionSource` earlier in this chapter.

In the example, the associated `Action` is stored in the `AsyncState`, and task status is manually set after some additional work following the `Action` invocation. This arrangement would be useful in situations in which a task is needed for a continuation (as in the example), but scheduling a task would not be desirable.

The string value is used to identify the task or `TaskCompletionSource`. The string could have been printed in a `Trace` statement or viewed in the Debugger. An application may have hundreds of running tasks. The string value may be useful for distinguishing tasks.

USING THE BLOCKINGCOLLECTION CLASS

Asynchronous messaging and isolation are ways to avoid shared state and to decouple parallel operations. Instead of modifying a common place in memory and invoking methods on each other, parallel operations pass copies of data. Concurrent operations may also operate at different speeds. Queuing messages is a common way to throttle processing disparities.

Figure 11-5 shows a typical internal asynchronous messaging solution with a queue.

An *actor/agent* is often used to characterize a parallel programming solution centered on messaging. A *producer/consumer* and *pipelining* both involve portions of a process that emit data and a portion that manipulates what is emitted. In each of the patterns, the solution involves two or more components coordinating their activities by exchanging data. If the data exchange is not efficiently done, it can become a bottleneck in a developer's code.

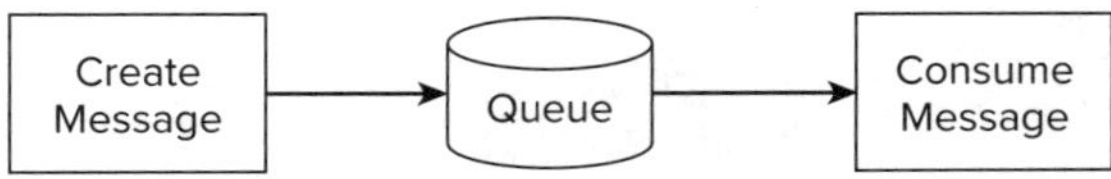

FIGURE 11-5: Asynchronous messaging

Writing and removing both modify the underlying data structure and require some means (such as a lock) to share access. Some code segments may take longer to process than other parts. Queuing helps, but some way to pause the producer, or allow the consumer to do something else while waiting for data, is essential to building flexible, efficient algorithms.

A `BlockingCollection` class has been built for handling all these scenarios.

The following code shows how to use a `BlockingCollection` class:

```csharp
var blockingCollection = new BlockingCollection<string>();
    //ConcurrentQueue is default

Task.Factory.StartNew(() =>
    {
        for (int n = 0; n < 10; ++n)
        {
            blockingCollection.Add(n.ToString());
            Console.WriteLine("Just added " + n.ToString());

            Console.WriteLine("Added " + n.ToString());
        }

        blockingCollection.CompleteAdding();
    }
);

Task.Factory.StartNew(() =>
    {
        foreach (var val in
            blockingCollection.GetConsumingEnumerable())
        {
            Console.WriteLine("Removed " + val);
            Thread.Sleep(1000);
        }

        Console.WriteLine("Done, CompleteAdding has been called.");
    }
);
```

Code file [Ch11_Code_Samples.zip] available for download at Wrox.com

`BlockingCollection` supports and offers a variety of ways to consume and add data. `GetConsumingEnumerable` is recommended over regular `foreach` iterations. As the method name implies, each iteration removes an item from the collection. `TryTake` enables optional timeouts if data is not present in a `TimeSpan`. `Take` blocks until data is present. However, `Take` can generate an exception when attempting a remove after the `CompleteAdding` has been called.

The following code snippet shows some other ways to access the `BlockingCollection`:

```csharp
var blockingCollection = new BlockingCollection<string>(5);
    //Capacity throttles process

Task.Factory.StartNew(() =>
    {
        for (int n = 0; n < 10; ++n)
        {
            while (!blockingCollection.TryAdd(n.ToString(), 300))
                { Console.WriteLine("Just did try add and failed " +
                    n.ToString()); }
            Console.WriteLine("Added " + n.ToString());
```

```
            }

            blockingCollection.CompleteAdding();
        }
    );

    Task.Factory.StartNew(() =>
        {
            var val = "";
            while (blockingCollection.TryTake(out val))
            {
                Console.WriteLine("Removed " + val);
                Thread.Sleep(1000);
            }


            Console.WriteLine("Done, CompleteAdding has been called.");
        }
    );
```

Code file [Ch11_Code_Samples.zip] available for download at Wrox.com

Adding a bounded capacity blocks the producing process and allows the consuming process to catch up. The preceding code is bound to five messages. A slight processing delay was added to the consuming side. Notice how the producer cannot proceed until space is made in the `BlockingCollection`. In fact, `TryAdd` repeatedly attempts to add until it succeeds.

By default, internally, a `BlockingCollection` uses a `ConcurrentQueue`, but anything supporting the `IProducerConsumerCollection` interface is supported. Following is an example using the `ConcurrentStack`:

```
var blockingCollection = new BlockingCollection<string>
    (new ConcurrentStack<string>());
```

With the `ConcurrentStack`, ordering in the `BlockingCollection` becomes Last-In-First-Out (LIFO). `BlockingCollection` has been optimized for performance and, internally, utilizes lightweight locking mechanisms.

Working with a BlockingCollection

As stated earlier, `BlockingCollection` supports scenarios centered around messaging. Earlier demonstrations showed how to configure the `BlockingCollection`. This section demonstrates an implementation from the `TPLContinuation` sample.

As stated earlier, the concurrent collections underpinning `BlockingCollection` can gracefully handle the contention often involved when disparate threads are adding data. The `DirectoryVisitor` class posts messages to the `BlockingCollection`. A `ProgressMessageCollector` class gathers the results, as shown here:

```
private IProcessorResults _processor;

public void Process(Task rootCompletion)
```

```
{
    var tryTakeFailedCount = 0;

    var task = Task.Factory.StartNew(() =>
        {
            try
            {
                ProgressMessage result = null;
                bool gotOne = false;

                while (!(rootCompletion.IsCompleted))
                {
                    gotOne = _processor.TryTake(out result);

                    if (gotOne)
                    {
                        switch (result.GetProgressType())
                        {

...

                        }
                    }
                    else
                    { tryTakeFailedCount = tryTakeFailedCount + 1; }
                }
            }
            catch (Exception ex)
            { Console.WriteLine("EXCEPTION " + ex.Message +
                ex.StackTrace); }

        }, TaskCreationOptions.LongRunning);

    task.Wait();

    Console.WriteLine("Total bytes == " + _totalBytes.ToString() + "
        try take failed count " + tryTakeFailedCount.ToString() +
        " times");
}
```

Code file [Ch11_Code_Samples.zip] available for download at Wrox.com

The whole arrangement looks much like Figure 11-6.

`DirectoryVisitor` classes call `TryTake` with a timeout. While developing the solution, the 10-millisecond timeout seemed to result in the fewest expiration failures. Although there was no recommended time limit in the TPL documentation, one of the overloads was geared specifically to milliseconds. Overloads like this normally imply that the most common scenario can be something less than a 1-second value.

The `ProcessMessage` class is a receptacle, as shown here:

```
public sealed class ProgressMessage
{
    public string Identification { get; private set; }
```

```
public Type PayloadType { get; private set; }

private object _value = null;
public void SetMessagePayload(object value)
{
    _value = value;
    this.PayloadType = value.GetType();
}

public T GetPayload<T>() { return (T)_value; }

public ProgressMessage(string identification)
{
    this.Identification = identification;
}
}
```

Code file [Ch11_Code_Samples.zip] available for download at Wrox.com

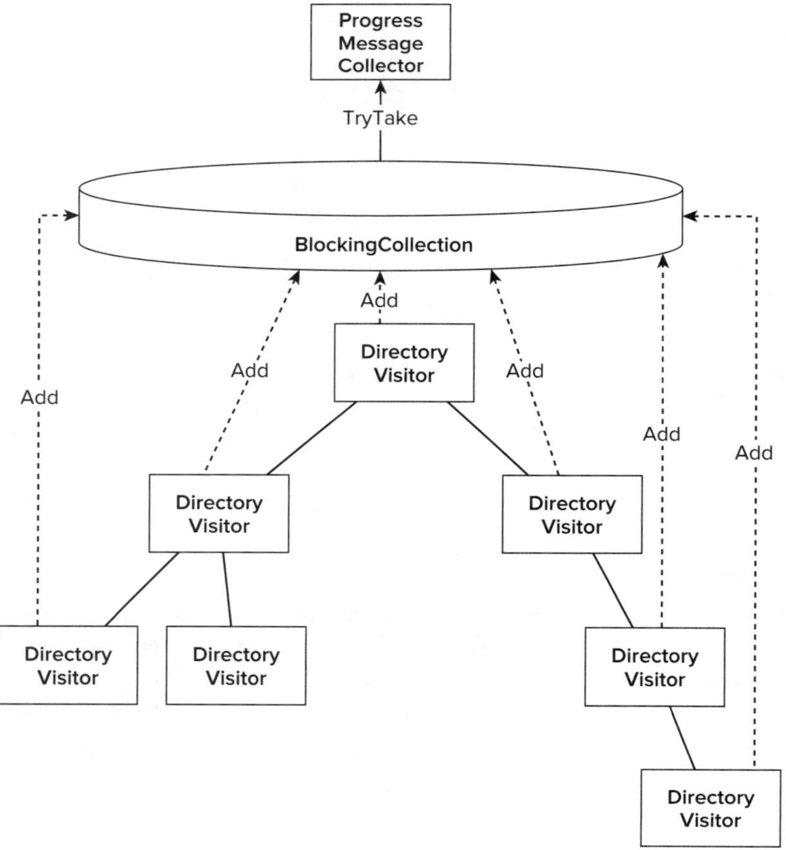

FIGURE 11-6: Visitor messaging

The message is a receptacle for a more specific payload. Separating the two parts allows for payload flexibility. Another portion gathering cancellation commands from user input also posts messages to the `BlockingCollection`.

`BlockingCollection` is hidden behind a class interface implementation, as shown here:

```
private class ProcessorResults : IProcessorResults
{
    private BlockingCollection<ProgressMessage> _resultsQueue =
        new BlockingCollection<ProgressMessage>(1024);

    public void PostResults(ProgressMessage result)
    {
        _resultsQueue.Add(result);
    }

    public bool TryTake(out ProgressMessage result)
    {
        return _resultsQueue.TryTake(out result, 10);
    }

}
```

Code file [Ch11_Code_Samples.zip] available for download at Wrox.com

Being a full-function data structure, it's often better to hide its usage behind a narrower set of options. Enabling full collection functionality means a developer could invoke methods that an architect never intended.

Understanding SpinWait.SpinUntil

`SpinWait` lives apart from the TPL in the `System.Threading` namespace. `SpinWait` is a code-blocking alternative to methods such as `Thread.Sleep` that skip its operating system timeslice, rather than telling the operating system to wake it up after a period of time. `SpinWait` has use across all TPL-based solutions. TPL solutions often need to block and check for some changing condition before proceeding. `SpinUntil` combines the blocking and checking in a single method. In addition, `SpinUntil` supports timeouts.

Following are some overloads of the `SpinUntil` method:

```
public static void SpinUntil(Func<bool> condition);
public static bool SpinUntil(Func<bool> condition, int millisecondsTimeout);
public static bool SpinUntil(Func<bool> condition, TimeSpan timeout);
```

Because this chapter's `SpinUntil` example utilizes the `BlockingCollection`, `SpinWait.SpinUntil` is introduced here. In the following `BlockingCollection` array extension function code example, `SpinUntil` blocks until data appears on any of the array's `BlockingCollections`:

```
static class TPLExts
{

    public static bool WaitForData<T>(this BlockingCollection<T>[]
        collections, int timeout)
```

```
    {
        var found = false;

        found = SpinWait.SpinUntil(() =>
            {
                return collections.Where(c =>
                    { return c.Count > 0; }
                ).Count() > 0;
            }
        ,timeout);

        return found;
    }


}
```


As stated earlier, `BlockingCollection` is built for performance, so this is efficient code. `SpinWait.SpinUntil` periodically calls the supplied function between yields. Applying `WaitForData` could work as shown in the following sample:

```
//Create an array of BlockingCollections
var collections = new BlockingCollection<string>[]
{new BlockingCollection<string>(),new BlockingCollection<string>()};

var found = false;
var indexWithData = 0;

found = collections.WaitForData(100);
Console.WriteLine("Was data found " + found.ToString());

collections[indexWithData].Add("Some data");

found = collections.WaitForData(100);
Console.WriteLine("Was data found " + found.ToString());

if (found)//Start Task to service the BlockingCollection
{
    Task.Factory.StartNew(() =>
        {
            Console.WriteLine("Service data " +
                collections[indexWithData].Take());
        }
    );
}
```


In the scenario envisioned in the previous code, a developer waits for data to appear before consuming it, delegating consumption to another task when one of the `BlockingCollections` contain data. `TryTake` removes data and, therefore, was not an acceptable solution.

Like `TryTake`, the `BlockingCollection.TakeFromAny` was also not an acceptable solution. Rather than creating multiple blocked tasks, each monitoring a single `BlockingCollection`, it was more efficient to create a single long-running task that monitors multiple `BlockingCollections`. In the example, the long-running task is the current thread. When data does appear, a task is created to service the `BlockingCollection`.

`SpinWait.SpinUntil` has a myriad of other uses. Many of the uses involve checking a property on a TPL class. The following list shows some other examples.

➤ Creating a continuation without creating a task (spinning and checking the `IsCompleted` property on an antecedent)

➤ Coupling waiting on a task with waiting on `BlockingCollection` data

➤ Waiting for a cancellation

SUMMARY

Learning the Task Parallel Library (TPL) starts with understanding a core set of classes. Most important of all the classes are tasks. Developers package code, configure, and submit tasks to the TPL. Tasks store the results of the executing code. Results can be some value, or even an exception.

When dealing with exceptions, the TPL utilizes the standard .NET exception handling. However, the nature of parallel tasks means that hundreds of tasks could generate hundreds of exceptions. An aptly named class called `AggregateException` simplifies the collection-and-handling process.

Aside from exceptions, tasks must deal with gracefully aborting what is being done. Cancellations provide mechanisms for stopping tasks. One of the TPL's greatest strengths is its capability to join completed or failed tasks to a new task. Joining a finished task to another task is called a *continuation*. Continuation composition is not restricted to a task, nor is it limited to just TPL-based parallel components.

The `TaskCompletionSource` can be helpful when working with asynchronous or other thread-based components of the .NET Framework. `TaskCompletionSource` enables a developer to control a task result. The TPL joins the old to the new in other ways.

Collections are everywhere in the .NET Framework. Collections present unique challenges when coupled with concurrency. The TPL includes concurrency-friendly collections. These underlying containers support another class called the `BlockingCollection`.

A `BlockingCollection` enables parallel components to share data using a messaging pattern often called actor/agent, producer/consumer, or pipelining. `BlockingCollections`, as well as all TPL classes, can benefit from some of the other new components in the .NET Framework — in particular, the `SpinWait` class.

ABOUT THE AUTHOR

Jeffrey Juday is a developer specializing in enterprise integration solutions utilizing SharePoint, WCF, WF, and SQL Server. He has been developing software with Microsoft tools for more than 15 years in a variety of industries, including military, manufacturing, financial services, management consulting, and computer security. Juday is a Microsoft MVP. When not writing or developing, he spends his time with his wife and daughter.

12

The WF Programming Language

by Vishwas Lele

Windows Workflow Foundation 4.0 (WF 4) is a programming language based on higher-level abstractions suitable for implementing business processes. Even though the WF 4 programs are likely to be authored using graphical tools (such as the Workflow Designer), developers must understand the fundamentals of the Extensible Application Markup Language (XAML) based declarative syntax to make the most of the features offered by WF 4.

This chapter starts with the notion of `Activity` as a basic construct of a WF 4 program. In this chapter, you learn about language fundamentals, including arguments and variables, scoping rules, expression support, and flow control constructs. In addition, you learn ways to extend the WF 4 framework by building domain-specific custom activities. Finally, this chapter examines hosting WF 4 programs in Windows AppFabric.

This chapter is designed for .NET developers who want to incorporate WF 4 into their solutions to ease the authoring of business processes. This chapter assumes that you have a good understanding of C# and .NET.

You can download all the code snippets illustrated in this chapter as part of the download package for this book located on this book's companion website (www.wrox.com).

GETTING STARTED

The key objective of any line-of-business (LOB) application is to implement the underlying business processes. As you can imagine, business processes come in all sizes and shapes. Interestingly, though, they exhibit two common traits:

➤ Business processes are *interactive*.

➤ Business processes are *long running*.

Given this commonality, it makes sense to provide a consistent framework to implement business processes. This is where Windows WF 4 comes in.

WF 4 is a part of the .NET Framework 4.0 designed to ease the implementation of business processes. It may be helpful to think of WF 4 as a language that raises the abstraction level for implementing interactive, long-running applications. Similar to a traditional software program assembled using language statements, WF 4 can be assembled using activities (units of work).

Consider a traditional execution environment where a program is executed. Again, the WF 4 runtime performs a similar role. The WF 4 runtime executes the workflow activities. In addition, it also provides a set of services, such as automatically loading and unloading long-running programs, persisting the state, and flow control.

Figure 12-1 shows a conceptual model of WF 4. WF 4 programs can be hosted with an operating system process. This includes hosting within a custom application process (referred to as *self-hosting*), or within a system-provided host such as Windows Process Activation Service (WAS). The runtime engine is responsible for executing a workflow program. WF 4 comes with a set of activities that is part of the base activity library. The most fundamental extensibility point of WF 4 is the capability to build custom activities.

In this chapter, the terms *WF 4 program* and *workflow* are used interchangeably. Both refer to a program composed of a set of activities.

Now start by writing a WF 4 program that is the same for all languages: print the words `hello, world`.

As mentioned, an activity is a building block for a WF 4 program. The WF 4 program, whatever its size, is a collection of activities. WF 4 programs are typically specified using the declarative XAML. Interestingly, the root element is also an activity. In other words, the WF 4 program is itself an activity.

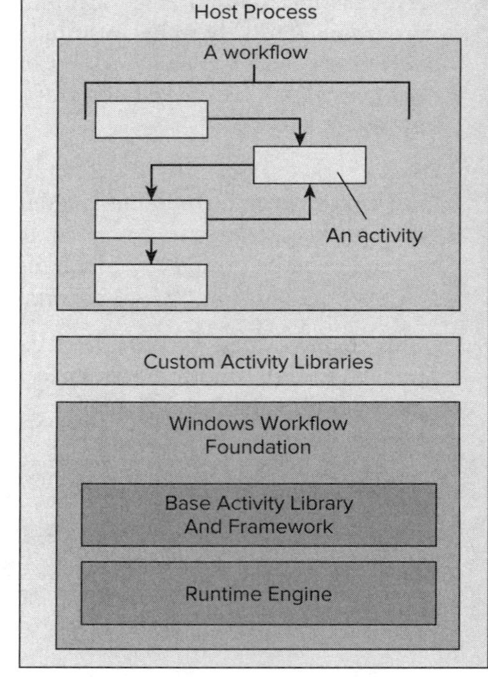

FIGURE 12-1: WF 4 conceptual model

In Listing 12-1, the parent activity is made up on a `Sequence` activity. A sequence activity, as the name suggests, is made up of a sequence of activities sequentially executed. In this example, the sequence activity consists of a single `WriteLine` activity responsible for writing the text `"hello, world"`.

LISTING 12-1: HelloWorld in WF 4

```
<Activity x:Class="ProgrammingWF4.HelloWorld"
    xmlns="http://schemas.microsoft.com/netfx/2009/xaml/activities"
    xmlns:x="http://schemas.microsoft.com/winfx/2006/xaml">
  <Sequence >
    <WriteLine Text="hello, world" />
  </Sequence>
</Activity>
```

Now that you have this WF 4 program ready, it is time to run it. Listing 12-2 shows a console program that runs the workflow.

LISTING 12-2: Running HelloWorld

```
static void Main(string[] args)
{
wf = new HelloWorld();
AutoResetEvent syncEvent = new AutoResetEvent(false);

WorkflowApplication wfApp = new WorkflowApplication(wf);

// Handle the desired lifecycle events.
wfApp.Completed = delegate(WorkflowApplicationCompletedEventArgs e)
{
    syncEvent.Set();
};

// Start the workflow.
wfApp.Run();

// Wait for Completed to arrive
syncEvent.WaitOne();


}
```

First, you create an instance of the `WorkflowApplication` class. This class acts as the host for a single WF 4 program instance. The constructor of `WorkflowApplication` class takes an instance of an activity as a parameter. As mentioned, the WF 4 program is also an activity. This enables you to pass an instance of the `HelloWorld` WF 4 program. After the `WorkflowApplication` instance has been created, you can simply run `HelloWorld` by calling the `Run` method.

You must wait for the workflow instance to complete before exiting the program. This is because the workflow instance is being run on a thread other than the main thread. So, even though the execution on the main thread is complete, the thread running the workflow may still be active.

You achieve this by subscribing to the workflow completion event. Within the workflow completion event handler, you set the event to a `Signaled` state, thus allowing the function `Main` to complete.

Relying on a host class (such as the `WorkflowApplication`) to run a workflow and to subscribe for completion events are patterns that are common across WF 4 programming. Later in this chapter, you learn about more advanced versions of the host class (such as `WorkflowServiceHost`) that support hosting of multiple WF 4 program instances.

WF 4 also supports a lightweight way to invoke workflow programs using the `WorkflowInvoker` class, as shown here:

```
wf = HelloWorldInCode();
WorkflowInvoker wi = new WorkflowInvoker(wf);
wi.Invoke();
```

Declarative Workflow Syntax

WF 4 offers a number of ways to author workflows. Workflows can be developed imperatively in code using a managed language such as C#. Workflows can also be written using declarative XAML. The program to print `"hello, world"` can be represented in code as shown here:

```
Activity wf = new Sequence
            {
                Activities =
                {
                    new WriteLine
                    {
                        Text = "hello, world"
                    }
                }
            };
```

However, the preferred authoring mode is the declarative mode. This is mainly because of the following:

➤ Declarative programs are easier to analyze and can be manually edited. Remember that the main reason for using WF 4 is to implement business processes. Authoring workflows in a declarative syntax makes it is easier for business analysts — the vast majority of them being nondevelopers — to follow the business logic.

➤ Declarative programs are easily transferable to different execution environments. For example, a XAML-based WF 4 program hosted within Windows AppFabric can be transferred to CRM 5.0 by a simple file copy operation.

➤ Because XAML is based on XML, you can represent the hierarchies in a human- and machine-readable way. For example, it is easy to represent a hierarchy of activities nested inside a parent activity.

➤ Declarative syntax makes it easier to author the workflow using a visual designer. Figure 12-2 shows the workflow designer view of the WF 4 program.

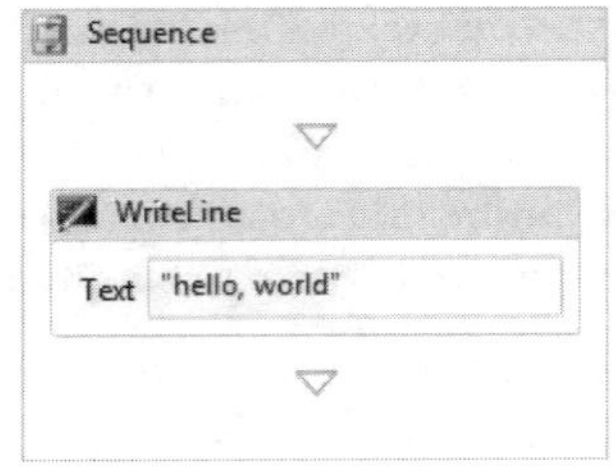

FIGURE 12-2: Workflow designer view of the example WF 4 program

Variables and Arguments

You can extend the example program to pass in parameters. For example, instead of hard-coding the text `"hello, world"` inside the `WriteLine` activity, you can pass a string as an argument. Listing 12-3 illustrates the use of parameters within a WF 4 program.

LISTING 12-3: Passing Arguments into HelloWorld

```
<Activity  x:Class="ProgrammingWF4.HelloWorld2"
           xmlns="http://schemas.microsoft.com/netfx/2009/xaml/activities"
           xmlns:x="http://schemas.microsoft.com/winfx/2006/xaml">
  <x:Members>
    <x:Property Name="argument1" Type="InArgument(x:String)" />
  </x:Members>
  <Sequence >
    <Sequence.Variables>
      <Variable x:TypeArguments="x:String" Name="var1" />
    </Sequence.Variables>
    <Assign >
      <Assign.To>
        <OutArgument x:TypeArguments="x:String">[var1]</OutArgument>
      </Assign.To>
      <Assign.Value>
        <InArgument x:TypeArguments="x:String">[argument1]</InArgument>
      </Assign.Value>
    </Assign>
    <WriteLine Text="[var1]" />
  </Sequence>
</Activity>
```

You declare an incoming argument called `argument1` of type `string`. Because this is an incoming argument, its value is set by the runtime before the activity is invoked. You have added a variable called `var1` under the `Sequence` activity. The scope of this variable is limited to the lifetime of the `Sequence` activity. So, when the `Sequence` activity completes its execution, `var1` cannot be accessed.

Next, you added an `Assign` activity that sets the value of `var1` based on the incoming argument. Finally, you have modified the `WriteLine` activity to print `var1`, instead of the hard-coded text. Notice that `var1` appears within square brackets. This represents an expression that must be evaluated. The result of the expression is stored in the `Text` property of the `WriteLine` activity.

Now that the WF 4 program includes the notion of an incoming argument, change the program that invokes it. Listing 12-4 shows how the parameters are passed in when a new instance of a WF 4 program is created.

LISTING 12-4: Passing Arguments into HelloWorld

```
Dictionary<string, object> arguments = new Dictionary<string, object>();
arguments.Add("argument1", "hello, world");
WorkflowApplication wfApp =
        new WorkflowApplication( new HelloWorld(),arguments);
```

Here you use an overloaded constructor of the `WorkflowApplication` that enables you to supply a WF 4 program instance and a dictionary of arguments.

Expressions

As mentioned, the square brackets represent an expression. By default, expressions can be literal values, or Visual Basic code that contains variables, arguments, constants, and so on, combined with operators to yield a value. Earlier, you saw an example of a literal value when you passed `"hello, world"` as the argument to the `WriteLine` activity.

The following code snippet shows two Visual Basic expressions. `[var1]` represents an expression in Visual Basic syntax that evaluates to the left side of the assignment expression. `[UCase(argument1)]` represents an expression in Visual Basic syntax that evaluates to the right side of the assignment expression.

```
<Assign >
    <Assign.To>
            <OutArgument x:TypeArguments="x:String">[var1]</OutArgument>
    </Assign.To>
    <Assign.Value>
            <InArgument
x:TypeArguments="x:String">[UCase(argument1)]</InArgument>
    </Assign.Value>
  </Assign>
```

Visual Basic expressions are compiled in-memory by the WF 4 runtime and included as part of the workflow logic. For the Visual Basic compiler to resolve the function `UCase`, you must import the appropriate assemblies, as shown here:

```
<Activity  x:Class="ProgrammingWF4.HelloWorld3"
    mva:VisualBasic.Settings="Assembly references
    and imported namespaces serialized as XML namespaces"
 xmlns="http://schemas.microsoft.com/netfx/2009/xaml/activities"
 xmlns:x="http://schemas.microsoft.com/winfx/2006/xaml"
 xmlns:mv="clr-namespace:Microsoft.VisualBasic;assembly=System"
 xmlns:mva="clr-amespace:Microsoft.VisualBasic.Activities;
    assembly=System.Activities">
```

Properties

You have now seen how to use parameters for passing values into an activity. Another way to achieve this is by setting any Common Language Runtime (CLR) properties exposed by an activity.

The limitation of this approach is that values passed into an activity are known at compile time. This also means that, for all instances of the WF 4 program, the property remains the same. This is different from the usage of arguments, where it is possible to pass a value at the time a WF 4 program is instantiated.

The following code snippet shows an example of a CLR property `MethodName` exposed by the `InvokeMethod` activity. The `MethodName` property is set to a method named `print` at compile time, and is the same for all instances of the WF 4 program.

```
<InvokeMethod DisplayName="Instance Method Call" MethodName="print">
  <InvokeMethod.TargetObject>
```

```
        <InArgument x:TypeArguments="msi:TestClass">[New
TestClass()]</InArgument>
      </InvokeMethod.TargetObject>
    </InvokeMethod>
```

This snippet also provides another example of a Visual Basic expression, as mentioned earlier. As the name suggests, the `InvokeMethod` activity can be used to call a public method of a specified object or type. In the previous example, Visual Basic expression `[New TestClass()]` instantiates the target object of type `TestClass`:

```
public class TestClass
  {
    public void Print ()
    {
        Console.WriteLine("hello, world");
    }
  }
```

The `InvokeMethod` activity then executes the method based on the value of the `MethodName` property.

"Dynamic" Properties

Properties and arguments enable data to be passed into a workflow. However, these values cannot be changed after the workflow execution starts.

To dynamically vary the passed-in data during the course of execution of the workflow, you can use the `ActivityFunc` activity. `ActivityFunc` is an activity that represents a callable method (delegate) that returns an argument. The delegate is defined by the workflow application, and passed into the workflow as a property. So, when the workflow references the property, the delegate gets invoked.

This pattern is illustrated in Listing 12-5.

LISTING 12-5: Dynamically Varying the Values Passed into a Workflow

```
<Activity>
<x:Members>
    <x:Property Name="Text" Type="ActivityFunc(x:String)" />
  </x:Members>
  <Sequence>
    <Sequence.Variables>
      <Variable x:TypeArguments="x:String" Name="PrintString" />
    </Sequence.Variables>
    <InvokeFunc x:TypeArguments="x:String" Result="[PrintString]">
      <PropertyReference x:TypeArguments="ActivityFunc(x:String)"
          PropertyName="Text" />
    </InvokeFunc>
    <WriteLine Text="[PrintString]" />
  </Sequence>
</Activity>
```

Here you declare a property called `Text` of an `ActionFunc` type. Notice the definition of the `Text` property. It is a type of a delegate that returns a string. Later, in the workflow definition, you invoke `ActionFunc` using the `InvokeFunc` activity. The `Result` is set to a workflow variable called `PrintString`. The last step of the workflow is to print the `PrintString` variable using the `WriteLine` activity.

Now that you have seen the workflow code, here is the code to invoke the workflow. You create the activity as part of the property initialization, and set the `Text` property to an instance of `ActivityFunc`.

```
Activity wf = new HelloWorld5
{
    Text = new ActivityFunc<string>
    {
        Handler = new TextGenerator
        {

        }
    }
};

WorkflowApplication wfApp = new WorkflowApplication(wf);
```

CONTROLLING THE FLOW OF EXECUTION

In the earlier sections, you saw how variables and properties can be defined within a WF 4 program. You also learned about the `Assign` activity that enabled you to define expressions, as well as set variables and properties.

Now look at activities that you can use to control the flow of execution of a WF 4 program. WF 4 supports two styles of flow control — *procedural styles* and *flowchart styles*. Now review each workflow style.

Procedural Style

The procedural style offers constructs similar to the ones offered by other procedural languages, such as the `while`, `if else`, and `switch`. Listing 12-6 shows an example of a procedural workflow.

LISTING 12-6: Procedural Style Constructs

```
<Activity>
  <x:Members>
    <x:Property Name="argument1" Type="InArgument(s:String[])" />
  </x:Members>
  <Sequence >
```

```xml
    <Sequence.Variables>
      <Variable x:TypeArguments="x:Int32" Default="[0]" Name="count" />
      <Variable x:TypeArguments="x:Boolean" Default="[false]" Name="finished" />
    </Sequence.Variables>
    <While Condition="[Not finished]">
      <Sequence >
        <If Condition="[count &lt; argument1.Length]" >
          <If.Then>
            <WriteLine  Text="[&quot;Hello &quot; &amp;
                argument1(count).ToString()]" />
          </If.Then>
          <If.Else>
            <Assign x:Key="0" >
              <Assign.To>
                <OutArgument x:TypeArguments="x:Boolean">[finished]</OutArgument>
              </Assign.To>
              <Assign.Value>
                <InArgument x:TypeArguments="x:Boolean">[true]</InArgument>
              </Assign.Value>
            </Assign>
          </If.Else>
        </If>
        <Assign >
          <Assign.To>
            <OutArgument x:TypeArguments="x:Int32">[count]</OutArgument>
          </Assign.To>
          <Assign.Value>
            <InArgument x:TypeArguments="x:Int32">[count + 1]</InArgument>
          </Assign.Value>
        </Assign>
      </Sequence>
    </While>
  </Sequence>
</Activity>
```

An array of a string is passed in as a parameter. The workflow is composed of a single `Sequence`. Within the scope of the `Sequence` activity, you define two variables — `count` and `finished`. The procedural steps nested within the `Sequence` activity are self-explanatory.

A `While` activity is used to loop over until the expression [Not Finished] returns `false`. Within each iteration of the loop, an `If` activity is used to check if the `count` variable is less than the length of the array passed in as an argument. If this is indeed the case, the `WriteLine` activity is used to print the greeting. Alternatively, if the count becomes equal to the length of the array passed in, the `Assign` activity is used to set the finished variable to `true`. Each iteration of the loop ends by incrementing the count variable by 1 using the `Assign` activity.

Because the code in Listing 12-6 is rather long, reviewing the equivalent WF designer view shown in Figure 12-3 may be helpful.

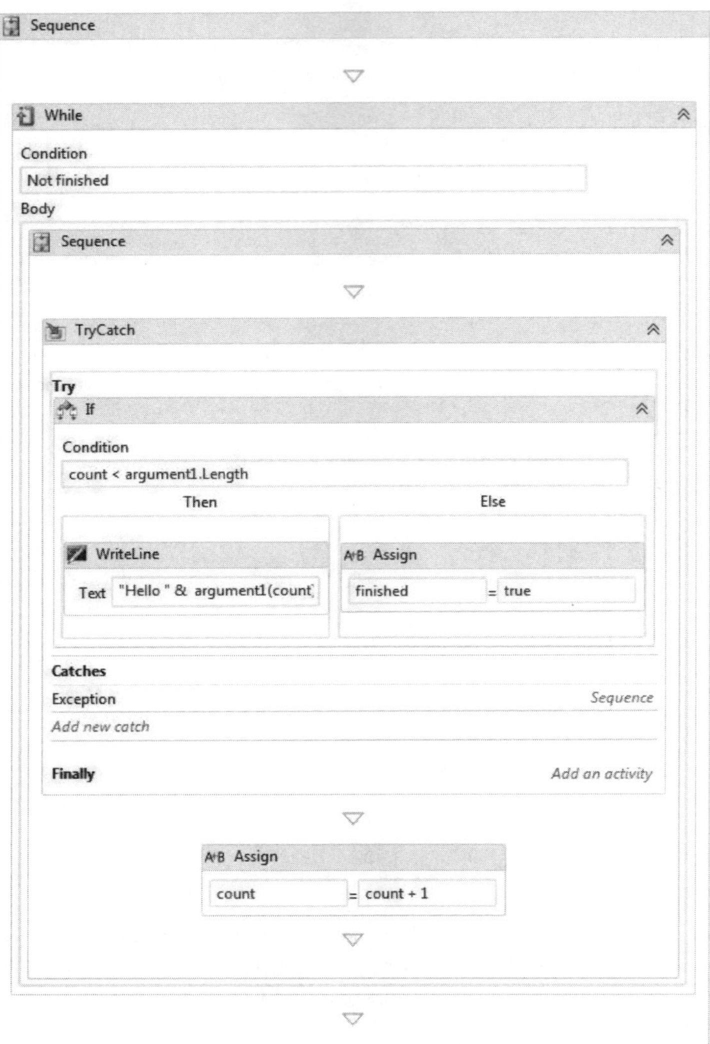

FIGURE 12-3: Procedural style in WF designer view

Exception Handling

Similar to other programming languages, WF 4 offers exception-handling constructs. As you learned earlier, most of the constructs in WF 4 are activities. Exception handling is no different. WF 4 provides the following activities for exception handling: `TryCatch`, `Throw`, and `Finally`.

You can easily extend the previous example to handle exceptions that may be thrown during the execution of the workflow steps. Listing 12-7 shows the use of the `TryCatch` activity to wrap the procedural steps discussed earlier.

LISTING 12-7: Exception Handling

```
<TryCatch >
    <TryCatch.Try>
      <If Condition="[count &lt; argument1.Length]" >
        <If.Then>
          <WriteLine  Text="[&quot;Hello &quot; &amp;
argument1(count).ToString()]" />
        </If.Then>
        <If.Else>
          <Assign >
            <Assign.To>
              <OutArgument x:TypeArguments=
                  "x:Boolean">[finished]</OutArgument>
            </Assign.To>
            <Assign.Value>
              <InArgument x:TypeArguments="x:Boolean">[true]</InArgument>
            </Assign.Value>
          </Assign>
        </If.Else>
      </If>
    </TryCatch.Try>
    <TryCatch.Catches>
      <Catch x:TypeArguments="s:Exception" >
        <ActivityAction x:TypeArguments="s:Exception">
          <Sequence >
            <WriteLine  Text="[&quot;Exception thrown&quot;]" />
            <TerminateWorkflow  Reason="exception thrown" />
          </Sequence>
        </ActivityAction>
      </Catch>
    </TryCatch.Catches>
  </TryCatch>
```

In case an exception is thrown, the `Catch` activity that takes an argument of the `Exception` type is invoked. The `Catch` activity, in turn, contains steps that are executed when an exception is caught. In Listing 12-7, the `WriteLine` activity is used to write diagnostic text to `console`, followed by calling the `TerminateException` activity to terminate the workflow execution.

Transaction and Compensation

WF 4 provides constructs to ensure the integrity of the data touched by the workflow program. This includes support for transactions and compensation.

WF 4 provides support for transactions in the form of the `TransactionScope` activity. The idea behind this activity is not different from the notion of transactions that developers are already familiar with. A WF program can embed one or more activities within the `TransactionScope` activity to ensure that they all execute as part of a single transaction.

Listing 12-8 shows an example of `TransactionScope` in action.

LISTING 12-8: TransactionScope

```
<Activity>
  <Sequence>
    <WriteLine>["    Begin workflow"]</WriteLine>
    <TransactionScope >
      <TransactionScope.IsolationLevel>3</TransactionScope.IsolationLevel >
        <TransactionScope.AbortInstanceOnTransactionFailure >true
</TransactionScope.AbortInstanceOnTransactionFailure>
      <Sequence>
        <WriteLine>["    Begin TransactionScope"]</WriteLine>
        <ntsa:PrintTransactionId/>
        <WriteLine>["    End TransactionScope"]</WriteLine>
      </Sequence>

    </TransactionScope>
    <WriteLine>["    End workflow"]</WriteLine>
  </Sequence>
</Activity>



   public sealed class PrintTransactionId : NativeActivity
   {
       protected override void Execute(NativeActivityContext context)
       {
//Access to the current transaction in Workflow is through the
//GetCurrentTransaction method on a RuntimeTransactionHandle
           RuntimeTransactionHandle rth =
               context.Properties.Find(typeof(RuntimeTransactionHandle)
               .FullName) as RuntimeTransactionHandle;
           Console.WriteLine("    TransactionID: "
             +rth.GetCurrentTransaction(context).
TransactionInformation.LocalIdentifier.ToString());
       }
   }
```

In this example, the `Sequence` activity is placed within the `TransactionScope`. The `Sequence` activity, in turn, contains two `WriteLine` activities and a custom activity called `PrintTransactionId` that prints the transaction identifier. The code for `PrintTransactionId`, taken from the MSDN WF 4 sample `NestedTransactionScopeSample`, is provided in the listing. The `PrintTransactionID` activity inherits from the `NativeActivity` base class. You learn about the `NativeActivity` base class later in this chapter.

Listing 12-8 also shows how additional properties can be set on the `TransactionScope` activity. For example, the isolation level is set to 3 (`ReadUncommitted` within the workflow designer). Additionally, the code indicates to the WF runtime that the workflow instance must be aborted in case the transaction fails.

You can also nest `TransactionScope` activities. Nested `TransactionScope` activities reuse the ambient transaction (as opposed to spawning a new transaction). However, nested `TransactionScope` activities should not cause a conflict with the outer `TransactionScope` activity.

For example, the nested `TransactionScope` should have the same isolation level as the outside `TransactionScope`.

As powerful as the `TransactionScope` activity is, it is not suitable for all scenarios. This is especially true for scenarios in which the duration of the transaction is long, thereby making it expensive to hold on to the resources participating in the transaction. In such situations, compensation — explicitly reversing an action — is more suitable. WF 4 provides rich constructs to help workflow authors model compensation logic into their workflows. The key construct related to compensation is the `CompensationActivity`. Listing 12-9 shows its usage.

LISTING 12-9: CompensationActivity

```xml
<Activity>
    <Sequence>
    <Sequence.Variables>
      <Variable x:TypeArguments="CompensationToken" Name="token" />
    </Sequence.Variables>

    <WriteLine>["Start of workflow."]</WriteLine>

    <CompensableActivity Result="[token]">

      <WriteLine>["CompensableActivity: Do Work."]</WriteLine>

      <CompensableActivity.CompensationHandler>
        <WriteLine>["CompensableActivity: Undo Work."]</WriteLine>
      </CompensableActivity.CompensationHandler>

      <CompensableActivity.ConfirmationHandler>
        <WriteLine>["CompensableActivity: Do Work Confirmed."]</WriteLine>
      </CompensableActivity.ConfirmationHandler>

      <WriteLine>["CompensableActivity: Do Work."]</WriteLine>

    </CompensableActivity>

    <Compensate Target="[token]" />

    <WriteLine>["End of workflow."]</WriteLine>

    </Sequence>
  </Activity>
```

In this example, the activity to be compensated is a `WriteLine` activity that prints the text `"Do Work"`. Now you must specify a `CompensationHandler` property that represents the undo activity that will be invoked when compensation is to be performed. In this example, the compensation handler is also a `WriteLine` activity that simply prints the text `"Undo Work"`.

In addition, you have another handler called the `ConfirmationHandler` that can be used to specify custom logic that will execute when a `CompensationActivity` is confirmed. The workflow has reached a point in which the compensation action associated with the `CompensationActivity` is no longer to be invoked. In this example, the `ConfirmationHandler` simply prints the text `"Do Work Confirmed"`.

In Listing 12-9, just below the `CompensationActivity`, is an activity called `Compensate` that is used to explicitly invoke the compensation handler. The `Compensate` activity takes as a parameter a token that points to the instance of the `CompensationActivity` whose action must be reversed. This token was populated by the outgoing parameter of the `CompensationActivity` called `Result`.

If you run this program, you can see the normal execution of the `CompensationActivity`, followed by the compensation action. If you had placed a `Confirm` activity in place of the `Compensate` activity, you would also see the normal execution of the `CompensationActivity`, followed by the confirmation action. As discussed, after the `ConfirmationHandler` has been invoked, calling `Compensate` would result in an error. This is to be expected because the invocation of the `Compensation` activity has already indicated to the WF 4 runtime that no further compensation is needed.

So far, you have been explicitly invoking compensation. This is not always needed because the WF 4 runtime can implicitly invoke the compensation behavior based on whether the workflow completed successfully. If there were an error in the execution of the workflow after the `CompletionActivity` successfully completed, WF 4 runtime invokes the compensation handler.

Parallel Execution

All the examples so far have been based on sequential execution. In other words, the WF 4 runtime executes the next workflow step only after the preceding step is complete. This begs the question about a scenario in which a parallel (or concurrent) execution would be needed.

As mentioned earlier, WF 4 is a language based on higher-level abstractions. This is why there are no built-in constructs to create and synchronize threads. In fact, the WF 4 runtime, by design, allows only a single workflow activity to execute at any given point in time. But that does not mean a WF 4 program cannot schedule more than one workflow activity for execution.

Listing 12-10 shows the use of the `Parallel` activity that makes it possible to schedule more than one workflow activity.

LISTING 12-10: Parallel Execution

```
<Activity>
  <Sequence >
    <Parallel >
      <Sequence >
        <WriteLine  Text="Parallel Path1 start" />
        <WriteLine  Text="Parallel Path1 end" />
      </Sequence>
      <Sequence >
        <WriteLine  Text="Parallel Path2 start" />
        <WriteLine  Text="Parallel Path2 end" />
      </Sequence>
    </Parallel>
  </Sequence>
</Activity>
```

As shown in the example, the `Parallel` activity is a collection of `Sequence` activities. The `Parallel` activity, acting as the parent activity, iterates over the collection of `Sequence` activities and schedules each of them for execution. As mentioned, only one of them gets to execute at any time. So, scheduling multiple activities is not actually doing any good. In effect, this program is going to execute sequentially.

To take advantage of the parallel execution, you need one of the executing activities to yield control back to the runtime. This typically happens when the executing activity is waiting for an event to complete.

For example, an activity that invokes a web service asynchronously can yield control back to the workflow runtime while it waits for its completion. When that happens, the workflow runtime can execute another activity that has been scheduled for execution.

Because this discussion has not addressed invoking web services up until now, try to simulate the "yield" behavior by invoking a `Delay` activity.

```
<WriteLine  Text="Parallel Path1 start" />
        <Delay Duration="00:00:01"  />
        <WriteLine  Text="Parallel Path1 end" />
```

As the name suggests, you can use the `Delay` activity to pause the execution of a workflow for a specified period of time. The paused activity, in turn, prompts the workflow runtime to execute another activity that has been scheduled for execution.

The order in which scheduled activities are executed is indeterminate.

Flowchart Style

As discussed, the procedural style mimics the common programming language constructs, such as conditionals, looping, and exception handling. This makes it easy to author well-structured business processes.

The concept of a well-structured process is familiar to developers — for example, they have been taught to use a looping construct when there is a need to return the flow of execution to an earlier location in the workflow. However, nondevelopers may find it difficult to accomplish this because it involves adding a looping construct, setting up a looping condition, and so on. They need an easier approach to alter the flow of execution.

This is where the flowchart style workflows come in. As the name suggests, this style mimics the well-known paradigm for designing programs. In a nutshell, a flowchart consists of nodes and arcs. Nodes represent the steps in a flowchart, whereas the arcs represent the potential path of execution through the nodes. In WF 4, the node maps to a `FlowStep` activity, and the arc maps to a `FlowDecision` or `FlowSwitch` activities.

Now take a look at an example that highlights the flexibility offered by the flowchart style. Implement a WF 4 program that mimics the business process shown in Figure 12-4.

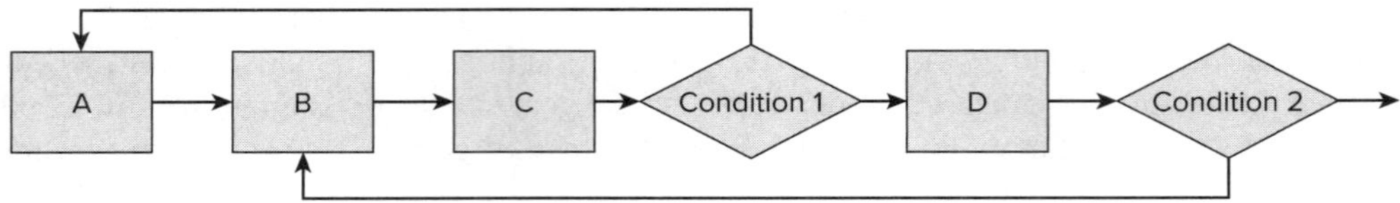

FIGURE 12-4: Business process suitable for flowchart style

Listing 12-11 shows the WF 4 program that implements the business process shown in
Figure 12-4.

LISTING 12-11: Flowchart Style

```
<Activity  ">
 <Flowchart >
   <Flowchart.StartNode>
     <FlowStep x:Name="__ReferenceID0">
       <Sequence >
         <WriteLine  Text="Step A" />
         <WriteLine  Text="Step B" />
         <WriteLine  Text="Step C" />
       </Sequence>
       <FlowStep.Next>
         <FlowDecision x:Name="__ReferenceID1" Condition="[True = True]" >
           <FlowDecision.True>
             <FlowStep x:Name="__ReferenceID2">
               <Sequence >
                 <WriteLine  Text="Step D" />
               </Sequence>
               <FlowStep.Next>
                 <FlowDecision x:Name="__ReferenceID3" Condition="[True = True]" >
                   <FlowDecision.False>
                     <x:Reference>__ReferenceID0</x:Reference>
                   </FlowDecision.False>
                 </FlowDecision>
               </FlowStep.Next>
             </FlowStep>
           </FlowDecision.True>
           <FlowDecision.False>
             <x:Reference>__ReferenceID0</x:Reference>
           </FlowDecision.False>
         </FlowDecision>
       </FlowStep.Next>
     </FlowStep>
   </Flowchart.StartNode>
 </Flowchart>
</Activity>
```

The `Flowchart` activity is like a container that can hold any number of `Flowstep` activities. Each
`FlowStep` activity models a step within the workflow. Notice the first `FlowStep` activity named
`__ReferenceID0`. It executes a sequence activity that contains steps A, B, and C from Figure 12-4.
There are two things to note about the `Sequence` activity.

First, you can mix procedural and flowchart styles. In this instance, the `FlowStep` activity is responsible for executing the `Sequence` activity. It is also possible to place a `Flowchart` within a `Sequence` activity.

Second, steps A, B, and C are placed within a `Sequence` activity. Although you could model each step as a distinct `FlowStep` activity, placing them inside a `Sequence` activity allows you to potentially narrow the scope. You can define variables that are visible only within the `Sequence` activity.

The `FlowStep.Next` property points to the next step in the flow chart. In this example, the `FlowDecision` evaluates an expression `True = True` (admittedly contrite to keep the example simple). If the expression evaluates to `true`, you execute another `Sequence` activity that, in turn, executes step D. Alternatively, if the expression evaluates to `false` (not possible in this example), it would cause the flowchart execution to return to the first `FlowStep` activity named `__ReferenceID0`.

The last step in the workflow is to add a `FlowDecision` activity after step D. Again, to keep things simple, you use a hard-code `true = true` expression. If the expression associated with this `Flow .Decision` evaluates to `false`, you would return to the `FlowStep` named `__ReferenceID0`.

Herein lies the most flexible aspect of the flowchart style — the capability to execute a workflow step by name, as shown in the following code snippet. This construct is what enables you to easily implement the business process shown in Figure 12-4.

```
<FlowDecision.False>
   <x:Reference>__ReferenceID0</x:Reference>
</FlowDecision.False>
```

You could have implemented the aforementioned business process by relying only on procedural constructs. Figure 12-5 shows an implementation based on procedural constructs. The complexity is evident from the block diagram — a XAML implementation would be more complicated.

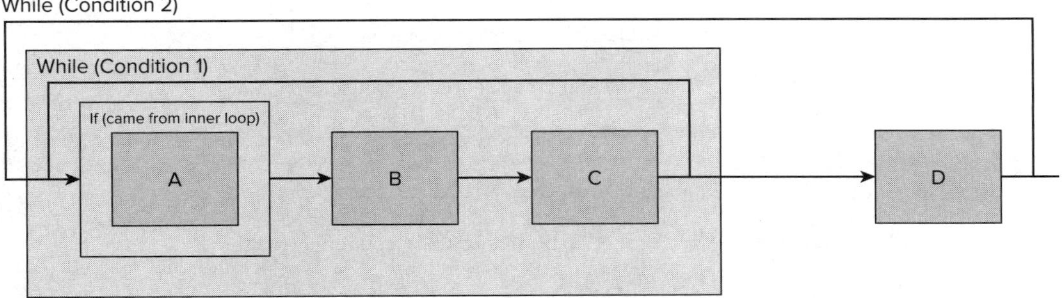

FIGURE 12-5: Implementation based on procedural style

Messaging

As you would expect, WF 4 provides messaging constructs designed to enable workflow programs to communicate with external entities. Consistent with the rest of the WF 4 theme, messaging constructs are also activities. These activities rely on Windows Communication Foundation (WCF) for providing the communication stack. Fortunately for the workflow authors, though, the messaging activities abstract many of the WCF details. For example, a WCF contract can be automatically inferred based on the set of messaging activities that make a workflow.

There are two core messaging activities — `Send` (used to send messages) and `Receive` (used to receive messages). In addition to the core activities, there are two additional activities, `SendReply` and `ReceiveReply`, that enable WF 4 programs to send and receive a response for a preceding invocation of `Receive` and `Send` activities, respectively. Together, these messaging activities enable workflow authors to model a variety of message-exchange patterns, including request-response, bidirectional, and one-way patterns.

Listing 12-12 shows an example of using `Receive` and `SendReply` activities. In addition, this example also illustrates the concept of *correlation* — a mechanism that associates activities based on a shared context.

LISTING 12-12: Receive and SendReply

```xml
<PickBranch Trigger="{x:Reference __ReferenceID0}">

  <p:SendReply >

    <p:SendReply.Request>

      <p:Receive x:Name="__ReferenceID0"  CanCreateInstance="True"
      CorrelatesWith="[TwitterIdHandle]"  OperationName="Hello"
      ServiceContractName="ISendGreeting">

        <p:Receive.CorrelatesOn>

          <p:MessageQuerySet>

            <p:XPathMessageQuery x:Key="TwitterId">

              <p:XPathMessageQuery.Namespaces>

                <ssx:XPathMessageContextMarkup>

                  <x:String x:Key="xgSc">http://tempuri.org/</x:String>

                </ssx:XPathMessageContextMarkup>

              </p:XPathMessageQuery.Namespaces>

              sm:body()/xgSc:Hello/xgSc:TwitterHandle

            </p:XPathMessageQuery>

          </p:MessageQuerySet>

        </p:Receive.CorrelatesOn>

        <p:ReceiveParametersContent>

          <OutArgument x:TypeArguments=
```

```
                    "x:String" x:Key="TwitterHandle" />

             </p:ReceiveParametersContent>

          </p:Receive>

       </p:SendReply.Request>

       <p:SendParametersContent>

          <InArgument x:TypeArguments="x:String"
              x:Key="Value">[NumOfRequests.ToString()] </InArgument>

       </p:SendParametersContent>

    </p:SendReply>

 </PickBranch >
```

The functionality implemented in this example is simple. It can receive a message, sent to it by an external entity. In response, it provides a count of requests received within a given context. In other words, it returns the total number of correlated incoming requests. Before reviewing the messaging code, however, let's consider one other concept used in this example.

This example provides an opportunity to look at another important control-flow construct called the `Pick` activity. The `Pick` activity is similar to the `Parallel` activity in that it enables creation of multiple parallel branches for workflow execution. However, it is specifically designed to wait concurrently for multiple event triggers. Each parallel branch represents an instance of `PickBranch` activity.

For example, consider the `Pick` activity that is modeled — one `PickBranch` waits for a delay trigger to arrive, while another `PickBranch` waits for the `Receive` activity to be invoked. Of course, given that workflow runtime ensures causality, only one `PickBranch` can execute at any given time. The `Pick` activity is useful when implementing a state *machine style workflow* — a workflow style in which the flow is based on a discrete set of states.

For simplicity, Listing 12-13 shows an elided view of the code that includes the code nested within the `PickBranch` activity.

LISTING 12-13: Messaging

```
<Activity>

  <Sequence >

    <Sequence.Variables>

       <Variable x:TypeArguments="x:Boolean" Default="[True]"
           Name="Running" />
       <Variable x:TypeArguments="x:Int32"  Name="NumOfRequests" />

    </Sequence.Variables>
```

```
<While >

    <While.Variables>

        <Variable x:TypeArguments="p:CorrelationHandle"
                                Name="TwitterIdHandle" />

    </While.Variables>

    <While.Condition>[Running]</While.Condition>

    <Sequence>
        <Assign >
            <Assign.To>
                <OutArgument
                    x:TypeArguments=
                        "x:Int32">[NumOfRequests]</OutArgument>
            </Assign.To>
            <Assign.Value>
                <InArgument x:TypeArguments="x:Int32">
                        [NumOfRequests + 1]</InArgument>
            </Assign.Value>
        </Assign>

        <Pick >
            Refer to Listing 12-12
        </Pick >
    </Sequence>
</While >
    </Sequence>
</Activity>
```

The `PickBranch` activity consists of two parts: a *trigger* and the *action*. In this example, the trigger that you are waiting on is a `Receive` activity with a name `__ReferenceID0`. This activity is responsible for receiving an incoming message. As stated earlier, based on the `Receive` activity attributes such as the `OperationName` and `ServiceContractName`, a WCF contract is inferred automatically.

The inferred WCF contract, combined with the WCF 4.0 feature to apply a default binding, means that there is no need for any WCF configuration (in code or in the configuration file) for this `Receive` activity. The `CanCreateInstance` attribute, when set to `true`, means that a new instance of the workflow can be created (if needed) to process the message received by the `Receive` activity.

The other two correlation-based attributes, `CorrelatesWith` and `CorrelatesOn`, need some explanation. Earlier you learned that correlation is about associating a set of activities. To understand why this is important, consider a scenario in which multiple external entities try to concurrently call the workflow program. As a result, multiple instances of the workflow program are created.

Now, it is up to the WF 4 runtime to deliver the incoming messages to appropriate instances. It does so by relating incoming requests that have a shared token (also referred to as the *correlation token*). Correlation, of course, is not limited to incoming messages; it could be about relating a request with a response. Correlation can be of two types:

➤ *Protocol-based correlation* relates messages based on data provided by the underlying infrastructure (for example, a token provided by the transport protocol).

➤ *Content-based correlation* relates messages based on the content of the message. (Listing 12-13 shows the use of content-based correlation.)

Now that you understand the notion behind correlation, continue the review of the remaining two correlation attributes.

Attribute `CorrelatesOn` specifies the part of the message content that will be used to relate the messages. In this instance, you rely on an XPath expression to specify the correlation token. The XPath expression points to the element `TwitterHandle` in the incoming SOAP request. So, if the SOAP request looked like the following example, the XPath expression would evaluate to `john`. Following is the value you correlate on.

```
<s:Envelope xmlns:s="http://schemas.xmlsoap.org/soap/envelope/">
    <s:Body>
        <Hello xmlns="http://tempuri.org/">
            <TwitterHandle>john</TwitterHandle>
        </Hello>
    </s:Body>
</s:Envelope>
```

The other attribute, `CorrelatesWith`, points to a workflow variable that stores the correlation token. The WF 4 runtime compares the result of the XPath expression to the variable pointed to by the `CorrelatesWith` attribute to determine where the message needs to be delivered.

Now that you understand the `Receive` activity, take a look at what's next in the workflow. The `SendReply` activity is responsible for sending a response to the caller. The most interesting part is the payload of the reply. You maintain a workflow variable `NumOfRequests` that is incremented each time you receive an incoming message. Listing 12-13 represents the overall flow of the workflow. As shown in Listing 12-12, the `SendReply` activity simply returns the current value of this workflow variable.

The last issue associated with messaging to examine is the client program used to call the workflow. Listing 12-14 shows the client code.

LISTING 12-14: Messaging Client

```
        BasicHttpBinding binding = new BasicHttpBinding();

        EndpointAddress address = new
    EndpointAddress("http://localhost:8080/HelloWorldService");

        ChannelFactory<ISendGreeting> factory = new
                        ChannelFactory<ISendGreeting>();

        ISendGreeting proxy =
            ChannelFactory<ISendGreeting>.CreateChannel(binding, address);

        using (proxy as IDisposable)
        {
            string res = proxy.Hello("john");
            res = proxy.Hello("john");
            res = proxy.Hello("mary");
            res = proxy.Hello("john");
        }
```

You use `ChannelFactory` to create a channel based on the endpoint information. Using the channel, you invoke the `Hello` method four times.

As discussed, the content-based routing scheme you have in place is based on a parameter being passed with the `Hello` method. This is why the first, second, and fourth calls (with parameter set to `"john"`) will all be associated to the same instance of the workflow. Consequently, the value returned upon the completion of the fourth call is 3. The second call (with parameter set to `"mary"`) causes a separate workflow instance to be spawned. As a result, the value returned upon the completion of the second call is 1.

BUILDING CUSTOM ACTIVITIES

So far in this chapter, you have learned about the use of built-in activities to author WF 4 programs. In addition to a rich set of built-in activities, WF 4 has also been designed to make it easy to develop and use custom activities.

As discussed, activities enable large workflows to be broken up into small steps that can be reused, thereby promoting reuse. Well-designed activities hide details of an operation from the workflow author. For example, a custom `SendMail` activity hides the implementation details associated with sending an e-mail. Workflow authors can simply add a `SendEmail` activity as a step within their workflow as needed.

Before looking at some code to create a custom activity, you need to recall that a workflow is also an activity. So, the examples of workflows you have seen so far can themselves be reused as activities by workflow authors (with adequate factoring of incoming and outgoing arguments). In other words, what you have seen so far are examples of custom activities declaratively assembled.

Building custom activities in this manner is a valid option. However, instances exist in which expressiveness of code is needed to building custom activities. The rest of this section focuses on building code-based custom activities.

WF 4 provides a set of base classes designed to accelerate the development of custom activities. Developers can select from this set, based on the type of activity being developed. Figure 12-6 shows the set of activity base classes provided by WF 4.

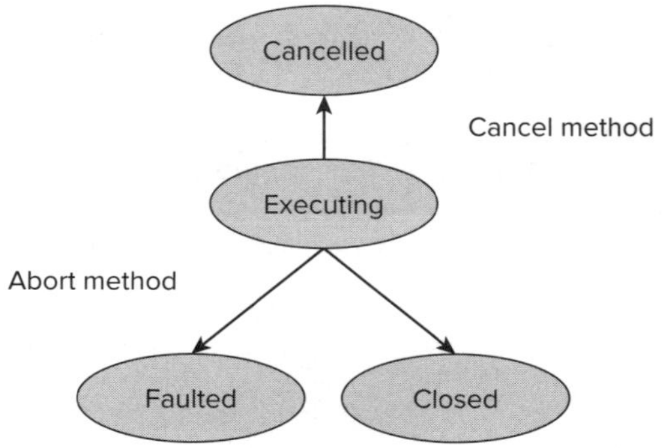

FIGURE 12-6: Activity base classes

Now look at each of these classes (`Activity`, `CodeActivity`, `AsyncCodeActivity`, and `NativeActivity`) in more detail.

Activity

`Activity` is an abstract base class that can be used to create activities using existing activities. You have already seen examples that use the `Activity` base class. The declarative workflows presented earlier had a root element of the `Activity` type. In essence, you simply added prebuilt activities (such as `While`, `Assign`, and `Sequence`) as needed to the `Activity` class. The `Activity` base class served as the composite or container class.

Now re-create the example from Listing 12-3 in which you declaratively authored a workflow. Use the `Activity` base class as a container, and rely on code-based constructs to re-create the workflow. Listing 12-15 shows the relevant code.

LISTING 12-15: Activity Base Class

```
public sealed class HelloWorld : Activity
{

public InArgument<string> argument1 { get; set; }public HelloWorld()
{
}
protected override Func<Activity> Implementation
{
    get
    {
        return () =>
        {Variable<String> var1 =
                new Variable<String> { Name = "var1" };
         return new Sequence
             {

                 Variables =
                  {
                      var1
                  },

                 Activities =
                  {
                      new Assign<String>
                      {
                          To = new OutArgument<string> (ac =>
                                               var1.Get(ac)),
                                        Value = new
                                            InArgument<string>
                                            (ac=> argument1
                                            .Get(ac))
                      },
                      new WriteLine
                      {
                          Text = new InArgument<string> (ac =>
                                               var1.Get(ac))
                      }

                  }
             };
        };
    }
    set
```

continues

LISTING 12-15 *(continued)*

```
        {
            base.Implementation = value;
        }

    }
}
```

The `Activity` base class has a property called `Implementation` that serves as the container for activities in the workflow. The `Get` accessor of the `Implementation` property defines the collection of activities that make up the workflow. Even though the initialization syntax is used to assemble the activities, the workflow logic is exactly the same.

You have a `Sequence` activity, which, in turn, contains an `Assign` activity that stores the incoming argument into a workflow `var1` variable. This is followed by a `WriteLine` activity that writes `var1` to `console`.

The only other noteworthy aspect of this listing is the pattern used to access the workflow variable and parameters. Rather than directly accessing the program properties (such as `argument1`), you must access them via the execution environment under which the activity is executing. Remember that the program is setting up only the workflow. The execution environment is accessed using the context (known as `ActvityContext`) provided by the `Activity` base class.

Now review an example of this pattern. To access the argument called `argument1` within the workflow, you must create an instance of `InArgument` `<string>` by passing in a lambda expression that takes the `ActivityContext` as a parameter and returns a string.

```
Value = new InArgument<string>(ac=> argument1.Get(ac))
```

In summary, this code-based example is similar to assembling a workflow declaratively — both rely on deriving from the base `Activity` class and setting the `Implementation` property. Another aspect is common to both; neither approach is about implementing code that executes as part of the custom activity. Rather, the custom activity logic is assembled using pre-existing activities.

Although the code-based approach based on the `Activity` class is more concise, it does come at a cost: additional complexity. Specifically, the manner in which activities must be stacked and then assigned to the `Implementation` property of the `Activity` class is not intuitive. Fortunately, WF 4 provides additional base classes that can simplify the development of custom activities.

CodeActivity

The `CodeActivity` base class is perhaps the simplest one to derive from. Custom activity classes that derive from `CodeActivity` are responsible for overriding the `Execute` method. In addition, they are responsible for implementing any arguments and variables as needed. Listing 12-16 shows an example of a custom activity that derives from the `CodeActivity` base class.

LISTING 12-16: Deriving from CodeActivity Class

```
public sealed class HelloWorld_CodeActivity : CodeActivity
{
    public InArgument<String> argument1 { get; set; }
    public OutArgument<String> result { get; set; }



    protected override void Execute(CodeActivityContext context)
    {
        private String _var1 = argument1.Get(context);
        Console.WriteLine(_var1);
        result.Set(context, _var1);
    }
}
```

The `Execute` method is overridden to supply an implementation for the custom activity. In this example, you store the incoming argument into a local variable called `_var1`. Notice that the incoming argument is of the `InArgument<String>` type. To access the value of the incoming parameter, you must invoke the `Get` method of the `InArgument`, and pass in the activity context. Setting a return value is similar, except you invoke the `Set` method, passing in the activity context and the value to be set.

You can now use the custom activity in the declarative workflow, as shown in Listing 12-17. The only difference from previous listings is that a namespace prefix called `"custom"` is added to include the namespace in which the custom activity is defined. This enables you to add the `HelloWorld_CodeActivity` to the workflow. The rest of the code is the same. The workflow has one incoming argument of type `string`, which, in turn, is passed to the `HelloWorld_CodeActivity`.

LISTING 12-17: Using Custom Activity within a Declaritive Worflow

```
<Activity  ..
          xmlns:custom="clr-namespace:ProgrammingWF4"
  <x:Members>
    <x:Property Name="argument1" Type="InArgument(x:String)" />
  </x:Members>
  <custom:HelloWorld_CodeActivity argument1="[argument1]" />
</Activity>
```

In summary, deriving from `CodeActivity` is straightforward. It requires providing custom execution logic via the `Execute` method of the base class. This approach is suitable for custom activities designed to perform short-lived, atomic operations.

AsyncCodeActivity

If a custom activity is designed for a long-running operation, it is advisable that it performs the bulk of its work on a separate thread. This ensures that workflow is not blocked while the long-running operation is completed. Recall the discussion of parallel activities earlier in this chapter. By moving the work to another thread, a custom activity yields control back to the WF 4 runtime. Based on this, the WF 4 runtime is now free to execute another activity that may have been scheduled to run in parallel.

To build long-running custom activities that perform asynchronously, WF 4 provides the `AsyncCodeActivity` base class. Now look at an example.

This time around, you do things a bit differently. In the previous section, the custom activity inherited from a `CodeActivity` class that was not generic. WF 4 provides generic versions of the activity base classes that are designed to further simplify the development of custom activities.

For example, by using the generic version, return types are predefined, based on a convention. For this example, build a custom activity that derives from the generic `AsyncCodeActivity<T>` base class. The code is shown in Listing 12-18.

LISTING 12-18: Deriving from AsyncCodeActivity Class

```
public sealed class HelloWorld_AsyncCodeActivity : AsyncCodeActivity<int>
{
        public InArgument<String> argument1 { get; set; }


        protected override IAsyncResult BeginExecute(
AsyncCodeActivityContext context,
AsyncCallback callback,
object state)
        {
            private String _var1 = argument1.Get(context);

            Func<string, int> LongRunningFunc = new Func<string, int>(DoWork);
            context.UserState = LongRunningFunc;
            return LongRunningFunc.BeginInvoke(_var1, callback, state);
        }


        protected override int EndExecute(
AsyncCodeActivityContext context,
IAsyncResult result)
        {
            Func<string, int> LongRunningFunc = (Func<string,
                int>)context.UserState;
            return (int)LongRunningFunc.EndInvoke(result);
        }

        int DoWork(string argument)
        {
            int WorkDuration = new Random().Next(10) * 1000;
            Thread.Sleep(WorkDuration);
            Console.WriteLine(argument);
```

```
        return WorkDuration;
    }

}
```

In an attempt to keep things simple, `Thread.Sleep` is combined with a `Random` class to simulate a long-running behavior. As you would guess, this is the portion of the code that will be executed on another thread. The custom activity, `HelloWorld_AsyncCodeActivity`, derives from `AsyncCodeActivity<int>`.

Defining arguments and variables is something you have seen already. In this example, you define an incoming argument called `argument1` and a local variable called `_var1` that is visible only inside the scope of the custom activity. Note, however, that you have not defined any return parameters. As mentioned, the benefit to using a generic base class is that the return value of type `int` activity is already defined for you. Furthermore, it is always consistently named `Result`.

Deriving from the `AsyncCodeActivity` requires you to override two methods from the base class: `BeginExecute` and `EndExecute`. Within the `BeginExecute` method, you create a delegate that points to the method that will be executed on another thread. You assign the delegate to the `UserState` property of the `AsyncActivityContext`. Storing the delegate reference within the activity context is what provides the continuity because the context is available throughout the execution of the custom activity.

The last step is to invoke the delegate and return control to the WF 4 runtime. At this point, `DoWork` is invoked on another thread. The interesting part about `DoWork` is that it does not have access to `AsyncActivityContext` because it is being executed on another thread. This is why you must pass the variable `_var1` as part of the `DoWork` invocation.

Also noteworthy is the direct access to the argument passed into the `DoWork` method. You treated it as CLR type. Unlike the incoming argument, `argument1`, you did not need to access the argument via the context.

The rest of the code within `DoWork` is quite mundane — sleep for a period of time based on a random number, print the passed-in argument to `console`, and return the sleep interval back to the caller.

When the `DoWork` method is complete, the WF 4 runtime invokes the `callback` function, defined as part of the `BeginInvoke` call. This callback location was passed into the `BeginExecute` method by the WF 4 runtime. This chain of events prompts the WF runtime to invoke the `EndExecute` method.

This is an opportunity for the custom activity to retrieve the results of the `DoWork` method. You achieve this by retrieving a reference to the delegate you stored within the `AsyncActivityContext` and calling the `EndInvoke` method on it.

You have just completed the asynchronous custom activity. What is interesting, however, is that the declarative workflow you saw in Listing 12-11 can be used to invoke this activity. As you would imagine, to the consumer of the activity it makes no difference whether the work inside the activity is done in a synchronous or asynchronous manner. However, as stated earlier, the consuming workflow would benefit from the asynchronous behavior only if the workflow scheduled more than one activity for execution — as discussed in the earlier section, "Parallel Execution."

NativeActivity

As you have seen in the previous sections, deriving from the `CodeActivity` base class is the easiest way to build a custom activity. However, the ease of development also means that the access to some of the more advanced WF 4 runtime services is not available. This is to be expected; hiding complexity is job one for a good abstraction.

So, when would you need to access some of the more advanced features of WF 4 runtime? One example would be an activity that is waiting for an external event, such as a task completion or a return receipt notification. The operative word is "external" — there are events arriving from outside the execution context of the workflow.

Observant readers are probably wondering why this requirement cannot be met by deriving from the `AsyncCodeActivity`. After all, the asynchronous method `DoWork` in Listing 12-12 can be modified to wait for an external event. As a result, the activity will yield control back to the runtime, thus facilitating the execution of another scheduled activity.

Although this line of thought is indeed correct, this approach has limitations. Remember that, by yielding control, you can make it possible for another activity within the workflow to schedule. For example, it will be possible for the WF 4 runtime to execute an already scheduled activity nested within another `Parallel` activity branch. However, as far the WF 4 runtime is concerned, the workflow instance is still active.

The reason this is important is because each workflow instance consumes WF 4 runtime resources. To scale, the WF 4 runtime should only expend resources on active workflows. As you saw a moment ago, even though the custom activity yielded control, overall, the workflow is still active — the `DoWork` method is actively waiting for an external event.

It would be better if the logic to wait for an external event were moved out of the custom activity and into the WF 4 runtime. This way, the entire workflow would yield control back to the runtime.

This would be an improvement over the behavior examined earlier in the context of an asynchronous custom activity, wherein an activity yielded control to another activity within the workflow. But because the asynchronous thread was busy working on the long-running task, the workflow as a whole could not yield control back to the WF 4 runtime.

WF 4 runtime provides a mechanism that enables activities to completely offload the task of waiting for an event. This way, the workflow can be completely passive during the wait. It is the runtime that is responsible for listening to any incoming events. As the events arrive, the runtime activates the appropriate instance of the workflow, passing in the payload associated with the event.

This mechanism is called a `Bookmark` in WF 4. To take advantage of this mechanism, custom activities must derive from the base class `NativeActivity`. As the name suggests, this base class enables custom activity developers to get closer to the native execution environment of the WF 4 runtime.

Listing 12-19 shows an example of a custom class that derives from `NativeActivity`.

LISTING 12-19: Deriving from NativeCodeActivity Class

```
class HelloWorld_NativeCodeActivity<TResult> : NativeActivity<TResult>
{
    public HelloWorld_NativeCodeActivity()
        : base()
    {
    }

    protected override void Execute(NativeActivityContext context)
    {
        context.CreateBookmark(Guid.NewGuid().ToString(),
new BookmarkCallback(this.Continue));
    }

    void Continue(NativeActivityContext context, Bookmark bookmark, object obj)
    {
        Console.WriteLine((string)obj);
        this.Result.Set(context, (TResult)obj);
    }

    // Must return true for a NativeActivity that creates a bookmark
    protected override bool CanInduceIdle
    {
        get { return true; }
    }

}
```

In previous examples, you passed in a parameter to the workflow at the time of invocation. In this listing, you use the `Bookmark` mechanism to pass data into a running instance of the workflow. You override the `Execute` method to create a `Bookmark`. The name of the `Bookmark` is set to a new instance of `Guid` class. You also pass in the callback delegate `Continue` that is invoked when the `Bookmark` is resumed.

At this point, the `Execute` activity blocks for the `Bookmark` to be resumed. By default, the activity blocks after creating a `Bookmark`. However, you can specify an alternative behavior.

For example, a custom activity may explicitly request a nonblocking behavior if it intends to create more than one `Bookmark` that is active concurrently. It should be noted that the `CreateBookMark` method is available to the custom activity because it derives from the `NativeActivity` base class. The `Bookmark` function is not available to the custom activities that derive from base classes you saw in previous sections, including `CodeActivity` and `AsyncCodeActivity`.

As discussed, it is useful to think of the custom activity's current blocking state as the one in which it is waiting for an external trigger. This is also the state in which the WF 4 runtime can idle the entire workflow instance. Notice that you have overridden the `CanInduceIdle` method to return `true`. When the external trigger does indeed arrive, the `Continue` method will be invoked.

Listing 12-20 shows the code that resumes the `Bookmark`. This code assumes that the external trigger comes in the form of some text entered by the user. In addition to the text, the user also needs the name of the `Bookmark` to be resumed. This is needed because, as discussed, there can be more than one active `Bookmark` created by a workflow.

LISTING 12-20: Resuming Bookmark

```
            Console.WriteLine("Enter the name of the bookmark to resume");
            string bookmarkName = Console.ReadLine();

            if ((!String.IsNullOrEmpty(bookmarkName)) )
            {
                Console.WriteLine("Enter the greeting '{0}'", bookmarkName);
                string bookmarkPayload = Console.ReadLine();

                BookmarkResumptionResult result !=
        application.ResumeBookmark(bookmarkName, bookmarkPayload);
                if (result != BookmarkResumptionResult.Success)
                {
                    Console.WriteLine("BookmarkResumptionResult: " + result);
                }
            }
```

Understanding When to Use Custom Activities

In summary, the `Activity` base class makes it is possible to develop custom activities declaratively using existing activities. This approach enhances reuse and, therefore, should be the preferred option. However, there are instances in which the activity must perform specialized work that requires the development of a code-based activity.

Based on the style of work, custom activities can derive from one of the three base classes:

➤ For work that is short-lived and can be completed without the need to yield control back to the runtime, deriving from the `CodeActivity` is recommended.

➤ For work that can benefit from being done on a separate thread asynchronously (such as invoking a web service), deriving from `AsyncCodeActivity` is recommended.

➤ For long-running work (such as waiting for an external event that can potentially take a significantly long time to complete), deriving from `NativeActivty` is recommended. In addition, deriving from `NativeActivity` is required for an advanced style of work, including creating nested activities, canceling or aborting child activity execution, and accessing custom tracking features.

Composite Activity

Although you have seen examples of prebuilt composite activities, (such as the `Sequence` activity that can contain other activities), you have not built a custom one yet. So, this section focuses on building custom composite activities.

Composite activities represent a parent-child relationship wherein the composite activities act as parents that can, in turn, invoke one or more child activities. The manner in which the child activities are invoked (serially or in parallel) and their order of execution (prioritized or by the order in which the child activities are stacked) is completely up to the author of the composite activity.

It is also common for a composite activity to serve as a control activity. Control activities can help control the order in which the activities are executed. Examples of control activities include `If`, `While`, and `ForEach`. Each of these activities, based on a condition, determine which child activities will be executed.

Because composite and control activities are closely related, now look at an example that combines the two. Build a composite activity called `HelloWorld_CompositeActivity`. This activity can contain zero or more instances of child activities. Additionally, to add a control flow aspect to the composite activity, support both sequential and parallel execution of child activities. Consumers of the `HelloWorld_CompositeActivity` can specify the execution mode by setting the property `IsExecutionSequential`.

The key aspect to develop a composite activity revolves around managing the life cycle of child activities. For all custom activities you have developed so far, you did not concern yourself with the life cycle of the custom activity — that is, the sequence in which the activity is created, scheduled for execution, and ultimately terminated. For the most part, you overrode the `Execute` method and relied on the fact that the WF 4 runtime would invoke it appropriately.

However, when building a composite (parent) activity, the activity author is responsible for managing the life cycle of the child activities. This includes scheduling the execution of child activities, reacting to their completion, and forwarding any cancellation or abort requests it receives on the child activities.

Life Cycle of an Activity

Figure 12-7 shows the life cycle of a WF 4 activity. An activity instance starts out in the `Executing` state. It remains in this state until all its pending work is complete including when it is persisted or unloaded. Upon successful completion, the activity instance transitions to a `Closed` state. If an exception is encountered during the execution, the runtime transitions the activity instance into a `Faulted` state. Likewise, if a cancellation is requested by the host, the runtime transitions the activity to the `Cancelled` state. All three states (`Closed`, `Cancelled`, and `Faulted`) are completion states. In other words, when an activity reaches a completion state, it cannot transition out of it.

Although all custom activities follow the aforementioned activity life cycle, there are differences in the level of control they can exert, based on the base activity class they derive from. For example, custom activities that derive from the `CodeActivity` base class cannot specify a cancellation or an abort handler — these handlers provide an opportunity for the custom activity to clean up before the activity is transitioned into the `Cancelled` or `Faulted` state.

Deriving from `NativeActivity` offers the most control by allowing the derived classes to supply a cancellation and abort handler. In addition, `NativeActivityContext` (an activity context available to activities that derive from `NativeActivity`) enables an activity to detect if a cancellation has been requested. Learning that a cancellation has been requested allows an activity in the `Executing` state to start a graceful shutdown of its ongoing work.

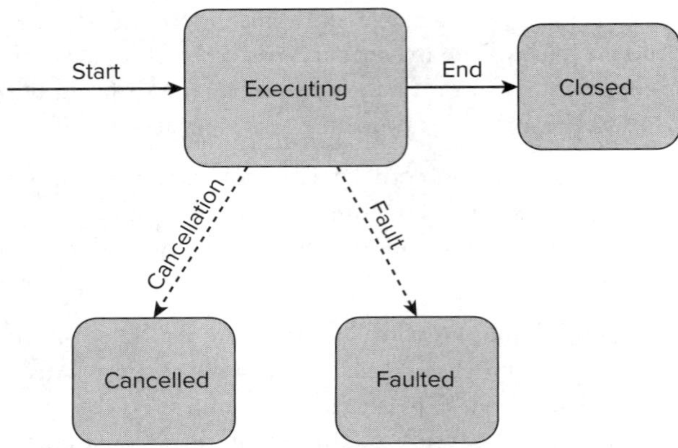

FIGURE 12-7: Life cycle of an activity

Access to the `NativeActivityContext` class also provides the capability to control the life cycle of a child activity. This includes a method for scheduling a child, canceling, and aborting a child activity.

Listing 12-21 shows the key aspects of a composite activity.

LISTING 12-21: Composite Activity

```
protected override void Execute(NativeActivityContext context)
{

        if (IsExecutionSequential)
        {
            // Schedule the first activity.
            if (this.Activities.Count > 0)
                context.ScheduleActivity(this.Activities[0],
                                    this.OnChildCompleted);}
        else
        {
            foreach (Activity child in this.Activities)
            {
                context.ScheduleActivity(child);}
        }
    }


    void OnChildCompleted(NativeActivityContext context,
        ActivityInstance completed)
        {// Calculate the index of the next activity to scheduled.
          int currentExecutingActivity = this.current.Get(context);
          int next = currentExecutingActivity + 1;
          // If index within boundaries....
          if (next < this.Activities.Count)
          {
              // Schedule the next activity.
              context.ScheduleActivity(this.Activities[next],
                                    this.OnChildCompleted);
```

```
            // Store the index in the collection of the activity executing.
            this.current.Set(context, next);
        }
    }
```

The `Execute` method is overridden as in the earlier custom activity examples. Using the local property `Activities`, you access the collection of child activities. Using the value of the `IsExecutionSequential` property, you know whether the consumer wants the child activities to be executed in sequence, or in parallel.

If a sequential execution mode is requested, `ScheduleActivity` is used to schedule the first child. As you would imagine, the parent waits for the currently executing child to complete before scheduling the next child.

The code to achieve this behavior is shown in the callback handler called `OnChildCompleted`. As the name suggests, this callback handler is invoked when the child activity completes. Inside the handler, you schedule the next child activity as needed. A noteworthy aspect of the `OnChildCompleted` method is the workflow variable called `current` that is defined inside the `HelloWorld_CompositeActivity`.

```
    Variable<int> current = new Variable<int>() { Default = 0 };
```

By virtue that `NativeActivityContext` is available inside the callback handler, you can get and set the value of this variable, like so:

```
    this.current.Set(context, next);
```

Alternatively, if a parallel execution mode is requested, all the child activities in the collection are scheduled immediately.

Listing 12-22 shows the code that creates an instance of a `HelloWorld_CompositeActivity` activity that contains two nested instances of `HelloWorld_NativeActivity` activities.

LISTING 12-22: Testing CompositeActivity

```
            return new HelloWorld_CompositeActivity
            {
                IsExecutionSequential = true,
                Activities =
                {
                    new HelloWorld_NativeActivity<string>() { },
                    new HelloWorld_NativeActivity<string>() { },

                }
            };
```

As you have seen, `HelloWorld_NativeActivity` uses a `Bookmark`-based approach to solicit the input from the `console`. In this example, you have set the `IsExecutionSequential` to `true` so that the child activities will be executed in sequence. Consequently, even if the resumption of `Bookmark` associated with the first child took a long time, the second child cannot be scheduled. Alternatively, if you set `IsExecutionSequential` to `false`, it would be possible to schedule the second child without waiting for the first child to complete.

USING PERSISTENCE

The previous section emphasized the benefit of placing a workflow in an idle state when it is waiting for an external trigger. But you have yet to see how the resources associated with an idle workflow can be reclaimed. This is where the persistence capability of WF 4 runtime comes in.

In a nutshell, persistence is about capturing the state of a workflow's instance and saving it in a durable store so that it can be re-created at a later time. After the workflow is persisted, it is possible to completely remove it from the host process, thus freeing up any associated resources.

Persistence has other benefits, too. For example, a persisted workflow can be re-created on a machine different from the one on which it was created. This capability derives from the fact that the workflow instance's captured state is bereft of any machine- or process-specific details. As you can imagine, the capability to re-create an instance on another machine can help with recovery in the event of hardware failure.

Although persistence is something that is, more often than not, initiated by the WF 4 runtime imperatively (when a workflow is idled, or when it completes the execution of a `TransactionScope` activity), it is also possible for a workflow to explicitly invoke persistence. This is achieved by invoking the `Persist` activity.

On the flip side, it is also possible for a workflow program to prevent persistence by using the *no-persist block*. (A no-persist block is actually a region of WF 4 code that sits between calls to `Enter` and `Exit` methods of the `NoPersistHandle` class.)

As you would guess, the WF 4 runtime needs a durable store to capture the workflow instance. The WF 4 runtime provides the `SqlWorkflowInstanceStore` class that is responsible for storing the workflow instance data to SQL Server. `SqlWorkflowInstanceStore` is an implementation of the abstract `InstanceStore` base class that represents an instance store. Here is the code to set up an instance store:

```
SqlWorkflowInstanceStore instanceStore =
new SqlWorkflowInstanceStore(
@"Data Source=.\SQLEXPRESS;Initial    Catalog=WFInstanceStore;Integrated
    Security=True;Asynchronous Processing=True");

        application.InstanceStore = instanceStore;
```

Based on where the workflow is hosted and the type of store, you can choose from a number of implementations of the `InstanceStore` class. Let's now take a look at the instance store provided as part of Windows AppFabric.

HOSTING WORKFLOWS INSIDE WINDOWS APPFABRIC

Windows AppFabric provides services for hosting and monitoring workflow programs. These services are built as extensions to the core Windows Server capabilities provided by Internet Information Server (IIS) and WAS. This section briefly describes how WF 4 developers can use these services.

All throughout this chapter, you have seen examples of WF 4 programs being hosted within a console application (also known as *self-hosting*). However, in a production setting, hosting the WF 4 programs within Windows AppFabric is generally preferable because of the benefits it offers, including auto-start, reliability, monitoring, and scalability. However, be aware that there are scenarios in which hosting within AppFabric may not be possible. For example, a workflow that relies on `WS-Discovery` cannot be hosted within the Windows AppFabric.

Earlier in the chapter, you learned how workflow instances that are idle can be persisted to a durable store. The earlier section, "Using Persistence," discussed the steps needed to enable persistence. Although the steps involved may not seem onerous at first, they can add up to be a significant overhead for the system administrator as the number of workflows grows.

Because a persistence store is part of Windows AppFabric installation by default, setting up persistence is easier. Furthermore, AppFabric provides a management UI to administer the persistence store. For example, there may be a need to configure multiple persistence database instances to avoid bottlenecks in the larger environments.

There is another aspect related to persistence that is worth mentioning here. Generally speaking, two types of events can cause a persisted workflow instance to be reloaded: the arrival of an external trigger (such as an incoming message) or the expiration of the elapsed time of a `Delay` activity. A workflow host must be active to process these events.

Fortunately, AppFabric can help with this as well. Workflow instances hosted within the AppFabric can automatically be started when a message arrives. This is a capability provided by WAS/IIS and is well known to developers. The handling of the expired `Delay` activities requires some additional explanation.

AppFabric installs a Windows service called the Workflow Management Service (WMS) that is responsible for monitoring the persistence store. It gets notified when a workflow is ready to be reloaded. Upon receiving a notification, it calls another AppFabric-provided WCF service called Service Management Service that is then responsible for reloading the workflow instance into memory.

Another store is associated with an AppFabric installation by default. This is the monitoring store. It is used for storing monitoring events emitted by the WF 4 runtime. Similar to the persistence store, the monitoring store can consist of multiple database instances. AppFabric provides tooling to aggregate the collected data that is helpful for performance monitoring and troubleshooting the workflow programs.

Another reason to host workflows within AppFabric relates to command queuing. The command queuing feature provides the capability to queue commands such as a cancellation to a running instance of a workflow program. In the self-hosted scenario, a cancellation request can be made by invoking the `Cancel` method on the class `WorkflowApplication`. As you would imagine, this approach requires some custom plumbing to be built for exposing the command queuing function to the system administrators. AppFabric reduces this burden by providing tooling to queue commands.

Finally, AppFabric offers the capability to set up a farm that includes multiple AppFabric servers. This enables handling of increased loads because the resources from multiple servers can be pooled together. One of the benefits of workflow persistence is that it enables for capturing the state of a workflow in a location-independent manner. (No information about the server executing the workflow is persisted.) This enables another node in the farm to resume the workflow at a later time. This means that a web farm can scale linearly by adding AppFabric nodes. Figure 12-8 shows the web farm made up to AppFabric nodes.

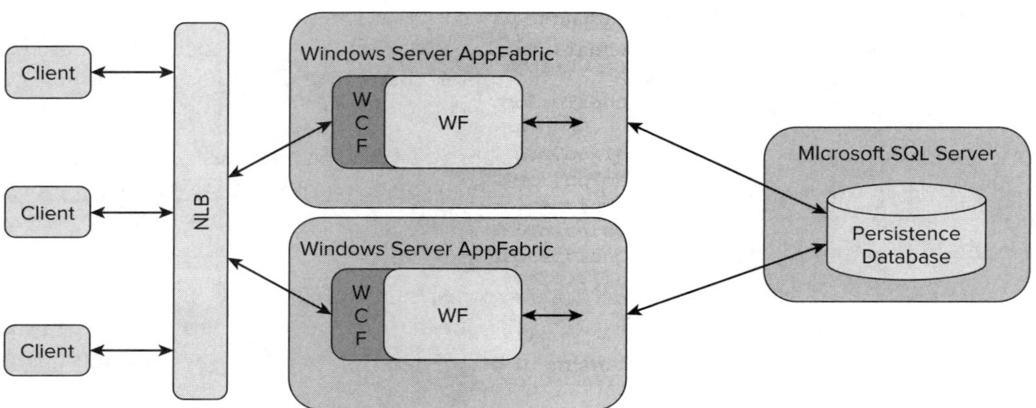

FIGURE 12-8: Scaling out AppFabric-hosted WF 4 programs

FURTHER READING

The primary target audience for this chapter is developers responsible for enabling the authoring of WF 4 programs. Typically, graphical design tools are used to author WF 4 programs. To assist developers in that goal, this chapter focused on the fundamentals of the WF 4 programming language — a behind-the-scene look at the code generated by the graphical design tools. Because of the focus on the language fundamentals, the aspects of the design experience were not explored.

For example, activity authors can build custom designers to make the authoring experience more productive. Another example of customizing the design experience is the capability to rehost the Workflow Designer tool inside a custom application.

As a next step, the following resources are recommended for developers looking to enhance the workflow design experience:

➤ *Custom activity designers* — You can find a collection of samples that use custom designers at `http://msdn.microsoft.com/en-us/library/dd759030.aspx`.

➤ *Designer rehosting* — A sample at `http://msdn.microsoft.com/en-us/library/dd699776.aspx` shows how to create the WPF layout to rehost the designer.

➤ *"Visual Design of Workflows with WCF and WF 4"* — In this article at `http://msdn`
`.microsoft.com/magazine/ff646977`, Leon Welicki offers tips for authoring workflows
within the Workflow Designer.

SUMMARY

In this chapter, you learned about the features of WF 4.0 from a perspective of a higher-level
programming language. You got a "behind the Workflow Designer" look at how WF 4.0 program
is structured and its core constructs, including the key `Activity` class. You learned about different
styles of WF 4.0 programs, including flowchart and procedural styles.

For WF 4.0 programs that need alternate flows of execution, you learned about sequential and
parallel flows of execution. You also built custom activities by inheriting from framework-provided
base classes, including `CodeActivity`, `NativeActivity`, and `AsyncCodeActivity`. And, finally, you
learned about hosting WF 4.0 programs in AppFabric.

ABOUT THE AUTHOR

Vishwas Lele is an AIS (`www.appliedis.com`) Chief Technology Officer, and is responsible for the
company vision and execution of creating business solutions using .NET technologies. Lele has more
than 20 years of experience and is responsible for providing thought leadership in his position. He
has been at AIS for 17 years. A noted industry speaker and author, Lele is the Microsoft Regional
Director for the Washington, D.C., area.

13

Practical WPF Data Binding

by Christian Nagel

This chapter provides practical information on data binding with Windows Presentation Foundation (WPF). It leads you on a journey to see various aspects of data binding and how you can use it. Simple object binding, as well as list binding (including validation and how to deal with large lists), are explained. Don't expect to see cool user interfaces (UIs) with WPF in this chapter. The UI is kept simple. Various features of WPF for styling, animations, and three dimensional (3D) are not discussed. This chapter focuses only on data binding with WPF.

SAMPLE APPLICATION

The sample application used in this chapter is based on a `Formula 1` database. Instead of just binding to in-memory data, a database with several tables and thousands of rows demonstrates data-binding features. You can download the database, along with the sample code for this chapter, on this book's companion website (`www.wrox.com`).

The database contains information about Formula 1 racers, circuits, and race results. With the application, racers can be queried and changed, and race results can be added.

Figure 13-1 shows the database structure. The `Circuits` table contains information about all Formula 1 circuits that have been raced on. You can find the race date for circuits in the `Races` table. Each record in the `Races` table connects to a list of records in `RaceResults`. An entry in `RaceResults` contains a link to one record in the `Racers` table and one record in the `Teams` table.

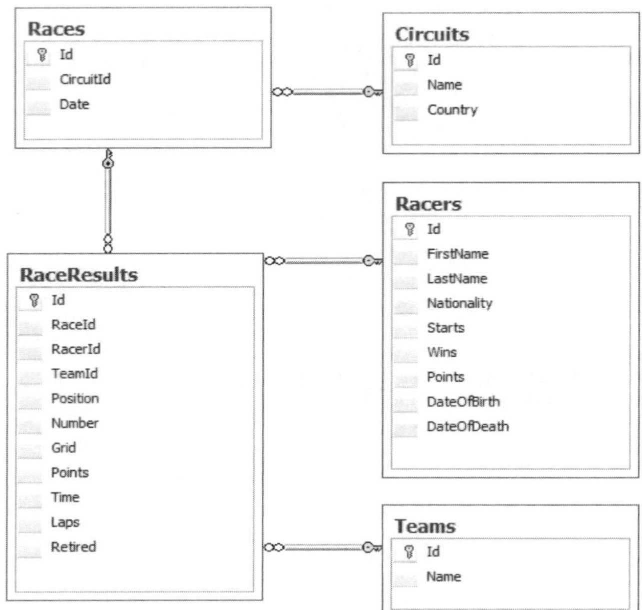

FIGURE 13-1: Database structure for sample application

Using MVVM

In WPF, with applications that are bigger, or ones that should be expanded over time, it is a good practice to make use of the Model-View-ViewModel (MVVM) pattern. This pattern is an adaptation of the Model-View-Controller (MVC) pattern that takes advantages of WPF features. And guess what? The WPF feature that this pattern is based on is *data binding*. That's why the sample code of this chapter makes use of this pattern as well.

With the MVVM pattern, the entities (Model) are separated from the presentation (View) with the help of the ViewModel. Figure 13-2 shows the architectural overview of this pattern. The Model represents the data classes. The View is the UI designed using Extensible Application Markup Language (XAML). The UI displays data, enables editing of data, and invokes methods of the ViewModel with the help of commands. The ViewModel is an adapter of the model to offer specific features for the View. It offers commands that are invoked by the View, and offers data that is read and written by the View.

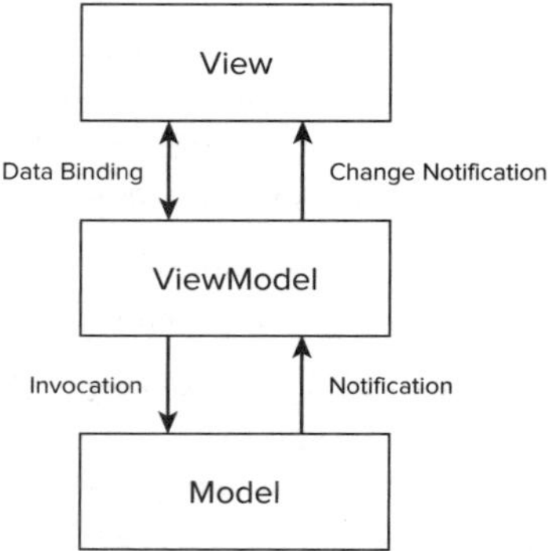

FIGURE 13-2: Architectural overview of MVVM pattern

Instead of using a command handler from the code-behind file of the XAML file, the separation done with the MVVM pattern enables easy *unit testing* of the functionality by writing test code for the ViewModel, and enables a *better separation between developers and UI designers*.

To use the MVVM pattern, you can use any of several available frameworks, such as Prism from Microsoft, which is available at `www.microsoft.com/prism`, the MVVM Light Toolkit (`www.galasoft.ch/mvvm/getstarted`) from Laurent Bugneon. This chapter doesn't make use of an MVVM framework, but you can easily adapt to any framework you prefer.

For more information on MVVM and the Prism framework, see Chapter 7.

Understanding the Sample Application Structure

To use the MVVM pattern, the classes of the solution must be structured into Model classes, ViewModel classes, and View classes. The sample solution makes use of separate `Model`, `ViewModels`, and `Views` folders within the project, as shown in Figure 13-3. These folders also have different namespaces for the classes that they contain.

You can also get an even bigger separation by splitting the parts of the pattern into different assemblies. This helps by not adding unwanted dependencies between the layers of the pattern. With Visual Studio 2010 Ultimate Edition, you can also use the Layer Diagram to verify the layer structure if just a single assembly is used.

The project also contains an `Infrastructure` folder that contains helper classes.

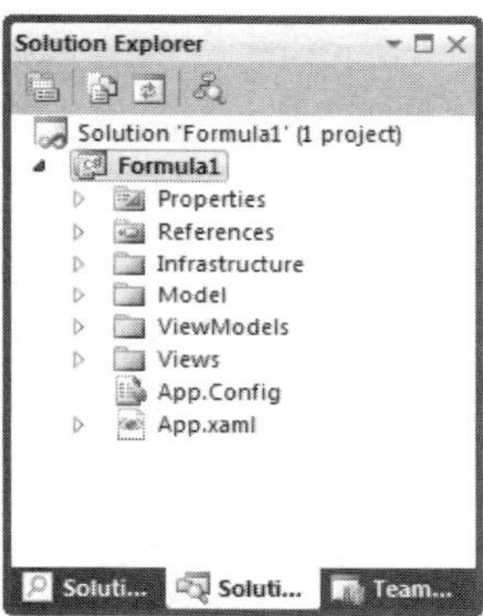

FIGURE 13-3: Folder structure for sample application

Understanding the Model

The Model contains entity classes. The sample application makes use of the ADO.NET Entity Framework (EF) because data needs to be retrieved and updated. For WPF data binding, it's actually not important what technology you use to read and update the data. You can use ADO.NET directly from the WPF application, or make use of a communication technology such as Windows Communication Foundation (WCF) or WCF Data Services. WPF data binding makes use of .NET objects to bind to, and that's no different than if ADO.NET, WCF, or WCF Data Services is used.

Figure 13-4 shows the EF data model used with the application. The model used here is a simple 1:1 mapping to the database. `Racer` and `Team` entities map to the `Racers` and `Teams` tables. Both `Racer` and `Team` have an association with `RaceResult` objects. `RaceResult` has an n-to-1 relationship with `Race`, and `Race` is associated with `Circuit`.

The designer creates partial classes that can easily be extended with custom code that is not changed when the designer re-creates the code. The `Racer` type is extended with a method `ToString` and a property `Name`, as shown here:

```csharp
namespace Formula1.Model
{
    public partial class Racer
    {
        public override string ToString()
```

```
        {
            return string.Format("{0} {1}", FirstName, LastName);
        }

        public string Name
        {
            get
            {
                return ToString();
            }
        }
    }
}
```

Code file [Model/Racer.cs] available for download at Wrox.com.

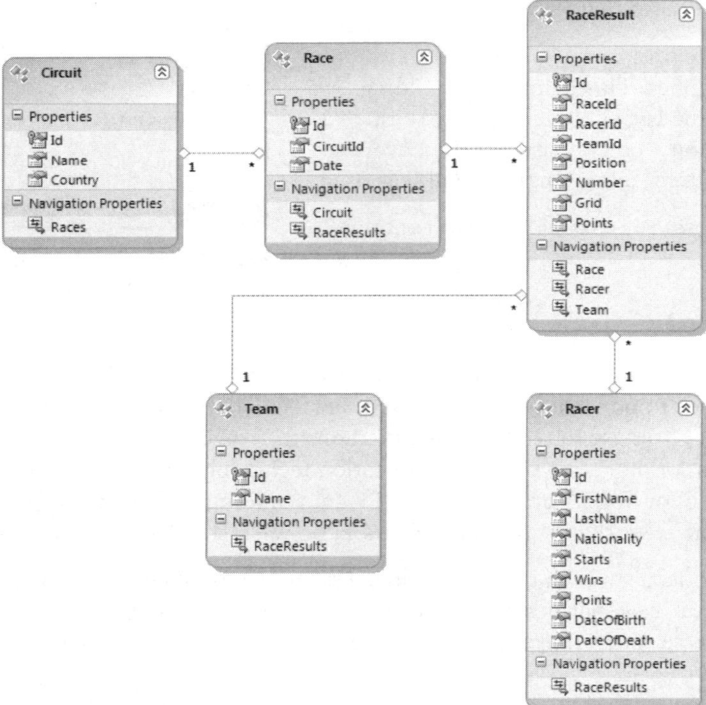

FIGURE 13-4: EF data model for sample application

Understanding the ViewModel

The ViewModel defines commands and properties that you can use for data binding. To notify the UI about changes to the properties, the `INotifyPropertyChanged` interface is implemented in the ViewModel classes. To get this functionality across all ViewModel classes, the base class `ViewModelBase` (shown in the following code snippet) implements this interface by offering the

`PropertyChanged` event. In addition to this interface, the base class also defines the `IsDesignTime` property. This property can be used to offer sample data for the Visual Studio and Visual Blend designers without accessing the database or a service.

The `ViewModelBase` class also provides an error-handling functionality that can be used to report errors to the View using the `HasError` and `ErrorMessage` properties, and the `SetError` and `ClearError` methods.

```csharp
public abstract class ViewModelBase : INotifyPropertyChanged
{
    public event PropertyChangedEventHandler PropertyChanged;

    protected virtual void RaisePropertyChanged(string propertyName)
    {
        PropertyChangedEventHandler handler = PropertyChanged;
        if (handler != null)
            handler(this, new PropertyChangedEventArgs(propertyName));
    }

    protected bool IsDesignTime
    {
        get
        {
            return DesignerProperties.GetIsInDesignMode
                (new DependencyObject());
        }
    }

    private bool hasError;
    public bool HasError
    {
        get { return hasError; }
        private set
        {
            hasError = value;
            RaisePropertyChanged("HasError");
        }
    }

    private string errorMessage;
    public string ErrorMessage
    {
        get { return errorMessage; }
        private set
        {
            errorMessage = value;
            RaisePropertyChanged("ErrorMessage");
        }
    }

    public void SetError(string errorMessage)
    {
        ErrorMessage = errorMessage;
        HasError = true;
```

```
        }

        public void ClearError()
        {
            ErrorMessage = null;
            HasError = false;
        }
    }
```

Code file [ViewModels/ViewModelBase.cs] available for download at Wrox.com.

A concrete ViewModel class derives from `ViewModelBase`. An example is the `ShowRacerViewModel` class. This class contains commands and properties used by the Views. The implementation of these will be explained soon during a discussion of data binding to commands and data binding to simple properties.

```
using System.Data.Objects;
using System.Linq;
using Formula1.Infrastructure;
using Formula1.Model;

namespace Formula1.ViewModels
{
    public class ShowRacerViewModel : ViewModelBase, IDisposable
    {
        // commands and properties for the view
    }
}
```

Code file [ViewModels/ShowRacerViewModel.cs] available for download at Wrox.com.

Understanding the View

Views are implemented with XAML. The following sample code makes use of user controls. The `ShowRacerView.xaml` file defines the UI representation for the view to display a racer.

```
<UserControl x:Class="Formula1.Views.ShowRacerView"
        xmlns="http://schemas.microsoft.com/winfx/2006/xaml/presentation"
        xmlns:x="http://schemas.microsoft.com/winfx/2006/xaml"
        xmlns:mc="http://schemas.openxmlformats.org/markup-
            compatibility/2006"
        xmlns:d="http://schemas.microsoft.com/expression/blend/2008"
        xmlns:utils="clr-namespace:Formula1.Infrastructure"
        mc:Ignorable="d"
        d:DesignHeight="300" d:DesignWidth="300">
    <Grid>
    <!-- user interface elements -->
    </Grid>
</UserControl>
```

Code file [Views/ShowRacerView.xaml] available for download at Wrox.com.

Using a Locator Class

The MVVM pattern does not define how the View matches with the ViewModel, nor how different Views can interact. Different frameworks use different techniques. One way to map the View and ViewModel is to use a locator class that knows about all the ViewModel types. Other approaches make use of the Managed Extensibility Framework (MEF) or a dependency injection/inversion of control container to reduce strong dependencies.

Because the various approaches don't make a difference on how data binding is done, the sample code in this chapter takes a simple approach that doesn't add complexity for this purpose.

The sample application uses a locator class that contains a collection of all the ViewModel types used by the main window, as is shown next. The `ViewModelInfo` class is used by the locator to have names to display inside the UI for every View, and a reference to the type `ViewModel`. The `ViewModel` property is of type `Lazy<T>` so that the ViewModel type is not immediately instantiated when the locator is instantiated, but only when the `Value` property of the type `Lazy<T>` is accessed.

```
public class ViewModelInfo
{
    public string Name { get; set; }
    public Lazy<ViewModelBase> ViewModel { get; set; }
}
```

Code file [ViewModels/ViewModelInfo.cs] available for download at Wrox.com.

The `Formula1Locator` class implements the `IEnumerable<ViewModelInfo>` interface to return an enumerator of the type `ViewModelInfo` that returns names and lazy types to instantiate the ViewModel types, as shown here:

```
public class Formula1Locator : IEnumerable<ViewModelInfo>, IDisposable
{
    private List<ViewModelInfo> viewModels;

    public Formula1Locator()
    {
        viewModels = new List<ViewModelInfo>()
          {
            new ViewModelInfo
            {
                Name = "Show Racer",
                ViewModel = new Lazy<ViewModelBase>(() => new
                    ShowRacerViewModel())
            },
            new ViewModelInfo
            {
                Name="Show Racers",
                ViewModel= new Lazy<ViewModelBase>(() => new
                    ShowRacersViewModel())
            },
            new ViewModelInfo
            {
                Name="Show Racers with Details",
```

```
                    ViewModel= new Lazy<ViewModelBase>(() =>
                        new ShowRacersWithDetailViewModel())
                }
                // ...more ViewModelInfo instances...
            }
        }

        public IEnumerator<ViewModelInfo> GetEnumerator()
        {
            return viewModels.GetEnumerator();
        }

        System.Collections.IEnumerator
            System.Collections.IEnumerable.GetEnumerator()
        {
            return GetEnumerator();
        }

        protected virtual void Dispose(bool disposing)
        {
            if (disposing)
            {
                foreach (var viewModel in viewModels)
                {
                    if (viewModel.ViewModel.Value != null)
                    {
                        IDisposable disp = viewModel.ViewModel.Value
                            as IDisposable;
                        if (disp != null)
                        {
                            disp.Dispose();
                        }
                    }
                }
            }
        }

        public void Dispose()
        {
            Dispose(true);
        }
    }
```

Code file [ViewModels/Formula1Locator.cs] available for download at Wrox.com.

The type `Formula1Locator` is globally instantiated and available as an application-wide resource in the `App.xaml` file with the key name `Locator`.

```
<Application.Resources>
    <viewModels:Formula1Locator x:Key="Locator" />
</Application.Resources>
```

Code file [App.xaml] available for download at Wrox.com.

The following XAML code snippet for the type `MainWindow` shows the main window. The `DataContext` property of the `Grid` control references the locator by its key with the help of the static resource markup extension `{StaticResource Locator}`. This makes it possible for all elements within the grid to bind to properties of the locator.

```xml
<Window x:Class="Formula1.Views.MainWindow"
        xmlns="http://schemas.microsoft.com/winfx/2006/xaml/presentation"
        xmlns:x="http://schemas.microsoft.com/winfx/2006/xaml"
        Title="Formula 1" Height="300" Width="300">
    <Grid DataContext="{StaticResource Locator}">
        <Grid.ColumnDefinitions>
            <ColumnDefinition Width="Auto" />
            <ColumnDefinition />
        </Grid.ColumnDefinitions>
        <TabControl Grid.Column="1" ItemsSource="{Binding}">
            <TabControl.ItemTemplate>
                <DataTemplate>
                    <StackPanel Orientation="Horizontal">
                        <TextBlock Text="{Binding Name}" />
                    </StackPanel>
                </DataTemplate>
            </TabControl.ItemTemplate>
            <TabControl.ContentTemplate>
                <DataTemplate>
                    <ContentControl Content="{Binding ViewModel.Value}" />
                </DataTemplate>
            </TabControl.ContentTemplate>
        </TabControl>
    </Grid>
</Window>
```

Code file [Views/MainWindow.xaml] available for download at Wrox.com.

The main UI consists of a `TabControl`, where every tab displays a separate view. The `ItemsSource` property makes use of the binding markup extension `{Binding}` to bind the complete list that is returned from the locator. Every item within the `TabControl` (defined with `ItemTemplate` and `ContentTemplate`) binds to a single item of the list. The `ItemTemplate` defines the header of the `TabItem` controls.

With the header, just the name of the view displays within a `TextBlock` binding the `Text` property to the `Name` property of the `ViewModelInfo` that is returned from the locator. The content of the `TabItem` controls displays only when the user clicks the tab header. Then a `ContentControl` displays that binds the `Content` property to `ViewModel.Value`. `Value` is a property of the type `Lazy<T>` that finally instantiates the type that derives from `ViewModelBase`, as defined by the locator.

The mapping from the ViewModel types to the views is defined in the `App.xaml` file with data templates. The following code snippet shows some of the mappings. For example, the `ShowRacerViewModel` type uses `ShowRacerView` as a UI representation. Accordingly, the `ShowRacersWithDetailViewModel` type uses the type `ShowRacersWithDetailView`.

```xml
<Application.Resources>
    <viewModels:Formula1Locator x:Key="Locator" />
    <DataTemplate DataType="{x:Type viewModels:ShowRacerViewModel}">
        <views:ShowRacerView />
    </DataTemplate>
    <DataTemplate DataType="{x:Type viewModels:ShowRacersViewModel}">
        <views:ShowRacersView />
    </DataTemplate>
    <DataTemplate DataType="{x:Type viewModels:ShowRacersCVSViewModel}">
        <views:ShowRacersCVSView />
    </DataTemplate>
    <DataTemplate DataType=
            "{x:Type viewModels:ShowRacersWithDetailViewModel}">
        <views:ShowRacersWithDetailView />
    </DataTemplate>
    <!-- ... -->
</Application.Resources>
```

Code file [App.xaml] available for download at Wrox.com.

With this mapping, the View type automatically has the data context assigned to the ViewModel type to which it is connected.

Figure 13-5 shows the main window of the application. Here you can see the `TabControl` with all the items that are returned from the locator, and the content of one of the Views is active.

You now have seen the main architecture of the application and some data binding in action. Now it's time to get into the details of data binding.

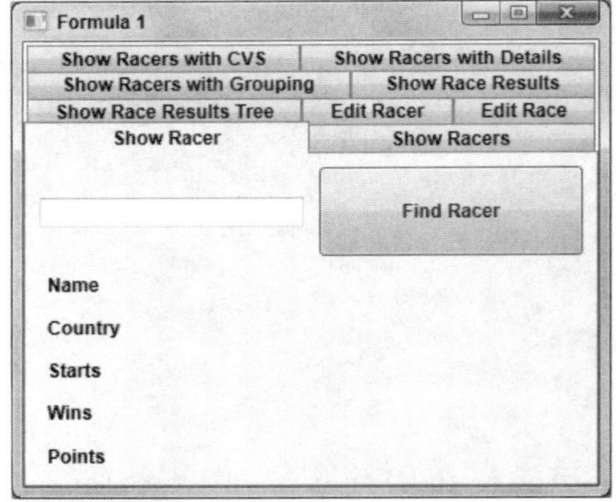

FIGURE 13-5: Main window of the sample application

DATA BINDING OVERVIEW

WPF data binding is based on the `Binding` class. With data binding, you can bind a dependency property of a UI element to a simple property of a .NET object. The `Binding` class connects a source (.NET object) and a target (UI element). The `Binding` class defines the `Source` property to define the source of the data, and the `Path` property, where the name of the property to bind to can be defined. The following code snippet shows binding with code-behind:

```csharp
var p1 = new Person { FirstName = "Matthias", LastName = "Nagel" };
var binding = new Binding { Path = new PropertyPath("FirstName"),
                            Source=p1};
text1.SetBinding(TextBox.TextProperty, binding);
```

First, an instance of the class `Person` is created. (This class defines `FirstName` and `LastName` properties.) The `Binding` instance assigns the `Path` property to the `FirstName` property name of the `Person` class, and the `Source` property to the `Person` instance.

To map the binding to the UI element, the `SetBinding` method of a `TextBox` named `text1` is invoked. The first parameter of `SetBinding` requires a `DependencyProperty`. The second parameter is an instance of a class that derives from `BindingBase`. With the following code, the `Text` property of the `TextBox` is bound to the binding variable that binds to the `FirstName` property.

To show data binding in XAML instead of code-behind, a `Person` object is instantiated and filled with values from XAML, as shown here:

```xml
<Window.Resources>
    <local:Person x:Key="p2">
        <local:Person.FirstName>Stephanie</local:Person.FirstName>
        <local:Person.LastName>Nagel</local:Person.LastName>
    </local:Person>
</Window.Resources>
```

With XAML, the `Binding` markup extension can be used to bind a `Text` property of a `TextBox` to the `FirstName` property and the source referenced using the key from the resources.

```xml
<TextBox Text="{Binding Source={StaticResource p2}, Path=FirstName}" />
```

`Path` is a default property for the `Binding` markup extension, and the XAML code can be simplified as shown here:

```xml
<TextBox Text="{Binding LastName, Source={StaticResource p2}}" />
```

In some scenarios, you must use the longer form of the XAML binding syntax. Instead of using an attribute, you can use an element as well, as shown here:

```xml
<TextBox>
    <TextBox.Text>
        <Binding Path="FirstName">
            <Binding.Source>
                <StaticResource ResourceKey="p2" />
            </Binding.Source>
        </Binding>
    </TextBox.Text>
</TextBox>
```

Understanding Data Context

Instead of assigning the source with the binding expression, the `DataContext` property can be assigned. In the following simplification of the previous version of code-behind, data binding assigns the `DataContext` of the `TextBox` named `text1` to the `Person` instance p1 before setting the binding of the `TextBox` with an overload of the `SetBinding` method that just requires a property name of the source with the second parameter:

```csharp
text1.DataContext = p1;
text1.SetBinding(TextBox.TextProperty, "FirstName");
```

Using data context has a big advantage in that it is used hierarchically. If the property `DataContext` is not assigned with the control that has the binding defined, the parent control is checked for a

`DataContext`. In the following code snippet, the `DataContext` is assigned to the `StackPanel`, and the `TextBox` controls within the `StackPanel` make use of the same data context. Checking the data context goes up through the complete hierarchy of the XAML elements.

```
<StackPanel DataContext="{StaticResource p2}">
    <TextBox Text="{Binding FirstName}" />
    <TextBox Text="{Binding LastName}" />
</StackPanel>
```

Understanding Element-to-Element Binding

The source for binding can be a UI element as well. Dependency properties of WPF controls can be accessed via normal property syntax, so this shouldn't be a surprise. Element-to-element binding is defined by using the `ElementName` property of the `Binding` class.

The following code snippet binds the `Text` property of a `TextBlock` element to the `Value` property of the `Slider` control that has the name `slider1`. Thus, the `TextBlock` displays the current value of the slider.

```
<Slider x:Name="slider1" Minimum="0" Maximum="100" SmallChange="1"
        IsSnapToTickEnabled="True" />
<TextBlock Text="{Binding ElementName=slider1, Path=Value}" />
```

Understanding Binding Modes

The direction of a binding can be defined by setting the binding mode. The `Binding` class defines a `Mode` property of `BindingMode` type.

`BindingMode` is an enumeration that defines if the values should be directed from the source to the target (`OneTime` and `OneWay`), from the target to the source (`OneWayToSource`), or both directions (`TwoWay`). The difference between `OneTime` and `OneWay` is that, with `OneTime`, the value from the source is read only once, and with `OneWay`, changes to the source values are taken care of in the UI.

The default value of the `BindingMode` enumeration depends on the target property and element. Although the `Text` property of the `TextBox` control is, by default, `TwoWay`, the `Text` property of the `TextBlock` has the default `OneWay`.

Binding Based on Interfaces

WPF data binding makes use of several .NET interfaces. This section examines the important interfaces for data binding.

To get changes from the source to the target, the source must implement the `INotifyPropertyChanged` interface. (Or the source must be a dependency property that has a similar notification feature.) With the sample code you've seen so far, the base class `ViewModelBase` implements `INotifyPropertyChanged` to notify the View of property changes.

To get information on a collection change, the `INotifyCollectionChanged` interface must be implemented with the collection. The `ObservableCollection<T>` class implements this interface.

An alternative to the `INotifyCollectionChanged` *interface that is of special interest when mixing WPF and Windows Forms applications is the* `IBindingList` *interface. This is supported by WPF for collection changes as well.* `IBindingList` *is implemented for collection notification with Windows Forms.*

In addition to dealing with exceptions, WPF supports the `IDataErrorInfo` interface to validate bound source objects. This interface enables checking properties for valid values. Later in this chapter, you learn more about this binding feature.

For converting values to be used with data binding, the `IValueConverter` interface can be implemented. The `IMultiValueConverter` interface enables converting multiple properties of a source to a single property of a UI element.

To bind collections, WPF uses the `IEnumerable` and `IList` interfaces. For filtering and sorting collections, the `ICollectionView` interface is used. You learn more about these interfaces later in this chapter in the "Binding to Lists" section.

Now it's time get into a bigger example that continues through all the following sections of this chapter. This example shows various binding features and how they can be practically used. Let's begin by looking at commands to interact with the ViewModel from the View.

USING BINDING COMMANDS

In addition to supporting .NET events and event handlers that are connected to the events, WPF supports commands. Commands offer a better separation from the source to the target.

For example, the `Button` class defines a `Click` event and a `Command` property. The `Button` class is a command source that invokes a command. With the `Click` event, a handler can be assigned that fulfills the requirements of the `RoutedEventHandler` delegate.

Using XAML 2006 with Visual Studio 2010, event handlers are tightly bound to the XAML. The event handler (in the code-behind file) must be available when the XAML code is compiled. With MVVM, a looser coupling is preferred. This can be achieved by using commands.

The `Command` property of the `Button` class enables assigning a command. A command must implement the `ICommand` interface. The .NET Framework offers some predefined commands in the `ApplicationCommands`, `NavigationCommands`, `MediaCommands`, `EditingCommands`, and `ComponentCommands` classes. The commands are defined using static properties.

For example, the `ApplicationCommands` class defines a static `Open` property that returns a `RoutedUICommand`. `RoutedUICommand` implements the `ICommand` interface. Such a command can be assigned to a `Command` property of a `Button` control, as shown in the following code snippet. With predefined commands, just the name of the command must be written to the XAML file, instead prefixing it with the class name. This shortcut is available in .NET 4 and later editions.

```
<Button Content="Open" Command="Open" />
```

What happens when the command is fired (when the button is clicked) is not defined by the command itself. Instead, command bindings bind commands to event handlers.

In the following code snippet, the `CommandBindings` of the `Window` define that, if the `Open` command is fired, the `OnOpen` method is invoked. The `CommandBinding` class defines `Executed` and `CanExecute` properties to define event handlers that are executed when the command is fired, and with `CanExecute` it is checked if the command is available. For example, if a file is opened and not yet changed, the `Save` command might not be available.

```xml
<Window.CommandBindings>
    <CommandBinding Command="Open" Executed="OnOpen" />
</Window.CommandBindings>
```

Command bindings are searched in a hierarchy. The `CommandBindings` property is defined with the `UIElement` class that is a base class of every WPF element. This way, controls can define command bindings and implement the handlers. Thus, it is necessary only to define the command source. The `TextBox` class implements handlers for `Cut`, `Copy`, `Paste`, and `Undo` commands, and it is necessary only to define command sources for these commands (for example, `MenuItem` elements).

Using MVVM and DelegateCommand

With the MVVM pattern, the command binding from within the XAML file is not helpful because, with the command binding, tight coupling to the command target is used. With MVVM, a command and the handler are defined by a ViewModel class, and loose coupling is done by binding the command.

To make this possible, an implementation of the `ICommand` is needed that invokes a handler defined by a delegate. An implementation is shown in the following code snippet. `DelegateCommand` implements the `ICommand` interface with the implementation of the `Execute` and `CanExecute` methods. The `Execute` and `CanExecute` methods invoke delegates assigned in the constructor of the class.

```csharp
using System;
using System.Windows.Input;

namespace Formula1.Infrastructure
{
    public class DelegateCommand : ICommand
    {
        private readonly Action<object> execute;
        private readonly Func<object, bool> canExecute;

        public DelegateCommand(Action<object> execute)
            : this(execute, null)
        {
        }

        public DelegateCommand(Action<object> execute, Func<object, bool>
            canExecute)
        {
            this.execute = execute;
            this.canExecute = canExecute;
        }
```

```csharp
        public bool CanExecute(object parameter)
        {
            return canExecute == null ? true : canExecute(parameter);
        }

        public event EventHandler CanExecuteChanged
        {
            add
            {
                CommandManager.RequerySuggested += value;
            }
            remove
            {
                CommandManager.RequerySuggested -= value;
            }
        }

        public void Execute(object parameter)
        {
            execute(parameter);
        }
    }
}
```

Code file [Infrastructure/DelegateCommand.cs] available for download at Wrox.com.

 *A class like the* `DelegateCommand` *is part of most MVVM frameworks.*

Creating a ViewModel

The first sample of the `Formula 1` application shows how the values of the `Racer` type can be shown on the user interface. The sample does not show any racer, but instead a racer who is queried for by the name of the racer. Starting the query is done by using a command.

The View to show the racer is `ShowRacerView.xaml`. The corresponding file that contains the ViewModel type is `ShowRacerViewModel.cs`. The class `ShowRacerViewModel` derives from the base class `ViewModelBase`.

```csharp
using System.Data;
using System.Data.Objects;
using System.Linq;
using Formula1.Infrastructure;
using Formula1.Model;

namespace Formula1.ViewModels
{
    public class ShowRacerViewModel : ViewModelBase
    {
```

Code file [ViewModels/ShowRacerViewModel.cs] available for download at Wrox.com.

This ViewModel class defines a command started from the user interface, as examined next.

Defining Commands with ViewModels

The previously defined `DelegateCommand` class can be used in ViewModel classes. The code snippet shown from the `ShowRacerViewModel` class offers the `FindRacerCommand` as a read-only property. This property can be used for data binding. The implementation of the `get` accessor returns the value of the `findRacerCommand` if it is not `null`. If it is `null`, a new `DelegateCommand` instance is created where a call to the `FindRacer` method is assigned to the constructor with a lambda expression.

```
private DelegateCommand findRacerCommand;
public DelegateCommand FindRacerCommand
{
    get
    {
        return findRacerCommand ??
            (findRacerCommand = new DelegateCommand(
                param => this.FindRacer(param)));
    }
}
```

Code file [ViewModels/ShowRacerViewModel.cs] available for download at Wrox.com.

As a reminder, `??` is the coalescing operator. The coalescing operator verifies if the preceding variable is `null`. If it is not `null`, just the value is returned. If it is `null`, the expression followed by the coalescing operator is invoked. The coalescing operator was invented with nullable value types and is useful with reference types as well.

The implementation of the `FindRacer` method makes a query using the ADO.NET EF and the object context that was created from the ADO.NET entity designer. The result of the query is assigned to the `Racer` property of the `ShowRacerViewModel` class. In the case of an EF exception, the `SetError` method of the base class is invoked to give some error information to the View.

```
public void FindRacer(object name)
{
    try
    {
        string filter = (string)name;
        using (Formula1Entities data = new Formula1Entities())
        {
            var q = (from r in data.Racers
                     where r.LastName.StartsWith(filter)
                     select r);

            Racer = (q as ObjectQuery<Racer>).
                    Execute(MergeOption.NoTracking).FirstOrDefault();
        }
    }
```

```
        catch (EntityException)
        {
            SetError("Verify the database connection");
        }
    }

    private Racer racer;
    public Racer Racer
    {
        get { return racer; }
        set
        {
            if (!object.Equals(racer, value))
            {
                racer = value;
                RaisePropertyChanged("Racer");
            }
        }
    }
```

Code file [ViewModels/ShowRacerViewModel.cs] available for download at Wrox.com.

The sample code offers a Racer *object directly with the* Racer *property. Instead, you could also offer* FirstName, LastName, Nationality... *properties directly from the ViewModel class. If the user interface needs properties that are somehow different from the entity type, it could be done this way. Here, the entity type fulfills all features needed by the UI and, thus, can be offered directly to the UI.*

Binding Commands from XAML Code

In the XAML code of the View, a Button can be defined that binds the Command property to the DelegateCommand instance of the FindRacerCommand property from the ViewModel class. Clicking the button results in the command being executed, and because this DelegateCommand references the FindRacer method, the method is invoked.

Because the FindRacer method has a parameter, a parameter must be sent to the command. This is done by assigning the CommandParameter property of the Button. The FindRacer method requires the name of the racer for returning a racer, so the value should be assigned dynamically from the UI. This again is done via data binding. The value of the parameter comes from the Text property of the TextBox that has the name textName.

```
<TextBox x:Name="textName" Grid.Row="0" Grid.Column="0"
        Margin="5" VerticalAlignment="Center" />
<Button Grid.Row="0" Grid.Column="1" Content="Find Racer" Margin="5"
        Command="{Binding FindRacerCommand}"
        CommandParameter="{Binding ElementName=textName, Path=Text,
            Mode=OneWay}" />
```

Code file [Views/ShowRacerView.xaml] available for download at Wrox.com.

Instead of using command parameters, you can also bind the property Text *of the* TextBox *to a property of the ViewModel class (for example, a* FindName *property) and use the property* FindName *within the method* FindRacer *instead of the parameter of* FindRacer*. Usually, this is just a matter of taste.*

When you bind the command to the UI, now the FindRacer method is invoked when the button is clicked. The FindRacer method then assigns the result to the Racer property. What's missing is a display of the racer. This is done next.

USING SIMPLE DATA BINDING

To display information on a racer, several TextBlock elements are created. The Text properties of the TextBlock elements are bound to Nationality, Starts, and Wins properties. These controls are within a Grid control that has the DataContext set to bind to the Racer property of the ViewModel.

Within the outer Grid control that binds directly to the ViewModel is a TextBlock with a red foreground that binds the Text property to the ErrorMessage property to display error information.

Another option without assigning the DataContext to a parent element would be to bind to Racer.Nationality instead of Nationality. Also, be aware that the command bound to the FindRacerCommand property is outside of the Grid with the DataContext and, thus, binds to the property of the ViewModel class directly.

```xml
<UserControl x:Class="Formula1.Views.ShowRacerView"
             xmlns="http://schemas.microsoft.com/winfx/2006/xaml/presentation"
             xmlns:x="http://schemas.microsoft.com/winfx/2006/xaml"
             xmlns:mc="http://schemas.openxmlformats.org/markup-
                 compatibility/2006"
             xmlns:d="http://schemas.microsoft.com/expression/blend/2008"
             xmlns:utils="clr-namespace:Formula1.Infrastructure"
             mc:Ignorable="d"
             d:DesignHeight="300" d:DesignWidth="300">
    <UserControl.Resources>
        <Style TargetType="TextBlock">
            <Style.Setters>
                <Setter Property="VerticalAlignment" Value="Center" />
                <Setter Property="Margin" Value="10,7,5,7" />
            </Style.Setters>
        </Style>
    </UserControl.Resources>
    <Grid>
        <Grid.RowDefinitions>
            <RowDefinition Height="*" />
            <RowDefinition Height="Auto" />
            <RowDefinition Height="Auto" />
        </Grid.RowDefinitions>
        <Grid.ColumnDefinitions>
            <ColumnDefinition />
```

```xml
                    <ColumnDefinition />
                </Grid.ColumnDefinitions>
                <TextBox x:Name="textName" Grid.Row="0" Grid.Column="0" Margin="5"
                        VerticalAlignment="Center" />
                <Button Grid.Row="0" Grid.Column="1" Content="Find Racer" Margin="5"
                        Command="{Binding FindRacerCommand}"
                        CommandParameter="{Binding ElementName=textName, Path=Text,
                            Mode=OneWay}" />

                <Grid Grid.Row="1" Grid.ColumnSpan="2" DataContext="{Binding Racer}">
                    <Grid.RowDefinitions>
                        <RowDefinition Height="Auto" />
                        <RowDefinition Height="Auto" />
                        <RowDefinition Height="Auto" />
                        <RowDefinition Height="Auto" />
                        <RowDefinition Height="Auto" />
                    </Grid.RowDefinitions>
                    <Grid.ColumnDefinitions>
                        <ColumnDefinition />
                        <ColumnDefinition />
                    </Grid.ColumnDefinitions>

                    <TextBlock Text="Name" Grid.Row="0" Grid.Column="0" />
                    <TextBlock Grid.Row="0" Grid.Column="1" />
                    <TextBlock Text="Country" Grid.Row="1" Grid.Column="0" />
                    <TextBlock Grid.Row="1" Grid.Column="1"
                            Text="{Binding Nationality}" />
                    <TextBlock Text="Starts" Grid.Row="2" Grid.Column="0" />
                    <TextBlock Grid.Row="2" Grid.Column="1" Text="{Binding Starts}" />
                    <TextBlock Text="Wins" Grid.Row="3" Grid.Column="0" />
                    <TextBlock Grid.Row="3" Grid.Column="1" Text="{Binding Wins}" />
                    <TextBlock Text="Points" Grid.Row="4" Grid.Column="0" />
                    <TextBlock Grid.Row="4" Grid.Column="1" Text="{Binding Points}" />
                </Grid>
                <TextBlock Foreground="Red" Text="{Binding ErrorMessage}" Grid.Row="2"
                        Grid.Column="0" Grid.ColumnSpan="2" />
            </Grid>
    </UserControl>
```

Code file [Views/ShowRacerView.xaml] available for download at Wrox.com.

The `TextBlock` showing the content of the `ErrorMessage` property should only be visible if there is an error. This is shown next.

VALUE CONVERSION

To display the `TextBlock` for the error message only in cases when there is an error, the `Visibility` property of the `TextBlock` can be bound to the `HasError` property of the `ViewModelBase` class. However, the `HasError` property is of type `bool`, and the `Visibility` property is an enumeration with three possible values: `Visible`, `Collapsed`, and `Hidden`. Binding such different types can be done by using a converter.

A converter as shown with the `VisibilityConverter` class implements the interface `IValueConverter`. This interface defines the `Convert` and `ConvertBack` methods. The `Convert` method is implemented to convert the Boolean input value from `true` to `Visibility.Visible`, and `false` to `Visibility.Collapsed`.

```csharp
using System;
using System.Globalization;
using System.Windows;
using System.Windows.Data;

namespace Formula1.Infrastructure
{
    [ValueConversion(typeof(bool), typeof(Visibility))]
    public class VisibilityConverter : IValueConverter
    {
        public object Convert(object value, Type targetType,
                                object parameter, CultureInfo culture)
        {
            bool input = (bool)value;
            if (input)
                return Visibility.Visible;
            else
                return Visibility.Collapsed;

        }

        public object ConvertBack(object value, Type targetType,
                                object parameter, CultureInfo culture)
        {
            throw new NotSupportedException();
        }
    }
}
```

Code file [Infrastructure/VisibilityConverter.cs] available for download at Wrox.com.

For using the `VisibilityConverter` type from within XAML code, the type is defined within the resources and can be accessed by using the `VisibilityConverter` key.

```xml
<UserControl.Resources>
    <utils:VisibilityConverter x:Key="VisibilityConverter" />
    <!-- ... -->
    </Style>
</UserControl.Resources>
```

Code file [Views/ShowRacerView.xaml] available for download at Wrox.com.

The definition of the `TextBlock` element can now be changed to bind the `Visibility` property of the `TextBlock` to the `HasError` property of the `ViewModelBase` type. The Boolean value is now converted to the `Visibility` enumeration by specifying the converter with the `Converter` property of the `Binding`. Without an error, the `TextBlock` stays collapsed and doesn't take any size in the View.

```
<TextBlock Foreground="Red" Visibility="{Binding HasError,
    Converter={StaticResource VisibilityConverter}}"
    Text="{Binding ErrorMessage}" Grid.Row="2" Grid.Column="0"
    Grid.ColumnSpan="2" />
```

Code file [Views/ShowRacerView.xaml] available for download at Wrox.com.

Now, what's missing is a `TextBlock` that displays the values of the `FirstName` and `LastName` properties. Using a single `TextBlock` to display a combination of multiple properties, `MultiBinding` can be used, which is shown next.

BINDING MULTIPLE PROPERTIES

If multiple properties of a source should be bound to one UI element, `MultiBinding` can be used.

The following sample shows how the `Text` property of a `TextBlock` is bound to both the `FirstName` and `LastName` properties of a `Racer`. The child elements of the `MultiBinding` element define all the properties used for the binding. How the properties are combined is defined by a class implementing the `IMultiValueConverter` interface. This is referenced by the `Converter` property of the `MultiBinding` element.

```
<TextBlock Grid.Row="0" Grid.Column="1">
    <TextBlock.Text>
        <MultiBinding Converter="{StaticResource NameConverter}">
            <Binding Path="FirstName" />
            <Binding Path="LastName" />
        </MultiBinding>
    </TextBlock.Text>
</TextBlock>
```

Code file [Views/ShowRacerView.xaml] available for download at Wrox.com.

The converter is defined within resources of the user control to reference the `NameConverter` class.

```
<UserControl.Resources>
    <utils:NameConverter x:Key="NameConverter" />
    <!-- ... -->
</UserControl.Resources>
```

Code file [Views/ShowRacerView.xaml] available for download at Wrox.com.

The `NameConverter` class implements the `IMultiValueConverter` interface in the following code snippet. `IMultiValueConverter` defines the `Convert` and `ConvertBack` methods. For one-way binding, just the `Convert` method is used. With two-way binding, the `ConvertBack` method must be implemented as well.

```
using System;
using System.Globalization;
using System.Linq;
using System.Windows;
using System.Windows.Data;
```

```
namespace Formula1.Infrastructure
{
    public class NameConverter : IMultiValueConverter
    {
        public object Convert(object[] values, Type targetType,
                              object parameter, CultureInfo culture)
        {
            if (values == null || values.Count() != 2)
                return DependencyProperty.UnsetValue;
            return String.Format("{0} {1}", values[0], values[1]);
        }

        public object[] ConvertBack(object value, Type[] targetTypes,
                                    object parameter, CultureInfo culture)
        {
            throw new NotImplementedException();
        }
    }
}
```

Code file [Infrastructure/NameConverter.cs] available for download at Wrox.com.

With the `Convert` method, the `values` parameter receives all the bound property values defined as children of the `MultiBinding` element. The return value is a single object built up from the input values. In a case in which the input values should be dealt with differently based on a parameter, the `parameter` argument is filled by assigning the `ConverterParameter` attribute to the `MultiBinding` element. For example, you could decide if the first name or last name should appear first.

Returning `DependencyProperty.UnsetValue` from the `Convert` method means that the `Convert` method didn't produce any value, and, thus, a `FallbackValue` should be used (if it is available), or a default value.

In the case in which binding multiple property values can be achieved by a format string, creating a class implementing `IMultiValueConverter` is not necessary. The following code snippet demonstrates how `MultiBinding` can be used to specify the `StringFormat` property to get the same result as before:

```
<TextBlock Grid.Row="0" Grid.Column="1">
    <TextBlock.Text>
        <MultiBinding StringFormat="{}{0} {1}">
            <Binding Path="FirstName" />
            <Binding Path="LastName" />
        </MultiBinding>
    </TextBlock.Text>
</TextBlock>
```

Code file [Views/ShowRacerView.xaml] available for download at Wrox.com.

With the `Racer` type as it is, there's another option instead of using `MultiBinding`. The `Racer` type overrides the `ToString` method to return the values of the `FirstName` and `LastName` properties as a single string. So, you can also bind the `Text` property of the `TextBlock` to do a default binding, and get the same result in this scenario.

```
<TextBlock Grid.Row="0" Grid.Column="1" Text="{Binding}" />
```

Running the application, a query for a racer can be performed to display the result, as shown in Figure 13-6.

FIGURE 13-6: Result of querying for a racer

BINDING TO LISTS

The next step is to bind a list of racers. This is done in the View type `ShowRacersView` with the ViewModel type `ShowRacersViewModel`.

Controls that derive from the base class `ContentControl` can only display a single item. To display a list of items, a control that derives from `ItemsControl` is needed. Examples of such controls are `ListBox`, `ComboBox`, and `TreeControl` classes. These controls have an `ItemsSource` property that can be used for binding a list. The next sample uses the `ListBox` and `ComboBox` controls.

The UI of this sample displays a list of racers. However, not all racers should be displayed in one list, but rather the list should be filtered. The sample enables filtering based on the country of the racers, or a year range when the racers were active, or both.

In the following code, the ViewModel class `ShowRacersViewModel` defines Boolean properties `FilterCountry` and `FilterYears` (if filtering on the country and the year should be active), the `Countries` property (which returns a list of all countries), and the `MinYear` and `MaxYear` properties (which return the range of available years). The `SelectedCountry`, `SelectedMinYear`, and `SelectedMaxYear` properties define the values selected from the UI. The ViewModel class also defines a command named `GetRacersCommand` that invokes (when fired) the `GetRacers` method.


```
using System;
using System.Collections.Generic;
using System.Linq;
using Formula1.Infrastructure;
using Formula1.Model;
```

```csharp
namespace Formula1.ViewModels
{
    public class ShowRacersViewModel : ViewModelBase, IDisposable
    {
        private Formula1Entities data;
        public ShowRacersViewModel()
        {
            if (!IsDesignTime)
            {
                data = new Formula1Entities();
            }
        }

        private DelegateCommand getRacersCommand;
        public DelegateCommand GetRacersCommand
        {
            get
            {
                return getRacersCommand ??
                    (getRacersCommand = new DelegateCommand(
                        param => this.GetRacers()));
            }
        }

        public bool FilterCountry { get; set; }
        public bool FilterYears { get; set; }

        private string[] countries;
        public IEnumerable<string> Countries
        {
            get
            {
                return countries ??
                    (countries = data.Racers.Select(
                        r => r.Nationality).Distinct().ToArray());
            }
        }
        public string SelectedCountry { get; set; }

        private int minYear;
        public int MinYear
        {
            get
            {
                if (IsDesignTime)
                    minYear = 1950;
                return minYear != 0 ? minYear : minYear =
                    data.Races.Select(r => r.Date.Year).Min();
            }
        }

        private int maxYear;
        public int MaxYear
```

```csharp
        {
            get
            {
                if (IsDesignTime)
                    maxYear = DateTime.Today.Year;
                return maxYear != 0 ? maxYear : maxYear =
                    data.Races.Select(r => r.Date.Year).Max();
            }
        }

        private int selectedMinYear;
        public int SelectedMinYear
        {
            get
            {
                return selectedMinYear;
            }
            set
            {
                if (!object.Equals(selectedMinYear, value))
                {
                    selectedMinYear = value;
                    RaisePropertyChanged("SelectedMinYear");
                }
            }
        }
        private int selectedMaxYear;
        public int SelectedMaxYear
        {
            get
            {
                return selectedMaxYear;
            }
            set
            {
                if (!object.Equals(selectedMaxYear, value))
                {
                    selectedMaxYear = value;
                    RaisePropertyChanged("SelectedMaxYear");
                }
            }
        }

        public void Dispose()
        {
            data.Dispose();
        }

        //...
    }
}
```

Code file [ViewModels/ShowRacersViewModel.cs] available for download at Wrox.com.

In the following code, the UI uses `CheckBox` elements that bind to the `FilterCountry` and `FilterYears` properties. A `ComboBox` displays all countries by binding the `ItemsSource` property to the `Countries` property of the ViewModel class. The selected item of the `ComboBox` is bound to the `SelectedCountry` property. `Slider` controls are used where the user can select the range of years for the racers. Sliders have a special feature to display a range within the complete range where values are bound to the corresponding slider element. Element-to-element binding is used here.

```xml
<GroupBox Header="Filter" Grid.Row="0">
    <Grid Grid.Row="0">
        <Grid.RowDefinitions>
            <RowDefinition />
            <RowDefinition />
            <RowDefinition Height="Auto" />
        </Grid.RowDefinitions>
        <Grid.ColumnDefinitions>
            <ColumnDefinition Width="Auto" />
            <ColumnDefinition />
        </Grid.ColumnDefinitions>
        <CheckBox IsChecked="{Binding FilterCountry}" Content="Country"
                Grid.Row="0" Grid.Column="0" Margin="5" />
        <ComboBox ItemsSource="{Binding Countries}"
                SelectedItem="{Binding SelectedCountry,
                    Mode=OneWayToSource}"
                Grid.Row="0" Grid.Column="1" Margin="5" />
        <CheckBox IsChecked="{Binding FilterYears}" Content="Years"
            Grid.Row="1"
            Grid.Column="0" Margin="5" />
        <Grid Grid.Row="1" Grid.Column="1" Margin="5">
            <Grid.RowDefinitions>
                <RowDefinition />
                <RowDefinition />
            </Grid.RowDefinitions>
            <Grid.ColumnDefinitions>
                <ColumnDefinition Width="Auto" />
                <ColumnDefinition />
            </Grid.ColumnDefinitions>
            <TextBlock Text="From" Grid.Row="0" Grid.Column="0"
                    VerticalAlignment="Center" />
            <TextBlock Text="To" Grid.Row="1" Grid.Column="0"
                    VerticalAlignment="Center" />
            <Slider x:Name="minSlider" Grid.Row="0" Grid.Column="1"
                    IsSelectionRangeEnabled="True"
                        IsSnapToTickEnabled="True"
                    TickFrequency="5" TickPlacement="BottomRight"
                    AutoToolTipPlacement="TopLeft" Margin="5"
                    Minimum="{Binding MinYear, Mode=OneTime}"
                    Maximum="{Binding MaxYear, Mode=OneTime}"
                    Value="{Binding SelectedMinYear}"
                    SelectionStart="{Binding MinYear, Mode=OneWay}"
                    SelectionEnd=
                        "{Binding ElementName=maxSlider, Path=Value,
                            Mode=OneWay}" />
            <Slider x:Name="maxSlider" Grid.Row="1" Grid.Column="1"
                    IsSelectionRangeEnabled="True"
```

```
                      IsSnapToTickEnabled="True"
              TickFrequency="5" TickPlacement="BottomRight"
              AutoToolTipPlacement="TopLeft" Margin="5"
              Minimum="{Binding MinYear, Mode=OneTime}"
              Maximum="{Binding MaxYear, Mode=OneTime}"
              Value="{Binding SelectedMaxYear}"
              SelectionStart=
                  "{Binding ElementName=minSlider, Path=Value,
                  Mode=OneWay}"
              SelectionEnd="{Binding MaxYear, Mode=OneWay}" />
      </Grid>
      <Button Command="{Binding GetRacersCommand}"
              Content="Get Racers" Grid.Row="2" Grid.ColumnSpan="2"
              HorizontalAlignment="Center" Margin="5" Padding="3" />
    </Grid>
  </GroupBox>
```

Code file [Views/ShowRacersView.xaml] available for download at Wrox.com.

As the filtering is done, the ViewModel class can return the filtered racers to the UI. In the following code, the `Racers` property is bound to the `ListBox` element. The `GetExpression` helper method used within the `get` accessor of the `Racers` property returns the filtered racers, depending on the `SelectedCountry`, `SelectedMinYear`, and `SelectedMaxYear` properties. From the `GetRacers` method invoked via the command, the UI just needs to be informed that the `Racers` property changed.

```csharp
private void GetRacers()
{
    RaisePropertyChanged("Racers");
}

private IQueryable<Racer> GetExpression()
{
    var expr = data.Racers as IQueryable<Racer>;
    if (FilterCountry)
    {
        expr = expr.Where(r => r.Nationality == this.SelectedCountry);
    }
    if (FilterYears)
    {
        expr = expr.SelectMany(
            r => r.RaceResults,
            (r1, raceResult) => new { Racer = r1, RaceResult =
                raceResult })
            .Where(raceInfo =>
                raceInfo.RaceResult.Race.Date.Year >= SelectedMinYear &&
                raceInfo.RaceResult.Race.Date.Year <= SelectedMaxYear)
            .Select(raceInfo => raceInfo.Racer)
            .Distinct();
    }
    return expr;
}
```

```csharp
public IEnumerable<Racer> Racers
{
    get
    {
        return GetExpression();
    }
}
```

Code file [ViewModels/ShowRacersViewModel.cs] available for download at Wrox.com.

A `ListBox` to display the filtered racers now must be bound to the `Racers` property.

```xml
<ListBox ItemsSource="{Binding Racers}" Grid.Row="1" />
```

Code file [Views/ShowRacersView.xaml] available for download at Wrox.com.

Running the application, racers can now be filtered, as shown in Figure 13-7.

FIGURE 13-7: Getting a filtered list of racers

Filtering with CollectionViewSource

Instead of filtering and sorting items in the database, WPF itself supports filtering and sorting with the help of the `CollectionViewSource` class. The disadvantage here is that all the data is needed with the UI layer that should be filtered and sorted. In many scenarios, both are required — filtering by retrieving only a subset of rows from the database, as well as filtering and sorting this subset for the UI.

The next sample is a variation of the previous sample in that all racers are read from the database, and the racers are filtered and sorted on the client side with `CollectionViewSource`.

The ViewModel class `ShowRacersCVSViewModel` gets the default `ICollectionView` for the racers collection inside the constructor. WPF always creates a collection View for a list that is bound, no matter if one is created explicitly. The View that is created automatically can be accessed with the

`CollectionViewSource.GetDefaultView` static method passing in the collection. This method returns an object that implements the `ICollectionView` interface.

This interface defines properties that can be used for filtering, sorting, and grouping. The `Filter` property is of the delegate type `Predicate<Object>`.

The following sample code applies a lambda expression to filter the racers based on the value of the `SelectedCountry` property. The `SortDescription` property is of type `SortDescriptionCollection`, where multiple `SortDescription` items can be added that will be used for sorting. If, with the first `SortDescription`, the items are equal, the second `SortDescription` applies. The sample sorts the racers based on the number of wins. If the number of wins is the same, the sort happens based on the last name.

```csharp
using System;
using System.Collections.Generic;
using System.ComponentModel;
using System.Linq;
using System.Windows.Data;
using Formula1.Model;

namespace Formula1.ViewModels
{
    public class ShowRacersCVSViewModel : ViewModelBase, IDisposable
    {
        private Formula1Entities data;
        private List<Racer> racers;
        public ShowRacersCVSViewModel()
        {
            if (!IsDesignTime)
            {
                data = new Formula1Entities();
                racers = data.Racers.ToList();
                ICollectionView cv =
                    CollectionViewSource.GetDefaultView(racers);
                cv.Filter = r => (r as Racer).Nationality == SelectedCountry;
                cv.SortDescriptions.Add(new SortDescription("Wins",
                                        ListSortDirection.Descending));
                cv.SortDescriptions.Add(new SortDescription("LastName",
                                        ListSortDirection.Ascending));
            }
        }
        //...
```

Code file [ViewModels/ShowRacersCVSViewModel.cs] available for download at Wrox.com.

The `SelectedCountry` property just needs a change to refresh the View when the property value changes, as shown here:

```csharp
private string selectedCountry;
public string SelectedCountry {
    get
    {
        return selectedCountry;
```

```
        }
        set
        {
            selectedCountry = value;
            CollectionViewSource.GetDefaultView(racers).Refresh();
        }
    }
```

Code file [ViewModels/ShowRacersCVSViewModel.cs] available for download at Wrox.com.

With this ViewModel class in place, from the UI, just bindings for the Countries and Racers properties are needed, and everything is in place.

```
<ComboBox ItemsSource="{Binding Countries}"
          SelectedItem="{Binding SelectedCountry, Mode=OneWayToSource}"
          Grid.Row="0" Margin="5" />
<ListBox ItemsSource="{Binding Racers}" Grid.Row="1" />
```

Code file [Views/ShowRacersCVSView.xaml] available for download at Wrox.com.

Running the application, you can see a screen similar to what is shown in Figure 13-8.

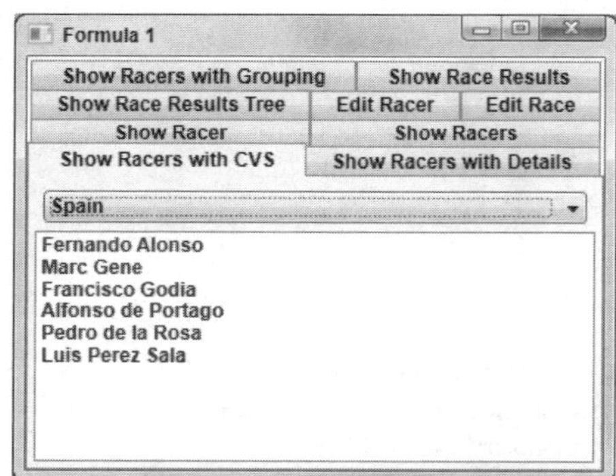

FIGURE 13-8: Racers sorted by the number of wins

Displaying Item Details of Lists

Displaying detail information of a selected item inside a list can be done easily with the help of a little magic. All that's needed here is the control displaying the list, controls displaying single-item content to access the same data context, and the list control setting the IsSynchronizedWithCurrentItem property to True.

The sample uses a ViewModel class with the same functionality as before, just a different View. The outer Grid control shown in the following code snippet has the DataContext set to the Racers property. Children within this Grid control are a ListBox and several TextBlock elements. Because they are all in the same grid, the same data context is used.

```xml
<Grid Grid.Column="0" Grid.Row="1" DataContext="{Binding Racers}">
    <Grid.ColumnDefinitions>
        <ColumnDefinition />
        <ColumnDefinition />
    </Grid.ColumnDefinitions>

    <ListBox ItemsSource="{Binding}" Grid.Row="0" Grid.Column="0"
             IsSynchronizedWithCurrentItem="True" />
    <GridSplitter Grid.Column="1" Grid.Row="0"
                  HorizontalAlignment="Left" Width="4" />
    <Grid Grid.Column="1">
        <Grid.ColumnDefinitions>
            <ColumnDefinition Width="Auto" />
            <ColumnDefinition Width="*" />
        </Grid.ColumnDefinitions>
        <Grid.RowDefinitions>
            <RowDefinition />
            <RowDefinition />
            <RowDefinition />
            <RowDefinition />
            <RowDefinition />
        </Grid.RowDefinitions>
        <TextBlock Text="Name" Grid.Row="0" Grid.Column="0" />
        <TextBlock Text="{Binding /}" Grid.Row="0" Grid.Column="1" />
        <TextBlock Text="Country" Grid.Row="1" Grid.Column="0" />
        <TextBlock Text="{Binding Nationality}" Grid.Row="1"
            Grid.Column="1" />
        <TextBlock Text="Starts" Grid.Row="2" Grid.Column="0" />
        <TextBlock Text="{Binding Starts}" Grid.Row="2" Grid.Column="1" />
        <TextBlock Text="Wins" Grid.Row="3" Grid.Column="0" />
        <TextBlock Text="{Binding Wins}" Grid.Row="3" Grid.Column="1" />
        <TextBlock Text="Points" Grid.Row="4" Grid.Column="0" />
        <TextBlock Text="{Binding Points}" Grid.Row="4" Grid.Column="1" />
    </Grid>
</Grid>
```

Code file [Views/ShowRacersWithDetailView.xaml] available for download at Wrox.com.

The `ListBox` control has the `ItemsSource` property bound to the data context (which is the `Racers` property because this is the first parent control that has a `DataContext` assigned), and the `IsSynchronizedWithCurrentItem` property is set. With `IsSynchronizedWithCurrentItem`, the selection of the `ListBox` sets the current item in the data context.

The `TextBlock` elements bind to properties of a single item: `Nationality`, `Starts`, `Wins`, and `Points`. The data context is a list of racers. However, because the racer collection doesn't have these properties, there's an automatic fallback. If the property is not available to bind to, WPF tries to bind to a property of the current item, and here this is successful.

The first `TextBlock` bound displays the name. Using just the markup expression `{Binding}` to get the result of the `ToString` method doesn't work because with `{Binding}` binding to the list is successful. This would just display the type name of the collection class. To get the default result of a single item, binding to / can be used. Accordingly /`Nationality` and /`Starts` can be used with the other binding expressions to bind to the properties of the current item.

Running the application gives the result shown in Figure 13-9.

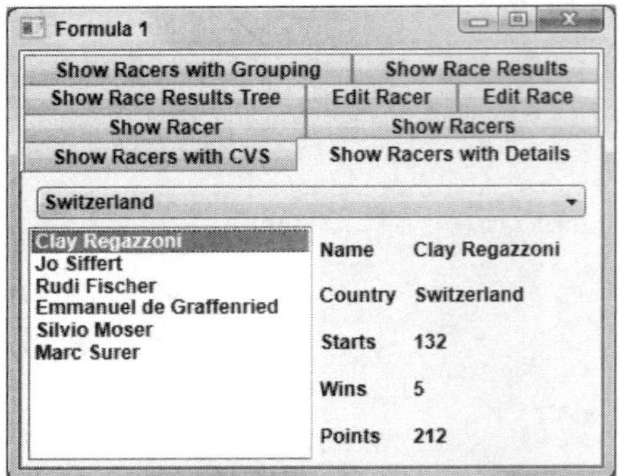

FIGURE 13-9: Displaying a detailed list of racers

Using Data Templates

The content of the `ListBox` so far has displayed the value returned from the `ToString` method of the `Racer` class. In the case when the `ToString` method is not overloaded or something different should be displayed, a `DataTemplate` can be created.

The following code snippet demonstrates using a data template within the `ItemTemplate` property of the `ListBox`. This way, every item displays with the elements used within the `DataTemplate`. Here, the property `Text` of the `TextBlock` binds to the default output of the bound item (the racer). It is possible to bind to any property of the `Racer` type within `ListBox` items.

```xml
<ListBox ItemsSource="{Binding}" Grid.Row="0" Grid.Column="0"
         IsSynchronizedWithCurrentItem="True">
    <ListBox.ItemTemplate>
        <DataTemplate>
            <StackPanel Orientation="Vertical">
                <TextBlock Text="{Binding}" />
            </StackPanel>
        </DataTemplate>
    </ListBox.ItemTemplate>
</ListBox>
```

Code file [Views/ShowRacersWithDetailView.xaml] available for download at Wrox.com.

In the case when a data template should be used with more than one control, it's advantageous to define it within resources. By defining data templates within resources, they can be either default ones (for a specific type) or named with a key (in which case, they must be referenced using the key).

This chapter already used default data templates to map the ViewModel class to the View. In the following code, a `DataTemplate` is defined within the application resources. This template is used

as a default template for the `ShowRacerViewModel` type. The UI representation for this type is the
`ShowRacerView`.

```xml
<DataTemplate DataType="{x:Type viewModels:ShowRacerViewModel}">
    <views:ShowRacerView />
</DataTemplate>
```

Code file [App.xaml] available for download at Wrox.com.

If multiple data templates should be used for the same type, a resource key can be specified. This
key is then referenced by using a `StaticResource` or `DynamicResource` markup extension.

*Similar to defining an item template, you can also define a content template for
elements that can display single content. Instead of using the `ItemTemplate`
property, these controls have a `ContentTemplate` property.*

Grouping

Lists can be grouped based on one or more properties. Grouping can be done with the
`CollectionViewSource` already used for filtering.

The following sample displays all racers grouped by country. The ViewModel class does nothing
other than offer a `Racers` property where all racers are returned. The `Racers` property is bound by
a `CollectionViewSource` defined within the XAML code. This `CollectionViewSource` defines
that the racers are sorted first by the `Nationality` property. If this is the same, then it is sorted by
`Wins`, and then by `LastName`. Grouping is defined by setting the `PropertyGroupDescription` to
`Nationality`.

```xml
<UserControl.Resources>
    <CollectionViewSource x:Key="RacersGroup" Source="{Binding Racers}">
        <CollectionViewSource.SortDescriptions>
            <comp:SortDescription PropertyName="Nationality"
                Direction="Ascending" />
            <comp:SortDescription PropertyName="Wins"
                Direction="Descending" />
            <comp:SortDescription PropertyName="LastName"
                Direction="Ascending" />
        </CollectionViewSource.SortDescriptions>
        <CollectionViewSource.GroupDescriptions>
            <PropertyGroupDescription PropertyName="Nationality" />
        </CollectionViewSource.GroupDescriptions>
    </CollectionViewSource>
</UserControl.Resources>
```

Code file [Views/ShowRacersWithGroupingView.xaml] available for download at Wrox.com.

The following `ListBox` code binds to the `CollectionViewSource`. Because grouping is defined
with the `CollectionViewSource`, the `GroupStyle` of the `ListBox` becomes active. The `GroupStyle`

element defines a custom template for the `GroupItem` type returned by grouping. In the template, an `Expander` control is used. Inside the header of the `Expander` control, the `Name` property (which represents the group) and the `ItemCount` property (which is the number of items in the group) are used for the display. The content of the `Expander` control is `ItemsPresenter`, which means that the `ItemTemplate` is used in that place for every item.

```xml
<ListBox ItemsSource="{Binding Source={StaticResource RacersGroup}}"
         Grid.Row="1">
    <ListBox.GroupStyle>
        <GroupStyle>
            <GroupStyle.ContainerStyle>
                <Style TargetType="GroupItem">
                    <Setter Property="Template">
                        <Setter.Value>
                            <ControlTemplate>
                                <Expander>
                                    <Expander.Header>
                                        <StackPanel Orientation="Vertical">
                                            <TextBlock Text="{Binding
                                                Name}" />
                                            <TextBlock
                                                Text="{BindingItemCount}" />
                                        </StackPanel>
                                    </Expander.Header>
                                    <Expander.Content>
                                        <ItemsPresenter />
                                    </Expander.Content>
                                </Expander>
                            </ControlTemplate>
                        </Setter.Value>
                    </Setter>
                </Style>
            </GroupStyle.ContainerStyle>
        </GroupStyle>
    </ListBox.GroupStyle>
    <ListBox.ItemTemplate>
        <DataTemplate>
            <Grid>
                <Grid.RowDefinitions>
                    <RowDefinition />
                    <RowDefinition />
                    <RowDefinition />
                </Grid.RowDefinitions>
                <Grid.ColumnDefinitions>
                    <ColumnDefinition />
                    <ColumnDefinition />
                </Grid.ColumnDefinitions>
                <TextBlock Text="{Binding}" Grid.Row="0" Grid.Column="0"
                        Grid.ColumnSpan="2" />
                <TextBlock Text="Wins:" Grid.Row="1" Grid.Column="0"  />
                <TextBlock Text="{Binding Wins}" Grid.Row="1"
                    Grid.Column="1" />
                <TextBlock Text="Starts: " Grid.Row="2" Grid.Column="0" />
```

```xml
            <TextBlock Text="{Binding Starts}" Grid.Row="2"
                           Grid.Column="1" />
        </Grid>
      </DataTemplate>
    </ListBox.ItemTemplate>
  </ListBox>
```

Code file [Views/ShowRacersWithGroupingView.xaml] available for download at Wrox.com.

Running the application, you can see the racers grouped as shown in Figure 13-10.

FIGURE 13-10: Racers grouped by country

Using Hierarchical Data Binding

You can use a `TreeView` control to display items in a hierarchical way. For hierarchical binding, use `HierarchicalDataTemplate` objects instead of `DataTemplate` objects to display the hierarchy.

The following code displays race results in a hierarchy. The first level is the years of the races. If you select a year, the races display. And, if you select a race, the race results display. For every level of a hierarchy, there's a ViewModel class. The `RaceResultHierarchicalViewModel` class represents the last level in the hierarchy. This class defines `Position` and `Racer` properties to display a race result.

```csharp
public class RaceResultHierarchicalViewModel : ViewModelBase
{
    private int position;
    public int Position
    {
        get { return position; }
        set
        {
            if (!object.Equals(position, value))
            {
                position = value;
                RaisePropertyChanged("Position");
            }
        }
    }
```

```
        }

        private string racer;
        public string Racer
        {
            get
            {
                return racer;
            }
            set
            {
                if (!object.Equals(racer, value))
                {
                    racer = value;
                    RaisePropertyChanged("Racer");
                }
            }
        }
    }
```

Code file [ViewModels/RaceResultHierarchicalViewModel.cs] available for download at Wrox.com.

The second level represents a race. The `RaceViewModel` class defines `Date` and `Country` properties. You define the `RaceResults` property to get to the race results from a race. To not load all race results initially, use the `Lazy<T>` type. The `RaceResults` property is of a `Lazy<IEnumerable <RaceResultHierarchicalViewModel>>` type. Passing a lambda expression to the constructor of the `Lazy` type, the lambda expression is invoked as soon as the `Value` property of the `Lazy<T>` type is accessed, but not with instantiation of the `Lazy` type. The `Value` property then returns `IEnumerable<RaceResultHierarchicalViewModel>`. The query returns all the race results for the date specified with the `Date` property.

```
        public class RaceViewModel : ViewModelBase
        {
            private DateTime date;
            public DateTime Date
            {
                get
                {
                    return date;
                }
                set
                {
                    if (!object.Equals(date, value))
                    {
                        date = value;
                        RaisePropertyChanged("Date");
                    }
                }
            }

            private string country;
            public string Country
```

```csharp
        {
            get
            {
                return country;
            }
            set
            {
                if (!object.Equals(country, value))
                {
                    country = value;
                    RaisePropertyChanged("Country");
                }
            }
        }

        public Lazy<IEnumerable<RaceResultViewModel>> RaceResults
        {
            get
            {
                return new Lazy<IEnumerable<RaceResultHierarchicalViewModel>>(() =>
                {
                    List<RaceResultHierarchicalViewModel> results = null;
                    using (Formula1Entities data = new Formula1Entities())
                    {
                        results = (from rr in data.RaceResults
                                   where rr.Race.Date == this.Date
                                   orderby rr.Position
                                   select new RaceResultHierarchicalViewModel
                                   {
                                       Position = rr.Position,
                                       Racer = rr.Racer.FirstName + " " +
                                           rr.Racer.LastName
                                   }).ToList();
                    }
                    return results;
                });
            }
        }
    }
```

Code file [ViewModels/RaceViewModel.cs] available for download at Wrox.com.

The first level of the tree is the `ChampionshipViewModel` that defines `Year` and `Races` properties. Similar to the `RaceResults` property, the `Races` property uses of the `Lazy<T>` type for lazy evaluation.

```csharp
public class ChampionshipViewModel : ViewModelBase
{
    private int year;
    public int Year
    {
        get { return year; }
        set
```

```
            {
                if (!object.Equals(year, value))
                {
                    year = value;
                    RaisePropertyChanged("Year");
                }
            }
        }

        public Lazy<IEnumerable<RaceViewModel>> Races
        {
            get
            {
                return new Lazy<IEnumerable<RaceViewModel>>(() =>
                {
                    List<RaceViewModel> results = null;
                    using (Formula1Entities data = new Formula1Entities())
                    {
                        results = ((from r in data.Races
                                    where r.Date.Year == Year
                                    select new RaceViewModel
                                    {
                                        Country = r.Circuit.Country,
                                        Date = r.Date
                                    }) as ObjectQuery<RaceViewModel>).Execute(
                                        MergeOption.NoTracking).ToList();
                    }
                    return results;
                });
            }
        }
    }
```

Code file [ViewModels/ChampionshipViewModel.cs] available for download at Wrox.com.

The ViewModel class that is directly bound to the View is `ShowRaceResultsTreeViewModel`. This class defines the `Years` property to return `ChampionshipViewModel` for every year.

```
        public class ShowRaceResultsTreeViewModel : ViewModelBase
        {
            public IEnumerable<ChampionshipViewModel> Years
            {
                get
                {
                    IEnumerable<ChampionshipViewModel> championShips = null;
                    using (Formula1Entities data = new Formula1Entities())
                    {
                        championShips = (from r in data.Races
                                         orderby r.Date.Year
                                         select r.Date.Year).Distinct()
                                         .Select(y => new ChampionshipViewModel
                                             { Year = y }).ToList();
                    }
```

```
            return championShips;
        }
    }
}
```


From the UI, a simple `TreeView` control is bound to the `Years` property of the ViewModel `ShowRaceResultsViewModel` class, as shown here:

```xml
<TreeView ItemsSource="{Binding Years}">
    <TreeView.Resources>
        <HierarchicalDataTemplate DataType="{x:Type
            vm:ChampionshipViewModel}"
                                ItemsSource="{Binding Races.Value}">
            <TextBlock Text="{Binding Year}" />
        </HierarchicalDataTemplate>

        <HierarchicalDataTemplate DataType="{x:Type vm:RaceViewModel}"
                            ItemsSource="{Binding
                                RaceResults.Value}">
            <StackPanel Orientation="Horizontal">
                <TextBlock Text="{Binding Country}" Margin="5" />
                <TextBlock Text="{Binding Date, StringFormat=d}"
                    Margin="5" />
            </StackPanel>
        </HierarchicalDataTemplate>

        <DataTemplate DataType="{x:Type vm:RaceResultViewModel}">
            <StackPanel Orientation="Horizontal">
                <TextBlock Text="{Binding Position}" Margin="5" />
                <TextBlock Text="{Binding Racer}" Margin="5" />
            </StackPanel>
        </DataTemplate>
    </TreeView.Resources>
</TreeView>
```


The first `HierarchicalDataTemplate` is used for the `ChampionshipViewModel` type returned from the `Years` property. The `ItemsSource` property of the `HierarchicalDataTemplate` defines the next level in the tree. This property is bound to `Races.Value`. `Value` is a property of the `Lazy<T>` type to invoke the lambda expression associated with this type. `IEnumerable<RaceViewModel>` is returned here.

The second `HierarchicalDataTemplate` is defined for the `RaceViewModel` type, and displays the country and the date binding to the `Country` and `Date` properties. Again, `ItemsSource` is defined to get an enumeration of `RaceResultViewModel` returned from `RaceResults.Value`. Finally, a `DataTemplate` is defined for the `RaceResultHierarchicalViewModel` type to display position and racer information.

Running the application, you can see the tree, as shown in Figure 13-11.

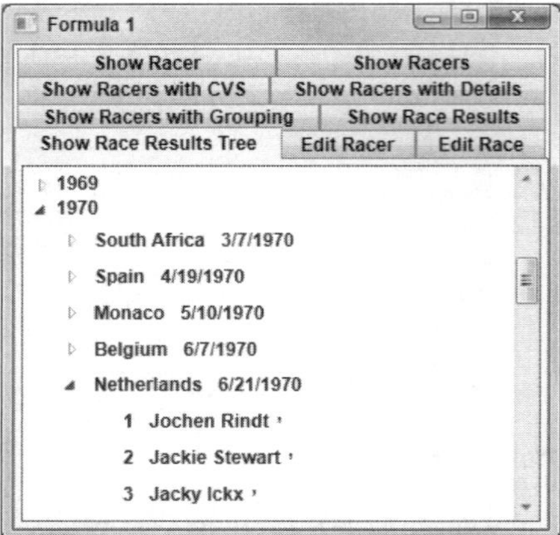

FIGURE 13-11: Hierarchical tree of racers

Binding Long Lists

Instead of binding long lists to a UI element, it's better to not return all records to the client. Rather, you should do filtering on the database side and just return a subset to the client. If this is not possible, filtering can be done with WPF with the `CollectionViewSource` as shown earlier. If there's still a specific reason to display a complete large list within a UI element, some performance can be tweaked.

The following sample code returns in the UI a list of all race results since the 1950s . A `ListBox` is used to display a long list of all race results. These are several thousand records to display and to scroll through. The implementation of the ViewModel class `ShowRaceResultsViewModel` returns a list of all race results, along with the information about the race, and the circuit linked to the information about the racer. All this information can be used from the UI with data binding.

```
using System;
using System.Collections.Generic;
using System.Data.Objects;
using System.Linq;
using Formula1.Model;

namespace Formula1.ViewModels
{
    public class ShowRaceResultsViewModel : ViewModelBase
    {
        private List<RaceResult> raceResults;

        public IEnumerable<RaceResult> RaceResults
        {
            get
            {
                if (raceResults == null)
                {
                    using (Formula1Entities data = new Formula1Entities())
                    {
```

```
            raceResults = data.RaceResults.Include("Race.Circuit")
                .Include("Racer").Execute
                    (MergeOption.NoTracking).ToList();
        }
    }
    return raceResults;
}
        }
    }
}
```

Code file [ViewModels/ShowRaceResultsViewModel.cs] available for download at Wrox.com.

With the UI, the `ListBox` control uses a `DataTemplate` to display information about race results. The issue for WPF performance is that for every item in the list, a data template must be created. Such templates can be fancy using cool WPF features that all consume resources such as memory and CPU and, in a long list, take up some time.

Available for download on Wrox.com

```
<ListBox Grid.Row="1">
    <ListBox.ItemTemplate>
        <DataTemplate>
            <DockPanel>
                <TextBlock DockPanel.Dock="Top"
                    Text="{Binding Race.Date, StringFormat='d'}"
                    HorizontalAlignment="Center" />
                <TextBlock DockPanel.Dock="Left"
                    Text="{Binding Race.Circuit.Country}" Margin="5" />
                <TextBlock DockPanel.Dock="Right" Text="{Binding Racer}"
                    Margin="5" />
                <TextBlock DockPanel.Dock="Right" Text="{Binding
                    Position}"
                    Margin="5" />
            </DockPanel>
        </DataTemplate>
    </ListBox.ItemTemplate>
</ListBox>
```

Code file [Views/ShowRaceResultsView.xaml] available for download at Wrox.com.

Luckily, by default, the `ListBox` makes use of the `VirtualizingStackPanel`. Virtualization is done in a way that only data templates shown in the `ListBox` (and a few more around the viewable area) are instantiated, but not all. With the setup of the UI as it is done next, you can see the effect of the virtualization, and you also see what more can be done.

In the following code snippet, the `ListBox` sets the attached `VirtualizingStackPanel` `.IsVirtualizing` property to a value selected by the `isVirtualizing` check box. The default setting is that this check box is checked because it is the default with the virtualization mode. If you deselect this check box, you can see that the list box behaves a lot slower, and much more memory is allocated by the application because every data template for every item in the complete list is instantiated.

```xml
<Grid>
    <Grid.RowDefinitions>
        <RowDefinition Height="Auto" />
        <RowDefinition Height="*" />
    </Grid.RowDefinitions>
    <Grid Grid.Row="0">
        <Grid.RowDefinitions>
            <RowDefinition />
            <RowDefinition />
            <RowDefinition />
        </Grid.RowDefinitions>
        <CheckBox IsChecked="True" x:Name="isVirtualizing"
            Content="IsVirtualizing"
                Margin="5" Grid.Row="0" />
        <ComboBox IsEnabled="{Binding ElementName=isVirtualizing,
            Path=IsChecked}"
                SelectedIndex="0" x:Name="virtualizationMode"
                Grid.Row="1" Margin="5">
            <ComboBoxItem>Standard</ComboBoxItem>
            <ComboBoxItem>Recycling</ComboBoxItem>
        </ComboBox>
        <CheckBox x:Name="isDeferredScrolling" Content="IsDeferredScrolling"
                Grid.Row="2" Margin="5" />
    </Grid>

    <ListBox VirtualizingStackPanel.IsVirtualizing=
            "{Binding Path=IsChecked, ElementName=isVirtualizing}"
        VirtualizingStackPanel.VirtualizationMode=
            "{Binding ElementName=virtualizationMode, Path=SelectedValue}"
        ItemsSource="{Binding RaceResults, IsAsync=True}"
        ScrollViewer.IsDeferredScrollingEnabled=
            "{Binding Path=IsChecked, ElementName=isDeferredScrolling}"
        Grid.Row="1">
        <ListBox.ItemTemplate>
            <!-- -->
        </ListBox.ItemTemplate>
    </ListBox>
</Grid>
```

Code file [Views/ShowRaceResultsView.xaml] available for download at Wrox.com.

Another option that can be set is `VirtualizingStackPanel.VirtualizationMode`. There are two possible values of the enumeration `VirtualizationMode`: `Standard` and `Recycling`. The default setting is `Standard`.

With the standard mode, as the user scrolls through the list, new data template objects are dynamically created, and the garbage collector (GC) can release the memory of the other ones not shown anymore. This is a lot of work for the runtime to allocate and release memory. Because the GC doesn't immediately release the memory, you can see that the memory consumption of the application increases as soon as the user scrolls through the list. After some time, when the GC runs, memory consumption reduces again.

A better-performing option is the recycling mode. Here, data template objects that are not needed anymore go into a pool and are reused from the pool as needed.

From the performance standpoint, there's even a better option that can be set: the `ScrollViewer.IsDeferred ScrollingEnabled` attached property. Setting this option to `true`, when scrolling, just the scroll bar moves, but the items in the list box don't. The data templates do not need to be created until the user completes the scrolling. From the performance standpoint, this is the best option, but not from the user experience — that's why it might not be feasible in most cases.

Running the application, you can see a View, as shown in Figure 13-12. To experience the differences with setting the various options, you need to run it. With the simple data template, you can experience big differences with the various settings. By having a more complex data template, the differences increase.

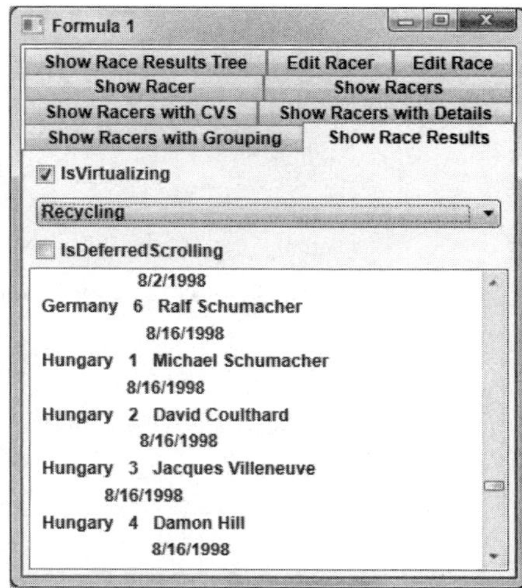

FIGURE 13-12: Displaying a list of racers with a scroll bar

EDITING DATA

The next samples step you through not only retrieving data for display, but also changing data to save changed information to the database. Here, you learn about editing single records, adding validation to changes, and, finally, using a `DataGrid` control to make more changes at once.

Updating Data

The following sample demonstrates how to edit and save a single item. For editing that allows cancellation, the `IEditableObject` interface can be implemented as is shown in the ViewModel class `EditRacerViewModel`. This interface defines the methods `BeginEdit`, `CancelEdit`, and `EndEdit`. The ViewModel class defines four commands: one to get a racer from the database (`GetRacerCommand`), and three commands that directly interact with the methods of the `IEditableObject` interface.

```csharp
using System.ComponentModel;
using System.Data;
using System.Linq;
using Formula1.Infrastructure;
using Formula1.Model;

namespace Formula1.ViewModels
{
    public class EditRacerViewModel : ViewModelBase, IEditableObject
    {
        private DelegateCommand getRacerCommand;
        public DelegateCommand GetRacerCommand
```

```csharp
    {
        get
        {
            return getRacerCommand ??
                (getRacerCommand = new DelegateCommand(param =>
                    this.GetRacer()));
        }
    }

    private void GetRacer()
    {
        using (Formula1Entities data = new Formula1Entities())
        {
            var racer = (from r in data.Racers
                        where r.Id == this.Id
                        select r).Single();

            RacerToVM(racer);
        }
    }

    private void UpdateRacer()
    {
        using (Formula1Entities data = new Formula1Entities())
        {
            Racer r = data.GetObjectByKey(this.key) as Racer;

            Racer current = VMToRacer();

            data.Racers.ApplyCurrentValues(current);

            data.SaveChanges();
        }
    }

    private EntityKey key;

    private int id;
    public int Id
    {
        get { return id; }
        set
        {
            if (!object.Equals(id, value))
            {
                id = value;
                RaisePropertyChanged("Id");
            }
        }
    }

    private string firstName;
    public string FirstName
    {
        get { return firstName; }
        set
```

```csharp
        {
            if (!object.Equals(firstName, value))
            {
                firstName = value;
                RaisePropertyChanged("FirstName");
            }
        }
    }

    private string lastName;
    public string LastName
    {
        get { return lastName; }
        set
        {
            if (!object.Equals(lastName, value))
            {
                lastName = value;
                RaisePropertyChanged("LastName");
            }
        }
    }

    private string nationality;
    public string Nationality
    {
        get { return nationality; }
        set
        {
            if (!object.Equals(nationality, value))
            {
                nationality = value;
                RaisePropertyChanged("Nationality");
            }
        }
    }

    private int? starts;
    public int? Starts
    {
        get { return starts; }
        set
        {
            if (!object.Equals(starts, value))
            {
                starts = value;
                RaisePropertyChanged("Starts");
            }
        }
    }

    private int? wins;
    public int? Wins
    {
        get { return wins; }
        set
```

```csharp
        {
            if (!object.Equals(wins, value))
            {
                wins = value;
                RaisePropertyChanged("Wins");
            }
        }
    }

    private int? points;
    public int? Points
    {
        get { return points; }
        set
        {
            if (!object.Equals(points, value))
            {
                points = value;
                RaisePropertyChanged("Points");
            }
        }
    }

    private void RacerToVM(Racer r)
    {
        this.key = r.EntityKey;
        this.Id = r.Id;
        this.FirstName = r.FirstName;
        this.LastName = r.LastName;
        this.Nationality = r.Nationality;
        this.Starts = r.Starts;
        this.Wins = r.Wins;
        this.Points = r.Points;
    }

    private Racer VMToRacer()
    {
        var current = Racer.CreateRacer(this.Id, this.FirstName,
            this.LastName);
        current.Nationality = this.Nationality;
        current.Starts = this.Starts;
        current.Wins = this.Wins;
        current.Points = this.Points;
        return current;
    }

    private DelegateCommand editCommand;
    public DelegateCommand EditCommand
    {
        get
        {
            return editCommand ??
                (editCommand = new DelegateCommand(
                    param => this.BeginEdit()));
        }
    }
```

```csharp
        private DelegateCommand cancelCommand;
        public DelegateCommand CancelCommand
        {
            get
            {
                return cancelCommand ??
                    (cancelCommand = new DelegateCommand(param =>
                        this.CancelEdit()));
            }
        }

        private DelegateCommand saveCommand;
        public DelegateCommand SaveCommand
        {
            get
            {
                return saveCommand ??
                    (saveCommand = new DelegateCommand(
                        param => this.EndEdit()));
            }
        }

        public void BeginEdit()
        {
            IsEditMode = true;
        }

        public void CancelEdit()
        {
            GetRacer();
            IsEditMode = false;
        }

        public void EndEdit()
        {
            UpdateRacer();
            IsEditMode = false;
        }

        private bool isEditMode;
        public bool IsEditMode
        {
            get { return isEditMode; }
            private set
            {
                if (!object.Equals(isEditMode, value))
                {
                    isEditMode = value;
                    RaisePropertyChanged("IsEditMode");
                }
            }
        }
    }
}
```

When the `GetRacerCommand` occurs, a racer is retrieved from the database, and properties of the ViewModel class are filled with the values of the `Racer` properties. The ViewModel class keeps a copy of these values to allow for direct data binding, and to keep it completely independent of the underlying data source.

The following three commands are related to the `IEditableObject` interface:

➤ `EditCommand` — On activation of the `EditCommand`, the ViewModel changes into edit mode by setting the `IsEditMode` to `true` property. This property can be used to change the UI to allow the user to edit values.

➤ `CancelCommand` — With `CancelCommand`, all values of the ViewModel properties are discarded, and the original values from the database are retrieved once more.

➤ `SaveCommand` — With the `SaveCommand`, properties of the ViewModel class are taken to store the information in the database.

With the UI, `TextBox` elements are used to allow the user to edit the data. With the `TextBox` elements, the `IsEnabled` property binds to the `IsEditMode` property to enable or disable interaction with the `TextBox`, depending on the mode. The `Text` property binds to the corresponding properties of the ViewModel class.

```xml
<Grid Grid.Row="1">
    <Grid.RowDefinitions>
        <RowDefinition />
        <RowDefinition />
        <RowDefinition />
        <RowDefinition />
        <RowDefinition />
        <RowDefinition />
    </Grid.RowDefinitions>
    <Grid.ColumnDefinitions>
        <ColumnDefinition Width="Auto" />
        <ColumnDefinition Width="*" />
    </Grid.ColumnDefinitions>
    <TextBlock Grid.Row="0" Grid.Column="0" Text="FirstName" />
    <TextBox IsEnabled="{Binding IsEditMode}"
             Text="{Binding FirstName}"
             Grid.Row="0" Grid.Column="1" />
    <TextBlock Grid.Row="1" Grid.Column="0" Text="LastName" />
    <TextBox IsEnabled="{Binding IsEditMode}" Text="{Binding LastName}"
             Grid.Row="1" Grid.Column="1" />
    <TextBlock Grid.Row="2" Grid.Column="0" Text="Nationality" />
    <TextBox IsEnabled="{Binding IsEditMode}"
             Text="{Binding Nationality}"
             Grid.Row="2" Grid.Column="1" />
    <TextBlock Grid.Row="3" Grid.Column="0" Text="Starts" />
    <TextBox IsEnabled="{Binding IsEditMode}" Text="{Binding Starts}"
             Grid.Row="3" Grid.Column="1" />
    <TextBlock Grid.Row="4" Grid.Column="0" Text="Wins" />
    <TextBox IsEnabled="{Binding IsEditMode}" Text="{Binding Wins}"
             Grid.Row="4" Grid.Column="1" />
    <TextBlock Grid.Row="5" Grid.Column="0" Text="Points" />
    <TextBox IsEnabled="{Binding IsEditMode}" Text="{Binding Points}"
```

```
                Grid.Row="5" Grid.Column="1" />
    </Grid>
```

Code file [Views/EditRacerView.xaml] available for download at Wrox.com.

The UI part that interacts with the commands is shown next. A `TextBox` is used to retrieve a racer with a specified identifier, and `Button` controls are defined to fire the commands available with the ViewModel class.

Available for download on Wrox.com

```
<Grid Grid.Row="0">
    <Grid.RowDefinitions>
        <RowDefinition />
        <RowDefinition />
    </Grid.RowDefinitions>
    <StackPanel Grid.Row="0" Orientation="Horizontal"
            HorizontalAlignment="Center" >
        <TextBlock Text="Id" />
        <TextBox Text="{Binding Id}" Width="80" />
        <Button Content="Get Racer" Command="{Binding GetRacerCommand}" />
    </StackPanel>
    <StackPanel Grid.Row="1" Orientation="Horizontal"
            HorizontalAlignment="Center">
        <Button Content="Edit" Command="{Binding EditCommand}" />
        <Button Content="Cancel" Command="{Binding CancelCommand}" />
        <Button Content="Save" Command="{Binding SaveCommand}" />
    </StackPanel>
</Grid>
```

Code file [Views/EditRacerView.xaml] available for download at Wrox.com.

Figure 13-13 shows the UI of the dialog running in edit mode.

What's not done yet is to check for false input by the user. Validation is added in the next section.

FIGURE 13-13: UI dialog running in edit mode

Validation

By default, if the user enters some data that is not accepted by the ViewModel, the properties of the ViewModel do not reflect the changes, and the user is not informed about the missing changes. Exceptions that occur from setting properties are, by default, just silently ignored. A red rectangle displays only if (before the properties are set in the code-behind) conversion fails from a string of the user input to the type of the property.

Supplying information to the user on failing validations can be easily resolved. WPF data binding includes validation rules that define what checking should occur. Validation rules derive from the base class `ValidationRule`.

The .NET Framework defines two concrete implementations:

- `ExceptionValidationRule` — This deals with exceptions from the ViewModel class.

- `DataErrorValidationRule` — With this implementation, it is necessary to implement the `IDataErrorInfo` interface.

The `Binding` class defines the `ValidatesOnExceptions` and `ValidatesOnDataErrors` Boolean properties that turn on these validation rules. Instead of using these simple properties, you can also define the validation rules using a longer binding term that is also needed with custom validation rules, as shown with the following code snippet:

```xml
<TextBox IsEnabled="{Binding IsEditMode}" Grid.Row="3" Grid.Column="1">
    <TextBox.Text>
        <Binding Path="Starts">
            <Binding.ValidationRules>
                <DataErrorValidationRule />
            </Binding.ValidationRules>
        </Binding>
    </TextBox.Text>
</TextBox>
```

The `EditRacerViewModel` ViewModel class is now changed to implement the `IDataErrorInfo` interface. This interface exposes the `Error` property and an indexer where a string is passed as an argument. Only this indexer must be implemented. With the indexer, the parameter receives a property name that should be validated. On error, a string containing the error message must be returned. If the validation is successful, `null` must be returned.

```csharp
string IDataErrorInfo.Error
{
    get { throw new System.NotImplementedException(); }
}

string IDataErrorInfo.this[string columnName]
{
    get
    {
        string message = null;
        switch (columnName)
        {
```

```
            case "Wins":
            case "Starts":
                if (Wins > Starts)
                    message = "Wins must be smaller or equal to Starts";
                break;
            default:
                break;
        }
        return message;
    }
}
```

Code file [ViewModels/EditRacerViewModel.cs] available for download at Wrox.com.

Running the application now and using the validation rule with every `TextBox` should be validated; nonvalid values are shown to the user with red rectangles surrounding the `TextBox`. Now take a look at how the UI can be changed for the error messages.

Displaying Errors

To display the error message that is returned via the `IDataErrorInfo` interface, you must create a custom style for the `TextBox` that contains a trigger. The trigger is active if the `Validation .HasError` attached property is `true`. With this trigger, the `ToolTip` property of the `TextBox` is set.

Now, binding is needed to access the value from the error message. To access the `TextBox` instance from the style, relative binding is used. `RelativeSource={x:Static RelativeSource .Self}` returns the `TextBox` instance where the style is applied. All the error messages can be read from the `Validation.Errors` attached property. This property returns a collection of active `ValidationError` objects. With `ValidationError`, the error message can be accessed with the `ErrorContent` property. `(Validation.Errors)[0].ErrorContent` returns the first error message.

Available for download on Wrox.com

```
<Style TargetType="TextBox">
    <Setter Property="Margin" Value="5" />
    <Setter Property="VerticalAlignment" Value="Center" />
    <Setter Property="Validation.ErrorTemplate"
            Value="{StaticResource validationTemplate}" />
    <Style.Triggers>
        <Trigger Property="Validation.HasError" Value="True">
            <Setter Property="ToolTip" Value="{Binding RelativeSource=
                {x:Static RelativeSource.Self},
                Path=(Validation.Errors)[0].ErrorContent}" />
            <Setter Property="Background" Value="Red" />
        </Trigger>
    </Style.Triggers>
</Style>
```

Code file [Views/EditRacerView.xaml] available for download at Wrox.com.

To display a different error view than the red rectangle around the failing `TextBox`, you can define a `ControlTemplate` referenced from the `TextBox` style previously shown. The style changes the

`Validation.ErrorTemplate` attached property to the template shown next. Instead of displaying a red rectangle, a big red ! is shown.

```
<ControlTemplate x:Key="validationTemplate">
    <DockPanel>
        <TextBlock Foreground="Red" FontSize="32" FontWeight="Bold"
                   Text="!" DockPanel.Dock="Left" />
        <AdornedElementPlaceholder DockPanel.Dock="Right" />
    </DockPanel>
</ControlTemplate>
```

Code file [Views/EditRacerView.xaml] available for download at Wrox.com.

Running the application, you can see the error display, as shown in Figure 13-14.

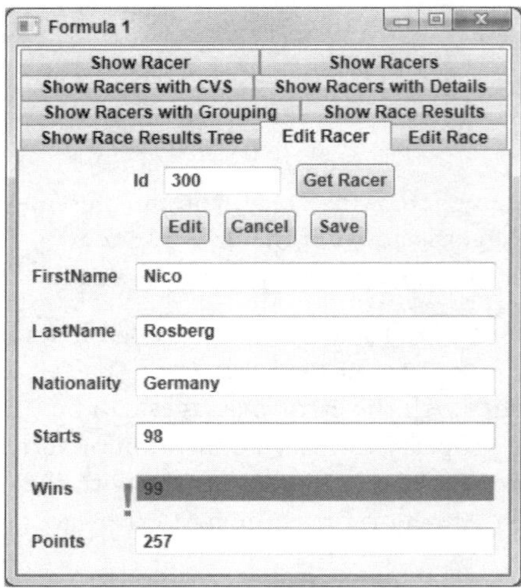

FIGURE 13-14: Displaying an error for inaccurate user input

Editing with a Grid

You use the `DataGrid` control when more than one record should be changed at a time. The last sample of this chapter demonstrates the use of the `DataGrid` control to add race results to the database.

The sample enables you to edit a race or to add a race. When adding a race, some records are pre-created and bound to the data grid to enable easy editing by the user. When the user has filled in the fields, the Save button can be clicked to store all the records.

The dialog contains buttons to add a race and to edit a race. These buttons are bound to `AddRaceCommand` and `EditRaceCommand`, as shown here:

```xml
<StackPanel Orientation="Horizontal" Grid.Row="0">
    <Button Content="Add a Race" Command="{Binding AddRaceCommand}"
            Margin="5" Padding="3" />
    <Button Content="Edit a Race" Command="{Binding EditRaceCommand}"
            Margin="5" Padding="3" />
</StackPanel>
```

Code file [Views/EditRaceView.xaml] available for download at Wrox.com.

The commands are defined with the ViewModel class `EditRaceViewModel`. When `AddRaceCommand` is fired, the `AddRace` method is invoked. This method changes the `AddRaceVisibility` property to `Visibility.Visible`. The default value assigned in the constructor is `Visibility.Collapsed`. Also, the `RaceDate` property is set to today to have a default value for the user to create race data.

`Circuits` is a property used by the View to retrieve a collection of `Circuit` objects defined by the EF designer. The `Circuit` type contains `Id`, `Name`, and `Country` properties.

```csharp
public class EditRaceViewModel : ViewModelBase, IDisposable
{
    private Formula1Entities data;

    public EditRaceViewModel()
    {
        AddRaceVisibility = Visibility.Collapsed;
        EditRaceVisibility = Visibility.Collapsed;
        RaceResultVisibility = Visibility.Collapsed;
        AddRacerVisibility = Visibility.Collapsed;

        if (!IsDesignTime)
        {
            data = new Formula1Entities();
        }
    }

    private DelegateCommand addRaceCommand;
    public DelegateCommand AddRaceCommand
    {
        get
        {
            return addRaceCommand ??
                (addRaceCommand = new DelegateCommand(
                    param => this.AddRace()));
        }
    }

    public void AddRace()
    {
        RaceDate = DateTime.Today;
        AddRaceVisibility = Visibility.Visible;
    }
```

```csharp
        private Visibility addRaceVisibility;
        public Visibility AddRaceVisibility
        {
            get
            {
                return addRaceVisibility;
            }
            set
            {
                addRaceVisibility = value;
                RaisePropertyChanged("AddRaceVisibility");
            }
        }


        private List<Circuit> circuits;
        public IEnumerable<Circuit> Circuits
        {
            get
            {
                if (!IsDesignTime)
                {
                    return circuits ??
                        (circuits = new List<Circuit>(
                            from c in data.Circuits
                            orderby c.Country
                            select c));
                }
                else
                    return null;
            }
        }
        //...
```

Code file [ViewModels/EditRaceViewModel.cs] available for download at Wrox.com.

The XAML code for the grid that has the Visibility bound property to the AddRaceVisibility property is shown in the next code snippet. The grid contains a DatePicker, where the SelectedDate property is bound to the RaceDate that is on display of the grid initialized to the current date. The user can change the date, and because of two-way binding, the information is written to the ViewModel class. A ComboBox is bound to the Circuits property. A data template defines TextBlock elements bound to the Country and Name properties available with the Circuit type.

```xml
<Grid Visibility="{Binding AddRaceVisibility}" Grid.Row="1">
    <Grid.RowDefinitions>
        <RowDefinition Height="Auto" />
        <RowDefinition Height="Auto" />
        <RowDefinition Height="Auto" />
    </Grid.RowDefinitions>
    <DatePicker Grid.Row="0" Margin="5" SelectedDate="{Binding
        RaceDate}" />
    <ComboBox Grid.Row="1" Margin="5" ItemsSource="{Binding Circuits}"
            IsSynchronizedWithCurrentItem="True">
```

```xml
<ComboBox.ItemTemplate>
    <DataTemplate>
        <StackPanel Orientation="Horizontal">
            <TextBlock Text="{Binding Country}" Margin="5" />
            <TextBlock Text="{Binding Name}" Margin="5" />
        </StackPanel>
    </DataTemplate>
</ComboBox.ItemTemplate>
</ComboBox>
<StackPanel Orientation="Horizontal" Grid.Row="2">
    <Button Content="Create" Command="{Binding CreateRaceCommand}"
            Margin="5" Padding="3" />
    <Button Content="Cancel" Command="{Binding CancelCommand}"
            Margin="5" Padding="3" />
    <Button Content="Save" Command="{Binding SaveCommand}"
            Margin="5" Padding="3" />
</StackPanel>
</Grid>
```

Code file [Views/EditRaceView.xaml] available for download at Wrox.com.

Starting the application and clicking the "Add a Race" button displays a dialog similar to Figure 13-15, where the user can define a date and select a circuit with the combo box.

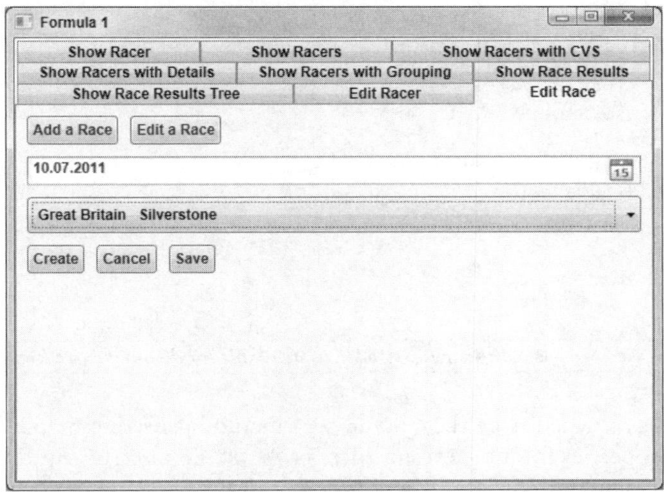

FIGURE 13-15: Dialog for user to define a date and select a circuit

Clicking the Create button invokes the `CreateRace` method with the help of the `CreateRaceCommand` command. This method fills some properties used by the `DataGrid` control for editing races. The `Racers` property is filled with racers who have results within the last ten years, and the `Teams` property is filled with all teams. The `DataGrid` control contains rows for each race result. The race results shown within a row of the grid are defined by the `RaceResultViewModel` type. Some values (such as position and points) are pre-filled in a loop. The `RaceResultViewModel` type is a simple ViewModel type designed in a similar way as the other ones to bind properties to the View.

```csharp
public void CreateRace()
{
    RaceResultVisibility = Visibility.Visible;

    // racers from the last ten years
    Racers = (from r in data.Racers
              from rr in r.RaceResults
              where rr.Race.Date.Year >= (RaceDate.Year - 10)
              select r).Distinct().OrderBy(r => r.FirstName).
                  ThenBy(r => r.LastName).ToList();

    Teams = (from t in data.Teams
             select t).OrderBy(t => t.Name).ToList();

    Circuit selectedCircuit =
        CollectionViewSource.GetDefaultView(Circuits).
        CurrentItem as Circuit;
    theRace = Race.CreateRace(0, selectedCircuit.Id, RaceDate);

    int resultId = -1;
    int[] points = { 25, 18, 15, 12, 10, 8, 6, 4, 2, 1 };
    for (int i = 0; i < 10; i++)
    {
        var raceResult = new RaceResultViewModel(this)
        {
            Id = resultId,
            RaceId = theRace.Id,
            Position = i + 1,
            Points = points[i],
            Racers = this.Racers,
            Teams = this.Teams
        };
        raceResults.Add(raceResult);

        resultId--;
    }
}
```

Code file [ViewModels/EditRaceViewModel.cs] available for download at Wrox.com.

The `RaceResultViewModel` type that is returned from the `CreateRace` method is used to map to race result values, and, thus, defines properties for a race result such as `RaceDate`, `Position`... The View supports not adding existing racers just by adding a string for the name, or selecting existing racers. This behavior is represented with the `SelectedRacer` and `NewRacer` properties.

```csharp
using System;
using System.Collections.Generic;
using System.Windows;
using Formula1.Infrastructure;
using Formula1.Model;

namespace Formula1.ViewModels
{
    public class RaceResultViewModel : ViewModelBase
```

```csharp
{
    private IEditRace editRace;

    public RaceResultViewModel(IEditRace editRace)
    {
        this.editRace = editRace;
        this.editRace.AddRacerVisibility = Visibility.Collapsed;
    }

    private DelegateCommand addRacerCommand;
    public DelegateCommand AddRacerCommand
    {
        get
        {
            return addRacerCommand ??
                (addRacerCommand = new DelegateCommand(param =>
                    this.AddRacer()));
        }
    }
    public void AddRacer()
    {
        this.editRace.AddRacerVisibility = Visibility.Visible;
    }

    private DateTime raceDate;
    public DateTime RaceDate
    {
        get { return raceDate; }
        set
        {
            raceDate = value;
            RaisePropertyChanged("RaceDate");
        }
    }

    private int position;
    public int Position
    {
        get { return position; }
        set
        {
            position = value;
            RaisePropertyChanged("Position");
        }
    }

    private int grid;
    public int Grid
    {
        get { return grid; }
        set
        {
            grid = value;
            RaisePropertyChanged("Grid");
        }
    }
```

```csharp
        }

        private int points;
        public int Points
        {
            get { return points; }
            set
            {
                points = value;
                RaisePropertyChanged("Points");
            }
        }

        private IEnumerable<Racer> racers;
        public IEnumerable<Racer> Racers
        {
            get { return racers; }
            internal set { racers = value; }
        }

        private string newRacer;
        public string NewRacer
        {
            get { return newRacer; }
            set
            {
                if (!object.Equals(newRacer, value))
                {
                    newRacer = value;
                    RaisePropertyChanged("NewRacer");
                }
            }
        }

        private IEnumerable<Team> teams;
        public IEnumerable<Team> Teams
        {
            get { return teams; }
            internal set { teams = value; }
        }

        private string newTeam;
        public string NewTeam
        {
            get { return newTeam; }
            set
            {
                if (!object.Equals(newTeam, value))
                {
                    newTeam = value;
                    RaisePropertyChanged("NewTeam");
                }
            }
        }

        public int Id { get; set; }
```

```csharp
        public int RaceId { get; set; }

        private Racer selectedRacer;
        public Racer SelectedRacer
        {
            get { return selectedRacer; }
            set
            {
                if (!object.Equals(selectedRacer, value))
                {
                    selectedRacer = value;
                    RaisePropertyChanged("Racer");
                }
            }
        }

        private Team selectedTeam;
        public Team SelectedTeam
        {
            get { return selectedTeam; }
            set
            {
                if (!object.Equals(selectedTeam, value))
                {
                    selectedTeam = value;
                    RaisePropertyChanged("SelectedTeam");
                }
            }
        }
    }
}
```

Code file [ViewModels/RaceResultViewModel.cs] available for download at Wrox.com.

The most important part of this section, of course, is the `DataGrid` control. The data grid contains UI elements for editing race results. This grid is shown only when the `RaceResultVisibility` property is set to `Visible` because of an outer grid control setting. The parent `DataContext` used by the `DataGrid` control is set to the `RaceResults` property of the ViewModel. `RaceResults` returns a collection of `RaceResultViewModel`. The data grid can now bind to properties of this type.

A simple configuration of the `DataGrid` control would be to set the property `AutoGenerateColumns` to `true`. This way, the data grid has default UI elements for every property of the bound item and displays the name of the property within the header.

In this scenario, this feature cannot be used. The `DataGrid` can also use types that derive from the base class `DataGridColumn` for displaying items. Examples are `DataGridTextColumn`, `DataGridCheckBoxColumn`, and `DataGridHyperlinkColumn` to display text, a check box, and a hyperlink, respectively.

`DataGridComboBoxColumn` displays enumeration data where the user can select from a list. The following sample code makes use of several `DataGridTextColumn` elements that bind to the `Position`, `Grid`, and `Points` properties.

```xml
<Grid Grid.Row="1" Visibility="{Binding RaceResultVisibility}">
    <Grid.RowDefinitions>
        <RowDefinition Height="Auto" />
        <RowDefinition Height="Auto" />
    </Grid.RowDefinitions>
    <Grid DataContext="{Binding RaceResults}" Grid.Row="0">
        <DataGrid x:Name="raceGrid" ItemsSource="{Binding}"
                AutoGenerateColumns="False" SelectionMode="Single"
                SelectionUnit="FullRow">
            <DataGrid.Columns>
                <DataGridTextColumn Width="Auto" Header="Pos"
                                Binding="{Binding Position}" />
                <DataGridTemplateColumn Width="*" Header="Racer"
                                MinWidth="210">
                    <DataGridTemplateColumn.CellTemplate>
                        <DataTemplate>
                            <StackPanel Orientation="Horizontal">
                                <ComboBox MinWidth="190"
                                    ItemsSource="{Binding Racers}"
                                    TextSearch.TextPath="Name"
                                    SelectedItem=
                                        "{Binding SelectedRacer,
                                        Mode=OneWayToSource,
                                        UpdateSourceTrigger=LostFocus}"
                                    IsEditable="True"
                                    Text="{Binding NewRacer,
                                        Mode=OneWayToSource,
                                        UpdateSourceTrigger=LostFocus}"
                                />
                                <Button Content="+"
                                    Command="{Binding
                                        AddRacerCommand}" />
                            </StackPanel>
                        </DataTemplate>
                    </DataGridTemplateColumn.CellTemplate>
                </DataGridTemplateColumn>
                <DataGridTemplateColumn Width="*" Header="Team"
                                MinWidth="120">
                    <DataGridTemplateColumn.CellTemplate>
                        <DataTemplate>
                            <ComboBox ItemsSource="{Binding Teams}"
                                TextSearch.TextPath="Name"
                                SelectedItem=
                                    "{Binding SelectedTeam,
                                    Mode=OneWayToSource,
                                    UpdateSourceTrigger=LostFocus}"
                                IsEditable="True"
                                Text="{Binding NewTeam,
                                    Mode=OneWayToSource,
```

```
                                    UpdateSourceTrigger=LostFocus}" />
                        </DataTemplate>
                      </DataGridTemplateColumn.CellTemplate>
                    </DataGridTemplateColumn>
                    <DataGridTextColumn Width="Auto" Header="Grid"
                                        Binding="{Binding Grid}" />
                    <DataGridTextColumn Width="Auto" Header="Pts"
                                        Binding="{Binding Points}" />
                </DataGrid.Columns>
            </DataGrid>
        </Grid>
```

Code file [Views/EditRaceView.xaml] available for download at Wrox.com.

For more flexibility, the `DataGridTemplateColumn` can be used. With this type, a template can be defined to use any WPF UI element for displaying the column. The data grid can be used in a read and an edit mode. For these differentiation settings, `CellTemplate` and `CellEditingTemplate` can be defined to have a different View, depending on the mode. With this code, the data grid is always used for editing, and, thus, only the `CellTemplate` is defined.

The cell template to display and enter the racer for a race result makes use of a `ComboBox` control bound to the `Racers` property. The `SelectedItem` property gives information to the ViewModel about the racer the user selected by binding it to the `Racer` property.

The `ComboBox` has an option to either select an existing item, or write a new item. Behind the scenes, the `ComboBox` makes use of a `TextBox` control for this option. This feature of the `ComboBox` can be enabled by setting the `IsEditable` property to `true`. Then, to retrieve the value that is added from the user, the `Text` property is bound to the `NewRacer` property.

The `Text` property is always set by the `ComboBox`, no matter if one element of the bound items is selected, or new text is added. This can be differentiated by checking the `SelectedItem` property. The `SelectedItem` property is `null` in case new text is added.

In the sample, the bindings of both the `SelectedItem` and `Text` property are configured with the mode `OneWayToSource`, and the `UpdateSourceTrigger` is set to `LostFocus`. `OneWayToSource` is configured because this binding should only be done from the UI control (the `ComboBox`) to the bound source (the `SelectedRacer` and `NewRacer` properties). The `UpdateSource` trigger is set because if the `ComboBox` is used within the template of the `DataGrid`, the trigger to change the source by default is only done explicitly from program code. Changing the value to `LostFocus` fires the change of the source on lost focus of the `ComboBox` control.

With this configuration of the `ComboBox`, the user can either select an existing racer, or add a new one. Another option for adding a new racer is the additional button that displays in the same column to create a new racer. With the `AddRacerCommand` command, a new dialog displays.

Running the application, it's now possible to add race results, as shown in Figure 13-16.

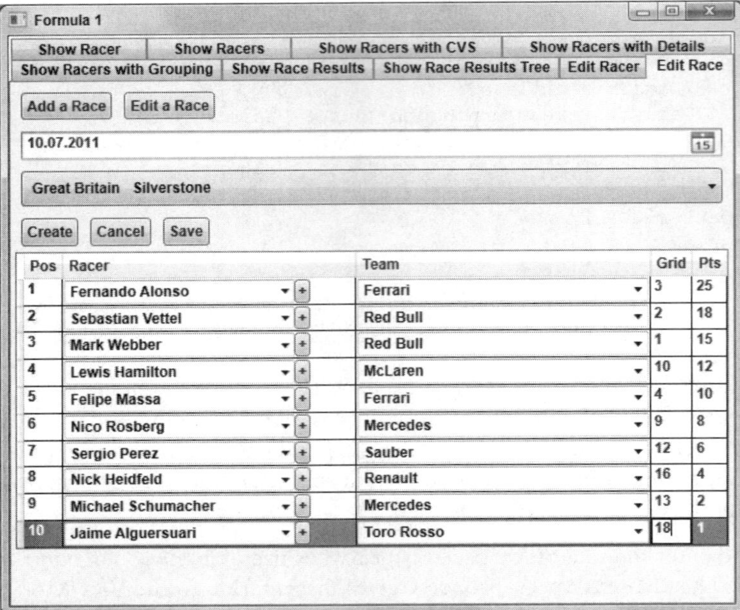

FIGURE 13-16: Adding race results

SUMMARY

In this chapter, you've learned about rich WPF data-binding features, starting with binding to simple properties, up to using data grids to edit data. You've learned how to bind lists in various ways with grouping, displaying hierarchical lists, and dealing with large lists in an efficient way. You've also learned about some features for editing data, including validation, and how to customize the UI for this.

ABOUT THE AUTHOR

Christian Nagel has worked with Microsoft .NET and created distributed applications with this technology since the first Beta in 2000. He is author of several .NET books, Microsoft Regional Director, MVP for C#, associate thinktecture, and offers training, coaching, and consulting services. He can be contacted at `www.cninnovation.com`, and via twitter `@christiannagel`.

14

Driving Development with User Stories and BDD

by Scott Millett

If I could offer you one piece of advice (apart from always wear sunscreen), it would be to do your utmost to understand your domain inside and out, share your stakeholder's visions and goals, and sit as close to your domain experts as possible. If you follow my advice, then you should find software development nice and easy. Okay, so you have to learn the framework and language syntax, but after you master them, everything else should be relatively simple.

So, if development is easy, why do so many projects get in trouble and fail to deliver what the business needs? The reason that projects fail is not because of a lack of programming ability or technical expertise, but rather because of a lack of understanding, communication, and business knowledge.

This lack of understanding stems from how developers capture knowledge of the problem domain they work in. Put another way, if developers and customers cannot effectively communicate, then even with the most accomplished programmers in the world, you ultimately cannot satisfy the needs of your customers.

This chapter is about refocusing efforts on how requirements of a system are captured, how customers communicate those requirements through user stories, how development can be driven from the language and features through behavior-driven development, and, ultimately, how software can be delivered to meet the needs and expectations of your customer.

CAPTURING REQUIREMENTS AS FEATURES WITH USER STORIES

A user story is typically one or two sentences, written in plain language on an index card, describing a feature of value to the business. You will learn that if you employ user stories to capture the features of a system as a direct replacement for more formal, all-encompassing requirements documentation, you can re-address the balance placed on communication during software development. The shift to emphasizing the importance on communication over detailed specifications can also help to commit and underline a customer's responsibility to the success or failure of the project.

Through regular and frequent conversations with the people the software is being built for, greater knowledge about the problem domain can be gained. This ultimately leads to a development team that is far more aligned and in sync with customer expectations and, therefore, capable of meeting the needs of the customer.

Before you can understand exactly what a user story is, you need to understand what problems they solve when compared to the traditional upfront requirements documentation.

Problems with Formal Requirements Documentation

In theory, extensive documentation is great. Gather all requirements up front, create a document detailing exactly what is needed, hand it all to the development team, wait 6 months, and have them deliver the product that you want. In reality, however, for all except the most rigid of projects, this process fails.

One of the most important artifacts of the upfront design approach to development is the requirements document — the Bible, if you will. A funny thing happens when all development is focused on what is contained within the requirements Bible. The document becomes the contract for the project. If it's not in the requirements document, it isn't done. The document controls development and prevents communication between the development team and the customer, which leads to issues and the famous phrase, "It's what I asked for, not what I need."

Following are some of the major problems with requirements documents:

➤ Documents are open to interpretation.

➤ Large requirements documents act as an incapacitating contract.

➤ Customers do not know what they want.

➤ Customers change their minds.

➤ Developers don't understand the requirements.

➤ Customers are not sure of the details of all requirements at the start of a project.

What is needed is a move away from trying to capture every conceivable piece of information before a project starts, and toward a development team that understands what the customer wants to achieve, who will work closely with the customer as it discovers the details, and who will adapt to the customer when requirements change as the project progresses and more knowledge is gained.

User stories shift the focus from writing large, upfront documentation (which can act as an inflexible and somewhat incapacitating contract), toward communication through talking, and talking often.

Using User Stories to Focus on Business Value and Promote Communication

In short, a user story is a short description of a unit of functionality that represents value to the customer. User stories are a more effective and lean way to capture requirements with just enough information to determine complexity and estimate effort to deliver.

The lack of details in user stories is one of the biggest benefits. Rather than trying to write down all requirements in one session, and hoping the customer has the answers to all your questions, you instead capture the essence of the feature, and commit to having a conversation with the customer at a later date to discuss the details.

User stories are typically captured on index cards following the template shown in Figure 14-1.

User stories must include the following:

- ➤ They are understandable by all and written in the language of the customer.

- ➤ They provide enough detail to estimate. When the story is worked on, a conversation is needed for the details.

- ➤ They are testable, enabling the development team to know when it is complete.

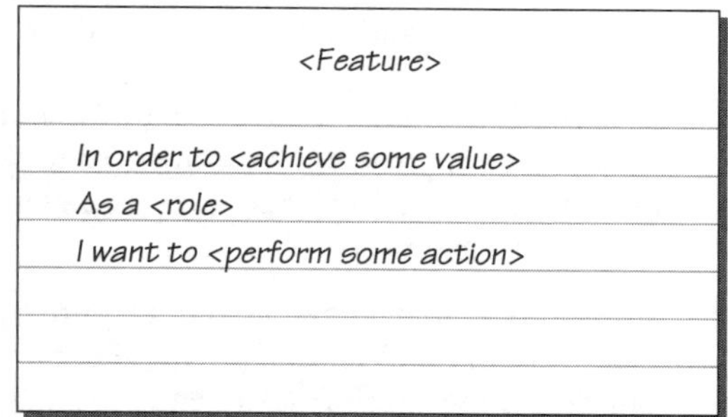

FIGURE 14-1: Example of user story captured on an index card

Later in this chapter, you will run through an exercise that utilizes user stories to capture requirements for a simple game of Tic-Tac-Toe.

For more information on user stories, see User Stories Applied: For Agile Software Development *(Boston: Addison-Wesley Professional, 2004) by Mike Cohn.*

User stories are great for capturing features, but to ensure the feature is developed and meets the needs of the customer, developers must understand the acceptance criteria of a business feature (in other words, how to know when a feature is done).

Feature Scenarios and Story Acceptance Criteria

When capturing requirements with user stories, it's a great idea to use the reverse side of the index card to jot down acceptance criteria and information that can assist you when working and talking to the customer at a later date.

After you note the initial acceptance criteria, you can produce acceptance scenarios to further confirm knowledge of the problem domain, and also use as tests to ascertain when the feature has been developed.

Scenarios are typically written in the "Given, When, Then" template, as shown here:

```
Given some initial context
When an event occurs
Then ensure some outcomes
```

Now apply the template to the "win a game" feature of Tic-Tac-Toe, and specifically the criteria that confirms a diagonal win.

```
Given that I have started a game of Tic-Tac-Toe
And the following moves have been played
```

```
        X  |  O  |
        ---------------
        O  |  X  |
        ---------------
           |     |
When Player X places a token at the coordinate 2, 2
Then Player X should be the winner
```

Because of the plain language that is used, describing acceptance criteria in this format makes it trivial for developers and customers to understand the features. It also makes it easy for the development team to know when it has completed a unit of work because it is simple for them to test against the clear acceptance criteria.

Now that you understand how to capture features using user stories, and how to define acceptance criteria, you can focus on turning those requirements into working software, safe in the knowledge that your development effort is driven with a mindset focused squarely on delivering value to the business.

But where do you start to develop? Maybe you should use TDD to drive out the system from the inside, starting with the smallest unit of functionality... or maybe there's a more effective way.

THE SHORTCOMINGS OF TDD

Test-Driven Development (TDD) is the methodology of driving the design of a system through writing a failing test, writing the code to get the test to pass, refactoring to a simpler design, and repeating until the application is built. TDD focuses on *unit testing*, which involves testing the smallest pieces of functionality. When driving design with this level of detail, you can easily become lost in the technical aspects of what you are trying to achieve, rather than focusing on the overall aim and behavior of the system.

TDD can place too much emphasis on the mechanics of a component in your application — in other words, how it does, rather than what it does. Developers must be disciplined when working with TDD to ensure that they always have the bigger picture in mind when they decide about the low-level technical details of a feature. For example, customers don't care about the intricate details of how data is stored, but rather that it is available when they use the system.

TDD still has a place in driving the development of a system. However, a more focused methodology is required to wrap the TDD process and emphasize the behavior of a system, rather than technicalities — or put another way, the "what it does" rather than "how it does it."

FOCUSING ON BEHAVIOR WITH BDD

Behavior Driven Development (BDD) has evolved from TDD, with a good dollop of *Domain Driven Design (DDD)* mixed in. BDD helps to keep focus on the behavior of a system by using the features of TDD, as well as the shared ubiquitous language of the business domain. BDD drives the design of a system using the desired features of the customer in a language that everyone can understand, and that clearly communicates the benefit and purpose of features under development.

With a better understanding of the domain through features, developers can incorporate this shared language into the code base, which further helps to concentrate efforts on what the system is trying to achieve, rather than how it will achieve it.

How the system will accomplish what it is designed to do (that is, the technical details) is still important, and this is where TDD comes in. Used together with BDD, they form "outside-in development."

Outside-In Development

Outside-in development is the process of driving the design of an application from the point of view of the customer. Customers typically measure the success of an application through the user interfaces (UIs) that they leverage to interact with it. With this in mind, outside-in development utilizes BDD to drive the design of the code from the UI (or the outside), and then employs TDD to discover the objects, services, and other code that form the domain of the application (or the inside).

Figure 14-2, the "BDD figure of 8" shows the process of BDD and outside-in development The "figure of 8" name comes from the two circles placed upon one another representing the life cycles of driving application and object behavior.

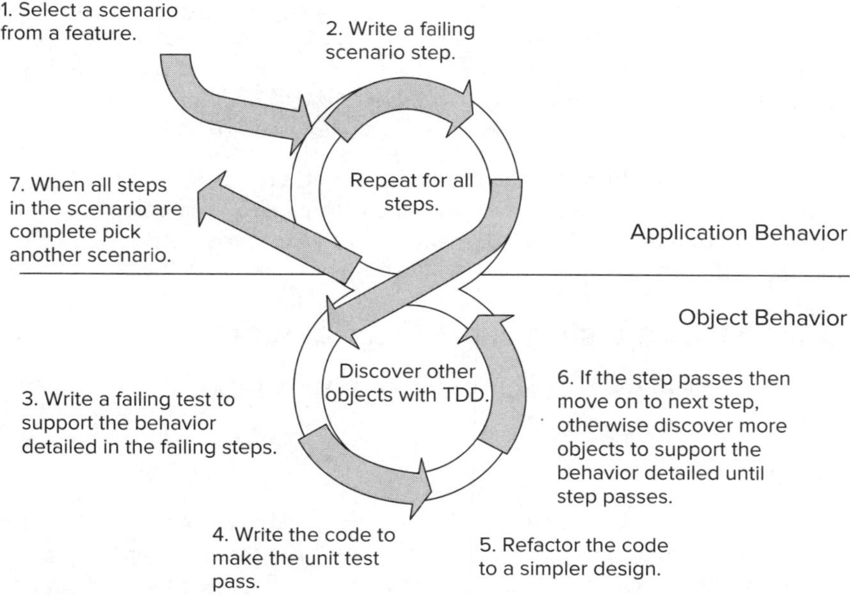

FIGURE 14-2: The "BDD figure of 8" diagram showing the process of BDD and outside-in development

The process of outside-in development begins with a feature selection, such as the following:

```
In order to place an order
As a customer
I want to add products to my basket
```

Then, a scenario is selected, such as the following:

```
Given I am on a product detail page for a hat costing $5
When I click the add to basket button
Then I should have 1 hat in my basket
And then basket total should be $5
```

The next action is to write a failing scenario step. In this instance, you would create code that confirms that the product detail page can display. For the page to display, you may discover that, in a web scenario, you need a new controller and controller action, and maybe a repository to retrieve the details of the product displayed.

You drive the design of the various components needed to display the page using TDD. After all the code is written to satisfy the scenario step, you can move on to the next step that handles the action of adding the product to the basket. Again, you drop down into TDD to drive the design and development of the low-level details that support the steps behavior.

This process is repeated until all steps of the scenario are passing, at which point you move on to the next scenario. After all scenarios are complete, you move on to the next feature until all features are complete.

Using the outside-in approach, you can quickly produce working code that is driven directly from the requirements and needs of the customer. This is achieved by working in vertical slices of functionality, rather than layers of responsibilities. Working from the outside in also enables customers to provide feedback on how the system behaves from an early stage, allowing developers to fine-tune the design and behavior of the system to better meet the needs of the customers. Leaner and more focused domain models built from features help to adhere to the "You Ain't Gonna Need It" (YAGNI) principle, and avoid unnecessary and overly complex domain hierarchies.

You should now have a good understanding of what BDD is all about. However, to use it to drive your development efforts, you must think about how you write your code. The simplest way to accomplish this is to use a BDD framework that guides you to turn your stories and acceptance criteria scenarios into working code.

Turning Features into Code Using BDD Frameworks

Some great frameworks support BDD in the world of .NET and beyond. Let's take a look at a couple of choice cuts.

Using NUnit in a BDD Style

NUnit is one of the most popular unit testing frameworks for .NET, and it's just as effective when used as a runner for BDD specifications. You can get NUnit by navigating to www.nunit.org/. The following code snippet is from the exercise that you tackle later in this chapter, which you can find in the code download on this book's companion website (www.wrox.com):

```
public class when_player_X_makes_the_first_move : with_a_TicTacToeGame
{
    public override void Given()
    {
        // No context to set up
    }

    public override void When()
```

```
        {
            SUT.place_token_at(new Coordinate(0, 1));
        }

        [Then]
        public void I_should_be_told_that_player_O_is_next_to_go()
        {
            Assert.That(SUT.next_player_to_move, Is.EqualTo("O"));
        }
    }
```

To align the NUnit specification code with the "Given, When, Then" syntax, an abstract base class can provide a template method. The SUT (System Under Test) property is created in the set-up method of the base class that initializes an instance of the TicTacToeGame object.

MSpec

MSpec is short for Machine.Specifications and is available from the project home page at https://github.com/machine/machine.specifications. According to the website, MSpec can be described as follows:

> *"…a Context/Specification framework geared towards removing language noise and simplifying tests."*

MSpec utilizes lambdas to produce code that is as free from noise as possible. When you get your head around the funny syntax, you will find MSpec to be a powerful BDD framework.

The following code snippet shows the equivalent MSpec version of the specification example used to demonstrate the NUnit code, which, in turn, is based on the exercise that you do later in this chapter (and available on this book's companion website at www.wrox.com):

```
    [Subject(typeof(TicTacToeGame), "Game Play")]
    public class when_player_X_makes_the_first_move : with_a_TicTaceToeGame
    {
        Because of = () => SUT.place_token_at(new Coordinate(0, 1));

        It should_say_that_player_O_is_next_to_go =
                    () => Assert.That(SUT.next_player_to_move, Is.EqualTo("O"));
    }
```

Reporting is a great feature of MSpec. When running the specs, MSpec produces some readable output, as shown in Figure 14-3, which can be handed straight to your customer for verification.

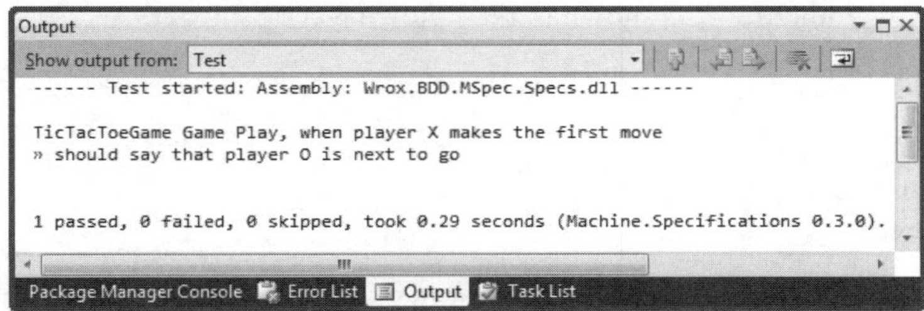

FIGURE 14-3: Output from MSpec

Ruby Cucumber and the Gherkin Domain Specific Language (DSL)

The Cucumber BDD tool for Ruby (`http://cukes.info/`) parses plain-text scenarios written in the Gherkin syntax form into code that runs step definitions that you produce. The following snippet shows an example of the Gherkin syntax that Cucumber understands:

```
Feature: Game Play
    In order to play a game of tic-tac-toe
    As a player
    I want to know the state of play


Scenario: Alternating moves
    Given that I have started a new game
    When Player "X" places a token at the coordinate "0","1"
    Then I should be told that player "O" is next to go
```

As a developer, your job is to create the step definitions that Cucumber requires to prove the acceptance criteria.

The following code snippet shows some Ruby code that defines the step definitions:

```
Given /^that I have started a new game$/ do
    pending
end

When /^player X places a token at the coordinate$/ do
    pending
end

Then /^I should be told that player O is next to go$/ do
    pending
end
```

Even though the Cucumber framework is for Ruby, it can still be utilized when working with .NET. Testers who have little programming experience and are verifying acceptance criteria may find it easier to learn the lean Ruby scripting language to run acceptance tests, rather than working in C#. Also, seasoned C# developers may want to leverage the mature Cucumber framework to verify that acceptance criteria have been satisfied.

SpecFlow

SpecFlow (available to download from `www.specflow.org/`) is the .NET version of the Cucumber BDD framework, which stays faithful to the Gherkin syntax. Features and scenarios are written in the exact same way as with the Cucumber tool, as shown in the following code snippet:

```
Feature: Game Play
    In order to play a game of tic-tac-toe
    As a player
    I want to know the state of play

Scenario: Alternating moves
    Given that I have started a new game
    When Player "X" places a token at the coordinate "0","1"
    Then I should be told that player "O" is next to go
```

SpecFlow uses a custom tool to parse the plain-text file into code that the .NET Framework can understand. The code produced by SpecFlow expects to find step definitions that match the steps of the plain-text scenarios. As with Cucumber, your job is to provide those step definitions and assert the behavior, as shown in the following code snippet:

```
[Binding]
public class GamePlaySteps
{
    [Given(@"that I have started a new game")]
    public void GivenThatIHaveStartedANewGame()
    {
        GameStorage.Current = new TicTacToeGame(new
            TicTacToeWinningCondition());

        Assert.That(GameStorage.Current.is_in_play, Is.True);
    }

    [When(@"Player ""(.*)"" places a token at the coordinate
        ""(.*)"",""(.*)""")]
    public void WhenAPlayerPlacesAToken(string player, int x_coordinate,
        int y_coordinate)
    {
        GameStorage.Current.place_token_at(
                                new Coordinate(x_coordinate,
                                    y_coordinate));
    }

    [Then(@"I should be told that player ""(.*)"" is next to go")]
    public void ThenIShouldShouldBeToldThatTheNextPlayerIs(string player_token)
    {
        Assert.That(GameStorage.Current.next_player_to_move,
            Is.EqualTo(player_token));
    }
}
```

SpecFlow is the best BDD framework for .NET when developing in the outside-in method. Its plain text (to describe the features and scenarios) becomes an artifact of the Visual Studio solution and ensures that it acts as living documentation of the behaviors of the system (which can be understood by customers with no technical knowledge).

To provide you with real-world experience of BDD, let's now work through a small code kata that utilizes the SpecFlow BDD framework.

The Tic-Tac-Toe BDD Kata

Now that you have read about the benefits of capturing feature requirements as user stories, and how by applying the BDD process you can drive your development and keep focus on delivering business value, it's time to see it in action. For this small code kata, you will develop an implementation of the classic game Tic-Tac-Toe (or naughts and crosses, if you're from my side of the pond). Pretend, however, that you have never heard of this game (even better if you haven't), and, as a diligent developer, your first course of action is to understand the domain better by capturing the features of the game.

 Code kata *is a term coined by Dave Thomas, co-author (with Andrew Hunt) of the book* The Pragmatic Programmer: *From* Journeyman to Master *(Boston: Addison-Wesley Professional, 1999), in a bow to the Japanese concept of kata in the martial arts. A code kata is an exercise in programming that helps hone your skills through practice and repetition.*

CAPTURING THE TIC-TAC-TOE FEATURES WITH USER STORIES

The best way to capture the features of a domain that you have no idea about is to talk to a domain expert, and your Tic-Tac-Toe expert is Mark.

You: "Hi Mark, I am going to be developing the Tic-Tac-Toe game. Can you tell me what your vision for the game is?"

Mark: "Sure. We want a simple console-based game for two players."

You: "Sounds great. Before we get into the details of the application, could you tell me how the game is played? I'm afraid I have never played before."

Mark: "Okay, no problem. Tic-Tac-Toe is a game for two players, played on a 3 × 3 grid. The first player to get three in a row wins."

You: "Three what?"

Mark: "Tokens. You have a player with an X token and a player with an O token."

You: "So, to win a game of Tic-Tac-Toe, a player must get three tokens in a line. Cool. That sounds like my first user story." (See Figure 14-4.)

You: "So, is this vertical? Horizontal? Or diagonal?"

Mark: "All of the above! As long as a player has three tokens in row, it doesn't matter if it's on a row, on a column, or from one corner to another."

Win a game

In order to win a game of Tic-Tac-Toe

As player

I must get 3 of my tokens in a row

FIGURE 14-4: User story describing the winning a game feature

You: "Ah, I understand. I will jot that down as acceptance criteria on the reverse side of the card for the user story." (See Figure 14-5.)

You: "Okay, what else do I need to know?"

Mark: "Well, you might want to jot down that you need a 3 × 3 grid to play."

You: "Ah, good call, I almost forgot. I will also draw a simple grid to visualize the game board." (See Figure 14-6.)

You: "So, can you place your token on top of another player's token and replace it?"

Mark: "No, that is not a valid move. Tokens can be placed only on empty squares within the grid."

You: "Okay, I will just make a note of that." (See Figure 14-7.)

You: "Okay, I think I have enough information on the rules of the game. How will the game start and how should we display the state of the game? Do you want players to be able to input their names?"

Mark: "Oh no, nothing as fancy as that. Perhaps just a little welcome message with some instructions on what to do could be displayed on the screen."

You: "Great, how about taking input from the players?"

Mark: "Can we just have them enter a grid reference or box number into the console?"

You: "Yes we can."

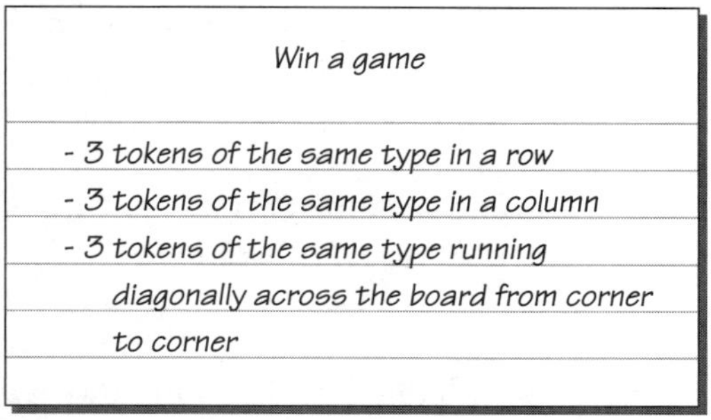

Mark: "Basically after every move we need to update the display on the console application, what we show to the players and how they interact is very important."

You: "I understand. I will capture that as another story." (See Figure 14-8.)

FIGURE 14-5: Acceptance criteria for winning a game feature

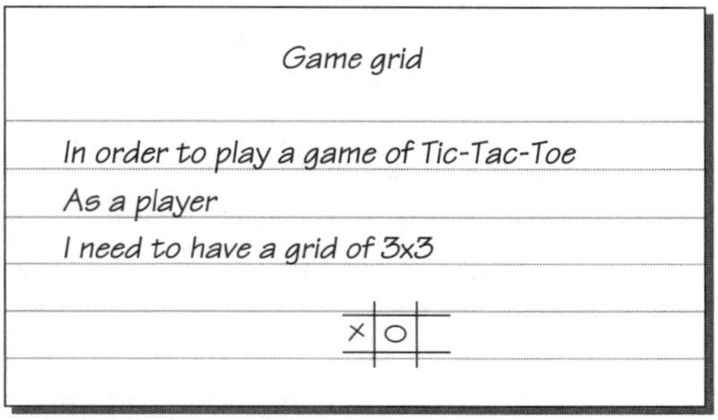

FIGURE 14-6: User story describing game grid feature

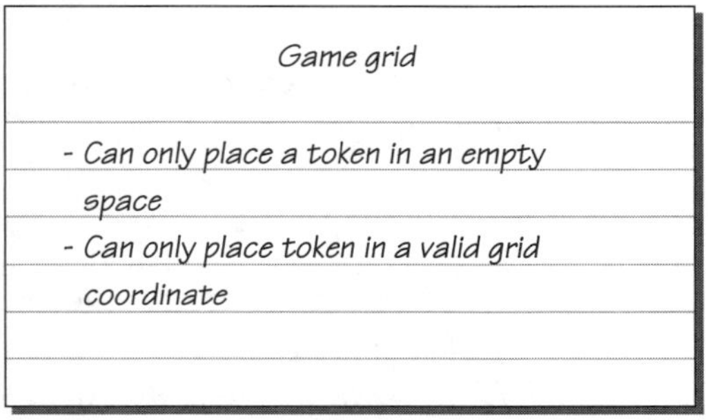

FIGURE 14-7: Acceptance criteria for game grid feature

You: "And I will add some notes to the back of the card on the welcome screen and inputting moves."

Mark: "Also, the players need to view the board so that they can plan their next move."

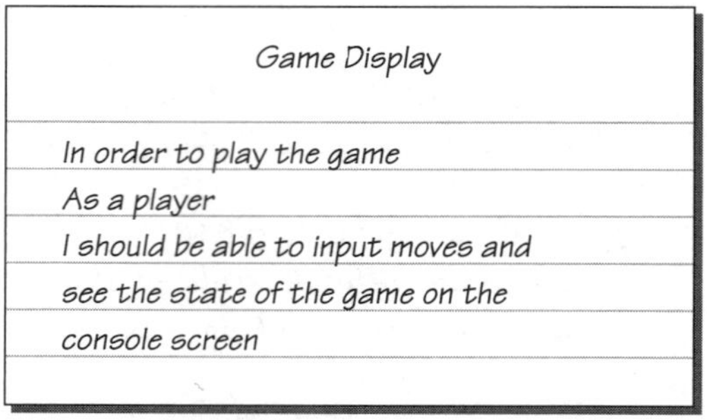

You: "Right, I understand. So, before each move they can take a look at the board so that they know where to place their next token. Cool! I will add that as more criteria for displaying the state of a game." (See Figure 14-9.)

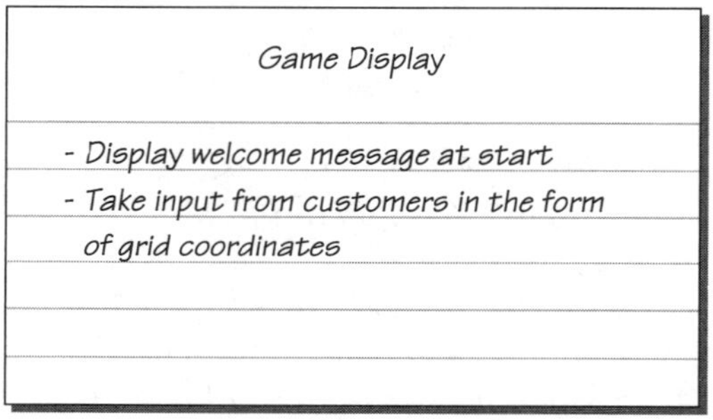

You: "Oh, one thing that I didn't ask when we were talking about the rules of the game was about drawing a game, is this possible?"

Mark: "Yes. It is possible to have a draw. If all spaces on the board are used, and no more tokens can be placed, then the game is a draw."

You: "Gotcha. I will capture that as another user story." (See Figure 14-10.)

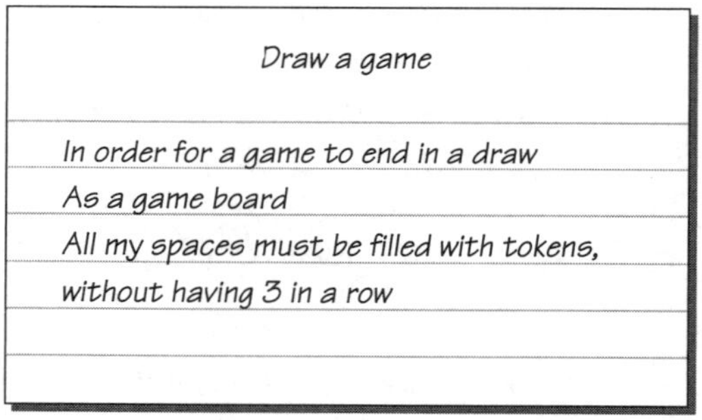

You: "Anything else?"

Mark: "Well, I guess for people who have never played the game before, it would be helpful to let them know whose turn it is."

You: "Yes, and they would also need to know if the game has a winner or has ended in a draw. I will add these points as notes on displaying the state of the game story." (See Figure 14-11.)

Mark: "Yep, that sounds good."

You: "So, who takes the first turn at the start of a game?"

FIGURE 14-8: Story describing the display of the game

FIGURE 14-9: Acceptance criteria for story describing the display of the game

FIGURE 14-10: Story describing the drawing condition of a game

Mark: "Traditionally player X is always the first to play."

You: "Brilliant! I will make a note of that." (See Figure 14-12.)

You: "Lovely. I think I have enough user stories to start to work. Can you think of anything else?"

Mark: "No, I think you have it all."

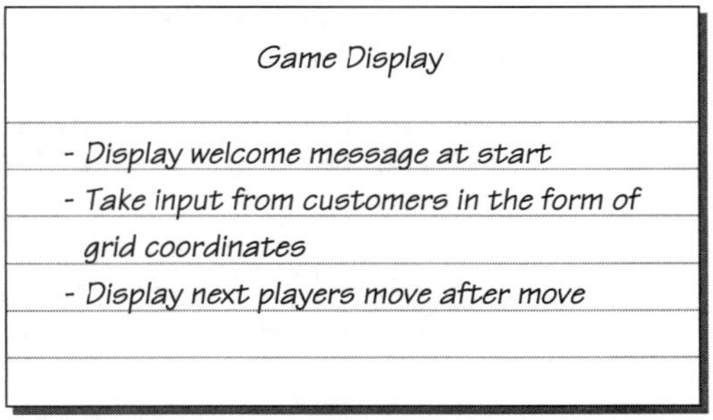

You should now have a much better idea of how you can use user stories to capture requirements. When capturing features as user stories, remember to do the following:

➤ Engage with the domain expert and capture features in the language of the customer, often referred to the *ubiquitous language*.

➤ Ensure that your stories are testable, can be estimated, and represent value to the business.

➤ Don't transcribe meetings. Capture just enough detail to understand a feature. Remember, user stories are reminders for conversations at a later date.

When you can't think of any more features, it's a good idea to go through some scenarios for each feature. This can help you to understand the feature at a more detailed level, as well as provide you with some acceptance criteria to test against.

FIGURE 14-11: More criteria for the story describing the display of the game

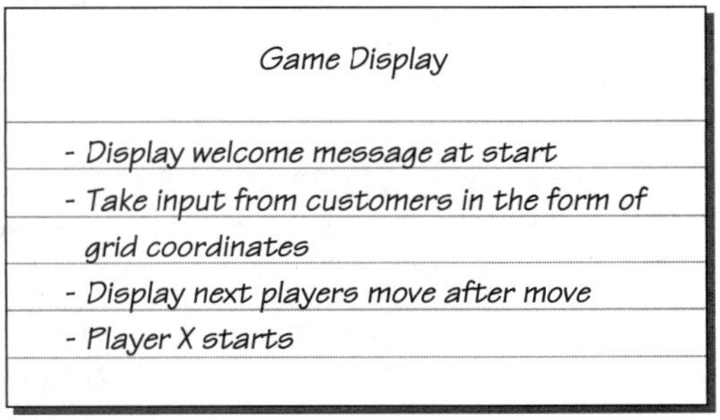

FIGURE 14-12: Even more criteria for the story describing the display of the game

GETTING STARTED WITH THE PROJECT

To start this project, the first thing you must do is install SpecFlow. SpecFlow integrates with Visual Studio to turn your Gherkin syntax into code that the .NET runtime can understand. Navigate to `www.specflow.org/`, download, and run the installation package.

With SpecFlow installed, fire up Visual Studio and create a new solution named `Wrox.BDD`. Add the following class libraries to the solution:

➤ `Wrox.BDD.Specs.UAT` — This will contain your SpecFlow specifications based on your acceptance criteria. The UAT acronym stands for User Acceptance Tests. This class library is specifying the behavior of your application.

➤ `Wrox.BDD.Specs.Core` — This will contain your MSpec specifications specifying the behavior of your objects that support the behavior of the application.

➤ `Wrox.BDD.Domain` — This project will contain the domain of the Tic-Tac-Toe game, including all of the rules and game logic.

➤ `Wrox.BDD.Ui.Console` — This project is a Windows console application project and will contain all the presentation for the game.

Next, you must reference NUnit and SpecFlow from within your `Wrox.BDD.Specs.UAT` project, and MSpec, NUnit, and Rhino Mocks (a Mocking framework) from within your `Wrox.BDD.Core` project. The quickest way to do this is to use the NuGet package installer.

NuGet (formerly known as NuPack) is a free, Open Source, developer-focused package management system for the .NET platform. It simplifies the process of incorporating third-party libraries into a .NET application during development. You can download it from `http://nuget.codeplex.com/`.

To set up NuGet, click Tools ⇨ Extension Manager from within Visual Studio. When the Extension Manager dialog box appears, select the Online Gallery tab, and enter **nuget** in the search box. When found, select NuGet Package Manager, and then click Download to install the tool.

After installation, you must restart Visual Studio. When restarted, pull up the Package Manager Console window by selecting Tools ⇨ Library Package Manager ⇨ Package Manager Console.

When the Package Manager Console is available, in the drop-down menu, select the `Wrox.BDD.Specs.UAT` project as the default project, as shown in Figure 14-13. Type in the following command:

```
install-package SpecFlow
```

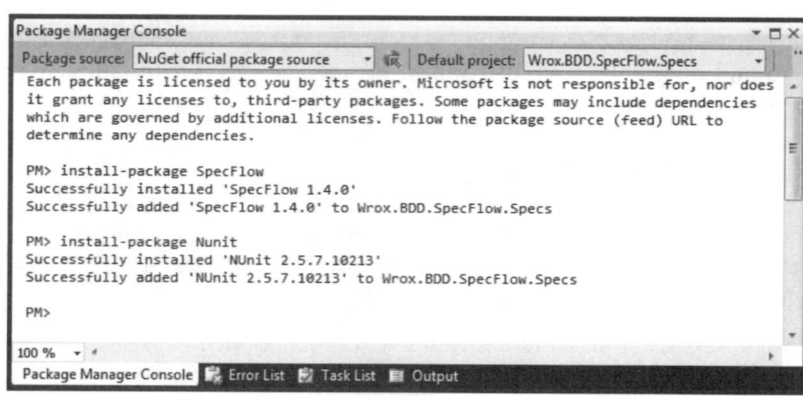

FIGURE 14-13: NuGet Package Manager Console dialog

Press Enter. After SpecFlow is installed, enter the following:

```
Install-package NUnit
```

NuGet pulls down the SpecFlow and NUnit packages to a local package folder at the root of your solution and also references the required assemblies in your `Wrox.BDD.SpecFlow.Specs` project.

Perform the same steps to add MSpec, NUnit, and Rhino Mocks to the `Wrox.BDD.Specs.Core` project by using the following commands.

For Rhino Mocks, use the following:

```
Install-package RhinoMocks
```

For MSpec, use the following:

```
Install-package Machine.Specifications
```

One last tool that is helpful when testing is TestDriven.NET from `www.testdriven.net/`. TestDriven.NET is an easy-to-use test runner that can run your `Wrox.BDD.Specs.UAT` project.

Scenario: Starting a Game

With your environment set up, you can start to work on your first specification. Create a folder within the `Specs.UAT` project named `Features` to store all of your features, and add a new feature named `GamePlay.feature` using the new template type that SpecFlow has installed. Then update the feature and scenario to match Figure 14-14.

The feature is written to describe the expected behavior of the game from the user's perspective. It is the presentation and user experience that is being specified at this point.

As mentioned before, the features, scenarios, and steps are written in the Gherkin language. You must write the specifications in this language because, as soon as you save the feature file, SpecFlow will parse it and create a matching code file that contains test fixtures that rely on step definitions you will create in a moment. With me so far?

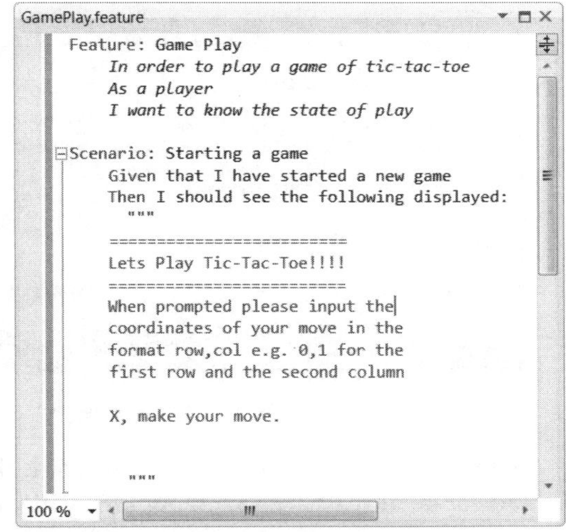

FIGURE 14-14: The scenario for starting a game in SpecFlow

Okay, maybe an example will help. If you run the SpecFlow specs with TestDriven.NET or with NUnit, you will see the output as shown in Figure 14-15.

What SpecFlow is telling you is that it was expecting to find methods for each of the steps in your scenario. If you think about it, that makes a lot of sense — you're expected to write the code and the step definitions to pass the scenarios. So, with this level-headed thinking, let's create some steps to satisfy SpecFlow.

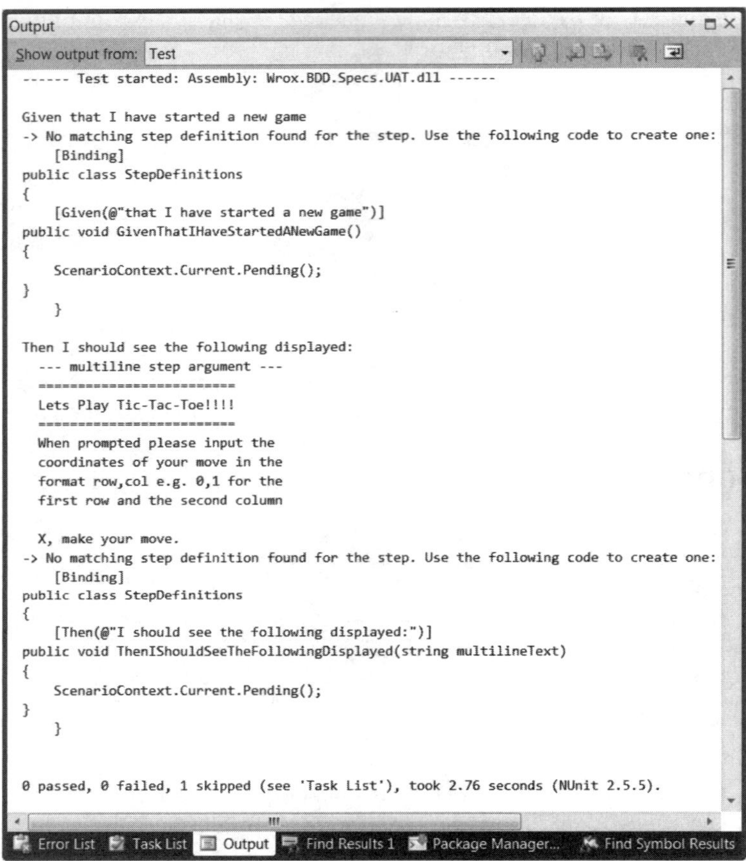

FIGURE 14-15: SpecFlow output showing the code template for the missing step definitions

Before adding code for the step definitions, let's pause for a moment to remind ourselves of the outside-in development methodology you will be following. You must drive development from the outside of your system — this means the presentation of the game of Tic-Tac-Toe. By driving design from this point of view, you will keep the development effort squarely focused upon application behavior. With that thought in mind, let's finally get to some coding.

It's a good idea to organize steps into logical groups, so add a new folder named Steps and a new class named GamePlaySteps. This will hold all steps relating to game actions. Copy in the code generated by SpecFlow, as shown in the following snippet:

Available for download on Wrox.com

```
using System;
using System.Collections.Generic;
using System.Linq;
using System.Text;
using TechTalk.SpecFlow;
```

```
namespace Wrox.BDD.Specs.UAT.Steps
{
    [Binding]
    public class GamePlaySteps
    {
        [Given(@"that I have started a new game")]
        public void GivenThatIHaveStartedANewGame()
        {
            ScenarioContext.Current.Pending();
        }

        [Then(@"I should see the following displayed:")]
        public void ThenIShouldSeeTheFollowingDisplayed(string multilineText)
        {
            ScenarioContext.Current.Pending();
        }
    }
}
```

Code file [GamePlaySteps.cs] available for download at Wrox.com.

Now, if you run the specs within your `Specs.UAT` project, you will find that they are skipped, and that you are told that one or more step definitions is not yet implemented. So, let's implement them.

To output the text to the screen, you must present a view of the game. Because this is a console application and, thus, stateful, unlike a web application, it makes sense to follow the Model-View-Presenter (MVP) pattern to organize the presentation logic.

Update the `GamePlaySteps` class with the following code. Remember that none of these classes exist. You are defining the API you want to work against from the outside in, or from the presentation to the domain.

```
using System;
using System.Collections.Generic;
using System.Linq;
using System.Text;
using TechTalk.SpecFlow;

namespace Wrox.BDD.Specs.UAT.Steps
{
    [Binding]
    public class GamePlaySteps
    {
        [Given(@"that I have started a new game")]
        public void GivenThatIHaveStartedANewGame()
        {
            var fake_game_view = new FakeGameView();
        }

        [Then(@"I should see the following displayed:")]
```

```
        public void ThenIShouldSeeTheFollowingDisplayed(string multilineText)
        {
            ScenarioContext.Current.Pending();
        }
    }
}
```

Code file [GamePlaySteps.cs] available for download at Wrox.com.

To start, you created a view, and, because this is a test environment, you create a fake view. The view will interact with a game presenter, and the game will start upon construction of the view. Now that you have an idea of how you want to drive the design of the system using the MVP pattern, you can create the presenter itself.

Add a new folder to the `Ui.Console` console project named `Presentation`. Within it, create a new class named `TicTacToeGamePresenter` with the following class definition:

```
using System;
using System.Collections.Generic;
using System.Linq;
using System.Text;

namespace Wrox.BDD.Ui.Console.Presentation
{
    public class TicTacToeGamePresenter
    {
        private readonly GameView _game_view;

        public TicTacToeGamePresenter(GameView game_view)
        {
            _game_view = game_view;
        }

        public void start()
        {

        }
    }
}
```

Code file [TicTacToeGamePresenter.cs] available for download at Wrox.com.

Next, add the missing view interface to the same presentation folder, as shown in the following code snippet:

```
using System;
using System.Collections.Generic;
using System.Linq;
using System.Text;

namespace Wrox.BDD.Ui.Console.Presentation
```

```
    {
        public interface GameView
        {
        }
    }
```

Code file [GameView.cs] available for download at Wrox.com.

You will need to update the `Specs.UAT` project to reference the `Ui.Console` project, and add a `using` statement for the presentation namespace.

> *You may have noticed the lack of the traditional `I` before the interface for the `GameView`. I have decided to drop the `I` prefix from my interfaces in order to discipline myself into thinking far more about the language I am using to convey an abstract concept in my domain. For years, I would blindly add an `IXXXService` to code without stopping to think about the language I was using. I now make it clear through language what is abstract and what is a concrete concept in my code base. Of course, a valid approach to prefixing an interface with an `I` might be to treat is as a verb (for example, `ICalculateIncomeTaxForEmployees`). It doesn't matter what naming convention you do or don't use. The most important point to remember is to make your code as readable as possible, and ensure that it communicates exactly what it does in the most natural manner.*

Now, the compiler will still be complaining about the undefined `FakeGameView`. To stop it from bothering you, create the missing class as shown in the following definition and place it in the root of the `Specs.UAT` project:

```csharp
using Wrox.BDD.Ui.Console.Presentation;

namespace Wrox.BDD.Specs.UAT
{
    public class FakeGameView : GameView
    {
        private TicTacToeGamePresenter _presenter;

        public FakeGameView()
        {
            _presenter =  new TicTacToeGamePresenter(this);

            _presenter.start();
        }
    }
}
```

Code file [FakeGameView.cs] available for download at Wrox.com.

If you run the specs now, you will find that the first step completes, but the second is still skipped. Okay, so now you have the game started. The next step definition requires you to confirm that the welcome message is displayed to the view.

To share the game presenter and the view between steps, you will use SpecFlow's scenario context. This simply means that objects can be shared across steps that could exist in separate step definition classes. Create a new folder named `StepHelpers` and add the following code:

```csharp
using Wrox.BDD.Ui.Console.Presentation;
using TechTalk.SpecFlow;

namespace Wrox.BDD.Specs.UAT.StepHelpers
{
    public static class GameStorage
    {

        public static FakeGameView game_view
        {
            get { return ScenarioContext.Current["View"] as FakeGameView; }
            set { ScenarioContext.Current["View"] = value; }
        }
    }
}
```

Code file [GameStorage.cs] available for download at Wrox.com.

The `GameStorage` class should be straightforward. If you're an ASP.NET/MVC developer, think of the `ScenarioContext` like the ASP.NET session object.

With the `GameStorage` class in place, you can update the `GamePlaySteps` class to save the fake view in one step, retrieve it in another, and use NUnit to assert that the expected text was displayed on the view.

```csharp
using TechTalk.SpecFlow;
using Wrox.BDD.Ui.Console.Presentation;
using Wrox.BDD.Specs.UAT.StepHelpers;
using NUnit.Framework;

namespace Wrox.BDD.Specs.UAT.Steps
{
    [Binding]
    public class GamePlaySteps
    {
        [Given(@"that I have started a new game")]
        public void GivenThatIHaveStartedANewGame()
        {
            var fake_game_view = new FakeGameView();

            GameStorage.game_view = fake_game_view;
        }

        [Then(@"I should see the following displayed:")]
        public void ThenIShouldSeeTheFollowingDisplayed(string multilineText)
```

```
        {
            var view = GameStorage.game_view;

            Assert.That(view.display(), Is.EqualTo(multilineText));
        }
    }
}
```

Code file [GamePlaySteps.cs] available for download at Wrox.com.

Again, you have added some behavior that makes sense, namely the display method that would return what has been output to the screen. You are comparing this to what you expect to be outputted.

The display method only makes sense on the fake view, because the real view will simply display any output to the console window. This is why you will not add the method to the `GameView` interface.

Update the `FakeGameView` to include the new display method.

Available for download on Wrox.com

```
namespace Wrox.BDD.Specs.UAT
{
    public class FakeGameView : GameView
    {
        private TicTacToeGamePresenter _presenter;
        private StringBuilder _display = new StringBuilder();

        public string display()
        {
            return _display.ToString();
        }

        public FakeGameView()
        {
            _presenter = new TicTacToeGamePresenter(this);

            _presenter.start();
        }
    }
}
```

Code file [FakeGameView.cs] available for download at Wrox.com.

Now that the IDE has stopped complaining about the missing display method, you can build and run the specs. You will find that you have your first logic error, hurrah! The welcome text that was expected is never written to the view. At this point, you can drop into the behavior of the objects (namely the presenter) to ensure that it is talking to the view as defined by the scenario step.

Before you start to code, what do you expect the presenter to do when it is told to start?

1. Display the welcome message on the view.

2. Prompt the player to make a move.

It's always a good idea to write out your assumptions and expectations before you start to write your specification within Visual Studio, so you can keep focused on behavior as you code.

Add a new folder named `Presentation_Specs` to the `Specs.Core` project, and then add a new class named `when_starting_a_new_game` with the following definition. You will need to add a reference to the `Ui.Console` project as well.

Available for download on Wrox.com

```csharp
using System;
using System.Collections.Generic;
using Machine.Specifications;
using Rhino.Mocks;
using Wrox.BDD.Ui.Console.Presentation;

namespace Wrox.BDD.Specs.Core.Presentation_Specs
{
    [Subject(typeof(TicTacToeGamePresenter))]
    public class when_starting_a_new_game
    {
        Establish context = () =>
        {
            game_view = MockRepository.GenerateStub<GameView>();

            SUT = new TicTacToeGamePresenter(game_view);
        };

        private Because of = () =>
        {
            SUT.start();
        };

        private It should_send_a_welcome_message_to_the_view = () =>
        {
            game_view.AssertWasCalled(x => x.write_line(Arg<String>.Is.Anything),
                                      a => a.Repeat.AtLeastOnce());
        };

        private It should_prompt_for_a_move = () =>
        {
            game_view.AssertWasCalled(x => x.get_coordinates_for_next_move());
        };

        private static TicTacToeGamePresenter SUT;
        private static GameView game_view;
    }
}
```

Code file [when_starting_a_new_game.cs] available for download at Wrox.com.

This is your first MSpec class. Let's quickly go through it so that you understand what's going on. First off, the class is decorated with an attribute that defines the subject under test. In this example, this is the `TicTacToeGamePresenter`. The subject is used when displaying the output of running the specs, which you will learn about later.

The `Establish` delegate, `context`, sets up the necessary classes and dependencies, and puts the system in a known state. This can be compared to `Given` in the template you used for the SpecFlow scenarios.

The `Because` delegate, `of`, performs the action on the system under test. Notice that the `TicTacToeGamePresenter` instance is named `SUT`, which stands for System Under Test. This again helps to focus on whose behavior you are defining.

Finally, the two `It` delegates (otherwise known as behaviors) perform the assertions that have taken place because of the action.

In this specification, you are providing a stub instance of a `GameView` and using Rhino Mocks to automatically generate it. Your expectations are that the presenter will write some lines to the view (the welcome message) and will prompt the view for the coordinates for the next move.

At the moment, however, the code will not compile, because neither the `write_line` or `get_coordinates_for_next_move` methods exist.

To stop the IDE from complaining, update the `GameView` interface to include the two new methods.

Available for download on Wrox.com

```
namespace Wrox.BDD.Ui.Console.Presentation
{
    public interface GameView
    {
        void write_line(string message);
        void get_coordinates_for_next_move();
    }
}
```

Code file [GameView.cs] available for download at Wrox.com.

To keep this chapter at a manageable size, and to communicate the concepts of BDD to you as succinctly as possible, I have jumped over an important step that I perform when designing a system behavior first. Typically, I will create all production code in the same class as the specification until such time as I am happy with my interface and class designs. The benefits of this are that I am able to work easily within one class that I don't consider to be production code. This important separation enables me to spike different design solutions easier than if I had my code spread out across a number of class projects, plus, subconsciously, I don't feel so precious about the code. So, I am more likely to try a number of designs until I am happy.

Again, remember that you defined these methods from the point of view of the user. You may not have realized it, but you have made a big design decision at this stage by asking for coordinates. You could have just as easily asked for a square number. Coordinates feel right at this stage, however, so let's stick with it.

With the `GameView` interface updated, you must also update the `FakeGameView` class.

```
namespace Wrox.BDD.Specs.UAT
{
    public class FakeGameView : GameView
    {
        private TicTacToeGamePresenter _presenter;
        private StringBuilder _display = new StringBuilder();

        public string display()
        {
            return _display.ToString();
        }

        public FakeGameView()
        {
            _presenter =
                new TicTacToeGamePresenter(this);

            _presenter.start();
        }

        public void write_line(string message)
        {
            _display.AppendLine(message);
        }

        public void get_coordinates_for_next_move()
        {

        }
    }
}
```

Code file [FakeGameView.cs] available for download at Wrox.com.

The `get_coordinates_for_next_move` method can remain empty. However, the `write_line` method will append each line to the display `StringBuilder` instance in order for you to be able to inspect within the step definition.

The class within the `Specs.Core` will now compile. But if you run the spec, it will fail because the `TicTacToePresenter` is not performing the expected behavior (that is, writing to the view and asking it to make a move).

Drop into the `TicTacToeGamePresenter` and update it with the following code:

```
namespace Wrox.BDD.Ui.Console.Presentation
{
    public class TicTacToeGamePresenter
    {
        private readonly GameView _game_view;

        public TicTacToeGamePresenter(GameView game_view)
        {
```

```
            _game_view = game_view;
        }

        public void start()
        {
            _game_view.write_line("===========================");
            _game_view.write_line("Lets Play Tic-Tac-Toe!!!!");
            _game_view.write_line("===========================");
            _game_view.write_line("When prompted please input the");
            _game_view.write_line("coordinates of your move in the");
            _game_view.write_line("format row,col e.g. 0,1 for the");
            _game_view.write_line("first row and the second column");
            _game_view.write_line("");

            prompt_for_next_move();
        }

        private void prompt_for_next_move()
        {
            _game_view.write_line("X, make your move.");
            _game_view.write_line("");
            _game_view.get_coordinates_for_next_move();
        }
    }
}
```

Code file [TicTacToeGamePresenter.cs] available for download at Wrox.com.

Notice how you have hard-coded the string X, make your move. You know that X will not be the only player allowed to move. However, you just want to get the spec to pass in the simplest way possible before adding more complexity like tracking whose turn it is.

Build the solution and run the specs. You should see the output displayed as shown in Figure 14-16.

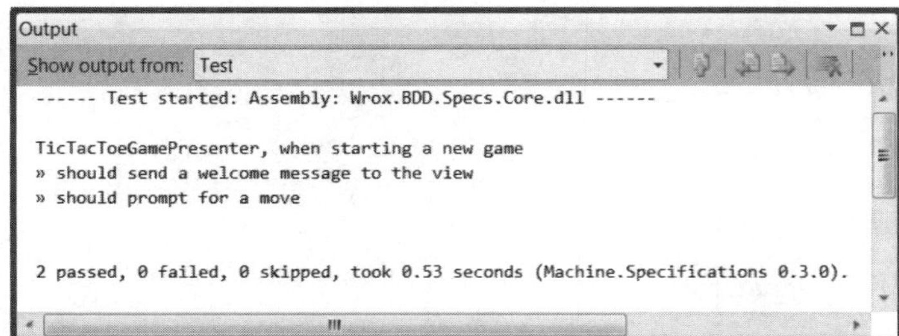

FIGURE 14-16: MSpec output showing the behaviors of the TicTacToeGamePresenter

Notice how the output reads like a set of requirements. Notice also how it matches your original expectations that you jotted down at the start of this section.

With no other behavior to add to the objects, jump back to the SpecFlow scenario in the Specs.UAT project and run the test. You should see that it passes, as shown in Figure 14-17.

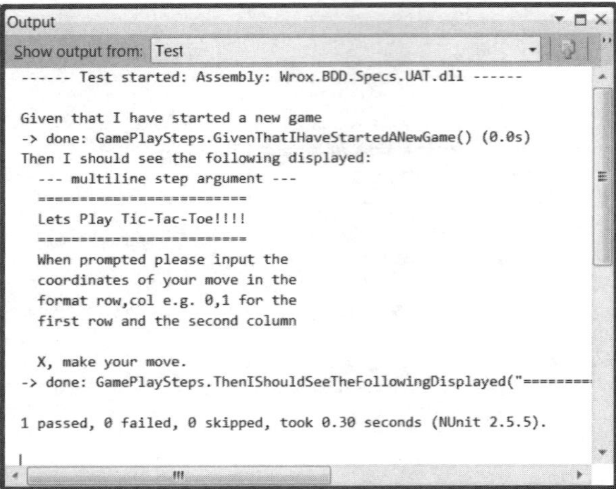

FIGURE 14-17: SpecFlow output showing the passing of the "start a game" scenario

Great! Your first scenario is working. However, all you have to show is a passing specification, which is no good to your customer, who counts success in terms of working software. Let's integrate this into a real console application before you add any more behavior so that you can demonstrate the first scenario to your customer.

Integrating the Starting a Game Scenario

To run the game in a console application, you first need to create a real implementation of the `GameView` that will output the game display to a console, rather than appending to a `StringBuilder`.

Add a new class named `ConsoleGameView` to the root of the `Ui.Console` project and update it to match the following code:

```csharp
using Wrox.BDD.Ui.Console.Presentation;

namespace Wrox.BDD.Ui.Console
{
    public class ConsoleGameView : GameView
    {
        private TicTacToeGamePresenter _presenter;

        public ConsoleGameView()
        {
            _presenter = new TicTacToeGamePresenter(this);

            _presenter.start();
        }
```

```
        public void write_line(string message)
        {
            System.Console.WriteLine(message);
        }

        public void get_coordinates_for_next_move()
        {
            System.Console.ReadLine();
        }
    }
}
```

Code file [ConsoleGameView.cs] available for download at Wrox.com.

A `ReadLine` call within the `get_coordinates_for_the_next_move` method has been added to ensure that the display is shown until you press Enter.

Lastly, create an instance of the `ConsoleGameView` class within the main method of the `Program` class so that the game can be started.

Available for download on Wrox.com

```
namespace Wrox.BDD.Ui.Console
{
    public class Program
    {
        static void Main(string[] args)
        {
            var game = new ConsoleGameView();
        }
    }
}
```

Code file [Program.cs] available for download at Wrox.com.

If you set the `Ui.Console` project as your startup project and press F5, you will see that a console application launches with welcome text, and a prompt for player X to make his move, as shown in Figure 14-18.

Fantastic! You already have something you can show the customer!

Scenario: Alternating Players

The second scenario to define the behavior of playing a game refers to the alternating of a player after a move has been made. Add the scenario as shown in Figure 14-19 to the `GamePlay.feature` in the `Spec.UAT` project.

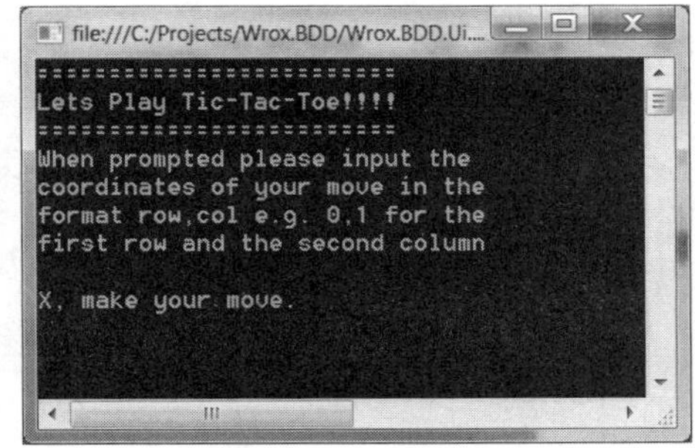

FIGURE 14-18: Console application showing the TicTacToe welcome message

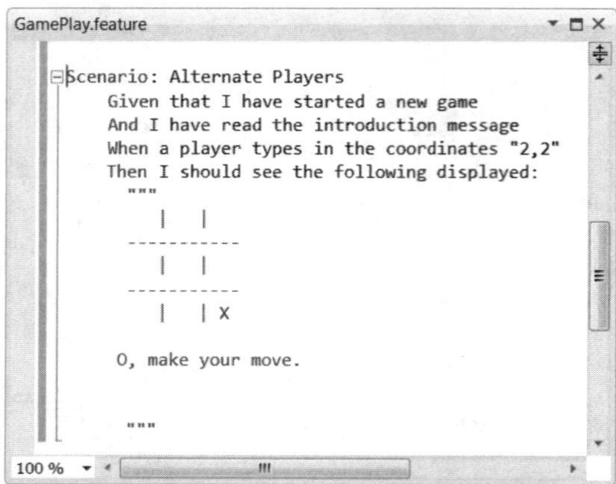

FIGURE 14-19: The SpecFlow feature file with the alternate players scenario

Because this scenario contains new steps, you can let SpecFlow auto-generate them for you by running the specs. Update the `GamePlaySteps` class with the new definitions and add the stub code, as shown here:

```
namespace Wrox.BDD.Specs.UAT.Steps
{
    [Binding]
    public class GamePlaySteps
    {
        [Given(@"I have read the introduction message")]
        public void GivenIHaveReadTheIntroductionMessage()
        {
            var view = GameStorage.game_view;
            view.clean_display();

        }

        [When(@"a player types in the coordinates ""(.*)""")]
        public void WhenAPlayerTypesInTheCoordinates(string coordinates)
        {
            var game_presenter = GameStorage.presenter;
            game_presenter.update_game_with_move(coordinates);

        }

        ......
    }
```

Code file [GamePlaySteps.cs] available for download at Wrox.com.

The first step is simply clearing the display of the view. This is only required during testing so that the scenarios can be kept to a manageable size, and so that you do not need to verify all of the text displayed on the view. The `clean_display` method will only be a method of the `FakeGameView` class, and will not be added to the interface, because this is only used in testing.

The second step receives the inputted coordinates from the user and passes them to the view. Again, note how you are defining the API of the presenter class from the view of its caller — in this case, it's the `GameView`.

You may have noticed that you now need to talk directly to the presenter, but currently you are not storing it in SpecFlow's context. To update this, amend the `GameStorage` class as shown in the following snippet:

```
using Wrox.BDD.Ui.Console.Presentation;
using TechTalk.SpecFlow;

namespace Wrox.BDD.Specs.UAT.StepHelpers
{
    public static class GameStorage
    {
        public static TicTacToeGamePresenter presenter
        {
            get { return ScenarioContext.Current["Presenter"] as
                                            TicTacToeGamePresenter; }
            set { ScenarioContext.Current["Presenter"] = value; }
        }

        public static FakeGameView game_view
        {
            get { return ScenarioContext.Current["View"] as FakeGameView; }
            set { ScenarioContext.Current["View"] = value; }
        }
    }
}
```

Code file [GameStorage.cs] available for download at Wrox.com.

You will need to store the presenter from within `FakeGameView`, as shown in the following snippet:

```
namespace Wrox.BDD.Specs.UAT
{
    public class FakeGameView : GameView
    {
        ......

        public FakeGameView()
        {
            _presenter = new TicTacToeGamePresenter(this,
                                            new TicTacToe());

            GameStorage.presenter = _presenter;
            _presenter.start();
        }
```

```
        ......
    }
}
```


While you have the `FakeGameView` class open, add the `clean_display` method as well.

```
namespace Wrox.BDD.Specs.UAT
{
    public class FakeGameView : GameView
    {
        ......

        public void clean_display()
        {
            _display.Clear();
        }

        ......
    }
}
```


Also, add the `update_game_with_move` method, but leave its body empty. Remember, you are only trying to get the code to a state where it complies and gives you a logic error.

```
namespace Wrox.BDD.Ui.Console.Presentation
{
    public class TicTacToeGamePresenter
    {
        ......

        public void update_game_with_move(string move_coordinates)
        {

        }
    }
}
```


With the IDE happy, you can now build your solution and watch the scenario unsurprisingly fail. With nothing more to do at the step-definition level, let's drop into the behavior of the presenter and the `Specs.Core` project.

So, how will you achieve the behavior described by the scenario? Let's write down some expectations for the behavior of the presenter to help drive the object design. The presenter should do the following:

1.   Ask the game for the next player to move.

2. Tell the game to place the current players token on a given square.

3. Display the game.

4. Display the next player to move.

Note how you are now talking about a game instance. This is where you start thinking in terms of the domain of the game and its responsibilities. You are rightly expecting a game to manage the current player, and to handle moves from the presenter.

Behavior 1: Ask for the Next Player

Let's begin by modifying the `when_starting_a_new_game` spec to add an additional behavior that expects the presenter to ask the game for the current player.

```
namespace Wrox.BDD.Specs.Core.Presentation_Specs
{
    [Subject(typeof(TicTacToeGamePresenter))]
    public class when_starting_a_new_game
    {
        Establish context = () =>
        {
            game_view = MockRepository.GenerateStub<GameView>();
            game = MockRepository.GenerateStub<Game>();

            SUT = new TicTacToeGamePresenter(game_view, game);
        };

        private Because of = () =>
        {
            SUT.start();
        };

        ......

        private It should_ask_the_game_for_the_next_player_to_move = () =>
        {
            game.AssertWasCalled(x => x.current_token());
        };

        private static TicTacToeGamePresenter SUT;
        private static Game game;
        private static GameView game_view;
    }
}
```

Code file [when_starting_a_new_game.cs] available for download at Wrox.com.

You have now introduced the concept of a `Game`. The `Game` interface will live in the `Domain` project, so ensure that you add a project reference to this from the `Specs.Core` project. The `Game` is responsible for the state and the logic governing the Tic-Tac-Toe game. The presenter, on the other hand, is responsible only for the presentation of the game, and handling user input.

With its single method, the `Game` interface should be added to the `Domain` project, as shown in the following code:

```
namespace Wrox.BDD.Domain
{
    public interface Game
    {
        Token current_token();
    }
}
```

Code file [Game.cs] available for download at Wrox.com.

The game returns a `Token` to represent the current player's token. Add the code to represent the `Token` to the `Domain` project, as shown in the following code:

```
using System;

namespace Wrox.BDD.Domain
{
    public static class Tokens
    {
        public static Token x_token { get { return new Token("X"); } }
        public static Token o_token { get { return new Token("O"); } }
    }

    public class Token : IEquatable<Token>
    {
        public string value { get; set;}

        public Token(string value)
        {
            this.value = value;
        }

        public bool Equals(Token other)
        {
            return this.value == other.value;
        }

        public override string ToString()
        {
            return value;
        }
    }
}
```

Code file [Token.cs] available for download at Wrox.com.

The `Token` is what is known as a *value object*. You have overridden the equality method because two value objects should be equal if their values are equal.

You could have used a simple enumeration to portray the concept of the X and O tokens in the game of Tic-Tac-Toe. However, by using smart enumerations in the form of immutable value objects, you can easily add behavior at a later date.

You will now need to modify the `TicTacToeGamePresenter` constructor to expect an instance of the `Game` as defined in the spec. Update the presenter as shown in the following code and ensure that you add a reference to the `Domain` project:

```
using Wrox.BDD.Domain;

namespace Wrox.BDD.Ui.Console.Presentation
{
    public class TicTacToeGamePresenter
    {
        private readonly GameView _game_view;
        private readonly Game _game;

        public TicTacToeGamePresenter(GameView game_view, Game game)
        {
            _game_view = game_view;
            _game = game;
        }

        ......
    }
}
```

Code file [TicTacToeGamePresenter.cs] available for download at Wrox.com.

You now have a bit of a problem. The presenter requires an instance of the `Game` in order to work. In specs, you can create stub instances using Rhino Mocks. However, you have already started to integrate the code, and also your `FakeGameView` requires a valid instance.

Update the `FakeGameView` and the `ConsoleGameView`, shown here, to include the as-yet-nonexistent `TicTacToe` implementation of the `Game` interface. Again, add a reference to the `Domain` project to the `Specs.UAT` project.

```
using Wrox.BDD.Ui.Console.Presentation;
using Wrox.BDD.Specs.UAT.StepHelpers;
using Wrox.BDD.Domain;

namespace Wrox.BDD.Specs.UAT
{
    public class FakeGameView : GameView
    {
        private TicTacToeGamePresenter _presenter;
        private StringBuilder _display = new StringBuilder();

        public FakeGameView()
        {
            _presenter = new TicTacToeGamePresenter(this, new TicTacToe());
```

```
                GameStorage.presenter = _presenter;

                _presenter.start();
            }

            ......
        }
    }
```



```
namespace Wrox.BDD.Ui.Console
{
    public class ConsoleGameView : GameView
    {
        private TicTacToeGamePresenter _presenter;

        public ConsoleGameView()
        {
            _presenter =
                new TicTacToeGamePresenter(this,new TicTacToe());

            _presenter.start();
        }

        ......
    }
}
```


You can now create the `TicTacToe` class within the `Domain` project. For the time being, just hard-code it to return an X token. You will update this when you have written a spec to define its behavior.

```
namespace Wrox.BDD.Domain
{
    public class TicTacToe : Game
    {
        public Token current_token()
        {
            return Tokens.x_token;
        }
    }
}
```


With the IDE happy, you now need to turn your attention to actually getting the spec to pass. Update the `TicTacToePresenter` so that it uses the `Game` instance to determine whose move it is.

```
using Wrox.BDD.Domain;

namespace Wrox.BDD.Ui.Console.Presentation
{
    public class TicTacToeGamePresenter
    {
        private readonly GameView _game_view;
        private readonly Game _game;

        public TicTacToeGamePresenter(GameView game_view, Game game)
        {
            _game_view = game_view;
            _game = game;
        }

        ......

        private void prompt_for_next_move()
        {
            _game_view.write_line(String.Format(
                        "{0}, make your move.", _game.current_token()));
            _game_view.write_line("");
            _game_view.get_coordinates_for_next_move();
        }

        ......
    }
}
```

Code file [TicTacToeGamePresenter.cs] available for download at Wrox.com.

With the behavior added, run all the specs. You will find that the spec you were working on now passes, as shown in Figure 14-20.

Behavior 2: Place the Token

For the next behavior criteria, you will need to create a new specification class that uses the `TicTacToePresenter` as its subject. Because you don't want to duplicate all of the setup code, you can refactor and move it all to a base class.

Add a new abstract class named `with_a_presenter` and move over all of the setup code from the `context` delegate of the `when_starting_a_new_game` class into the constructor so that both classes match the code shown here:

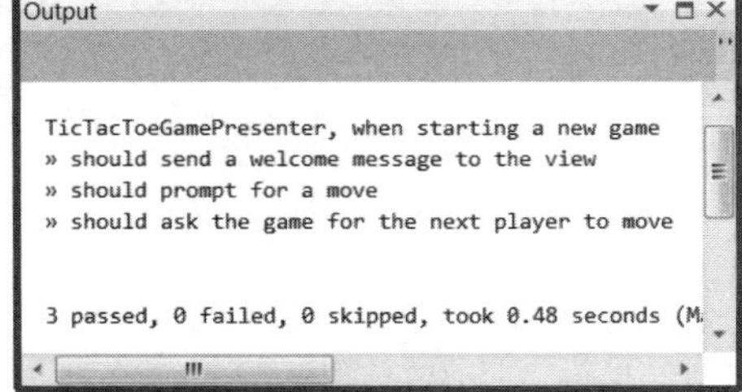

FIGURE 14-20: The MSpec output showing the behaviors of the TiacTacToeGame Presenter

```
using Rhino.Mocks;
using Wrox.BDD.Ui.Console.Presentation;
using Wrox.BDD.Domain;

namespace Wrox.BDD.Specs.Core.Presentation_Specs
```

```
    {
        public abstract class with_a_presenter
        {
            public with_a_presenter()
            {
                game_view = MockRepository.GenerateStub<GameView>();
                game = MockRepository.GenerateStub<Game>();

                SUT = new TicTacToeGamePresenter(game_view, game);
            }

            protected static TicTacToeGamePresenter SUT;
            protected static Game game;
            protected static GameView game_view;
        }
    }
```

Code file [with_a_presenter.cs] available for download at Wrox.com.

```
namespace Wrox.BDD.Specs.Core.Presentation_Specs
{
    [Subject(typeof(TicTacToeGamePresenter))]
    public class when_starting_a_new_game : with_a_presenter
    {
        Establish context = () =>
        {

        };

        ......

        //protected static TicTacToeGamePresenter SUT;
        //protected static Game game;
        //protected static GameView game_view;

    }
}
```

Code file [when_starting_a_new_game.cs] available for download at Wrox.com.

You can now create a new spec class that inherits from the `with_a_presenter` base class, as shown in the following definition that defines behavior number two as shown in your list:

```
using Machine.Specifications;
using Rhino.Mocks;
using Wrox.BDD.Ui.Console.Presentation;
using Wrox.BDD.Domain;

namespace Wrox.BDD.Specs.Core.Presentation_Specs
{
    [Subject(typeof(TicTacToeGamePresenter))]
    public class when_a_player_places_a_token : with_a_presenter
```

```
    {
        Establish context = () =>
        {
            coordinate_text = "1,1";
            coordinate = Coordinate.parse(coordinate_text);
        };

        private Because of = () =>
        {
            SUT.start();

            SUT.update_game_with_move(coordinate_text);
        };

        private It should_tell_the_game_to_place_a_token = () =>
        {
            game.AssertWasCalled(x => x.place_token_for_current_player_at(
                            Arg<Coordinate>.Matches(c =>
                                c.Equals(coordinate))));
        };

        private static Coordinate coordinate;
        private static string coordinate_text;
    }
}
```

> *Code file [when_a_player_places_a_token.cs] available for download at Wrox.com.*

The spec expects that the presenter will take input from the view, convert it to a coordinate, and then pass it to the game. In this spec, you have introduced the notation of a coordinate object to represent a location on the game grid.

Like `Token`, the `Coordinate` class is an immutable value object. Add it to the `Domain` project by matching the following code definition:

```
namespace Wrox.BDD.Domain
{
    public class Coordinate : IEquatable<Coordinate>
    {
        public Coordinate(int x, int y)
        {
            X = x;
            Y = y;
        }

        public int X { get; private set; }
        public int Y { get; private set; }

        public bool Equals(Coordinate other)
        {
            return this.X == other.X && this.Y == other.Y;
        }

        public override string ToString()
```

```
        {
            return string.Format("{0},{1}", X, Y);
        }

        public static Coordinate parse(string move_coordinates)
        {
            var coordinates = move_coordinates.Split(',');

            return new Coordinate(int.Parse(coordinates[0].ToString()),
                                  int.Parse(coordinates[1].ToString()));
        }
    }
}
```

Code file [Coordinate.cs] available for download at Wrox.com.

You didn't have to create a class to represent a coordinate. You could have simply passed two integers around, and had a helper method convert strings into integers. However, by creating a value object, you are representing an important concept in the domain. This will make it easy for other developers to understand the code, and easy for you when you must work on the codebase at a later date.

As mentioned, a value *object is a small, simple object that represents a concept or concern in a business domain. Typically, value objects have no identity and are immutable. The value objects that you have used up to now have represented a coordinate on the game board, and a game token. It's a good idea to use value objects in place of simple parameter types in order to better express the concepts of the problem domain. It's also easier to add behavior and validation to value objects when needed, rather than adding procedural or transcript code around simple types. Value objects can also help to clarify complex entities by moving behavior to single-responsibility value objects that better convey the concern. You can learn more about value objects by reading* Domain-Driven Design: Tackling Complexity in the Heart of Software *(Boston: Addison-Wesley Professional, 2003) by Eric Evans.*

To get the IDE to compile, you must update the Game interface with the new place_token_for_current_player_at method, as shown in the following code snippet:

```
namespace Wrox.BDD.Domain
{
    public interface Game
    {
        Token current_token();
        void place_token_for_current_player_at(Coordinate coordinate);
    }
}
```

Code file [Game.cs] available for download at Wrox.com.

And, in turn, you must update the `TicTacToe` implementation. Again, just leave it blank for the time being.

```csharp
namespace Wrox.BDD.Domain
{
    public class TicTacToe : Game
    {
        public Token current_token()
        {
            return Tokens.x_token;
        }

        public void place_token_for_current_player_at(Coordinate coordinate)
        {

        }
    }
}
```

Code file [TicTacToe.cs] available for download at Wrox.com.

To get the spec to pass, you must add the expected behavior to the presenter.

```csharp
namespace Wrox.BDD.Ui.Console.Presentation
{
    public class TicTacToeGamePresenter
    {
        ......

        public void update_game_with_move(string move_coordinates)
        {
            var coordinate = Coordinate.parse(move_coordinates);

            _game.place_token_for_current_player_at(coordinate);
        }
    }
}
```

Code file [TicTacToeGamePresenter.cs] available for download at Wrox.com.

If you run the specs now, you will find that they pass! But you may have noticed that you added some behavior on the `Coordinate` class without a spec to verify it. This is fine to do as long as you remember to add a spec to verify behavior before you go on to specify another piece of behavior in the system.

To verify the behavior of the `Coordinate` class, add a new folder named `Domain_Specs` to store the spec related to coordinate, and add to it the following class listing:

```csharp
using Machine.Specifications;
using Wrox.BDD.Domain;
using NUnit.Framework;

namespace Wrox.BDD.Specs.Core.Domain_Specs
{
```

```
[Subject(typeof(Coordinate))]
public class when_parsing_a_valid_coordinate
{
    private Because of = () =>
    {
        x_coordinate = "2";
        y_coordinate = "1";
        coordinate = Coordinate.parse(
            String.Format("{0},{1}", x_coordinate, y_coordinate));
    };

    private It should_be_able_to_correctly_parse_the_coordinate = () =>
    {
        Assert.That(coordinate.X, Is.EqualTo(int.Parse(x_coordinate)));
        Assert.That(coordinate.Y, Is.EqualTo(int.Parse(y_coordinate)));
    };

    private static Coordinate coordinate;
    private static string x_coordinate;
    private static string y_coordinate;
}
}
```

Code file [when_parsing_a_valid_coordinate.cs] available for download at Wrox.com.

Now you have two of the presenter steps taken care of and are ready to move on to number three.

Behavior 3: Display the Game

Behavior number three deals with the displaying of the game. Add a new behavior to the `when_a_player_places_a_token` specification class, as detailed here:

```
namespace Wrox.BDD.Specs.Core.Presentation_Specs
{
    [Subject(typeof(TicTacToeGamePresenter))]
    public class when_a_player_places_a_token : with_a_presenter
    {
        Establish context = () =>
        {
            coordinate_text = "1,1";
            coordinate = Coordinate.parse(coordinate_text);
        };

        private Because of = () =>
        {
            SUT.start();

            SUT.update_game_with_move(coordinate_text);
        };

        ......

        private It should_render_the_game = () =>
        {
```

```
                board_renderer.AssertWasCalled(x => x.render(game));
            };

            private static Coordinate coordinate;
            private static string coordinate_text;
        }
    }
```


You have now been introduced to the concept of a `board_renderer`. The responsibility of this object is to render the state of a game instance.

Update the `with_a_presenter` base class to include the `board_renderer` as a dependency of the presenter.

```
namespace Wrox.BDD.Specs.Core.Presentation_Specs
{
    public abstract class with_a_presenter
    {
        public with_a_presenter()
        {
            game = MockRepository.GenerateStub<Game>();
            game_view = MockRepository.GenerateStub<GameView>();

            board_renderer = MockRepository.GenerateStub<BoardRenderer>();

            SUT = new TicTacToeGamePresenter(game_view, game, board_renderer);
        }

        protected static TicTacToeGamePresenter SUT;
        protected static Game game;
        protected static GameView game_view;
        protected static BoardRenderer board_renderer;
    }
}
```


The interface for the `BoardRenderer` is very simple, and contains a single method that returns a string.

```
using Wrox.BDD.Domain;

namespace Wrox.BDD.Ui.Console.Presentation
{
    public interface BoardRenderer
    {
        string render(Game game);
    }
}
```

To match the expected behavior, you must update the `TicTacToeGamePresenter` to accept a `BoardRenderer` as a constructor argument, and ensure that it calls its `render` method passing the instance of the game.

```
namespace Wrox.BDD.Ui.Console.Presentation
{
    public class TicTacToeGamePresenter
    {
        private readonly GameView _game_view;
        private readonly Game _game;
        private readonly BoardRenderer _board_renderer;

        public TicTacToeGamePresenter(GameView game_view, Game game,
                                      BoardRenderer board_renderer)
        {
            _game_view = game_view;
            _game = game;
            _board_renderer = board_renderer;
        }

        ......

        public void update_game_with_move(string move_coordinates)
        {
            var coordinate = Coordinate.parse(move_coordinates);

            _game.place_token_for_current_player_at(coordinate);

            display_game();

            prompt_for_next_move();
        }

        private void display_game()
        {
            _game_view.write(_board_renderer.render(_game));
            _game_view.write_line("");
        }
    }
}
```

Code file [TicTacToeGamePresenter.cs] available for download at Wrox.com.

You have introduced a new `write` method on the view, which simply writes text straight to the console without adding a line. This extra `write` method is required because the view of the game will not be able to be represented on a single line. Update the `GameView` interface as shown in the following code snippet:

```
namespace Wrox.BDD.Ui.Console.Presentation
{
    public interface GameView
    {
```

```
        void write_line(string message);
        void write(string message);
        void get_coordinates_for_next_move();
    }
}
```


In order for the code to compile, you must supply a concrete instance of the `BoardRenderer` for use within the `FakeGameView` and the `ConsoleGameView`.

Add a new class called `PlainTextGameBoardRenderer` to the `Presentation` folder of the `Ui.Console` project. Remember, this is a presentation concern, and that's why you are adding this to the presentation layer of your application.

```
using Wrox.BDD.Domain;

namespace Wrox.BDD.Ui.Console.Presentation
{
    public class PlainTextGameBoardRenderer : BoardRenderer
    {
        public string render(Game game)
        {
            var squares = new string[3,3];
            squares[2, 2] = "X";

            var grid_display = new StringBuilder();
            var row_seperator = "";

            for (int row = 0; row <= 2; row++)
            {
                if (!String.IsNullOrEmpty(row_seperator))
                    grid_display.AppendLine(row_seperator);

                var pipe = "";
                var row_display = new StringBuilder();

                for (int column = 0; column <= 2; column++)
                {
                    row_display.Append(string.Format("{0} {1} ", pipe,
                                pad_if_square_empty(squares[row, column])));
                    pipe = "|";
                }

                grid_display.AppendLine(row_display.ToString());
                row_seperator = "-----------";
            }

            return grid_display.ToString();
        }

        private string pad_if_square_empty(string value)
        {
```

```
                return String.IsNullOrEmpty(value) ? " " : value;
            }
        }
    }
```

Code file [PlainTextGameBoardRenderer.cs] available for download at Wrox.com.

There is a fair bit going on in this class. From a 1,000-foot view, it simply generates a string representation of a 3 × 3 grid using a string multi-array to define where the tokens are on that grid. You should note that the scenario expects an X token to be displayed at position 2,2. You have hard-coded this in the `PlainTextGameBoardRenderer` class because you have no method of asking the `Game` instance where the tokens are. This will obviously be altered in upcoming specs, but for now, you just want to get the scenario passing.

With an instance of the `BoardRenderer` in place, you can update the `FakeGameView` and `ConsoleGameView` to instantiate an instance of the `PlainTextGameBoardRenderer` and pass it in as an argument to the presenter, as well as include the implementation for the new `write` method.

Available for download on Wrox.com

```
namespace Wrox.BDD.Specs.UAT
{
    public class FakeGameView : GameView
    {
        private TicTacToeGamePresenter _presenter;
        private StringBuilder _display = new StringBuilder();

        public FakeGameView()
        {
            _presenter = new TicTacToeGamePresenter(this, new TicTacToe(),
                                        new PlainTextGameBoardRenderer());

            GameStorage.presenter = _presenter;

            _presenter.start();
        }

        ......

        public void write(string message)
        {
            _display.Append(message);
        }
    }
}
```

Code file [FakeGameView.cs] available for download at Wrox.com.

```
namespace Wrox.BDD.Ui.Console
{
    public class ConsoleGameView : GameView
    {
```

```
        private TicTacToeGamePresenter _presenter;

        public ConsoleGameView()
        {
            _presenter =
                new TicTacToeGamePresenter(this, new TicTacToe(),
                                    new PlainTextGameBoardRenderer());

            _presenter.start();
        }

        public void write_line(string message)
        {
            System.Console.WriteLine(message);
        }

        public void get_coordinates_for_next_move()
        {
            System.Console.ReadLine();
        }

        public void write(string message)
        {
            System.Console.Write(message);
        }
    }
}
```

Code file [ConsoleGameView.cs] available for download at Wrox.com.

Build and run your specs, and they should all pass. That's another one crossed off the list.

Now, check to see how far you are with the scenario. Cool, it's displaying the grid, but the scenario still fails because of the missing line prompting the next player to make a move — which is number four on the list. Let's deal with that now.

Behavior 4: Display the Next Player

The behavior of supplying the next player to move is the responsibility of the Game. At the moment, it's hard-coded in the TicTacToe instance to always return token X. Because the TicTacToe class is the subject of your spec, and because you are likely to have more behaviors to verify against it, let's create an abstract base class for use with the specifications.

```
using Wrox.BDD.Domain;

namespace Wrox.BDD.Specs.Core.Domain_Specs
{
    public abstract class with_a_tictactoe_game
    {
        public with_a_tictactoe_game()
        {
            SUT = new TicTacToe();
        }
```

```
            protected static Game SUT;
        }
    }
```


With the base class in place, create a new specification class, again in the `Domain_Specs` folder of the `Spec.Core` project.

```
using Machine.Specifications;
using Rhino.Mocks;
using Wrox.BDD.Domain;

namespace Wrox.BDD.Specs.Core.Domain_Specs
{
    [Subject(typeof(TicTacToe))]
    public class when_placing_a_token_on_the_board : with_a_tictactoe_game
    {
        Establish context = () =>
        {
            coordinate_text = "1,1";
            coordinate = Coordinate.parse(coordinate_text);
        };

        private Because of = () =>
        {
            SUT.place_token_for_current_player_at(coordinate);
        };

        private It should_alternate_the_player = () =>
        {
            player_tracker.AssertWasCalled(x => x.finish_players_move());
        };

        private static Coordinate coordinate;
        private static string coordinate_text;
    }
}
```


Your specification expects that a call should be made to a `player_tracker` instance after a move has been made. The responsibilities of `player_tracker` are to simply remember whose turn it is, and to alternate after the `finish_players_move` method is called. Remember, this code doesn't exist. You are simply thinking about the most logical and straightforward way of determining whose turn it is.

It makes sense that this `player_tracker` is a dependency of the `Game`. Update the `with_a_tictactoe_game` base class to include the new constructor dependency, as shown in the following code:

```
using Wrox.BDD.Domain;
using Rhino.Mocks;

namespace Wrox.BDD.Specs.Core.Domain_Specs
```

```
    {
        public abstract class with_a_tictactoe_game
        {
            public with_a_tictactoe_game()
            {
                player_tracker = MockRepository.GenerateStub<PlayerTracker>();

                SUT = new TicTacToe(player_tracker);
            }

            protected static Game SUT;
            protected static PlayerTracker player_tracker;
        }
    }
```

Code file [with_a_tictactoe_game.cs] available for download at Wrox.com.

Now you must create the new interface within the `Domain` project, as shown here:

```
namespace Wrox.BDD.Domain
{
    public interface PlayerTracker
    {
        Token current_player();
        void finish_players_move();
    }
}
```

Code file [PlayerTracker.cs] available for download at Wrox.com.

Notice that the `current_player` method has been added. You have not previously specified this behavior. However, experience has shown that this should be the responsibility of the `PlayerTracker` and not the `Game`.

Modify the `TicTacToe` class to accept an instance of the `PlayerTracker` via its constructor. Replace the hard-coded token X in the `current_token` method with a delegation to the `PlayerTracker`. Finally, add a call to the `PlayerTracker` to finish the player's move after a token has been placed. This is all shown in the following code:

```
namespace Wrox.BDD.Domain
{
    public class TicTacToe : Game
    {
        private PlayerTracker _player_tracker;

        public TicTacToe(PlayerTracker player_tracker)
        {
            _player_tracker = player_tracker;
        }

        public Token current_token()
        {
            return _player_tracker.current_player();
        }
```

```
    public void place_token_for_current_player_at(Coordinate coordinate)
    {
        _player_tracker.finish_players_move();
    }


    ......

}
}
```


You must now create an instance of the `PlayerTracker` to supply to the `FakeGameView` and `ConsoleGameView`. Add a new `TokenTracker` class with the following definition:

```
namespace Wrox.BDD.Domain
{
    public class TokenTracker : PlayerTracker
    {
        private Token _current_playing_token = Tokens.x_token;

        public Token current_player()
        {
            return _current_playing_token;
        }

        public void finish_players_move()
        {
            _current_playing_token =
                    (_current_playing_token.Equals(Tokens.x_token))
                                            ? Tokens.o_token :
                                                Tokens.x_token;
        }
    }
}
```


`TokenTracker` simply stores a single token and, starting with token X, alternates it when a call to `finish_players_move` is made.

You can now update the `FakeGameView` and the `ConsoleGameView`.

```
namespace Wrox.BDD.Specs.UAT
{
    public class FakeGameView : GameView
    {
        private TicTacToeGamePresenter _presenter;
```

```
        private StringBuilder _display = new StringBuilder();

        public FakeGameView()
        {
            _presenter = new TicTacToeGamePresenter(this,
                                      new TicTacToe(new TokenTracker()),
                                      new PlainTextGameBoardRenderer());

            GameStorage.presenter = _presenter;

            _presenter.start();
        }

        ......

    }
}
```

Code file [FakeGameView.cs] available for download at Wrox.com.

```
namespace Wrox.BDD.Ui.Console
{
    public class ConsoleGameView : GameView
    {
        private TicTacToeGamePresenter _presenter;

        public ConsoleGameView()
        {
            _presenter =
                new TicTacToeGamePresenter(this, new TicTacToe(new
                    TokenTracker()),
                                        new PlainTextGameBoardRenderer());

            _presenter.start();
        }

        ......

    }
}
```

Code file [ConsoleGameView.cs] available for download at Wrox.com.

Build and run all of your specs. All passing? Great. That was the last expected piece of behavior. Now, if you run your scenarios, you should see them all passing, as shown in Figure 14-21.

With the code all working under testing, let's integrate it and see if it works for real.

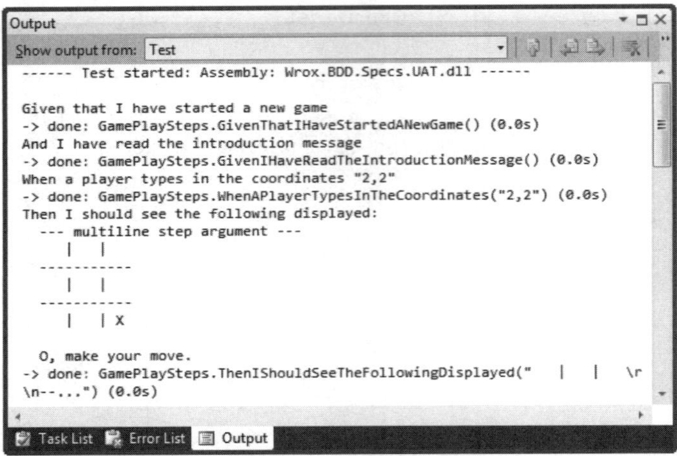

FIGURE 14-21: The SpecFlow output showing the passing of the alternate player scenario

Integrating the Alternate a Player Scenario

The only modification you need to make to get the code integrated is to wire up the input, as shown in the following code:

```
namespace Wrox.BDD.Ui.Console
{
    public class ConsoleGameView : GameView
    {
        ......

        public void get_coordinates_for_next_move()
        {
            var coordinates = System.Console.ReadLine();

            _presenter.update_game_with_move(coordinates);
        }

        ......
    }
}
```

Code file [ConsoleGameView.cs] available for download at Wrox.com.

You should now be able to run the code and input a coordinate as shown in Figure 14-22. Remember to input it using the valid syntax because you have not added code for the non-happy-day scenarios. Also, note that whatever coordinate you input, the screen will always display an X token at grid reference 2,2. Hmmm, that's not great, but the system is coming along.

The next scenario to tackle is displaying the game after a series of moves. This should help to display a true representation of the moves that the player has made.

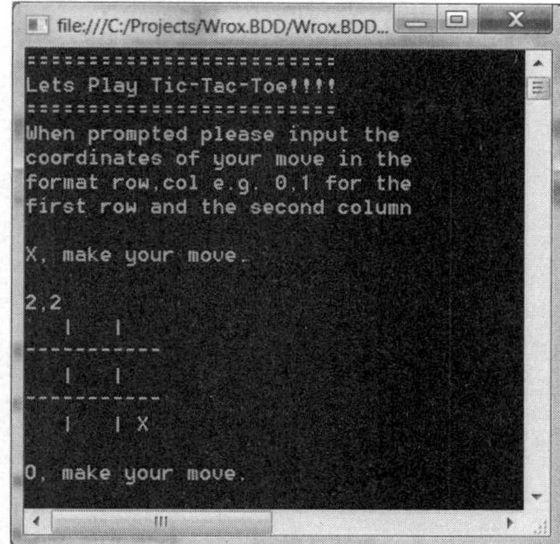

FIGURE 14-22: The Console application showing the game welcome message and prompt for player O to move

Scenario: Displaying the Game

Figure 14-23 shows the scenario for displaying a game after a series of moves. This scenario should be added to the `GamePlay.feature` file.

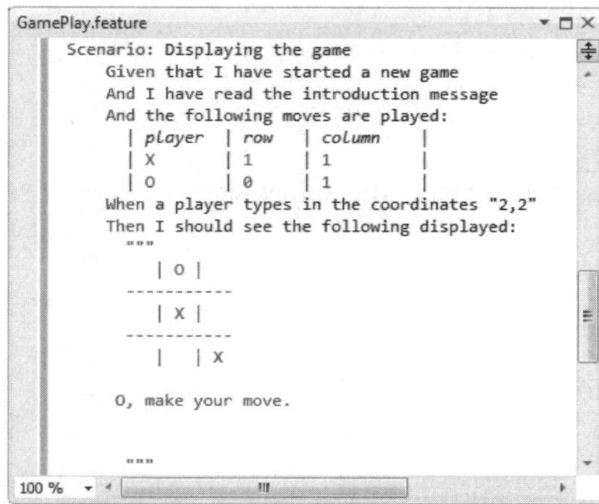

FIGURE 14-23: The GamePlay feature showing the scenario for displaying the game

With the new steps that play a series of moves, a new step definition must be created. Add the following code to the `GamePlaySteps` class:

```
namespace Wrox.BDD.Specs.UAT.Steps
{
    [Binding]
```

```
public class GamePlaySteps
{
    ......

    [Given(@"the following moves are played:")]
    public void GivenTheFollowingMovesArePlayed(Table table)
    {
        foreach (var row in table.Rows)
        {
            GameStorage.presenter.update_game_with_move(
                string.Format("{0},{1}", row["row"], row["column"]));
        }

        GameStorage.game_view.clean_display();
    }
}
}
```

Code file [GamePlaySteps.cs] available for download at Wrox.com.

To support the display of the game, you must dive into the behavior of the objects that support the application in terms of rendering a game and handling the placement of tokens. Let's make a list of the behaviors you must add:

1. The Game should place the token on a square on the grid.

2. The Game should be able to confirm placement of token.

3. The Game rendered should be able to obtain a read-only view of the grid for rendering.

Behavior 1: Placing the Token on the Grid

Update the when_placing_a_token_on_the_board spec to match the following code:

```
namespace Wrox.BDD.Specs.Core.Domain_Specs
{
    [Subject(typeof(TicTacToe))]
    public class when_placing_a_token_on_the_board : with_a_tictactoe_game
    {
        Establish context = () =>
        {
            coordinate_text = "1,1";
            coordinate = Coordinate.parse(coordinate_text);
            player_tracker.Stub(x => x.current_player()).Return(Tokens.x_token);

        };

        private Because of = () =>
        {
            SUT.place_token_for_current_player_at(coordinate);
        };

        private It should_place_a_token_on_the_grid = () =>
```

```
        {
            tic_tac_toe_grid.AssertWasCalled(x => x.place_token_at(
                Arg<Coordinate>.Matches(c => c.Equals(coordinate)),
                Arg<Token>.Matches(c => c.Equals(Tokens.x_token))));
        };

        ......

        private static Coordinate coordinate;
        private static string coordinate_text;
    }
}
```

Code file [when_placing_a_token_on_the_board.cs] available for download at Wrox.com.

Notice that you must mock the behavior of the `player_tracker` in the context delegate so that it will correctly return token X as the current player.

The new behavior defines that the `TicTacToe` game should pass the coordinate onto a `tic_tac_toe_grid`, along with the current playing token.

The `tic_tac_toe_grid` will represent the underlying board grid that the game is based upon. The grid is essential to the game, and, thus, should be a dependency of the game supplied at construction. Amend the `with_a_tictactoe_game` base class to add the new grid as a parameter to the construction of the `TicTacToe` instance, as shown here:

```
namespace Wrox.BDD.Specs.Core.Domain_Specs
{
    public abstract class with_a_tictactoe_game
    {
        public with_a_tictactoe_game()
        {
            player_tracker = MockRepository.GenerateStub<PlayerTracker>();
            tic_tac_toe_grid = MockRepository.GenerateStub<Grid>();

            SUT = new TicTacToe(player_tracker, tic_tac_toe_grid);
        }

        protected static Game SUT;
        protected static PlayerTracker player_tracker;
        protected static Grid tic_tac_toe_grid;
    }
}
```

Code file [with_a_tictactoe_game.cs] available for download at Wrox.com.

It's important to keep the grid and the game separate to support the single responsibility principle, and to reinforce domain concepts. The grid looks after everything to do with the playing board (for example, placing tokens and knowing what tokens are where). The game class knows (or at least knows who to talk to) about implementing the rules of the game of Tic-Tac-Toe, such as whose turn is next, and if the game is in a winning or drawn state.

Create the `Grid` interface in the `Domain` project with its single method.

```
namespace Wrox.BDD.Domain
{
    public interface Grid
    {
        void place_token_at(Coordinate coordinate, Token token);
    }
}
```

Code file [Grid.cs] available for download at Wrox.com.

Now, update the `TicTacToe` class by adding the `Grid` to its constructor, and by implementing the expected behavior.

```
namespace Wrox.BDD.Domain
{
    public class TicTacToe : Game
    {
        private PlayerTracker _player_tracker;
        private Grid _grid;

        public TicTacToe(PlayerTracker player_tracker, Grid grid)
        {
            _player_tracker = player_tracker;
            _grid = grid;
        }

        public Token current_token()
        {
            return _player_tracker.current_player();
        }

        public void place_token_for_current_player_at(Coordinate coordinate)
        {
            _grid.place_token_at(coordinate, current_token());

            _player_tracker.finish_players_move();
        }
    }
}
```

Code file [TicTacToe.cs] available for download at Wrox.com.

To run the specs, you must create an instance of the `Grid` in order to supply to both the `FakeGameView` and `ConsoleGameViews`. For the time being, the grid instance will contain no behavior. Add a new class named `NineSquareGrid` to the `Domain` project that implements the `Grid` interface.

```
namespace Wrox.BDD.Domain
{
    public class NineSquareGrid : Grid
    {
```

```
        public void place_token_at(Coordinate coordinate, Token token)
        {

        }
    }
}
```


You can now update the `FakeGameView` and `ConsoleGameView` with the new constructor dependency.

```
namespace Wrox.BDD.Specs.UAT
{
    public class FakeGameView : GameView
    {
        private TicTacToeGamePresenter _presenter;
        private StringBuilder _display = new StringBuilder();

        public FakeGameView()
        {
            _presenter = new TicTacToeGamePresenter(this,
                              new TicTacToe(new TokenTracker(),
                              new NineSquareGrid()),
                              new PlainTextGameBoardRenderer());

            GameStorage.presenter = _presenter;

            _presenter.start();
        }

        ......

    }
}
```



```
namespace Wrox.BDD.Ui.Console
{
    public class ConsoleGameView : GameView
    {
        private TicTacToeGamePresenter _presenter;

        public ConsoleGameView()
        {
            _presenter =
                new TicTacToeGamePresenter(this,
                              new TicTacToe(new TokenTracker(),
                              new NineSquareGrid()),
                              new PlainTextGameBoardRenderer());
```

```
            _presenter.start();
        }

        ......

    }
}
```


You will now be able to compile your code and then test the specs. Great! You have another passing specification.

Behavior 2: Confirming Placement of a Token

Okay, now you must create some specifications with the `Grid` as the subject. Add a new class named `when_checking_for_a_token_on_the_grid` and update it with the following code:

```csharp
using Machine.Specifications;
using Wrox.BDD.Domain;
using NUnit.Framework;

namespace Wrox.BDD.Specs.Core.Domain_Specs
{
    [Subject(typeof(NineSquareGrid))]
    public class when_checking_for_a_token_on_the_grid
    {
        Establish context = () =>
        {
            coordinate_with_token = Coordinate.parse("1,1");
            coordinate_without_token = Coordinate.parse("2,2");
            SUT = new NineSquareGrid();
        };

        private Because of = () =>
        {
            SUT.place_token_at(coordinate_with_token, Tokens.x_token);
        };

        private It should_contain_a_token = () =>
        {
            Assert.That(SUT.contains_token_at(coordinate_with_token), Is.True);
        };

        private It should_not_contain_a_token = () =>
        {
            Assert.That(SUT.contains_token_at(coordinate_without_token), Is.False);
        };

        private static NineSquareGrid SUT;
        private static Coordinate coordinate_with_token;
```

```
        private static Coordinate coordinate_without_token;
    }
}
```

Code file [when_checking_for_a_token_on_the_grid.cs] available for download at Wrox.com.

This specification defines that a grid should be able to retain the placement of a token. To start to add the behavior, first amend the `Grid` interface to match the following code:

```
namespace Wrox.BDD.Domain
{
    public interface Grid
    {
        void place_token_at(Coordinate coordinate, Token token);
        bool contains_token_at(Coordinate coordinate);
    }
}
```

Code file [Grid.cs] available for download at Wrox.com.

Next, implement the new method in the `NineSqureGrid` implementation of the interface.

```
namespace Wrox.BDD.Domain
{
    public class NineSquareGrid : Grid
    {
        public void place_token_at(Coordinate coordinate, Token token)
        {

        }

        public bool contains_token_at(Coordinate coordinate)
        {
            return true;
        }
    }
}
```

Code file [NineSquareGrid.cs] available for download at Wrox.com.

If you run the specs now, only one will pass. This is because you have hard-coded the `contains_token_at` to always return `true`. Let's update the `NineSquareGrid` to match the expected behavior.

```
namespace Wrox.BDD.Domain
{
    public class NineSquareGrid : Grid
    {
        protected readonly Token[,] _squares;

        public NineSquareGrid()
```

```
    {
        _squares = new Token[3, 3];
    }

    public void place_token_at(Coordinate coordinate, Token token)
    {
        _squares[coordinate.X, coordinate.Y] = token;
    }

    public bool contains_token_at(Coordinate coordinate)
    {
        return _squares[coordinate.X, coordinate.Y] != null;
    }
  }
}
```

Code file [NineSquareGrid.cs] available for download at Wrox.com.

You have elected to store tokens in a multiple array. Notice again that you aren't bothering to check if the coordinate is within the boundaries of the array. You will add this to the running list of edge cases to deal with after you have the happy-day scenarios passing.

Run the specs and all should now be passing. You are making some good progress now!

Behavior 3: Obtaining a Read-only View for Rendering

The final piece of behavior on the list is for the `BoardRenderer` to obtain a view of the game grid for rendering. You want the game to only expose a read-only view of the grid, because you are allowing access from the presentation layer, and you don't want the presentation code to bypass any logic and muddle with the data. With this in mind, create a specification with the `PlainTextGameBoardRenderer` as the subject named `when_rendering_the_game`, as shown in the following code:

```
using Machine.Specifications;
using Wrox.BDD.Domain;
using Wrox.BDD.Ui.Console.Presentation;
using Rhino.Mocks;

namespace Wrox.BDD.Specs.Core.Presentation_Specs
{
    [Subject(typeof(PlainTextGameBoardRenderer))]
    public class when_rendering_the_game
    {
        Establish context = () =>
        {
            var square_array = new string[3, 3];
            game = MockRepository.GenerateStub<Game>();
            game.Stub(x => x.get_game_view())
                        .Return(new GridView() { squares = square_array });
            SUT = new PlainTextGameBoardRenderer();
        };

        private Because of = () =>
        {
```

```
            SUT.render(game);
        };

        private It should_ask_the_game_for_a_readonly_view = () =>
        {
            game.AssertWasCalled(x => x.get_game_view());
        };

        private static PlainTextGameBoardRenderer SUT;
        private static Game game;
    }
}
```

Code file [when_rendering_the_game.cs] available for download at Wrox.com.

You will now need to update the `Game` interface and add the new method call that will return the yet undefined `GridView` class.

```
namespace Wrox.BDD.Domain
{
    public interface Game
    {
        Token current_token();
        void place_token_for_current_player_at(Coordinate coordinate);
        GridView get_game_view();
    }
}
```

Code file [Game.cs] available for download at Wrox.com.

Next, create the `GridView` class itself.

```
namespace Wrox.BDD.Domain
{
    public class GridView
    {
        public string[,] squares { get; set; }
    }
}
```

Code file [GridView.cs] available for download at Wrox.com.

You could have just as easily returned a multi-string array, but wrapping it in the `GridView` class helps to convey the concept of a view of the grid in a clearer way.

With the addition to the `Game` interface, you will now, of course, need to update the `TicTacToe` instance to implement the new method. Simply have it return a new instance of the `GridView` populated with an empty multi-dimensioned string array, as shown in the following code:

```
namespace Wrox.BDD.Domain
{
    public class TicTacToe : Game
    {
```

```
......

        public GridView get_game_view()
        {
            return new GridView(){ squares = new string[3,3]};
        }
    }
}
```


To meet the expected behavior, you must ensure that a call is made to obtain the GridView during the render method of the PlainTextGameBoardRenderer class.

```
namespace Wrox.BDD.Ui.Console.Presentation
{
    public class PlainTextGameBoardRenderer : BoardRenderer
    {
        public string render(Game game)
        {
            var squares = game.get_game_view().squares;
                    var grid_display = new StringBuilder();
            var row_seperator = "";

            for (int row = 0; row <= 2; row++)
            {
                if (!String.IsNullOrEmpty(row_seperator))
                    grid_display.AppendLine(row_seperator);

                var pipe = "";
                var row_display = new StringBuilder();

                for (int column = 0; column <= 2; column++)
                {
                    row_display.Append(string.Format("{0} {1} ", pipe,
                            pad_if_square_empty(squares[row, column])));
                    pipe = "|";
                }

                grid_display.AppendLine(row_display.ToString());
                row_seperator = "-----------";
            }

            return grid_display.ToString();
        }

        private string pad_if_square_empty(string value)
        {
            return String.IsNullOrEmpty(value) ? " " : value;
        }
    }
}
```

You should now be about to build your code and run your specs. However, the responsibility of creating a read-only view of the grid should not rest with the game, but instead the grid instance should be able to produce a read-only view of itself. Let's create another spec with the `NineSquareGrid` as the subject and add this behavior.

```csharp
using Machine.Specifications;
using Wrox.BDD.Domain;
using NUnit.Framework;

namespace Wrox.BDD.Specs.Core.Domain_Specs
{
    [Subject(typeof(NineSquareGrid))]
    public class when_generating_a_readonly_view_for_rendering
    {
        Establish context = () =>
        {
            coordinate_with_X_token = Coordinate.parse("1,1");
            coordinate_with_O_token = Coordinate.parse("2,2");
            SUT = new NineSquareGrid();
        };

        private Because of = () =>
        {
            SUT.place_token_at(coordinate_with_X_token, Tokens.x_token);
            SUT.place_token_at(coordinate_with_O_token, Tokens.o_token);

            result = SUT.generate_grid_view();
        };

        private It should_have_the_X_token_in_the_correct_position = () =>
        {
            Assert.That(result.squares[coordinate_with_X_token.X,
                                coordinate_with_X_token.Y],
                        Is.EqualTo(Tokens.x_token.value));
        };

        private It should_have_the_O_token_in_the_correct_position = () =>
        {
            Assert.That(result.squares[coordinate_with_O_token.X,
                                coordinate_with_O_token.Y],
                        Is.EqualTo(Tokens.o_token.value));
        };

        private static GridView result;
        private static NineSquareGrid SUT;
        private static Coordinate coordinate_with_X_token;
        private static Coordinate coordinate_with_O_token;
    }
}
```

Code file [when_generating_a_readonly_view_for_rendering.cs] available for download at Wrox.com.

Now, add the new method to generate the grid view to the `Grid` interface.

```
namespace Wrox.BDD.Domain
{
    public interface Grid
    {
        void place_token_at(Coordinate coordinate, Token token);
        bool contains_token_at(Coordinate coordinate);
        GridView generate_grid_view();
    }
}
```

Code file [Grid.cs] available for download at Wrox.com.

Next, update the `NineSquareGrid` itself by adding the code that will build the read-only view.

```
namespace Wrox.BDD.Domain
{
    public class NineSquareGrid : Grid
    {
        ......

        public GridView generate_grid_view()
        {
            var readonly_squares = new string[3,3];

            for (int row = 0; row < 3; row++)
                for (int column = 0; column < 3; column++)
                    readonly_squares[row, column] =
                                    _squares[row, column] == null ?
                                    "" : _squares[row, column].value;

            return new GridView() {squares = readonly_squares};
        }
    }
}
```

Code file [NineSquareGrid.cs] available for download at Wrox.com.

With the responsibility now with the grid to produce the read-only view, you can update the `TicTacToe` class to delegate the view creation to the grid.

```
namespace Wrox.BDD.Domain
{
    public class TicTacToe : Game
    {
        ......

        public GridView get_game_view()
        {
            return _grid.generate_grid_view();
        }
    }
}
```

Code file [TicTacToe.cs] available for download at Wrox.com.

Run your specs and all should pass. Now, with all the behavior added in the objects, your scenario should now pass, as shown in Figure 14-24.

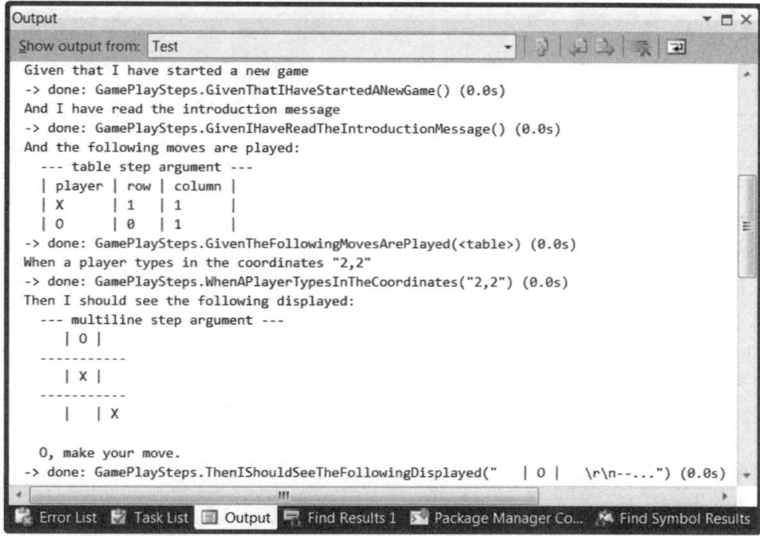

FIGURE 14-24: SpecFlow output showing the passing of the scenario to display a game

Brilliant! You can now display the grid. Let's see what it looks like when you run the game for real.

Integrating the Displaying a Game Scenario

If you run the game, you see that whenever you make a move, the grid display is updated and the current player alternates. There is one problem, however. The game will go on forever because there is no check for a winning line!

Another issue found is that there is nothing to stop a player from placing a token on a square that is already occupied. You'd better add this to this list of behaviors to verify later on.

Scenario: Winning the Game with Three in a Row

In order for a game to finish, you must check for a winning condition. A win is three of the same token in a line. Add a new feature named `PlayerWinsAGame.feature` to the features folder of the `Specs.UAT` project, and update it to match the scenario in Figure 14-25.

As luck would have it, you don't need to add any more step definitions because this scenario reuses all of your existing steps.

Let's jot down some initial steps that must occur for the view to display if a player has won.

1. The presenter should end the game if the current player is the winner.

2. `Game` should check for a winning line.

3. Presenter should display the winner to the view.

```
PlayerWinsAGame.feature                        ▾ ▢ ✕
      Feature: Win A Game
          In order to win a game of Tic-Tac-Toe
          As player
          I must get 3 of my tokens in a row

      Scenario: Diagonal Win
          Given that I have started a new game
          And the following moves are played:
            | player | row | column |
            | X | 1 | 1 |
            | O | 0 | 2 |
            | X | 0 | 0 |
            | O | 1 | 2 |
          When a player types in the coordinates "2,2"
          Then I should see the following displayed:
          """
          X |   | O
          -----------
            | X | O
          -----------
            |   | X

          X has won the game!

          " " "
100 %  ▾  ◂           |||              ▸
```

FIGURE 14-25: The SpecFlow PlayerWinsAGame.
feature with the diagonal win scenario

Behavior 1: End the Game if There Is a Winner

The first behavior on the list defines that in order for the presenter to display if a player has won the game, it must check with the game instance if the game has been won by the current player after each token placement. Add a new behavior definition to the when_a_player_places_a_token specification to verify that a check is made after a token is placed.

```
namespace Wrox.BDD.Specs.Core.Presentation_Specs
{
    [Subject(typeof(TicTacToeGamePresenter))]
    public class when_a_player_places_a_token : with_a_presenter
    {
        ......

        private It should_check_if_the_current_player_has_won_the_game = () =>
        {
            game.AssertWasCalled(x => x.the_current_player_has_won_the_game());
        };

    }
}
```

Code file [when_a_player_places_a_token.cs] available for download at Wrox.com.

The specification defines that the presenter should call a method on the Game interface to determine if the game has been won. Add this to the Game interface, as shown in the following code:

```
namespace Wrox.BDD.Domain
{
    public interface Game
```

```
        {
            Token current_token();
            void place_token_for_current_player_at(Coordinate coordinate);
            GridView get_game_view();
            bool the_current_player_has_won_the_game();
        }
    }
```

Code file [Game.cs] available for download at Wrox.com.

With a change to the interface, there must also be a change to the `TicTacToe` class that implements it. For the moment, simply hard-code a `false` return.

```
namespace Wrox.BDD.Domain
{
    public class TicTacToe : Game
    {
        ......

        public bool the_current_player_has_won_the_game()
        {
            return false;
        }
    }
}
```

Code file [TicTacToe.cs] available for download at Wrox.com.

In order to get the specification to pass, you must update the `TicTacToeGamePresenter` to match the expected behavior by checking with the game for a winner.

```
namespace Wrox.BDD.Ui.Console.Presentation
{
    public class TicTacToeGamePresenter
    {
        ......

        public void update_game_with_move(string move_coordinates)
        {
            var coordinate = Coordinate.parse(move_coordinates);

            _game.place_token_for_current_player_at(coordinate);

            display_game();

            if (!_game.the_current_player_has_won_the_game())
                prompt_for_next_move();
        }

        ......
    }
}
```

Code file [TicTacToeGamePresenter.cs] available for download at Wrox.com.

Run the specs and all should pass. Now, what's next on the list?

Behavior 2: Check for a Winning Line

To get the `Game` instance to check for a winning line, first create a new specification with the `TicTacToe` class as the subject.

```
using Machine.Specifications;
using Wrox.BDD.Domain;

namespace Wrox.BDD.Specs.Core.Domain_Specs
{
    [Subject(typeof(TicTacToe))]
    public class when_checking_if_the_current_player_has_won_the_game :
                                                with_a_tictactoe_game
    {
        private Because of = () =>
        {
            SUT.the_current_player_has_won_the_game();
        };

        private It should_tell_the_game_to_place_a_token = () =>
        {
            line_checker.AssertWasCalled(x =>
                    x.contains_a_winning_line(tic_tac_toe_grid));
        };
    }
}
```

Code file [when_checking_if_the_current_player_has_won_the_game.cs] available for download at Wrox.com.

You have now introduced the concept of a `line_checker`. This class will be responsible for determining if the grid contains three tokens in a row. Because you need this for the game to function correctly, add it as a constructor dependency and update the base specification class.

```
namespace Wrox.BDD.Specs.Core.Domain_Specs
{
    public abstract class with_a_tictactoe_game
    {
        public with_a_tictactoe_game()
        {
            player_tracker = MockRepository.GenerateStub<PlayerTracker>();
            tic_tac_toe_grid = MockRepository.GenerateStub<Grid>();
            line_checker = MockRepository.GenerateStub<LineChecker>();

            SUT = new TicTacToe(player_tracker, tic_tac_toe_grid, line_checker);
        }

        protected static Game SUT;
        protected static PlayerTracker player_tracker;
        protected static Grid tic_tac_toe_grid;
```

```
        protected static LineChecker line_checker;
    }
}
```


Create the new interface for the winning line checker.

```
namespace Wrox.BDD.Domain
{
    public interface LineChecker
    {
        bool contains_a_winning_line(Grid tic_tac_toe_grid);
    }
}
```


As you probably noticed, the code won't compile, so update the `TicTacToe` class to accept an instance of the `LineChecker` and also delegate to the `LineChecker` the responsibility of checking if the current player has won.

```
namespace Wrox.BDD.Domain
{
    public class TicTacToe : Game
    {
        private PlayerTracker _player_tracker;
        private Grid _grid;
        private readonly LineChecker _line_checker;

        public TicTacToe(PlayerTracker player_tracker, Grid grid,
                         LineChecker line_checker)
        {
            _player_tracker = player_tracker;
            _grid = grid;
            _line_checker = line_checker;
        }

        ......

        public bool the_current_player_has_won_the_game()
        {
            return _line_checker.contains_a_winning_line(_grid);
        }
    }
}
```


In order for the code to compile, the `FakeGameView` and the `ConsoleGameView` must be supplied a concrete implementation of the `LineChecker`. Because you are only interested in the diagonal line, add a new class named `DiagonalWinningLineChecker` to implement the interface, hard-coded with a negative response.

```
namespace Wrox.BDD.Domain
{
    public class DiagonalWinningLineChecker : LineChecker
    {
        public bool contains_a_winning_line(Grid tic_tac_toe_grid)
        {
            return false;
        }
    }
}
```

Code file [DiagonalWinningLineChecker.cs] available for download at Wrox.com.

Now, update the `ConsoleGameView` and the `FakeGameView`.

```
namespace Wrox.BDD.Ui.Console
{
    public class ConsoleGameView : GameView
    {
        private TicTacToeGamePresenter _presenter;

        public ConsoleGameView()
        {
            _presenter =
                new TicTacToeGamePresenter(this,
                        new TicTacToe(new TokenTracker(), new NineSquareGrid(),
                                new DiagonalWinningLineChecker()),
                        new PlainTextGameBoardRenderer());

            _presenter.start();
        }

        ......

    }
}
```

Code file [ConsoleGameView.cs] available for download at Wrox.com.

```
namespace Wrox.BDD.Specs.UAT
{
    public class FakeGameView : GameView
    {
        private TicTacToeGamePresenter _presenter;
        private StringBuilder _display = new StringBuilder();

        public FakeGameView()
```

```
        {
            _presenter = new TicTacToeGamePresenter(this,
                new TicTacToe(new TokenTracker(), new NineSquareGrid(),
                            new DiagonalWinningLineChecker()),
                new PlainTextGameBoardRenderer());

            GameStorage.presenter = _presenter;

            _presenter.start();
        }

        ......

    }
}
```

Code file [FakeGameView.cs] available for download at Wrox.com.

Build and run your specs. They all pass!

You have now introduced some more behavior in the form of a new object, the `LineChecker`. You can add a fourth responsibility to your list that specifies that the job of the line checker is to determine if there is a winner, based on the state of the game grid.

Behavior 3: Displaying the Winner to the View

The next behavior on the list deals with the presenter announcing the winner by updating the view. Add a new spec with the `TicTacToeGamePresenter` as the subject, and add the following code to the class:

Available for download on Wrox.com

```
using Machine.Specifications;
using Wrox.BDD.Domain;
using Wrox.BDD.Ui.Console.Presentation;
using Rhino.Mocks;

namespace Wrox.BDD.Specs.Core.Presentation_Specs
{
    [Subject(typeof(TicTacToeGamePresenter))]
    public class when_a_player_gets_3_tokens_in_a_row : with_a_presenter
    {
        Establish context = () =>
        {
            coordinate_text = "1,1";
            coordinate = Coordinate.parse(coordinate_text);

            game.Stub(x => x.current_token()).Return(Tokens.x_token);
            game.Stub(x => x.the_current_player_has_won_the_game()).Return(true);
        };

        private Because of = () =>
        {
            SUT.start();

            SUT.update_game_with_move(coordinate_text);
```

```
    };

    private It should_announce_that_he_has_won_the_game = () =>
    {
        game_view.AssertWasCalled(x => x.write_line("X has won the game!"));
    };


    private static Coordinate coordinate;
    private static string coordinate_text;
  }
}
```

Code file [when_a_player_gets_3_tokens_in_a_row.cs] available for download at Wrox.com.

Because the presenter already has the `Game` as a dependency, all you must do is amend the `TicTacToeGamePresenter` to check for a winner, and then announce that the current player is the winner.

```
namespace Wrox.BDD.Ui.Console.Presentation
{
    public class TicTacToeGamePresenter
    {
        ......

        public void update_game_with_move(string move_coordinates)
        {
            var coordinate = Coordinate.parse(move_coordinates);

            _game.place_token_for_current_player_at(coordinate);

            display_game();

            if (_game.the_current_player_has_won_the_game())
                announce_current_player_as_the_winner();
            else
                prompt_for_next_move();
        }

        private void announce_current_player_as_the_winner()
        {
            _game_view.write_line(string.Format("{0} has won the game!",
                            _game.current_token()));
        }


        ......

    }
}
```

Code file [TicTacToeGamePresenter.cs] available for download at Wrox.com.

If you run the specs after that small amendment, they should all pass!

Behavior 4: Check the Grid for a Winner

Now, let's move on to the last behavior for this scenario — adding the behavior to the `DiagonalWinningLineChecker`.

Before getting into the nitty-gritty of the `DiagonalWinningLineChecker`, let's think about how you want to communicate with the grid in order to ascertain whether there are three of the same token in a diagonal line.

The following code is some pseudo-code to visualize how you would like the `DiagonalWinningLineChecker` to query the grid. You are trying to create a fluent interface that reads easily from left to right.

```
namespace Wrox.BDD.Specs.Core.Domain_Specs
{
    [Subject(typeof(DiagonalWinningLineChecker))]
    public class when_checking_if_game_has_a_3_in_a_diagonal_line
    {
        private It should_check_for_3_O_tokens_from_right_to_left_diagonally
            = () =>
        {
            grid.square_at(coordinate_0_1).contains_token_matching(Tokens.o_token);

            grid.square_at(coordinate_1_1).contains_token_matching(Tokens.o_token);

            grid.square_at(coordinate_2_2).contains_token_matching(Tokens.o_token);

        };
    }
}
```

The code should read as close possible to plain English from left to right. To make this fluent interface work, the grid must return an object that is capable of determining if the square at the coordinate contains a token that matches the token given. It makes sense that the object is a square.

Now that you have an idea of what the end result should look like, let's create the spec.

```
using Machine.Specifications;
using Wrox.BDD.Domain;
using Rhino.Mocks;
using NUnit.Framework;

namespace Wrox.BDD.Specs.Core.Domain_Specs
{
    [Subject(typeof(DiagonalWinningLineChecker))]
    public class when_checking_if_game_has_a_3_in_a_diagonal_line
    {
        Establish context = () =>
        {
            grid = MockRepository.GenerateStub<Grid>();
            square = MockRepository.GenerateStub<Square>();

            coordinate_0_0 = new Coordinate(0, 0);
            coordinate_1_1 = new Coordinate(1, 1);
```

```csharp
            coordinate_2_2 = new Coordinate(2, 2);

            square.Stub(x => x.contains_token_matching(
                Arg<Token>.Matches(c => c.Equals(Tokens.x_token)))).Return(true);

            grid.Stub(x => x.square_at(Arg<Coordinate>
                    .Matches(c => c.Equals(coordinate_0_0)))).Return(square);
            grid.Stub(x => x.square_at(Arg<Coordinate>
                    .Matches(c => c.Equals(coordinate_1_1)))).Return(square);
            grid.Stub(x => x.square_at(Arg<Coordinate>
                    .Matches(c => c.Equals(coordinate_2_2)))).Return(square);

            SUT = new DiagonalWinningLineChecker();
        };

        private Because of = () =>
        {
            result = SUT.contains_a_winning_line(grid);
        };

        private It should_check_for_3_X_tokens_from_left_to_right_diagonally
            = () =>
        {
            grid.AssertWasCalled(x => x.square_at(
                    Arg<Coordinate>.Matches(c => c.Equals(coordinate_0_0))));
            grid.AssertWasCalled(x => x.square_at(
                    Arg<Coordinate>.Matches(c => c.Equals(coordinate_1_1))));
            grid.AssertWasCalled(x => x.square_at(
                    Arg<Coordinate>.Matches(c => c.Equals(coordinate_2_2))));

            square.AssertWasCalled(x => x.contains_token_matching(
                    Arg<Token>.Matches(c => c.Equals(Tokens.x_token))),
                                o => o.Repeat.Times(3));
        };

        private It should_find_a_winning_line = () =>
        {
            Assert.That(result, Is.True);
        };

        private static DiagonalWinningLineChecker SUT;
        private static Grid grid;
        private static Square square;
        private static bool result;
        private static Coordinate coordinate_0_0;
        private static Coordinate coordinate_1_1;
        private static Coordinate coordinate_2_2;
    }
}
```

Code file [when_checking_if_game_has_a_3_in_a_diagonal_line.cs] available for download at Wrox.com.

To make the fluent API work, you have introduced the concept of a `Square`. This represents the location for a given `Coordinate`.

The `Square` interface has a single method that determines if a given token matches the token that is occupying the square.

```
namespace Wrox.BDD.Domain
{
    public interface Square
    {
        bool contains_token_matching(Token token);
    }
}
```

Code file [Square.cs] available for download at Wrox.com.

The `Grid` also has an additional method added to its interface that returns a `Square` for a given `Coordinate`.

```
namespace Wrox.BDD.Domain
{
    public interface Grid
    {
        void place_token_at(Coordinate coordinate, Token token);
        bool contains_token_at(Coordinate coordinate);
        GridView generate_grid_view();
        Square square_at(Coordinate coordinate);
    }
}
```

Code file [Grid.cs] available for download at Wrox.com.

With the modification to the `Grid` interface, you must also update the implementation, the `NineSquareGrid`. It needs to return an instance of the `Square`, so add a call to instantiate an as-yet nonexistent class.

```
namespace Wrox.BDD.Domain
{
    public class NineSquareGrid : Grid
    {
        ......

        public Square square_at(Coordinate coordinate)
        {
            return new PlayingSquare();
        }
    }
}
```

Code file [NineSquareGrid.cs] available for download at Wrox.com.

Now, create the implementation of the `Square` interface and default the `contains_token_matching` to return `false`.

Available for download on Wrox.com

```
namespace Wrox.BDD.Domain
{
    public class PlayingSquare : Square
    {
        public bool contains_token_matching(Token o_token)
        {
            return false;
        }
    }
}
```

Code file [PlayingSquare.cs] available for download at Wrox.com.

You can now update the `DiagonalWinningLineChecker` to use the new methods of the `Grid` and `Square` in order to match the expected behavior, as specified in your spec class.

Available for download on Wrox.com

```
namespace Wrox.BDD.Domain
{
    public class DiagonalWinningLineChecker : LineChecker
    {
        public bool contains_a_winning_line(Grid tic_tac_toe_grid)
        {
            var coordinate_0_0 = new Coordinate(0, 0);
            var coordinate_1_1 = new Coordinate(1, 1);
            var coordinate_2_2 = new Coordinate(2, 2);

            if (tic_tac_toe_grid.square_at(coordinate_0_0)
                        .contains_token_matching(Tokens.x_token) &&
                tic_tac_toe_grid.square_at(coordinate_1_1)
                        .contains_token_matching(Tokens.x_token) &&
                tic_tac_toe_grid.square_at(coordinate_2_2)
                        .contains_token_matching(Tokens.x_token))
                return true;

            return false;
        }
    }
}
```

Code file [DiagonalWinningLineChecker.cs] available for download at Wrox.com.

If you run the specification classes, all should pass.

By now, you should have noticed that I write a method's name in lowercase with underscores to separate words. This is a design decision that I have taken to increase the readability of code, borrowed a little from Ruby as well. I have also thought hard about how I have named my methods in order to convey the behavior of the object to users of it. Remember, by creating code in a test-first process, you are able to create the best API you can, so I advise you take time to play with language in order to better communicate the behavior of objects in your solution.

You now must check that the implementation of the `Grid` interface can correctly return a `PlayingSquare` that confirms the existence of a token.

Update the `when_checking_for_a_token_on_the_grid` with a new behavior that confirms the placement of a token.

```
namespace Wrox.BDD.Specs.Core.Domain_Specs
{
    [Subject(typeof(NineSquareGrid))]
    public class when_checking_for_a_token_on_the_grid
    {
        ......

        private It should_be_able_to_match_the_token = () =>
        {
            Assert.That(SUT.square_at(coordinate_with_token)
                            .contains_token_matching(Tokens.x_token), Is.True);
        };


        ......
    }
}
```

Code file [when_checking_for_a_token_on_the_grid.cs] available for download at Wrox.com.

The `NineSquareGrid` can now instantiate a `PlayingSquare` and pass in the `Token` at the given coordinate. Remember, this is only the happy-day scenario you are dealing with here, so you are not adding code to cover edge cases.

```
namespace Wrox.BDD.Domain
{
    public class NineSquareGrid : Grid
    {
        ......

        public Square square_at(Coordinate coordinate)
        {
            return new PlayingSquare(_squares[coordinate.X, coordinate.Y]);
        }
    }
}
```

Code file [NineSquareGrid.cs] available for download at Wrox.com.

A `PlayingSquare` is another immutable value object, add a constructor that takes a token, which it then uses to perform an equality check with the passed-in token. Once the `PlayingSquare` is created, it cannot be modified.

```
namespace Wrox.BDD.Domain
{
    public class PlayingSquare : Square
    {
        private readonly Token _token;
```

```
        public PlayingSquare(Token token)
        {
            _token = token;
        }

        public bool contains_token_matching(Token token)
        {
            return _token.Equals(token);
        }
    }
}
```

Code file [PlayingSquare.cs] available for download at Wrox.com.

Your spec should pass. Now, let's get back to the edge case. What happens if there is no token for a given coordinate? Let's write a new behavior to verify what should happen.

```
namespace Wrox.BDD.Specs.Core.Domain_Specs
{
    [Subject(typeof(NineSquareGrid))]
    public class when_checking_for_a_token_on_the_grid
    {
        ......

        private It should_not_match_a_missing_token = () =>
        {
            Assert.That(SUT.square_at(coordinate_without_token)
                    .contains_token_matching(Tokens.o_token), Is.False);
        };

        ......

    }
}
```

Code file [when_checking_for_a_token_on_the_grid.cs] available for download at Wrox.com.

If you run the specs now, the code will throw an exception because there is no token at that coordinate that you can pass to the `PlayingSquare`.

You know the code is doing what you'd like to, so amend the `NineSquareGrid` class to check for a `Token` at the given coordinate, and, if no token exists, you can use a design pattern named the Null Object Pattern to create an `EmptyPlayingSquare` using a parameterless constructor.

```
namespace Wrox.BDD.Domain
{
    public class NineSquareGrid : Grid
    {
        ......

        public Square square_at(Coordinate coordinate)
        {
            return contains_token_at(coordinate) ? (Square)
```

```
                              new PlayingSquare(_squares[coordinate.X, coordinate.Y]) :
                              new EmptyPlayingSquare();
            }
        }
    }
```

Code file [NineSquareGrid.cs] available for download at Wrox.com.

The `EmptyPlayingSquare` simply returns `false` for a match on a token, and saves you from checking for `null`s throughout your code.

Available for download on Wrox.com

```
namespace Wrox.BDD.Domain
{
    public class EmptyPlayingSquare : Square
    {
        public bool contains_token_matching(Token o_token)
        {
            return false;
        }
    }
}
```

Code file [EmptyPlayingSquare.cs] available for download at Wrox.com.

This completes the list of behaviors for the scenario.

Run the specs and all should pass. Now, you should be done with this scenario, so let's run the UAT specs to see if you are good. Ooops! Looks like you have an error!

You were expecting player X to win, but the output is that player O has won. It looks as though the current player is being updated even though the game has ended. Let's write a spec to ensure that the `TicTacToe` game doesn't update the current player in the event of the player winning.

Available for download on Wrox.com

```
using Machine.Specifications;
using Wrox.BDD.Domain;
using NUnit.Framework;
using Rhino.Mocks;

namespace Wrox.BDD.Specs.Core.Domain_Specs
{
    [Subject(typeof(TicTacToe))]
    public class when_placing_a_winning_token_on_the_board : with_a_tictactoe_game
    {
        Establish context = () =>
        {
            coordinate_text = "1,1";
            coordinate = Coordinate.parse(coordinate_text);

            line_checker.Stub(x =>
                        x.contains_a_winning_line(Arg<Grid>.Is.Anything))
                            .Return(true);

            player_tracker.Stub(x => x.current_player()).Return(Tokens.x_token);
```

```
        };

        private Because of = () =>
        {
            SUT.place_token_for_current_player_at(coordinate);
        };

        private It should_not_alternate_the_player = () =>
        {
            player_tracker.AssertWasNotCalled(x => x.finish_players_move());
        };

        private static Coordinate coordinate;
        private static string coordinate_text;
    }
}
```

Code file [when_placing_a_winning_token_on_the_board.cs] available for download at Wrox.com.

And now, simply implement the behavior in `TicTacToe` class.

```
namespace Wrox.BDD.Domain
{
    public class TicTacToe : Game
    {
        ......

        public void place_token_for_current_player_at(Coordinate coordinate)
        {
            _grid.place_token_at(coordinate, current_token());

            if (!the_current_player_has_won_the_game())
                _player_tracker.finish_players_move();
        }

        ......
    }
}
```

Code file [TicTacToe.cs] available for download at Wrox.com.

Run all of you specs. Great! They all pass! Let's see the code in production.

Integrating the Winning a Game with Three in a Row Scenario

There's nothing extra you must do in terms of integration, apart from simply running the game. If you put three X tokens in a diagonal line from left to right, you will find that the game ends. However, no other winning variations will cause the game to finish, and there is nothing to stop tokens from being placed on top of each other, or on invalid squares.

You have added a fair bit of behavior for the game thus far, and even though you have a lot left, the most important thing is that your customer can see the progress you've made. He can start to play the game and get a feel for the software. By choosing to build vertical slices of functionality rather than layers, you can get working software in front of the customer quickly for valuable feedback.

Completing the Game

Unfortunately, this is where this chapter leaves the `TicTacToe` code kata. However, as an exercise, I strongly suggest that you complete the game by adding the remaining features in the manner you have been shown.

Along with the code download that accompanies this chapter, I have also added the complete source code for the finished game that you can use to compare against how you may have designed the remaining features.

MOVING FORWARD

You should experiment more with code katas to better understand BDD and the importance of focusing on the language of the domain you work within, all of which can help you become a better developer.

Figure 14-26 shows the Agile Manifesto, the four principles that are the cornerstone to producing better software. After reading the manifesto, you should see how user stories and BDD support a more agile development process.

Manifesto for Agile Software Development

We are uncovering better ways of developing
software by doing it and helping others do it.
Through this work we have come to value:

Individuals and interactions over processes and tools
Working software over comprehensive documentation
Customer collaboration over contract negotiation
Responding to change over following a plan

That is, while there is value in the items on
the right, we value the items on the left more.

Kent Beck	James Grenning	Robert C. Martin
Mike Beedle	Jim Highsmith	Steve Mellor
Arie van Bennekum	Andrew Hunt	Ken Schwaber
Alistair Cockburn	Ron Jeffries	Jeff Sutherland
Ward Cunningham	Jon Kern	Dave Thomas
Martin Fowler	Brain Marick	

FIGURE 14-26: Agile Manifesto

SUMMARY

This chapter dealt with the need to focus on the behavior of a system under development, rather than its technical details, to meet and exceed the needs of a customer. To better capture the behaviors of a system under development, you were introduced to user stories that emphasized the communication between the development team and the customer, as an alternative method to the traditional requirements gathering, which places more value on written documentation.

User stories enable you to capture just enough about a feature so that you can estimate complexity and have a conversation with the customer about the details of the feature at a later date. From user stories, acceptance criteria are born using the "Given, When, Then" template, which enables the details of features to be explored and verified.

The second part of this chapter introduced you to Behavior Driven Development (BDD), which has evolved out of a need for Test-Driven Development (TDD) to take a step back to avoid losing focus on what the system under development wants to achieve. Outside-in development further emphasizes the need to drive development from features that a customer can benefit from, and when used with TDD, can be a powerful force for software development.

In the final part of the chapter, you worked through the capturing of features for a Tic-Tac-Toe game via user stories and the development of it using SpecFlows BDD framework for specifying application behavior, and MSpec for specifying object behavior. This exercise underlined the effectiveness of BDD and user stories in software development to produce quality software.

By applying the techniques found in this chapter, in conjunction with listening to your customers and working with them to understand their visions and goals, you will be in a better place to write software that exceeds their expectations, which will make your job a whole lot easier.

ABOUT THE AUTHOR

Scott Millett works in London, England, for `Wiggle.co.uk`, an e-commerce company specializing in cycle and triathlete sports. He has been working with .NET since version 1.0, and was awarded the ASP.NET MVP in 2010, and again in 2011. He is the author of *Professional ASP.NET Design Patterns* (Indianapolis: Wiley, 2010) and the co-author of *Professional Enterprise.NET* (Indianapolis: Wiley, 2009). When not writing about or working with .NET, he can be found relaxing and enjoying the music at Glastonbury and all of the major music festivals in the United Kingdom during the summer. If you would like to talk to him about this chapter, anything .NET, or the British music festival scene, feel free to write to him at `scott@elbandit.co.uk`, or by giving him a tweet @ScottMillett.

15

Automated Unit Testing

by Caleb Jenkins

As a consultant, development mentor, and agile coach, I've worked with many dozens of organizations and hundreds of developers who have struggled through the realities of implementing automated unit tests. Most developers have at least heard of unit tests. They even believe that implementing automated tests would be a good idea and would make their code better, even if they're not sure exactly how or why — or rather, they're not fully convinced that the added time and complexity of writing tests can make their code better.

If you are a developer, you already know how to write code — you probably get paid for it — and won't tests just slow you down? Won't they give you more code to write and maintain? If you've ever struggled with these notions about writing tests, know that you're not alone! If you have these concerns now, you will probably be a better test writer in the long run.

This chapter lays the right foundation for your tests, and gives you the practical skills and tools to make unit testing a natural part of your coding activity.

UNDERSTANDING UNIT TESTS

At their core, *unit tests* are just code you write to test code that you wrote — or, better yet, code that you are going to write. With automated unit tests, you can run and rerun hundreds, or even thousands, of tests with the click of a single button, or have the test run automatically on the server whenever a developer checks in new code to source control.

Scope, LEGOs, and Connected Parts

Think of software development in terms of building with LEGO blocks (the classic children's interlocking building bricks), except that you must individually build most of the blocks. A LEGO block is like a class, and, as you build your software, you assemble the various parts.

Thinking about software this way is helpful. It is also a bit sobering when you realize that you are responsible for building the blocks, and for making sure that they fit together and function properly.

Understanding Test-Driven Development

It has been said that the worst word in Test-Driven Development is the word *test*. Why is that? Because when you think of a test, it is often something that is done after that fact.

For example, when you build a house, you have an inspector come after that house has been built to confirm that it is structurally sound and stable. Compare that to the role of the architect who originally designed and built the house. He wrote *specifications* that the builders then had to follow.

In Test-Driven Development (TDD), think of your tests as *executable specifications*, and not as *after-the-fact* tests. By writing the tests first, you in essence tell your code what it is supposed to do, and you tell it in such a way that you can easily execute and confirm that it does what you told it to do!

The basic workflow to TDD is simple enough, but it is also a powerful practice if your team embraces it. As Yoda might say, "The tests are my ally, and a powerful ally they are."

Following are the four basic steps for TDD:

1. Write the test.

2. Run the test and watch it fail.

3. Write code to pass the text.

4. Refactor the code.

> *This process can be summarized as red, green, refactor — rinse and repeat.*

The first step is easy. Write the test that tells your code what it should do.

Next, you run your test and watch it fail (red). Of course, it *should* fail — you haven't written the code to make it pass yet! It's important to see your test fail to ensure that it can. I've worked with far too many systems that had passing tests — tests that would and could never actually fail. Simply put, as tests, systems, and scenarios grow in complexity, it is all too easy to get caught in the weeds, and inadvertently write a passing test (one that will never fail). So, ensure that your tests can fail, okay?

Then write just enough code to pass your tests. This is actually more difficult than it sounds. For developers, it is too easy to get caught up in the moment and the momentum of where the code is going. "We know what it should do next; I'll write the tests later."

The problem is that this is often where scope creeps its way into your systems. Use the power of the tests to help guide and push your code where you want it to go. Write *just enough* code to pass your test (green). I know, I know, you are probably thinking that the code is ugly, it's a hack, and it just does the minimum to pass. Yep — and that is why you have Step 4.

In Step 4, you refactor your code to make it perform better, as well as ensure that it is maintainable and readable. Basically, Step 4 is a cleanup step. Now that you have a passing test, you can refactor and test, refactor and test, and so on, and have a level of confidence that the refactoring you do here isn't breaking something else. Then, when you have it all cleaned up, you write another test!

UNDERSTANDING THE BENEFITS OF A TEST-FIRST APPROACH

I'm not saying that everyone must always write tests first before any code is written (although that is preferred). The argument could be made that fast proto-typing and mock-ups are an example of when that might be overkill. But take a quick look at several of the direct benefits of following a *test-first approach*.

Testable Code

Although I am not a stickler on having massive test coverage in every scenario, I am a huge stickler when it comes to writing *testable* code. If you find that your code is difficult to test, writing your tests first can dramatically help your ability to write testable code. Most people who start down this path soon realize that they like it so much that it becomes uncomfortable to not have tests first. Give it a try!

Self-Documenting Code

Do you find yourself coming back to your code after the fact, and trying to explain it to other developers? Wouldn't it be great if you had a whole host of example code that showed exactly how to use your library?

Defensive Code

Do you work with other developers who check in code without asking first? (I'm being a little facetious here. Of course, they don't ask for permission to check in code — and you wouldn't want them to!) Having your unit tests already in place is the best way to ensure that other developers (or yourself, for that matter) aren't breaking your code.

Maintainable Code

Some people try to argue that writing tests slows down development and increases the cost of software. However, at this point in our industry, it is a statistically established fact that the cost of software *creation* is pennies on the dollar when compared to the cost of software *maintenance*.

In other words, the real problem with quick-and-dirty is that *dirty* always outlasts *quick*. Having a healthy suite of automated tests is quite possibly the single largest and fastest thing that any team could do to decrease the cost of software maintenance, decrease the fragility of its code, reduce the risk of future change, and lower the total cost of software ownership.

Code Smell Detector

If you find that your code is increasingly difficult to test, that is a huge smell indicating that it will be difficult to use. Think of writing your tests like dogfooding your own code — you know, eating what you make to see how it tastes. Writing tests is a way to use your own code early and often.

Writing software is often about writing useful pieces of functionality that then gets chained together for a larger need of functionality. The larger need (although necessary to software development) is often obscured from view when smaller pieces break. Unit tests enable you to quickly test at the smallest level of usefulness.

GETTING ORIENTED WITH A BASIC EXAMPLE

Okay, enough with the chitchat — let's code! Let's start by taking a look at a simple (albeit contrived) example.

Assume that you are going to write a library to manage account balances. You want to withdraw funds, add funds, and get the current balance. What would the class for that look like? Check out the following:

```
public class Account
{
    public int Total { get; set; }
    public void Withdraw(int amount)
    {
        Total -= amount;
    }
    public void Deposit(int amount)
    {
        Total += amount;
    }
}
```

That's simple enough, right? But can it do what you need? Does it work as expected? Can you spot any issues with the code? How would you test to see if the code can do what you want it to do?

You could do a simple test of this code with something like this:

```
var testAccount = new Account() { Total = 100 };
testAccount.Deposit(10);
bool passed = (testAccount.Total == 110);
```

But then you have to ask yourself, "How am I going to run this test code?" Back in the day, you might have whipped up a quick Windows Form application, drawn a button, double-clicked it, written your test code in the event handler, and ended with a big `MessageBox` telling you that it worked! Don't laugh. It's sad, but many developers "unit" test their code that way, and, frankly, at least it is a unit test.

Later in this chapter, you learn about automated unit tests and using mocking frameworks and test runners to make your life easier and more productive. But first, look at the fundamental components that make up every bit of test code — "The Three A's."

ASSIGN, ACT, ASSERT

Aside from being a catchy homily, the "Three A's" do help to ensure that you write appropriate tests. Now dig a little deeper into what each means.

Assign

The *assign* section is basically the setup for the test. This is where you assign your starting values for your test. In the earlier example pseudocode, I created the test account and then *assigned* the property `Total` to `100`.

In many cases, it makes sense to move the starting position (or assign section) for a test to a common method that gets called before every test — especially if you group your tests together by common scenarios.

Act

The *act* (or *action*) section is the method or event that you test. In the previous example, it was the *act* of depositing `10` into the account that was the action.

It's tempting to cram multiple scenarios and actions into a single test, but that's actually just a headache waiting to happen, which can lead to confusion and uncertainty when the tests fail. It's a much better practice to adhere to "one act per test."

Assert

The *assert* statement is what tells your test if it has passed. *An assert statement is always a Boolean expression* — you either pass or fail, and nothing in between. In the preceding example code, I set the result to a `bool` (passed) and left what I was going to do with that `bool` up to the imagination.

If you wrote a Windows Form application, you'd be tempted to do a `MessageBox` at this point with the message, "It passed!" If you wrote a `Console` app to handle your unit tests, you would have done a `Console.Write` to display the result of your test. But, again, you have better options. You have moved on. You have embraced the unit testing framework.

A unit testing framework is like having a test application for your code already in place. You leverage the testing framework as infrastructure to host your code, and run your tests against your code.

CODE, TESTS, FRAMEWORKS, AND RUNNERS

If you think about it, there are just four major components to an automated unit testing environment:

➤ Code

➤ Tests

➤ Testing framework

➤ Test runner

Now take a look at each of these components.

Code

This is simply the code that you wrote or are going to write, and that you want to test.

Tests

This is the code that tests your code. (This is what was discussed earlier in this chapter.)

Testing Framework

The *testing framework* is what makes the whole automated unit testing environment possible. The testing framework that you use will be an enabler to the whole process. Testing frameworks are available for almost every language and environment.

In the .NET world, nUnit has been around the longest. It's freely available (`http://nunit.org`), and is completely Open Source. Also, Microsoft's VS Test is included with all versions of Visual Studio Professional and up, so it's also extremely ubiquitous and readily available (`www.microsoft .com/visualstudio/en-us/solutions/software-quality`). Other testing frameworks are available, but this discussion focuses on nUnit and VS Test. As a consultant and agile coach, these are the two that I run into more with clients than anything else in the field.

> **CHOOSING A TESTING FRAMEWORK**
>
> In my experience as a consultant, Microsoft VS Test is typically used at companies that are new to testing (it is the easiest to adopt if you are already using Microsoft Visual Studio), or have made the complete shift to Microsoft Team Foundation Server and Microsoft Team Build as a build server and for Continuous Integration (CI).
>
> nUnit is typically used at companies that have been unit testing longer than Microsoft has officially supported it, or in combination with other Open Source tools and non-Microsoft build servers. For example, Hudson, Team City, and CruiseControl .NET are all build server/CI environments that play nicely with nUnit.
>
> If you use Team Foundation Server, VS Test integrates nicely out-of-the-box. (This isn't to say that you can't mix and match these, but they might require more effort to configure.)
>
> nUnit and VS Test are not the only testing frameworks available in .NET. Following are a couple of others worth looking at:
>
> ➤ xUnit.NET (`http://xunit.codeplex.com/`)
>
> ➤ MbUnit (`http://mbunit.com/`)

Microsoft's testing framework is composed of multiple pieces:

➤ MS Test (`MSTEst.exe`, the Microsoft Test Runner console application)

➤ Visual Studio Testing Framework (`Microsoft.VisualStudio.QualityTools .UnitTestFramework.dll`)

➤ Visual Studio Test Professional (the version of Visual Studio that specifically incorporates all the testing features from Microsoft)

I refer to the Microsoft collections of unit testing features as VS Test. Fortunately, automated unit testing is included in all versions of Visual Studio from Visual Studio Professional on up, not just the Test Professional version.

The testing framework provides a set of APIs and attributes that your test runner can use to execute your tests, and your tests can use to notify the test runner of your test results. For example, if you were to write the test code shown earlier with VS Test, it might look something like this:

```
[TestMethod]
public void TestDeposit()
{
    var testAccount = new Account() { Total = 100 };
    testAccount.Deposit(10);
    Assert.Equals(testAccount.Total,110);
}
```

Did you notice the `[TestMethod]` attribute? That is the part of the testing framework that tells the test runner that this is a test that must be executed. You should also notice that the method is public and returns `void` (`Public Sub` in Visual Basic). All tests need to be public `void`s.

If you were using nUnit instead of VS Test, then you would have used the nUnit `[Test]` attribute instead, as shown here:

```
[Test]
public void TestDeposit()
{
    var testAccount = new Account() { Total = 100 };
    testAccount.Deposit(10);
    Assert.That(testAccount.Total.Is.EqualTo(110);
}
```

You might also notice that nUnit offers the `Assert.That` method. nUnit also has the `Assert .Equals` method that was used in the VS Test snippet. You could have moved your test code over and only changed the attribute. It is a matter of preference and readability as to whether you prefer `Assert.Equals()` or `Assert.That()`.

Test Runner

Running a single test with a Windows Form or `Console` application would not be that big of a deal — maybe even running r or 5 tests. But what happens when you have 20, 30, 100, or 500 various automated tests that you want to run all at once? This is where the *test runner* comes in.

Figure 15-1 shows an easy-to-use test runner included with nUnit. Figure 15-2 shows a VS Test test runner integrated directly in Visual Studio.

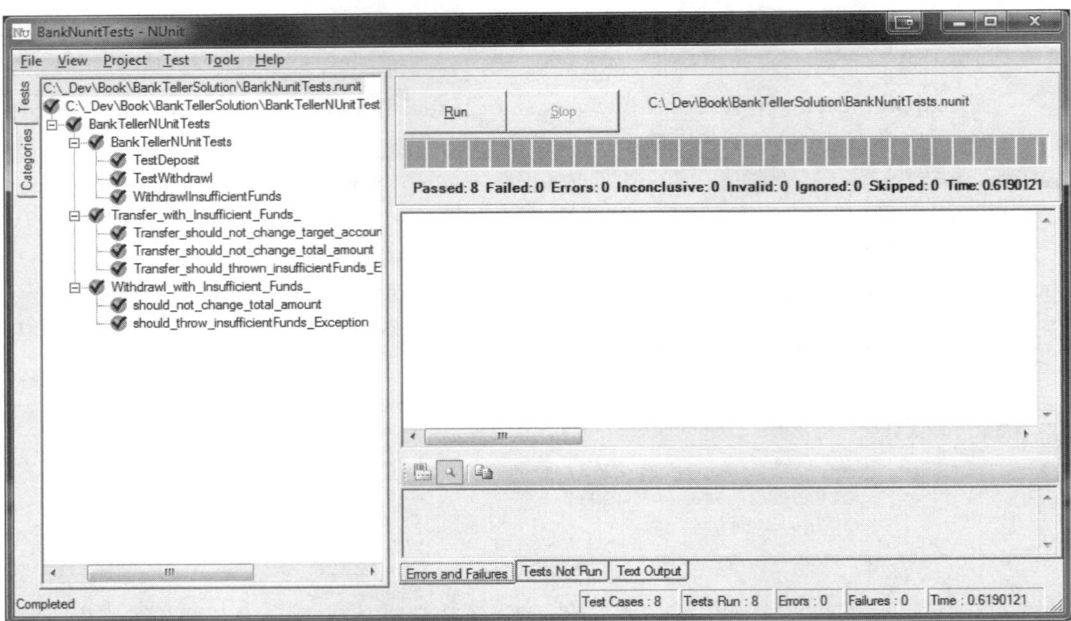

FIGURE 15-1: Test runner in nUnit

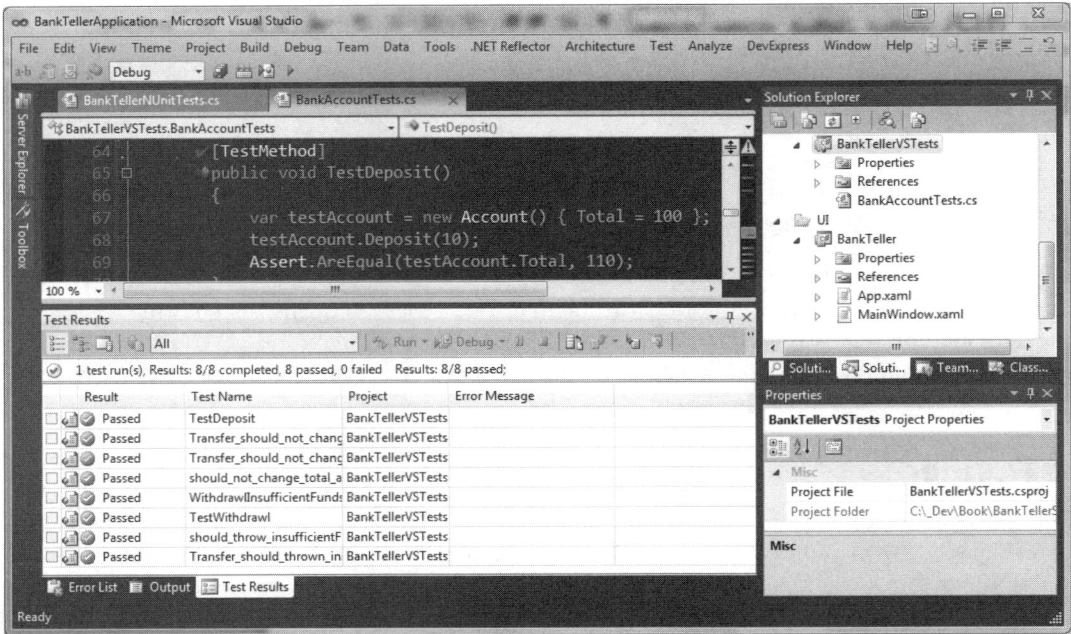

FIGURE 15-2: Test runner in VS Test

It's easy to think of the test runner as being synonymous with the testing framework. I try to make a distinction between the two because you will probably use other test runners from time to time, and you might prefer some of those.

For example, if you use Team Foundation Server for Continuation Integration (CI), then Team Build will be your build server and Team Test would actually be the piece executing your tests. If you use Nant as a build server, then you might use Cruise Control.NET for CI and have a Nant script to run your nUnit tests.

Other examples of test runners include the following plug-ins for Visual Studio:

➤ Test Driven .NET (`www.testdriven.net/`)

➤ ReSharper (`www.jetbrains.com/resharper/`)

➤ CodeRush (`www.devexpress.com/Products/Visual_Studio_Add-in/Coding_Assistance/`)

Other test runner plug-ins for Visual Studio are available, but these three tend to be the most common and most popular. (I use the integrated test runner included with CodeRush from DevExpress.) What I like about all these is that you end up with a consistent testing environment and test execution workflow, regardless of the testing framework. As a consultant, I use whatever testing framework the client happens to use. So, using a test runner that spans multiple test frameworks helps reduce my friction switching between projects.

Using CI Servers and Source Control

Now take a moment to clarify exactly what CI servers are, and how they fit into the overall mix. The basic workflow is this:

1. A developer checks code into a source control server.

2. Your CI server monitors the source control for check-ins and grabs the latest source, pulls it to a known location, and engages a build server (such as MS Build or Nant) to compile the code and run the unit tests.

3. In a good CI environment, the results of the build, the unit tests, and any other metrics tools that you include post to a report view of some kind.

With Team Foundation Server, all this is included out-of-the-box (although it does need to be configured properly). Other well-known CI servers worth looking at include Jet Brain's Team City, Hudson CI, and Cruise Control.

At this point, you should have a good grasp on the major players or the big-picture items in unit testing (your code, your tests, testing frameworks, and test runners), and, more important, why these are all important pieces in your testing environment. Take a minute to dig in to some important specifics, such as the overall organizational structure of the solution/project.

SOLUTION/PROJECT STRUCTURE

If you use Visual Studio's VS Test, then you can simply right-click in your code and select Generate Unit Tests. This creates a new Test Project, makes the appropriate references, and does a lot of the wire-up details for you. Figure 15-3 shows the result of this approach.

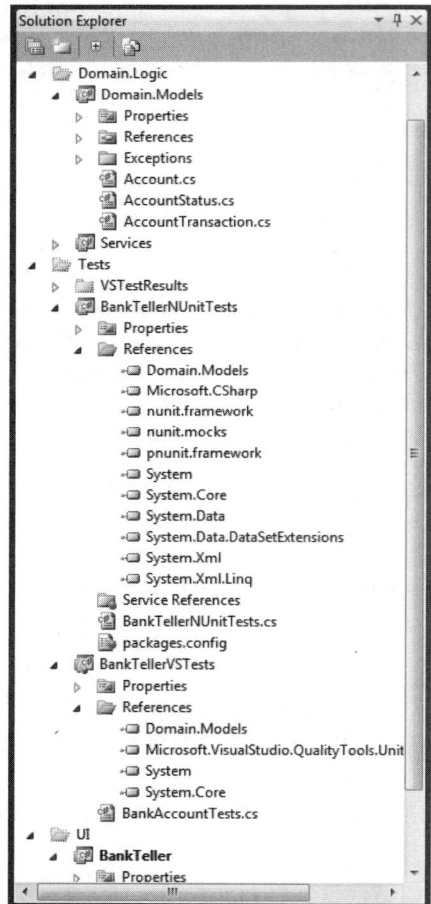

FIGURE 15-3: VS Test file and directory organization

There are times, however, when you might want to configure your tests in a specific way, or use other testing frameworks (such as nUnit), so take a quick look at some important details:

➤   Your code and your tests should be in separate assemblies (projects).

➤   The projects with your tests should reference your testing framework and the project that you want to test. (In VS Test, this is a Visual Studio Test Project; if you use nUnit, then it's just a C# or VB Library.)

➤   The code that you test should never reference your test code. This may seem obvious, but it's an important step to keep the direction of dependencies in the right order. Keep in mind that you want this separation because you never want to ship your tests in your production code.

USING NUGET TO BLEND NUNIT AND VS 2010

In the past there were certain challenges using tools and libraries that weren't included with Visual Studio "out-of-the-box." These challenges might include knowing what libraries could be trusted, downloading the latest versions and their dependencies, and then repeating this for every project.

As mentioned several times, VS Test is included with Visual Studio. It's also worth mentioning how easy it is to add nUnit's testing framework to your solution with Microsoft's new Open Source NuGet tool. As noted on the official NuGet website (`www.nuget.org`), "NuGet is a Visual Studio extension that makes it easy to install and update open source libraries and tools in Visual Studio." In other words, NuGet makes working with third-party Open Source libraries a breeze.

To add NuGet to Visual Studio, follow these steps:

1. In Visual Studio 2010, go to Tools ➪ Extension Manager.

2. Select Online Gallery, and search for "NuGet."

3. Select NuGet Package Manager and click Install.

To add nUnit from NuGet, follow these steps:

1. Create a class library for your nUnit tests.

2. Right-click the class library project, and select Add Library Package Reference.

3. In the search bar, type **nUnit**.

4. As shown in Figure 15-4, select the nUnit package, and click Install,

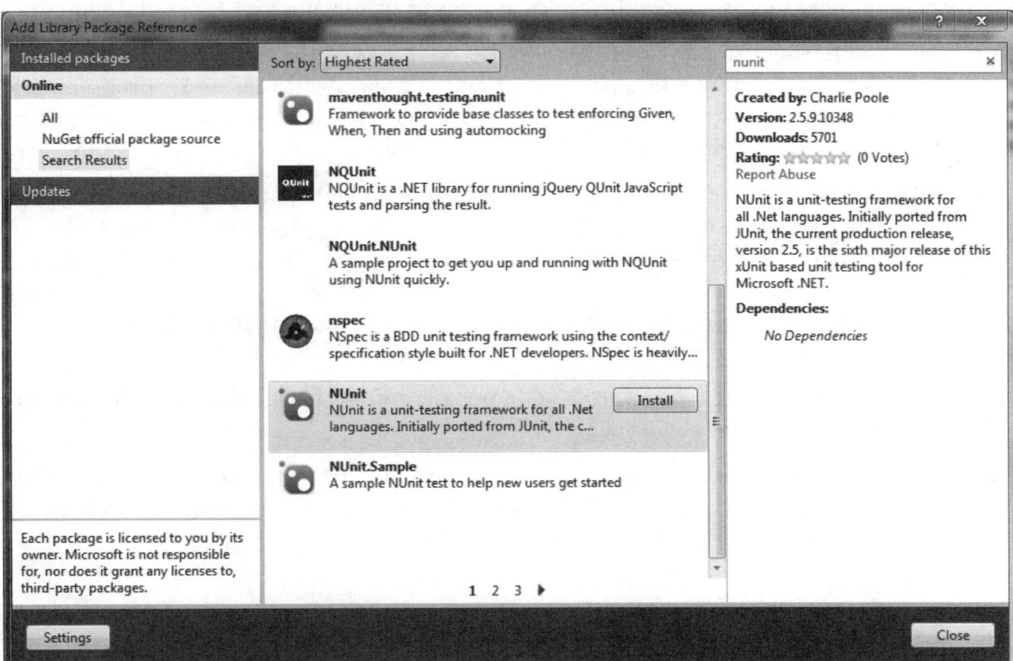

FIGURE 15-4: Adding nUnit from NuGet

METHODS WITH FAKES AND MOCKS

Earlier, you learned how it is desirable to fully test each code block or class so that you know that it fits properly and behaves as it should. Some parts are easier to test than others. For example, a method that takes in parameters and returns a value with no other dependencies is easy to test, but what about more complicated software applications? For example, what about the kind that actually connects to other areas of your application and has dependencies and connections to other methods and classes?

Faking with Dependency Injection

The single greatest thing to that you can do to make your code more testable and healthy is to start taking a *Dependency Injection* (*DI*) approach to writing software. The full breadth of DI is beyond the scope of this chapter, but, simply put, DI enables you to inject objects into a class, as opposed to the class creating the object. A quick example may help to put this into context.

Start with a common scenario. Say that you are inside of your business layer and you need to make a call to your data layer. Sound familiar? What does that code look like?

```
// Some business layer code where I'm doing business logic stuff …
IMyAwesomeDataLayer data = new MyAwesomeDataLayer();
data.update(someData);
// more business layer stuff…
```

Setting aside the lack of error handling, does that code snippet look about right? Now, think about how you will test that call. How will you test how the business layer responds to an exception from the data layer — in other words, how will you force an error at this point?

Note that you're not testing the data layer. Right now you're testing the business layer that is supposed to call the data layer, with certain parameters and in a specific scenario. At this point in your test, you don't care if the data layer actually exists. You are not testing that the data layer is doing its awesome thing. You care only that the business layer is calling it when and how it's supposed to.

In this example code snippet, you have an interface-backed data layer (`IMyAwesomeDataLayer`), but you have a hard dependency on the instantiation of a specific implementation of that interface. One testing solution would be to introduce a simple abstract factory and call that instead of specifically "newing" up your class in code. Unfortunately, an abstract factory would solve one problem and introduce a whole new one. You'd have a new dependency to your class that would then resurface as an issue in less obvious ways later. So, what else would work?

What if you simply told your class that you need an instance of `IMyAwesomeDataLayer` without telling it where to get it? How could you do that?

You could simply add it as a constructor parameter, or a property that gets set before you call your method. (Without going in to the religious DI debate, I'll just say that I prefer constructor injecting on anything that is a required dependency.)

Moving to a DI style of software development can help you make your code more modular, easier to test, and easier to maintain. A number of available DI frameworks exist (including Windsor from the Castle Project, Microsoft Unity, Ninject, Structure Map, and others) that use a dependency style of code that is easier to work with and maintain. However, those are beyond the scope of this chapter, and, typically, those are also outside of your unit tests.

Now that you have a way to get your specific implementation of the `IMyAwesomeDataLayer` into the class, you have the capability to create implementations that you can specifically use for testing. For example, what if you want to test how the business layer handled various exceptions that the data layer could throw, you now could create a class that implemented the `IMyAwesomeDataLayer` interface, but that always threw a specific exception whenever you called the update method.

```
public class FakeDataLayerForTest : IMyAwesomeDataLayer
{
    public void Update(Account account)
    {
        throw new InvalidAccountNumberException();
    }
}
```

A *fake class* like this would be useful only for testing that specific scenario, but think how useful a scenario that could be to test! So, now what do you do? You end up writing (and maintaining) a new set of fake classes for every possible scenario.

Take a minute to consider the types of fake classes that you would want to build for various scenarios. Maybe you could build a validation fake class that always returned true, a data class that always returned the same exact record, or even a networking class that always acted like the network was down.

This chapter began with a comparison between writing code and building with children's LEGO bricks. Like building with LEGO bricks when the pieces rarely sit by themselves, building software requires multiple moving parts to all work together, as shown in Figure 15-5.

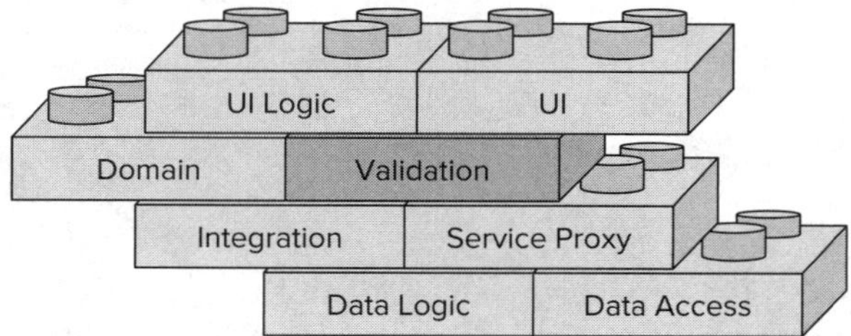

FIGURE 15-5: Thinking of building software applications as building with LEGO bricks

In this scenario, you need something to represent what the UI sends to the Validation piece, plus you need something to act as the Integration and Service Proxy pieces that talk back to the Validation component. It's nice to know that you don't need to re-create the entire application to isolate the Validation piece, just the parts that touch it. Figure 15-6 shows this process.

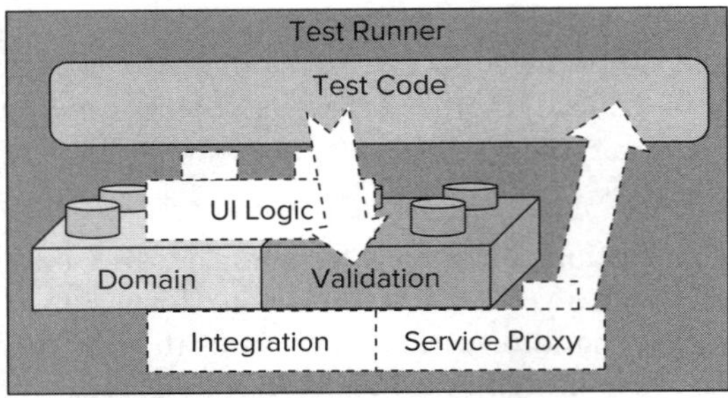

FIGURE 15-6: Validation process

Although creating fake classes for each component is possible (and can work well), as you add fake classes to your test suites, your tests become less readable. Or to be more specific, to understand what and how a test behaves, you end up looking inside of each fake class that you created, and discerning its purpose and behaviors to understand exactly what the test is doing, and why. It doesn't take long for the large number of fake classes for specific scenarios in your test suites to build up. This is why I prefer using mocking frameworks instead of fake classes.

Mocking Frameworks

A *mocking framework* enables you to create fake classes on-the-fly and in line with your test code. That may be a bit of a simplification. Mocking frameworks use a combination of emits, reflection, and generics to create runtime instance implementations of .NET interfaces. In other words, they create fake classes on-the-fly!

> **CHOOSING A MOCKING FRAMEWORK**
>
> A number of popular mocking frameworks are worth looking at, including the following:
>
> ➤ Rhino Mocks (`http://ayende.com/projects/rhino-mocks.aspx`)
>
> ➤ MoQ (`http://code.google.com/p/moq/`)
>
> ➤ nMock (`www.nmock.org/`)
>
> Rhino Mocks has been around the longest. It is probably the most mature and most used mocking framework for .NET, so that's what is used in this chapter. You can use the same instructions provided earlier in this chapter for installing nUnit with NuGet to add any of these mocking frameworks.

Now look at some test code with a mocking framework. First, get a mock object that matches the interface, as shown here:

```
loggerMock = MockRepository.GenerateMock<ILog>();
```

Remember, you're not testing the ILog object. You're testing something that has a dependency on it, and so you use a mock to fake the expected interactions.

Next, you tell the mock object what you expect, as shown here:

```
loggerMock.Expect(x => x.Error("Error Happened")).Repeat.Once();
```

In this case, you expect the method that you call to need to log some error, specifically the message, "Error Happened." Obviously, this would not be a useful message in real code, but it makes things nice for this example. You also tell the mock that you expect this method to get called, with this parameter, and that you expect it to be called once, and only once.

Now that you have set up your mock, let's "new up" the class that you actually want to test, and pass in the mock as a dependency. Here is the constructor:

```
public AcmeBankingService(ILog logger)
```

This enables you to inject the dependency (or in the case of this test, the mock instance), as shown here:

```
var serviceUnderTest = new AcmeBankingService(loggerMock);
```

Finally, you perform your action and then verify your expectations, as shown here:

```
var tx = serviceUnderTest.CashWithdraw(Account_Number, amount_withdraw);
loggerMock.VerifyAllExpectations();
```

In this simple example, the only thing that you ask the mock to do is receive a method call a certain number of times, with a certain parameter being passed in to it. Even with this basic example, you verify quite a bit!

By using mocking frameworks, you can go much deeper into the interactions that your code is expected to have with its dependencies. Also, by using a mocking framework, you can expect method calls, return specific values, throw exceptions, and raise events. Your mocks can quickly become quite complicated; although, that should also be a bit of a code smell. Remember, if it takes a tremendous amount of work to test a single class, you might be trying to do too much in one place.

CLASS ATTRIBUTES, TEST ATTRIBUTES, AND SPECIAL METHODS

Testing frameworks provide attributes that you will use in your tests to let the test runner know what it should do. For example, the test runner will need to know which classes contain your test methods, and then which public methods are the actual tests. You might also have supporting methods that you'll want the test runner to call at specific points in the testing. Wouldn't it be nice if you could say, "run this method before anything else — it sets up the test environment," or "run this same method before each test in this suite." And this is where your special test (attributes) will be used.

If you use VS Test, not only do you start by creating a Test Project, but also Visual Studio starts you off with an "example" unit test, including placeholders for several attributes that you will probably never use or need. Now take a look at the attributes that will be the most helpful to you.

Earlier in this chapter, you learned about the Three A's in unit testing: assign, act, and assert. It doesn't take too many tests to realize that you seem to be using the same sort of "assign" repeatedly in your tests. Remember, the "assign" section of your tests is where you set up the starting values that you are going to test against.

So, if you were testing some sort of validator, the setup might include initializing the validator, setting some values on the test object that you are going to validate, and so on. If you were using mocks, you would typically register your mocks with the mocking framework and set up your expectations here as well.

The testing framework infrastructure recognizes this common pattern (using a single method to set up the majority of your tests), and provides helpful attributes for your use. With nUnit, you mark a method with `[TestFixtureSetUp]`, and with VS Test you mark a method with `[ClassInitialize]`. Like tests, what you actually name these methods is irrelevant, as long as they return `void` and are public.

By marking a method with the appropriate attribute, the test framework promises to call that method one time before it runs any of the tests. Inversely, you can probably quickly figure out what `[ClassCleanup]` (VS Test) and `[TestFixtureTearDown]` (nUnit) do. They run at the end of all the tests in that class. This would be useful if, for example, you were running unit tests against a database, and you needed to reset some of the test data to a known state, or to reset any system environmental variables that you might have changed during the tests.

> *I am a huge proponent of isolated unit tests and leveraging mocking frameworks to reduce those sorts of dependencies. I almost never have a need for the tear-down attributes.*

What about times when you need to do a certain amount of setup before each unit test, not just before the class of unit tests? Well, if you use Microsoft's VS Test, you can mark a method with `[TestInitialize]`. If you use nUnit, then `[SetUp]` can do the job. I end up taking this approach more often than not. You will probably start with a certain setup that spans all your tests and needs to be done only once. Quickly, though, you'll find the improved quality of your tests by running each test in isolation.

TESTING THE HARD TO TEST — PUSHING THE EDGES

So far, this discussion has focused on the interactions and tests with libraries and utility functions. On one hand, this makes sense because the majority of your application should live in the business logic of a class library. On the other hand, libraries and utility functions are easy to demonstrate in an automated unit test — so this is where most examples stop. However, now take a look at some of the hard-to-test areas.

The edges of your application are always the hardest to test. Think about your normal three-tier application with a UI, Business and Data layers, as shown in Figure 15-7.

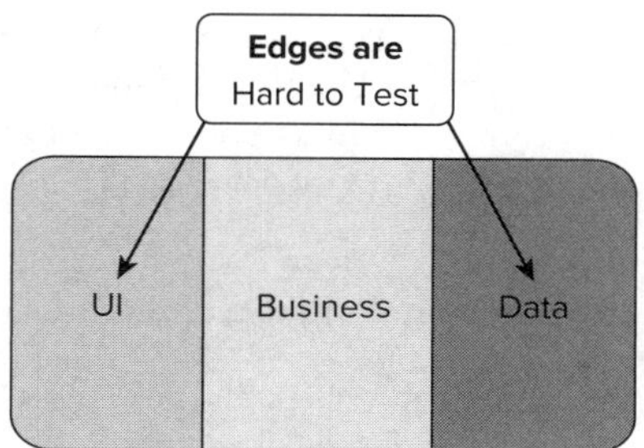

FIGURE 15-7: Normal three-tier application

The edges of your application are always the hardest to test. Even if this basic diagram doesn't fit your application's model, the edges of your application are still hard to isolate in a unit test. Are you working on writing a device driver? The edge is easy to find there. What about a web service? The edge is an obvious service endpoint, and it would be easy to point to the many record and playback web tools out there for testing web services. However, those would not be unit tests, but instead would be full integration tests, or at a minimum, functional tests that would require the entire application to be up and running to test. Remember, you're not testing applications; you're testing the bricks that they are built from.

So, what is the solution? Make the edge as wide as possible, and increase your testable area, as shown in Figure 15-8. Several new UI and data patterns have emerged (though not that new, "new in popularity" might be a better way to say it) that help achieve this goal.

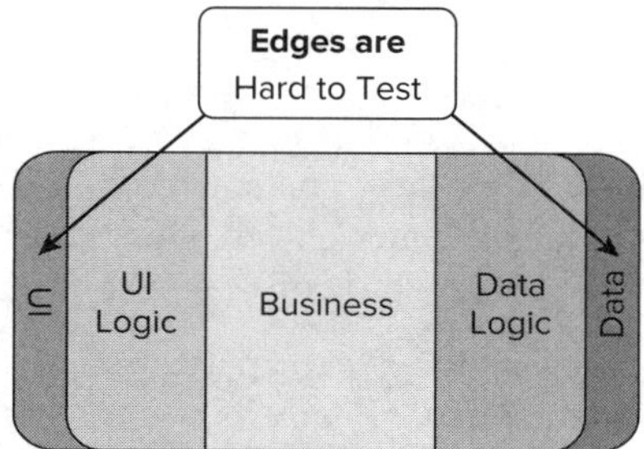

FIGURE 15-8: Increasing the testable area

By separating the UI and data logic from the actual edge implementation, you gain the benefit to increase your testable area, and creating a better separation between your UI and data implementations with the rest of the application. One way to achieve this separation is to use a trusted UI pattern framework.

Three UI patterns surface as being notable for unit testing:

➤   Model-View-Controller (MVC)

➤   Model-View-Presenter (MVP)

➤   Model-View-ViewModel (MVVM)

In each of these, a model represents an application model, or simple data object. A model holds data, but other than that, should be dumb. The same holds true with views. They should look pretty and be dumb as rocks. Why? Because you want those views to be as thin as possible so that as much of your UI logic as possible can be pushed in to the controller (MVC), presenter (MVP), or ViewModel (MVVM).

Although each of these models is touched upon in other chapters of this book, take a glance at each in the context of unit testing.

Model View Controller (MVC)

With MVC, your controller is where your UI logic should live. In MVC, all input is routed to a controller. The controller decides what actions to take, what classes to call, and what view to display. This is ideal for certain web scenarios, in which all input essentially goes straight to the web server where it gets processed.

MVC separates the UI "edge" from the UI logic, with the controller giving you a nice clean place to add automated unit testing to your UI layer.

Take a look at Microsoft's latest ASP.NET MVC Framework for examples on using MVC as a proven pattern.

Model View Presenter (MVP)

In an MVP approach, a presenter object contains all your UI logic. Your view implements an interface that enables you to mock your view when you want to test your presenter object. This is a helpful pattern where the view itself is rich enough to actually bubble up its own events.

Contrast a rich client Windows Form/WPF screen with a button linking to a web application. In a rich client application, the button is componentized enough that it actually owns its own event handler and initiates its own click event. With an ASP.NET Web Form application, the click event actually results in an HTTP request going across to a web server, where it bubbles up through a managed pipeline leveraging `View State` to eventually end up in an event handler.

This artificial pipeline in ASP.NET Web Forms makes the MVP pattern a good fit in ASP.NET Windows Form Web Form scenarios, as well as rich client applications.

When using MVP pattern, make sure that your presenter objects go in a separate class library from your main UI application. This isn't as critical with Windows applications, though it's always a good idea. In web applications, you want that separation to keep your unit test lightweight. You don't want to spin up a whole web server just to run your unit tests!

MVP separates the UI "edge" from the UI logic with the presenter object, making it the ideal place to unit test the UI logic in your UI layer.

Model View ViewModel (MVVM)

In the MVVM (or simply ViewModel) approach, your UI architecture is broken in to three key pieces. Like the previous two patterns, your application Models hold your application data, and your Views display the data. But with MVVM, you have View-specific models called ViewModels.

MVVM takes advantage of the rich data binding available in Microsoft platforms such as Silverlight and WPF, so that, instead of having a presenter that manipulates your view like a puppet master, you have a single ViewModel that exposes properties and event handlers that are bound to the View. Think of the View as a thin shell that gets wrapped around the ViewModel. All the UI logic and behaviors are rolled in to the ViewModel, which can easily be tested.

MVVM separates the UI "edge" from the UI logic with the ViewModel object, so that's where your unit test should focus.

Table 15-1 provides a summary for the use of these three patterns.

TABLE 15-1: UI Patterns for Unit Testing

UI PATTERN	USEFUL SCENARIO	TESTABLE UI LOGIC
MVC	Web and non-componentized Windows applications	Controller
MVP	Windows and Web Forms applications	Presenter
MVVM	Rich client application with strong data binding (Silverlight/WPF/some JavaScript frameworks)	ViewModel

Now that you understand some of the common approaches to making the hard-to-test scenarios easier to test, let's look at some strategies for dealing with really difficult (or even impossible) code to test.

USING SENSING VARIABLES TO REFACTOR NONTESTABLE CODE

Every developer has "inherited" some hard-to-test code from time to time. For example, this might have occurred after the umpteenth time that a new release broke some part of the code, and it was obviously time for a change.

To solve this problem, you add some unit tests to protect this code from other changes in the system. And while a complete refactoring might be in order, there might be some simple steps that you could take to quickly achieve a level of testability.

Start seeing how this could be done by looking at the following example:

```
private int qualifiedPoints;
public void ValidatePoints(decimal amount, AccountType accountCategory)
{
    if (amount > 100 && accountCategory == AccountType.Business)
        qualifiedPoints += 4;
    else if (amount > 100 && accountCategory == AccountType.Personal)
```

```
            qualifiedPoints += 2;
        else if (amount <= 100 && accountCategory == AccountType.Business)
            qualifiedPoints += 1;
        else
            // nothing for Personal account < 100
    }
    public void UpdatePoints()
    {
    if(qualifiedPoints  > 0)
    {
        var data = new AccountData();
            data.UpdatePoints(accountNumber, qualifiedPoints);
            qualifiedPoints = 0;

    }
    }
```

In this code snippet, the first thing you should notice is that there seems to be a lot of business logic tied up in the `ValidatePoints` method, and there is not an easy way to test it. After you toss in an expense, you must add 3 points, or 4 points, or 2 points, or no points, depending on whether this was a Personal Account or a Business Account, and depending on how large the transaction was.

This is the sort of code that changes frequently, and yet you have no easy way to validate the logic and functionality. One approach could be to mock the data layer and then test how many points were pushing through it. Of course, that would lead you to only checking the final output, and not easily checking that the logic in `ValidatePoints` was actually correctly working.

This introduces the need for a sensing variable. A *sensing variable* (or method) is simply a way to peak at the internal state of an object. This would be immediately useful for testing this object. What would that look like? What if you simply added a read-only property to give you the current number of qualified points?

```
    public int QualifiedPoints
    {
        get { return qualifiedPoints;}
    }
```

And just like that, this class just became a whole lot easier to test.

Now that you are starting to refactor your code to make it testable and using your tests to drive better coding practices, you might be asking, "now that I have tests, what can I do — I mean, beyond running those tests?" Let's take a look at how having automated unit tests build a foundational layer for many of the other engineering practices that will help reduce your technical debt, and improve the quality of your code.

USING AUTOMATED UNIT TESTING WITH OTHER PRACTICES

As an agile coach, I work with teams of developers all over the world, and one of the things that I enjoy about embracing automated unit tests is not only what they do for an individual's code, but also what having a suite of tests can do for a team of developers working together. Automated unit tests make up one of the core staples in reducing technical debt, and improving a team's overall code quality.

One of the key benefits to build up your automated units is the multiplier effect that your tests can have with the additional services and metrics of code health that you can now take advantage of.

As your code base and team grow, it becomes more challenging to ensure a consistent practice around unit testing. Although nothing can replace solid development practices like code pairing to help ensure higher code quality, you can look at several metrics to help monitor quality practices within larger teams.

Code coverage is a measurement of what percentage of your code that your unit tests cover. Although some people might want to hit some artificial number of code coverage (such as 80 percent, or 30 percent, or whatever), I'm usually more interested in the trend of coverage than any specific number. I want to see the coverage going up, or at least remaining steady. Otherwise, I know that new code is being added without test coverage.

Coverage isn't everything. As all developers know, not all code is created equal — as in importance or criticalness. So, for example, I typically don't unit-test getters and setters on properties for simple data transfer objects (DTOs). (You could, but is there value there?) Rather, I'd want to ensure that the critical and complex areas of my code have the most coverage.

In addition to covering the most important areas, I also want to ensure that I'm accounting for the various scenarios within a specific section of code. So, instead of relying on code coverage to be everything, I also want to ensure that my number of unit tests continues to grow over time.

NCover is a product that integrates with multiple unit testing frameworks and CI servers to provide code coverage metrics. Microsoft's VS Test features include code coverage metrics that work with MS Test, and integrates out-of-the-box with Team Foundation Server and Team Build for a CI solution.

MICROSOFT'S WORK WITH AUTOMATED UNIT TESTING

Microsoft is doing some incredibly interesting work with automated unit testing in its research group. It developed a couple of tools that do a good job figuring out your existing code and generating a high number of high-quality unit tests. This is significant work to develop a useful tool to add to your utility belt (although not a replacement for consistent TDD). This is especially useful for those applications that you inherit, that you need to refactor, and just need a safety net of sorts added to the code before you start working on it.

Check out Microsoft Research's Pex & Moles projects. Pex is the tool that actually automatically creates the unit tests. Moles is a separate tool (that Pex uses — and that you can just use directly yourself) that enables your tests to "mock" objects that can't normally be mocked, similarly to Isolator (a product worth looking at from a company called TypeMock).

Although no tool can (or should) replace the solid coding practice and separation that TDD typically leads to, having a broad set of tools on your belt should be helpful!

SUMMARY

This chapter discussed the fundamentals of automated unit testing. You learned about the Three A's — Assign, Act, and Assert. The discussion broke down automated unit testing into its four major components — code, tests, testing framework, and test runners. You learned a bit about Dependency Injection and working with mocking frameworks, and then about some of the added benefits of having automated unit tests — code metrics, continuous integration, and code coverage. Finally, you learned about some of the leading-edge work that Microsoft Research is doing, and you were encouraged to go beyond the basics so that you may continue to grow your unit testing developer skills.

ABOUT THE AUTHOR

Caleb Jenkins is a practicing agile coach for the largest global software company in the airline and travel industry. He is a development mentor who cares deeply about software craftsmanship, as well as improving and maturing the practice of software development. He has worked for Microsoft as a Developer Evangelist, was the lead software architect for Six Flags Corporation, and built his own consulting company in Dallas, Texas. Jenkins is a Microsoft MVP for ASP .NET, and a national speaker for the International .NET Association. He frequently presents at various conferences, and is well-known for his engaging speaking style, depth of knowledge, and creative energy. Jenkins lives in the Dallas area where he continues to date his beautiful wife and busies himself playing Candy Land and Xbox 360 with their four incredible children. You can follow Caleb on Twitter (`http://twitter.com/calebjenkins`) or find out more about him through his blog at `http://developingUX.com`.

INDEX